Orthodoxy

Orthodoxy

The American Spectator's
20th Anniversary Anthology

R. EMMETT TYRRELL, JR.
Editor

1817

HARPER & ROW, PUBLISHERS, New York

Cambridge, Philadelphia, San Francisco, Washington
London, Mexico City, São Paulo, Singapore, Sydney

Designer: C. Linda Dingler

Indexer: Judith Hancock

Library of Congress Cataloging-in-Publication Data

Orthodoxy: the American spectator's 20th anniversary
  anthology.

  Includes index.
  1. Tyrrell, R. Emmett. II. American spectator
(Arlington, VA)
AC5.O77 1987   051   87-45082
ISBN 0-06-015818-2

Contents

II. Americana   69

III. The Sexes   137

VI. Conservatives   381

Introduction

R. EMMETT TYRRELL, JR.

What hath motivated mankind from those incunabular days in the caves, the garden Eden, or wherever the scientific community eventually fixes our point of departure? There are various theories. All, however, are quite unsatisfactory; except, of course, for that of Dr. Marx, which is totally convincing at least for those whose ultimate goal is to knock off millions of fellow citizens or to join the faculty of the Harvard Law School. The primary deficiency with all recorded theories of human motivation is that they overlook the obvious, the great unacknowledged mainspring of human action, to wit: boredom. Those scholars who have assayed great lives probably recognize boredom's place in history, but who would respect these scholars if they were to lay the great deeds of a Napoleon, a Niels Bohr, a T. Boone Pickens, to mere boredom? Nonetheless, the cognoscenti must recognize that there is plenty of evidence confirming that Alexander the Great left Macedonia because the place was getting on his nerves, that Chaucer wrote *The Canterbury Tales* to fill his vacant days, that had Richard Nixon starred on the golf team at Whittier College he would not have given politics a moment's thought, so delighted would he have been with the capacities of a #1 wood.

Having established this much about the motives of history's great men, surely you will not mistake me for a humble man if I tell you in the well of our friendship that I founded *The American Spectator* twenty years ago out of boredom. Since then through every editorial day I have been preceded by little children throwing flowers. But before this charming pageant began I was 23 and bored.

The year was 1967, and whatever future historians might make of that it was sheer luck. I might have done the same thing in 1767 and been hung by the Red Coats. In 1967, though, a historic inflammation was beginning to afflict America's latest Old Order. The last time this happened to an American Old Order the year was 1929, and the Old Orderites were leaping out windows. This time the Old Orderites were growing bushy sideburns and leaping into beds, often with their daughter's girl friends, occasionally with their daughter's boy friends, but most often they were leaping into bed *sans copain;* and alone they commenced to dream.

The Old Order was no longer resolute in defense of liberty, reason, and intelligent thought. As the years staggered by, its recumbent stalwarts dreamed on as though nothing was changing, as though their liberalism was still liberal: rational, tolerant, freedom-loving, and audacious in defense of good causes. In truth, by the 1980s liberalism was none of the above. It had become reactionary, a religion without cathedrals, a theocracy of high priests self-appointed.

While liberalism slept the magazine that I founded, then called *The Alternative,* grew from an off-campus magazine at Indiana University to become a national anti-radical journal, part of a network of anti-radical students with representatives at Harvard, the University of California at Berkeley, and the University of Chicago. It embraced much that was once right with historic American liberalism as well as what was increasingly right and relevant with the emerging conservatism of the late Twentieth Century. By the early 1980s over 30 of its associates were serving high in the Reagan Administration, and a former legal and literary advisor of mine, William J. Casey, was the head of America's world-wide network of intelligence officers.

In 1977 we changed the name from *The Alternative* to *The American Spectator.* I would like to say that a shrewd marketing decision was behind the change, say an attempt to attract sports fans, but the fact is that the word "alternative" had come to be associated almost exclusively with radicals and with their way of life. We changed the magazine's name for no other reason than to discourage unsolicited manuscripts from the clinically insane.

Surrendering the name *Alternative* was not our last cultural loss to the 1960s radicals. Their greying, withering band has for two decades had things pretty much its own way with everything but nature. Their bogus claims gained wide credibility in our culture, though most of these claims were stupendously false, for instance the claim that they typified 1960s youth (the majority of whom voted for Richard Nixon in 1972), that the totalitarian conquest of Southeast Asia vindicated their protests, that drugs and zoo sex were an advance for civilization. Today, after their bouts at drug therapy centers, on Dr. Freud's couch, in the clutches of various mountebanks of personal growth or far eastern flapdoodle, and—it must be said—at certain federal institutions for moral rehabilitation, the 1960s radicals are still bragging and pontificating. Surprisingly they are still extolled as moral and intellectual colossi. Their livers have prematurely turned into useless little stones, their teeth are falling out, their own children mutiny, and the IRS closes in. The vast majority of Americans regard them as vessels of misfortune. Yet they show no sign of smartening up, and the keepers of American culture only slowly grow suspicious of the radicals' shortcomings.

Well, such is life. An increasing variety of evidence demonstrates that *The American Spectator* has been right about the major public issues of its time. Wherever the radicals' foreign policy prescriptions have touched ground the corpses have accumulated and rotted in the fields. Wherever the radicals' social panaceas have been perpetrated pathologies multiply. What follows is not a chrestomathy of the best of *The American Spectator* but a sampling of its positions

in the intellectual battles of the past two decades. That position is best characterized as American orthodoxy, not the orthodoxy that has sozzled the Republic's
intelligentsia recently but the orthodoxy established during two hundred years
of American history. For an American intellectual to defend that orthodoxy
today is admittedly quite unorthodox, but the writers and readers of this magazine have never been intimidated by the trends of the hour. Given the choice
of dining with Madison and Jefferson or the Rev. Jesse Jackson we would pass
up the air conditioning and dine with the old fellows.

Harvey Mansfield, Jr.'s splendid 1974 essay "Defending Liberalism"
shows that we anticipated liberalism's troubles, and Malcolm Muggeridge's
"Operation Death-Wish" demonstrates that we suspected that they would con-
duce to flights into the irrational. The diversity of writers in this volume bespeaks the varied sources from which we have drawn strength, from Europe and
from North America, from conservatives, libertarians, social democrats, occasional liberals, and from neoconservatives. This brings me to one of the most
significant achievements of this magazine. *The American Spectator* was the first
intellectual review to bring together the traditional conservatives and those
liberals who would eventually be called neoconservatives. For some reason
those who have written about neoconservatives have usually missed this fact. I
wish they would note it, for bringing the conservatives and neoconservatives
together was not easy. I have scars on my person where conservatives pummeled
me for allowing dangerous radicals like Irving Kristol aboard. And I bear other
scars where the neoconservatives throttled me for being so reactionary. They
did this when they were still called liberals. Now some of them throttle me for
being insufficiently conservative. At any rate both groups are now happily to the
right, and I suppose it is my good manners that prevent me from reminding the
colleagues of my prophetic vision and enduring moderation.

In the pages of this magazine we have scotched much sham and ignorance
(see Peter Rodman's superb piece). We have resisted the politicization of what
should remain unpolitical (note particularly section three) and resolutely opposed the last threat of totalitarianism in this century (see section four). We have
provided a setting for writers to develop their talents, and many have gone on
to become major popular writers, for instance an early Washington correspondent by the name of George Will, and our only literary editor, Roger Rosenblatt.
Others have gone into government and academe. Finally *The American Spectator*
has remained what it set out to be, an American magazine, alive with the vitality
and humor of the American people. That is perhaps our most unforgivable
achievement. In a time when American intellectuals mistake being earnest for
being serious *The American Spectator* has dared to snicker. Well, that is the
American way, and it beats boredom.

But before you go let me tell you that we owe this volume especially to
a small army of loyal staff who have served this magazine incomparably and to
a varied group of financial supporters who have helped with the bills. They are
the Medicis of the Age. We owe special thanks to Wladyslaw Pleszczynski, our
managing editor and an invaluable aid with this volume. Finally let us thank
The American Spectator's Assistant Publisher, Lou Ann Sabatier. She makes the
deals.

I
Media, Books, and Criticism

The Function of Criticism
at the Present Time

(1972)

ROGER ROSENBLATT

When I was a college senior debating whether to apply to law school or graduate school in English, my prospective father-in-law advised law school, and so I applied to graduate school. The first place that accepted me was Michigan, and when I told my prospective father-in-law he said that's fine, but it isn't the East. Next I was accepted by NYU. He said that's all right, but it's not the Ivy League. When Columbia came through, he told me that it wasn't Harvard, Princeton, or Yale. When I got into Princeton, he said it wasn't Harvard or Yale. When I got into Yale, he said it wasn't Harvard. When I got into Harvard, he said it wasn't law school.

Things trouble me more at a later stage than they do most people. I seem to catch on to the fact that a problem exists in a certain area at just about the time its solution is imminent. Luckily, my zeal at these discoveries is so wholehearted that people mistake it for a long-running, passionate commitment which has recently peaked, and therefore congratulate me on my stamina. It took me three years in graduate school to wonder what I was doing there. Between teaching assignments, taking exams, learning three languages, writing a dissertation, taking out the garbage, losing my jump shot, noticing that my wife had given up teaching to raise two children, apparently ours, discovering an inability to stay awake past midnight, acquiring charge accounts, electrical appliances, and a few other things which signaled my future death, I gradually began to consider towards what profession my graduate student friends and I were supposed to be heading. (Most of these friends had actually considered this problem two years earlier, and are now in legal practice, earning a bundle.) One thing was certain; I had no skills. This, in the eventuality of universal draft, seemed an advantage.

As long as I kept to my own constituency, this matter of what I was doing never came to a head. All of us graduate students were in the same boat (no one wanted to make waves), and at parties—there were many, all of them desperate—we behaved like characters in Thomas Mann's short stories, unconsciously decking out our own burial ships (we English teachers can go on like this forever), without even the tacit admission that we were all at sea. The only hope we had to go on was the fact that our mentors, the professors whom we were to become, were alive and seemed content. It was reasonable to conclude that if we behaved ourselves, we too would grow up to be alive and content, yet our elders never said exactly why they were content or what they were doing with their lives. Even had I been brave enough to put the question directly, no purpose would have been served. In university circles, the question, "what are we doing here?" is the signal to break up the party.

Modern times have not really affected this silence because we teachers are too busy reforming the curriculum to explore the existing profession. The good in this is that it preserves one area within the university where there is no danger of fist fights. On the outside, however, it is a different story, as it always is, because no matter how naturally adept or practiced you are in social evasion, there must always come a moment, after the soup, a gap in the lunch time hilarity or in the shared melancholy over world crises, when your (businessman, cop, doctor, architect, pimp, engineer, commercial artist, forest ranger) friend will look straight into your shifty eyes from the steady security of his own, and ask what it is precisely that you do. I usually try to get around this rudeness first by simply naming the courses I teach, skillfully tossing in literary jargon (ana-goge, Skeltonics) in hopes that my accuser will not wish to appear ignorant before me and drop the subject. This rarely works, as the presence of a college professor like no other stimulus on earth seems always to encourage confidence in even the shakiest people. I will then try merely stating the classes I teach, again being careful to indicate that I guide graduate students and honors candi-dates as well as the regular run, implying by so doing that my work is really too advanced for lay comprehension. Failing these two ploys, I tell the truth, always an error. I gulp and simply say that my job is to read books and talk and write about them, to determine and demonstrate what these books mean, where they fit into the history of facts and ideas, and why or why not they are worth reading. After I make this declaration there is an excited pause while my companion searches my expression for a sign that I'm kidding.

I won't say that there isn't some compensation for leading this mystery life, because there is. First of all, it's a great advantage with women, or so I'm told through hearsay by distant acquaintances in foreign universities. Of course, there are those who, when you tell them your work, split your sides and theirs by exclaiming, "Well, I'd better watch my grammar," but for every one of these there are five others who glow all over at the mere mention of literature, and who wriggle furiously at the drop of "poetry." Throw in Modern or Romantic, and watch out. To these women it makes not the slightest difference that they don't know what it is you do. Whatever it is, you've got to be very sensitive to do it. There is no doubt that the academic attachment to poets is the next best thing to being there. I tell women I teach Robert Browning, and immediately they begin talking in sonnets.

With men, however, you can barely strike up a conversation if they know what it is you do. Once you get past the "Well, I'd better watch my grammar" line, a special and eerie quiet comes over the scene, one in which the stranger is occupied in guessing whether you're a fairy, and you in retaliation are trying to strike poses which would indicate that you're not. It never fails that if I am cloistered with a businessman to whom I've just revealed my profession, my next move inevitably is to mention something about sports, especially football.

If it would help matters I would probably tell a traveling salesman joke and wear chaps, but it wouldn't. Even by the time I've proven I'm straight I've talked so much sports that I sound like a one-track jock.

Occasionally you meet someone who has either majored in English himself (but who since law school has seen his error and now would take his conversion out on you), or whose child who majored in English is now selling lanyards in Majorca. These people are unusual in that although they do not know what you do, they do not like it and seek a fight. In the long run their hostility is easier to deal with than the bafflement of the general, because you can always pit your sense of beauty against their crass materialism. Of course, beauty will beat materialism every time, the equalizing factor being that it envies what it conquers, but for the moment of the struggle you have the advantage of their not understanding the function of literary criticism, your knowledge that this lack of understanding is ubiquitous, and your consequent disregard for a hundred forensic devices with which a seasoned debater would string you up. You therefore conduct the contest on the ethereal plan which is the English teacher's native ground, using the universal ignorance of your function the way a cuttlefish uses his own smoke (a mixed metaphor, though pretty).

In balance, however, the fact that almost no one knows what I do for a living must be considered a handicap. Working in a university one has certain general privileges associated with teaching such as the freedom to meander on Madison Avenue in the middle of the day in the middle of the week, but except for observing obsequious acts of deference performed by publishers' text book representatives who seek your editorship of selected essays by animals, there is no particular external advantage to the teaching of English, and more than a fair share of particular drawbacks. Unlike our colleagues in more flashy disciplines we are not invited to serve in government, primarily I suppose because, excluding JFK, no recent U.S. President seems to have needed English. And except for the unearthing of the Sutton Hoo burialship (these things keep coming up) in 1939 and the identification of a new Shakespearean source and a Joyce manuscript a couple years ago, there aren't many news events on which English scholars are asked to comment. I would like to say that our insularity has sharpened our wits, but this essay speaks for itself. The fact is that although we know what evil lurks in the hearts of men, we have clouded men's minds so that they cannot see us (an allusion).

The most painful situation where the employment question develops is with students themselves, a situation more delicate and potentially embarrassing than dealing with one's contemporaries, and one which illustrates the wisdom of teachers avoiding students whenever possible. At Harvard this situation occurs around the middle of the freshman year, when in an effort to decide on their areas of concentration, students will seek out faculty members of the various departments and ask them to advertise their trades. It is a small consolation to recognize that ninety-nine per cent of the students are insincere in this quest, wanting either to start working up an elaborate network of self-exonerations (when later, in retrospect, they decide they've chosen the wrong major), or simply to kill time (yours) or, in the case of my colleagues, to meet a famous man. Most Harvard men and women usually know in what they wish to specialize from birth. At the age of eighteen what they want to learn from you is are they going to be happy, to which I always answer yes, one fraud to another.

It's the one sincere percent, as usual, who cause all the trouble—not the little orphans Annie combing English for relevance (for these I have a prepared speech packed with quotations from Hooker and Sidney which, by the time it has mounted to its boring peroration, has left the kid's heart set on Social Relations)—but the others, the ones who genuinely wish to discover if the study of literature would be a decent way to spend three and a half years of schooling. Once these people are in the program, they pose no problem. Like insects to fire, they become what they sought to investigate. But at the start of things, when these trouble makers honestly want to know why English, that's when I begin to wish I were in economics. In those instances, instead of reciting the law, I would much prefer to read the students "To His Coy Mistress," "The Vanity of Human Wishes," the ode "To Autumn," "Lucifer in Starlight," something of Addison and Johnson, of *Paradise Lost,* a Shakespearean soliloquy, a paragraph from Jane Austen, one from Hardy, one from Conrad, passages out of Arnold, Melville, Thoreau, lines from *Troilus and Criseyde,* the Thomas villanelle, short stories of Hawthorne, Twain, O'Connor, etc. etc., deep into the night, only to look up afterwards into the same innocent and ignorant, though maybe by now tearful or flushed, faces I greeted at the opening of the interview. Therefore I do state the law, hoping that somewhere in my recitation they catch the fact that I enjoy my work, and are attracted at least by that.

For these students and their heirs, for my lunch time companion and his, for my father-in-law and his Wall Street cronies, for my own father, an internist who has politely wondered these past years why I too am called doctor, but primarily for Mr. and Mrs. English Graduate Student and all the ships at sea, I have decided to decide publicly what it is I do. I know this is a risk, that at the end I may discover that what I do is nothing, but if only for the sake of the children, I have to face this thing. Naturally, if I should find out that what I do is nothing, I will scrap this piece, not because it is better to thrive in ignorance, but because other English teachers would do me violence. (If at this point you pure and social scientists are beginning to feel comfortable, let me remind you that English, whatever it is, commands the attention and loyalty of more undergraduates in this nation than any other discipline, and if English departments go, colleges go, and so go you, government grants and all.) Indeed, with tens of thousands of students majoring in English, with dozens of university presses publishing hundreds of new critical works each year, with the current Ph. D. market overrun with would-be teachers of English, with a seemingly endless number of quarterly publications made up of literary notes and questions and answers, with many of these same publications and certain societies as well devoted to the celebrations or anatomy of particular authors, with these and the plain fact that in every high school and college curriculum the single absolute and indispensable requirement for an educated individual is the study of English, we must be doing something, right? Right!

(Don't panic.) I start with a working definition a little narrower than the general designation of literature as written work of enduring importance. For the teacher of English who deals directly or indirectly with people, literature too must deal with people, and it must be good. Literature, then, is the beautiful and orderly expression of human activity in written words. It deals with people, and it does something good. In the highest uses of language it shows our common heroism, cruelty, capacity for gentleness and stupidity, our resilience, friability, magnanimity, selfishness, our blunderings and grace. In short, among the arts it is the most comprehensive expression of our humanity. Accordingly, literary criticism is the instrument by which such expression may be made clear or clearer (clarity not being necessary to beauty or order), made known or more widely known. What beauty may mean I leave to the proving power of the individual critic. The larger point is that literature does something good, and that literary criticism also does something good, though it is not the same good.

The operation of literary criticism is divided into five parts. (It is always a good idea to number one's items in an essay, even if, as in this case, the writer is not certain that he has enough distinctions to fill his quota. Had Poe used numbers in "The Philosophy of Composition" no one ever would have noticed that there are no ideas in the piece, and if it weren't for Empson telling you that there are seven types of ambiguity, you'd swear that each was worth one seventh. I've also always suspected that there are fewer than thirteen ways of looking at a black bird, more than ten commandments, and that there are actually three *Quartets,* but judge for yourself.) The number five is a memorable number, and therefore there are five operations in literary criticism. They are as follows: 1) the expansion of literature, 2) the revealing of patterns, 3) the recognition and admiration of excellence, 4) the demonstration of precision, 5) the recognition of the distinction between literature and life.

Of the five the first is the easiest, although it can appear the most remarkable. All that it takes to open up a literary work is study—in the case of *Finnegan's Wake* about ten years which prove not to be worth it, in the case of Joyce's "Clay," about ten hours which make the difference between a dim apprehension of personal sadness and the clear vision of a whole dead world. The expansion of the story, "Clay" depends on a familiarity with the map of Dublin around 1910, some facts about the city laundries, the rules of one Halloween game, and the words and tune of Balfe's song, "I Dreamt that I Dwealt"—nothing more. Add to these one's own sense of the mixture of pitiable and irritating qualities in certain old people, and the story fans out completely. The expansion of literature is detective work at its best. It encourages appreciation of compression and selectivity, for the art of being able to see human activity in terms of little things like symbols and images, but best of all, it urges the mind to assault the seemingly invulnerable, to shake up and poke around until one begins to see things sharply and with a cool intelligence.

The revealing of patterns takes a wider range of study than the expansion operation, but it's a similar process of placing a literary work into one or another perspective, and enjoying it the more for that placement. In *Go Tell It on the Mountain,* the patterns one ought to know are the patterns of the black migration north in the United States, the patterns of black education and of black Christianity, as well as the more universal patterns of sexual guilt and the relationship between fathers and sons. These patterns are historical, cultural, spiritual and psychological in nature, and it takes an understanding of all of them to know what Baldwin is talking about. There are personal patterns worth knowing too, ones which indicate where a work or a line fits into a writer's own scheme of thought, and there are patterns of convention, form, theme and myth—to get into Robert Graves' Ulysses, look at Homer's, Dante's, Shakespeare's, Daniel's and Tennyson's. Sometimes the most important part about revealing patterns is to discover the discrepancies, the places where a man changes his mind and the pattern in which he functions changes shape. In that is a version of the whole struggle between human invention and restriction, not always a pleasant business to watch, but our own.

I come to the recognition and admiration of excellence, an elitist notion if there ever was one, and one bound to exasperate those who prize the Scott and Helen Nearing crowings from the wilderness over *Walden.* No exertion of energy is likely to dissuade such readers because, like the *New York Times,* they confuse contemporaneousness with life (unlike *Life* which confuses contemporaneousness with the *New York Times*), but the effort is still a central operation of literary criticism. This is not to suggest that a critic ought to stop using the word "perhaps" and to cease apologizing for his own existence because these are our tools of the trade, but after or under all the gestures of self-depreciation the cold truth is that the product of an enormous amount of reading, of a thousand comparisons of the ways in which feelings and ideas are expressed, is taste, and to mean something taste must be passed on, even if it may be regarded as an imposition. If it is so regarded, the trick is to make the student prove that it is an imposition, and should he do so effectively, the worse for you, but the better for criticism. The achievement of a sense of discrimination is more painful in literature than in one's social life because it takes time, but in the long run it saves time, which cannot be said of any social decision.

The demonstration of precision in literature could justifiably be incorporated under the recognition of excellence, but to do so would obscure its independent value, to say nothing of reducing the number five. If you remember, I am talking about the function of criticism at the present time, and there is no time like the heavy, drag, and out o' sight present to demonstrate precision of language. (This, by the way, is not a swipe at slang, as every age has its slang, language managing to flourish with or in spite of it. What scares me about our own age is the apparently willful desire for inarticulation, which can only be an off-shoot of the desire to avoid discriminations in a larger striving, I suppose, for the equality of man in deaf muteness.) In Eliot's "Sweeney Erect," Sweeney wipes "suds" around his face as he prepares to shave. Why suds instead of shaving cream? Because shaving cream would break the rhythm of the line, and it adds nothing to it. Why suds instead of cream? Because with cream the action may be misunderstood. Why suds instead of soap? Because soap suggests cleanliness and conveys a less vivid picture. Why suds instead of foam? Because Sweeney is a comic character as well as lecherous. Why suds? Because Sweeney is comic and lecherous and grotesque and potent, and because the sound is right. The difference, said Twain, between the word and the right word is the difference between the lightning bug and the lightning.

The fifth operation, the recognition of the distinction between literature and life, applies to a potential pitfall of all the arts, but particularly to literature because literature is the most explicit. Because it is the most explicit, even those people who appreciate the meaning of a literary work, recognize its patterns, its general excellence and manipulation of language, can and do make the mistake of comparing literary activity, especially the activity of fictional characters, to their own. The practical purpose in pointing this out as a mistake is the deflation of their self-esteem, as no one ever compares himself to a mean or low character—all those fathers moaning about serpents' teeth—but the greater usefulness in the recognition of the distinction between literature and life is that it provides a reminder of one's own wonderful and terrible human sloppiness. Literature is the beautiful and orderly expression of human activity in written words, but most of the time real human activity is neither beautiful nor orderly, and to see this is not merely to see that one's children are more grateful than Lear's, but, in a wider view, to see the importance of endurance as a virtue, and to appreciate that in real life it is our dogged perseverance alone which carries our familial tragedies and comedies beyond the final act. Literature orders life, and life goes on. To recognize this is to think the more of both.

It is inevitable, and I know that all of you who are still awake have already perceived this, that the five kinds of operations described above easily become forms of advocacy. I said before that literary criticism does something good. To disclose the secrets of a work of literature is to see something clearly for its various components; to know its patterns is to see something steady and whole; to recognize its worth is to make informed evaluations; to appreciate its precision is to appreciate the act of saying what one means; to understand that what you're reading is not what you're living precludes your corruption of either. Done right, literary criticism teaches these things, and the learning of them in turn reminds some people at least that such revelations and processes are not inborn, but must be continually coaxed from us, restated and rehearsed, lest we once again convince ourselves of our latent divinity. The function of criticism at the present time—are you ready?—is the advocacy of common sense. If that isn't doing something good, I'll go to law school.

Nietzsche hated academics, and being one himself he had a right to. I confess enormous pleasure in being able to cite Nietzsche, not because he was so deep a thinker, but because of his great name. There are few pleasures in criticism equal to the dropping of exotic names. Poe (king of an exotic name himself) advised writers for *Blackwood* magazine to toss in a line of Greek whenever possible for sheer effect, and admittedly there is a certain shimmer about any page of prose that frames such a line, even if the translation turns out to be "I see the blue duck," but nowadays that particular pretense is exposed, not thanks to Poe, but to the hordes of pretenders themselves who overdid a good thing. Names, however, still have an immense impressive power, so immense in fact that one day a man's entire intellectual or artistic value may be determined solely by the spelling of his name, a phenomenon already being born in the celebrations of Levi-Strauss and Sontag. These two are fine names and should be cited very often, though not as often as Kafka, Goethe, Hegel, Schlegel, Jung or Nietzsche. I also like Proust, Camus, Sartre and Gorki, but not as much as the Germans, the very letters of whose names send readers hurtling against doors. Critics should be very grateful that essays didn't begin and end with Johnson and Burke. One well-placed Kierkegaard is worth a hundred Johnsons, comparative intelligence notwithstanding.

Nietzsche hated academics for their lack of "nobility," for the fact that they do not "dominate," are not "authoritative," for their "industriousness" and "patient acceptance of place." Except where these characteristics would mean that a person would not fight for his rights of free citizenship or those of someone else, I would judge such attributes to be both admirable in themselves and worth instilling in others. In a world of ever increasing sentimentality it is essential to know how to probe, unravel, and evaluate all sorts of grand constructs, and in so doing to be able to recognize one's proper relationship to them. This is the basic sanity of literary criticism. Literary critics may all be mad as hatters, but the work itself is okay; it makes sense.

Now here would be a fine point to launch into a professional hymn of praise, and God knows we deserve one, but this was not my intention, and such a hymn would probably be premature by a few months anyway. The purpose of this essay was to report that a literary critic and teacher does something. That done, I leave to others the task of determining that among the various walks of life ours is the most enlightened, the most humane, the most scrupulous and intelligent, and the most essential to national security. For the moment it is enough to note that in the history of human communications there have been relatively few men and women who have heightened our language and the account of our thoughts and actions to a degree where we would look upon ourselves with as much fear and wonder as we would look upon the gods. Then there are some others whose commonplace job it is to remind us that we are only human, a condition complicated and tough enough in itself without seeking higher office, and at times quite splendid, almost satisfactory. These others are saints. One does not ask a saint what he does for a living.

How to
Read *Newsweek*

(1974)

JAMES GRANT

(Baltimore) Journalism is an inherently imperfect craft. To write on deadline is to understand the elusiveness of truth. There is never enough time or knowledge, it seems. Facts, the journalist's bane and glory, pass from source to reporter to editor, from one sieve to the next, and so to the printed page.

Competence is the newsman's standard, not perfection, and the most demanding test of competence is convincing those who know first-hand. In the reader's eye, truth is indivisible. If a story about Baltimore is wrong, how can a Baltimorean believe what he reads about Watergate? And when gross inaccuracy is joined by willful distortion, a journal no longer deserves to be read.

For these sound if provincial reasons, I have renounced *Newsweek* magazine. An account of the two-week strike by Baltimore municipal workers (July 1–15) was so sensationalized that it missed the point of what really happened here. And last year, in another article referring to Maryland, *Newsweek* deliberately distorted the truth. Willful distortion is a grave charge to make against a journal that purportedly deals in fact, yet *Newsweek* itself admits the truth of the charge.

That story, which appeared on April 30, 1973, concerned male prostitution and included the following sentences: *"One Maryland politician who had run for office on a law and order platform was collared recently while prowling for boys in the Times Square area. 'He once promised to build a boys' home in his state,' recalls Manhattan patrolman Anthony Mercaldi . . ."*

It was with intense disappointment that *The Sun* (Baltimore) discovered the truth. The hapless pederast, alas, was not in fact from Maryland. As *Newsweek* explained it, the story's authors felt bound to protect the politician's identity, so they tacked the name Maryland to his. Why Maryland? Why any state? *Newsweek* says it does not know. Perhaps the reporters thought the Free State so corrupt that no one would notice.

"It was the wrong thing to do," Hal Bruno, *Newsweek*'s deputy bureau chief in Washington, conceded recently. "A mistake was made. A reporter and writer chose the wrong means to protect a confidential source. If they had just said 'a politician' and let it go at that, it would have been okay. I don't think it was done for a malicious reason," he added. "The people responsible for this have had their error pointed out to them and have been warned it had better not happen again."

Lou Panos, a Baltimore *Evening Sun* columnist who first exposed the story, reported then that an explanation "is expected to be printed in the next issue in the form of an editor's note replying to a letter from a reader." The correction never appeared. Mr. Bruno pointed out that *Newsweek* confessed its sins to inquiring reporters as soon as the article ran. The confessions, however, were evidently offered sotto voce. Mr. Bruno, prior to my call and his own check with New York, had never heard of the incident.

Newsweek's most recent assault on Maryland was its story ("The Dump"; July 22) on the Baltimore police and garbage strike. Accompanying the article was a dramatic picture of Negroes looting a store.

"It was a city under siege," Newsweek began. *"Sprawling heaps of garbage sent a sickening stench into the humid mid-summer air; the city's jails and schools were undermanned; the public-health officer warned of an outbreak of bubonic plague; the streets were safe only for muggers, looters and the ever-burgeoning population of rats. And for the crisis-weary residents of Baltimore, there was no end in sight last week."*

There was no siege, of course. Garbage accumulated in parts of the city, but private enterprise and the public's cooperation kept much of Baltimore clean. *"Sprawling heaps of garbage,"* which suggests a city awash in swill, is the phrase of an unbridled imagination. A week before *Newsweek* went to press, the public-health officer, Dr. Robert E. Farber, ruled out the near-term possibility of plague. Indeed, no sickness has been directly linked to the strike. The claim *"the streets were safe only for looters, muggers and the ever-burgeoning population of rats"* is a fabrication. It might be noted, too, that the gestation period for rats is twenty-five days; the strike lasted only two weeks.

"A strike by some of the city's sanitationmen started it all three weeks ago, after Mayor William D. Schaefer declared wage negotiations had reached the bottom line," the story continued. *"The city had offered a wage increase of 5.5 percent, but it wasn't enough—and last week the garbage was piled everywhere. The city coped for a while: a volunteer squad of several hundred white-collar trash men supplemented private haulers, and the remaining heaps were sprayed with chlorine to keep the smell down and the rats away. But in last week's soaring temperatures, tempers also ran high; radical unionists spoke of 'shutting down the whole goddam city to get our demands,' and a protest rally at city hall triggered twelve arrests by policemen with nightsticks flailing."*

Newsweek's account of the initial walk-out is inaccurate and incomplete. The mayor did not declare that negotiations had reached *"the bottom line."* On June 30, the day before the garbage men bolted, Local 44 of the American Federation of State, County and Municipal Employees (AFL-CIO) voted to accept a one-year contract providing wage increases of 5½ percent. That vote bound every union member, including the sanitation men. The garbage, of course, was not *"piled everywhere."* Nor did the city's resistance perceptibly weaken as the strike wore on. *Newsweek,* however, did spell Mayor Schaefer's name correctly.

"The next night," Newsweek concluded, *"police themselves went on strike for higher pay. Even though about half the force remained on duty, looting and vandalism broke out all over the city, police bands were jammed by calls, one suspected looter was*

*killed by a non striking policeman and on Friday state police had to be called in to quell
an outbreak of racial violence. Jail guards, city zoo keepers, and janitors for the public
schools were refusing to cross the growing number of picket lines.*

*" 'This city will go crazy,' said one East Baltimore woman. 'It's just about crazy
now.' Sanity returned at the weekend, with tentative settlements of both strikes. But
Baltimore was a shaken city, and a pall of smoke from the burning garbage still hung
over the sweltering streets."*

Newsweek again refused to qualify its claims. Looting and vandalism did
erupt after news spread of the police walk-out, but the damage was localized.
(That *"about half the force remained on duty"* seems to have been true for the first
night of the police strike.) In two hours of reporting that night for *The Sun,* I
did not see a single act of looting. Most of Baltimore, including the downtown
business district, was left unscathed. State police, who were called in as a show
of force, assisted in quelling racial trouble (in an area that had experienced it
long before the police strike). They were not, however, summoned specifically
for that assignment.

"Sanity returned at the weekend," a phrase which appears in the final paragraph, directly contradicts the last sentence in the second paragraph: *"And for
the crisis-weary residents of Baltimore, there was no end in sight last week."* The *"East
Baltimore woman" Newsweek* quoted is probably a woman who happened to be
standing on East Baltimore street. That, at least, is how the same quotation
appeared in *The Sun.*

Baltimore was undoubtedly a shaken city as the strike reached a close. It
was also a proud city, having survived and functioned for two weeks in the
absence of key government services. "The people of Baltimore would not let
our city become paralyzed," proclaimed Mayor Schaefer, and the mayor was
right.

Newsweek's Mr. Bruno, who that week directed the magazine's reporting
in Maryland, agreed that the story, in places, was exaggerated. "In parts there
should have been some qualifying words," he said, "but I'm not prepared to
agree that it was all that inaccurate." *Newsweek* relied on a "stringer," a part-
time correspondent in Baltimore, for most of its information on the strike. That
stringer, Mr. Bruno said, neglected to call the magazine prior to deadline in
order to check the finished story against the facts he submitted. To this charge,
the stringer—one of *The Sun's* best reporters—pleads guilty.

That helps explain some of the errors. But, it does not explain why *Newsweek* proceeded so boldly with information it had not been able to verify. A
magazine does not rise or fall on two articles. Yet within eighteen months, two
Newsweek stories I had first-hand knowledge about turned out to be false; one
of them was intended that way. These might have been flukes, but how can we
be sure?

George Jean Nathan:
Mencken's Gunnery Mate

(1976)

WILLIAM H. NOLTE

Though he has not been awarded a niche in the pantheon of Great American Writers, George Jean Nathan certainly deserves a place in the annex of that sacred hall. I seriously doubt that many in our literate minority remember him at all. Try reciting his name to the average Harvard graduate and see what response you get. The few super-literates who do remember him are by now bent and gnarled by the spinning years and hence enjoying the skimpy usufructs of a life well (or badly) spent—such rewards, for example, as hardening of the arteries, senile dementia, transient ischemic attacks, visceral prolapse, the blind staggers, and a wonderful wondering as to what the hell it's all about. Before my favorite quack informs me that I have been thus blessed by my Maker, I want to pay this small tribute to dear Nathan, wherever he may now reside.

I daresay that most people who remember him at all remember him as the gunnery mate of Henry Mencken, who has long since been anointed, warts and all, and seated at the table with such indecorous savants as Rabelais, Swift, Voltaire, and Mark Twain. If that anointment makes a few of the Pure of Heart and the Earnest Strivers grumble and cry foul, then so much the better. I take almost as much delight from their discomfort as I do from seeing Mencken get his just desserts. Not only is the Baltimore Sage still very much with us, he is the most widely quoted of all our literati—and by a country mile. I sometimes wonder who occupies second place. Mark Twain? Emerson? Thoreau? Henry James? It's hard to say. I by no means intend to imply that mere quotability is the sole criterion for bestowal of the laurel; I simply point to the obvious fact that Mencken is still being read and attended to, and not just gathering dust on the shelf.

While on the subject of posthumous fame, I should remark the somewhat different courses the reputations of Mencken and Nathan took over the years. From the day they met, probably in May of 1909, and began their twenty-year editorial partnership, first on *The Smart Set* and then on *The American Mercury,* Mencken was the dominant figure in the relationship, both in his influence on Nathan and his visibility on the national scene. It was he, not Nathan, whom the *New York Times* editorial writer called "the most powerful private citizen in America." In his delightful "Introductory Reminiscence" in *The Smart Set: A History and Anthology* (1966), the late S.N. Behrman wrote that Mencken's

14

reputation, as early as 1915, was "massive, overwhelming and tantalizing." He referred to the Sage of Baltimore as "Socrates in easy wedlock with Rabelais, a one-man Academe swimming sturdily in Pilsener." In the penumbra of such a reputation, Nathan "played an irreverent obbligato."

Behrman described Nathan as an incredibly handsome man: "Posters of him sprouted all over town as if he were a matinee idol appearing in a Broadway show." But, I think, he accurately assessed Nathan's stature when he said: "I knew Nathan and took him in my stride. He was amusing enough but after all, when you come right down to it, he was only a drama critic who had been abroad. . . . Mencken was something else again. I thought him (and still do) a great man."*

If Nathan's stock never rose so high, neither did it sink so low as Mencken's did in the Great Depression when it became a favorite pastime among the proletarians, Marxists, and New Dealers to attack him as one of the false gods of the marketplace. Mencken always drew a crowd, of course, and many of its members did not like what they heard, which is understandable enough since he purposely antagonized entire groups of complacent and self-assured Americans. All of his writing, he once wrote, whether it took the form of burlesque, serious criticism, or mere casual controversy, sought "to expose a false pretense, to blow up a wobbly axiom, to uncover a sham virtue." In the teens and twenties he was violently attacked as being un-American (a charge to which he readily pleaded guilty), but in those decades his assailants were defending the status quo against his ribald mockery of the insularity and cheapness of what he called American snivelization; during that heady period he echoed the Nietzschean call for a transvaluation of values.

Ironically, his revilers in the thirties attacked him as an apologist for the capitalist system which they sought to overthrow. One writer, for example, sneered at him for still holding to the outlandish belief that Adam Smith said anything remotely applicable to modern economics. Where the leftists defended democracy for its egalitarian tendencies, Mencken, as a Federalist in spirit, opposed it for leading, particularly in hard times, to a tyranny of the majority. The leftists and Mencken were in agreement on only one thing: that capitalism and democracy must be essentially at odds with one another. It would be an oversimplification, though not an untruth, to say that Mencken rejected Roosevelt's New Deal (he once compared FDR's concept of government to "a milch cow with 125,000,000 teats") because its economic theory was founded on deficit spending in perpetuity.

More to the point of his fall from grace, Mencken opposed FDR (after voting for him in 1932) as strongly as he had opposed Woodrow Wilson. The true believers laughed with him as he debunked the three clowns who reigned between the two Saviors. It was one thing, however, to mock a Harding; quite another to gouge a Roosevelt. Mencken was doubtless correct in his belief that

*Behrman concludes his little essay with a wildly funny story (much too long to recount here) about his first meeting with Mencken. Harold Ross, who evidently idolized the Sage, had invited Behrman in the early thirties to have dinner with him and Mencken at 21. That evening Mencken told Ross a tale, by way of pulling his leg, that makes me laugh every time I think of it. Fetch a copy of the book and have a look.

"The liberation of the human mind has been best furthered by gay fellows who heaved dead cats into sanctuaries and then went roistering down the highways of the world, proving to all men that doubt, after all, was safe—that the god in the sanctuary was a fraud." One should add that there has never been an iconoclast who has escaped public opprobrium.

Much of Mencken's ill repute, as well certainly as his popularity, may be attributed to his having possessed to an extraordinary degree the two qualities that most of us take for granted but few possess—honesty and courage. Moreover, he seemed to have been born without illusions, which made him, in the eyes of those who are constantly moving from one certitude to the next, something of a monster. A final note: if Mencken was so severely chastised and pummelled, so shot at from both the Left and the Right, if he was such anathema to all right-thinking men, then how did he survive? And not only survive, but actually thrive? Why would readers, properly forewarned, keep going back to his articles and books? I give only one of the possible answers, and perhaps not the most important one, but one that tickles my midriff: to wit, his enemies too often made the fatal mistake of quoting him. Those critics intent on burying him, and there still are many such, would be well advised to employ paraphrase in their denunciations but to avoid at all costs direct quotation.

Nathan suffered no such decline in reputation during his lifetime; only after he was gone did the light dim, and our collective memory fade. Although he was, so far as I can make out, just as honest and courageous as Mencken, and just as fond of thumbing his nose at pomposity and affectation, he really cared no more about political matters, or social justice, or manners and morals, or the national interest, or what delusions the people cherished, than did the average alley cat. Again and again in his books and articles he insisted that he was interested only in "the surface of life: life's music and colour, its charm and ease, its humour and its loveliness." But nowhere did he express his hedonism better than in the foreword to *The World in Falseface* (1923): "The great problems of the world—social, political, economic and theological—do not concern me in the slightest. I care not who writes the laws of a country so long as I may listen to its songs. I can live every bit as happily under a king, or even a Kaiser, as under a President. One church is as good as another to me; I never enter one anyway, save only to delight in some particularly beautiful stained-glass window, or in some fine specimen of architecture, or in the whiskers of the Twelve Apostles. If all the Armenians were to be killed tomorrow and if half of Russia were to starve to death the day after, it would not matter to me in the least. What concerns me alone is myself, and the interests of a few close friends. For all I care the rest of the world may go to hell at today's sunset. . . . On that day during the world war when the most critical battle was being fought, I sat in my still, sunlit, cozy library composing a chapter on aesthetics for a new book on the drama. And at five o'clock, my day's work done, I shook and drank a half dozen excellent apéritifs."

I can admire what Nathan wittingly reveals here—that he knows what he wants from life and has no illusions about his essential selfishness. Bluntly and candidly, he viewed life as an aesthetic experience devoid of moral meaning—in fact, lacking any meaning whatsoever, save that which humans impose upon it.

A good deal, I believe, can be said for such a view. But the credo also reveals, unwittingly, a man firing blank cartridges at a target that doesn't exist. Remove the rather exotic flowers from that tapestry of prose and you will see right through it and into the front parlor of most dwellings, high or low. Far from setting himself apart by his admitted egotism, Nathan has simply confessed that he is like most other people, but without the moral fustian that some employ to hide their tracks as they move from one attained (or unattained) goal to the next.

Unfortunately he was not content with that one avowal of self-interest. Reading various of his books recently I was struck by his preoccupation with himself, with his apparent need to flaunt his rather hollow-sounding hedonism in the reader's face. In *The Autobiography of an Attitude* (1928), he informs us that the older he becomes the more he is "persuaded that hedonism is the only sound and practical doctrine of faith for the intelligent man." Not content with that sweeping generalization, he adds that he doubts if "there ever has lived an intelligent man whose end in life was not the achievement of a large and selfish pleasure." From there he moves to the view that altruism is itself a form of hedonism, that it is, indeed, "the highest flowering of selfishness." If all of us are hedonists, I see no reason for either bragging or complaining about the fact. Nathan is least interesting when discoursing on his favorite subject—that is, himself.

There were other interests, of course—primarily, his abiding and, to me at least, baffling love for the theatre, or more precisely for drama, since, as Nathan pointed out, much of what comes under the heading of "the theatre" has little to do with plays or drama. I have little doubt that Nathan's narcissism helps explain that enduring interest. In an essay on Nathan, in *Prejudices: First Series,* Mencken wondered what could keep so intelligent a man returning night after night to the theatre, "breathing bad air nightly, gaping at prancing imbeciles, sitting cheek by jowl with cads." Perhaps it was "a secret romanticism—a lingering residuum of a boyish delight in paste-board and spangles, gaudy colors and soothing sounds, preposterous heroes and appetizing wenches." But more likely it was simply a sense of humor, a delight in spectacle that was "infinitely surprising, amusing, buffoonish, vulgar, obscene." To this he added a final peradventure: "The theatre . . . is not life in miniature, but life enormously magnified, life hideously exaggerated. Its emotions are ten times as powerful as those of reality, its ideas are twenty times as idiotic as those of real men, its lights and colors and sounds are forty times as blinding and deafening as those of nature, its people are grotesque burlesques of every one we know. Here is diversion for a cynic."

With such a description (some would call it an indictment) of the drama, and of the nightflies attracted to it, Nathan offered no complaint. Rather, indeed, a corroboration. He considered all art as being artificial life, which was itself artificial. Back to Platonism: the artifice of an artifice of the Real, whatever the Real might be; certainly Nathan never claimed to know. While such a view helped him keep an open mind concerning art, keep an objective distance between the viewer and the thing being viewed, it also prevented him from ever taking the theatre too seriously. It enabled him to see the shallowness of ideological drama and "message" plays of playwrights like Clifford Odets, Robert Sherwood, Maxwell Anderson, T.S. Eliot, Arthur Miller, and other assorted special pleaders. When he took his aisle seat in a theatre he carried with him one of the most finely-tuned crap-detectors of his time. Of Eliot's message in *The Cocktail Party,* which was widely hailed as a masterpiece, he wrote, "Eliot's religious philosophy, insofar as one can penetrate its opium smoke, here suggests that of a sophomore Methodist boning up for examinations in Catholicism, and his sexual philosophy is no less that of a man whose dalliance with women seems to have been confined to hand-holding in an ivory tower." He complained of Odets' inviting us "to believe that neuroticism and talent are one and indistinguishable." When the New York Critics' Circle Award for best play of the year was given to Miller for *All My Sons,* Nathan reminded his reader that the same season had seen the first production of O'Neill's *The Iceman Cometh* and then, using those two plays for evidence, delivered a withering little lecture on the difference between timeliness and timelessness. In a devastating piece on Sartre's *No Exit,* much admired by those who had never seen all his shopworn borrowings in print before, Nathan first identified the source of the plagiarisms and then offered this closing reminder:

"That such and similar worn ideas should be regarded as noteworthy mental achievements is, nevertheless, not surprising. Even at their most familiar and obvious they are tablets from the mount in comparison with much of what passes for mentality in the drama of Broadway. After a starvation diet, even a slightly senescent pork chop seems pretty wonderful. We should not forget that Ibsen shook the claptrap reasoning of the English-speaking stage off its feet with ideas which, while strange to the theatre, were not materially above the intellectual level of a popular novelist. Nor should we forget that Shaw subsequently shook Ibsen off his feet in turn by heaving himself into the latter's domain and at the very outset staggering audiences far and wide with, for the first time from a stage, a facile parroting of doctrines culled from Schopenhauer, Nietzsche, and Marx.

"A Sartre, of course, is no remotest, faintest Ibsen or Shaw, but he seems to be onto the trick of rubbing one platitude against another and producing what the credulous see as brilliant sparks."

What Nathan says here needed saying—even though it, too, is a parroting of what Mencken had written about Shaw and Ibsen some forty years before. Indeed, I was astonished in going through Nathan's books to note the pervasive influence of Mencken on all aspects of Nathan's thought.

When not writing about the drama, Nathan churned out thousands of words on such favorite subjects as women, marriage, sex, doctors, vacations, his more famous friends, everything in fact that in any way occupied his time or attention. Writing was as much a part of his daily existence as breathing. Needless to say, particularly since various others have pointed it out, Nathan was extremely repetitious; what he liked he wrote about over and over, and often in almost the same words. Strangely enough, he never mastered the essay form. I say strangely since one would expect a writer whose talent was critical in nature to have organized his thoughts in some kind of progressive manner, to have begun with a thesis, then supported it in a hierarchical fashion that led inevitably, logically to a conclusion that at least came within waving distance of where he began. After overcoming an early tendency toward prolixity, and at times turgidity, he became an adept craftsman in the making of sentences that glitter and sting. I suspect that La Rochefoucauld taught him much about the making of aphorisms, as I know Nietzsche did. He could never resist stretching an analogy until it snapped in his hand, and in the reader's face, as here: "It is possible a man may love only one woman in his life. So, for that matter, is it equally possible that a man get through life with only one pair of trousers." Or this: "Marriage is based on the theory that when a man discovers a particular brand of beer exactly to his taste he should at once throw up his job and go to work in the brewery." Those "work" well enough, but this one draws a blank: ". . . such is the baffling drollery of human nature that a man's wife ever seems to him a virgin." Here's one from Nietzsche's waste basket: "Beware the sexlessness of those who talk most of sex!" If you've heard a politician speak lately this should ring a bell: "All that is necessary to raise imbecility into what the mob regards as profundity is to lift it off the floor and put it on a platform." This one requires a double-take: "God is just. He has reserved most of the prettiest legs for homely women." One that I wish I had thought of: "The argument most often advanced for the abolition of capital punishment is that it has not successfully deterred and doesn't deter persons from committing murder. One might with equal logic therefore argue for the abolition of all forms of punishment in that none so far devised has succeeded in deterring persons from committing theft, perjury, arson, assault, bigamy, hold-ups, rape, or anything else." My favorite, though, is one that he shares with some anonymous wag: "In the words of a friend of mine, I drink to make other people interesting."

On at least two or three occasions in the middle fifties, Nathan called Henry and his brother August, who still resided at the old 1524 Hollins Street address, to inform them that he was nearing the end and to wish them a fond farewell. The two brothers were doubtless shaken by the first calls, but their anxiety turned to mirth in 1955 when they learned of Nathan's decision to marry. Two years later he was baptized in the Roman Catholic Church. His parents, incidentally, were part Jewish, but his mother had been a practicing Catholic. When asked why he thus renounced his agnosticism for the Church of Rome, he is reported to have answered, ever the pleasure-seeker, "Because I want to go to Heaven." In the end his selfishness turned to Glory. Well, I hope he made it.

Sally Quinn
and the Telegenic Intellect

(1975)

PHILIP TERZIAN

Don't get me wrong. Being a celebrity is not entirely tedious. I like being called to do a piece for the Atlantic. *I like being interviewed by* Time. *I like making money. I have returned from television to discover that I have a magnified reputation that does get in the way. But I am not a failure. I am not a loser.*
SALLY QUINN,
Time, *July 17, 1975*

The philosophers of weight-watching insist that inside every fat man is a thin one yearning to get out. An interesting theory, and not without its general application, for I have long believed that by the same token inside every metropolitan newspaper is a *National Enquirer* champing at the bit.

About a year ago the hostess of a morning television show in Florida committed suicide by shooting herself on the air. The *Washington Post* sent down Sally Quinn—hitherto the chronicler of receptions at the Honduran Embassy, interviewer of George Wallace's mother-in-law—to get the details ignored by the wire service accounts. Sally sent back what has since remained a classic of its kind: a long, loving description of the path of the bullet through the woman's brain, the blood splattering onto the camera lens, the contorted face, the stricken technicians. This was a stylistic departure for Sally, but instructive in what it showed about her, about the newspaper that provided her abundant columns of space, about the putrefaction that lies festering in the souls of Washington's movers and shakers.

Sally Quinn is a reporter for a supplement of the *Post* called "Style"—as opposed to substance, to be sure—and was for a time the sensationally unsuccessful co-hostperson of something called the CBS Morning News. It is said that when she was hired she admitted to the *Post*'s editor, Benjamin Bradlee, that she had never written anything before.

"Nobody's perfect," smiled Ben, who ought to know, author as he is of the recent *Conversations with Kennedy.*

This is the sort of job interview every journalism graduate dreams about, the eager novice, willing to work, plucked from obscurity to try his hand at what is usually reserved for more seasoned, experienced folk. A Lana Turner of the linotype come to life.

In her recent reminiscence of her days at CBS, *We're Going to Make You a*

Star (Simon and Schuster, $7.95), Sally denies this particular version of the story, but it rings true. Her career, such as it is, has been founded on the *Post*'s predilection for missing the point of what it sends its troops to cover, for splashing the moronic and the contemptible across its ample pages as the heroes of our time. Who, after all, cares whether Henry Kissinger is a swinger, secret or otherwise? What rock star, speaking frankly into Sally's microphone between gigs, has anything to say? This is largely the complaint of a Washingtonian who must put up with it every morning jostling on the bus. But it is disheartening that she and her newspaper lust so vigorously after the second-rate, that so many newsworthy opportunities are missed—or worse, ignored—that so vacuous and uninteresting a figure as Sally should be its selling point, a force to be reckoned with in the capital of the Western world.

Nor, might I add, is the Sally syndrome a passing phenomenon. Trendiness in all its guises has crept slowly but inexorably into the surrounding pages, a temperamental virus that is not so easily shaken off. And Sally needn't worry about fading influence or lack of space. She now co-habitates with Bradlee, and as the editor settles into an undignified old age, he no doubt has the satisfaction of knowing the torch of banality has been passed, and passed with a vengeance.

My subject, however, is Sally's book, trumpeted by her publisher as a "hilarious" account of her misadventures at CBS. Hilarious it is, like a painting by a schizophrenic—crude, artless, yet matchlessly revealing.

Of course, it goes without saying that Sally can't write very well. ("The only person I met who has no fear at all is Hughes Rudd. Hughes is the most fearless person I ever met. His lack of fear . . . kept me going.") However, her prose has a piquant quality to it that is difficult to convey, impossible to duplicate. She can speak shamelessly of how delightful she is. She refers persistently to her Smith education while betraying no evidence of it.

She wanders off the track in many and revealing ways. One morning, leaving her apartment building, she encountered a CBS photographer at the front door. She thought he was the man who hounded Jackie Onassis in much-publicized ways a few years ago. Hysterical, Sally ran away screaming, but the wheels of the Barbie Doll mind were grinding nevertheless inside: "My mind raced to what I would wear in the courtroom when I sued Ron Galella to stay at least fifty yards away from me."

Her flat mind can but relate stories as she alone experienced them, her inane presence the axis around which events revolve. Had she stood along the Via Dolorosa we would know what she was wearing, where she ate dinner after the unpleasantness and the freshness of the thorns in Christ's crown. Men are either handsome or ugly, cities exciting or dull, jobs well-paid or ill-paid. Sally also has a peculiar inability to convey personalities, except her own, and that only by inference. Her portraits rely upon adjectives strung imaginatively together that could apply interchangeably, or to a dog. Barbara Walters is "warm, generous, loyal, dignified, humorous"; Walter Cronkite "easy, natural, unaffected, smart, gentle and funny"; Mrs. Hughes Rudd a "feisty, gutsy, bright, funny dame who doesn't mince words." Sometimes, indeed, the characteristics Sally treasures are mysterious. The movie star Warren Beatty is "bright, sensitive and serious and has a clearer understanding of his environment than most people I know in any situation.'' I always thought an understanding of your environment had something to do with knowing to come in out of the rain.

Sally's thesis is that she was cruelly unprepared for the task of reading news stories into a camera. Undoubtedly television news requires some skill, a facility for looking up from the warmed-over AP dispatches now and then and projecting sincerity, shock, impatience, or whatever. It is mostly a matter of show business, however, with the attendant importance of clothes, hairdo, winning smile, mastery of the difficult names of foreigners, keeping a straight face in the wake of the men and events that shape our times. Sally seems not to have been able to do this. It is her contention that CBS should not have unleashed her without some elocution lessons, without learning the minutiae of television production.

What she doesn't realize is that CBS's error of omission was more than likely her own fault. Someone who could virginally sit down at her *Post* desk and type her way to glory is naturally expected to duplicate the feat under other circumstances.

That Sally failed so miserably, then, is explained only two ways: either television news-reading is a much more difficult craft than anyone suspected, or Sally's flair rests soundly in the lap of the *Post*'s vulgarity, and could not be adapted to the outside world. Unhesitatingly, I choose the latter. Sally, as might be expected, takes a different view; that is understandable. To make an ass of oneself in the presence of millions is doubtless an unpleasant experience, and that, together with Sally's natural emptiness of mind, led her to seize what was for her the only conceivable rationale.

She has no sense of perspective, no humor, no sense of the absurdity of her situation, no inclination to review her debacle with a measure of irony. She is instead tormented by predictable demons: jealous newspaperwomen, rapacious, sexist CBS executives, a cruel recurrence of her acne, insensitive people to the left and right of her. This is where the fun begins. Sally speaks frequently of herself as a clever, mordant observer of the passing circus. But she is primly, ferociously indignant when other clever, mordant observers train their eyes on her. O injustice! She can dish it out, as they said at Smith, but she can't take it. As an illustration of the biter bit—and if the reader is willing to indulge that view—the book is incomparable.

It is educational, too, telling us more than we ever wanted to know of Sally's personal tastes, romantic life, her scorn for sham, cowardice, hypocrisy, the military-industrial complex, women with moustaches. It is funny—unintentionally, of course—although Sally's humor is an acquired taste. Likewise, Sally's candor, while selective, is intense and wide-ranging; but it can get out of hand and be not just disarming but excruciating as well. Several pages, for instance, are devoted to a lurid description of her bout with constipation. Who among us can countenance the image that passage conjures up—Sally's toothy visage hunched over the toilet in an agony of frustration, exhorting her reluctant bowels to do their stuff? Certainly not I. Anyway, if, as Freud suggests, our physical ills are sometimes transferred in place from one part of the body to the other, this book may very well be Sally's solution to that problem.

De mortuis nil nisi bonum. So much for Sally and broadcast journalism. She left CBS, ostensibly to join the Washington bureau of the *New York Times,* until she discovered how insensitive Clifton Daniel can be. Now she is back at the *Post,* her spiritual home, the womb of inconsequence from which she strayed and to which, like the prodigal daughter, she has returned.

Excited gossip has it that she is working on a Washington novel. It should be good, perhaps as good as Tom Wicker's or Willie Morris'. The literature of self-aggrandizement is a field both broad and fertile, and even the *Post* recognizes that it cannot go on publishing Watergate sanctimony forever.

Sally Quinn, meanwhile, is regaining her land legs. She was away for awhile and things have happened, new faces have arisen, embassies have opened and closed, prostitutes, transvestites, professors of sociology, homosexuals are there to be interviewed. And Sally will be there, pencil in hand, hand on hip, hip against the street lamp of Illumination, a wad of gum stuck firmly to the roof of her mouth.

Oh, Violence!
Please, Violence!

A Plea for Malice in Book Reviewing
(1979)

RHODA KOENIG

"I never read a book before reviewing it," said the Reverend Sydney Smith. "It prejudices a man so." I am sure the reviewers of Bernard Malamud's new novel, *Dubin's Lives,* have read it attentively, but they seem to have retained an impartial determination to consider it a wonderful book. "Searing," they call it, "marvelous," and "brilliant." "What a lovely story this is," coos Peter Prescott in *Newsweek.* "One must toast the vital specificity of the characters," commands Christopher Lehmann-Haupt in the *New York Times.* "A book a reader must live with for a long time," decrees Roger Sale in the *New York Review of Books.* So why is it that, despite this great weight of opinion and the high place the book occupies on the best-seller lists, I cannot see *Dubin's Lives* as anything but an immense bore?

William B. Dubin—certainly not the "hero"; indeed, the phrase "epony-mous protagonist" was made for him—is a vaguely Jewish biographer of Lincoln, Twain, and Thoreau, now 56 and restless with his career and his 25-year marriage. Dubin, who seems to be looking for aggravation, takes on a life of D.H. Lawrence and an affair with Fanny Bick, a 22-year-old college dropout who is briefly the Dubins' "cleaning person." The only other character of importance is Kitty, Dubin's Gentile wife, who, with her relentless analyzing and earnest sensuality, seems more Jewish than he.

For about 300 pages, the plot consists of Dubin going to bed—or almost going to bed—with Fanny, Dubin writing his Lawrence biography, and Dubin talking to his wife about the meaning of life. Now, this material could have been the basis for a funny story—the distinguished author makes a fool of himself over a girl less than half his age; his sex adventures parody the ones in Law-rence's novels; and he analyzes philosophical problems in bed with his wife, while having one short, unphilosophical word on his mind. Or it could have been turned into a serious novel about the conflicting claims of life and art, love and responsibility. But, as Malamud said in a *New York Times* interview, this is his "significant" novel, explaining what his "experience" has "totaled up to," and "the texture of it, the depth of it, the quality of human experience in it is greater than in my previous books." And you can be sure that when significant comes in the door, serious as well as funny fly out the window.

Not surprisingly, Dubin, like his creator, has a very high opinion of himself. At one point, when his wife is on vacation, the telephone rings, and "Kitty was on the phone, her voice affectionate. Though he had been expecting her call Dubin was displeased to have it come as he was lying in bed with Fanny." Fanny, however, seems to have a softening effect on the arrogant, mean-spirited Dubin. She inspires him to poetic flights ("You're a little larger than life, Fanny. I mean you make life seem larger. I felt that before you tossed your underpants at me"); she heightens his awareness ("I'm sorry I didn't respond more appropriately to your needs"); and she introduces him to hitherto unknown pleasures ("Is this what is called footsie?"). None of this newfound sensitivity, however, prevents Dubin from telling his wife that he has slept with one of her friends, or from sneaking out to the barn behind the house for a roll in the hay with Fanny.

Fanny is an appropriate match for this courtly lover. In a grand seductive gesture, Dubin takes her to Venice, but the expensive and elaborate consummation is delayed by Fanny's recurrent bouts of nausea and diarrhea. Then, after Dubin has endured two nights of sleeping chastely next to Fanny, he walks into their hotel room to find her underneath a gondolier. "He's young," explains Fanny, "and I like his ass."

Fanny's vocabulary is about as deficient as her moral sense. She says things like "Jesus, I had this mind-blowing god-awful dream" and "I've read *Walden.* Some chapters turn me on." Oddly, Dubin, the respected writer, never winces at this kind of talk. Malamud even falls into it himself, telling us that Dubin "regretted his stiff-assed frigid letter to her basically warm one," that Fanny's "orgasm, she swore, spaced her," and that "she had this thing about cola drinks—they gave her hives." Fanny's attraction to Dubin is simply incredible—and, unlike her, I do not mean that as a compliment. Why does a lively young girl seek the caresses of a tedious, elderly academic? Apparently, Dubin's great mind exerts a powerful spell over the popsy. "I like the vibes you have with what you're doing," she tells him, and later admits that she contrived to meet him because she was impressed by a section in one of his biographies ("That part wiped me out"). Although Dubin keeps saying that Fanny "teaches" him about sex, he is plainly the one in charge in this stale version of a teacher-student affair. "Could you specifically say," she writes to him, "what I ought to be thinking about in the way of a job or career, or recommend books that might be helpful?"

It's ironic that Malamud should have told the *Times* interviewer that he has been influenced by the women's movement and that his daughter "raised my consciousness," for Fanny seems to exist only for Dubin's convenience. When he wants to be rejuvenated, she is the Life Force; when he wants to be wise and paternal, she is Troubled Youth. Indeed, these two forces tend to cancel each other out. Fanny's undiscriminating sex life makes it impossible to take her search for order very seriously, and her coarseness and naiveté repeatedly trivialize her sexuality.

In the last 40-odd pages of the book, fate, as Lorelei Lee put it, keeps on happening. Dubin's grown son and daughter—who have made only a couple of brief appearances—get into terrible trouble; Dubin himself is almost killed; Kitty discovers the affair; Fanny inherits some money and decides to become a lawyer—and suddenly the book is over. Since none of the characters has changed (Fanny's sudden career decision is as unconvincing as everything else about her), we are left to imagine Fanny telling a colleague that his brief really wiped her out, and Dubin inviting eager young Lawrence scholars for dirty weekends in Sun City.

What, then, are we to make of the critics who have praised *Dubin's Lives* to the heavens? A friend of mine suggests what I know many people believe: "They just want to keep being invited to those literary cocktail parties." This may be a motive, although I have assisted at a number of these orgies and found, as Dorothy Parker did 50 years ago, that "the place was filled with people who looked as if they had been scraped out of drains."

More to the point, I think, is that the critics at *Newsweek* and the daily *Times,* and the others who write regularly, have to read an enormous number of books each year, or, to put it another way, their jobs consist of shoveling mountains of crud. And the periodicals who use different reviewers with every issue give most of their "important" books to the same few people. So when a book comes along that's not too hard to write about, that seems to be about something, and that has the appearance of literacy—especially if it's by a large and glowing name—the regular critics fall upon it with the enthusiasm of lifers baying after the warden's ugly daughter.

These demoralized souls bear little resemblance to the popular stereotype of the reviewer as a gleefully malicious imp. They take such a beating each week that they are easily impressed by someone who writes, not an 800-word column, but—a book! with a shiny cover! and a number on every page! I am told that, at a meeting of the judges of the National Book Critics Circle awards last year, one tenderhearted member protested the exclusion of a very silly title thus: "Oh, but it's such a *brave* book!" Reviewers for the more sophisticated journals may know how to disguise this kind of deference in print, but in a paper like the *Minneapolis Tribune* one sees it in its most naked form. A review in that paper's book section recently said, "I always try to approach a book sympathetically—realizing how damn difficult it is to write even a bad book." (That line says even more about the editors who let it stand than it does about the reviewer.)

When reviewers do rouse themselves to find fault with large, important books, they often apologize for their remarks, or sweep them away, in the same review. Robert Towers gets almost to the end of his long, favorable review of *Dubin's Lives* in the *New York Times Book Review* before confessing, "The book, as a whole, eluded me." Then he winds up, "But if flawed, it is also a rich book, generous in what it offers." Writing in the *Washington Post,* John Gardner admits that Malamud "frequently abandons verisimilitude and psychological credibility," but says that he does so "because he cares more about ideas than about how people really talk." And Richard Locke, in the *Saturday Review,* ended his penultimate paragraph, "Some book—ill-written, self-serving, morally obtuse, narratively and psychologically crude." The next paragraph begins: "But this is excessive."

Twenty years ago Elizabeth Hardwick wrote for *Harper's* an article entitled "The Decline of Book Reviewing." "Sweet, bland commendations fall everywhere upon the scene," she lamented. "A universal, if somewhat lobotomized, accommodation reigns. A book is born into a puddle of treacle; the brine of hostile criticism is only a memory. Everyone is found to have 'filled a need,' and is to be 'thanked' for something and to be excused for 'minor faults in an otherwise excellent work.'" Not long after Miss Hardwick wrote that, she helped to found the *New York Review of Books,* which for years carried long, thoughtful, sometimes mischievous essays. And Francis Brown, the nonentity at the *Times Book Review* of whom she complained in her piece, was succeeded by John Leonard, who made the *Times Book Review* more lively and more literary. But now the *New York Review* carries a great many pedantic essays, on books you haven't heard of and don't want to—some of them in languages other than English. And the man currently in charge of reviews at the *Times Book Review* lacks the capacity or the will to make it interesting. Both publications seem in the cold, dead grip of academe. The *Times Book Review* keeps assigning reviews to college professors ("experts in their field"). And the *New York Review* announces in its classified section that over 40 percent of its readers are teachers or graduate students. This cannot be good.

I wonder and worry about the nonacademics who consult book reviews before heading for a store, the people who are simply intelligent and interested in books. What do they think after reading a leaden book that has been hailed as the masterpiece of the month? Do they believe that they are insensitive, like those readers of *Cosmopolitan* who, not knowing what magic can be achieved with a bit of surgical tape, think the models' breasts much more beautiful than their own? Are they disappointed and angry, having been gulled into buying a very expensive flower press? Or do they get past the first few pages at all?

I wonder if the gentlemen at the book reviews think they're helping these readers any more than the people who write jacket copy. And I dearly hope that they will snap out of it and stop being so amiable about so much of what comes their way. A little more thought would be nice, a little more discrimination, but at least they could stop being so gentlemanly. The maddening affability of too many reviewers these days makes one want to stand and scream, like the young wife in *Who's Afraid of Virginia Woolf?,* "Oh, violence! *Please,* violence!"

Keeping Disinformed

(1980)

MICHAEL LEDEEN

No, there will be no comment here about television coverage of the great "dream ticket" escapade in Detroit. Instead, this space will be devoted to two stories that never made it into the American press, even though many of the Most Important Persons at the *Washington Post, New York Times, Wall Street Journal,* and elsewhere knew about them. That neither story got space is a disgrace. Both deserve the fullest possible coverage and discussion, for both involve the use of the press for nefarious purposes by our national enemies.

The first story comes from *L'Express* in a signed article by Jean-François Revel in the 12 July edition. Two months earlier a pair of reporters from *L'Express* and a correspondent from the Sygma news agency had been smuggled into Sanandaj, the capital of the province of South Kurdistan in Iran. At the time the city was under siege by the Khomeini forces, and the three journalists spent considerable time in the city's "hospital of the martyrs," which was under the direction of a 30-year-old female doctor named Chahin Bavafa. She showed them around the hospital, observing that the main operating room had itself been struck by a 120-millimeter shell, that ambulances had been fired upon by Khomeini forces, and that the hospital lacked blood serum, antibiotics, anesthetics, and even bandages.

Chahin Bavafa implored the French journalists to write in detail of these events, and she asked them to promise that they would cite her name as a source of information, so that there could be no possible doubt about the accuracy of their reportage. They objected, fearing that the supporters of the Ayatollah might attempt to punish her, but she insisted. Thus *L'Express* ran a story in which Chahin Bavafa was quoted as imploring the journalists: "Cry out about what you have seen. And demand, I beg of you, that your government intervene to bring an end to this butchery."

Later in the month Chahin Bavafa was arrested and brought before an Islamic Tribunal to face two charges: sabotage in her work and "publication of an insurrectionary and counterrevolutionary appeal in a foreign magazine." Found guilty, she was killed by firing squad on 17 June.

It's quite a story. And Jean-François Revel—to whom we already owe a great debt for *The Totalitarian Temptation*—spells out the consequences:

First, one cannot explain away this execution as the result of uncontrollable revolutionary fervor. The murder of Chahin Bavafa was carried out in cold blood.

Second, "Agents of Khomeini's SAVAK are at work in the Iranian Embassy in Paris—and hence in all Iranian Embassies abroad—reading the foreign press coverage of Iran. . . . All criticism of the regime by Iranians, wherever it is published, means the death of the critic."

Third, "If the death [of Chahin Bavafa] had taken place under the shah's regime, we would have seen an outburst of petitions and petitioners." The Iranian Embassy might even have come under occupation, like the Spanish Embassy in 1975 after the last of the Francoist political trials. "I hope that the demonstrators and petitioners will remember," Revel writes, "that a cadaver is always a cadaver, even when the murderer is right-thinking."

Fourth, "The Third World dictators have for years been conducting a campaign to stifle the free flow of information. The Ayatollah has found an absolute weapon: kill his opponents quoted in the free press."

Why did no one pick this up? I personally called editors and editorial writers, sent photocopies around to journalists I know, urged people to reprint the article or to look into the matter in greater detail. A regime that declares it a crime to speak the truth to a journalist is one that every American newspaper ought to condemn in the strongest possible terms. Instead there is silence.

There is silence as well about another spectacular development, this time in France, carried in striking detail by *Paris-Match,* the week of 11 July. It is the story of the first western journalist to be sent to jail because he worked as a disinformation agent of the KGB. His name is Pierre-Charles Pathé, the bastard son of Charles Pathé, the great French cinema mogul of the early twentieth century. Pierre-Charles Pathé was not one of the most important journalists in the country, but he had a fairly impressive set of credentials, having written for *France-Observateur, Libération, Le Nouvel Observateur, Realité, Option, Vie Ouvrière,* and others. He often wrote under a pseudonym: Charles Morand. In addition, he had his own publication, financed directly by covert funds from the KGB *residentura* in Paris: a bulletin under the letterhead of the "Center for scientific, economic and political information."

Pathé's career is fascinating for those who wish to familiarize themselves with Soviet techniques. He began by writing some highly pro-Soviet articles and books, works that brought him to the attention of the Soviet Embassy in Paris. Over the course of several years he received training, financing, and information from the KGB, thus permitting him to acquire financial stability and to create a name for himself as a first-class journalist with access to highly confidential information. In this phase he was not used to disseminate "disinformation." More recently, however, he was used as a channel for passing systematically misleading information about French politics and about Russian intentions and activities. For this task the KGB helped him start a new newsletter in 1976, entitled "Synthesis." This bi-monthly publication had restricted circulation to the French elite, reaching 41 journalists, 299 members of the Chamber of Deputies, 139 Senators, 14 Embassies, and 7 others. In April of that year the magazine *Realité* called Pathé "an independent sociologist and economist, for many years an analyst of the problems of the modern world, having formulated various observations and propositions that have often impressed French and European leaders."

He was tracked down by French security officials, his contacts with the KGB were watched, an air-tight case was established. He was sentenced to five years in prison, a sentence, according to M. Jean-Pierre Van Geirt of *Paris-Match,* that is not very severe. But then, as Van Geirt rightly observes, Pathé did not turn over national security information to the Russians:

He created filing cards on journalists who might have been subject to Soviet recruitment. He gave information concerning an official of the S.d.e.c. [the French CIA] whom he knew to the K.G.B. But, above all, he succeeded in influencing the shapers of the written press, arriving at a position from which he could spread all around the ideas of the Soviets.

For many years now, there has been a great hue and cry in this country and elsewhere about the nefarious role of the CIA in recruiting American journalists for clandestine activities. Congressional committees have published thousands of pages dealing with this question, hundreds of editorials have warned about the dangers of overly-close relationships between the press and the American intelligence community. The Director of Central Intelligence has recently been attacked for even considering the use of journalists in intelligence missions. Yet the activities of the "other side" do not attract attention.

The Pathé case is remarkable for another reason: It comes right out of the pages of *The Spike,* the best-selling novel by Arnaud de Borchgrave and Robert Moss. These two gentlemen are often accused of "Cold Warism" and extreme political paranoia. Yet in this case their concerns are amply justified. There most certainly are Soviet disinformation agents in the West. It would be astonishing if there were none in this country. Does no one care? Or has the fear of defending one's own country become so strong that a spectacular story from Paris is totally "unnewsworthy" for our leading newspapers and magazines? Why will no one write of these things in the United States? Mr. Rosenthal, are you listening? Mr. Bradlee? Mr. Cronkite? Roone Arledge? Is any one home?

Whoring After
the New Thing

E.L. Doctorow and the Anxiety of Critical Reception
(1981)

BRYAN F. GRIFFIN

"Loon Lake tells us about love and sex and money and desire," wept young Christopher Lehmann-Haupt of the *New York Times,* and the older boys and girls winked knowingly at one another. It had been a hard-fought battle, but Mr. Lehmann-Haupt had finally surrendered his innocence to a new novel by E.L. Doctorow, and things would never be the same again: "It tells us as much about ourselves as Theodore Dreiser did," sobbed the disillusioned lad, and nobody had the heart to ask the little chap to please speak for himself. Pop-philosopher Susan Sontag handed the boy a dry copy of the *New York Review of Books,* and tried to persuade him that she'd liked *Loon Lake* even more than he had: "the best American book *I* have read in several years," sniffed Ms. Sontag, just daring anybody to poke fun at her reading habits. A few overeducated louts started to do just that, and an embarrassing situation was only averted by the noisy arrival of some subsidiary philosophers from *Vogue* magazine, who began dancing around a fashionable little pot and insisting that Mr. Doctorow was "a magician." "His images haunt you," chanted the girls from *Vogue:* "words crash up against each other like loose atoms." The whole room seemed to be swaying: "You can never be sure what you saw," shrieked the literary dancers, "mind can hardly keep up with matter." Things were beginning to get a little scary, but just then the bell rang and everybody had to sit down in their assigned seats. *Publishers Weekly* muttered something about "a splendid achievement," and the *New York Review of Books* noted dutifully that Mr. Doctorow was "one of the bravest and most interesting of modern American novelists," but most of the real excitement seemed to be over. Everybody was just about to go back to sleep when the reviewer from *Time* magazine raised his hand and asked if he could get any extra credit for saying that *"Loon Lake* tantalizes long after it is ended." Suddenly the juices began to flow, and it was almost like old times. "Tantalizing," repeated Robert Towers of the *New York Times Book Review* thoughtfully. "Fascinating," he added somewhat tentatively, and everybody nodded. "E.L. Doctorow is an astonishing novelist," said Mr. Towers, a little louder now. There were scattered bursts of applause, and the speaker got to his feet. "Concentrically expanding ripples of implication," he said; "contemplative

stasis, acquisitive action; Yin and Yang; duality contained within a circle." The tension in the literary community was almost palpable. By Jove, "the implications seem endless," roared Mr. Towers, and all hell broke loose. The implications were indeed endless, and the competition to produce the most sweeping statement about *Loon Lake* lasted far into the night.

In the end, it was left to Anthony Burgess to give the game away, and he did so in the pages of *Saturday Review*. Mr. Burgess was convinced that Mr. Doctorow was somehow "superior to most of his American fellow-novelists," not because Mr. Doctorow had anything particularly interesting to say, but because he was so darn good at "expanding the resources of the genre." Mr. Burgess didn't say for what purpose this thing was being done, but he didn't much care, either: "I am happy to learn that *Loon Lake* is already a popular book," he continued artlessly, "in that it is a Book of the Month Club choice and eighty-odd thousand copies have already been printed." Mr. Burgess was happy because "serious students of the novel" (for which read "Anthony Burgess") "must recognize here a bracing technical liberation," and—thank goodness—"such a recognition is being forced upon a readership probably happier with *Princess Daisy*." The red-faced fellow tried to cover up his slip with some fast chatter about "epistemological agonies" and "convincing spacetime continua," but it was an awkward moment for all concerned: The unavoidable implication was that Anthony Burgess was only happy when readers were not, and for a minute it looked as though "serious students of the novel," like fans of *Princess Daisy*, might be far more interested in sales figures and "technical liberations" than in real books or genuine ideas.

If Matthew Arnold had been in the room he might have reminded Mr. Burgess that a serious man values ideas and reason above all else, "in and for themselves, irrespectively of the practical conveniences which their triumph may obtain for him" (or for anyone else). But then he would have gone on to point out that "the man who regards the possession of these practical conveniences as something sufficient in itself, something which compensates for the absence or surrender of the idea, of reason, is . . . a Philistine"; and Mr. Burgess wouldn't have liked that at all. In any event, Matthew Arnold was no longer around, and *Loon Lake* was, and there was excitement in the air.

To an unhappy visitor from the real world, the reason for all the excitement would not have been immediately apparent. Edgar Laurence Doctorow is not, after all, a particularly impressive figure, intellectually or otherwise. Lately he has been spending a lot of time giving interviews, and in those interviews he generally talks about "fictional renderings of experience," and "integrating fiction into people's lives," and that kind of thing—pretty standard stuff, in other words. Mr. Doctorow is pretty standard stuff in other ways as well: He has, in Alfred Kazin's phrase, "a nostalgic, deeply felt revulsion against capitalism," and so of course he also has long grey hair and a beard and a National Book Critics Circle Award. Like everybody else on the American literary campus, he likes to dress up in manly footgear and laborers' trousers and lovingly pressed, unbuttoned work shirts, and when it is time for photographs he appears in uniform and smiles quizzically at the cameras in a sardonic, working-class sort of way. He thinks that James Baldwin and Norman Mailer are great writers, and he publishes his own work in *Playboy* magazine. It is not necessarily a criticism of Mr. Doctorow to say that he does seem to be a bit of a type, or to suggest that he resembles, in many ways, the sort of lower-middlebrowed, middle-aged English teacher who is likely to write scatological political novels in his spare time. That's exactly what he is, as a matter of fact: a fifty-year-old English teacher who likes to write scatological political novels. Unfortunately, he is a teacher with a difference: In 1975, one of his novels accidentally turned into a particularly raucous Publishing Event, and some folks are still celebrating.

The saga of Edgar Doctorow is as representative as its hero. Like almost everybody else in the faculty lounge, Mr. Doctorow had long nursed visions of literary grandeur—"I thought of myself as a writer for many years before I wrote a thing"—but he was having trouble getting the critical horses excited, perhaps because of his insistence on "writing without knowing what you're going to write about." "One of my working principles," he explained recently, "is not to know too clearly or too objectively what I'm doing." This conviction constituted an apparently insurmountable obstacle to popular success until late in 1970, when Mr. Doctorow suddenly decided to revise an old manuscript about Julius and Ethel Rosenberg, the Americans who were executed in 1953 for conspiring to give atomic secrets to the Soviets. "Decided" may be too strong a word: "I sat down at the typewriter recklessly and irresponsibly, full of rage and frustration and despair, and just to do something, almost in mockery of the pretense of writing, I began to type something," Mr. Doctorow recalled a little while ago. "I didn't even know what it was."

Neither did anybody else, of course, but Mr. Doctorow's timing couldn't have been better: Nobody had published a mockery of the pretense of writing for several days, and there hadn't been a sympathetic book out about the Rosenbergs for more than a month. Mr. Doctorow arrived, so to speak, in an intellectual vacuum, and the consequences were predictable and instantaneous. Novelist Joyce Carol Oates, who also teaches English at Mr. Doctorow's college, let it be known that the Rosenberg book was "a nearly perfect piece of art." Under the circumstances, this must have come as something of a surprise to Mr. Doctorow, but he kept a straight face about it: "Write the book you find yourself writing," the nearly perfect artist told an interviewer, "and after it's done you look around for a rationale for it." Mr. Doctorow didn't have to look very far, either: The editors of *Contemporary Literary Criticism* were ready with the suggestion that his "major fictive concerns" might be "the cyclical nature of history and ways of knowing." This sounded pretty good to Mr. Doctorow, and he didn't make a peep when *Partisan Review* announced that the whole world was "in awe" of the way in which he "managed to handle historical figures fictively." The book was "a brilliant achievement," and "the best contemporary novel" the partisan reviewer had stumbled across in one heck of a long time. By the time it was all over, the Rosenberg novel had become, in the hushed words of movie critic Stanley Kauffmann, "the best American political novel in a generation," and it stayed that way for more than ten days, thus establishing a new record.

Now, Professor Doctorow may have been "reckless and irresponsible" when it came to writing books, but he knew a good thing when he saw one, and he scampered right back into his study to work up another big load of "rage and frustration and despair." But let him tell it in his own words: "I was in my study staring at the wall. So I started writing about the wall. It was in a house built in 1906. Then I started writing about the house itself. And I was off and running." Well, Mr. Doctorow typed and raged and despaired just as hard as he knew how, and after a little while he came out, grinning from ear to ear and carrying a big new book called *Ragtime*. It was this book that became the Publishing Event of 1975, and it was this book that really started all the trouble.

Ragtime was a typical example of the novel sans emphasis, which is to say that it was an example of the novel that seeks, or happens, to render all human experience meaningless simply by virtue of an aggressively monotonous prose style. In the stylistic sense—as distinct from the political sense—Doctorow's big novel relied for its impact upon two very old tricks (or three, if we are mean enough to count the inevitable presence of Dr. Freud and other "fictionalized" characters). The first gimmick is creaky but always effective: no punctuation, other than the period. As *many* periods as possible, please, particularly in the middle of what should be sentences, but nothing else.

The second gimmick is slightly more subtle in nature, but when handled properly, it can impart a grim and pseudo-ironic mood to every page in the book, and that's what we're after in this business. Not just to some pages, mind you: to *every* page. The way to do this is to drop any event of significance (particularly if it's violent, and it always is) right into the middle of a paragraph of unrelated trivia, so that the Awful Thing seems no more or less important than the everyday things which surround it. The dumping must be done more or less at random (chronology is definitely out), and if you're the sort of stick-in-the-mud who insists on cluttering up the book with any real development of character or plot, it's a good idea to conceal such development from the more persistent readers by tucking it away among a series of long paragraphs of detailed descriptions of supremely uninteresting localities. (It can be done the other way around, too: Trivia may be unloaded haphazardly onto non-trivia, but it's not quite so much fun that way, because it means you have to write out all that important stuff before you can get to the trivia.) It's all quite simple, really, almost as simple as unbuttoning the top buttons of your Bloomingdale's work shirt: First you put tape over the punctuation keys on your typewriter, and then you add a shot of the reliable old Sophisticated Irony, and before you know it, you too can turn out paragraphs positively pregnant with well-hidden significance and concentrated boredom. Just like Mr. Doctorow's:

But we were in New York and we had no money. We needed money for a railroad ticket and for a gun. And that's when I put on embroidered underwear and walked 14th Street. An old man gave me two dollars and told me to go home. I borrowed the rest. But I would have done it if I had to. It was for the *attentat*. It was for Berkman and the revolution. I embraced him at the station. He planned to shoot Frick and take his own life at his trial. I ran after the departing train. We only had money for one ticket. He said only one person was needed for the job. He barged into Frick's office in Pittsburgh and shot the bastard three times. In the neck, in the shoulder. There was blood. Frick collapsed. Men ran in. They took the gun. He had a knife. He stabbed Frick in the leg. They took the knife . . .

And so forth, for two pages. The passage becomes even more awe-inspiring when we realize that it is intended to represent a monologue by the late Emma Goldman, who was, in real life, the author of such works as *The Social Significance of the Modern Drama,* which means that she was not a fundamental illiterate. But then, even the mildest attacks of literacy can prove fatal to a publishing event, and *Ragtime* was more than an event: It was the sum total of all human experience to date. It reminded the *Village Voice* of Dostoevsky, and of course it reminded *Newsweek* of *The Great Gatsby* (everything reminds *Newsweek* of *The Great Gatsby*). The *New York Review of Books* figured it was "a combination of Pynchon, Edward Gorey, and William Appleman Williams," and the *New Yorker* thought it was "not unlike Auden's 'Musée des Beaux Arts' " (which was odd, because Publishing Events usually remind the *New Yorker* of something by Céline). *"Ragtime* reminds *me* of Hart Crane's *The Bridge,"* grumbled Stanley Kauffmann, and the party was complete.

Critic Walter Knorr delivered the invocation: "Doctorow," said Mr. Knorr, "evokes in his readers an 'anxiety of critical reception,' a fear on our part that we might not be getting all of his signals, as if to balance off his own 'anxiety of influence.' " For some reason all of this anxiety made Mr. Knorr worry about "the value of literary scholarship," because, you see, such scholarship was really "a dismantling and reconstruction of an individual work within all of the possible modes of allusion: synchronic (contemporary), diachronic (historical), metachronic (archetypal), literary (imaginative variations of the archetypal), and non-literary (documentary)." By this time Mr. Knorr was almost in tears, but he didn't know how to stop: "the natural affinities among historical recurrences—to speak in Vico and Joyce's terms—are ultimately part of the rhetoric of fictional and biographical characterization," he whispered helplessly, "of a self's justification for its own vectors." An awed silence fell upon the room, and we all stared guiltily at our feet, trying to forget about our vectors, and not succeeding. "Nothing quite like it has ever been written," muttered Mr. Doctorow's blushing publishers, as they passed a note to the *New York Review of Books.* "No one has written a book quite like it," confirmed the *Review,* crumpling up the note. The *New York Times Book Review* tried to keep things going by saying that Mr. Doctorow's sentences were "the verbal equivalent of ragtime." "Plink a plink," said the *Times.* "Plink a plink, a-plink-plink, a-plink-plink." Everybody got the giggles, and the big Event was adjourned until the following week.

It's true that trick novelists tend to attract trick reviewers. But if certain boys and girls in the back row were making fools of themselves, it wasn't entirely the fault of Mr. Doctorow. To be sure, *Ragtime* wasn't a particularly good book—but then, its author had never pretended that it was. On the contrary, he had taken pains to persuade all his friends that he'd really wanted his Event to appeal to semi-educated, "working-class" people: He didn't like literary elitism, he said, and he was eager to restore the "popular interest" in fiction (or anyway, in Edgar Doctorow's fiction). Concluding on a rather bizarre note, the man of the people explained that he wanted his book to be "accessible" to gas station attendants. This caused a brief flurry of confusion in the American petroleum industry, but it turned out to be an empty threat, and calm was soon restored to the pumping stations.

In any case, Mr. Doctorow's slightly strained cover story had been forgotten by the end of 1980, and all that remained was the vague memory of past days of glory. Doctorow. *Ragtime.* Publishing Events. The very words summoned up images of the Golden Age, and once more the cry went up: Find Doctorow. Doctorow did it before and he can do it again. Find Doctorow, and praise him, and all may yet be as it was on the campus of Philistia.

And so the wise men went to find Doctorow; and lo, when they saw him he carried in his arms a big new book, and it was a scatological novel of politics called *Loon Lake,* and it was good. It was more than good, it was fine, as fine as *War and Peace.* It was better than *War and Peace . . .* it was the best book anyone had ever written . . . it was . . . it was better than *Ragtime*! Why, it was so good that some people knew it was good even before they'd had a chance to look at it: The *Washington Star,* for instance, somehow guessed back in the middle of the summer that *Loon Lake* would be "September's leading fiction title." And a month before they'd even assigned the book for review, the literary astrologers from the *Washington Post* just *knew* that *Loon Lake* would turn out to be "dazzling." Also "skillful," and "alive with passion, brutality, power, violence and corrupting success," which are all good things to be alive with, over at the *Post.* Outsiders observed that Mr. Doctorow was already scheduled to hype his forthcoming novel at a $10-a-ticket *"Washington Post Book and Author Luncheon"* to be held in October, and those same twisted souls were still making snide remarks when the *Post* proceeded to feature not one, or two, but three adoring articles about the author of *Loon Lake.* Which just goes to show how cynical some people can be when it comes to art.

Still, nobody was too terribly surprised when the *Post* finally got around to reviewing the book and discovered that it was just as dazzling as the paper had been predicting. It was an occasion for dancing in the streets, because *Loon Lake* was, among other things, "an odd cross" between *The Grapes of Wrath* and— you guessed it—*The Great Gatsby.* "A comparison with *Moby Dick* may seem excessive," said the *Post*'s determined reviewer, "but that's the league Doctorow is playing in." Oh, sure, there were a few un-Melville-like flaws, but on the whole the book was "one verbally dazzling solo performance after another," because Mr. Doctorow was "one of the most courageous and interesting writers around," and it was hard to imagine him writing *anything* "lacking in courage and interest." Nobody could figure out what all that courage had to do with anything, but the *New York Review of Books* had already ruled that Mr. Doctorow was indeed "one of the bravest and most interesting of modern American novelists," and it would have been tacky to ask too many questions.

The Washington papers were joined in their astonishing prescience by the editors of the *Nation,* who predicted that current thinking about "the tools of contemporary political repression" would be "enriched by the forthcoming publication of an important new work of the literary imagination, E.L. Doctorow's *Loon Lake.*" As a matter of fact, the editors were so high on Mr. Doctorow that they asked him to write an analysis of the moral character of Ronald Reagan. Mr. Doctorow did so with characteristic gusto, revealing, among other things, that it was only after the end of the Second World War that "Reagan's life began to attach to the nonfictive structure of things." Nobody was quite sure what that meant, but it sounded awfully sexy, and so a few weeks later the *Nation* decided to print an entire fictive chapter from *Loon Lake,* which was a pretty big step for all concerned: "As far as we can determine," said the editors, *"The Nation* has never published an excerpt from a novel." There was an awed silence which threatened to become embarrassing until the fellows remembered to explain that Mr. Doctorow "transmuted emanations of historical events into novelistic meditations," which meant that he wrote leftist political novels. Everybody glanced at the excerpt and nodded politely and tried to move on to other things, but the editor of the *Nation* was waiting for them in the pages of the *New York Times Book Review,* where he was interviewing . . . E.L. Doctorow. People were beginning to get a bit annoyed, especially when Mr. Doctorow started talking about "accommodating the complexity of fiction, which as a mode of thought is intuitive, metaphysical, mythic." The editor of the *Nation* kept pestering him about *Loon Lake,* and Mr. Doctorow finally got mad and said that his book was "discontinuous and mind-blowing." "The convention of the consistent, identifiable narrative is one of the last conventions that can be assaulted," said Mr. Doctorow, and he was pretty damn sure he'd assaulted it: Hell, "I think it has now been torpedoed," guffawed the talkative fellow, who added that he'd also torpedoed "the basic compact between narrator and reader." "Here you don't know who's talking so that's one more convention out the window," explained Mr. Doctorow; "that gives me pleasure."

One man's pleasure can easily be another man's boredom, and by this time people were getting pretty sick of the rather peculiar arrangement between the *Nation* and Mr. Doctorow. The editors of the paper finally crossed the line when they printed a two-page tribute to *Loon Lake* by still another English teacher. This one had the feeling that the Doctorow style was "like a chorus of the blues played by Dizzy Gillespie," and he was especially hard hit by certain enchanting passages written "in a kind of semilyric computerese." "A tone, a mood, an atmosphere, a texture, a poetry, a felt and meditated vision of how things go with us," hummed the *Nation*'s reviewer, which is Critic Talk for "I can't think of the word I want, but by Gosh this is a favorable review." It wasn't exactly a new tune (five years earlier the same teacher had been saying that *Ragtime* was "cool, hard, controlled," and "all we could ask for in the way of texture, mood, character and despair"), but this time the gang had gone too far: Someone finally looked at the small print and discovered that Mr. Doctorow was . . . an editorial advisor to the *Nation.* And suddenly there was a kind of light.

Loon Lake itself is not a particularly interesting novel. It is poorly written, and hardly structured, but there is nothing especially new or shocking in its awfulness. It is, to be sure, a determinedly squalid book (much more so than *Ragtime*), but it is surprisingly old-fashioned in its squalor: Mr. Doctorow is one of those timid American male writers who is afraid to use a grown-up word where a four-letter one will do, and if the result is undeniably sleazy, it is also undeniably stale—much more likely to elicit a surreptitious yawn than a disciplinary grimace. "You travel from orgasm to political organization along an arbitrary morpheme," says Anthony Burgess, perhaps disapprovingly. "It is Doctorow's way." It was also everybody else's way, about 15 years ago, and unfortunately for Mr. Doctorow, there are no new sights to be pointed out during the hike: *Loon Lake* is merely one more in a thinning line of "grotesquely socio-erotic epics," and as such it is—we hate to say it—more than a little old hat.

Like all excessively familiar objects, it is rather difficult to describe. There is no attempt at historical, narrative, or psychological coherence, and accordingly there is no real plot (which is perhaps just as well). There are, however, periodic references to the melodramatic adventures of a boy named Joe, who runs away from home to visit the Great Depression. Alas, Joe, like his creator, is a rather dull and ill-educated boy:

I climbed firescapes and watched old women struggle into their corsets, I joined a gang and carried a penknife I had sharpened like an Arab, like a Dago, I stuck it in the vegetable peddler's horse, I stuck it in a feeb with a watermelon head, I slit awnings with it, I played peg with it, I robbed little kids with it, I took a girl on the roof with it and got her to take off her clothes with it,

and so on. Some people pretend to enjoy this kind of thing—it has "hypnotic force," if you work at *Time* magazine—and Mr. Doctorow can turn the stuff out by the yard, when he's in the mood, and he always is. Well, our Joe has problems of an intimate nature ("alone at night in the spread of warmth waking to the warm pool of undeniable satisfaction p----d from my infant c--k into the flat world of the sheet and only when it turned cold and chafed my thighs did I admit to being awake, mama, oh mama"), and he also suffers from religious doubts, which come to a head one afternoon as he is, in his boyish way, robbing the church poorbox: "God the Father the Son and That Other One really p-----g them off with my existence I twist turn kick the Father has b---s they don't cut off their own b---s they don't go that far the son of a bitch—spungo!" Joe is able to resolve his doubts by discussing them with a friendly clergyman—"red apoplectic face I know the feeling Father but you're no father of mine he is on his hands and knees on the stone he is gasping for breath You want your money I scream take your f--king money"—but the experience marks him for the next 252 pages as a boy without punctuation. (The experience also did something funny to Michael Kernan of the *Washington Post,* who received the Unmitigated Gall Award for saying that "the sentences are clean and tight, even if they don't have any commas in them, and sometimes no periods.")

Eventually Joe joins a carnival to find those parts of himself which he has not already found, but his studies are soon interrupted by a party of unenlightened workingmen who proceed to rape and then murder the carnival's Fat Lady. This makes Joe very angry, in a symbolic sort of way: "I felt betrayed by her, as by life itself, the human pretense. I became enraged with her! In my nostrils, mixed with the sharp fume of booze, was an organic stench, a bitter foul smell of burning nerves, and s--t and scum." Momentarily distracted by the unexpected presence of so many commas, the lad catches a glimpse of a naked girl whizzing by in a private train (an extremely common sight during the Great Depression) and takes off in hot pursuit. Naturally he winds up on the enormous estate of a millionaire oppressor of the workers, where he is set upon and almost eaten by a pack of wild and presumably capitalistic dogs, and then—*please* sit still, this is very serious—then he runs into a union-busting gangster named

Crapo and his lovely and talented gun moll Clara, who take turns teaching him how to oppress workers. He also meets an alcoholic expert in Oriental religions who wants to murder the millionaire oppressor, and since the expert is also a poet, the happy encounter gives Mr. Doctorow an opportunity to unload some of his unused words, which he is only too happy to do:

> Come with me
> Compute with me
> Computerized she prints out me
>
> Commingling with me she becomes me
> Coming she is coming is she
> Coming she is a comrade of mine
> Comrades come all over comrades
> Communists come upon communists
> Hi. Hi.

By an astonishing coincidence, the poet was also once attacked by a pack of wild dogs, just like Joe! The two have other things in common as well: They were both fascinated, as young boys, by the sight of little girls urinating, and they both have exactly the same prose style. (If Robert Towers of the *Times* was willing to admit that the alcoholic Orientalist was "a singularly undistinguished poet," that was all he was willing to admit: "Whether Doctorow intended him to be so is not clear," said Mr. Towers, shutting his eyes tight and pretending it was too dark to see anything.) Presumably Mr. Doctorow's characters would like to talk with one another about all the piles of accumulated symbolism, but things are just too hectic: A female aviator who looks a lot like Amelia Earhart keeps landing and taking off from the estate in her hydroplane (her search for "higher altitudes" corresponds to the poet's search for "the ineffable in Zen," according to Towers of the *Times*), and Joe himself has to steal a Mercedes and rescue the gun moll and get a job in an auto plant so that he can organize the workers to bring social democracy to the Adirondacks. "Doctorow *is* a story-teller, a mythmaker," wails *Newsweek,* sounding just a bit desperate about the whole thing. The mythmaker is also a terribly sensitive fellow, of course, and he gets a chance to exhibit great wads of his sensitivity when he suddenly finds himself reminiscing about Joe's first crush:

I was enraged by the flaws of her, the unnatural cleft of her left hip, one buttock was actually atrophied, the raised veins behind the knees, the hanging breasts like deflated balloons, the yellowed face with loosened folds of skin at the neck, rising in parallel rows as she turned her head from me this stinking Hungarian hag this thieving crone bitch with the gall to think she had me for her toy boy her lover chuffing now like a f--king steam engine I brought the tears to her eyes she would acknowledge nothing she resisted . . . the lying c--t in the Pine Grove Motor Court,

and so on and on, into the tiresome night. One keeps having to remind oneself that the words were in fact typed by a middle-aged father of three who has been hired by a not-disreputable university to teach teenaged Americans about the purposes of literature. "His prose is so clean and precise," sighs the critic Wilfrid Sheed, "even when it seems to ramble, that the details stand out sharply and form an abiding picture in the mind." Well, yes, in a way: "At one point," chortles Doctorow-as-Joe, "the coins sticking to the wet a-s, the wet belly, I invented a use of [a woman] so unendurable to her that with the same cry that must have come from her the day she fell twisting from the trapeze, she flung herself off the bed—a moment's silence, then the sickening shaming sound of bone and flesh slamming into the floor, a grunt." Ah, yes, the literary grunt. Well, young love is indeed wonderful, but class is dismissed—all except for Mr. Sheed, who will please remain in his seat.

Actually, Wilfrid Sheed has an excuse, of sorts. He is serving as head critic for the Book-of-the-Month Club these days, and *Loon Lake* is one half of a Double Selection. It would be asking too much of Mr. Sheed to insist that he stand up in front of the class and admit that Edgar Doctorow is a rather tacky novelist, completely devoid of talent. Still, when Mr. Sheed starts saying that Mr. Doctorow's novels constitute a picture of "nothing less than 20th-century America itself," and that "our stock of imaginings is increased, and the American experience has itself a new legend," chances are he'd rather not be taken too seriously (people who talk about "imaginings" and "the American experience" almost never want to be taken seriously). On the other hand, some of the juniors and seniors can remember a time when Wilfrid Sheed wrote real criticism, a time when he was still able to say that "cultural conservatism is becoming in an older writer; anything else is cosmetics anyway. If he whores after the new thing, he will only get it wrong and wind up praising the latest charlatans, the floozies of the New."

Apparently Mr. Sheed wasn't referring to himself. Perhaps he was thinking of Peter Prescott of *Newsweek,* who has managed to persuade himself that E.L. Doctorow is "a connoisseur of American literary myth," the sort of connoisseur who spends his afternoons "swimming securely in the main current of American literature" (apparently without getting wet). But then, Prescott of *Newsweek* also has a vested interest in the matter: He has never been able to live down some hasty remarks he made ten years ago about Mr. Doctorow's Rosenberg book. The memory must haunt him still: It was a slow day at *Newsweek,* and Mr. Prescott got to feeling silly, so he said that the book was "more deeply felt than all but a few contemporary American novels." "The year is not half spent," he continued happily, "and a better American novel may yet appear, but I doubt it." It may have seemed like a good joke at the office, but the consequences for Mr. Prescott have been awful: He helped to create the beast, so to speak, and now he must keep feeding the creature in order to preserve a certain reputation. That is the tragic lot of the professional critic, and it is one reason why so many nice guys end up—in Mr. Sheed's characteristically graceful phrase—"whoring after the new thing." What they never seem to realize is that, in our century, the New Thing is always the same New Thing: Fall for it once, and you're stuck for life.

Five or ten years ago, Mr. Doctorow was very much the New Thing. As a matter of fact, he was attached to a whole school of New Things, all of whom spent their time writing scatological political epics and issuing vague statements about the arrogance of power. Kurt Vonnegut was enrolled in the school, as were Joseph Heller, Robert Coover, William Styron, and a few others. Some of the students were better writers than others (Styron had the largest vocabulary), and some were more repulsive than others (Coover wrote a series of explicit short stories about raping small girls), but they all shared a common attitude towards life: They didn't like it much. "Part of the trick for people my age," Mr. Vonnegut told *Playboy* magazine recently, "is to crawl out of the envying, life-hating mood of the Great Depression at last." It is extraordinarily hard to love literature if you hate life, which may be why the Vonneguts of our time have such a hard time describing what they like to think of as their creative processes: "It isn't really up to me," maintains Mr. Vonnegut; "I come to work every morning and I see what words come out of the typewriter." He sounds an awful lot like Mr. Doctorow, who sat down at the typewriter, "began to type something," and "didn't even know what it was."

The trouble with typewriter-art, of course, is that typewriters have good days and bad days: "I wasn't even getting reviewed," recalls Mr. Vonnegut, as if that were something to complain about. "I was also noting the big money and the heavy praise some of my contemporaries were getting for their books, and I would think, 'Well, s--t, I'm going to have to study writing harder.' " And so he did, in a manner of speaking: "What the hell," he says today, looking back on it all: "I was building a power base anyway, with sleazo paperbacks. This society is based on extortion, and you can have anything you want if you have a power base. The computers of my paperback publishers began to notice that some of my sleazo books were being reordered," and the rest is history. Pretty soon Mr. Vonnegut, like Mr. Doctorow, had his very own collection of "big money" and "heavy praise." His first hit was, as he recalls with some excitement, "an Alternate Selection for Literary Guild," and his first Publishing Event was "a Primary Selection for Literary Guild, Saturday Review Book Club, and Book Find Club." This was success, in Mr. Vonnegut's terms: "If we aren't the establishment," he remembers saying at the time, "I don't know who is." But then, that is the fate of all conscientiously new things: They become Old Things almost before they know it. And if they are not especially deep New Things—if their newness was all they ever had to offer in the first place—they quickly become vulnerable, and then scared: "In order to have enough things to talk about," frets the Establishment's representative, "I may finally have to become an educated man." And then, in a sudden explosion of shy-making candor: "My career astonishes me. How could anybody have come this far with so little information, with such garbled ideas of what other writers have said?"

Mr. Vonnegut wasn't speaking for the rest of the faculty, but he might as well have been. His plea raises certain awkward questions about the intellectual stature of the school as a whole, and in addressing those questions we may expose the core of the problem. What we are talking about, not to put too fine a point on it, is literary intelligence, or the lack of it. Alfred Kazin pointed the way when he devoted a recent column to an analysis of "Doctorow's intellectual shortcomings." It is a delicate subject, and we don't want to be too rude, but . . . well, put it this way: None of these guys—Doctorow, Vonnegut, Heller, Styron, etc.—is ever going to make Head of the Department. In the end, it is this immunity from intellectual promotion that links them most securely together as a single historical and artistic unit; and if nobody around here is talking too raucously about the literature of stupidity, it is only because people around here are so extraordinarily polite.

Still, there are limits to tolerance, and if Mr. Doctorow and his colleagues give too many more interviews, those limits will almost certainly be tested. A series of interviews can reveal a lot about the mental and spiritual equipment a writer brings to the job. Too much, sometimes: It was Doctorow himself who recently told an interviewer that *Loon Lake* was an "accessible" effort because "anyone who watches television news for five minutes knows how to read this book." Even Mr. Doctorow must have suspected that he'd said a bit too much, because by the time the next interviewer showed up he'd changed his mind: If *Loon Lake* was a "confusing" book, well, that was okay, because, "you know, a little confusion isn't a bad thing." After all, "it's better to be ahead of a reader than behind him," said Mr. Doctorow sulkily, inadvertently giving away a closely-guarded trade secret. There was an uncomfortable silence, and then everybody went scurrying over to look at William Styron, who was talking, as so often before, about Sex and the American Novel.

Mr. Styron was telling the world that he "was plainly trying to work on several levels in terms of sex," as if the world cared much. His latest hero and heroine, for example, "would have had it beautifully made on the sexual level had there not been a madness in their relationship," and so forth. Mr. Styron told a female interviewer that he was also making what he insisted was "an interesting side point," which was that "there was a lot of sexual frustration existing on the cultural scene in the late '40s." Apparently Mr. Styron was very close to the cultural scene in those days: "I mean girls just weren't putting out yet in those years, right?" If Mr. Styron's ramblings didn't seem to have much to do with books, he was at least making more sense than poor Mr. Vonnegut, who had managed to get sex and literature all mixed up with the American space program: "It's a tremendous space f--k, and there's some kind of conspiracy to suppress that fact. . . . How would the taxpayers feel if they found out that they were buying orgasms for a few thousand freaks within a mile of the launch pad? And it's an extremely *satisfactory* orgasm," said Mr. Vonnegut with considerable enthusiasm. "I understand," he concluded sweetly, "that there are certain frequencies with which you can make a person involuntarily s--t with sound."

If there is a certain sameness to these professorial musings, it is only because there is a certain sameness to the professors. Inevitably, the whole exercise gets most embarrassing when the boys try to talk about real books and real writers. Mr. Doctorow remembers Nathaniel Hawthorne, for instance, as the one American author who "really holds up in my mind as someone very important," which must be a source of enormous comfort to the ghost of Nathaniel Hawthorne. And Mr. Vonnegut likes to recall that although he "wasted eight years building model airplanes and [masturbating]," he nevertheless found time to read some science fiction: "conservative stuff—H.G. Wells and Robert Louis Stevenson, who's easily forgotten, but he wrote *Jekyll and Hyde,*" explains Mr. Vonnegut, in the manner of one confiding a little-known fact of English literature.

Understandably annoyed, our English cousins fought back through novelist Graham Greene, who ran out into the front yard, said that Kurt Vonnegut was "one of the best living American writers," and then ran back inside and slammed the door, giggling all the while. Unfortunately, Mr. Vonnegut believed him: "I started out writing for a large audience," recalled one of the best living writers, "and if I did a lousy job, I caught a lot of s--t in twenty-four hours. It just turned out that I could write better than a lot of other people. Each person has something he can do easily and can't imagine why everybody else is having such trouble doing it. In my case it was writing." Nobody trusted themselves to say anything, and after a few minutes Mr. Vonnegut went away again.

Mr. Doctorow, on the other hand, almost never goes away. Every now and then he remembers that he's supposed to be an English teacher, and the consequences can be absolutely catastrophic, as they were the other day when he brought the conversation around to his only subject, politics and literature. "It's the old Matthew Arnold idea," he declared airily. "He said great writing needs the power of the man but it also needs the power of the moment." And indeed, it must have been an extremely old Matthew Arnold idea, since, as every freshman is supposed to know, Arnold spent the whole of his adult life attacking the concept. Over and over, a dozen different times in a dozen different places, he called on writers to "remember the plain and simple proceedings of the old artists, who attained their grand results by penetrating themselves with some noble and significant action, not by inflating themselves with a belief in the pre-eminent importance and greatness of their own times." And while Professor Doctorow is acquainting himself with the thought of Matthew Arnold, he might note that genuine artists "do not talk of their mission, nor of interpreting their ego, nor of the coming poet; all this, they know, is the mere delirium of vanity." Arnold knew what the Doctorows can never know, that in order to discover art in their own time, artists require "great actions, calculated powerfully and delightfully to affect what is permanent in the human soul; that so far as the present age can supply such actions, they will gladly make use of them; but that an age wanting in moral grandeur can with difficulty supply such, and an age of spiritual discomfort with difficulty be powerfully and delightfully affected by them." Which is to say that Mr. Doctorow's "old Matthew Arnold idea" was really nothing but a new Edgar Doctorow idea dressed up in a better man's clothes. Kurt Vonnegut came back to sum up the situation: "I get more respect for Truman Capote as the years go by," he said, "probably because he's becoming genuinely wiser all the time. I saw him on television the other night, and he said most good artists were stupid about everything but their arts." Cried Mr. Vonnegut: "I want to stop being stupid in real life. I want to stop being clumsy offstage." It was all a little sad, but the cheers from this quarter were deafening: After all, if things improve offstage, it stands to reason that they'll get a little better onstage as well.

Which leaves us with Mr. Vonnegut's original enquiry: How *could* these fellows have come so far, "with so little information"? And now we see that the question answers itself. They have come so far precisely because they have so little information. They are successful, in certain circles, not because they have anything to do with the purposes of art, but because they happen to serve the political, cultural, and professional ambitions of other people. And if a new book by E.L. Doctorow constitutes remarkably barren ground, intellectually and artistically, well, that is the point of the whole exercise: Empty art exists so that empty critics will have some place to hang their hats. Though he didn't know it, this is what Mr. Doctorow was talking about when he told the editor of the *Nation* that the text of a book, rather than the author's intention, was the proper focus of literary criticism. The editor noted, with some satisfaction, that the novelist always qualified his comments about his own work with an "anyway, that's my theory," or an "as I see it." "Mr. Doctorow makes it quite clear," reported the editor, "that . . . his theories about his books are no more qualified than anyone else's." Well, of course not: Mr. Doctorow's popular reputation can survive only so long as he doesn't pretend to know what he's writing about.

He would be well-advised to take empty-lessons from William Styron, who's an old hand at the game. Recently a wayward book reviewer from the *Washington Post* asked Mr. Styron if his latest book could be seen as a sequel to the previous book, "in the sense that they deal with two levels of slavery." "Yes," replied Mr. Styron, "I guess it can." There was a long silence, followed by a little chatter about slavery, and then the reviewer asked if the book had anything to do with oppression. "Yes," said the novelist, "absolutely." There was another long pause, and then the reviewer suggested that Mr. Styron's central theme might be that of "victims turning into oppressors." "Oh absolutely," replied the novelist, wagging his intellectual tail and smiling helpfully. This went on for a while, and the nice woman from the *Post* began to get a little desperate. She pointed out that there was enormous significance in the fact that Mr. Styron had awarded the same first name to two of his "central victim-oppressor figures." Mr. Styron was pleasantly surprised: "I hadn't even thought of it until you mentioned it. And no one's mentioned it," he added indignantly, sticking his finger into the heart of the matter. He was glad, however, to have the information: "The choices of names," announced Mr. Styron, "often have curious subconscious significance." Well, he'd repeated the magic word, and before anybody knew what was happening the reviewer was asking him if he would please "compare this periodic density of evil to the new concept of black holes in physics." Yes indeedy, said Mr. Styron, "I think that's a very good analogy." He went on to say some complimentary things about black holes, and pretty soon his interviewer was encouraged to ask him if he was making a "universal statement about sin in the human condition." Replied Mr. Styron: "Yes." Which was exactly the right thing to say.

What we are talking about, of course, is party-fiction. Which is what the genuine critic Jonathan Raban was talking about five years ago when he said that Mr. Doctorow's *Ragtime* was "a splendid book to talk *about*—a big, party-sized idea." "There will be a very large number of people," predicted Mr. Raban, "who know little, and care less, about either the novel or history, who will see *Ragtime* as the most dazzlingly sophisticated exploration of both the novel and history that they have ever read." He was right, of course: Such people are always with us, always bored out of their skulls, and always ready for another party. That's why they were all so relieved to see *Loon Lake:* "It is a book I want to discuss and argue about with my friends," confessed Robert Towers of the *New York Times,* breaking out the faded balloons; "I hope they will quickly get around to reading it." And if Mr. Towers sounded a bit nervous, it was because so many of the best people had pleaded prior engagements. The novelist Mark Harris, for instance, sent his regrets in the form of a superb essay in the *New Republic:* He was sure, he said, that *Loon Lake* would give the kids "plenty of work looking up allusions and interpreting symbols and writing papers describing their findings," but he didn't want to join in the fun. "I do not believe this book will snap open surprisingly to the exertion of our minds," Mr. Harris explained gently, "nor do I expect that it will receive the corroboration of time." That's the sad thing about parties: They must always come to an end. And when they do, honest writers and critics must be ready to take advantage of the fleeting opportunity to throw open the windows and clean up the mess and make the place habitable again.

If *Loon Lake* is not a particularly interesting book, it is because its creator is not a particularly interesting man. It is not quite true, as Alfred Kazin says, that "Doctorow the novelist is not so smart as he is talented." The statement betrays a fundamental misconception about the nature of talent, and it is a rather popular misconception. Talent is divisible from intellect only in theory, rarely in fact: Literary intelligence cannot really be said to exist without the presence of the complementary talent that gives it form. By the same token, ability itself is only as real as the intellectual and moral guidance it receives: "Talent," as Lowell said, "is that which is within a man's power." The talent of a great soul is great because the soul is great, and the talent of a small soul can never outgrow its parent. As truth feeds beauty, so does intellect feed talent; as beauty defines truth, so does ability serve thought. It is all part of the same elixir, which is what Charles Rollin meant to imply when he said, almost three centuries ago, that "talents constitute our very essence." We have forgotten the wisdom, as we have forgotten Charles Rollin. He knew what our century does not: that genuine art can grow and survive only in those forests where talented intelligence seeks moral splendour, and that such forests are not so common as we think. The equation, then, is a simple one: If we cannot speak of "moral splendour" and *Loon Lake* with the same breath, then we will not find a connection between E.L. Doctorow and literary purpose. And where words exist without purpose, there is excruciating boredom. The poet Shelley must have seen Mr. Doctorow coming:

> Peter was dull; he was at first
>   Dull,—oh, so dull—so very dull!
> Whether he talked, wrote, or rehearsed—
> Still with this dullness was he cursed—
>   Dull—beyond all conception—dull.
>
> Even the Reviewers who were hired
>   To do the work of his reviewing
> With adamantine nerves, grew tired;—
> Gaping and torpid they retired,
>   To dream of what they should be doing.

All for Love: Europe in the Springtime

Love Dopes the Western World
(1982)

JOHN P. SISK

If love be not in the house there is nothing.
—EZRA POUND

The great days of the Shakespeare and Company bookstore, when it was located at 12 Rue de l'Odeon on the Paris Left Bank, may be behind it, but in its present location across the Seine from Notre Dame Cathedral it is still a place where one can browse in an atmosphere that connotes a legendary past. Here in early June we could buy the *New York Review of Books* and the *Village Voice.* The latter featured a piece by John Berger on Modigliani, then the subject of the exhibition we had recently seen at the Museum of Modern Art in Paris. "The paintings are so widely acknowledged," Berger wrote, "because they speak of love," and in case we had forgotten, the editors reminded us in a footnote: "Paris in the springtime is for love, as we know." Given the subject of his recent books, we would not have been surprised if Norman Mailer's contribution to the *New York Review,* announced on the cover as "A Vision of Hell," had taken off on the same subject. However, it turned out to be the introduction to *In the Belly of the Beast* by that ill-starred ex-convict, Jack H. Abbott. In it one finds this not very loving statement: "We are all so guilty at the way we have allowed the world around us to become more ugly and tasteless every year that we surrender to terror and steep ourselves in it."

There were moments in Modigliani's last years when he probably would have agreed with Mailer, but it is hard to see the effect of such moments in his paintings, so many of which suggest a man who had not lost faith in an erotic utopia. Thinking of them, not Mailer, my wife and I left that place and walked along the Seine to a point where, on the approach to Pont Neuf and oblivious of the noonday traffic, two clutched-together young lovers had obviously chosen Modigliani over Mailer. But this was not odd for we too had discovered that not only Paris but Europe generally, in the springtime or anytime, was for love of one sort or another, either in present fact or in recollection.

We saw lovers strolling hand-in-hand through the Modigliani exhibit or the Louvre, or ducking under the turnstile in the Rue du Bac metro station and kissing afterward. They kissed between sips of Coca-Cola or Fanta as they sat on the banks of Lac Inferieur in the Bois de Boulogne, or as they stood in line on the Champs-Elysées to see Paul Newman in *Le Policeman.* Young motorbiking lovers startled us with their temerity as they held hands traveling side by side on Rue Bonaparte, and young thespian lovers charmed us with their optimism at a Friday evening in Maggi Nolan's Celebrity Services office, where not too many Friday evenings previously the late William Saroyan had charmed everyone. On the train to Paris we shared a couchette with a young couple so intoxicated with one another that they had no need of the Scotch we offered to share with them and seemed unaware that the car, in the best tradition of Italian railroading, had been dispatched from Rome without water and with unflushable toilets.

Goethe wrote of his first experience of Venice that "nowhere does one feel himself more solitary than in a crowd." This is the way it is with lovers also. We saw them in their amorous isolation in Venice among the pigeons and the tourists of all nations in St. Mark's Square, in Rome at the Trevi Fountain, and in the Colosseum. In Siena we saw young lovers kissing as they came hurrying hand-in-hand down the narrow and treacherously cobbled Via di Citta. In the Roman ruins at Fiesole, one of D.H. Lawrence's Etruscan Places, we and other Sunday visitors stepped respectfully around lovers lying abstracted out of time in the long grass—as were those other lovers who lay in one another's arms in the open middle section of Ponte Vecchio in Florence, where the lost children of the world gathered with bedrolls, backpacks, and guitars around the bust of Benvenuto Cellini, himself a proper patron for lovers.

Nobody says that London in the springtime is for love, but even in London there was an ambiance of romance that took the edge off the news of strikes, riots, and IRA starvation in Northern Ireland. It seems to us that when the weather was right, which wasn't too often, lovers lay in the grass in Russell Square in unprecedented numbers. Perhaps the forthcoming royal wedding was a factor. *Paris Match* estimated that 1600 items decorated with pictures of the loving-couple were being offered for sale in British stores.

Of course, not all love is happy love, as the poets know. Mendicant troubadours sang of lost love in the square in front of the Georges Pompidou Center in Paris, in the metro tunnels and metro trains, and happy lovers contributed to them generously, perhaps out of a realization that happy love can be a good story only when lost love is a possibility. On the steps of the church of San Gaetano in Florence two young lovers—German, we guessed—held hands and cried together, and on the Ponte Vecchio among the lost children of the world a bedraggled girl cried in the arms of a bedraggled boy. Two handsome young Japanese cried with their arms around each other in the Colosseum. In London, the *Sunday Observer* featured somewhat belatedly the lost love of Jean Harris for Dr. Herman Tarnower. Meanwhile, the American musical *Pal Joey,* enjoying a successful London revival, featured the erotic adventures of the aging socialite, Mrs. Vera Simpson, who is "bewitched, bothered, and bewildered" to find herself in love again and happy only when she is in love no more. No doubt D.H. Lawrence, who has left his mark all over Europe, would say of her, as of Jean Harris, that she suffered from sex in the head and was therefore doomed to bewitchment and botheration.

But love in the springtime takes many forms. In Rome we lived near the Spanish Stairs, beside which Joseph Severn once nursed the dying Keats and at the top of which, in the opening of Tennessee Williams's *The Roman Spring of Mrs. Stone,* stands that menacing drifter who in due time will possess the aging beauty—who may also suffer from sex in the head. On a newsstand in the Rome railroad station pornography was on display beside *Flash Gordon, Walt Disney,* and books by and about the Pope. In the Bargello Museum in Florence Michelangelo's statue of Bacchus has been rendered perhaps permanently obscene for many viewers because some vandal had broken off its penis. It is not easy to find a McDonald's in Paris but sex shops are no problem; some of them, as we first noticed in Rue des Lombards near the Pompidou, even honor Visa cards. In London's Leicester Square, sex shops were as numerous as electronic games arcades, and Basil Seal was complaining in the *Tattler* that "at a recent count, central Soho contained more than 150 establishments offering some sort of filth." Our copy of *Where to Go: The London Guide* included a supplementary "Adult Guide" that indicated where one might engage Antoinette, Samantha, Sandie, Natasha, Candy, or Natalie (professional virgins retired out of Barbara Cartland romances, perhaps) to escort, pamper, anoint, or massage you (TV lounge and free drinks included) or relax you with "enemas Victorian and modern." In bookstores it was not unusual to find *Charles and Diana: A Royal Love Story* competing for attention with Gay Talese's *Thy Neighbor's Wife,* as if the management had decided that even royal romance could benefit from a second perspective.

One can assume that the Pope looks on Talese's kind of loving as something that belongs in the second circle of Dante's Hell. Indeed, not so long ago the Pope startled the world with the announcement that it was wrong to lust after one's own wife, let alone someone else's—intending, perhaps, to clear up some of the confusion about sexual love that had resulted from the earlier papal announcements on the subject by Wilhelm Reich, Norman O. Brown, and Alex Comfort. In any event, we arrived in St. Peter's Square the Sunday after the assassination attempt in time to hear the Pope say in his taped statement: "I pray for the brother who shot me, and I sincerely forgive him." Appropriately enough, inside the Basilica the Mass of the day began with this prayer: "God our Father, look upon us with love. You redeem us and make us your children in Christ."

The Pope was speaking out of charity, in Christian terms the highest form of love. But the would-be assassin, Mehmet Ali Agca, must be given his charitable due. He had acted out of no personal desire, only a burning need to protest the silence of the world about the hundreds of thousands of victims of Soviet and American imperialism. So he too was a kind of lover—no less than was John Hinckley who devoted his attempted assassination of President Reagan to the movie star, Jodie Foster. Agca's shooting of the Pope, like Dante's love of Beatrice, was only a means to higher things. Indeed, he was a version of that most dangerous kind of lover, the armed idealist. One of his kind, Peter Sutcliffe, "The Yorkshire Ripper," would soon be sentenced in England to life imprisonment for the brutal slaying of thirteen women during a five-year reign of terror, the judge not having been persuaded by the Ripper's argument that he had a divine mission to rid the world of prostitutes.

We remembered Agca in Paris as we visited the prison in the Conciergerie where in the Chapel of the Girondins you may see such mementoes of that earlier Terror as Marie Antoinette's crucifix and a guillotine blade. Danton and after him Robespierre are said to have been detained before execution in one of the small cells opening off the chapel. Robespierre the Incorruptible and passionate lover of the Republic of Virtue speaks for Agcas and Pol Pots yet unborn when the playwright Georg Büchner has him say in *Danton's Death:* "Vice must be punished. Virtue must rule through the Terror." His utopian vision having been sharpened by the censorship of fanaticism, he can say quite honestly: "The number of scoundrels is not great; we have only to lop off a few more heads and the country is saved." Who would have understood better the words of that armed Libyan idealist, Mu'ammar al-Qaddafi, which we had read the day before in *Time:* "The duty of the revolutionary committee is to practice revolutionary violence against the enemies of the revolution"?

St. Peter's Square—indeed, all of Vatican City—was an exciting place those days. Something had happened. Terrorists, as Walter Laqueur has said, are the super-entertainers of our time because "they will always have to be innovative." What greater innovation than to shoot the Pope while he was mingling fraternally with people who were in effect his guests? Of course, most people were sorry for the Pope, and many admired his charitable forgiveness of his brother. But surely there were some who understood very well that brother's kind of loving and secretly sympathized with it, having come to believe (usually from a safe distance) that there is something vital and honest in it that is directed, however extremely and confusedly, against the ugliness of the world that so discourages Norman Mailer.

Keats dying beside the Spanish Stairs could only dream of Venice, where Wagner, himself a fabulous lover, finished that fabulous love story, *Tristan and Isolde.* There one day we ate lunch at a standup bar close to where Byron once lived above the shop of a draper, with whose young, dark-eyed wife he promptly began an affair. Indeed, now free from his own wife, "that virtuous monster, Miss Milbanke," he enjoyed various Venetian ladies from one of whom he picked up gonorrhea. Here too he met Countess Teresa Guiccioli and became her faithful *cavalier servente,* a role he continued to play later in Ravenna, where he established himself with his famous menagerie. Yet dying in Missolonghi a few years later it was not his fulfilled love for Teresa that he celebrated in what was probably his last poem but his unfulfilled love for the handsome Greek boy, Loukas, who had become his page.

D.H. Lawrence, whose *Lady Chatterley's Lover* was written and first published in Florence, defined love in terms of a romantic obliteration of personality, and one consequence is that not only do the women in Lawrence, Byron, and Shelley have a tendency to sound like clones off the same original, but there is a sameness in the language of passionate abandon that they inspire. In their presence we are too often embarrassingly close to the erotic ecstasies of the tabloids, and old-fashioned movie magazines. The ecstasy is the problem. To be denied ecstasy in this post-Enlightenment world is to be denied that other prelapsarian birthright, Utopia. The Air Afrique ad in the Paris metro stations, featuring Ideal Beauty as a seductive girl in a white bikini, offered both at once to all who would fly away with it and her to La Fête Du Soleil—there to experience the time-stopping transcendence of what Shelley in "Epipsychidion" calls "passion's golden purity."

The Air Afrique lady may be to us a familiar incarnation of a cultural Muse, but she is not the kind of Muse Etienne Gilson writes about in *A Choir of Muses*. His Muses "are primarily divinities invented by the Greeks to account for the ordered design which confers upon certain of the ideas and works of man a super-human loveliness." They are "the women who have inspired men to write," for they reveal "the living unity between love, art and religion." They elicit the demand that all must be sacrificed to the absolute beauty they reveal so that the poet may sing the better. This is the way it was with Dante and Beatrice, about whom we often thought as we walked along Via del Corso in Florence where they may have met, and this is the way it was with Petrarch and Laura, though Petrarch being more of a modern man had a harder time putting down his carnal impulses.

In the chill, crepuscular catacombs of the French Pantheon where we went one morning there are great writers enough but Muses are in short supply. Voltaire is there, sharing a place of honor across the corridor from Rousseau, from whose tomb a hand holding a torch protrudes as if a man trapped inside a doghouse were trying to burn his way out. In life at least no love was lost between these two. Rousseau disparaged Voltaire as a playwright, and in an anonymous pamphlet Voltaire called Rousseau a heartless father for having abandoned the bastards produced for him by Thérèse le Vasseur. Voltaire also thought the success of *La Nouvelle Heloïse* one of the infamies of the century. If such sentiments do not suggest a personality so vitriolic no Muse could tolerate it, then his own successful novel *Candide* does. A Muse would have to tend her own garden, not his, and this is not what Muses are supposed to do.

Hugo is there too, sharing a cell with Zola. He loved many women, but none of them qualifies as a Muse—surely not Juliette Drouet who at age twenty-six began a half century's devotion to him as a mistress. She served him as a nurse, secretary, and confidante, in the process writing him 17,000 letters, and tolerated his many infidelities, one of which almost landed him in jail. At her funeral August Vacquerie referred to her as a heroine with "a right to her part in the poet's glory, having shown her loyalty in the time of testing." Hugo's own funeral procession was witnessed by more than a million people, was attended by rolling drums, booming cannons, and twelve wagonloads of flowers. Edmond Goncourt reports in his *Journal* that the women from the brothels had celebrated the occasion the night before with "a tremendous copulation," offering themselves "to all comers on the grass along the Champs Elysées."

Muses tended to disappear in Hugo's century in proportion as the secular spirit made it hard to believe in a love that moves the heavens and all the stars. After Darwin, Marx, Nietzsche, and Freud, potential Muses had to settle for domestic bliss, become call girls, or learn to administer enemas Victorian and modern to narcissistic males who idolized their own passions. Flaubert, for whom the world was as ugly as it is for Mailer, had literature as his idol and thus no more needed a Muse than Joyce did. And it would be a brave Muse indeed who would venture with Lawrence into the dark forest of his soul, which in *Studies in Classic American Literature* he opposes to the lighted clearing in which Benjamin Franklin's "venery" takes place. Certainly Frieda was not his Muse any more than she was John Middleton Murry's, and when the latter two became lovers after visiting Lawrence's grave at Venice one could only hope that the dead man still exercised enough spiritualizing power over both of them to keep their love from being mere venery.

Only the Pope has a Muse that Dante and Petrarch would understand. According to a *Newsweek* we read in Florence, the hospital room in which he lay recovering from his wounds was decorated with a picture of his beloved Black Madonna of Częstochowa. As he lay there, certain personal effects of Marilyn Monroe, including a 36D pink mesh bra, were auctioned off at Sotheby's in London. The purchaser of a strapless evening gown promised to resell it later for children's charity—and charity, as the Pope should know, is love.

For Byron as for so many romantics the ideal lovers' enclave is an island, where the syphilis that plagued nineteenth-century writers is as unlikely as *Dr. Spock's Baby and Child Care* is unnecessary. This compelling island idea, so closely linked to the idolization of art and sexual love, has its political analogue, as the *International Herald-Tribune* kept reminding us while we roamed about Europe. The armed idealists with their fierce and uncompromising charity, and fired with their own kind of passion's golden purity, were just as busy obliterating personality in the interest of their grand themes as their predecessors were two centuries ago when Western Civilization first became intoxicated with the idea of Utopia and began to experience its tradeoff in disgust with the ugliness of the given world. Now we no more expect negotiable demands from terrorists than we expect true love to be put off by fear of adultery or true art to result if the artist is afraid to sacrifice wife and children to it. Lawrence thought *Ulysses* was a dirty book, but it was the product of the same non-negotiable heroics as his own *Chatterley*. And when was Robespierre, the fanatic idolator of the Republic of Virtue, more their heroic fellow artist than when he refused to be distracted from his grand objective by a squeamish reluctance to chop off a few more heads?

Modigliani whose paintings speak of love was of this company. He died of tuberculosis in the nuns' charity hospital on Rue Jacob, home street for us in Paris as it had been earlier for Wagner, Sherwood Anderson, and Hemingway. One beautiful Sunday early in June, such a day as makes old lovers young again, we went looking for him in Père-Lachaise cemetery. We found him in the Jewish section in the corner of which is the heartbreaking memorial to those six hundred thousand French who in World War II died for France as deportees in the German work force or as fuel for the ovens of Auschwitz. Modigliani shares the grave with his mistress, Jeanne Hébuterne, she having earned her place, the headstone told us, because in her devotion to him she had made the extreme sacrifice. While a Goodyear blimp, sounding like a distant motorboat on a mountain lake, drifted below cotton puff clouds, we thought of the final act in that sacrifice: her suicidal leap from a fifth-story window in her parents' apartment the morning after Modigliani's death.

Jeanne Hébuterne, says the biographer Pierre Sichel, was Modigliani's only great love. No other woman "would have subjected herself to Modi's whims." She "had the capacity to give herself totally to him," and she "gave gladly, without thinking" for they were "well matched, a perfect couple," all of which makes her sound like a woman Lawrence would have approved of. She gave him one child and was nine months pregnant with another when she died, so her extreme sacrifice may have had some desperation in it. The whims she had subjected herself to had been aggravated by drugs, alcohol, poverty, lack of recognition, and deteriorating health; often he treated her in the best tradition of the totally committed and half-maddened artist, which is to say that he often treated her abominably. "He believed in himself and his art," says Sichel, "and, truly, nothing else ever mattered." What Sichel does not say is that Modi had been anticipated by that political artist, Robespierre the Incorruptible, who never hesitated to offer a few more heads on the altar of the Republic of Virtue.

This willingness of the artist to sacrifice all, including his own mental and physical well-being, on the altar of art guarantees him an authentically eventful biography. This is why we sometimes felt sorry for such part-time Florentines as Hawthorne, Longfellow, and Browning, whose biographies, especially in their love relationships, are so old fashioned—one might even say inartistic. As young men they were not rebellious hell-raisers, they married the women they loved, having courted them properly first, and as husbands they were faithful and loving. They were law-abiding citizens, paid their debts, honored their contracts. They were relatively free from that obsession with the ugliness of the bourgeois that was beginning to validate the lives of literary intellectuals.

Hawthorne, who fought the Florentine mosquitoes with as little success as we did and who once visited the Brownings at Casa Guidi for tea and strawberries, certainly had the wrong biography for Lawrence, just as America had the wrong history. In his cranky if sometimes shrewd study of *The Scarlet Letter* he admires the "blue-eyed darling of a Nathaniel" for having in "perfect duplicity" written the "most colossal satire ever penned" about an American that, being a phallic disaster, cannot know its women darkly in the blood. Lawrence seems to be implying that Hawthorne was so crippled by his culture that he was unable to write an American *Lady Chatterley's Lover*—an implication agreeable to many American readers.

Longfellow was a fine teacher and an important transmitter of European literature to America, as well as a poet whose marvelous ear and instinct for technical experimentation should have impressed Ezra Pound, who was said to be his grandnephew. But who reads him now? Whenever in Florence we walked by the building in which he had lived on the Piazza di Santa Maria Novella, I thought how unwisely he had ordered his life. If like Lawrence he had run off with someone else's wife, if like Stendhal he had come away from his first sexual encounter with a venereal disease that plagued him the rest of his life, if like Hugo he had remained avid of nymphs into old age, if after the trauma of his beloved wife's accidental death by fire he had become an alcoholic instead of picking up his life like the man of character he was—if he had done at least one of these things we might take him more seriously as a poet today. We might even be tempted to read "Hiawatha" and "Evangeline" as duplicitous surfaces beneath which frustrated dark phallic forces surge.

Sometimes we strolled into Browning's neighborhood near the Pitti Palace, always crossing on the Ponte Vecchio where, it was easy to believe, the lost children of the world were preparing their own brief and sad biographies. Browning was and is a great poet; even Ezra Pound had to live with that fact. He was great without the biographical advantages that have almost become the certain signs of the authentic artist. He loved a splendid woman all the days of their life together and was loved by her in turn, and when she died he was devastated, but being like Longfellow a man of character he picked himself up and went back to being a great poet, which itself suggests a quality of loving about which Byron and Shelley had only heard rumors.

Browning, in any event, made the better approach to the brilliant London revival of *Oklahoma!* which we saw one afternoon as our wanderings came to an end. No doubt, there were far more patrons in the sex shops of Leicester Square that afternoon, submitting themselves to the darkness in their blood, than there were in the Palace Theater. There are those who describe *Oklahoma!* as a sentimental love affair with a lost America, if not an America that never existed at all. But it is *Pal Joey,* which we had seen a few nights before, that is both sentimental and cynical—even Byronic in its denial of the world of true romance in which musical comedy belongs. Romance in *Oklahoma!,* thanks to the inspired collaboration of composer, lyricist, and choreographer, has a psychological and moral complexity without ever losing sight of the life-supporting distinction among kinds of loving that characterizes Dante's *Commedia* and Shakespeare's *As You Like It.* Once the pornographic imagination of Jud has been vanquished we expect the lovers Laurey and Curly to enjoy their honeymoon, their island out of time, but we know that their wished-for destiny is not the utopia of passion's golden purity but life as husband and wife in the human, time-bound community. Basically, one might say, it is a very Victorian story. Byron would have had as much fun with it as with the royal wedding had it been available as grist to feed into the mill of his *Don Juan.*

And so then, with Browning and *Oklahoma!* still in mind, to Westminster Cathedral on Trinity Sunday, the day on which is celebrated, as Dante celebrates it in the last canto of the *Commedia,* the divine collaboration of Father, Son, and Holy Ghost—the Holy Ghost whom Lawrence always celebrated, if in terms that would have given little comfort to the now convalescing Pope. Here, depicting their own pageant of love, are Eric Gill's great Stations of the Cross. And here on this day we heard these words from St. Paul's Second Letter to the Corinthians: "Live in peace, and the God of love and peace will be with you. Greet one another with the holy kiss."

What was this if not a charitable injunction to a world confused perhaps no less than ours by the conflicting imperatives of love?

Media Smears:
One Man's Experiences

A Noted Economist Fires Back
(1982)

THOMAS SOWELL

In the movie, *Absence of Malice,* lives are damaged and even destroyed by irresponsible reporting—and the law offers no real protection. In real life as well, the most damaging, unsupported, and inaccurate statements about an individual can be written and broadcast coast to coast, without the law's offering any meaningful recourse. Judges have so watered down the laws on slander and libel that only in special cases can you nail those who are being irresponsible, vindictive, or even outright liars.

I know. As one who has taken controversial stands on various issues, I have been the target of a smear campaign for more than a year. Demonstrably false statements have been made about me in the media and positions attributed to me that are the *direct opposite* of what I have said for years in my own published writings. And yet a lawsuit would probably do nothing but waste months of my time, at the end of which the smear artists could slip out through one of the many loopholes—and proclaim themselves vindicated and their charges substantiated.

Instead, let me submit some examples to the court of public opinion—some merely irresponsible, and others more vicious.

Wrong "Facts"

The most staggering of many false charges was made by CBS correspondent Lem Tucker on that network's morning television program. According to a broadcast by Tucker on October 13, 1981, my viewpoint "seems to place him in the school that believes that maybe most blacks are genetically inferior to whites." For a charge as sweeping and inflammatory as genetic inferiority of a race—*my* race—you would think there would have to be some speck of hard evidence. But you would be wrong. For ten years, I have repeatedly and extensively argued *against* the genetic inferiority theory—in four books, two newspapers, two magazines, and various lectures. These included a feature article I wrote on I.Q. in the *New York Times Magazine* of March 27, 1977. There I pointed out that European immigrants had the same I.Q. scores as blacks when they lived under conditions similar to blacks, and cited massive amounts of data I had collected on the subject.

Anyone who wanted the facts about my position could easily have found them. Lem Tucker chose instead to broadcast sensational rhetoric coast to coast. The closest thing to factual evidence that he had was a newspaper interview in which another reporter had asked where my personal "stubbornness and isolation" came from, and I suggested that these traits were probably inherited, since some of my relatives had similar personalities. How one gets from this to genetic inferiority is a mystery only Lem Tucker can solve.

False statements in the press can have serious consequences, even when they are not smears. In the *Washington Post* of February 5, 1981, Herbert Denton reported that I had formed an organization "which was incorporated this week in California under the name Black Alternatives Association, Inc." This organization never existed, even though the *Washington Post* story was carried coast to coast in other newspapers. It is a matter of public record when an organization is incorporated, so anyone can check the incorporation records for that week—or any other week—and find no "Black Alternatives" organization incorporated by Thomas Sowell.

Although the organization was nonexistent, the results of the story were quite real. For weeks an avalanche of mail and telephone calls came to my office and my one secretary. We struggled day in and day out to get our regular work done, to organize a conference that was scheduled, and to proofread the galleys for my book, *Ethnic America*—all the while being interrupted every few minutes by phone calls from people wanting to join the non-existent organization, or from reporters wanting a detailed blueprint of its far-flung operations, as reported in the *Washington Post.*

In order to try to keep up with our regular work despite incessant interruptions, my secretary and I began coming in to work earlier and earlier in the morning, and leaving later and later at night. We still fell behind. Eventually exhaustion caught up with us. She took a week off. My doctor put me on medication and I stayed home for two weeks. Our conference was cancelled, and other commitments and deadlines had to be left unmet.

What was the basis for the *Washington Post* story? Some friends and I were *thinking* of establishing an organization, but its specific activities had not been worked out, nor any money collected, nor an office rented or stationery printed. One of my associates reported his own speculations to Denton, who turned them into "facts"—and headlines—about *my* plans. When Denton phoned me for verification, I told him that there was already enough misinformation in the world, without his printing such a story. Apparently he disagreed.

Ironically, my staying home led to another fictitious story. *Jet* magazine reported that I was hospitalized in Palo Alto. Actually, I have not been hospitalized in more than a decade, and do not even know the location of a hospital in Palo Alto. But again, a fictitious story had real consequences. A member of my family on the East Coast read the *Jet* story and became alarmed. Having heard nothing about hospitalization from me, she concluded that I must be so gravely ill that the family was keeping the news from her because of her own serious heart condition. Her worst suspicions seemed to be confirmed when she phoned my home while I was out. I was at a local pool, swimming 500 yards while supposedly "hospitalized."

Among the many false charges in the media, the one that most piqued my curiosity was that I had "castigated" Vernon Jordan. Dorothy Gilliam of the *Washington Post* was the source of this charge, later repeated by others. I could not for the life of me remember mentioning Vernon Jordan, much less attacking him. I first went through two articles of mine that Gilliam was denouncing. No Vernon Jordan. Then I started going through the indexes of my books. Still no Vernon Jordan.

Finally, I wrote to Vernon Jordan. He had never heard of any such attack either, and advised me to "pay it no mind."

Not all demonstrably false statements can be attributed to political bias or personal animosity. Some media statements have been miles off base without being either favorable or unfavorable. For example, I have been repeatedly identified as a Republican, on television and in newspapers. In reality, I have never been a Republican, nor even addressed a Republican gathering. It has been a decade since I was a registered member of any party, and then I was a Democrat. The only partisan gathering I have ever addressed was an informal luncheon sponsored by the Libertarian Party.

Unsupported Insinuations

After the 1980 election, stories began to appear in many newspapers that I was going to become a Cabinet member in the Reagan Administration. Some papers said Secretary of Labor, others Secretary of Education, or of Housing and Urban Development. Some said Chairman of the Council of Economic Advisers. They all sounded very sure of their facts, though obviously one man could not be holding all these jobs.

I of course knew all along that I was not about to go to Washington for any job. I had declined offers of presidential appointments in previous administrations, and saw no reason to change now. But since no one in the new administration had asked me, it would have been a gratuitous insult to the incoming President to have said so. Finally I was asked, declined politely, and figured that was the end of that.

Not as far as the press was concerned.

Opinions that I had been expressing for more than a decade were now suddenly depicted as opportunistic statements echoing the Reagan Administration in order to get me a job in Washington. On January 31, 1981, the *Pittsburgh Courier* said: "Like flies chasing a garbage truck, opportunists of all stripes (and colors) are scrambling to align themselves with the new Reagan administration." Among these were "Thomas Sowell of the notorious Hoover Institution." Columnist Carl Rowan likewise said, "Sowell parrots the Reaganites," and included me among the "supplicants" for Administration largesse. None of those who wrote this way ever found it necessary to show where I had ever gotten a dime from the Reagan Administration.

The most they could come up with was my unpaid position as a member of a committee that met occasionally, had no powers, and could only offer outside advice to the Administration. Even this position I gave up after one meeting, when it became clear that the combination of jet lag and long meetings created medical problems for me.

But some newspapers would not give up the idea that I was part of the Reagan Administration, even after it was public knowledge that I was not. The Baton Rouge *Community Leader* called me "the most prominent Black policy maker," even though I never made a policy in my life. Lee Daniels in the *New York Times* called me "the Administration's favored black spokesman," even though I had never spoken a word for the Administration, had gone for months without saying anything publicly on any subject, and had turned down innumerable requests for interviews. How one can be a spokesman without speaking remains a mystery.

In a similar vein, a book reviewer in the *New York Times* called my *Ethnic America* a book "to be feared—as a signpost pointing to the probable future direction of the present national administration regarding minorities." Not a single policy is recommended in *Ethnic America,* which is a history book. It was begun in 1978 and completed before the 1980 elections, which is to say, before there was a Reagan Administration. Even now, I have no hard information that anybody in the Administration has ever read it.

The really ugly insinuations concern money. A writer in the *Sacramento Observer* depicted an article of mine as showing a "soul sold for a little money." *What* money was of course never specified. Money also figured prominently in the *Washington Post* story about my non-existent organization—$100,000 which unnamed corporations and foundations had "promised" to contribute. I wish I knew who made those promises, because I have not seen a penny materialize.

There is an irony for me in the constant emphasis on money. As one who quit his job as an economic analyst for the world's largest corporation to become an academic, I was hardly following a course of action likely to maximize my income. Moreover, even within the academic world, there was far more money to be made, over the past 20 years, saying the direct opposite of what I said. Large lecture fees, foundation grants, directorships of minority programs (and of major corporations) went to those who shouted and shook their fists and demanded special programs. Those of us who questioned that whole approach were at best tolerated. At more than one university during the 1960s, I lived in cramped, rented quarters while "militant" black academics owned spacious homes. And they drove Mercedes while I drove a Volkswagen. Yet innuendoes about selling out were directed toward me, but never toward them. The blatant facts of the situation seemed not to make the slightest difference. Nor did it seem to occur to critics that no one sells out to the lowest bidder.

Even in today's changed climate of opinion, a number of blacks at the other end of the political spectrum make several times my income. Again, the media never question whether what they say might be influenced by what they receive from the very programs they champion.

Personal Attacks and Double Standards

For much of the decade of the 1970s, I engaged in research on American ethnic groups. What I discovered often conflicted with prevailing views in the media and among politicians and civil rights leaders. For example, I discovered that group differences in income had many causes, some of them with much greater impact than employer discrimination. A close look at the data also showed that school busing and "affirmative action" policies not only failed to achieve their goals, but generally ended up making the disadvantaged even more disadvantaged. Some of these facts were surprising to me, and forced me to change some of my own thinking. I expected them to be surprising to others, and probably, not very popular.

What I did not expect was that the facts would be so widely and totally disregarded, and that so much of the response would consist of purely personal attacks on me—and that the press would apply a double standard in the controversies that followed.

For example, in December 1980, *Washington Post* reporter Herbert Denton told me that an NAACP official had called me by the vile epithet, "a house nigger." When I threw the charge back in his face, the headline in Denton's story proclaimed *my* attack on the NAACP as "house niggers." You would have to dig quite a ways into the story to find out who attacked and who replied. A later story by Denton called me "vituperative" in my "attacks" on the civil rights organizations.

When former Cabinet member Patricia Roberts Harris proclaimed that I did not know what poverty was, no one questioned what basis she had for that statement, or what relevance it had to the facts about public policy. It so happened that I grew up in such poverty that I was eight years old before I lived in a home with hot running water. Patricia Roberts Harris, though black, grew up in a middle-class home and in college belonged to a sorority too snobbish to admit dark-skinned women. When I reported these facts, there was a storm of outrage in the press—and claims that I was attacking Mrs. Harris for being light-skinned! The lady herself played this theme to the hilt, saying that it was a "use of South African apartheid concepts of racial gradations, combined with an exotic infusion of Marxist class warfare notions." By and large, the press bought her version.

The behind-the-scenes story of this controversy was more of the same double standard. Editor Meg Greenfield of the *Washington Post* tried repeatedly to get me to water down or eliminate various criticisms—including that of Patricia Harris—in a pair of articles I wrote for that paper. I challenged her to find a single misstatement of fact in my articles, but she complained instead of the harshness of what was said. After her many phone calls, weeks of delay, and heated words between us, Meg Greenfield finally agreed to print what I had said—but with a weary air of being much put upon.

No such standards applied to the many articles which the *Post* then printed denouncing my position. For one thing, they appeared much too quickly for Meg Greenfield to have engaged in weeks of agonized discussions and hand-wringing. Neither harshness, nor irrelevance, nor inaccuracy stopped them from being published. If someone wanted to refer to my "blackface sociology" or to my non-existent castigation of Vernon Jordan, that was fine. If they had no specific facts but only vague innuendoes about "selling out," that was fine. If later Carl Rowan wanted to say that I did more harm to blacks than Quisling did to his fellow-Norwegians under Nazi rule, the *Post* was ready to print it.

Apparently, it all depends on whose ox is being gored.

I have not been the only target of such unsupported innuendoes or such double standards. Various black writers have emerged in recent years to challenge some of the prevailing assumptions of the civil rights establishment and have encountered personal attacks rather than substantive criticism of their work. Sociologist William Julius Wilson of the University of Chicago produced a widely read study that questioned whether racial economic differences today were nearly as much due to racial discrimination as in the past. Economist Walter Williams of George Mason University wrote a prize-winning article on numerous government programs that harm minorities—including some programs, such as the minimum wage law, that are ostensibly intended to be beneficial. Former civil rights attorney Derrick Bell, now dean of the law school at the University of Oregon, questioned whether massive busing was really in the interest of black children. Professor of psychiatry Gloria Powell of UCLA published a massive study which failed to show any clear pattern of psychological gains by black children who had been "integrated" in the public schools, despite what was widely expected, promised, or claimed.

Several things are remarkable about this group of people. They arrived at their conclusions by research, independently of each other, and without a common social or political position. They are academics with neither a financial nor a political stake in one conclusion rather than another. Yet they have all been accused of seeking personal gain or political advancement, or of being too affluent to understand the ghetto. Yet the press has seldom used the same standards when judging their critics. The *New York Times,* for example, asked NAACP Executive Director Benjamin Hooks whether Walter Williams's middle-class status and income did not undermine Williams's positions on racial issues, without ever considering whether Hooks's own background was not far more middle class than Williams's or his current income far higher—and dependent on the very programs he advocated. Carl Rowan's innuendoes that people were taking certain public positions on issues to get political appointments for themselves centered on two academics (Williams and myself) who have never been politically appointed to any job—though Rowan himself has. Nathaniel Jones of the NAACP publicly questioned whether Derrick Bell was not trying for personal career gain by opposing busing, though in fact the real gains were to be made by taking Jones's position—which gained him a federal judgeship through appointment by President Carter, while Bell remains an academic.

If facts about issues are to be subordinated to speculations about personal motives, then at least the standards can be the same for those on opposite sides of the issues.

"Real" Meanings

When there is nothing that can even be lifted out of context to support a damaging interpretation, some writers resort to reporting your "real" meaning. "Real" meanings require no evidence whatever, and can never be disproved. They are ideal for smears.

According to book reviewer Paul Buhle in the *Nation,* the real purpose of *Ethnic America* was to offer "economic and historical justification" for "gutting social services." Nowhere in the book is any social service mentioned as requiring reduction. According to St. Clair Drake in the *Palo Alto Weekly,* the real purpose is to "put forward a conservative agenda"—though no agenda at all is put forth in the book—a fact which other reviewers (including those in *Time* and *Newsweek*) complained about. In the same vein, David Herbert Donald declared in the *New York Times* that "Mr. Sowell is really less interested in the past than in the present and the future," even though the book is a history, with almost no discussion of current policies.

Among the "real" meanings discerned was one presented by Carl Rowan in such a way that unwary readers might think it was a direct quote from me about my career: "I did all this on my own, with hard work, so I don't want government to give any lazy bastard anything." What I actually said about my own career was written a decade ago in *Black Education: Myths and Tragedies:*

It would be premature at best and presumptuous at worst to attempt to draw sweeping or definitive conclusions from my personal experiences. It would be especially unwarranted to draw Horatio Alger conclusions, that perseverance and/or ability "win out" despite obstacles. The fact is, I was losing in every way until my life was changed by the Korean War, the draft, and the GI Bill—none of which I can take credit for. I have no false modesty about having seized the opportunity and worked to make it pay off, but there is no way to avoid the fact that there first had to be an opportunity to seize.

Words lose a lot in translation when other people start reporting your "real" meaning. Lem Tucker on the CBS morning program had me claiming "that he alone, almost without bootstraps, pulled himself out of the ghetto through Harvard and the University of Chicago." Others have depicted me as advising other blacks to emulate my example, though they could never seem to come up with any specific quote from when I had done so. It would of course be a ridiculous piece of advice, for luck was an important element, and there is no way to emulate luck. What I have urged is that other disadvantaged people be allowed more options—school vouchers as just one example—and less advice from "experts."

Responsible Journalism

Any discussion of irresponsible or malicious statements in the press is itself misleading if it does not mention that there are fair, honest, and intelligent journalists as well. But it takes relatively few individuals to keep a smear campaign going. And once certain distortions are repeated often enough, they become "facts" to many readers and even to other writers.

People are constantly telling me how surprised they are at reading something I have written, because it is so different from what they have been led to believe by the media. But the problem is much bigger than me or my ideas. If I were going to let smears stop me, I would have stopped years ago. What is far more important is that an atmosphere of character assassination is not one in which there is a widespread clash of opposing views. It is not even a question of which view is right. No single individual or set of "leaders" has a monopoly on understanding. Even the truth may be an incomplete truth, and need additional perspectives that lie beyond one person's vision. In short, the process of airing different perspectives is even more important than the question of which is closest to the truth.

Implicit in much that is said about the emotional subject of race and ethnicity is the presumption that *no honest disagreement is possible* on the orthodoxy promoted by the civil rights leaders and liberal politicians. "Lay not that flattering unction to your soul," Hamlet warned. It is a warning that is as timely today as it was centuries ago.

Historically, people who have looked at things differently have always been seen as a threat—in science, religion, the military, and every other field of human concern and commitment. Even the most advanced nations in Western Civilization—including the United States—burned women alive as witches within the past three centuries. Where feelings run deep, rationality has often broken down. Moreover, the time pressures of the media and the need for excitement to attract readers and viewers promote the creation of stereotypes, bogeymen, and scapegoats. But surely it is time we learned from history that the particular victims and scapegoats are not the only losers in an atmosphere of witch-hunting. We all lose when we stifle the diversities of opinion which alone give us some hope of understanding complex and difficult social issues.

High Life/Low Life
by Jeffrey Bernard and Taki

(1982)

TOM WOLFE

Jeffrey Bernard and Taki are two of the hottest tickets in British journalism. They write for the *Spectator* of London, in whose venerable ecru pages they stand out like a couple of yobbos looking for a brawl. They approach BritLit's favorite medium, the essay, with the instincts of a Westbrook Pegler. They throw open the door and blurt it out. This may explain why they are so popular in a country that produces graceful and witty essayists in job lots but very few exciting ones.

Taki—he uses only the one name—writes a column called "High Life," based on his ongoing adventures as the playboy younger son of one of the Greek shipping tycoons, John Theodoracopulos. Bernard writes the complementary column, "Low Life," based on his adventures as a drunk, a debtor, a cad, a sloth, a loser, a failure. He does it so well, however, to such applause, he may be writing himself out of a role.

Both writers subvert the customary literary approaches to the upper and lower orders. Taki tells his readers that, contrary to what they may have read in the *New Statesman,* the *Spectator*'s IngSoc (English Socialist) rival, rich people are on the whole more pleasant and more admirable than other people. He cheerfully reports that his own family, the Theodoracopuloses, are worth much more than the 200 million pounds mentioned in Nigel Dempster's gossip column.

True, Taki indulges in the perfectly conventional British sport of ridiculing the *nouveaux riches,* but he has no use for the standard British weapons of subtlety, irony, and the snigger. Taki prefers hyperbole and outrageous directness. In "High Life" rich Italians are fat and cowardly. Taki's fellow rich Greeks are fat and gauche and have repulsive fat children. Americans—or rich Americans in London, at any rate—are thin and stringy. They have grown prematurely old from jogging every morning at dawn, imitating the speech and dress of the English upper classes all day, and cringing every night before their own hideous snarling wives, who free-base testosterone.

At Taki's favorite seaside resort, Vouliagmeni, ten miles east of Athens, once the very picture of quiet luxury, he now finds himself shank to flank with rich Arabs "who keep spitting in front of my cabana as if it were a spittoon.

Their children do biggies in the swimming pool and the place has to be drained after every meal.''

Every daughter of the rich wears ''a pair of tight jeans with pencil-thin legs, a hot-green tube top, a purple belt, a yellow plastic bracelet, high-heeled shoes, frizzy hair and two bright spots of pink rouge on her cheeks. She could be the daughter of a duke or a postman. One could never tell them apart.'' All of them, young, old, Arabs, Greeks, Englishmen, Americans, the lot, are sinking into the ooze of their own rhinal catarrh, thanks to the only thing in the world they are willing to die for: cocaine. No sane person, says Taki, goes into the lavatory of a chic nightclub anywhere in the West without ''a surgical mask as if in an asbestos plant during an explosion. Masses of humanity sniff, snort, sneeze, cough and expectorate. One popular London club has even taken out the toilet bowls as redundant.''

Clubs and resorts are Taki's favorite settings. Through them scamper such characters as Bianca Jagger, who he insists is ancient, Halston, whom he calls ''Dracula,'' Diane von Furstenberg, who he says is a nonentity from Belgium who trades (in the rag trade) on the name of the ''gay prince'' she married, and John Aspinall, a gambling club operator and wild animal tamer whom he admires. In fact, Taki relishes it all, and his hyperbole often takes off into marvelous deliriums reminiscent of Céline's *Death on the Installment Plan* or a Gillray tableau.

But through the caricature runs a cold vein. There is a touch of Mishima about Taki (who named the yachts his father gave him *Bushido I* and *Bushido II*). After long nights of wrenching his reticular formation out of shape at Annabel's and Xenon, he is in a mood to insist on patriotism and the warrior virtues of honor, courage, manliness, physical prowess, and chivalry. Taki is himself a karate adept and tennis star who has represented Greece in both sports in international games. In 1980, at the age of 43, he fought in a New York Athletic Club boxing tournament in the middleweight division.

He is one of the few highly vocal foes of feminism outside the ranks of the Upland Baptists. Last year his article in *The American Spectator* called ''Ugly Women''—arguing that ugly thoughts and shrill voices turn the good looks of women like Jane Fonda and Shirley MacLaine into revolting masks—provoked feminist groups to protests and manifestos. In Taki's book the ultimate decadence of people of wealth and power consists of caving in to feminism, pacifism, or other forms of Left chic rather than defending their own values or even their own class interests. To Taki the question of what, besides cocaine, the rich people of the West might be willing to die for is not funny. An underlying fury at the sight of the West suffocating in its own flab puts iron in the soul of his wild gift for farce and insult.

Meantime, Jeffrey Bernard's ''Low Life'' is scarcely what Orwell, Steinbeck, or the proletarian novelists had in mind when they wrote about being down and out in the 1930s. Bernard often makes note of his own appearance. His hair is ''the color of man-made ice'' and loaded with dandruff, and a dentist has informed him that all of his top teeth will have to come out on March 20. ''When I think of what my body and I have gone through over the past 45 years,

I should have thought it would have the decency to hang on a little longer—at least until the hot weather started. It is not a pretty sight. Starting at the top, the memory banks are now completely empty, the concentration fuses have blown and only a few basic animal instincts remain. Fleeting moments of lust and greed occasionally threaten to turn the motor over but the spark is weak."

Many columns begin with our half-toothless hero sitting in a saloon in the middle of the day. The most ordinary barroom touches irritate him, starting with the sign behind the bar: "You don't have to be mad to work here, but it helps." The regulars at the bar are saying: "Squire—neck of the woods—ding dong (for Bells whisky)—my better half—tincture—at this moment in time—gee and tee—long time no see—I've only got one pair of hands—similar?—don't tell my bank manager—cold enough for you?" The barmaid is saying: "Plenty of work about for you, Jeff? No? I should have thought you'd be doing very well. But it's the same for all of us really, isn't it? I mean there just isn't the money about, is there? Mind you, it's all right for some, I dare say; farmers and such like. No, when you think what a pound's worth today, well. Funny though, I should have thought those magazines and things you write for, I should have thought they'd pay very well. No? Of course, you know what you ought to do? I'll tell you. You should write a book. I'll tell you what. If I could write I'd sit down and write a book. God, the stories I could tell."

Then the "TV commercial boys" come in and start saying, "Yes, I know, love, but if we cut it there—bang, bang—we wouldn't have to hold him in long shot coming down those stairs looking so dreadfully bored. Let's face it, loves, we're here, basically, to sell the wretched stuff." "I couldn't agree more. No, Basil's right. Cut it and let's scrap the dissolve. Incidentally, did you see Richard Three last night? My God. Of course, basically, it's a really boring play, particularly if it isn't done well, but I thought . . ."

For some reason this drives him to the edge. "For the umpteenth time in six months I make a mental note to ask some bright spark like Bron Waugh to write a piece actually attacking those people who keep using the word basically when it's not necessary. . . . It makes me think they're all talking a different language which, at this moment in time, basically, is what it's all about. I mean, I know you've got to let it all hang out and stay loose which is quite incredible and absolutely amazing in a basic sort of way, basically, that is, but it's really beginning to bug me. Basically, I'm pretty tolerant but if I go on hearing that word I think I might flip. I mean it's really draggy and, basically, out."

Then it dawns on you that you have been skillfully drawn into the mental atmosphere of a man with a terrific hangover. Like most aching drunks he tries to transform what is really troubling him into those demons, Other People, the people who say "Similar?" when they mean "Have another?" and "basically" when they mean "I dare say." Every so often, however, comes a column in which Bernard—or the main character of "Low Life" he has turned himself into—confronts himself directly. He tells about the moment, the final five or ten minutes, in which he breaks up with a girlfriend of long standing. What troubles him most of all is his inability to summon up any emotion. After she left "I felt strangely ashamed at not being more upset so I put some Mahler on the record player to see if that would provoke the appropriate misery. Nothing. In fact, I sat there listening to the syrup feeling distinctly irritated."

What Bernard has done is create a low life that is more dreadful to the readers of the *Spectator* of London (or Bloomington) than visions of the slums or the Third World. His world is that of the failed middle-class intellectual. His columns are like slices of the novel he says he is going to write and keeps cadging advances for and never sits down to. He has taken the intellectual's gamble—cut his ties with conventional life in favor of dreams of low-wattage glory—and lost. He is finally cut off even from the commonplace emotions that would let him feel properly sorry for himself.

It is here that Bernard's low life and Taki's high life converge. Both are writing about the *homo novus* of the twentieth century, the smart number who is too befuddled and deracinated to fight back, even when pushed to the wall. The remarkable thing, in England, is to find two gifted writers who are able to bring that character alive in such an uninhibited way.

But Taki and Bernard have an advantage over their colleagues: Neither has ever attended a major English university. Most bright young writers in England go to universities such as Oxford and Cambridge, which operate on the tutorial system. Every week the student writes an essay and then reads it out loud to his tutor, his don, a figure of maturity, sophistication, and certified wisdom. Nothing is more embarrassing, when prose is read aloud—particularly in England, to a don—than purple passages, leaps of the imagination that fall flat, elaborate word play, leg-slappers, slang, sentiment, personal revelations, obvious emotions, or excessive effects of any sort. The mooncalf intellectual is soon operantly conditioned, as the psychologists say, to avoid such areas altogether. After three years of it he is likely to turn into a polite essayist of consummate grace and wit who will never embarrass himself or a publisher in print for the rest of his days. His chances of becoming a good novelist or a lively journalist, however, are remote. The field demonstration of the above is the past eighty-two years of British history. In this century there have been scarcely half a dozen British novelists or playwrights of the first rank who have come from out of the great tutorial universities. After John Galsworthy and Evelyn Waugh the list peters out rapidly. Orwell, Shaw, O'Casey, Joyce, Lawrence, Maugham, Pinter, Burgess, Behan, and Conrad, like Dickens, Hardy, and Kipling before them, were spared the opportunity.

Jeffrey Bernard, who dropped out of Britain's Naval College, and Taki, who bounced around schools in Europe and America, are English journalism's latest evidence of the exuberant literary life just over the buttressed walls.

Seasick

(1982)

GEOFFREY NORMAN

NBC reporter Robert Bazell went to sea in a fourteen-foot aluminum boat. His wife and two daughters were with him in the boat. He ran out of gas. The boat began to drift out to sea. Bazell jumped overboard and swam for help. It took him about three hours to reach shore. A search was launched but it was three days before the boat was found. Bazell's family was safe, if mightily inconvenienced, and that was that. A happy ending to a minor drama, I thought when I first read the one paragraph item in the morning paper.

But I forgot that we were dealing here with a television newsman, a species that has been bred for both ignorance and arrogance. When you line breed intensively, something is inevitably lost. For example, collie dogs have been bred for long-pointed heads and it has gone so far that there isn't enough room in the animal's head for everything it needs. Most of them have detached retinas. TV newsmen have lost all sense of proportion somewhere in their breeding.

Those thoughts came to me as I read one of those rare follow-up stories in my morning paper. Seems that Mr. Bazell, upon being reunited with the family, charged that the Coast Guard had been lax in launching a search for his boat and dependents. Now I don't know a lot about reporting what is loosely called the "news" on television, but I know something about small boats and the Coast Guard. And I like to think I know a little about humility and a sense of proportion. I know for sure that I wouldn't go to sea in a fourteen-foot boat and run out of gas. And if I did and then had to swim for help—not such a good idea, by the way—I would be a little shy about having my picture in the paper and being quoted about what a poor job the Coast Guard did in coming to my rescue. You see, I might think I'd done a damnfool thing. I'd be too ashamed to find fault with anyone, especially the people who'd saved my family at some inconvenience to themselves and for pay that TV newsmen would no doubt consider indecent.

As for the Coast Guard, they have a problem with finding able recruits since they have been loaded down with all the equal opportunity baggage of the last decade's social progress. Most of the people who enlist have spent too much time watching television and don't know how to do technical things such as read a book. But while seamanship has declined, the demographics are better. There might be a story there for Mr. Bazell. He could dress up like Mike Wallace in a suit of indignation and interview a recruit from Detroit on how to tie a sheepshank.

Now since Mr. Bazell, like Mr. Wallace and virtually everyone else on television, feels competent to judge everything except his own performance, someone will have to do that for him. I will take on that heavy burden.

First, you don't as a rule go out in big water in a little boat. If you do, you ought to have a radio and some distress signals because even if you are smart enough to leave with enough gas, you may lose power for any number of other reasons. Friend of mine, for instance, ran over a shark and tore up his prop. He carried a spare, however, and had the problem corrected in a few minutes. All by himself.

But let's say you've spent too much time in front of the television to know how to repair a motor, even though you are smart enough to know they burn gas. Well, if you have a radio, you can call for help which beats swimming every time. And if you don't have any navigational aids so that you can give your rescuer your exact position, then you fire a flare, which can be seen from great distances, to aid him. It helps if you have an anchor aboard. You tie a line to one end (don't forget that) and throw it over the side and that will keep your boat from drifting to sea if you have lost power for some reason such as running over a shark. (Nobody runs out of gas.)

There are other rules of safe seamanship that might be helpful to Mr. Bazell. But he won't learn them watching television. Nor, obviously, by committing television. So Mr. Bazell might want to enroll in a small boat safety and seamanship course with the Coast Guard. If the NBC limo doesn't take him to class and he has to drive his own car, he might want to remember to put some gas in the tank. Or perhaps that is the responsibility of the Highway Patrol.

II
Americana

Vermillion (with two ll's),
South Dakota

(1970)

JOHN R. COYNE, JR.

South Dakota calls itself "the land of infinite variety," and no place in the state better epitomizes this variousness than Vermillion. Vermillion is easy to find, lying as it does half-way between Elk Point and Yankton, about eight miles off Route 29, the main road between Sioux City, Iowa, home of the nation's ninth largest stockyard, and Mitchell, South Dakota, famous for the Mitchell Corn Palace, a structure constructed entirely of corn cobs.

Vermillion's three major motels, the Wigwam, the Tomahawk, and the Prairie, adequately serve the unfortunately limited tourist trade. Of these, the Prairie is perhaps the best, for it offers not only a striking view of corn fields but also a fine restaurant and bar which adjoin a twelve-lane bowling alley. Here the traveler sinks deep into a narrow corafoam chair, sips his Grain Belt beer, and watches through a plate-glass partition the fierce competitions among members of the local bowling leagues. The Prairie epitomizes that quality South Dakotans call "class," a term admittedly hard to pin down but which might be defined as that sophisticated but lighthearted spirit which led the managers of the Prairie to paint the words "Bulls" and "Heifers" on the restroom doors.

Another establishment with class is the Charcoal Lounge in the heart of downtown Vermillion. Like the Prairie it is frequented by faculty from the University of South Dakota and young executives from the J.C. Penney Store and the alf-alfa plant, and like the Prairie it serves hearty meals of well-done beef and, to the delight of the gourmet, salads prepared in the great midwestern fashion, delectable combinations of cottage cheese, bananas, jello, canned fruit salad, shredded coconut, pineapple and whipped marshmallow. But the greatest single attraction of the Charcoal Lounge is Ronnie, the only bartender in the midwest with a gouty big toe. Ronnie can spin many a good yarn about his affliction, and if you ask about it, stranger or not, he will regale you with stories far into the night. ("See? I had to cut this here hole in my best shoes," Ronnie will say, hoisting his foot up onto the bar and wiggling the fabled toe.)

But, as seasoned travelers know, one wishes not only to frequent those places with class, for by so doing one fails to meet the "real people," for Vermillion is most compact, consisting as it does of about thirty weatherbeaten, dirty, old buildings facing one another across Main Street. And it is just across

71

from the Charcoal Lounge, on the south side of Main Street, that one encounters the "real people" at play.

The best place to get to know the natives is Hogan's, a quaint old tavern with a utilitarian bar, an enormous plank dance floor, some old wooden tables, and a juke box which boasts one of the best collections of Ernest Tubb records in the world. The mood is simple and heartwarming at Hogan's, where farmers, truck drivers, drunken agency Indians, and the boys from the alf-alfa plant congregate nightly. The talk is boisterous but good-humored: "I seen who YOU was with last night." "Hee-haw," they shout, and slap their legs and stamp their feet. "You never!" The stranger need feel no apprehension, for he is soon made a part of the fun: "What the hell YOU looking at, Dude?" "Hee-haw." "How'd you like a good stompin?"

Ladies are treated chivalrously at Hogan's ("There's that Ellie that works up to the diner. I'd like to get me some of that.") and the proprietor, a diminutive man whose solemn demeanor cloaks a fun-loving nature ("Old Squint would murder his mother for a nickel"), delights in serving up lady-like drinks, the favorite being Seagram's and Dr. Pepper. The men, most of them traditionalists, prefer the customary shot and beer, although on festive occasions they will order coke-highs (bourbon and Coca-Cola).

Hogan's doesn't specialize in haute cuisine, as do the Prairie and the Charcoal Lounge, but one can always enjoy a tasty, pre-cooked, cellophane-wrapped ham and cheese sandwich which Old Squint expertly heats in a small aluminum oven. And the Beer Nuts at Hogan's are justly famous. "Gimme some of them there Beer Nuts, you miserable old bastard," the jocular cry rings out nightly.

The numerous other attractions of Vermillion are too various to detail here: the public library, which contains a complete collection of the novels of Frank Yerby and autographed first editions of the works of Badger Clark, South Dakota's Poet Laureate; and the handsome new building of the Wesley Foundation on the USD campus, where on Sundays one can enjoy tea with Preem, peanut-butter cookies, and good, clean conversation. The movie theater in Vermillion regularly reruns the best of the Doris Day films, and occasionally there is an old Jane Withers or Judy Canova for the connoisseur. And don't think that the electronic revolution has by-passed South Dakota. McLuhan himself would be impressed with the impact of radio station WNAX in Yankton on the area. The wizardry of radio keeps Vermillion residents informed of exciting local news stories (one of the most gripping of these recently recounted how a farmer from Sweat lost his life when his head was caught in the power takeoff of his John Deere tractor) as well as of more important national news, such as the daily reports of hog prices from the Chicago Livestock Auctions. WNAX also carries a wealth of educational and cultural programs, such as Lifeline and The Singing Lady.

And finally, no description of Vermillion would be complete without an appreciation of the scenery it offers. Perhaps most striking of all is the view of the small brown hills of Nebraska that can be injoyed from a bluff on the west edge of town. (For the convenience of the nature lover, the city has thoughtfully placed a green bench atop the bluff. One should sit with caution, however, for the bench has been there a long time and nature's erosive processes have sharply heightened the danger of splinters.) There are times, admittedly, when the prospect is somewhat obscured by smoke belching from the alf-alfa plant which nestles in a gulch just below the bluff. In fact, the traveler might be well advised at such times to remove himself quickly, for to the uninitiated the smell of burning alf-alfa may prove unpleasant and may even cause mild gasping and choking.

Nevertheless, stenches aside, Vermillion, South Dakota, should definitely rate a visit by that traveler through "the land of infinite variety" who possesses sophisticated sensibilities and an appreciation of the exotic and colorful.

Booze and Pot:
The Metaphysical Distinction

(1973)

E.T. VEAL

Suppose you enjoyed breaking the legs of small dogs. You live in a society notorious for cynophilia, so your neighbors might object. Indeed, they might haul you before a municipal court on some such unlibertarian charge as "cruelty to animals," threatening to separate you for a time from both canine and human society. How would you defend your freedom?

There are (barring a plea that mutilation of animals is symbolic speech protected by the First Amendment) two available courses. One is to explain straightforwardly to the jury why you like to break dog's legs. You might appeal to the musical sound of slowly cracking bones or to the sense of personal fulfillment to be found in mastering another being's fate or to the need for rebellion against an Establishment that employs dogs in its military operations.

Such arguments might save you from prison—by convincing your neighbors that you belonged in an asylum.

However, you might argue differently, and, I suspect, with greater prospect of success. Instead of explaining, *reclassify.* Announce that you are engaged in "scientific research," not, admittedly, of the customary, hide-bound sort, but research nevertheless. Point out that acknowledged scientists infect small dogs with painful diseases, subject them to dubious surgeries, and even, sometimes, break their legs. If society does not punish *those* researchers, why should it punish *you?* Your case may not carry the day, because the common men on juries often possess a *quantum sufficit* of common sense, but you will surely impress the judge or the Court of Appeals (for judges are educated men after the twentieth century fashion, and therefore more impressed by Classes than by Things). Thus, you may eventually win in the higher tribunals and be able to return to your individual pursuit of happiness. Maybe you will end up as an "historic case in the struggle for civil liberties," and be invited to address a banquet of the ACLU.

Putting Things into Classes is the beginning of reason. Imagining that this process alters the Things is the beginning of silliness. And silliness is not a rare affliction. It is not limited to madmen who establish a common ground between torture and medical research. Everyday politicians and publicists seize on the farthest-fetched analogies between A and Z to prove that placing these letters

74

at the opposite ends of the alphabet is an illiberal prejudice that society can no longer tolerate.

This is the error that permeates most present discussion of marijuana. Both marijuana and alcohol, used in sufficient quantity, cause marked changes in behavior, most strikingly a decline in what our sober selves would call "rationality." From this point of resemblance, it has become an assumption of most debate that marijuana is simply the counter-culture's version of the martini. A favorite juxtaposition of movie and television script-writers is the booze-squiffing parent and the pot-smoking child. The implication is that between alcohol and marijuana, there is merely a distinction without a difference, and that Daddy is a fascist hypocrite for supporting laws that jail Sonny's friends and suppliers. The title of a recent pro-legalization-of-pot book, *Marijuana: The New Prohibition,* states the argument concisely.

In various forms, this argument has been stated so often that everyone seems to have overlooked a point that at once springs to mind as soon as one steps back and looks at the implications of the equation: it tells as heavily against pot as for it. The Old Prohibitionists, after all, were not wrong when they claimed that liquor has many effects that society would be better off without. Broken homes, barroom brawls, DT's, and hangovers were not spawned by Carrie Nation's fancies. What defeated Prohibition was not a paucity of solid arguments against alcohol's use, nor a considered decision that the use was worth the abuse, but the fact that strong drink is too firmly rooted in the affections of western man to be abolished by legislative *fiat.* Where Bacchus is not so much at home, as in the Moslem lands, governments have been able to restrict his worship and hew down his altars. American oil company employees in Saudi Arabia have discovered that they must erect clandestine stills; the *gendarmerie* has dried up the bootleg traffic in spirits.

Despite the blossoming of the counter-culture, its favored intoxicant is still no stronger here than liquor in Saudi Arabia. Confining its use to the fringes of society presents no insuperable difficulties. Ninety-five percent of Americans have no strong affection for pot. They will submit to regulation, leaving the dissenters as fish in a desert.

With no reason to fear a massive backlash of civil disobedience such as Prohibition inspired, one can make a pretty good case for depriving Sonny of his quasi-martini. Only a mad sense of fair play would say that the existence of one evil justifies the existence of all others. Because some murderers will never be caught, we don't free the ones who are (at least we didn't used to). If the rescue party arrives after half the passengers on the sinking ship are already drowned, it doesn't abandon the rest out of a sense of equity. A man who can stop an arsonist is not persuaded to refrain on the ground that the building next door has been destroyed by lightning. Similarly, on the basis of the argument we are considering, marijuana has no claim to legality just because no one has figured out an effective way to ban alcohol.

Some readers have probably already come up with an answer to my inversion of their standard debating point. They are muttering to themselves, "This fellow writes so glibly about logic, yet he's no master of the art. Look at the silly error that he's just now committed." And what, pray, is my mistake? "You assume that alcohol and marijuana have the same effects. But they don't, so your sophistical little inversion is irrelevant."

Yes, that is the proper reply. My inverted argument proceeds from a false premiss. *But I have taken that premiss from the argument that I am inverting.* If alcohol and marijuana have substantially different effects, then they are different Things belonging in different Classes. There is no more reason to accord them the same treatment than there is to give medical research grants to animal torturers. Marijuana must stand on its own, not lean on the legal privileges of liquor.

Outside the debating room, the friends of marijuana are well enough aware that its resemblance to alcohol is remote. They never apply to the use of pot the restraints that drinkers apply to liquor as a matter of course. I fancy that the most ardent friend of bourbon would have felt it somewhat inappropriate for me to imbibe a flask of that beverage at my Yale graduation ceremony. But some of my classmates were "turning on" at the same ceremony, with no visible reprobation from their pro-marijuana comrades. As a consumer of alcohol, I should not be gleeful to learn that junior high school students were sneaking to the lavatories for shots of brandy between classes. Have you ever heard an advocate of marijuana deplore its use by teens and sub-teens?

As the final proof, why, except because they believe that the two substances are fundamentally different, should those who favor cannabis be so outrightly hostile toward liquor? Their writings seethe with sneer at the besotted older generation, unfavorably contrasted with their own upstanding selves. Sometimes they go further than literary attack, as when the *Yale Daily News* tried, two years back, to interest the New Haven Police in closing down Mory's. Men do not draw distinctions so bitterly unless they imagine that some real distinctions exist to be drawn.

The first obvious distinction—it may seem superficial, but it springs from something deeper—is a difference in number. Alcohol has many uses. Some men do drink to escape the world. But others drink to join it more firmly. A proper drinking party with old jokes and songs and old friends (whom you may have met only an hour ago) is, as the Greeks knew, a lifeline pulling us back to the world of things and men from the realm of introspective solitude into which it is so easy to slip (into which the solitary drunk, with his eternal, egoistic reveries, *has* slipped). This sort of drinking is not confined to festive occasions. The quiet beer after work, the quarter-hour that dissipates our narrow, fiendish concentration and prepares our spirits to receive what the world has next to offer us, is also a "social drink," though no one may be nearby. Nor should I forget that beer and wine and brandy and whiskey can be drunk from a mere liking for their aromas and tastes. If they were suddenly to lose all their physiological effects, wine would still be taken with meals and beer with snacks. Brandy would still be just the thing to round off a banquet, and whiskey would remain a noble accompaniment to the evening.

Now, marijuana may be excellent for its own peculiar use, but it has only one. It affects the mental processes. It gives rise to what its users call "new perceptions." It permits men to fly from the mundaneness of their everyday senses into a realm of "sensitivity." But this is all. No one goes to a pot party simply for a sociable evening with the boys. No one puffs a non-intoxicating quantity of grass for relaxation. Never do you hear of pot-and-pretzels or of a hostess searching for the right variety of cannabis to enhance her dinner nor of anyone eulogizing the flavor of vintage reefers. Consciousness-changing is marijuana's only trade.

Its users find this trade well worth the imposts. Given encouragement, they will devote many unstoned hours to praising the pleasure, enlightenment, and insight that they find in their "new state of consciousness." They express pity for the rest of us. How much happier and wiser the world would be if everyone turned on!

Alcohol has never promised so much. Bacchus too will rescue you from the "light of common day" if you let him. He, however, says frankly that his method is to blot out the dull light, not to provide a superior illumination. If you ask him for a less drastic remedy, he points back at the world, at the very tiresomeness that you wanted to get away from. He turns your face towards the human being next to you, toward the bench you are sitting on, toward the taste and feel of the glass in your hand. *In vino veritas*—which means, truth is found *in* Things, not away from them. *In vino, in rebus, non in te ipso!*

No one should be surprised that western philosophy began in *symposia*, drinking parties, nor that the philosophy with such roots has always had as its central assumption the existence of an objective universe to which individual speculations must conform. The whole West, divided on everything else, unites to shout the great axiom, that thinking does not make it so.

This is not an axiom congenial to marijuana. The pot-smoker receives his "insights" by peering into himself, not by fixing his attention on the world, and he regards his inspirations as private truths. He rejects any notion of objective verification. Generously, he will allow other persons to have other truths, all these private revelations being not so much contradictory as incommensurable.

No wonder there is such hot warfare between the followers of Bacchus and the worshippers of the hempen gods from the East. The subject of their quarrel is only the universe.

The quarrel is not such as we of the West are accustomed to. It is not like the division between Plato or Aristotle or between Descartes and Kant or between any other schools of western thinkers. For these disputants could dispute. They all agreed that propositions about the universe are either true or false (or badly stated, but that is a different problem). No one suggested that contradictory ideas were both entirely correct, or that there was no way for their proponents to debate.

The metaphysics fostered by marijuana cannot dispute. Debate among the holders of private visions is not even conceivable. What would they argue about? If truth is an individual affair, how can anyone argue, except in the manner of people "arguing" about their favorite colors?

The chasm is complete. Every time one side begins an argument by pointing to the universe, the other will reply by pointing to himself, and each will be firmly convinced that his antagonist is fatuous.

This is why marijuana has such deadly import for the survival of society.

It is the missionary of falsehood. It provides an irrational tug toward the abandonment of the western axiom of a real universe. Where reason is speechless, moods and emotions are powerful orators. We have good reason to fear these orators. Long before Freud, the West knew that the pit of man's soul is not a garden of delights; it rots with delusions and devils. We do not want the truths dredged from that mire.

In the deepest folds of Bacchus, men see pink elephants. They are, to the eye, funny creatures, more likely to raise a smile than a whiff of terror. But today marijuana is encouraging men to release those elephants from their cages and ride them pell-mell through the world. It may prove that what looks pink at a distance is really not so lovely.

Confessions of a Cigar Snob

(1975)

ARAM BAKSHIAN, JR.

Author's note: Since the Great American Saloon Series has run dry due to the milksop nature of most Alternative contributors, a few nonsaloon pieces on pleasant indulgences might be in order. If no one else steps forward in the next few issues, the author threatens, time allowing, to follow this short essay with further confessions of a liqueur snob, a book snob, a pipe snob, a snuff snob, a beer snob, a hotel snob, a food snob, a political snob, and—if a less frowzy periodical can be lined up—a magazine snob. You have been warned, so pick up your spoon handles or crayons and get cracking.

A dear old Viennese friend, now in his nineties but still a great smoker, once confided to me that he knew the Weimar Republic was doomed when he began noticing too many good cigars falling into the hands of the wrong sort of people.

It's not a bad rule of thumb. Something is seriously wrong with any society in which too many pimps can afford Lincoln Continentals and too many pipsqueaks can afford Havana Coronas. And, sooner rather than later, the quality of both the Coronas and the Continentals begins to skid.

Fortunately for those of us who are more interested in creature comforts than mobility, cigars seem to have avoided their grand climacteric longer than the American automobile—despite the zealous efforts of *Playboy* propagandists and others bent on popularizing and plasticizing the good life. We can probably thank the big city political bosses of a generation ago, who were usually caricatured with large, fuming stogies clenched between their teeth, for keeping the cigar from becoming a status symbol for smart young moderns. God bless the ward heelers.

There are, it is true, hundreds of garbage brands, usually sold over drugstore counters, but this is hardly a new development. Rubbishy cigars have always been with us, from the foul green cheroots smoked by Paraguayan peasant women (and occasionally their brats) for at least three centuries, to the *Tijuana Smalls,* tasting more of paper than tobacco, that came on the market at about the same time that a number of jaded, middle-aged trendies were developing a morbid interest in a different sort of smoke with a similar sounding name—which must have occurred to the ad agency writer who christened these legal but highly offensive pseudocigarillos.

Unfortunately, the bulk of mass-produced American cigars are not pure tobacco products. A small note on most of the popular labels shamelessly confesses that the cigars "are made predominantly of tobacco with significant amounts of nontobacco material added," which is rather like a Mother Superior explaining that the nuns in her charge are primarily virgins but with substantial amounts of nonvirgins tossed in. An honorable exception on the domestic market (unless they have made a recent policy change) is the *Antonio & Cleopatra* line of cigars produced by American Brands. In particular, their maduro (dark) wrapper version is a full, even smoke. As I recall, they use African Cameroon leaf which provides a good, spicy aroma and flavor. *Rum River Crooks,* another and even more modestly-priced American cigar, is still, I believe, pure tobacco—Pennsylvania or Connecticut leaf most likely. But the leaf is not particularly noble and the rum flavoring and aroma put off many smokers. Still, they deserve an honorable mention amidst so many synthetic monstrosities.

A vanishing phenomenon on the cigar scene is the small local or regional American manufacturer. There used to be dozens of these, some of them very nice, but as with local breweries they are either folding or being absorbed. A few still remain, a good example being the Ibold Cigar Company of Cincinnati, Ohio, which puts out a modestly priced line of smokable mass manufactured cigars. These may not win any awards in international competitions, but they are a surviving specimen, little the worse for wear, of what was once a thriving and diverse selection of domestically made cigars. Worthy of individual mention are two of their maduro wrapped items, their *Brevas* and their *Black Peters,* which are very much in the old American stogey tradition.

For sheer, unabashed shoddiness, however, a foreign product of nearly a century ago is still without peer. Anyone familiar with the not-so-glorious history of the old Royal Italian Army knows that it was riddled with corruption and jobbery. One result was the humiliating massacre at Aduwa, where a large, modernly-equipped Italian force was wiped out by primitive Abyssinian levies—an event that seems to have traumatized an impressionable lad named Mussolini, who tried to get even some years later.

A less historically significant symptom of corruption was Italy's army-issue cigar in the reign of Victor Emmanuel I. The crooked contractors who produced it stopped at nothing, adding vast quantities of alien material including straw and mud—items better suited for raising earthworms than for rolling cigars. According to tradition, there were even times when the Italian Army cigar achieved the complete opposite of the ideal—the most ingenious of the grafters somehow managed to concoct a cigar that was 100 percent tobacco-free! No doubt the anticancer lobby, had it been around at the time, would have loudly applauded.

If, for old time's sake, you ever feel the urge to savor something akin to the old Italian Army cigar, you can still find Tuscan-style cigars in some Italian-American grocery stores. One firm, *Barodi,* even produces them in the States. However, such a course is only recommended to the most masochistic of nostalgia enthusiasts.

At the other end of Western Europe, in Spain (more precisely, in the sun-drenched Canary Islands), one finds cigars of a much higher order. The tobacco trade in the Canaries dates back to the sixteenth century when early Spanish explorers introduced tobacco plants from the New World and made the first attempts at cultivating them in the Old.

The Canary Islanders are still at it today, and with the help of a number of anti-Castro émigrés—many of them the former heads of old Cuban cigar firms who brought seeds and expertise with them—they are producing some of the finest cigars available in the world today. *Casa Buena, Don Sancho,* and *Flamenco* are all good lines, available in a wide range of shapes and sizes including, in the case of *Flamenco,* the once familiar but now rather rare "torpedo."

The mass exit of the old proprietary and managerial classes from Cuba has created a curious cleavage in the cigar world. Most of the old, revered Havana brands—*Punch, Bolivar,* and *Upmann* to name a few—now fly under two flags, each using the same name but with different assets and liabilities. Exile *Punches,* for example, are produced by the old management in Tampa, Florida, while the Cuban government still exports cigars under the same brand name. The tobacco in the Tampa *Punches* is Havana seed grown elsewhere and not quite up to original Havana standards which require that special blend of soil, sun, and soul unique to Cuba. However, they are made with a measure of care and quality control that is absent from all but the most expensive Castro-era Cuban cigars. Other émigré firms hold forth in Honduras, Nicaragua, and Mexico.

The best available Cubans are sold in London, Moscow, and other foreign capitals, but these usually cost an arm and a leg. In London, it is not unheard of to pay a pound for a good corona-sized Havana, well-wrapped, well-preserved, and made of prime leaf. That comes to $2.40 a throw, which is rather steep by any standard.

The best course for those who enjoy good smoking but would just as soon avoid bankruptcy is to cultivate a taste for out-of-the-way cigars that, if not masterpieces, are at least good examples of regional taste and craftsmanship.

For those with robust appetites, there are the dark, strong sun-cured tobaccos of Brazil, available from *Seuerdieck* and *Dannemann,* firms that grow and handmake their own cigars in Bahia. These are genuine but a little risky—sometimes loosely wrapped and with an occasional hair that betrays the scarcity of depilatories among the buxom Negresses who roll the cigars on their thighs. They are good, coarse, reactionary cigars from a good, coarse, reactionary part of the world. For some reason, they are particularly popular with Germans. Even Walter Ulbricht, the late Communist boss of East Germany, found them irresistible, despite their fascist taint.

Far milder in taste (though not in aroma) are the delicate cigars of the Philippines. These too date back to the early years of Spanish exploration and conquest. *Isabella* leaf, a special strain developed in the Philippines and named after Spanish royalty, goes into the best of them, hand-made and marketed by firms like *Alhambra.* Brazilian and Sumatran leaf also go into most of the best small Dutch and Danish whiffs—brief, tasty smokes suitable for occasions when one can't really do justice to a full-fledged cigar. *Schimmelpenninck, Ormond, Karl I,* and *Larsen* are all old houses that turn out a good variety and there are also several sound English imitations (*Mannikins* springs to mind). Like good Sherry, the best whiffs are invariably dry—sometimes too much so for American palates.

The best the British Empire (may it rest in peace) had to offer came from Jamaica. The late Sir Winston Churchill, perhaps as much for political reasons as out of real preference, always favored *Royal Jamaicans,* still made and widely exported along with several less expensive but worthy brands like *Mario Palomino.* Jamaican cigars have less character than Havanas but they are even, light, and usually well-made. The Dominican Republic, endowed with most of the right natural elements, also exports cigars—good raw material but finished products that are uneven at best.

For the really sentimental imperialist, however, the most appropriate smoke of all is a Burma cheroot—a dark, slender cigar chopped off at both ends and specially cured. As the economy of independent Burma slowly sinks back into the stone age, the supply of cheroots to the outside world dwindles. But several creaky old firms still manage to deliver an occasional batch of plantation bundles to the wharf which ultimately find their way to smart London tobacconists like Bewlay's and Green's.

Green's has dubbed its cheroots *Call of the East* and, with their wafting, almost incense-like fragrance, that is exactly what they are—a very pleasant change of pace, especially for retired Blimps, former tea planters, and readers of Kipling.

Having taken your pick from the above array, you really should choose a decent cigar clipper. If it is good it will probably have been made in Solingen, West Germany, although some interesting examples (usually more eye-catching than functional) are also produced in Sweden and Italy. Strange people, the Germans—they produce both the worst cigars and the best cigar clippers in the world. Favorites from my own collection are an enormous monstrosity made of ramshorn and silver, and a brass and pewter piece with a sharp, wedge-shaped blade surmounted by a constellation of Baroque *putti* in bas-relief, not one of them so much as puffing on a cigarillo.

All that remains now is the purchase of a nice, solid mahogany humidor (cedar-lined) and the mapping out of a cigar zone somewhere in the house. Opposition from the fair sex may be formidable—at the turn of the century, when he was already well into his fifties, the Prince of Wales (later Edward VII) still had to waddle off and smoke behind some particularly wide palace pillar whenever old Queen Victoria put in an appearance. After she died, he made up for so many lost smokes that his lungs soon gave out.

However, assuming that the General Directress of your own household is somewhat more pliant, and a territorial treaty can be signed, have a few friends over who are capable of enjoying a decent smoke and are also up to a good night's tippling and conversation. As Thackeray observed in one of his minor essays, "Honest men, with pipes or cigars in their mouths, have a great physical advantage in conversation. You may stop talking if you like—but the breaks of silence never seem disagreeable, being filled up by the puffing of smoke—hence there is no awkwardness in resuming conversation—no straining for effect. . . ."

A bit later on, the creator of *Vanity Fair* sums it up for all of us who have known the pleasure of a really good cigar. "I vow and believe," he concludes, "that the cigar has been one of the greatest creature-comforts of my life—a kind companion, a gentle stimulant, an amiable anodyne, a cementer of friendship. May I die if I abuse that kindly weed which has given me so much pleasure!"

Actually, those of us who are overfond of it are much more likely to pay the ultimate price than its detractors. Sigmund Freud, U.S. Grant, and Emperor Friedrich I of Germany (Kaiser Wilhelm's unfortunate father), all cigar devotees, literally croaked from various forms of mouth and throat cancer. But there's a price tag on everything and, besides, as the air gets more and more foul, abstinence is less and less likely to buy much extra time from the grim reaper.

At any rate, when the old gentleman does come for you, I hope you'll have the decency to offer him a cigar.

In Defense of Smoking

(1979)

WALTER GOODMAN

The heat is on. In theaters, airplanes, and restaurants, the smoker is already at bay, and the pursuit has lately moved into office and home as well. Hostesses put out little cards as centerpieces on their dinner tables, with this message: "You may smoke if you wish, but most people don't." Or the guest may find at his place a plastic stick figure in the act of breaking a realistic-looking cigarette and the snide line, "Thank you for not smoking." There are reports of people who actually commit violence on the offending object, extinguishing it in one's very mouth. Acquaintances go out of their way to let smokers know how revolting they are. These days, as I light up an occasional cigar in the privacy of my office, I can be pretty sure that somebody will take the trouble to stop by for the purpose of telling me the place stinks.

Everyone understands that cigarette advertisers put their wholesome-looking models in the vicinity of sky and sea in order to suggest that, no matter what unpleasant things the Surgeon General has to say, smoking and a robust constitution go together like Marlboros and a horse. These young chain-smokers clearly have lungs that could carry them across the Atlantic. Lately, however, the ads evoke a different image: the lone smoker, driven from civilization into the free outdoors where, Thoreau-like, he or she can inhale until the chest bursts with pleasure or something else. The habit adopted by many in adolescence as an aid to enduring the pains of socialization has become anti-social, a bar to friendly intercourse. Smokers already occupy the rear of the airplane, and who knows what lies ahead before the Office of Civil Rights comes to the defense of this latest chivvied minority.

Just as non-smokers insist on attributing the "addiction" of smoking to some need, that is to say weakness, of those who do it, so we must look to the psyche of the non-smoker to understand the current vendetta. Given the overwhelming evidence that cigarettes are killers, a case can be made for banning them on grounds of their high social cost—lost work days, health insurance payments, survivors benefits, and so forth. But nobody knows better than Secretary Califano, who used to require three packs a day to help him assist certain trade groups enhance their interests in Washington, that a ban is not feasible given economic and political realities. All the fuming of the virtuous cannot get Congress to raise the tax on cigarettes by a mill or eliminate federal loan programs that make the lives of tobacco growers more comfortable. Their frustrations are therefore turned on the smoker. In the case of ex-smokers, the attack may be a form of self-defense. I know one former heavy smoker whose tactic is to burst into a fit of furious coughing whenever anyone lights up in her presence. It is not that she is offended by the smoke, but rather that, like those Victorian gentlefolk who used to hound prostitutes, she is so attracted by it that it threatens her own virtue.

I no longer ask the woman next to me at a dinner party if she minds my cigar for fear that she will tell me she does. That would not necessarily deter me, but it could make conversation awkward. What would I do if my companion went into a coughing fit at my first puff? Well, I might suggest she change seats.

For 20 years, I have participated in a monthly poker game that has never known a serious dispute: Lately, a couple of the players' wives have made remarks about the disgusting pall we leave behind in their living rooms—and *windows have been opened.* A sense of strain has insinuated itself into our cordially thick atmosphere. The attack, long repressed, is obviously against the instinct for male-bonding, and I fear for the future.

The assault on the smoker, although it may offer an outlet for the frustrations, aggressions, and fears of the non-smoker, has its peculiar side. After all, smokers are victims—of their own weakness if you will—but victims withal. Cigarette smokers are killing themselves. They may be as foolish as people who drink a lot or drive fast (though perhaps not as costly to society), but as things go in this world they are not sociopaths; they are harming mainly themselves and their loved ones. (Until the Surgeon General rules that smoking is dangerous to the health of the person sitting next to you, let us treat that figment of the anti-smoker's nightmares with the scorn it deserves.) The smoker's predicament ought to call forth compassion. Instead, it has called forth a declaration of war. The potential victims are treated as active sinners.

There is a streak of Fundamentalism here. The Lord did not give man lungs in order that he should pollute them. If the body is a temple, then one ought to treat it with reverence; and it one does not, let him be damned. But that line isn't popular anymore. In fact, sin is not popular. It's damnably hard to find a good sin in a time when such formerly sure-fire items as abortion, homosexuality, and adultery are celebrated as expressions of liberation. Enlightenment has struck—but morality does not love a vacuum.

The idea of sin is powerful, both in attraction and repulsion. To point at a wrongdoer and lament that he is an unfortunate product of an inequitable society, or that he has had the misfortune to have been born with his genes askew, is milk and water stuff compared to the satisfactions of pointing at him and announcing, there, by God, goes a *sinner*! At a time when sin is in such short supply and the pure-in-lung are jogging four miles a morning, flossing, avoiding eggs, and drinking Perrier with lime, the sinner is he who refuses to abide by the commandments of the health-obsessed. A large number of saints, notoriously careless of their bodies, would today be hellbound. So the need for sinners is being satisfied at the expense of smokers—and not just cigarette smokers who are courting catastrophe, but pipe smokers who are known for their erudition and cigar smokers who are known for their good humor and longevity.

People who dedicate themselves to stopping other people from jeopardizing their immortal souls are, in the nature of things, disruptive of civility, the glue of the liberal community. One may respond, so what . . . some communities are better off coming unstuck—witness Sodom and Gomorrah. But those who take a more benign view of our condition will wish to weigh the costs of disruption. One gets the feeling today that a lot of people would much rather insult a smoker than redeem him, rationalizing perhaps that the insult is the first step toward redemption. That sort of behavior is not designed to promote civility.

It may, for one thing, incite resistance. I have not yet been accosted by one of those people who reportedly carry with them implements to snuff out a cigarette or cigar as it is being enjoyed, but if such a one were to attack my after-dinner Havana ($2 a shot), no jury of my peers (cigar smokers) would convict me for any mayhem that ensued. If necessary, I would bring forward a psychiatrist to testify to the psychic cost of such an assault on my expression of virility.

Suppose that the present attack on smokers not only shames us into taking our detestable pleasure only in the toilet, but actually works—and we all stop. What would be the cost in wife abuse, husband abuse, child abuse, and similar ills that we are told daily demand our most earnest attention? How many heart attacks would result from the consequent obesity? What would be the cost in dental bills for teeth damaged by excessive nail-biting? How many new wars would be started by irritable reformed smokers? Chairman Mao was too pure to smoke, and wrote terrible poetry instead. The fact that Vice Premier Teng is a chain-smoker may prove of enormous benefit to his people and the whole world, even if it did stunt Mr. Teng's growth. The man who smokes, Edward Bulwer-Lytton observed, "thinks like a sage and acts like a samaritan." The observation would be more persuasive had Joseph Stalin not spent his life with a pipe between his teeth—but probably it was hired for propaganda purposes, like those kids whose heads he used to pat.

Secular societies, let us be grateful, do not deal with the notion of sin; that is beyond them and ought to remain there. They do sometimes punish "crimes" against one's body—the use of narcotics, for example, or attempts at suicide. Whatever the merits of these contested matters, so far smoking is not a crime and cigarettes are not legally prohibited except in selected places like elevators. That does not mean that individuals or groups may not, on their own behalf, try to discourage smoking. But as long as the act is lawful, then the issue becomes one of balance, like most issues in a peaceable community. In the interests of such a community, a Smoke Ender dropout I know, who coughs as heavily as she smokes, has trained herself to sit soundless at the theater, saving her explosions for intermission. I fear to estimate what her sacrifice for the common good costs this exemplary citizen. Can we ask less of the non-smoker?

Here we are at a dinner party. Someone lights a cigarette, someone makes an adverse comment. Is the displeasure of the non-smoker of greater weight than the need of the smoker? That depends. Maybe the non-smoker is a pregnant asthmatic, in which case the smoker must bow or at least retreat to a far corner. On the other hand, maybe the non-smoker just doesn't like the person who is smoking, in which case the smoker may wish to puff up a storm. When disagreement strikes in society, the parties need not wrestle it out; they may reach an accommodation or separate. I am put off by the odor of cigarettes and heavy perfume, yet I often endure both because I like some people despite their nasty habits. The hostess who is offended by cigar butts need not invite me to dinner—or if she invites me with a stipulation that I leave my cigars at home, I need not accept. But if she invites me knowing that I will smoke, then she must weigh the charms of my presence against the vileness of my pleasure. Or I must weigh the lack of the evening's final satisfaction against the joys of her cooking.

Such choices are commonplace, made daily at modest cost and no ripping of the social fabric. My physician, who gave up smoking about a year ago, exemplifies the nondoctrinaire approach. One is greeted at the entrance to his office by a bold American Cancer Society command not to smoke. But within, for those who never need a cigarette more than in a doctor's waiting room, are conveniently-placed ashtrays. No-smoking signs in elevators and in assigned sections of restaurants and airplanes are reasonable restraints; the imposition on the smokers' pleasures are temporary or partial. (Let us avoid the word "rights," whether in regard to smokers or non-smokers; it has been run into the ground by the lawyers and polemicists and is scarcely fit any longer for anything but parody.) Attempts like those by a group of federal workers, on the other hand, to bar smoking wherever a non-smoker complains of discomfort, are a form of vigilantism; they are flagrantly unjust, will probably subvert productivity (although that may not matter in federal offices), and are bound to breed guerrilla warfare. No free society can satisfy those who insist on their purity, or their pleasure, at the total expense of others.

Now, if you don't mind, I am going to have a cigar. If you mind I'll have one anyway.

Why Not the Most?

(1979)

THEO LIPPMAN, JR.

As mid-term approached, my political and popular support were dismally low. The polls had me running behind Senator Edward Kennedy. My "approval rating" was almost as low as Richard Nixon's and Harry Truman's had been. Yet I had accomplished so much! It wasn't fair! "What can we do," I asked Rosalynn at a Cabinet meeting, "besides pray?"

She said the problem wasn't that I wasn't a good president. It was that the press was not reporting the truth to the people. "We need an image communicator," she explained. So we hired an advertising man and one of the best friends I ever had, Jerry Rafshoon. His job was to get the true story of the Jimmy Carter presidency to the people.

I was saddened to note that he failed. In the first months after hiring him, my standing in the polls and with traditional Democratic interest groups fell.

To perk up my spirits, Rosalynn hired a new pastry chef for the White House, Albert Kumin of Windows on the World, a three-martini café in New York. Mr. Kumin is a genius with chocolate, and Rosalynn knew what was then a well-kept secret. I am a chocolate freak. Of course, with my extraordinary resolve, I had till then limited myself to only one dessert a week. I didn't need a Jerry Rafshoon to tell me that fat politicians were seldom successful.

Mr. Kumin's first night on the job, he prepared peanut brittle supreme, with chocolate filling in the peanuts themselves. It was a touching tribute to the Carter family heritage. I cried. We called Chef Kumin in from the kitchen and prayed together. I ate four helpings.

The second night Mr. Kumin prepared his own specialty, chocolate velvet cake. I ate the whole thing. "Rosalynn," I exclaimed, "let's have dessert every night. The way the polls are, I don't have to worry about my image anymore. It looks like we're headed back to Plains in 1981. Let's go back fat and sassy."

Chocolate ice cream with cinnamon, chocolate fruit tarts, chocolate pound cake . . . there was no end to Chef Kumin's imagination. By the fall of 1979 I weighed 200 pounds. None of my clothes fit anymore. I no longer could button my trousers. I hadn't made a public appearance since June. Rafshoon was horrified. But the polls leveled off.

On Christmas Eve, I felt I had to make a public showing. For me no

American tradition is more hallowed than Christmas. "But you weigh 235 pounds," said Rafshoon. "You're a mess."

I insisted, and on Christmas Eve, from the new Prayer Room of the White House, I addressed the American people on the war in the Holy Land. The networks naturally placed their cameras so that I was seen in the most unflattering poses. But to everyone's surprise, the public response was positive. My "approval rating" rose five points. I couldn't understand this. Neither could Rafshoon. Neither could Rosalynn. When I ventured out again, to walk the streets of Plains for the first time in a year (I had stayed away because of the trial—see Chapter XII), I was warmly cheered by townsfolk, tourists, and family members alike. It was gratifying, if mystifying.

All the best brains in the administration worked to understand this development, to no avail. Meanwhile, the dessert regimen—tarts, tartlets, compotes, bombe—continued. By New Hampshire primary day, I was a rotund 250. Too fat to campaign, but just fat enough to win. I edged out Teddy Kennedy, 52 percent to 48 percent. Teddy weighed in at 233. He had gained 26 pounds in the last week of the campaign, on the advice of a secret memo from Arthur Schlesinger, Jr. This memo later fell into our hands. Mr. Schlesinger advised Kennedy that the American people's tribal memory of the good times before World War I—the last years of American innocence and irresponsibility—had been evoked by my fatness. I looked like William Howard Taft.

But Kennedy had started too late. I had that 17 pounds on him by March 1, and I am, of course, much shorter. He dropped out of the race in early May, kayoed, he later admitted, by my promise to "outweigh William Howard Taft" by Inauguration Day, and by my slogan, "Why Not the Most?"

With only Jerry Brown between me and renomination, I stepped up the pace. Instead of speechwriters, Chef Kumin and his staff traveled with me in Air Force One. Sorbet, chocolate truffles, genoise cakes soaked in kirsch . . . The week before the California primary, I was over the 270 mark and fattening. Brown had taken the opposite approach at first; he began the campaign with a fast. But as I gathered momentum, he found himself reduced to a minimum of organized support—marathon runners, Weight Watchers, and the Americans for Democratic Action, none of whom vote. In one of his characteristic reverses, he announced that he had been secretly fat all along. He released a doctor's statement that his cholesterol level was over 300. "Inside, I'm fat," he proclaimed.

It didn't work. We celebrated my California victory with triple helpings of chocolate mousse all around. "I pledge to you a government as fat as its people," I said on television from the convention the next month, when I was nominated by acclamation.

The Maharishi Effect

(1979)

JOHN O'SULLIVAN

A few years ago I arrived at Chicago's airport late, harassed and groaning under too many suitcases. It was probably inevitable under these circumstances that I should promptly be accosted by a lunatic, or, as I now suspect, by someone posing as a lunatic. He was wearing that fixed sweet smile of overwhelming charity that skeptics like myself call double-beatific vision, and he asked me whether or not I was saved.

"Yes," I replied briskly, hoping to avoid him. "Also I am in danger of not getting to San Francisco. Kindly step aside."

But there had apparently been some hitch in my salvation. At any rate, the evangelist pointed out that saving souls was a tricky business, often bungled by well-meaning amateurs. But I need not despair. His own sect had fortunately perfected a foolproof method of avoiding hellfire which could be communicated to me for a modest sum. And from his robes he produced a book containing this essential formula.

My reaction was swift and, I hoped, terrible. I threatened that, if he did not get out of my way and the San Francisco plane left without me, then I would seek him out and put his theory of salvation to the ultimate test. His blood, however, remained uncurdled. Instead he smiled—a smile of such repellent sweetness that it could have cloyed a lemon at 60 paces. Then he cooed.

"Thank you for sharing your anger with me," he said.

That episode festered long in my memory, proving the shrewdness of Lincoln's remark: "Love your enemies—they'll hate it." It returned to unsettle me a month or two ago as I motored through the English countryside to Mentmore Towers, the stately Victorian pile that belonged until recently to the Marquis of Roseberry, to attend a banquet given by English followers of the Maharishi Mahesh Yogi, its present owners and occupants.

Would the place, I wondered, be packed with loonies smiling aggressively? And what on earth, so to speak, was the World Government of the Age of Enlightenment, which we guests had been invited to celebrate? Would the evening include speeches of the length and dullness usually associated with the phrase "World Government" or of the obscurity suggested by the word "Enlightenment"?

On the other hand, the formal invitation card—black italic lettering on stiff white cardboard—bred considerable confidence in its recipient. In response to its instructions, I had donned, if not the full soup-and-fish, at least a rather stylish green velvet dinner jacket and butterfly bow. A strikingly pretty girl was by my side, grateful for the prospect of Lucullan entertainment for which others were paying. And had not the invitation distinctly promised a banquet—a word redolent of many courses, sorbets to cleanse the palate in between, excellent claret, 30-year-old brandy, beautiful immoral women, and other delights not often provided in tin-roofed salvation sheds?

Immediate impressions were reassuring. We entered the reception hall, an indoor piazza green with potted plants, surrounded by pillars, and set under a windowed roof that shed soft summer light over small groups of elegant middle-class English people in conventional evening dress, all chattering politely away and accepting drinks from liveried flunkies. It was a scene of fashion and affluence, rather like an advertisement for an up-market menthol cigarette. A young man came across to welcome us. Admittedly, he had traces of that dread smile; but it had been captured a while before and was by now thoroughly domesticated.

"How do you do," he began agreeably. "I'm the Minister for Research and Development and All Possibilities." I was tempted for a moment to reply that I was a homicidal psychopath, just escaped from Broadmoor, to see who blinked first. But—and this was a portent for the rest of the evening—my intention quailed before his evident niceness. So, after the briefest of pauses, we murmured the usual pleasantries and were handed a Maharishi cocktail: a glass of orange juice, with any transcending done under your own steam.

The Minister for R&D&AP was host for the evening with other guests to greet. So a fairly junior Minister took us in tow for a guided tour of Mentmore, explaining as we went along the value of Transcendental Meditation as a sort of psychological equivalent of jogging. Business organizations encouraged their executives to try it; doctors recommended it as therapy for nervous illnesses; it was a scientifically validated program.

But I had heard rumors that advanced meditation techniques, known as the "TM-Sidhi Program," were supposed to endow adepts with astonishing powers, *viz.,* the ability to fly, to become invisible, to walk through walls, to materialize objects out of thin air by sheer mental power, in short to amuse your friends and be a hit with the girls. Was it really the case, I wondered politely, that fully accredited yogis could, well, fly?

"Oh, *that,*" replied my guide dismissively. "Well, it's scarcely worthy of the name of flying as yet. We can't control it properly as yet, move forward and back at will, you know, and we manage to stay in the air for only brief periods. So flying is a *bit* of an exaggeration. As a matter of fact, among ourselves we call it 'hopping.'"

This diffident reply disarmed me mortally. Only an utter cad, I felt, would bring up the subject of walking through walls. ("As a matter of fact, among ourselves, we call it 'squeezing.'") Fortunately, at that moment, a red-coated flunky announced that dinner was served and we were ushered into Mentmore's sumptuous dining hall for the banquet.

Over the vegetable pie, Mr. Peter Warburton, the Minister for Information and Inspiration, a tall, dark, handsome, and earnest young man wearing impeccable dinner clothes and the sincere frown of an idealistic young doctor in a soap opera, explained matters further. Studies showed, he said, that if one percent of a city's population practiced TM, then accidents declined, hospital admissions decreased, crime fell, creative activities flourished, and industrial productivity soared beyond our wildest imaginings. These benefits had been given the technical name of "the Maharishi effect," a spreading influence of orderliness and harmony in the collective consciousness of the whole society.

This was indeed inspiring stuff. But perhaps Mr. Warburton was simply doing his job? It seemed not. There clung about him, as about his Cabinet colleagues, the impression of a mild, unassuming, but determined belief that made one reluctant to ask brutal questions and yet made the most obvious enquiries seem, somehow, dreadfully brutal. Nevertheless, I rallied myself sufficiently to ask if there was an unambiguous example of this Maharishi effect working on cue.

Mr. Warburton gave me a smile—but a different sort of smile, and I'm-glad-you-asked-that-question kind of smile. Yes, there was such an example. One hundred top meditators had flown—conventionally—into Nicaragua at the height of the first round of fighting in the civil war and booked into the Managua Intercontinental Hotel, there to meditate full-time. And lo and behold, the fighting had come to a halt.

"But keeping 100 top spiritual leaders in a luxury hotel was an expensive business," went on the Minister sadly, "and after a while we had to pull them out. So, of course, the violence started up again."

"Yes," I said weakly, hoping that it would come out, "no," but too cowed and in the grip of social embarrassment to manage a clear denial. "Well, p'raps, you never know, stranger things in Heaven and Earth, Horatio, and all that . . ."

But, in striking a mystical note, I had entirely missed the point. This was all strictly scientific, no-nonsense, feet-on-the-ceiling stuff. Back in the piazza for an after-dinner lecture, we heard the Minister for All Possibilities disavow any similarity to cults and express an old-fashioned, almost Wellsian faith in the scientific method and its validation of TM. Studies showed that crime fell, creativity soared, hospital admissions plummeted, etc. Slides were shown to demonstrate that TM was more effective than sleep at producing really deep relaxation. Comparative tests of heartbeats and pulse rates were cited. Pictures of brain waves were triumphantly pointed at. It had been established that TM, in addition to its other benefits, also rendered its practitioners youthful in appearance.

Behind the lecturer, apparently themselves scientific validation of this claim, were the Ministers of This and That and The Other and Everything Else, all suave and glittering in their evening clothes, every one a debutante's delight, a battalion of Dorian Grays. Had a dowager entered the room at that point, she would have wired instantly to her unmarried daughters: "Come at once. There *is* a Maharishi Mahesh Yogi."

It was at the same moment, as the young men smirked and looked bashful, that a terrible conviction came over me. Suddenly, everything fell into place. I turned to my pretty companion.

"We're on Candid Camera," I said. "It's all a hoax. Someone will come bounding out from behind the arras any minute and ask us to sign a release form. We shouldn't have been so polite. We'll look gullible fools."

But she was, as ever, femininely matter-of-fact.

"Don't be silly," she replied. "Who would go to all this expense, just to make a fool of *you*?" Thus reassured, I relapsed into polite acquiescence and began to enjoy myself. When ushered later into a room covered with mattresses and told that it was "the flying room," I merely mumbled something along the lines of, "Ah, the flying room, quite so, for flying I imagine, well you have a fine room for it." And since my hosts were themselves charming even in the face of skepticism, we ended the evening on the friendliest of terms. Eventually we were seen off by virtually the entire Administration of World Enlightenment and Transcendental Hopping, all waving cheerily, and returned bemused to that other world of "telegrams and anger."

But there is a postscript to this curious tale. Some weeks later, the *Guardian* newspaper reported that a number of TM disciples had left the movement, disillusioned that it had failed to produce the spiritual and physical uplift promised. "It's just bouncing around on your bum," complained one bitterly.

And Miss Hester Fishberg, "a 31 year-old London lawyer," described the scenes of meditation thus: "You saw people leaping around the room like frogs, shaking, screaming, babbling. The movement calls this 'unstressing,' but I intuitively began to wonder what was happening to me." I like the word "intuitively" in the last sentence. A sharp one, that Hester. No pulling the wool over *her* eyes.

Let me declare that, perhaps over-influenced by the diffident eccentricity displayed at the banquet, I have little sympathy for the disillusioned yogis. If London lawyers of mature years are silly enough to join quasi-religious sects in the hope of learning to fly or mastering ancient techniques of materializing a black forest *gâteau* out of thin air, then they deserve to end up bouncing around on their bums.

Are not the really dedicated levitationists altogether more sympathetic? I like to think of the Minister for R&D&AP earnestly photographing brainwaves; of the apprentice hoppers carefully laying out the mattresses each morning, just in case of a crash landing from a great height—"Pilot error, old boy, sudden loss of faith, pranged down on the *chaise longue*"; of the Minister for Information and Inspiration explaining . . . But why speculate? In response to the *Guardian*'s story, Mr. Warburton actually extruded an unanswerable piece of scientific logic: "If you spoke at random to more people who have learned to fly, you would not get such a bad response." There is, as they say, no answer to that.

My only serious quarrel with yogis is a patriotic one. Why have they got involved with mysterious Oriental fakirs and foreign types when there is a perfectly serviceable English tradition on which they could base their activities—the tradition of mad squires and country house eccentricity?

It is evening at Totleigh Towers. In the library, the butler is laying out drinks and mattresses for post-prandial relaxation. Upstairs, in his room, Gussie Fink-Nottle is busily photographing the brain waves of newts. On the lawn, Madeline Bassett is correcting her thesis on the statistical correlation between the wails of babies and the birth rate among fairies.

"Ah, Jeeves. Lay out my white mess jacket with the brass buttons and my flying helmet, would you? I am in the mood for parlor-nautics. It is of no avail to frown, Jeeves. Your young Master is determined. White mess jackets are all the rage in Cannes this year."

The Jersey Shore

(1981)

JOE MYSAK

The first attraction of the Jersey Shore is the beach, stretching for mile after unbroken mile along the Atlantic. The second is drinking.

Not drinking in the conventional, convivial sense, for the Jersey Shore is not exactly inhabited by sane people. I am speaking here of your basic collegiate, gut-wrenching guzzling, of fabulous and fantastic drinking contests, of sheer stupendous quantity battling with bottomless capacity, of colossal hangovers. I am speaking of virtual orgies of self-destruction and alcohol abuse, of blind staggers, dry heaves, the basic shakes, the heebie jeebies, and ultimate *delirium tremens.* I am speaking of morning-after scenes that resemble nothing so much as Shiloh. I am speaking of drinking done by those in search of the First Real Hangover, of drinking as done by the young, by those just learning, and by those desperately trying to reach their peak consumption level, which, as we all come to know, declines rather drastically after age 25.

In other words, the stuff of stories told in premature old age, of things we don't even now actually quite believe we did then, even though then is not so very many years ago.

The whole Shore thing surpasses even such events in the Jersey kid's life as getting a license or going to the prom. For one thing, the Shore is kid fantasy land, forever populated with males and females aged 16 to 28. Sure, there are rich homeowners whose gorgeous oceanfront piles dot the windswept bluffs, whose manses make up such burgs as Spring Lake, Deal, and Long Branch. But they are not the Shore. Nor are the occasional families—as seen in the typical automobile ad, the kinds who adorn their rented cottages with plaques done up with woodburning sets: THE KENNEDYS—no, they are not the Shore either. At the Shore, such conventional Americans look out of place . . . gross . . . bizarre . . . even pathetic.

No, the Real Shore is kid heaven, thousands of white, upper and middle-class bluejeaned kids on a mammoth, summer-long bender, in cars, awash in beer, the Beach Boys, and Bruce Springsteen. There is no mystery about it. The parents know exactly what is happening, and the kids admit as much when they leer at a friend's parents with a look that says, "Imagine the worst, and know in your heart of hearts that it's all really happening." Instead of panic, the typical parental response is one of studied unconcern. The kid announces that this weekend he's going to the Shore, Beach Blanket Animal House, and the parent says, "Have a nice time at the beach, dear."

The Shore is affectedly low-rent in appearance, although its inhabitants gladly fork over about $1,000 a bedroom for summer bungalows that would not look out of place in Appalachia, suburban Pittsburgh, or the Blue Ridge. Shore towns are planned by the same fellows who laid out Hong Kong, and are bleached white under a fierce sun and a cloudless sky. At the Shore there are no trees. There is no grass. There are no front yards, and there is no ozone layer. The ground, when it is not part of the Garden State Parkway, is sand, blacktop, chipping concrete, splintery grey wood, broken glass almost exclusively from beer bottles, and bottle caps. The Shore is, in a word, unrelieved. The beach is interrupted only by vast plastic and neon palaces of garish design and vulgar appeal, known quaintly as boardwalks.

The boardwalks, which are only sometimes made of boards and more often of asphalt, have provided the state's only contribution to the architect's vocabulary: Shore Gothic, best described as an agglomeration of structural summer designs dating from 1870 through 1958, when all construction apparently ceased. Nothing at the Shore is ever torn down, ever—but in some rare cases it is moved from one spot to another. The only way to kill it is to blow it away in a hurricane, which happened in 1938, or to dynamite it. Even then, it is never really gone, but rather towed out to the 4000 Loran Line, where it provides homes for tilefish and Big-Eye tuna.

A number of distinct styles have emerged from Shore Gothic, but are known only to experts. There is vintage Cape May, which is Victorian run amok, Asbury Park, variously known as Newark-by-the-Sea or Big Arcade Slum, and Atlantic City, which, before the steel and glass revival of the Casino Age, was Ocean Art Deco.

The Shore also has a population of millions of cars, whose existence is separate and distinct from the thousands of tender delinquents who apparently own them. Here we have the better kid cars: Corvettes, Trans-Ams, Firebirds, Camaros, Mustangs, Triumphs, BMWs, and Volkswagens—as well as the miscellaneous ancient wrecks usually driven by the young.

Now that the stage is set, follow a typical group through a Shore road trip. Consider, for a heroic but hardly unusual example, the Cranford Athletic Club, which in its more exuberant years rented a house in the notorious Shore ghetto of Manasquan. Five, sometimes ten, but no less than three members would storm the Shore after a Thursday night consisting of three hours of softball in the Cambodian heat of central New Jersey, followed by four hours of heavy-duty beer drinking in the 35-degree reaches of the famed Frenchy's beer hall, previously described in these columns. As many ACs as were going down would pile into one car, preferably the '69 Cadillac convertible with the 470 engine, and roar down the beautiful and picturesque Garden State Parkway. They would roll into Manasquan around 2 A.M. Friday morning and collapse.

Friday they would go to the beach, watch the girls, swim, watch "My Three Sons" on television over lunch, comment on the absence of the really good early episodes featuring William Frawley as Bub (because those were shot in black and white), discuss the sinister aspects of Fred MacMurray ("he showed his true colors in *The Caine Mutiny"*), and tackle such favorites as cars, girls, war, What They Will Do, possible salaries, Everyone Else, sports, Sunday's double-header, and the transcendental qualities of the ocean. And they would drink.

In the waning twilight hours, one of them might begin car-fighting, a sport inspired by Jean Shepherd and by Ernest Hemingway's *Death in the Afternoon*. In car-fighting, the matador steps in to the street with a shirt or tartan plaid blanket, waves it, and executes several passes against automobiles, at times on his knees. Amateurs usually choose cars with dimensions of cabin cruisers, while more advanced matadors readily challenge smaller, more maneuverable Toyotas and Datsuns. The bigger autos make more of an impressive show, but the smaller ones take more skill to fight.

But this goes so far and no further. The boys drink. And drink, case after case of Michelob, Budweiser, Heineken, Miller, Schlitz, Schmitz, and Shaefer. Some of the more lasting records of prodigious consumption include 34 cans in an eight-hour stretch, and 21 in less than three hours. At one point, it was estimated that every five seconds somebody on the Shore is knocking down a brew. Experts have noted that the Jersey Shore consumes more beer, from May to September, than does the continent of Australia in a year. The reasons are complex, and probably understood only by Aleuts and Swedes, who have delved into the effects of environment upon alcohol consumption at great length, most notably in Bergman films and in the carved scenes on walrus tusks. A few psychologists have opined that most of those who occasionally visit the Shore are hell-bent for alcohol, while those who rent houses there are so bored out of what is left of their minds that they try to drink themselves to death, the same way Eskimos will during a party pull the pin on a grenade and grin, Tibetans commit self-immolation, or South Carolinians repair stock-car engines while pulling on corn cob pipes.

An essential part of Shore drinking is watching the passing show, particularly the summer police, who patrol their beats as assiduously as lawmen sitting in speedtraps. The constabulary, who are rumored to be responsible for 77 percent of many Shore communities' budgets, nightly write tickets for drinking on the sidewalk, flaunting controlled substances, making too much noise, parking in five-minute parking zones, and car-hood riding. In the morning they give summonses to those who refuse to buy beach badges, those who sleep on front porches, and those unfortunates who insist on breaking the town ordinances on overoccupancy of bungalows. The men in blue are an essential part of any Shore summer. The Cranford Athletic Club, for one, has paid some $250 in assorted fines.

There are no great American saloons on the Jersey Shore, because they are neither necessary nor appreciated. There are saloons, such as Legget's Sand Bar in Manasquan, which serves up bottles of the Pride of Old Latrobe, Rolling Rock, for a dollar, and whose premises are usually suitably filled with tanned and toothsome young wenches.

And there are rock clubs. These will never figure prominently in a hit movie, unless it be called Saturday Night Dead Drunk. For one thing, they have cover charges, usually of three dollars; for another, most of the patrons arrive already drunk, having economically filled up at home or in cheaper places along the road; for a third, there is no dancing. What dancing there is is usually done between bouncers on vacation from the Green Bay Packers and fist fighters whose egos have been abused. At times, these gentlemen show the unruly the door even for such minor offenses as breaking glasses and singing louder than the band.

A few misguided souls think they can go to such places as the Osprey Hotel in Manasquan and Jimmy Byrne's Sea Girt Inn in nearby Sea Girt to pick up girls, but this is a myth. Some think they go to hear the band—this can hardly be avoided, for the sound level of a Shore bar can best be approximated by standing in a closed hangar at Newark International Airport with your head resting against the engine cowl of a 747 revving up. As ever, the real reason for visiting such places is to savor the choice libations regularly served up.

There are two: the velvety concoction known as the Kamikaze, which might be better known as the Kiss of Death, and the Screwdriver. The Kamikaze consists of two ounces of vodka, a dash of lime juice, and a touch of Triple Sec. At times the thing is made with gin, but in all cases it is meant to be dropped down the chute, not sipped. It is not even an actual drink, but a method of getting drunk, not to say sick, in a hurry, sort of a liquid hand grenade.

The Screwdriver is not the obvious potation familiar to all. Screwdrivers at rock clubs at the Shore are not made with vodka. They are mixed with some kind of rocket fuel liquid nitro, camouflaged by just enough orange juice to turn the thing not orange, but a kind of grey. In all seriousness, I have seen people light the things up with matches. (They make superb Molotov cocktails when thrown.) The bartenders get mad if you finish one and ask for another, and those who do are acknowledged by all to be Really Asking For It.

What it all leads to is the technicolor yawn, brain damage, death, and tales of Getting Really Sick at the Shore. But that is what it's all about. That is what happened, has happened, happens, and will happen. It is also why you rarely hear of anybody drowning in the gentle Jersey surf.

The Metaphysical Martini

(1981)

WERNER J. DANNHAUSER

I have never met a martini I did not like. Under no circumstances would I assert that any martini is as good as any other; my mind may be soaked, but not in rampant egalitarianism. I am willing to argue, however, that while the best martini demands to be called "perfect," the worst is nevertheless passable, and far better than no martini at all.

Surprisingly enough, so wondrous a drink has failed to spawn much of a literature that celebrates its wonders. It may well be that most sane men would rather drink martinis than read about them and would rather read about them than write about them. Yet that tempting explanation fails to satisfy, simply because martinis can be held in one hand, so that anyone who can talk and chew gum at the same time can just as well teach himself simultaneously to sip a martini and to read or write about it.

Nor will it do to contend that the absence of a library of works on the martini constitutes an undisguised blessing because writing about them would resemble what Leo Strauss once called "the loathsome business of explaining a joke." That was in another context and besides the great man's imposing list of virtues did not include a love of martinis. A mystique surrounds martinis, to be sure, but it does not suffer from an attempt at articulation. Indeed, for many of us the joy of drinking martinis is enhanced by talking about the joy of drinking martinis.

What, then, can the matter be? The safest explanation takes into account the drink's youthfulness. The martini was born in the nineteenth century and has flourished—perhaps peaked—in ours. The occurrence of phenomena necessarily antedates their comprehension, as Hegel might have remarked, and no wise man tries to hurry history, as Adlai Stevenson did in fact maintain, so true understanding may have to await the fullness of time, to borrow Martin Luther's felicitous phrase.

The patience we need while hoping for the appearance of the martini's philosopher (not to be confused with the philosopher's martini) will surely be strengthened by a reading of Lowell Edmunds' *The Silver Bullet: The Martini in American Civilization.* It can hardly be called the definitive book on the subject, but it is a pioneering work in the best sense. It abounds with information, including the above tidbits about the age of the martini; it luxuriates in insights educing the shock of recognition; it promulgates bold postulates demanding reflection and attempts at verification; in short, it performs an invaluable service and puts all of us in the author's debt.

I learned a great deal from this book. For example, I found out that Franklin D. Roosevelt changed not only the face of America, but the contents of the traditional martini—by adding fruit juice. I was taught almost more than I could absorb about vermouth, that most necessary of evils required to make a good martini—it is a "fortified wine." I discovered poetry by Auden, *New Yorker* cartoons, pictures of various permissible glasses, and a bibliography that will enable me to begin research on Scotch and other estimable beverages should the spirit ever move me to study spirits.

I mention the above matters to convey something of this slender volume's richness, not to suggest that Professor Edmunds devotes himself primarily to the collection of intriguing trivia. Nothing could be further from the truth. After the briefest of introductions, the author at once turns to the task of giving an adequate account of the martini. He attributes the perennial fascination the martini exerts to three fundamental ambiguities surrounding it and constituting "the source of its symbolic power." First of all, the martini comes across as both civilized and uncivilized. On the one hand, it is consumed by solitary drinkers who become nasty and brutish, if not short; on the other hand, it serves as the centerpiece of various social and communal experiences that make for better living in this blessed land, and others emulating our ways. It can act as a spur both to love and hate.

Secondly, the martini appears both in the guise of the classic and the individual. For Professor Edmunds, a distinguished classicist, the classic denotes the unitary and perfect, as opposed to the sickly romantic. One suspects he would subscribe to Winckelmann's beautiful description of the ancients as characterized by "noble simplicity and serene grandeur." That can be said of martinis as well, at least half the time. The other half, the martini provides a lovely playground for idiosyncrasy and eccentricity. Some spend a happy lifetime pursuing the ideal perfect martini, a drink unsullied by anything merely personal, while others use the cocktail hour as a fine vehicle for creativity and self-expression.

Finally, according to Edmunds, the "Martini is in itself both sensitive and tough." It was adored by the sensitive W. Somerset Maugham as well as the tough James Bond, and the sensitive Auden sang of its toughness in sensitive verse.

The author obviously has a taste not only for martinis but for ambiguity; at any rate he does not directly attempt to reconcile the opposites he documents. Instead, he goes on to detail the "simple, unambiguous messages" conveyed by the martini, propositions which "function as the propaganda, as it were," for the martini and "play on several common prejudices." The reader never quite knows whether and to what extent Professor Edmunds shares those prejudices. Be that as it may, the seven messages sent out by the martini are that it is American and nothing else, urban rather than rural, upper class, a man's and not a woman's drink, optimistic and not pessimistic, for adults and not children, of the past, albeit of the living past, and not the present. These propositions are obviously debatable, but they are stated so reasonably one finds himself wishing he could discuss them with the author, over a martini, of course.

Having provided the reader with ample drink for thought, Professor Edmunds concludes on a profound note by relating the martini's nickname, "Silver Bullet," to its deepest meaning. He ingeniously connects it with the Lone Ranger, who also "embodies all the characteristically American ambiguity" by being gentle and tough, a loner in the service of the common good.

Such a skeletal outline necessarily violates the book on which it reports, for which I apologize, especially since I must now divulge some differences I have with the author. The book is admirable, but good books deserve and demand the toughest possible criticisms. Here, then, are mine.

Let me begin with trifles. Like any pioneering work, his book omits a bit of needed information here and there. Two examples must suffice. Many of us do not really know what bitters are and the author fails to tell us. What is more serious, in his generous selection of martini drinkers from American literature the author fails to include Melville Godwin, from John P. Marquand's *Melville Godwin, U.S.A.* Rumor has it that the character was modeled on Eisenhower, in which case his predilection for ever drier martinis as the years went by would take on added significance. Moreover, his inclusion might well shed light on a question that vexes me at least once a year: Is Marquand worth reviving?

This is as good a point as any to introduce some methodological reservations about the author's approach. For mysterious reasons of his own, the author relies too much on examples from literature instead of real life, an especially problematic procedure inasmuch as most of the fiction and authors he cites must be described as second rate. To put it bluntly, this little jewel of a book contains too many references to Bernard De Voto. It would be churlish to blame the author for the martini's inexplicable failure to find its Homer, but one does feel that Professor Edmunds might have concentrated on consumers instead of producers.

By that I do not mean to imply that his study lacks historical perspective. On the contrary, at times the author almost falls into the dastardly pit of historicism, the insidious doctrine that one can explain things only in the light of their origins. He is saved above all by his familiarity with classical philosophy, as a passing reference to Aristotle's distinction between nature and history (in the *Poetics*) suggests, but he is not saved often and radically enough. The reader finds too many anecdotes of the past and too few of the scintillating generalizations of which Professor Edmunds is quite capable. I commend to him Marion Magid's sage observation that one cannot order a martini at the bar of history.

In the absence of a poet, what the martini needs above all is a philosopher. This study, however, forthrightly settles for less, declaring itself as belonging to "the field of bacchanology." Now science surely has its uses and some of my best friends are scientists, but a work owing even a tiny bit, as this one does, to Roland Barthes errs on the side of being too chic in its scientific bent. The author realizes as much by sounding suitably embarrassed when mentioning matters like "the semantics of material culture." The science yearns to be more than science but Professor Edmunds tends to shy away from what is above science by virtue of being its queen. He avoids philosophy.

Now for most of us the avoidance of philosophy is a matter of self-under-standing and suitable modesty; philosophers are hard to find and we simply realize that we do not belong to the world's most exclusive club. But Professor Edmunds does not strike me as a humble man. I have no intention to give umbrage and I suspect Professor Edmunds will not take it, being familiar with Aristotle, who thinks of humility as a vice. I do not think he feels he is below philosophy, because I fear he thinks himself above it. He writes like a genuine member of a genuine nobility, for whom philosophy is a mere game. He is, in short, a perfect gentleman. I have nothing at all against gentlemen, and if so few of my best friends can be called that it is because gentlemen shun me and not because I avoid them. But the author's nobility does at rare times tinge his excellent book with a bit of dubiousness, and since I must love truth more than I love Edmunds I must also force myself to mention two shortcomings.

The first of these is what might be called false purism. Believing as I have already confessed that there is no such thing as a bad martini, I also would not hesitate—in fact I don't—to use tap water for making ice cubes to pour in the vermouth in a cavalier if sparing way, scorning measurement, and in madcap moments experiment recklessly. What is more I would drink warm martinis out of dixie-cups without blinking or blushing. Rather than continue with a cata-logue of what some would call crimes—I have more, much more to confess—I will add a base truth about drinking martinis, one which the author is too noble to accentuate: Martini drinkers drink to get drunk, or at least to get high. One does not denigrate martinis in the least, I insist, by emphasizing the efficiency with which they do the job we assign them. Let no one sneer at the power of our national cocktail. We vote as many, but we drink as one. And let nobody deny that martini drinkers show great interest in what alcohol does to us. I have met many martini drinkers and loved not a few, but I have yet to encounter one who drinks *only* martinis.

Probity, always exacting, also demands that I take issue with Professor Edmunds over a second and closely related matter. One does him no injustice to call him a martini elitist. Now let me make one thing perfectly clear. In general, I admire elitists. In democracies they are absolutely essential to combat leveling tendencies and to return to the word "discrimination" its pristine sense. But it is no less true that for the health of democracy we elitists share as many of the fine things of life with the many as possible. That ennobles democracy and safeguards us elitists at one and the same time. Some things must always remain beyond the ken of the many, alas, but not martinis. Making them can be taught to the meanest capacities and enjoying them to the coarsest palates. We who are true conservatives should prize magnanimity very highly, and that virtue demands of us that we reach out to bring the uncommon martini to the common man.

But I have no wish to engage in unseemly disputations with Professor Edmunds. His book brought me great pleasure and I am grateful to him. In a small way it even resembles Aristotle's *Ethics.* Reading it one is bound to think of happy times in one's life. Even as I write this my mind becomes warm with tender recollections.

I remember many a communal rite of a pre-dinner martini or two. The occasions have varied from reunions with dear friends to ceremonies before dinner parties. I love the preparation, the toast, the first cool, bracing sip. In some ways I am especially partial to the toast. My favorite is *l'chayyim*—to life—which I proffer to all friends who are Jewish or would like to be. But I am graced with courtesy of the heart when it comes to toasts. As a good host I suit the words to the situation. For example, when I drink with my students I love to salute their triumphs, for I am made happy by their happiness. It ought to go without saying, but it doesn't, that I enjoy drinking with my students. On those joyous occasions I may even have taught some of them something more valuable than drinking martinis—a tall order. In any event, my students and I constantly expose as foolish prattle the ideas one sometimes hears bandied about concerning teaching as a power relationship.

I remember also the martini of the relationship. I think of sitting in peace with my beloved. Call her Jenny. We sit together, talk of common plans, let speech suffuse itself in love, feel blessed in our closeness, safe in trust; the very air grows intimate.

I remember, finally, the solitary martini. I put away my work, the daily drudgeries. Relaxing, I prepare my drink with loving care. Then I sit back and think of once and future deeds and speeches, but mostly of the past. I summon up the living and the dead, rehearse old scenes of tenderness and wit. Then time melts slowly as betrayals lose their sting. My friends and I are young again, alive with hope. Grace smiles on me as Mr. Death assumes a modest stance, and all the while martinis make the music for my memories.

Second Wife City

Sunning with the Sad Sacks of Hollywood
(1982)

BEN STEIN

I have reached a few new conclusions about life in Southern California. Life here spreads itself in front of me like statistical data on the incidence of mortgage foreclosures, and I cannot stop myself from drawing conclusions about the life I see day by day. Like a mad, short-circuited sociologist among the producers and the starlets and the tax-shelter attorneys, I keep coming into the living room with a new analysis of California life. My wife tells me to go back to sleep, but I cannot help myself.

Take the Malibu Beach Colony, for example. It is a small row of oceanfront houses in Malibu, protected from the mobs at the public beaches by a guard dog and chain-link fences with barbed wire on top. Houses here start at one-and-a-half million each, and that's generally for a tear down that needs complete reconstruction. The houses are on tiny lots right next to each other, with each household's five Mercedes crowding up against the next household's five Mercedes.

We rented a house here for the summer and I sat at the junction of sand and surf and saw what I could see. First, I noticed that the modal inhabitant of the Colony is a Jewish man of about fifty with a thin waist and a tortured look (only thinly masked by a beard). Every one of these men, at some point during the day, emerges from his house with a woman about half his age, so thin that she makes Lauren Hutton look like a hippopotamus. Both the man and the woman set their faces grimly and stride along the beach as if showing the world that they can suffer the fate of living at the Colony and come back for more each day. The women are, of course, second or third wives or girlfriends. My wife and I have come to call the Colony "Second Wife City," which does not amuse the neighbors at all.

Now, as a mad sociologist, I have to wonder:

(1) Why do all these men have little gray beards? It would show far more individualism to have no beard, so perhaps the object of the exercise is to show conformity. If so, where did the model come from, since only in Biblical times did all Jewish men wear beards. Could it be that I am witnessing the classic

104

California phenomenon, rigid conformity to a code mindlessly believed to display originality and daring?

(2) What happened to all the first wives? Sarah and Trudy have long since been displaced by Heather and Kelly, but where are Sarah and Trudy? The answer to this question explains another startling California, or Los Angeles, fact. In a city of substantially less size than New York City, about ten square miles are given over exclusively to the display and sale of furniture, carpets, and interior design fixtures. Now, everyone knows that interior design shops are to well-off middle-aged, divorced Jewish women what Elba was to Napoleon, so perhaps as the phenomenon of second and third wives spreads, and with it the number of discarded Sarahs and Trudys grows, the asymptotic result will be the entire development of Los Angeles as an interior design center for the Pacific Basin.

(3) Why do all the wealthy men and women on the beach look so pained? I recall from my youth that on beaches in the East, primarily Rehoboth Beach, Delaware, sunbathers looked quite pleased to be on the beach, even if they were poor. Why do rich beachcombers look so miserable? Here, I am at a loss to explain. But the thought occurs to me that the thinness of the men and women in the Colony must have something to do with the looks of pain and suffering under the hundred-dollar haircuts and above the five-thousand-dollar silicone jobs. To stay as thin as a whippet well into middle age requires an exercise of will power, a never-ending attention to diet, exercise, health, and appearance that is quite literally the equivalent of living with one's own internal NKVD. This could explain the men's appearance. In turn, the general ill-humor of the men could have some effect on the women's state of mind.

And then there is the complaining. In my thirty-seven years, I have lived in neighborhoods of lower middle-class people, middle-class people, and even upper middle-class people. The epoch in the Colony is the first and only time I have lived among truly rich people. But I have never heard so much complaining about the general state of the world as I have here, except for one brief semester in law school when I worked as a legal aide at a poverty law office in the middle of an all black, completely impoverished public housing project in New Haven. And even there, the complaining had an end when the complainers would tearfully thank the attorney for getting back their lost welfare checks.

But here, the complaining knows no bounds, either religious or economic or of age or time. The wife of the family across the street, a maniac in tight toreador pants at the age of forty-five, like a ghastly recall of Shelley Winters in the movie of *Lolita,* strolled over almost every day to complain that her daughter was a slut, her husband had ". . . overgrown his sexuality . . ." (whatever that might mean), and that she needed ". . . new outlets for the physical me. . . ." (I knew what that meant: Run and hide.)

The writer-producer who lives next door (with his second wife and his little beard) drops in at night to complain that he has been cheated by a large studio and cannot possibly make more than eight hundred K this year, as opposed to the one point three mil he made last year, and that he is sick and tired of being ". . . pissed on . . ." and made to feel like a bum.

The commercial office-space mogul who lives two down (with the little beard and the pinched-face twenty-five-year-old wife) was and is hysterical because the school where his three year old, Jason, goes to nursery school, at forty-five hundred per year, has just fired his favorite teacher. The woman had been in charge of a course called "character building," had been young, pretty, and had been busted by the Beverly Hills P.D. last weekend for turning tricks out of an apartment on Camden Drive when she was not at work teaching character building.

A TV executive who is about to marry the daughter of a German billionaire is bitter that the father-in-law has not already altered his will to provide for him. "Am I supposed to live on my salary while my wife clips coupons?" he asked me. "What the hell's the point of that? I might as well have married the checkout girl at the Colony Market."

Why do these people complain constantly? By almost any standard, they are dramatically well off. In general, relative to their age, they are uncommonly healthy. And, of course, many of them have wives half their age.

My theory is that the complaining has totemic significance, to ward off the evil eye of failure. It would be much the same as if primitive man asked the deity to have pity on his miserable self, fearful that boasting would tempt a fall. But in that case, why do the same people flaunt the fancy cars and the (second) wife's jewelry? Can it be that the same stringent diets are causing so much unhappiness that even men who are paid a million dollars for eight weeks' work cannot think of a kind word about their own lives? Or does the totemic significance attach only to spoken communications on the assumption that a malevolent deity is blind or does not know how much a BMW 633csi costs and that there will be no retribution for that visible hubris?

In any event, there is rich material here. For my next analysis, I am going to try to understand why any grown man or woman would allow his or her child to be an agent.

The Love Song
of James Earl Carter

(1983)

LEWIS H. LAPHAM

This is very special. The winner of our J. Gordon Coogler Award for the year's worst book is a former President of the United States of America. The thing was inevitable. Jimmy was President. He wrote his memoirs. As Georg Wilhelm Friedrich Hegel used to say, Timothy Dickinson tells me, what is had to be.

Yet you ask. Why have Lewis Lapham review this work? Why did I not take on the ceremony myself? In 1976, as editor of Harper's *magazine, Lewis Lapham was present at the creation, so to speak, and for four years he was duly indignant. Few shared his insight. In point of fact, only one other editor and one other magazine approached his astuteness and persevered in abominating the ignoble high jinks of Jimmy Carter throughout the rogue's brief and absurd public life. Humility and good taste restrain me from mentioning the editor and his magazine.*

Though Lyndon Johnson's presidency may have been the most disastrous of the century, it is now irrefutable that Jimmy Carter was the century's worst President. Nonetheless through all his shabby pratfalls only Harper's *and that other magazine that I shall not mention continued to jeer and to gasp. Others came to Lapham's position, but slowly; and few maintained the watch to the end. Most pundits remained silent, and they remain silent still. Toward the end, Lapham and that other editor who must remain anonymous were frequently being rebuked by the mature adults among the intelligentsia. "Come, come," they would be told. "He is the only President we have," or "He is soooo smart," or "We all know about Carter. Pick another ax to grind." Well, if everybody knew about Jimmy's pathetic presidency, why is no one writing about it today? Why to the contrary do so many persist in rolling out the same dubious conventional wisdoms about the scamp? In the* New York Times Book Review's *assessment of Jimmy's memoirs, the* Times's *former White House correspondent even repeated the tired myth that this transparent fraud is "an enigma."*

Well, of course Jimmy was the Times's *candidate. In fact, he was the candidate of all polite pundits, and by endlessly repeating the old fables about his prodigies they can spare themselves the pain of self-indictment. The pundits live in a fantasy world where all is bliss and gorgeous celebrity. The jolly times never end. Thus when Jimmy shambled out from the boondocks the giants of our time would not see him for the fantastic figure he was. He intoned their platitudes, and they were reassured. To this day the giants of our time cannot and will not recognize the damage he did. Mr. Lapham, it is your show.*

—RET

During his four years in the White House Jimmy Carter kept a faithful diary. An eager and voluminous diary. A lover's diary five-thousand pages long and bound in eighteen precious volumes. He made so many notes that it is a wonder he had time to do anything else. Apparently he was forever writing in a corner, jotting down his thoughts and observations, preserving his impressions of historic moments. An idealist or a Republican might say that this was not a proper occupation for the President of the United States, but so stern a judgment would fail to make sympathetic allowance for the Wagnerian magnificence of Mr. Carter's passion. He was writing about himself, and the subject so captivated him, so consumed him with the fires of love, that he abandoned himself to it in the way that lesser men abandon themselves to their enthusiasms for stamps or butterflies or Civil War cannon.

Now that Mr. Carter has made a book of his diary, an adoring memoir entitled *Keeping Faith,* the notes read like a collection of letters sent from scout camp. Arranged in chronological sequence, they tell the story of a boy and his mirror. The young and upright Jimmy Carter goes north to Washington, and there among the cruise missiles and the cherry blossoms, he has a wonderful time. He meets wonderful and important people; he thinks wonderful thoughts (some of them statesmanlike, others merely warm and human); he travels to romantic, far-off lands; he lives in an old and famous house; sometimes he is sad, but most of the time he is happy and brave. Once or twice he saves Western civilization.

The book continues in this voice for 596 pages, and except for Jimmy Carter's mother I don't know who could bear to read the whole of the correspondence. Presumably it is his mother that Mr. Carter has in mind as his perfect reader, and I'm sure that she also enjoyed looking at the candid snapshots (Jimmy in the Oval Office, Jimmy at Camp David, Jimmy among dignitaries, etc.) stuffed into the pages like blurred photographs of the camp baseball and swimming teams. For the purposes of a review, it is enough to read the first sixty-two pages (all of them introductory and advertised under the heading, "A Graduate Course in America"), and then to look at random through the rest of the collection. The tone never varies, nor does the scout's unfailing ability to achieve a subtlety of perspective comparable to that seen on a postcard of the Lincoln Memorial.

The scout concedes in his preface that he has no wish to write "a history of my administration." Not only would this be too difficult and boring a task, but, even worse, it might interrupt the diarist's elegiac contemplation of himself. Instead of a history he writes what he calls "a highly personal report of my own experiences" because he wants to share (certainly with his mother and maybe with a few other ladies in Plains, Georgia who wonder how he's doing up there in Washington) the "feelings of gratitude and pleasure" that he has gathered as keepsakes during his visit to the nation's capital.

The opening chapter is meant to be a dramatic account of Mr. Carter's last few hours in office. It is the morning on which his agents arrange to transfer almost $8 billion through the Bank of England in return for the release of the American hostages in Teheran. Given the events in question, another writer might have endowed the scene with liveliness and force. Mr. Carter reduces it to dullness by the simple expedient of staging the action in the theatre of his emotions. What is important is the play of the scout's feelings, not what is happening in Algeria, England, Germany, or Iran. Nobody else in the room attains the status of reality, and before he has gotten to page eight, Mr. Carter has reverted to extensive quotation from his beloved diary. At 1:50 A.M. he begins "jotting down some rough notes." The presidential stenography continues unabated for four pages until 10:45 A.M., when, "from Rosalynn: 'Jimmy, the Reagans will be here in fifteen minutes. You will have to put on your morning clothes and greet them.' "

During the intervening eight hours and fifty-five minutes Mr. Carter has jotted down twenty-five dutiful notes, and the reader is left to ask who, if Mr. Carter was serving as recording angel, was acting the part of President? The notes reveal the temper of the scout's mind. As for example:

7:55 A.M. . . . I am personally receiving reports on radio traffic halfway around the world—between the Teheran airport control tower and three planes poised at the end of a runway. The airport is on the outskirts of the capital city of Iran, and only a few months ago it was one of the busiest in the world.

I would like to think that Mr. Carter revised this entry when getting it ready for the printer, augmenting the excitement of "I am personally receiving reports" with the geopolitical dimension provided in the phrase, "The airport is on the outskirts of the capital city of Iran," but I'm afraid that the notation appears as Mr. Carter wrote it that morning in the White House, holding the telephone in one hand and scribbling notes with the other in order that his mother should be apprised of momentous events until the very end, until finally Rosalynn had to come and tell him that scout camp is over and that it is time to go home.

I quote the passage at length because it offers a fair example of Mr. Carter's method as well as the sound of his complacence. Whenever possible, he mistakes the novelties of technology for the substance of diplomacy; because he can listen to an air traffic controller "halfway around the world," he thinks he has become fully informed across the entire spectrum of Islamic affairs.

On page 19 the scout establishes the major key of pious self-approbation in which he composes the rest of his ballad to the lost loveliness of the Carter Administration. He is describing his wonderful, wonderful inauguration day, and as he and his wife "approached our new home," he remembers the following colloquy:

I told Rosalynn with a smile that it was a nice-looking place. She said, "I believe we're going to be happy in the White House." We were silent for a moment, and then I replied, "I just hope that we never disappoint the people who made it possible for us to live here." Rosalynn's prediction proved to be correct, and I did my utmost for four solid years to make my own hope come true.

On page 23 he completes the sentiment:

As we walked through the living quarters on my first day as President, we were properly awestruck—but comfortable, and at home.

Within the span of the next thirty-nine pages the scout effectively destroys his credibility as a witness to anything other than his own innocence. He compares himself, flatteringly, to President Wilson, and then, a few pages later, he expands the comparison to embrace Presidents Jefferson, Madison, and Jackson. He confides to his diary the thrilling experience of seeing his first movie in the White House; he admires his humility as exemplified in his wanting a policy of "no Ruffles and Flourishes or honors being paid to me"; feeling slightly sheepish, he confesses to the pleasure in hearing the military bands play "Hail to the Chief." The technological luxuries available to the President move him to little cries of wonder and delight. He is as pleased with "the quality of the notes" (i.e., the memoranda prepared by the household clerks) as he is with "the procedures for responding to nuclear attack." The same Christmas shopper's mentality animates his discussion of the men whom he chooses to serve on his staff and in his Cabinet. Into none of their characters does he evince the least glimmering of an insight. Ham and Jody and Charlie and Bert, of course, he knows from the old days in Georgia; these wonderful fellows professed their belief in Jimmy Carter before he was elected President, and so obviously there can be no question about their worth and talent. His Cabinet officials he looks upon as items of elite merchandise. He chooses them because of their titles and credentials, because he has seen them advertised in the pages of the *New York Times* and the catalogues published by the Trilateral Commission, the Aspen Institute, and the Council on Foreign Relations. The scout collects the ornaments of the policy-making establishments in the way that twelve-year-old boys collect the portraits of baseball heroes found in packages of bubble gum. He thinks of them as giants, as leaders, as Very Important People who have been to NATO and the Bohemian Grove. It never occurs to him that he is dealing, almost without exception, with the personifications of the same toadying mediocrity that distinguished the administrations of Presidents Nixon and Ford. Impressed by the merit badges sewn on the sleeves of the older scouts, the diarist marvels at their sophisticated banter with the camp counselors. He conceives of Zbigniew Brzezinski as "a first-rate thinker" and a master of expository prose. Mr. Brzezinski undoubtedly possesses many talents, but thinking and writing, at least in English, are not among them. To the scout this is unimportant. He believes what he reads on the labels, and it is enough that Brzezinski can find Czechoslovakia on a map.

By the time he comes to page 54 the scout has persuaded himself that he knows most of what needs to be known about "history, politics, international events and foreign policy." He tells his diary that he likes nothing better than to sit around with "Ham and Jody and Zbig," talking wonderfully important talk about the fate of mankind. He's been at camp for little more than a month, hardly time enough to unpack his catcher's mitt, but already he can "disagree strongly and fundamentally" on questions of state; already he has become the peer of Kissinger and Castlereagh, and guess what, Mama, these Very Important People, these veteran scouts who can read a menu in French, they nod and smile and listen to what he has to say. All of it is pretty big-time stuff, Mama, for a boy who, before coming north, thought that history was for girls.

"Next to the members of my family," he explains in one of his letters home, "Zbig would be my favorite seatmate on a long-distance trip; we might argue, but I would never be bored."

And then, of course, there was Fritz and Cy—the most expensive objects displayed in the catalogues. Wonderful, wonderful Fritz Mondale who was a man of such stature, and Cy, good old decorous Cy. About Cy, the scout can't say enough.

Among all the members of my official Cabinet, Cy Vance and his wife, Gay, became the closest personal friends to Rosalynn and me. He and I were to spend many good times together—talking, fishing, skiing, playing tennis—as well as the less enjoyable hours negotiating a Middle East settlement and praying for the hostages.

Later in the camp term the scout humiliates Cy in a particularly nasty and mean-spirited way, but this is Cy's fault, and by that time the scout has taken to referring to him simply as Vance.

On page 39 the scout briefly addresses the dilemma of nuclear war and responds with his customary self-satisfaction:

I wanted to understand our defense organization . . . and my myriad special responsibilities in the control and potential use of atomic weapons. This is a sobering duty of the chief executive of our country, and every serious candidate for this office must decide whether he is capable of using or willing to use nuclear weapons if it should become necessary in order to defend our country. Under those circumstances, I was ready to perform this duty.

That's about as far as the scout gets with the question, which, fortunately for all concerned, doesn't exceed the moral capacities required of a first-year camper. Nor does the scout have much trouble making decisions. On page 57 he explains that once he had found his way to the lake and athletic fields, he felt pretty confident with the camp routine.

I realized that my ability to govern well would depend upon my mastery of the extremely important issues I faced. I wanted to learn as much as possible and devoted full time to it, just as I had done as a young submarine officer, a businessman, a governor and a political candidate running against enormous odds to be elected President.

Because he "devoted full time to it," the scout assumes that he has reached complete understanding. How could it be otherwise? The scout believes that his time is not like other men's time, that he has been blessed with omniscience and grace. He also enjoys a close and long-standing acquaintance with God, to whom he "prayed a lot—more than ever before in my life." The alliance between his own sublime competence and God's political tips removed from his mind "any possibility of timidity or despair." Thus he could make quick work of the business of state ("option papers describing the choices I had to make rarely stayed on my desk overnight") and get back to the more urgent and poetic task of writing bulletins to his diary.

It isn't that Mr. Carter perjures himself in the first sixty-two pages of his memoirs but rather that he shows himself so incapable of self-knowledge that his words lose all hope of relation to the events he chooses to describe. Except as the odd expression of mind afflicted with terminal narcissism, how is it possible to accept the testimony of a man who believes that the White House is a fun and comfortable place, that Zbigniew Brzezinski is a first-rate thinker, that the arts of government devolve automatically, with the desk and the telephone system, on the occupant of the Oval Office?

If any doubts remain as to Mr. Carter's delusions of moral grandeur, he puts them to rest with the repeated references to himself as "a populist," i.e., a humble man of the people winning the prize of the presidency against the all but insuperable obstacles raised against him by the northern and eastern establishments. This is so ludicrous a misstatement of the facts that it changes the venue of Mr. Carter's self-serving fictions from the arena of political chicanery to the amphitheatre of clinical pathology. As a populist, Mr. Carter was a fraud. In the campaigns of 1976 he enjoyed the full faith and backing not only of the northern media but also of the eastern financial interests. He was the candidate boomed by the *New York Times,* by *Time* magazine, by David Rockefeller's Trilateral Commission, by the entire apparatus of eager Democratic office-seekers who hoped for nothing better than a chance, after eight years of eating nuts and berries in the Republican wilderness, to return to the picnic tables of federal patronage. The Democrats that year lacked the moral and intellectual energy to go to the trouble of staging even the pretense of debate. What difference did it make? What was there to say except that it would be nice to be back in Georgetown? Against Gerald Ford, the heir presumptive to Richard Nixon's disgrace, the Democrats figured they could win with any candidate willing to spend the required period of time in Holiday Inns. Carter would do as well as anyone else, largely because the media had become enchanted by a fairy tale of their own invention in which Jimmy Carter appeared as the avatar of the old-fashioned rural virtues believed (at least among city folks) to reside in small towns. It was the bicentennial year, and the media were in a mood to listen to homespun sermons and country guitars. To the editors of *Newsweek* Jimmy Carter looked like the political analogue of the Beverly Hillbillies and the Nashville Sound. The scout passed his preliminary examinations with people like Cyrus Vance and Douglas Dillon and Paul Austin, persuading those fine gentlemen on the admissions committee that he possessed the traditional southern qualities that William Faulkner attributed to the Snopes family—small-minded and mean, only too eager to do what he was told in order to protect the Yankee investment in the cotton fields. Two years later, after it became painfully obvious that the scout also believed his Sunday-school nonsense, the media turned away from him in scorn and disgust. By the autumn of 1979 Mr. Carter had become so peripheral a figure in American politics that he had to push his way into the locker room at the end of a World Series game in order to attract the notice of the television cameras. In November of that year he was rescued from oblivion by the divine intercession of Allah.

The chapter headings of *Keeping Faith* indicate that beyond page 62 the scout discusses China and Bert Lance and human rights and the energy crisis and the Panama Canal and Camp David and God knows how many other topics of pressing concern. I couldn't force myself to read the text. Neither would I willingly listen to a narrative of the Wilderness Campaign told to me by some poor soul imagining himself to be Ulysses S. Grant.

Glancing at the diarist's notes that continue throughout the book, I see that the scout persists with his relentless discovery of the obvious. Sometimes he marks the spot with an exclamation point. He learns that the press is irresponsible, that the Congress puts its private interests ahead of the public interest, that the Arabs and the Jews don't like each other, that the Russians have a lot of guns. Whenever something goes wrong, it is invariably somebody else's fault. Sen. Edward Kennedy prevents him from giving the country a wonderful, wonderful health-care program; Walter Sullivan, the American Ambassador in Teheran, causes him to suffer the agony of the hostage crisis; the Ayatollah deprives him of re-election in 1980; the American people fail him throughout his Administration because they concentrate too much on their own selfish interests and refuse to understand that he had come among them as their saviour and redeemer.

All in all, despite the world's ingratitude, the scout still manages to have a wonderful time. Toward the end it gets a little hard to find enough people who properly appreciate the gift of his person. During his last week in the White House he presides at a banquet for the happy few who remain loyal to his vision of a world that might have been. The evening is a wonderful, wonderful success. After dinner the guests go into the ballroom to listen to John Raitt sing hit songs from *Carousel* and *Oklahoma!;* several of the guests come forward to whisper compliments into the scout's eager ear. Of these flatteries "the most memorable of all" is presented by Slava Rostropovich, the cellist recently arrived in the United States as an exile from the Soviet Union. The scout thinks the phrasing especially fine because Rostropovich is "a courageous man . . . and special friend of ours" who has suffered the cruelties of a police state and therefore knows what life is all about. The praise of Rostropovich is worth ten thousand times the praise of the *Washington Post.* So delighted is the scout with the music of the cellist's "heavily-accented" voice that he must have found it difficult to wait until everybody left before rushing upstairs to tell his diary the wonderful, wonderful news. The entry deserves to be quoted in its entirety:

Slava Rostropovich gave an excellent little speech at our table, pointing out that the masses of people were often wrong—that what was significant was the personal relationship that developed between leaders or performers or artists and others. He said that we had meant more than anyone in the United States to him and his family when they came here from the Soviet Union. He pointed out that the masses made a mistake on November the 4th, as they had when they rejected Beethoven's Ninth Symphony, rejected *La Traviata,* and in the first performance of *Tosca* the audience reacted against it so violently that they couldn't even raise the curtain for the third act. He said history was going to treat my administration the same way they did Verdi, Puccini, and Beethoven. It was beautiful.

Diary, January 13, 1981

This notation all but ends the scout's reverie; it appears on pages 593 and 594, in the place that a musical composition would reserve to the coda. Nothing more needs to be said about the deranged melody that Mr. Carter plays on his two-string banjo. I'm told that the book was accorded respectful reviews in the *New York Times,* the *New York Review of Books,* and a number of other journals supposedly interested in the direction of American politics. If this is true and not merely a vicious rumor put about by right-wing extremists, then the nation probably can look forward within the next few years to the election of a President capable of composing even crazier music for drums, cymbals, and atomic bomb.

Iacocca: An Autobiography

(1985)

P.J. O'ROURKE

You see the poor bastards at every airport in the country and all the Ramada Inns, Avis counters, and Beef-and-Blank restaurants. They have shoes with metal dingles, vinyl briefcases, Seiko watches. They're dressed in poly-blend vested suits and don't know not to wear a belt with the vest. Horrible Yves Saint Laurent buckles peek out the bottoms of the waistcoats. They are America's young management meatballs. And every man jack of them has a copy of *Iacocca: An Autobiography* under his arm. It is the *New York Times'* number one nonfiction bestseller. It has overtaken *In Search of Excellence* as the nation's most popular business book. Over 1.4 million copies have been printed, and each is being read by someone who painfully traces his way down the page with a finger and moves his lips.

The secret is in there. The meatball knows it. If he can just read carefully enough he'll crack the code: "How I turned personal failure, corporate debt, the two-bit K-car, and a goofy last name into glory, fame, and worldwide respect."

Lee Iacocca is a hero for our time—a conceited, big-mouth, glad-handing huckster who talked the government into loaning his company piles of money. And *Iacocca: An Autobiography* is literature for our time. That is, it stinks. My copy looks like some origami instruction manual, it is so dog-eared from marking idiocies.

First, there is the beastly style, coarse, disorganized, repetitious, and bulked with oatmeal filler:

During that time the factories were simply not operating, which meant that both the machinery and the workers were idle.

John Riccardo and his wife, Thelma, were two of the finest people I've ever met. Unfortunately, the crisis at Chrysler was so severe that I never really got to know them.

To say the least, testifying before congressional and Senate committees has never been my idea of fun and games.

But then came the Depression. No one who's lived through it can ever forget.

Also, there's the earthy wit:

This was probably the greatest jolt I've ever had in my business career. When I thought about it, I was bereft. (That's a euphemism for feeling lower than whale shit!)

115

This much can be blamed on the amanuensis, William Novak, who should know better and ought to be held by his heels and shaken until his brains run out his ears and some more useful innard slides down and fills his skull.

The rest of the problems are Iacocca's own. He is a paranoid egomaniac. But those are not the terms. They are too clinical and blame-evading. We need older, stricter words. The man is consumed by pride and besotted with vanity. Every nitpick in his life must be of compelling interest to us, his co-adulators:

When I was in sixth grade there was an election for captain of the student patrol. The patrolmen all wore white belts with a silver badge, but the lieutenant and the captain got to wear special uniforms with special badges. . . . I loved the idea of wearing that uniform, and I was determined to be the captain.

. . . a number of journalists have reported (or repeated) that my parents went to Lido Beach in Venice for their honeymoon and that I was named Lido to commemorate that happy week. It's a wonderful story, except for one problem: it's not true.

There is persistent name-dropping done mostly with a degree of deftness thus:

Once, at a private dinner with Vince Lombardi, the legendary football coach and a friend of mine . . .

And every now and then we are treated to a passage of the following kind:

Once [Henry Ford] and his wife, Cristina, came to our house for dinner. My parents were there, too, and Henry spent half the night telling them how great I was and that without me there wouldn't be a Ford Motor Company. On another occasion, he took me to meet his good friend L.B.J.

Of course, self-love cannot be displayed in full bloom without a leafy green background of hatred for others. Chapter ten begins with the sentence, "In 1975, Henry Ford started his month-by-month premeditated plan to destroy me."

Darn that old Henry Ford, anyhow. And he'd just got done telling Lee's mom and dad what a swell kid they'd raised, too. Well, Lee is not going to take this lying down, not when he's got a whole book of his own to say things in. Iacocca launches a rhetorical assault the likes of which has not been heard since Cicero accused Marc Antony of screwing the pooch. Rapier thrust follows rapier thrust: Lee wanted a signed photograph of Henry Ford, but Henry never got around to signing it. Henry sold the company plane to the Shah of Iran for five million dollars and "The company lost a bundle on the deal." Henry used tax shelters. Henry told his executives to ". . . get off your asses and do what needs to be done for the black community," then later that day used the word "coon." And Henry Ford and women?

Actually I always thought he hated women—except for his mother. When Henry's father died, Eleanor Clay Ford had taken over the family and put her son Henry in charge. She also kept him somewhat in line.

But when she died in 1976, his whole world came tumbling down.

One sick bunny, that Henry Ford. What's more, he likes to have a few shooters and get wide:

Henry tried to be sophisticated and European. . . . But it was all a facade. After the third bottle of wine, all bets were off.

(With Iacocca in the next office, his head as large as a haystack and barbering from nine to five about what a big lasagna he is, who wouldn't need a drink?)

Anything can be excused by genius, and Iacocca has been called one. But where's this genius parked?

Iacocca's book is filled with managerial balloon juice. "The only way you can motivate people is to communicate with them." ". . . the speed of the boss is the speed of the team." "In addition to being decision-makers, managers also have to be motivators." "To sum up: nothing stands still in this world."

He exhibits general ignorance of business principles. "A couple of months after I arrived [at Chrysler] something hit me like a ton of bricks. We were running out of cash!" He berates the Federal Reserve Board for being primarily concerned with banking. He blasts America as "a nation enamored with investing in paper" as though the cash represented by stocks, bonds, and certificates of deposit were all jammed in a sock under Carl Ichan's mattress. He discusses the overseas retail prices of Japanese cars without reference to Value Added Tax, indicts the Japanese for exporting unemployment to the United States (How do they pack it? Does it spoil?), and he claims this for the United Auto Workers' reaction to his ballyhooed 1980 salary of $1 a year:

From that day on I was their pal. The union loved me. . . . They said: "This guy is going to lead us to the promised land."

Moreover, Iacocca exhibits *specific* ignorance of the automobile business. He says, "Now, it's true that you can't make money on small cars—at least not in this country." But Honda does, at its Marysville, Ohio plant. And General Motors is investing 1.5 billion dollars in a new domestic small car division, presumably not for kicks. Iacocca calls the Mustang II "a terrific design." It sucked. He says, "The K-car is a sensational product." It is adequate. He claims the Chevrolet Vega had a "pancake aluminum engine." It had nothing of the kind. And he proudly takes credit for the stupid seatbelt interlock ignition system that appeared on 1973 cars and disappeared as quickly as owners could unhook it.

Iacocca's idea of engineering:

The [Mercury] Marquis had achieved . . . the softest, plushest ride in the world.

His idea of design:

My plan was to create a new car using the same platform, engine, and even the roof, but to make enough changes so that the car really *looked* new and not like a spinoff of the T-Bird.

And the following explains better than John Stuart Mill himself could what it is Lee Iacocca does for a living:

. . . on the island of St. Thomas, we unveiled the new Cougar. At a beach lit by clusters of brilliant torches, a World War II landing craft pulled up to the shore and lowered its ramp. The audience was breathless as a shining white Cougar drove onto the sand. The door opened, and out stepped singer Vic Damone, who began to entertain.

But let's be fair. The man works hard. He took a risky job at a troubled company and managed to put it in the black. He . . . Oh, let's *not* be fair. This book is rubbish. The meatballs in the airports would be better off reading the phone book. Check under Brooks Brothers. A banker-grey two-piece chalk stripe with a button-down shirt and a pindot tie and at least you'll "really *look*" like you've got some sense.

As for Lee Iacocca, he's being bruited about as a 1988 Democratic presidential candidate. The man deserves no better.

Remembering the Kingfish

(1985)

VIC GOLD

Who built the highway to Baton Rouge?
Who put up the hospital and built your schools?
Who looks after shit-kickers like you?
The Kingfish do.
It's the Kingfish, Kingfish,
Friend of the working man,
Kingfish, Kingfish,
The Kingfish gonna save this land.
— RANDY NEWMAN
(Warner Bros. Records, 1974)

Speaking of memorable dates—as who isn't in this year of commemorative excess?—September 10 will mark the 50th anniversary of the death of the most dynamic American politician of the twentieth century. Alternative historians, take note: It was on that day in 1935 that the Kingfish—Senator Huey Pierce Long of Louisiana—died, thirty hours after having been shot while leaving the marbled state Capitol he built, and which still stands, in Baton Rouge.

I was only six years old at the time, but well remember the last news photo taken of Huey, which appeared on the front page of the New Orleans *Times-Picayune* the morning after the shooting. It showed him perched, arms akimbo, against the Speaker's rostrum in the Louisiana House. He was open-coated in his white double-breasted summer suit, with a Kingfish-cocky grin on his face as he put the legislature through its paces in a special session.

That was the way Huey had run the state when he was governor, and so long as the trains traveled from Washington to Louisiana and back, it was the way he would run it as United States Senator. "Now this bill here," he would explain, urging passage of a particular piece of legislation, "is just good govern-ment." And the House would pass it, no further explanation needed. As for the sitting governor—a hand-picked surrogate aptly named O.K. Allen—whatever the Kingfish wanted, the Kingfish got. "A leaf flew in the window of O.K.'s office," a critic of good government once commented. "He signed it." Intended as a dig at Huey's iron-fisted control of state politics, the remark was taken as a side-splitter, because most folks in Louisiana wanted things run that way in those days. Louisiana, by god, was Huey Long's domain, his fiefdom, his base of operations for the Great Campaign to come, the one to save this land. "I may

119

be the smartest politician in the country," the Kingfish told a Washington reporter. "I know damn well I'm the smartest in Loozyana."

In the spring of 1935, Huey wrote a book titled *My First Days in the White House.* Wrote it himself, no ghosts needed. A few years before, he had written the lyrics to his political anthem, "Every Man a King." I remember the song blaring through the family Philco as a prelude to his radio talks.

"Folks," he would begin, "this is the Kingfish. Now before I get into my speech tonight, do your neighbors a favor. Open a window or go next door and tell 'em Huey Long is on the air and he has something to say they ought to hear." Then the Kingfish would pass time telling a story—maybe the one about LeJeune the Cajun and the drowning drummer—before launching into one of his hell-raising spiels against Wall Street.

But first came the song:

> Why weep or slumber, America,
> Land of brave and true?
> With castles and clothing and food for all,
> All belongs to you.
> Every man a King, every man a King,
> For you can be a millionaire . . .

Oh yeah, as Huey's younger brother Earl used to say, the Kingfish knew how to work a crowd, in person or by radio. He knew the words and music that folks wanted to hear those Depression years, not only in populist Louisiana but in populist Peoria. By 1935—only two years after arriving in Washington—he was more than a regional phenomenon, he was a national figure. A secret poll taken by the Roosevelt White House showed that the Kingfish, running as a third party candidate in 1936, could siphon off enough Democratic votes to elect a Republican President. And according to the poll, Huey's "Share Our Wealth" program had as many prospective voters in the industrial cities of the East as it did in the rural South and Midwest.

That was about the way the Kingfish had it figured, too. He saw 1936 as his first time around, just as he had run for governor in 1924 and lost. Then, in 1940, he would run for the presidency and win, just as he had done in Louisiana in 1928. And then . . .

My First Days in the White House was Huey's projection of how, as President, he would bring to Washington the same principles of governance he had brought to Baton Rouge. Were there hard times in weeping, slumbering America? Just leave everything to the Kingfish. Hadn't he said, "If it weren't for being part of the United States, Louisiana would never have known a Depression"? Oh yeah. If anybody knew how to dry those tears and wake the sleeping giant, it was the Kingfish:

CHAPTER 1

It has happened. The people had endorsed my plan for the redistribution of the wealth and I was President of the United States. I had just sworn upon the Bible . . . to uphold the Constitution and to defend my country against all enemies, foreign and domestic. Yet standing there on the flag-draped platform erected above the East Portico of the Capitol, delivering my inaugural address, it all seemed unreal. I felt I was dreaming. The great campaign which was destined to save America from Communism and Fascism was history. Other politicians had promised to re-make America; I had promised to sustain it.

Keep in mind, those were the words of a first-term senator, a mere back-bench Democrat from a backwater state. We now live in purportedly free-spirited times, but can one imagine even a tenured senator with known presidential ambitions—say, a Gary Hart or a Bill Bradley—publishing that sort of scenario? Not on your high-tech, button-down life. But such was Huey Long's style: cornpone and chutzpah. He was brash, pushy, disdainful of the Establishment; which meant not just the established structure, but the established way of doing things. He had taken on, and whipped, the Baton Rouge crowd; he would take on, and whip, the Washington crowd.

Not that there wouldn't be a proper place in a Long Administration for an ex-President of Franklin Roosevelt's stature. The former President would become Huey's Secretary of the Navy. And there would be a place for Roosevelt's predecessor as well. Other Democrats could scorn Herbert Hoover, but the Kingfish would make room for him in the Cabinet—as Secretary of Commerce.

Oh, that Huey. He really knew how to cut the high-and-mighty down to size. But *My First Days* (published, as history would have it, after the author's death) wasn't written simply as an exercise in political whimsy. Rather, it was the calculated ploy of an outlander who had come to Washington both unawed and certain of his mission; an anti-Establishmentarian who had nothing but contempt for the Senate Club and who, at age 42, envisaged an American future that would one day find him perched against the Speaker's rostrum in the U.S. House, putting Congress through its paces.

Huey was crude. There is no denying it. He fancied silk pajamas and gave lessons in the proper mixing of a Ramos Gin Fizz, but two drinks and he was just another coarse redneck come to the big city. Impatient to get to the men's urinal in a Long Island night club, he tried to finesse the matter through the legs of the man in front of him. The effort cost him a much-publicized black eye, but his populist constituency was understanding. Out in the fields, when you gotta go, you gotta go.

On a higher plateau of expediency, however, the Kingfish could not be charged with the meaner crudity associated with Southern populists like Mississippi's Theo Bilbo and Georgia's Gene Talmadge. He did not ply the politics of race. On the contrary, considering the standards of his time and region, he was a moderate on the issue. Asked by a newsman how he would treat Negroes if elected President, he replied, "Treat them the same as anybody else, give them an opportunity to make a living." He despised the Ku Klux Klan, and when informed that the Imperial Wizard planned to come to Louisiana for a speaking engagement, the Kingfish called a special press conference to tell reporters that "that Imperial bastard will never set foot in Louisiana, and . . . when I call him a son-of-a-bitch I am not using profanity, but am referring to the circumstances of his birth." If the Wizard did venture into the land of the Kingfish, warned Huey, he would leave it with "his toes turned up."

Crude, crude, crude. On being served a gourmet dish at *haute cuisine*

Antoine's in New Orleans, Huey forked a bay leaf, held it up, and asked the waiter, "What's this wood? Bring me a steak." And when the commander of a visiting German cruiser dropped by his Roosevelt Hotel suite to pay respects, the Kingfish greeted him in green pajamas covered with a red and blue lounging robe. The German consul was outraged. "My country," he said afterward, "has been insulted." Huey was nonplussed. "Hell of a note," he was reported as replying. "It looks like war between Germany and Loozyana."

It was incidents like that—crude, yes, but audacious—that set Huey Long apart from other politicians, and forever defined, for me, the term "populist"; which is why, let me confess, I am less than impressed with contemporary politicians and would-be movement leaders who would claim the label for themselves. Populism, for anyone who remembers the original article, was as much a matter of political style as substance. And that style embraced a willingness (if not eagerness) to be less than "respectable" in the eyes of a critical press, to risk giving offense to Establishment sensibilities. None of the so-called "neo-populists" on today's political scene—given their propensity for button-down shirts and furrow-browed lectures on macro-economics—even comes close.

> The Boss regarded the fine paneling of the closed door for a couple of minutes.
> Then he said, "You know what Lincoln said?"
> "What?" I asked.
> "He said a house divided against itself cannot stand. Well, he was wrong."
> "Yeah?"
> "Yeah," the Boss said, "for this government is sure half slave and half son-of-a-bitch, and it is standing."
> "Which is which?" I asked.
> "Slaves down at the legislature, and the sons-of-bitches up here," he said. And added, "Only sometimes they overlap."
>
> —ROBERT PENN WARREN
> All the King's Men

In this age of docudrama, in which art and life are scripted to overlap in prime-time network mini-series, it would figure that when the name Huey Long is mentioned to some member of the under-40 generation the usual response is, "Right, I've read the book (or seen the movie)." Meaning not T. Harry Williams's definitive biography of the Kingfish, but Robert Penn Warren's novel. Indeed, the fictional voice of Warren's protagonist, Willie Stark—the Boss—resonates with that of the real Kingfish, and his rise and fall closely parallel Huey's, right down to being assassinated in the state Capitol by an idealistic doctor. "Why did he do it to me?" asks Willie; virtually the same words that Williams attributes to the Kingfish as he was being rushed to the hospital in Baton Rouge: "I wonder why he shot me?"

The wonder, really, is that Huey should have wondered. For years he had constantly talked about threats to his life and compulsively carried with him a retinue of bulky, gun-toting bodyguards for protection. Only two months before his death he had taken the Senate floor to announce he had uncovered a plot to kill him. "Does anyone doubt," he asked his fellow Senators, with rhetorical flourish, "that President Roosevelt would pardon the man who rid the country of Huey Long?"

In the event, Huey's assassin was riddled beyond hope of any presidential pardon, real or imagined. No fewer than fifty-nine bullet holes were found in the body of Dr. Carl Austin Weiss. In their frenzy, Huey's bodyguards thus silenced the only voice that might have answered, with certainty, Huey's last question.

The most reasonable theory advanced for Weiss's action at the time, and fifty years later, holds that the Baton Rouge doctor shot the Kingfish for personal, if idealistic reasons. Weiss's father-in-law was Judge Benjamin Pavy, an independent state jurist who had given the Long machine problems over the years. Pavy was up for reappointment to the bench, and the machine, which preferred pliant judges who owed their tenure to Huey's patronage, had marked him for early retirement. So Weiss took matters into his own hands.

Or so the theory goes. It makes as much sense as any assassination theory, yet to this day Huey's son Russell believes that Weiss did not act alone, motivated by a personal grievance, but as part of a larger conspiracy. Whose conspiracy? Russell won't say. However, there are several schools of thought on the subject in Louisiana, a state whose Byzantine politics lends itself to conspiracy theories. One school has it that Huey was eliminated by his longtime enemies, the old state political ring. A more ambitious theory holds that the orders to kill Huey came from Franklin D. Roosevelt himself; an unbelievable postulation, unless one has spent enough time in the state to appreciate what Louisianians, then and now, are capable of ingesting as truth.

The prime example of that credulity can be found in the ongoing speculation about what happened to "the box" Huey allegedly kept, the one containing millions in cash set aside for his presidential campaign. Rumors about "the box" surfaced shortly after Huey's death. It was reported—and T. Harry Williams confirms this in his biography—that the Kingfish's closest friends pressed him as to the whereabouts of the box even as he lay dying. Huey told them nothing. Did such a treasure actually exist? To the Louisiana political mind, there can be no doubt. The proof? What more proof of the box's existence is needed than the fact that it has never been found?

Fifty years after his assassination, the larger historical questions asked about Huey Long have to do more with the how and why of his life than the how and why of his death. To the Louisiana political and economic establishment he took on and whipped, the Kingfish is remembered as a radical leftist; if not a card-carrying Communist, the next worst thing. But the prevailing liberal Zeitgeist of the 1930s—and this is the view taken by contemporary historians, the late Professor Williams excepted—held that Huey Long was a would-be American Hitler, the fascist model for Sinclair Lewis's novel, *It Can't Happen Here*.

The New Orleans writer Harnett Kane, a Long critic who leaned toward the latter view, concluded in his book, *Louisiana Hayride,* that Huey was neither Communist nor fascist, because he had no "central philosophy." He was simply, wrote Kane, "pure dictator." And yet:

"He took Louisiana out of the mud," continued Kane. "He threaded her flat lands and her hill country with magnificent, if expensive, roads; crossed her bayous and rivers with towering high-cost bridges. Under his influence the concept of a state's services to its citizens underwent a sharp change for Louisiana and for some of the other Southern commonwealths. He made possible a broad expansion of the schools, of daytime facilities for the children, night classes for the adults. He could claim that he had increased enrollment more than 25 percent by his free textbooks, and had taught 100,000 of the state's 238,000 illiterates to 'read, write and cipher.' He improved hospitals and set up new ones. He provided employment to tens of thousands on his public works. He granted tax exemption on part of their property to rural and urban small-home owners. He eliminated the poll tax. . . ."

And more: For the Kingfish was a man of direct action, the sort of action that would exact the attention of his constituents and excite the imagination of at least one pre-teen political animalcule growing up on the streets of New Orleans.

Was there a disastrous run on Louisiana banks? Huey would get a $20 million loan from the RFC. But the money couldn't be cleared until Monday. If the banks opened Saturday, on schedule, a wipe-out would occur. What the state needed was a bank holiday. Let's see now, what happened on February 4, any year? Nothing. As Harnett Kane put it, February 4 proved to be the most uneventful day in human history. Ah, but what about February 3? On that date in 1917, the United States severed diplomatic relations with Germany. Surely, thought Huey, such a momentous event must have had a one-day overlap. So it was that Louisianians woke up the morning of Saturday, February 4, 1933, to learn that their banks would be closed because of a legal holiday, never before (or since) celebrated. They reopened, with deposits secure, on Monday.

Did Barnum & Bailey insist on bringing a circus to Baton Rouge on a Saturday afternoon the LSU Tigers were scheduled to play football? The Kingfish called the circus owners to ask them to delay their show until the game was over. It would hurt attendance at Tiger Stadium. Not a chance, said the circus. Oh, really? said Huey. "Brother, we got health laws in Loozyana, and the way I interpret 'em, every one of your animals will have to get dipped in sheep dip before they cross the line." Barnum & Bailey's decided a night show would be dandy, and the LSU Tigers played their game before a capacity crowd.

Oh, yeah, that Huey, he knew how to get things done.

But now, alternative history: What would have happened had Huey Long lived? Folks still ask that question in Louisiana, despite the fact that the issues he dealt in during his years of power and prominence have long since been forgotten, save by terminal Depressionacs who deliver keynote speeches at Democratic conventions.

Yet, half-a-century after Huey's death and forty years removed from his fiefdom, I, too, still find myself engaged by his possibilities as a leader destined to "save this land." Because—for all his lumpen socialist "Share Our Wealth" babble—the Kingfish was to this conservative what FDR was to the conservative who now spends his days in the White House: He was my political coryphaeus, the distant mentor of my younger days.

So I wonder. What would have happened, I ask myself, if the Kingfish hadn't been assassinated? What destiny awaited him? I wonder; then recall the answer a fellow Louisianian gave to the same question in 1940. "That's easy," replied Harnett Kane. "He'd have been assassinated."

Chuck Colson
vs. the Fundamentalists

(1986)

MALCOLM GLADWELL

Chuck Colson, the Nixon hatchetman turned evangelist, and Jerry Falwell, the Lynchburg preacher playing statesman, are brothers in Christ. But they're hardly close friends. They might have been—after all, one of Colson's tasks as a young secular humanist in the Nixon White House was to be the administration's liaison with the religious community—but somehow history got in the way. Falwell was still grounded in Lynchburg, excoriating the ghost of Martin Luther King for mixing religion and politics, when Colson was wooing religious leaders from the White House. By the time Falwell had his celebrated epiphany on the road to Washington, Colson too had changed, finding God and in the process turning his back on everything he had stood for in the past. "I wondered," said the transformed Colson, "how I could have spent three and a half years in the White House and missed so many things that really matter." Colson left power and politics for God. His autobiography, *Born Again,* sold in the millions, but he would seek none of the trappings of evangelical stardom—the television show, the crystal cathedral. He became a prison preacher, a minister to the hopeless and forgotten, working as closely with those who wield no power as he once did with those who do.

Today the two men are at odds. There is little doubt who Colson is referring to when he calls for "sober soul-searching" in the evangelical community because "worldly power—whether measured by buildings, budgets, baptisms, or access to the White House—is more often the enemy than the ally of Godliness." He has mocked the ascent of TV evangelists—"Some preachers, especially a few I've seen on television, sound like they've just hung up from a private session with Him before going on the air"—and questioned their pretensions to authority: "The quiet, often unnoticed actions of ordinary Christians . . . speak far more loudly than all the bombast of so-called religious leaders." Nor is there much doubt about whether the man who has quipped that "the Kingdom of God will not arrive on Air Force One" thinks Pat Robertson should run for President. "The presidency would not be something a Christian leader could run for, but something he'd be drafted for, and there is only one Person who could do the drafting." In other words, no.

It has always been true, of course, that some of the bitterest critics of the newly politicized evangelists have been other evangelists. Bob Jones (of Bob

126

Jones University) has said that Falwell's involvement with politics makes him the greatest instrument of Satan in America today. But no one's criticisms carry the weight of Colson's. In the fundamentalist panorama men have repented from crime or alcoholism or even—as in the case of Pat Robertson—a bad case of secular humanism. But never has a man been redeemed from something of the symbolic enormity of Watergate. "A religion based on conversion," Garry Wills has said of fundamentalism, "tends to measure the height of a man's rise by the depth of his fall." By this standard, Colson is a giant, whose power as an evangelist is owed entirely to the sinfulness of his political past. Bob Jones's quarrel with Falwell is theological; Colson speaks from personal experience. For his political sins he was sent to prison where, he remembers, "surrounded by despair and suffering, I began to see through the eyes of the powerless. I began to understand why God views society not through the princes of power, but through the eyes of the sick and the needy, the oppressed and the downtrodden. . . . I learned that power did not equal justice."

Chuck Colson is not simply the most powerful internal critic of the religious right. He is also, in a sense, the most sophisticated. Unlike so many of Falwell's detractors, he does not issue a blanket condemnation of all forms of political activity. In fact, through his prison ministry, the organization known as Prison Fellowship, he has become involved with criminal justice movements across the country. Colson explains that his own experiences with "the injustices in our courts, and the barbarisms in our prisons," inspired him to action. Today Colson the prison preacher is also Colson the prison reformer, an outspoken critic of capital punishment and prison conditions. He is for criminal restitution and innovative sentencing for nonviolent offenders. He has spoken and continues to speak directly to state legislatures in support of reform legislation because, as he puts it in his most recent book, *Who Speaks for God?*, "the only way to combat the demagoguery which so inflames public passions [about crime] is for Christians to work for laws which apply biblical standards to criminal justice issues."

Colson has even added to Prison Fellowship a registered political lobby group called Justice Fellowship, which, since its founding in 1983, has been involved in everything from the fight against Congress's recent Crime Control Act to the drafting of the 1983 Nunn-Armstrong "Sentencing Improvement Act." For Colson these were serious, critical battles. In fact, when the Nunn-Armstrong bill was tabled by the Senate, Colson reacted by including the addresses of the White House, the Senate, and the House of Representatives in his Prison Fellowship newsletter. Sound like a good lobbyist? "One thing about a democracy is clear," Colson wrote, exhorting his readers to action. "In it the people will get the government they deserve . . ."

There is a substantial difference, however, between Colson's political activity and that of the fundamentalists he criticizes. Unlike groups such as the Moral Majority with their broad emphasis on electoral politics, he sticks closely to single-issue lobbying. "We don't expect to be able to usher in the Kingdom of God," says Justice Fellowship director Daniel Van Ness, "but there are biblical principles we think we can apply to the specific question of criminal justice." Nor does Colson make political endorsements, urging Christians to vote only for men and women of demonstrated integrity. Justice Fellowship is careful to steer a neutral course. Armstrong and Nunn approached Colson in the drafting of their crime bill, not the other way around, and Van Ness stresses the symbolic importance of the bill's bipartisan sponsorship. On the state level, Justice Fellowship avoids the endorsement and support of organizations and interest groups, preferring instead to set up state caucuses of concerned individuals. The contrast between this narrow mandate and the Moral Majority is obvious.

Colson has a very clear sense, in other words, of the limits of his political activity. Even as he works for prison reform he recognizes that "penal institutions can't deal with the ultimate problem: the human heart. That's why the gospel of Christ is the only real answer." At the center of Colson's ministry is his individual work with prisoners. Through Prison Fellowship he has set up a highly acclaimed rehabilitative and support network that today uses local volunteers and professional counselors to minister to thousands of convicts, ex-convicts, and convicts' families. Justice Fellowship is simply conceived as a complement to this work. Michael Cromartie, one of Colson's early aides, explains that "Chuck set up Justice Fellowship to authenticate his concern for prisoners. He couldn't go in there and gain their respect if he weren't doing something for them on the outside." Even Colson's political conclusions—which essentially form a "liberal" agenda on criminal justice and prison reform—seem to have been reached less for explicitly ideological reasons than because of his firm religious conviction that "even a modest effort by Christians at evangelizing a prison can do more to reduce the crime rate than building twenty new fortresses."

Indeed, even though Colson uses the political process to advance certain of his goals, he seems to have little respect or patience for it. Drawing heavily on the work of French legal philosopher Jacques Ellul, Colson often argues that political power is an illusion, that the governing institutions are incapable of dealing effectively with human problems. An activist by temperament—"Jesus forgave sin *and* fed the hungry. . . . Can an obedient follower do less?"—Colson is frustrated by politics. "One of the major things that led to my conversion," he recalls, "was that when I walked out of the White House I realized most of the problems I had worked on there were worse when I left power than when I had begun." The religious right, he says, is in the grip of this political illusion: "Many evangelicals have sought to solve our culture's problems from the top down, by 'taking dominion over America.' Such rhetoric may make us conspicuous in the news, but for the most part we are also conspicuous by our absence from the day-to-day battles where human problems are most acute."

On occasion Colson will even sound like a radical when he talks about modern Christianity's evasion of social responsibility. He can be biting on the subject of the "middle class church"—that "attractive edifice in a location near a growing suburb and as far away from crime-infested downtown as possible . . . [with] committees organizing concerts, covered-dish suppers, Bible studies, slide shows, and the like." Once, on Jim Baker's television show "PTL Club," Colson stunned the audience by suggesting that the word of God was more real in the prisons where he took his ministry than there in the TV studio. As he remembers the moment: "I looked at the smiling, white, scrubbed-clean faces of the audience . . . the ladies with puffed-up coiffures that looked like spun candy; but my mind saw expressionless men in dirty brown, marching in cadence along steel and concrete ramps. For me this was reality . . ." Colson feels called to work among the "powerless and the oppressed." "Christians must no longer sit idly by," he says, in another context. "We must, if necessary, defy immoral authority."

Those who know Colson don't take this rhetoric too literally. He may sound off against the middle-class ethos, but the Prison Fellowship has its headquarters in an old mansion in Reston, Virginia, an "attractive edifice in a location near a growing suburb and as far away from crime-infested downtown as possible." Ladies with puffed-up coiffures that look like spun candy probably form the backbone of Prison Fellowship's financial constributors. As for defying authority and working outside of the system, Colson's ministry with inmates is possible only because of a special dispensation from Norman Carlson, director of the Federal Bureau of Prisons.

The point is that Colson uses the language of radical Christianity simply for effect, to shake up the traditional fundamentalist passivity toward social problems that manifest itself either in narrow evangelism—one Oral Roberts aide described his organization's prison ministry to me as "distributing 100,000 bibles and bible cassettes free of charge"—or, on the political level, as an arid "law 'n' order" mentality. There is absolutely no indication that because Colson borrows from the left he feels bound to it in any larger sense. This is a man who has taken communion from evangelicalism's most prominent radical—Jim Wallis of *Sojourner's* magazine—but who also once silenced a hostile college audience asking about Watergate by stating flatly: "Richard Nixon is my friend, and I don't turn my back on my friends." Political terms and the implications of ideology seem to have little meaning for Colson. Because, ultimately, he seems to hold the capabilities of politics in disdain, he seems to be above it, unfettered by its restrictions. This is the freedom Colson has found in being born again. The power broker for Nixon is now a power broker for Jesus. Colson doesn't feel beholden to any ideological standards save those of his conscience.

This apparent contempt of Colson's for politics and political institutions is at the heart of his debate with the religious right. Tim LaHaye, who as head of the American Coalition for Traditional Values (ACTV) and a founding board member of the Moral Majority, has just recently moved from the fundamentalist backwaters to a Washington office overlooking the Capitol, sounds more hurt than anything else when he says: "I think it would be disastrous for our country if all Christians adopted Colson's attitude." Another evangelical within the Administration speaks sharply of Colson's refusal to provide Christians in politics with guidance about how to square faith with secular responsibility: "I will tell you for a fact that if I were in any way uncomfortable with the use of power I wouldn't survive. Colson gives me no help in how to use political power in a place like the White House." Colson is so dismissive of the whole issue that when it comes to providing role models for the Christian use of power he will only make vague references to the English parliamentary reformer Wilberforce and render recondite theological distinctions that usually involve Mother Teresa—"she has no power in the worldly sense . . . but she has enormous authority."

The fundamentalists, above all else, want their struggles to be taken seriously. The purpose of the historic founding meeting of the Moral Majority was, according to its organizer Robert Billings, no less than "to draw up a plan to save America." LaHaye claims Colson has no sense of urgency. "His was a comfortable position when we enjoyed a Christian consensus," says LaHaye, "but that's been eroded by secular humanists." As LaHaye put it in an earlier interview: "They have us in a stranglehold. There are only 275,000 of them, but they control everything—the mass media, government, and even the Supreme Court. . . . Either the church is going to become morally active and set moral issues as the dominant standard for its elected officials or we will be overrun by humanist thought by 1990." For LaHaye, times have changed. Cautious lobbying must give way to voter registration, religious agendas, and Christian candidates. "Almost everything is political these days," he continues. "We've begun to realize that government is the most powerful human force in the world."

LaHaye and the Moral Majority have a point. Nathan Glazer, among others, has argued that the agenda of the religious right was only a response to the success of secular and liberal forces in America. Richard John Neuhaus, in an essay for *Commentary* entitled "What the Fundamentalists Want,"* portrays the fundamentalist entry into politics as an understandable response to an assault on their cultural and religious values. Does Colson appreciate this? Sometimes it's not clear that he does, and he seems to criticize fundamentalists for something that they themselves did not do willingly.

But it is one thing to say that the fundamentalists arrived at the public square reluctantly, and another thing to say that once they got there their inhibitions remained. This is what the fundamentalists' defenders have tried to argue. "At heart, Falwell remains a country preacher," wrote Dinesh D'Souza in his recent biography. Glazer too argues that the fundamentalists are engaged in a "defensive offensive" with limited aims. "If we withdraw from imposing the views and the beliefs of the cosmopolitan elite on the whole country," he concludes, "we will find the new fundamentalism returning to its modest role in the American kaleidoscope." Neuhaus, although he concedes that the activist fundamentalists "are not going to go back to the wilderness," stresses the modesty of their eventual goals: ". . . the country cousins have shown up in force at the family picnic. They want a few rules changed right away. Other than that they promise to behave, provided we do not again try to exclude them from family deliberations."

This is a seductive argument, especially for those with an interest in quieting what Neuhaus calls the "increasingly hysterical and increasingly hollow alarm" over the religious right. Yet—and this is Colson's strongest point—it does not ring true, not so long as Jerry Falwell turns from TV evangelism to

*Available in reprint from the Ethics and Public Policy Center, 1030 15th St, NW, Suite 300, Washington, D.C. 20005.

international ambulance chasing or Pat Robertson hungrily awaits word from God on whether to run for the presidency. There is simply too much eagerness in fundamentalist political activity—the exploitation of direct mail, the proliferation of PACs, the slick and lavish promotional efforts. They may have been pushed into politics, but now they like the game an awful lot. Tim LaHaye has on the cover of his monthly "Report from the Nation's Capital" a picture of himself on the Senate steps. Is he troubled? Is he tight-lipped? No, he's smiling, and somehow that seems entirely appropriate.

The fact is that in some sense fundamentalism has always been a political movement waiting to happen. Historian Edwin Orr points out that the appeal of modern evangelicalism is for "enlistment, not repentance"—in other words, that evangelists have always exploited Christianity's populist characteristics, its potential as a social movement, at the expense of the more demanding aspects of Protestant theology. Even as it has been in reaction to secular America, fundamentalist culture has shown a marked ability to adapt to social trends. Evangelical historian George Marsden calls this a historic propensity to respond to secularization "by bless[ing] its manifestations—such as materialism, capitalism, and nationalism—with Christian symbolism." In the fifties that meant that Oral Roberts, in preaching to a largely rural and poor audience, recast the gospel into a variation of the American dream. His text was John 3:2—"I wish above all things that thou may prospereth and be in health, even as thy soul prospereth"—not the book of Job. And today? Consider the two rules from Pat Robertson's 1982 manifesto *The Secret Kingdom.* This is yuppie theology: "First, there is absolute abundance in the kingdom of God. Second, it is possible to have total favor with the ruler of that abundance. . . . If a person is continuously in sickness, poverty, or other physical or mental straits, then he is missing the truths of the Kingdom." As Notre Dame historian Nathan Hatch sums up the modern evangelists: "[They] spoke the language of peace of mind in the 1950s, developed a theology of 'body-life' and community in the wake of the 1960s, and are currently infatuated with a gospel of self-esteem that correlates precisely with the contemporary passion for self-fulfillment."

In other words, it shouldn't come as a surprise that the fundamentalists have taken to the political process so quickly and completely. That strain in fundamentalism that believes in an abundant God, what Colson calls the notion of God as a "rich and benevolent uncle," has easily adapted to modern America's emphasis on acquiring and using political power. If prosperity is the gift of God, then so must be the political clout that comes with it. Do the fundamentalist meek still inherit the earth? Pat Robertson, the Christian entrepreneur made good, doesn't seem to think so. "God uses oak trees," he says, somewhat obscurely, "not mushrooms." For Tim LaHaye, making it in America means making it in Washington. Power is a Christian birthright. "If we comprise thirty percent of the people in this country," he maintains, "we should hold thirty percent of the elected offices."

This is a dangerous attitude for the Christian witness. For some on the religious right, advancing a political agenda has come to take precedence over even the most basic ethical considerations. A number of years ago, University of Chicago historian Martin Marty pointed out that the Moral Majority's evaluation scale for politicians would have given then Congressman Paul Simon, a committed Christian, zero, and Florida Rep. Richard Kelly, who was fingered in the Abscam investigation for pocketing a $25,000 bribe, a perfect rating. Does this mean that Christians should still vote for Kelly over Simon? Yes, says Tim LaHaye: "If I had to choose between a rascal like Kelly and an antimoralist, I would be inclined to vote for the rascal . . ."

In the fundamentalist world, ideological considerations have begun to color fellowship with other Christians. Just as Falwell found Bishop Tutu a "phony," Tim LaHaye expresses puzzlement at the fact that Sen. Mark Hatfield can be a liberal *and* a Christian. "He's a real enigma to us," says LaHaye. "He must be a melancholy temperament. Melancholy temperaments are such supersonic idealists that they are often highly impractical." And what of born-again Jimmy Carter? This time LaHaye is certain: "I shook hands with him twice and got absolutely no spiritual response."

Colson's objections to this politicized Christianity are not particularly radical, nor are they particularly new. In fact, these arguments have long been made against the religious left. Who remembers what Richard Neuhaus said of the political activism of the National Council of Churches just four years ago? "At stake, most ominously, is fidelity to the gospel of Christ. Chesterton said the great sin is to call a green leaf gray. It is the dullest gray to call salvation politics. The political task is urgent but it is one among many. Yet the imperiousness of the political in our culture is such that for many Christians the actual state of fellowship, how they relate to other Christians, is determined more by what one thinks of Ronald Reagan than by what one thinks of God." Today, as some of the fundamentalists are guilty of these same sins, it is left to Chuck Colson, the Nixon hatchet-man turned evangelist, to sound the alarm—not over what a politically ascendant fundamentalism is doing to the rest of America, but over what it is doing to itself.

Making It

(1986)

BRUCE BAWER

Standing in line at the supermarket checkout recently, I was intrigued to notice that the cover of the current issue of *Vogue*—a periodical to which I ordinarily do not pay a great deal of attention—boasted a "special report" on my hometown, little old New York. How could I resist? Eschewing the diverse attractions of the latest *Newsweek, TV Guide,* and *National Enquirer,* I grabbed *Vogue* and found my way to the "special report."

Alas, the report turned out to be less than special. It offered little more than the usual superficial survey of trendy restaurants, fashionable department stores, and high-toned hostelries. But leading off the whole thing was a keynote piece that I found myself reading all the way through, and then (since the man in front of me was buying enough groceries to stock a fallout shelter) reading all the way through again. Written by one Joan Juliet Buck, it was entitled "New York: Life at the Center of the World," and it went—in part, at least—like this: "Today, any man who is a real man has to measure himself against New York City, and that goes for any woman, too. To refuse is to be a pacifist, a coward, and a ninny." Indeed, "the duty of everyone alive is to participate in its existence . . . to stay away from New York is to live in the past and to refuse the challenge of opportunity." For "the past century has made New York America's capital, no matter what the official truth is: and the last five years have made New York the center of the world."

The center of the world! As I slipped the magazine back into its rack, it occurred to me that I'd run across a lot of pieces like that lately. They all had that same breathless, hyperbolic quality, as if the writer were trying desperately to convince himself that, yes, New York in the eighties *is* Mecca, Camelot, and Shangri-La rolled up in one. Why, I wondered, was it so important for them to believe this nonsense? Shouldn't the important question be whether living in a given place contributes to one's happiness and sense of fulfillment?

It's not, after all, as if the city has, in the past five years, become the center of anything that it was not the center of before. It is, as it was a generation ago, the headquarters of American garment production and of publishing, the home of the stock market, the location of great art museums and theaters and the New York Public Library and the United Nations. It is, as it was a generation ago, the city that young Americans migrate to in order to make their lives a little more interesting.

What's changed, though, is that these young Americans—who are now coming, as Miss Buck observes, in greater numbers than ever—are no longer drawn to Gotham so much by its real attractions as by the unprecedented and unrealistic hype of a hundred Miss Bucks. What started it all? Maybe it was Frank Sinatra's 1980 recording of "New York, New York," the song of the immortal if meaningless line: "If I can make it there, I'll make it anywhere." Or maybe it was Woody Allen's shamelessly romantic 1979 film *Manhattan;* or maybe it was the 1977 election of Ed Koch, that nauseating stereotype of a New Yorker who has become something of a one-man ad campaign for the Big Apple.

Wherever it began, the upshot is that hordes of young Americans, convinced that New York is The Only Place To Be, have swarmed into town, their determination to Make It There pathetically imprinted on their faces. Their other identifying characteristics are equally unmistakable. They refuse to live in Brooklyn or Queens or the Bronx (indeed, they make a point of boasting that they don't know their way around those dull Outer Boroughs). They laugh at tourists. They sport T-shirts that say "Welcome to New York—Now Go Home." They hang on their walls a copy of that *New Yorker* poster depicting a Manhattanite's view of America, with everything west of the Hudson exceedingly vague. They reside in sections of the city that used to be known as slums but have now turned into high-rent districts because these onetime out-of-towners are willing—nay, eager—to live there, among the chic New York rats and cockroaches, the chic muggers and pushers, the chic falling plaster and smell of urine in the hallway. One day a year or so ago I was standing with one of these new New Yorkers on the grimy front steps of his crumbling apartment building when he proudly nodded in the direction of a prostitute who was plying her wares not ten feet from us. "That's our local hooker," he boasted. "They don't have *those* back home!"

Most of these young immigrants come to New York boasting that they are artists of some kind—painters, poets, singers, musicians, dancers, actors, novelists. (Sometimes all seven at once.) To be sure, most of them support themselves by working as waiters, secretaries, and the like, but even if they never actually get around to creating anything, they persist in considering themselves to be artists and feel no qualms about identifying themselves as such. They would not get away with this back home, or even try to—but New York is different. It's not the real world to them but is, rather, an Emerald City, a Fairyland, a place to live out their dreams. They perceive New York's dirty streets, dangerous subways, and armies of street people not as real problems but as colorful fantasy problems, like the nasty apple trees, evil monkeys, and sleep-inducing poppies that Dorothy encountered on her trek down the Yellow Brick Road. The city's one big movie set to them; watching them walk down its streets, one has the feeling that they spend each day imagining that a camera is on them, tracking their passage up Fifth Avenue, past the Plaza Hotel, into Central Park. It is the presence of the imaginary camera, one senses, that gives their lives meaning. They are at the Center of the World, and the world is watching. (But of course it isn't.)

"I've conquered New York," an immigrant from one of the loveliest towns in the Midwest told me recently—meaning not that he had prospered or found contentment on the banks of the Hudson, only that he had survived. He was chain-smoking, was pale and nervous and tired, was living in a horribly over-priced East Village loft in what looked from the outside like an abandoned building—but, hell, he was still here! He'd *made* it.

III
The Sexes

The Woman Problem

(1970)

GEORGE F. WILL

Earlier this year America faced the tedious prospect of a new decade without a new oppressed group to liberate. But in one swell fell swoop our Yankee ingenuity conjured into existence a gaggle of downtrodden persons to uplift. We discovered that women need liberating and this discovery has liberated us from creeping ennui.

This oppressed majority will gain Uhuru come Hell or low hemlines. Just ask Barney Rosset, pornographer. Rosset runs Grove Press, an establishment guided by his philosophy: "What's wrong with exciting people? Our whole society—television, movies, fashion—is built on exciting people." The Women's Liberation Front recently added a new dimension to the exciting business of pandering to prurient interests.

The WLF sat in at Grove Press to protest commercial "sexism." The men at Grove Press are fierce opponents of repression, but they take a businesslike approach to mixing business and pleasure. They had the WFL protestors arrested. This was good for the Grove Press property rights but bad for its revolutionary reputation. The WLF promptly announced that Grove Press has "the same mentality as Judge Hoffman" and demanded an end to "one-dirty-old-man-rule" at the Press. This reference to Rosset was less than fair. He is only forty-seven.

Most men know that struggling women need dramatic tactics, like bra burning, for it manifests the liberated woman's escape from the roles and stereotypes of a male-dominated society. Hence most men would suffer death, or at least a mild blister, in defense of every American's right—regardless of race, color, creed, national origin or sex—to burn bras.

Yet regrettably this form of bodily witness, so helpful in eliminating false consciousness, causes air pollution. Recent studies reveal that if every women in America were to burn three slightly padded bras there would develop an enormous increase in air pollution and an enormous glut in Manhattan's garment district.

This is acceptable. As Lenin said, you shouldn't break eggs without making an omelette. Besides, the First Amendment is precise and unambiguous: Congress shall make no law abridging the right of even the most flamingly symbolic speech. If men have the right to burn draft cards, then the principle of sexual reciprocity stipulates that women have the right to burn bras.

Some male Neanderthals thought female suffrage would suffice to end female servitude. This was rank sociological naivete. Advanced thinkers understand that we must use compensatory programs to correct the terrible legacy of centuries of unbridled male tyranny.

We need an ambitious program to salvage those young women who suffer the cultural deprivation of attending predominantly female colleges. Such a program could be called Upward Curtsey, and could use Federal funds to send (say) Bryn Mawr graduates to Atlanta, Georgia, for a two year hitch in the robust and rehabilitating atmosphere of Georgia Tech. Upward Curtsey would affirm the basic principles of the American Dream by guaranteeing any American girl the chance to grow up to be a Rambling Wreck from Georgia Tech.

It would be even better to directly attack what the "Mrs. Kerner Commission" calls "institutional male chauvinism." Let us begin by distinguishing between *DeJure* and *De Facto* discrimination.

DeJure discrimination is that which is established by law, or by the deliberate acts of public officials; such is the ban which bars women from the New York Mets' locker room. *De facto* discrimination results from community customs or mores, such as the practice of giving a lady your seat on the subway. The Constitution is not only color blind but sex blind, and it is immoral to tolerate laws or customs that take notice of another human being's sex.

Fortunately women have not fallen victim to the wretched condition denoted by the wretched noun "ghettoization." As a result of dumb luck (that is, without HEW guidelines), women are spread evenly across the nation. Balanced residential patterns reduce the need for forced busing to achieve sexual balance in schools. Nevertheless, some busing is needed to eliminate pockets of impacted sexual imbalance.

For example, there was a time when Smith College, Northampton, Massachusetts, actually boasted about being the nation's largest all-female college. Although this "peculiar institution" is becoming co-educational, the pace of Smith's progress is unacceptable. Under the guise of "deliberate speed," Smith is substituting tokenism for meaningful change.

The government must mount a determined attack on all such "private" institutions. Their so-called "privateness" is an illusion which must not insulate them from public control. After all, every autumn the students get to these colleges by driving over public highways. Therefore the students are engaging in interstate commerce and the colleges are permeated with public aspects.

Such colleges must be compelled to conform with the law of the land, which is that every school must have a sexual composition identical with that of the surrounding community. The Justice Department should seek a court order requiring Smith to bus males from (say) Amherst until the Smith student body has the same sexual composition as the town of Northampton. Forced busing is awkward, but no one can take seriously the disingenuous argument that Smith women and Amherst men will get together without Federal compulsion.

Advanced sociological thinking supports the justice of such busing. Federal officials will soon release the "Mrs. Coleman Report." This is the fruit of a multi-million dollar research project which proved what it set out to prove, namely, that when young men and women study together they learn some things they might not otherwise learn in school. Therefore, it is monumental hypocrisy to attack *de jure* sexism while leaving the *de facto* form untouched. It is time to opt for minimum standards saying "Never!" to deliberate speed, letting the chips fall where they may, and pausing only to pluck the blossom equality from the nasty nettle sexism.

Now after forced busing achieves integration at all schools, we must recognize the justice of women's demands for creative sexual separatism. We must acknowledge the independent dignity of "female culture" by establishing "female studies programs" that will cleanse the sex-bias from our hairychested university curricula.

The "historical sexism" that lavishes attention on Napoleon while downgrading the contributions of Catherine d'Medici and Katherine von Bora must end. We must demand that the time devoted to Catherine the Great be proportionate to the real uniqueness of her behavior. Fairness demands that if Faulkner is studied, there must be equal time for Eudora Welty. The principle of literary sex parity requires trade-offs between Sinclair Lewis and Ayn Rand, or Norman Mailer and Taylor Caldwell. And breathes there a woman with a soul so dead, who never to herself has said, "One Hemingway deserves a Willa Cather?"

Some persons worry that women's liberation will distract us from the all-important task of fending off environmental apocalypse. But that worry betrays an insufficiently systemic view, for the new science of "issue ecology" teaches that every issue is related to every other issue in this troubled biosphere.

Dr. Mary Calderone, director of the Sex Information and Education Council of the United States, recently demonstrated awareness of this when she told the Women's National Democratic Club that, "The primary ecological system that all other systems need to serve is the relationship between a man and a woman. It, too, is subject to pollution." Clearly there are more forms of pollution under the sun than appear in the Sierra Club's philosophy.

Dr. Calderone understands the charm of "environment" as a political issue. One cannot turn around (or roll over in bed) without rubbing up against environment. This is deliciously egalitarian. Anyone with a grievance is relevant now that "environmental concern" is the measure of relevance.

Fastidious people may claim that Dr. Calderone is contributing to semantic pollution in order to make her cause congruent with this month's priorities. But it is tolerant to believe that pollution is in the eye of the beholder. Anything that bothers you is a pollutant of your environment.

Of course, when we sweep every one of the world's disagreeable features into the "environment crisis" we turn the term "environment" into a classification that doesn't classify. But while the term loses precision, it gains an ability to make one feel au courant, which is how I feel when I can classify bad books, shoddy arguments and Senator Fulbright as "pollutants" and ecological disasters. Women liberators must feel relevant twice over—as freedom fighters and environment cleaners.

Female assertiveness is going to have some dramatic effects on American life. If women shun jobs to which they were once relegated, who will be airline stewardesses? The day may come when the traveler slumps wearily into his seat, only to hear a rich baritone voice asking "Coffee, tea or milk?" Thus the women's liberation movement may rescue the railroad passenger business. Women may break the sex barriers in many occupations. Someday a woman may play tight end for the Baltimore Colts. Then imagine the spectator interest that would arise over a 15-yard penalty for illegal use of the hands and arms?

Finally there is the stigma of servitude attached to the exclusive use of women in the *Playboy* centerfold. Equity demands a color centerfold of Joe Namath, stapled in the navel. This will give men a sample of the shame and horror women feel when they are cast in the role of pliable sex objects.

There is one basic reason why women are victims of capitalism, male chauvinism, institutional sexism, imperialism, objectification, Hugh Hefner, psychological deformation, moral mutilation and physical exploitation. The reason? Women have nice bodies, and fortunately, government cannot do much about that.

We are much in need of a conspicuous problem which clearly cannot be solved by government. Some Americans do not believe such a problem exists. But the soft, warm, intractable fact about women's problems may teach these Americans an invaluable lesson about the very finite capabilities of government.

Women's liberation will not be a gift of government. Women must save themselves. Most important, they must not be betrayed into servility by "Aunt Toms," those collaborationists who trade their birthrights for a mess of service. No woman will be free until all women are willing to step on cockroaches. This is a stern test, but as the philosopher said, if women can't stand the heat they should stay in the kitchen.

Men Without Women

Meditations on the Half-Life of the Homosexual
(1978)

MICHAEL NOVAK

A peculiar paradox emerges from recent debates about homosexuality. On the one hand, proponents of homosexuality speak of "sexual preference" and "alternative choices." On the other hand, they speak of being "trapped," of "having been given a different nature." So there are really two different possibilities involved. First, if homosexuality is a matter of choice or preference, it lies in the realm of freedom. The argument then concerns whether such choices ought to be encouraged or discouraged; whether, in a word, homosexuality is a good choice. Second, if homosexuality is a matter of nature, it lies in the realm of necessity. The argument then does not reach so high a moral level. Those involved are not really free to choose an alternative. They suffer from a diminished range of freedom.

The moral argument about this second alternative is sometimes simply expressed as "Do what comes naturally," or "To yourself be true." In other moral traditions, however, the limitation of freedom involved in this alternative constitutes a moral defect, like kleptomania, pyromania, or other "natural" psychic flaws. Few human bodies fulfill classical possibilities of form; so also few human psyches. Each of us carries serious flaws. In some traditions, homosexuality is such a flaw. It makes people suffer, but does not make happiness or moral courage impossible.

It is probably important to distinguish between male and female homosexuality. Male infants have a hurdle to jump—I speak as a nonscientist—which females do not have to jump: *viz.*, a transference of their sexual identity away from their mother, with her sensual closeness, to their father. A distance must be established between the male and the mother, and an identification made with the father. One must appreciate the fact that, in a percentage of cases, this transition will be handled very rudely. In addition, one anticipates the probability that the natural endowment—hormonal, neural, emotional, whatever—of a certain percentage of children will not follow the norm. Aristotle pointed out long ago that nature does not work flawlessly, but only "for the most part," i.e., with considerable looseness and randomness, producing a spectrum of individu-

143

als from the nearly flawless to the seriously aberrant. None of us ever chose our nature. Yet we each do become responsible for what we make of it.

When the male infant does not make a successful transfer in sexual identity to the father, the male is attracted to other males. Females may even seem to him repulsive, surrounded by an aura of conflict or disinterest. In past ages, such homosexuality was sometimes construed as a danger to the human race because it meant (a) a decline in population, or (b) a decline in those masculine qualities essential for survival. What happened in the socialization of the young male was perceived to be of greater significance, and of greater risk, to the race than what happened to the female. Unless I am mistaken, even today society is in a more troubled state about male homosexuality than about female homosexuality. Lesbianism may suggest infantile pleasure and regression, but it does not threaten the public, at least not to the same extent that male homosexuality does. Female handholding, public exchanges of tenderness, and the like indicate that females are permitted a more relaxed attitude than males with members of their own sex. Female homosexuality seems somehow more natural, perhaps harmless. Male homosexuality seems to represent a breakdown in an important form of socialization.

The point may need elaboration. Recent publicity about women has served to shield us from an event of far greater significance: the decline of value, status, and the need of "masculine" qualities. In modern corporate life, "mother bureaucracy" swallows the strong ego. Rewards do not come from taking risks, being aggressive, speaking out. In the rationalized, smooth world of government and corporate life, "going along to get along" wins more certain rewards.

The rules of corporate bureaucracy may be more decisive in altering sex roles than the pill. These rules weaken masculine qualities in obvious ways. Yet the male spirit leads one to put one's own body at risk; a degree of occasional physical danger is as necessary for male living as air. The modern era suffocates the male principle. (I say "male" rather than "masculine" to emphasize the high animal spirits involved, the instinctual base on which culture works.) The deep and wide-ranging changes in our experience of maleness have been too little explored. They have certainly induced vast sexual confusion.

They may also—in an odd way—help to cast light on at least part of the inexplicable rage among contemporary women. Suppose that some women, unconsciously, seek the male principle and cannot find it realized in the corporate men around them. What a vast disappointment there seems to be among women today about the men of their acquaintance. They *tell* us that we are "male chauvinist pigs." But what if they *mean* that we are not even males, that they can have no respect for us? The fact that so many men cave in before the rhetoric of militant feminists must only increase the rage, by proving its unconscious point.

Is it true that the number of homosexuals is multiplying in our day? Who could marvel if it were? Men find it perplexing to be male. Seeking the male principle, some women are trying to supply it themselves. It is not just that "sex-role stereotypes" are breaking down. Rather, basic systems of identity have been profoundly altered by the technology and organization of modern life. Personal confusion abounds. The problem is deeper than that of homosexuality alone.

Society has a special stake in the development of married family life. Without strong, enlightened, spiritually nourishing families, the future of society looks bleak indeed. The family is the original, and still the most effective, department of health, education, and welfare. If it fails to teach honesty, courage, a desire for excellence, and a whole host of basic skills, it is exceedingly difficult for any other agency to make up for its failures. Who would trust politicians to do the job?

More than that, society has an important stake in nourishing that special wisdom and powerful realism learned in marriage in the battle between the sexes. For thousands of years, masculine culture and feminine culture have been quite different. It is not easy for men and women to understand each other, or to learn to be honest with each other. "Honesty" may mean something different to males and to females.

In addition, the raising of children is morally demanding in a special way. Most of what one learns is failure. A raw realism develops. The brute demands of running a house, of keeping order, of teaching all that one must teach, and of encountering the daily struggles of self-will and self-assertion on the part of each parent and each child are of great moral significance. Sometimes the moral life of families is taken to be conventional and easy. It is not. Moral health must be won against great odds by each couple and each family, starting from scratch, and battled for over and over. We are learning in our generation how many social supports are necessary to make family life successful. We are learning the hard way. In the *hubris* of pursuing "progress" through affluence, mobility, and the promotion of individual hedonism on a vast scale, we have destroyed most of these supports.

I must add here that I am a Catholic—not to say that other traditions do not have analogous concerns, but only to give my own comments moral concreteness. Morals do not come down to us in some universalist language of the lowest common denominator, but in the concrete rituals, voices, affects, and symbols of long historical traditions, internalized by individuals who carry them. To my mind, the human body is a dwelling place of God, and the joining of a man's and a woman's body in matrimony is a privileged form of union with God. The relationship is not merely that of a mechanical linking, putting genitals here or there. It is a metaphor for (and an enactment of) God's union with mankind. Marital intercourse thus reenacts the basic act of creation. It celebrates the future. It acts out in the flesh a communion of two separate persons who are not, at the beginning of their marriage, or at their fifteenth or any other anniversary, nearly as united in fact as this symbol pledges them to become.

There is no doubt that women can truly love women, and that men can have profound love for other men. (Aristotle, indeed, argued that men could only be true friends with men, not with women, because friendship depends on equality, and men and women did not have equality.) In some ways, friendships are indeed easier between persons of the same sex. Sexual relations between men and women are enormously complex, so that one short lifetime is normally insufficient to plumb even one such relationship. Heterosexual relations are full of terror. They are not as rosy and cheerful as *Playboy* and *Penthouse* would puff for our infantile fantasies.

Men have done most of the world's writing, so we are well informed about how little, and how poorly, men understand women. It would be foolish to believe—all experience tells against it—that women understand men any better. (In a secret area of bias, I confess to believing that men, at least sexually, are simpler to understand. The truth is so simple, I think whimsically, that many women cannot bring themselves to believe it. They keep looking for deeper, more complicated explanations.)

Society has a great—an overwhelming—interest in the battle between the sexes, and in its successful negotiation by its millions of couples. Even given the full social supports of an economic and cultural and spiritual system, such as we do not now have, not all couples can be expected to be successful. In a system as fantastically successful, rich, and centrifugal as ours, the casualties must be many. Democratic capitalism necessarily develops powerful contradictions, as Daniel Bell has spelled out. It is the freest system ever devised by mankind. But it sends individuals off every which way, in general moral incoherence. The effort to nourish strong families in such a system places huge burdens upon each solitary couple.

Great strides have been made in recent years—strides which I welcome—in winning tolerance for homosexuals. Tolerance for individuals does not entail moral approval, however. In a democracy, one must live and let live. But one is free to argue against. From my point of view, homosexuals absent themselves from the most central struggle of the individual, the struggle to enter into communion with a person of the opposite sex. That is the battle most at the heart of life. Excluded from this struggle, whether by choice or by psychic endowment, the homosexual is deprived of its fruits. Those fruits are a distinctive honesty, realism, and wisdom taught by each sex to the other: that complementarity in which our humanity is rejoined and fulfilled. Apart from this civilizing struggle there is a lack, an emptiness, a loss of realism. On the other hand, God knows, there are compensating riches of the spirit. Often those deprived in one way are the most sensitive and creative in others. Fulfillment does not depend on being heterosexual, or married, or familial. But the marital ideal nourishes every other ideal we have.

Psychiatrists have ceased calling homosexuality a sickness, or a lack, but one is not sure that they—or others—have ceased thinking that way about it (or that they should). There are three features in the very structure of homosexual life that tell against it. The first is a preoccupation with one's own sex. Half the human mystery is evaded. The second is the instability of homosexual relationships, an instability that arises from the lack of the full dimension of raising a family. Apart from having and raising children, a couple can hardly help a degree of self-preoccupation. The structure of family life—the same onerous structure that feels like a "trap"—places the married couple in a context larger than themselves, shields them from one another, so to speak, and opens up new avenues of realism and honesty. It is an especially important experience to exercise the authority of a parent, having rebelled against mother, or father, or both, for so many years. Only thus does one see things from the other side.

Thirdly, the homosexual faces a particular sort of solipsism, which is difficult to escape simply through companionship. Homosexual love is somehow apart from the fundamental mystery of bringing life into the world, and sharing in the birth and death of the generations. It is self-centered in a way that is structural, independent of the goodwill of the individual. Marital love has a structural role in continuing the human race that is independent of the failures of the individuals who share it.

There are also particular dangers in homosexuality. If it is true that the homosexual is lacking something that nature usually intends, then that lack is bound to be felt, at least unconsciously. A certain rage against nature is likely to be felt, and perhaps internalized and directed at the self. Of course, it is often argued that nature has made no mistake, that the homosexual is fully endowed, and that it is *society* that is the cheat. The rage will then be directed against society. Yet even in this case, one will expect to see the rage turned inward, and one will not really expect it to be assuaged by public approval. Indeed, the more the public might seem to approve of homosexuality, the more one would expect homosexuals to begin punishing themselves. For the source of this rage is not merely an anger at being different; it is deeper than that. One knows one has been left out of something. One wishes to be accepted for what one is. But one does not wish to be told lies in the process. One can make something heroic out of a flaw in oneself, but not by lying.

In fact, the climate of the last ten years—just the years in which tolerance and "understanding" have been growing in unprecedented ways—has encouraged the growth of rage among homosexuals. First, it has become conventional to rage against society. Negativism and hostility are in the air. For homosexuals, however, rage against society will not alleviate rage against the self. That rage must be dealt with by the self. Self-fulfillment is at stake. (This does not mean mere self-expression, or doing what one feels like doing.) Self-fulfillment is doubly difficult for the homosexual; it is hard enough for everybody. But the married person with family has so many demands made by others upon the self that many painful blows are struck from outside-in, so to speak, and this is an inestimable advantage. (Edward Albee's hideous play about a marriage, *Who's Afraid of Virginia Woolf?*, only appeared to be about a man and wife; the dialogue was unmistakably that of the soul in rage against itself. The play is an almost perfect metaphor for the rage of the homosexual against himself.)

Second, a peculiar sickness fell upon the rhetoric of blacks during the past decade. It was duly reported by the media as authentic. Incredible poses were struck, rage was faked, pantomime was acted out. Instead of seeing this charade for what it was, many good liberals employed a double standard: Blacks act "funny," so this play-acting must be true. Then everyone who wished to gain the benefits accruing to the "oppressed" through the media began aping militant blacks of that period (now already out of style). "The student as nigger" was the first act. "Women's liberation" was the second. "Gay Power" came third upon the stage. Howsoever poignant the stories to be told, they now come out as canned, bowdlerized, third-rate imitations. Can anyone doubt the inevitable result if this charade continues, long after the public has seen through the symbolic form? Demonstrations of fist-waving homosexuals carrying placards fulfill stereotypes in the public mind surrealistically.

The politicizing of almost everything—I call it "Nixonizing"—is a symptom of civil corruption. Politics is a clumsy instrument for the teaching of tolerance or the spreading of moral enlightenment. Other social forces (the arts, the schools, the churches) can do such things; not politics. Not only is politics a blunt and destructive instrument, supplanting precise reason with slogans, stereotypes, namecalling, and other campaign necessities. It is, in addition, an awakener of fierce counteraction. If one is seeking tolerance and solid shifts in underlying values, politics defeats one's efforts by stimulating and crystallizing opposition. Politics awakens irrational forces. It is not a wholly rational sphere.

That there are, and always will be, homosexuals among us (among our friends, in our families, among those we work with, throughout society) is certain. That they are often among our most talented, creative, and successful citizens is obvious. Yet the homosexual condition offers rather more inner suffering and sorrow, even with its normal quotient of human happiness, than I would wish for my children or for others. Heterosexuality is the full and complete human ideal. Homosexuality is not a preference of equal moral weight. Still, it would be good for laws specifically aimed against homosexuality to be stricken from the books, so that the coercions of the state do not enter into private life. Similarly, no one should be coerced by the state into giving approval for a way of life of which he does not approve. The state should be kept as much as possible outside such questions.

Homosexuals have psychic desert enough without adding to it. As often happens in life, their own inner sources of adversity are often transformed by courage into unusual creativity. Homosexuals know that powerful social pressures may induce behavior otherwise not freely chosen. Yet no social system completely determines behavior, and in any healthy social system there must be room to experiment and to live in many different ways. Society has a strong interest, in private and in public, in encouraging heterosexuality and in discouraging homosexuality. To do so without injuring those homosexuals who are without choice, and to establish conditions in which their lives may be tolerably creative and satisfying, is an important social task. I am in favor of a tolerant and open system. I am not in favor of one that treats heterosexuality and homosexuality as equals, or as matters of indifference. Individuals (and societies) can make their own moral vision clear without undue coercion upon those who do not, or who cannot, share it. For the good of all of us, homosexuals included, it is well that society should prefer heterosexuality and specially nourish it. The future depends on it. But it is also good for all of us to lighten the burdens of homosexuals, as we would have them lightened for ourselves.

A Handbook for Maidens

(1980)

JOHN SIMON

What, one might well ask, does the sacrifice of a few words matter as long as the social fabric is strengthened thereby? Bear in mind, however, that no change ever stops *there,* wherever the particular *there* may be. Take the case of feminist English and its demands from, and depredations on, Standard English. Take, for example, the war on the masculine pronoun in its all-encompassing sense. Whole treatises have been written by feminists to prove the enormous psychic damage done to women by the grammatical masculinity of *everyone* and *anyone*—by our saying, for instance, "Everyone was in his place" or "Anyone can make up his own mind," and the like. Such usage has allegedly convinced countless women through history that they were second-class citizens, excluded from full participation in humankind or, as male supremacists through the ages have called it, mankind. If I were frivolous, I could remark that at least half of such statements carry a negative value, and that women might count themselves lucky to be excluded from such asseverations as "Everyone is dumber than he ought to be" or "Anyone can become the victim of his gullibility." But let me be strictly serious.

In the just-published *Handbook of Nonsexist Writing,* Casey Miller and Kate Swift—two journalists who previously collaborated on the book *Words and Women*—have a relatively long chapter on "The Pronoun Problem." I shall address my remarks chiefly to this; to attempt to refute the *Handbook* point by point, I would have to write a book myself and stoop so low as to debate the authors about why I still prefer "manhole cover" to their "utility-hole cover," the kind of casuistry I'd just as soon put a lid on.

Miller and Swift's first point in the representative chapter under discussion is that when the early English grammarians used masculine pronouns in a seemingly bisexual way, they were actually writing "grammars . . . for male readers in an age when few women were literate." This use, therefore, "did not reflect a belief that masculine pronouns could refer to both sexes," our authors claim, on what evidence they do not choose to state. Grammarians, they continue, later invented the so-called "generic" *he* in an attempt to change the long-established English usage (as Miller and Swift call it) of "*they* as a singular pronoun," of which they give quite a few examples from good writers, e.g., Lord Chesterfield's remark, "If a person is born of a gloomy temper . . . they

149

cannot help it." It is not till 1850, however, that "an Act of Parliament gave official sanction to the . . . 'generic' *he*. . . . The new law said, 'words importing the masculine gender shall be deemed and taken to include females.' " The authors conclude that "as a linguistic device imposed on the language rather than a natural development arising from a broad consensus [is there such a thing as a narrow consensus?] 'generic' *he* is fatally flawed."

Miller and Swift then refer to "several recent systematic investigations of how people of both sexes use and understand personal pronouns." They do not tell us, however, how and by whom these investigations were conducted; if by committed feminists, the results would most likely reflect what the investigators set out to prove. And who but a committed feminist would conduct such an investigation? The outcome allegedly showed that "at all levels of education people whose native tongue is English seem to know that *he, him,* and *his* are gender-specific [lovely word!] and cannot do the double duty" of representing both men and women.

Well, I could go out into the street right now to do a little questioning of my own and find contrary evidence aplenty. For much as our embattled authors advocate such constructions as "I shouldn't like to punish anyone, even if they'd done me wrong" (this from George Eliot), the construction is manifestly illogical and grates on any ear connected to a thinking brain. I do not care how many good writers have at times fallen into such illogic—there simply is no way in which any*one* or every*one* can suddenly multiply, as if it were a rabbit, into a *they.* And not even rabbits could produce parthenogenetically a litter between a main and a subordinate clause. In fact, a logical mind might be thrown by Eliot's sentence, and go looking for some antecedent to *they* other than that inappropriate *anyone.* But, along with like-minded feminists, Miller and Swift insist that "like 'generic' *man,* 'generic' *he* fosters the misconception that the standard human being is male." Isn't it odd that in no non-English-speaking country have women's groups found it necessary to quarrel in this mode with the language for psychopolitical (or is it psychopathological) reasons?

But it isn't odd at all that the only authority of any kind whom Miller and Swift actually quote by name in this section of their book is not a grammarian, linguist, writer, or other word-oriented person, but an obscure psychologist now called Wendy Martyna, though in a book she edited in 1972 she was still Wendy Martin. In their previous collaboration, *Words and Women,* our crusading authors wrote:

At a meeting of the Modern Language Association the story was told of twin girls who came home from school in tears one day because the teacher had explained the grammatical rule mandating the use of *he* when the referent is indefinite or unknown. What emotions had reduced them to tears? Anger? Humiliation? A sense of injustice? It is unlikely that any woman can recapture her feelings when the arbitrariness of that rule first struck her consciousness: it happened a long time ago, no doubt, and it was only one among many assignments to secondary status.

Now, I ask you, who shall prevail? Those unnamed twins whose eyes brimmed over with tears of anger, humiliation, or righteous indignation at such organized grammatical misogyny, or the tradition of good English that has functioned for centuries, that accords with other Indo-European languages, and that, despite the unrecapturable feelings of any woman, did not condemn her to secondary status, but allowed her to become Jane Austen or George Eliot, or even Casey Miller or Kate Swift. Note, however, the inconsistency of the latter two when, in *The Handbook of Nonsexist Writing,* they argue that *because* in the past the prescriptive grammarians permitted the plural *you* to become singular as well and displace *thou,* nowadays the plural *they* should be allowed, *in spite of* the grammarians, to become singularized when necessary, or when the feminists deem it so. And what, pray, has happened to the "broad consensus" that was said to be required to justify such a change? Superseded, perhaps, by a consensus of broads.

We would not be in serious danger from Miller, Swift, and their sorority if we still had prescriptive grammarians, if the vast majority of linguists and lexicographers were not of the descriptive and permissive persuasion that abrogates the right to pronounce one usage correct and another incorrect. The reason is political. One wants to be the champion of progressive causes, repressed minorities—in short, the People—and so takes it out on the English language. One cannot get remuneration, votes, or even a pat on the back from the language; but there is abundant recognition and remuneration for taking up the cudgels for the People and bludgeoning the language, logic, even mere common sense, with them. What Miller and Swift conveniently overlook is the price we have paid for losing our second-person-singular pronominal form. Both in life and in literature, the switch from *you* (formal) to *thou* (informal and intimate), or back again, carried enormous emotional impact. Gone, all gone!

Although Miller and Swift are perfectly satisfied with the singular *they,* another solution also holds evident appeal for them. They cite at length and with palpable approbation recent attempts to coin "a new sex-inclusive singular pronoun." From "myriad suggestions," they adduce *co, E, tey,* and *hesh;* as well as *na,* from a novel by June Arnold, and *person* or *per,* from a book by Marge Piercy. They even reach back to the nineteenth-century eccentric Charles Converse, who proposed *thon* (a contraction of *that one*), and approvingly mention the new supervisors' guide of American Management Associations, published by AMACOM (which sounds like some dreadful film from Fellini's artistic dotage), in which *hir* is used "as a common-gender pronoun meaning he or she." "In a cogent introductory statement," our authors report, "the publishers explain the purpose of the innovation and the reasons for their selection of *hir.*"

Consider now a simple sentence, say, "Everyone must do his duty," which could become, "Everyone must do *co* [or *E, tey, hesh*] duty." Or it could become "everyone must do *na* [or *person, per, thon, hir*] duty." I can envision a time when someone casually saying "na duty" to someone who usually says "hesh duty" will be overheard by someone else who uses "tey duty" in the presence of yet another accustomed to "hir duty"—and the result will, of course, be Babel. Unless perhaps an Act of Parliament, or some other such legislation, mandates (or, more properly, womandates) one of these pronouns into law. But since Miller and Swift are against such legislation, could this happen? Possibly, because it is in the nature of radicals who bitterly oppose laws that disagree with them to foist equally or more restrictive laws on people of another persuasion.

Still, you might interject, where is the danger in making a few footling concessions if the result is peace in the republic? The danger is in that small concessions lead to big ones, that a few concessions lead to many, that one type of concession may encourage demands of quite a different type, and that the result will be chaos. Remember the great couplet from Pope's *Essay on Criticism:* "Our sons their fathers' failing language see,/And such as Chaucer is, shall Dryden be." Do you grasp the full implications of this? Thanks to changes in our language—some in the cause of simplification, but many more based on political interest or sheer ignorance—Shakespeare is already beyond the reach of most people, Chaucer has to be read in second-rate modernizations, and Dryden, for the amplitude and elegance of his rhetoric, is not read at all.

There are two further problems with Miller and Swift's position. One is self-contradiction and consequent wishy-washiness. Take the question of *girl* versus *woman.* Miller and Swift first define their attitude thus: "A person may appropriately be called 'a girl' until her middle or late teens. After that, although her family and close friends may go on calling her a girl with impunity, most red-blooded women find the term offensive." This, even aside from ending with a sentence that does not parse, is curious. Why wouldn't a girl of twenty or twenty-two, regardless of the color of her blood, exult in her girlhood, than which there is no lovelier condition known to humanity? Think only of what poets, novelists, painters, and sculptors—male and female—have done to glorify the term "girl"; if the word becomes synonymous with "child," all their works will lose much of their meaning and beauty. The only reason "boy" is not coextensive in age with "girl" is that, unfortunately, there are pressures on males to go out and make a living before they have had the time to become "men," and they duly turn into charmless, premature adults lacking that sense of the child in man that Nietzsche rightly admired. That a female could remain much longer like unto the lilies of the field—having, perhaps, to spin a little, but, with luck, not toil at all—was, and still can be, a piece of good fortune for the loss of which the title "woman," with its real or implied responsibilities, is hardly adequate compensation.

But if "girl" applied to a person of nineteen or more is indeed something that makes red blood boil (blue blood, clearly, is immune to this demotic disorder)—if, in other words, it is an insult, an indecency, why is it all right for friends and kinfolk to use such filthy language to a woman of twenty? A few pages later, though, our authors go back even on their "late teens" deadline and cite with approval a reference to "young women in the thirteen-to-sixteen-year age-group." Clearly, this is the same kind of upgrading that turns undertakers into funeral directors, garbage collectors into sanitation workers, maids into household technicians—in other words, part of that self-serving, unrealistic procedure that tries to exalt the humdrum, and thus contributes to the confusion of meanings, debasement of values, and erosion of notions of excellence. And all this for a chimera; the workman who collects garbage will smell no sweeter even if it becomes compulsory to call him Philosopher King.

Inconsistency is everywhere. The feminine ending *-ess* is not acceptable to women who, it seems, must be called actors and sculptors, not actresses and sculptresses; but *alumnae,* with its feminine ending, is a must to women who would feel discriminated against if subsumed under *alumni.* "Goddess" is not only permissible, however, but may indeed become preferable to the Christian God with his chauvinistic maleness. Yet if women consider themselves included under "actors" and "Sculptors," why do they feel excluded by "everyman" or "journeyman" or other such no longer masculine endings? Contradictions proliferate; even Saint Joan is no longer to be known as a heroine but as a hero. Poor girl—or woman: The Inquisition forced feminine clothing on her thus exposing her to the lust of her jailers; now the sisters are foisting a masculine ending on her, thus depriving her of the double glory of being simultaneously a female and a leader.

Finally, Miller, Swift, and their likes have no sense of euphony, of the sound words make. They wonder what is wrong with "repairer" for repairman and "launderer" for laundryman. You have to be pretty monomaniacal and tone-deaf to ignore the ugliness of *repairer* and of the *erer* in *launderer. Laundress* is presumably unacceptable because of the feminine ending. It is hard to resist the conclusion that feminists either hate their femininity or smart under their lack of feminine comeliness—unhealthy situations both.

However that may be, by allowing irresponsible alterations in the language, we are not only losing the necessary touch with the glories of our literary past, we are also inviting a linguistic turmoil that must lead to the breakdown of everyday communication in the not so distant future.

One Baby for You,
One Baby for Me

(1981)

TUNG TUNG

The following is a slightly edited translation of a Chinese story that appeared in Anti-Revisionism House (Fan Hsiu Lou), *a collection of short stories published in 1979 by a group of former Red Guards in Hong Kong. The author of the story, pseudonymously Tung Tung, was formerly a leader of a major Red Guard faction in Shanghai. Like the other contributors to the book, he has sought to write honestly and accurately about life as he experienced it in the People's Republic of China, using a thin fictional cover. The story is thus based on a true incident in a Shanghai factory. All the characters bear striking resemblance to living persons, who still mingle somewhere with the throng in China's greatest industrial city. The practice of birth control as described here has been confirmed by the Chinese Communist press—for example, by the Hong Kong newspaper* Ta Kung Pao *on June 11, 1980, which also disclosed that couples in Kwangtung Province who wish to have a child must now first obtain a "birth permit."*

Nothing—alas, nothing in this story has been exaggerated.

—Miriam London and Ta-ling Lee

The sky was overcast and a whistling north wind slashed at the faces of people waiting, huddled together at the trolley stop. Slowly the No. 21 trolley bus approached the Heng Pin Bridge stop on Szechuan North Road, its two flying-pigtail contact poles now and then spitting blue-white sparks. Even before it drew close, people swarmed forward to board. Ch'ien Ssu-ming, young and strong, went into action, applying a long-perfected technique. He elbowed his way through the crowd and quickly boarded the trolley. Then, clutching a side rail with his left hand and jamming his left foot against the closing door, he pulled his slow-moving companion, Ma Kuei-ts'ai, inside with his free right hand and kicked his right foot back once, hard. The kick caught those pressing behind him by surprise, tumbling them backward, while Ch'ien Ssu-ming withdrew his entire body into the car. Then, with his right hand, he removed the pancake and fried cruller clenched all the while in his teeth and roared out a command, "Let's go!" The door clanged shut.

Squeezed next to Ch'ien Ssu-ming, like sardines in a can, Ma Kuei-ts'ai shook his head and said, "Little Ch'ien, if I hadn't run into you, I'd never have made it."

"You got to be tough these days," Little Ch'ien said through a mouthful of pancake and cruller. "Be polite and people take advantage of you."

After the trolley passed the Ni Ch'eng Bridge, Ma and Ch'ien were finally able to find seats and sit down. Ch'ien Ssu-ming, however, seemed preoccupied today, unlike his usual sociable self. He just sat in silence, staring out the window.

Ma Kuei-ts'ai nudged him with an elbow. "What's the trouble, Little Ch'ien? Why the long face? Have a fight with the little lady?"

"No, it's just that planned parenthood meeting yesterday. Every time I think of it I get mad. Where does it say you got to have a vasectomy after the second child?" His face darkened with anger.

"Oh, but it's supposed to be for your own good! And besides, it's the state plan." Ma Kuei-ts'ai tried to smooth things over a bit.

"State plan?! Which central document says you got to have a vasectomy after two kids? Isn't it enough I make a point of practicing birth control on my own? I wouldn't have a vasectomy, even if they held a knife to my throat!" Ch'ien Ssu-ming was really mad.

"Come on, Little Ch'ien, you're past thirty, you're grown up now. You should know better than to try to break a rock with an egg. Being pig-headed will only land you in trouble. All you need is to be shut up in a few study classes* and you'll go along, like it or not."

"I'm not afraid of that. My family are factory workers three generations back and my own record has always been good. I don't give a damn what those jerks have to say about me behind my back!"

"You're right, I guess. Not like me. I'm just a hunk of dough. They can make me round or flat, just as they like."

"It's your tough luck—you've got that 'small businessman' background. Director Chiang said, didn't she, that couples with two kids who belong to the four classes† have absolutely got to have a vasectomy. But people from the working class just have to be mobilized to get up the enthusiasm, right? So, you had no choice. And by the way, Master Ma,‡ I heard your vasectomy didn't go too well. Is that right?"

Ma Kuei-ts'ai was rocked by the question. "Where'd you hear that?" he asked quickly.

"Never mind, never mind! Just some rumors. But what happened?" Ch'ien Ssu-ming noticed his companion's nervousness and pressed him.

---

*A Mao Tse-tung Thought Study Class. A worker found guilty of ideological sin could be confined to such a class—actually a prison-like room within the factory—under heavy psychological pressure, usually for a period of one week to two months, but in some cases much longer.

†The four social categories originally stigmatized during the Mao era were the former "landlords, rich peasants, counterrevolutionaries and bad elements" and their descendants. However, the term "four classes" came to be applied loosely to all members of an expanding list of "bad categories."

‡Shih-fu, a polite manner of address for a skilled craftsman. The use of "master" in conversation here implies, however, that Ch'ien Ssu-ming retains a slight distance between himself and the socially "inferior" Ma Kuei-ts'ai. On the other hand, the ingratiating Ma adopts the more friendly "Hsiao (Little) Ch'ien" in addressing his companion.

"Well, uh . . . better not talk." Ma Kuei-ts'ai barely got out the words and waved the subject away with a despairing gesture of one hand.

"Why so hesitant? You can tell *me,* can't you?"

"Well, to tell the truth, Little Ch'ien, stay away from vasectomy if you can avoid it. I feel now like someone deaf and dumb who's taken bitter medicine—I can't even talk out the bitterness," Ma Kuei-ts'ai said, sighing.

"But, Master Ma, what was it, what happened?" Ch'ien Ssu-ming asked a little impatiently.

Ma Kuei-ts'ai glanced about furtively and then spoke in a low voice directly into Ch'ien's ear: "Little Ch'ien, they forced me to go to a hospital for a vasectomy and guess who did the operation on me—a young girl of 16–17!"

"A young girl?!" Ch'ien Ssu-ming stared at Ma incredulously, eyes wide.

"Yes, a barefoot doctor just up from Ch'uan Sha County for job training."

"How can this be? How could they be so shameless to let a young girl do *this* kind of operation?" Ch'ien Ssu-ming was at a loss to understand.

"What could I do?" Ma said in a pitiful voice. "Others refused, but not me. With my bad background, what right had I to speak up? Otherwise they'd pin a label on me for 'opposing revolutionary new-born things,' for 'opposing barefoot doctors.' So, I got up the strength to follow her into the operating room, I closed my eyes and put myself at her mercy."

"Well, you seemed to have pulled through all right."

"Pulled through? The worst possible thing happened!" Ma slapped his thigh heavily with one hand.

"The worst?" Ch'ien asked, bewildered.

"The day after the operation I felt something was wrong. My belly got all swollen, just as if I had a ball inside. I felt burning down there, but I just couldn't piss."

"Some infection? Because of poor sterilization?"

"Infection? It would've been simple if it were only that!" Ma Kuei-ts'ai became visibly more excited as he talked. "Finally, I just couldn't hold out any longer. My belly was all swollen and painful. I couldn't stand or sit. So, I went back to the hospital to look up Dr. Liu in the surgery department."

"And what did Dr. Liu say?"

"Nothing. He just examined me. And then he sighed and shook his head and ordered me to go immediately to the operating room."

"Another operation?" Ch'ien Ssu-ming burst out.

"Not that. The first operation had been just like a blind man trying to light a candle—a waste of wax. That barefoot doctor tied the wrong tube!"

"What? The wrong tube?"

"Right, she tied my urinary canal!" Ordinarily Ma Kuei-ts'ai did not show his emotions readily. But now he was puffing with rage.

"Oh, good heavens, this is like playing games with human life!" Ch'ien Ssu-ming said, shaking his head, indignant and moved almost to laughter at the same time.

At that moment, the trolley swerved sharply at high speed, throwing most of the passengers off balance. The canvas "soft section" connecting the two cars fanned out like an accordion, making it possible for the long, awkward conveyance to navigate the turn. Trolley No. 21 had reached its last stop.

Within days the story of how a barefoot doctor tied someone's urinary canal snowballed through the entire factory. The workers got scared and nobody wanted a vasectomy. All this worried Chiang Feng, director of the Planned Parenthood Office at the factory. Before the Cultural Revolution, Chiang Feng had been an ordinary cleaning woman. With the rise to prominence, however, of Chairman Mao's wife, Chiang Ch'ing, she—Chiang Feng—had also begun a new career at the factory. The reason was that she not only shared the same surname, but like Chiang Ch'ing, had also a single given name. Even more important, she was from Chiang Ch'ing's native province, Shantung—an asset, without a doubt. Thus, whenever she spoke at meetings, large or small, she never failed to mention the name of Chiang Ch'ing. By the time the Revolutionary Committee was set up in the factory, she became a natural choice for a post on the new staff.

A long banner stretched the length of the factory mess hall: "Use Class Struggle as the Key Link. Resolutely Strike Down Class Enemies Who Try to Sabotage the Work of Planned Parenthood!" Presiding over the struggle meeting on the platform was Chiang Feng.

"Comrades," she began, "we in Shanghai represent the vanguard of our country in the work of planned parenthood. But our class enemy will never give up the ghost. Lately, they've blown up an evil wind in our factory, trying to sabotage the work of planned parenthood. This handful of class enemy has infiltrated the different shops. They're stirring up the lower ranks, they're hatching secret plots. They're spreading rumors to smear one of the Cultural Revolution's 'new-born things'—the barefoot doctor—in an attempt to put down the accomplishments of the Cultural Revolution. This is not just some isolated thing. No, it's all connected with that current 'rightist wind to reverse earlier verdicts'—meaning, it's the new direction of the current class struggle. Today, we're going to criticize and struggle** a reactionary capitalist—Ma Kuei-ts'ai. Drag Ma Kuei-ts'ai up on the platform!" Chiang Feng furiously barked the command.

Head bowed low, Ma Kuei-ts'ai was led on stage by two militiamen. He stood at one corner of the platform, hunched forward almost 90 degrees, like a jumbo shrimp.

"Ma Kuei-ts'ai, why are you spreading rumors to sabotage planned parenthood work?" Chiang Feng demanded angrily.

"Director Chiang, I . . . but I never spread any rumors," Ma Kuei-ts'ai timidly ventured in his own defense. "That barefoot doctor really did tie my urinary canal . . ."

The audience roared.

Embarrassed by the audience's reaction, Chiang Feng quickly cut in, "Ma Kuei-ts'ai, who told you to say this? You've got to tell us your real motives. Isn't it true you deliberately tried to sabotage . . ."

**To "struggle" someone is to interrogate for the purpose of inducing a confession and often involves physical coercion.

"Oh, no! Oh, no! . . ." Ma Kuei-ts'ai stuttered in his haste to explain. "Director Chiang, it was all unintentional what I said on the trolley the other day."

"Unintentional? To hear you talk, it was all so simple! Then why didn't you choose some other time or place? You picked a time on the trolley when everyone was going to work so they could all hear you."

"Well, . . . uh . . . uh," Ma Kuei-ts'ai was at a loss to add a single word. He was in shock, his mouth fallen wide open.

"This is class struggle! This is the trick our class enemy uses! I hereby announce: From now on, Ma Kuei-ts'ai will be put under supervised labor in the factory. Take him away!"

Ma Kuei-ts'ai wiped the sweat off his forehead with his hand. Secretly, he was glad to have been spared a beating.

Chiang Feng picked up a large sheet of red paper from the lectern: "Comrades, on behalf of the Factory Party Committee and the Planned Parenthood Office, I now announce the names of couples of child-bearing age in our factory permitted to have children in 1976. According to the quota allotted our factory by the higher authorities, we are allowed two child-bearing couples for this year. After discussion by the masses and review by the Party Committee, it has been decided that the quota will be filled by Comrades Yu Hung-wei and Niu Erh-ch'iang."

"Director Chiang!" Niu Erh-ch'iang, a strapping but slow-witted fellow, raised his right hand for permission to speak.

"Yes, Comrade Niu Erh-ch'iang, what do you want to say?

Niu Erh-ch'iang scratched the back of his head. "First of all," he began, "I thank the Party for being so kind to give me one of the two births in the quota for the whole factory."

Chiang Feng was in a good mood, pleased with the response to her efforts. Evidently fearing, however, that Big Dummy Niu might not be able to express himself properly, she interrupted, gently, to ask that he speak slowly.

Such encouragement from Director Chiang was a shot in the arm to Niu Erh-ch'iang, who went rattling on: "Comrade Ch'ien Ssu-ming—now he had two daughters in a row and he's really wanted a son. My wife's in the village, you know—she gets not too many work points. So, with my wage of 30 yuan or so, I barely get by. So, the two of us talked it over and we decided not to have kids for the time being. We'll wait until our financial situation gets a little better to have kids. So . . . I'd like to loan my baby for getting born to Ch'ien Ssu-ming and I'll wait till . . ."

Here Big Dummy Niu brought down the house, but he insisted on finishing the last sentence: "I'll wait till the next time to get my quota back and get my own baby."

Chiang Feng was between laughter and tears. She shouted, "No, a quota cannot be loaned to anyone else! If you don't have your own baby this year, it means you voluntarily give up the quota." Thereupon, she hastily dismissed the meeting.

It was 1977 and the "Big Red Roster" of planned parenthood for the year had just been posted. As in the previous year, it was posted on the main bulletin board, right at the front gate of the factory. In addition to the usual information listed after each name—age, class background, number of children, year for which birth was planned, year for which birth was approved, etc.—the Factory Party Committee and Planned Parenthood Office had added a new item for 1977, contraceptive measures used. There were two reasons, so people said, behind this move to disclose publicly the contraceptive measures used by every couple: to mobilize the masses for exchange of experiences and to enable them to watch over one another.

Niu Erh-ch'iang had tried his best during the year, but his wife failed him—she did not bear him a child. Thus the quota was wasted. On the other hand, Ch'ien Ssu-ming's wife was pregnant again.

At the sound of the quitting bell, everyone ran to the Big Red Roster, quite curious to learn how others practiced contraception. One wicked fellow read aloud: "Ch'ien Ssu-ming, condoms, pills . . ."

Before he could go on, Old Tang, the office messenger, rushed into the crowd and yelled: "Is Ch'ien Ssu-ming around? Telephone from home.‡ Go to the hospital immediately. Your wife is having a baby!"

"Wow! Ch'ien Ssu-ming is really tops when it comes to producing babies! Even double insurance didn't help!"

The crowd burst into laughter. Redfaced, Ch'ien Ssu-ming hopped on his bicycle and quickly rode away.

At the hospital he tiptoed into the ward, where he saw his wife lying in bed, looking very worn. He gently touched her face with his hand.

"Hsiu-ying, it's a son, right?" Ch'ien Ssu-ming asked, full of hope.

Hsiu-ying opened her weary eyes, took one timid look at her husband and then silently closed them again.

"Another girl? Oh, you . . . how can you be such a no-good . . ."

"Ssu-ming, how can you blame me? I wanted a son just as much as you! But . . . maybe the next . . ." Tears rolled from the corners of her eyes onto the pillow.

"The next? We don't even know what to do with this one!"

He took it all out on Hsiu-ying: "We won't be able to get her a residence permit and there won't be any ration! You won't have maternity leave and we'll have to pay the delivery and hospital fees! And, yes, there'll be criticism the minute I return to the factory. Big character posters will sure to be out tomorrow. You've lost all my face for me!"

He sat on the edge of the bed. Burying his head in his hands, he talked to himself: "This is the end. I'm going to die this time. They're going to make me have a vasectomy!"

The room was still, the bed was still—except for Hsiu-ying's soft sobbing. All the other patients in the ward watched them silently.

Ch'ien Ssu-ming stared at the floor. A strange thought crossed his mind: How nice it would be if a T'angshan earthquake hit Shanghai at this very moment, so that he could fall into a crack in the earth, never have to face anyone again or have any worries anymore.

‡This is not a private home telephone, but one on the street near the workers' apartment house.

Ugly Women

(1981)

TAKI

Remember the old joke about the Russian diplomat visiting New York and having a prostitute sent to his room courtesy of his contacts at Amnesty International? The Soviet biggie starts to undress her, but as soon as he has a glimpse of her calf he complains about the lack of hair. "What, no wool?" he moans. He gets more annoyed when he realizes that she even shaves her armpits. "Why no wool? I like wool," he keeps repeating. Finally, after his groaning has reached a fever pitch, the hooker has had enough. She turns toward the representative of the United Soviet Socialist Republic and tells him: "Hey Bud, what do you want to do, knit or f--k?"

I used to think this joke was funny, and indicative of the ugliness of Russian women, whom I always considered among the ugliest, if not the ugliest in the world. As painful as this confession may be, however, I must admit that I was wrong. And as if this weren't enough, guess who I have concluded are the ugliest? Yes, horror of horrors, the Americans. As incredible as it may sound, my opinion is based on scientific research, not emotions. After all, my anti-Communist credentials are impeccable. But before anyone starts to throw stones, let me explain how I arrived at my findings.

It is an accepted fact that true beauty is a combination of body and spirit. Just as true is the fact that a woman lacking femininity cannot possibly be considered beautiful in the true and classical sense of the word. In fact I'll go further than that. A good figure and regular features detract from, rather than enhance, the appearance of a woman lacking femininity. How does one define femininity? Easy. A feminine woman possesses qualities which make her as different from a man psychologically as she is physically. That is, she is passive, cunning, patient, motherly, a homebody, monogamous, etc. Furthermore, a feminine woman defines herself almost exclusively by her relationship to man, and is sculpted accordingly. If this sounds far-fetched, it shouldn't. Four-hundred million years of field experiments have proved that the female is sculpted differently from the male for the above reasons.

Thus the human's closest species, the macaque, is bigger than his female counterpart, stronger, and the one who decides if and where they will move their breeding grounds. The male will respond to outside dangers, while the

160

female remains unconcerned. She will continue feeding the young or grooming herself while the male stalks the enemy. She knows the male is responsible.

Does this sound familiar? Of course it does. That's how it was until a few ugly women who could not get men to like them decided to change something that is as unchangeable as, well, for lack of a better example, man and woman. John Aspinall, the English sage who breeds wild animals in his two private zoos in Kent, believes that a woman's trust consolidates the man's dominance. Without it, the male tends to lose his masculinity. One does not have to be a scientist or an anthropologist to see that this makes sense. Look what is happening now. Ever since women decided not to trust men, that men were almost expendable, there has been a marked increase in pederasty. The phenomenon has been widely observed.

Aspinall contends that every male has a 70 to 30 percent hormone count. Seventy percent male hormones, thirty percent female. Every female is the opposite. (Again, before anyone starts to shout, these are rough estimates. Exact figures are for jargon-artists trying to mislead through statistics.) As the state has taken over the male (or father) role, the male species has come to feel disrobed, his position usurped. The only function left to him by the omnipotent state is to pay bills and attend to the occasional derelict relative. Even his old familiar role as warrior has been challenged. Some women, although I doubt their hormone count is 70 to 30, now try to compete by being soldiers. America now has 44 percent more female soldiers than all the world's other armies combined.

Which brings us to the subject of why some women are unique. Like Mrs. Thatcher, whose male hormone count has risen dramatically ever since she found herself surrounded by males without enough male hormones. Looking at the state of Small Britain today I am not surprised. Mrs. Thatcher, unlike Cleopatra or Elizabeth I or Catherine the Great, all of of whom inherited their fathers' dynastic strength, entered a vacuum left by males suffering from a very low testosterone count. (Socialists, trade union leaders, intellectuals, are notoriously effete.)

Mull this over for a while, and I believe you will agree that despite outward appearances a woman can be truly ugly. Take Jane Fonda and Shirley MacLaine. That harshness, those granite glares, the shrillness of their rhetoric—it makes one want to shriek at their ugliness. This is less true when one is confronted with the ruins of remarkable ugliness, as in the case of Lillian Hellman. (See what I mean about good figures and regular features detracting from rather than enhancing one's appearance? Hellman's revolting features do not make her any uglier than her ugly rhetoric and pathetic lies. In Fonda's case and MacLaine's, they do.)

Maggie Scarf, the female science writer, has proved beyond any reasonable doubt that John Bowlby's "attachment theory" is correct. Bowlby, an Englishman, says that a female needs to connect through emotional bonding. This she manages through a behavioral mechanism, a trait that has found its way into the female genetic code. Scarf points out that emotional bonding, once a key to survival for the weaker sex, now causes nothing but trouble as women are caught between the demands of their genes—to be feminine, obedient, married—and a society telling them that they are equal and independent. Feminists are not only making women become uglier, but unhappier as well. Feminism is a brutal hoax.

So, now that we have established once and for all that America's liberated women are the ugliest, precisely which of these ugliest is ugliest? Bearing in mind that I am far more experienced in esteeming European and Middle Eastern women, I will attempt a short—and certainly incomplete—list for the loyal readers of *The American Spectator*. But remember. It is not important who is ugliest, but what makes her ugly.

Not to include leading Women libbers among the ugliest would be like leaving the corn out of Kansas. Gloria Steinem, Marge Piercy, Adrienne Rich, Phyllis Chesler, Susan Brownmiller, the aforementioned Fonda and Warren Beatty's sister, as well as some others too ugly for me to want to recall. Then there are Bella Abzug and Diane Von Furstenberg, that nice Jewish girl from Belgium who married her gay prince and made millions selling clothes under his name, though she now tells us that electing Ronald Reagan was a crime. (Diane recently wrote a letter asking in a rhetorical manner what happened to the generation of the 1968 barricades. She is referring to the Paris riots. Unfortunately for her she includes herself in that generation. Even more unfortunate for her is the fact that I remember what she did during the time of the barricades. She drove with me to Geneva because Regine's had closed down and she needed to hook her future husband. So much for the angry young woman.) Let me also add Kate Millet, Shirley Chisholm, Barbra Streisand. The list is endless.

But it is not long enough. The more I think on it the longer the list becomes. But not long enough to prevent the American male from making a comeback. All he has to do is try to behave a bit more like his ancestor, the macaque. Put the little woman on a pedestal, spoil her by protecting her, not by taking any back talk. Oppress her. She'll love it. Force her to be obedient and feminine and even her genetic traits will start responding again. That will bring her instant happiness. Even the bills will be reduced, what without valium to buy and shrinks to pay. Be jealous. Nothing works like a little bit of jealousy to bolster the female ego.

Finally, never be brutal, but be very firm. The Japanese beat their wives symbolically every day on the assumption that even if they don't know why they do it, their wives will understand. Japanese women—with the exception of Yoko Ono—have always been extremely happy. Let's take an example from the land of the rising sun. If Detroit had we wouldn't be in the economic mess we're in today. Ditto where sex is concerned. And I know that Americans prefer sex to cars.

Cosmo's Aging Vixen

(1983)

RACHEL FLICK

The title of Helen Gurley Brown's recent book of advice for ambitious young women is *Having It All,* and "it," not surprisingly, turns out to mean everything Brown has. She has fantastic success in her work; Helen Brown is the editor who brought *Cosmopolitan* magazine from the brink of extinction to one of the largest circulations in America. She has "Johnny Carson Show" celebrity. She is rich. She has—as she eagerly confesses—all of that beauty which money can buy. She has the vigorously won appearance of youth, despite her 59 years. She has a long-standing and happy marriage to an equally successful man. In short, she has all the things you can neither take with you nor leave behind, in any enduring way.

Having It All is a how-to book of wide range—how to organize a day efficiently, write a résumé, apply cosmetics to tiny lines and wrinkles, snag a husband—and it is considerably more interesting than such books usually are. For one thing, the advice is almost uniformly excellent, and so—as wise advice about practical things is wont—it indirectly illuminates large matters as well as small ones. For another, its authoress is a rare and fascinating woman, and the book gains as much from what her anecdotes and occasional reflections reveal about herself as it does from its revelations about dinner table conversation and disorganized closets.

What is most rare about Brown is a personal quality perhaps best called by its Greek name, *thymos,* loosely definable as a combination of anger, spirit, and ambition. Although Brown believes this characteristic is hers by nature—she has felt "different" almost since she can remember—she also insists that the material conditions of her childhood molded the distinctive spirit with which she was born. Brown grew up in a poor, backward part of the world and cannot remember a time when she was not consumed by the longing for more. She considers this early deprivation to have been, in a way, her good fortune—the original stimulus behind everything she has attained. She writes:

I *never* liked the looks of the life that was programmed for me—ordinary, hillbilly, and poor—and I repudiated it from the time I was seven years old, though I didn't have many means of repudiation. I didn't like my little-girl cousin who peed in the creek in front of a lot of other people. I didn't like all my cousins saying "ain't" and "cain't" and "she give five dollars for that hat."

They were, and are, dear, lovely people who lead honorable lives in the Ozark Mountains, but I wanted something else. And so I began to feel and be "separate."

The "something else" was the life recorded in movie magazines, and it was consequently on this world that she fixed her considerable energy and desire. The rest, as they say, is history.

Brown is frankly delighted with her present station in life. Her success is an enormous credit to her, the triumph of her discipline and fortitude, and she knows this and relishes it. Yet she manages to avoid the usual up-from-the-ghetto cant. She has no shame about where she's come from, but no false pride in it either, for she understands that it is also responsible for what she is not. She appears to understand that it has left her forever without what she at one point calls "elegance." Brown knows the deep-running importance—the importance to character—of having been born to money and sophistication, and the impossibility of ever transcending the fact she was not. After twenty years of success, she is still not "used to" where she is, and never will be. "If you are practicing *up* for elegance," she lets on, "one of the secrets is that you practice when you're alone, not just for company." And she adds that she is never ("never!") going to get the hang of this.

Brown makes it absolutely plain that she has the vices of a woman born poor: she fights a lingering, persistent miserliness, and is the victim of what she calls "a crush on rich people." ("Rich, powerful men who run empires are my idols," she writes. "Just let me sit at their feet and hear how they cornered soybeans.") Most important of all, she is an unabashed social climber. "It's *better* up there," she explains, "in almost every way."

An ambitious person of no substance may be a fool, but an ambitious person of some real excellence is not, and Helen Brown is no fool. Whatever reservations one may have about her work, she is indisputably the mistress of a certain slick, effortless, chatty writing for women. The fast-food voice that her *Sex and the Single Girl* introduced in 1963 is widely imitated but seldom equaled. (Even *Cosmopolitan* does not often employ this voice as well as does Brown when she is speaking for herself.)

The voice is systematically conversational and intimate. Brown writes exclusively in the first person. She punctuates not according to standard usage but to the pattern of speech used by the women she is addressing—her writing is heavy on dashes, exclamations, and catty asides; it has a real, gossipy swing. Her trademark, though, is unquestionably her early sixties ladies-lunch vocabulary ("How to begin?" Brown asks. "Well, on little pussycat feet you just pad *into* it").

It may be cheap, but like most commercial products this voice is highly effective. *Having It All* establishes a marvelously persuasive air of confidentiality. By the end, the reader truly feels as if she and Brown have become girlfriends, so to speak. Moreover, it's an affectionate intimacy; Helen Brown has created for herself an immensely *likable* persona.

Indeed, it's all so artfully achieved that if not for the book's countless sound and often subtle insights, one would think *Having It All* was intended purely as a money-making venture. Now, *Cosmopolitan* may be trash, but *Having It All* reveals a Helen Brown both intelligent and breathlessly, heartrendingly genuine.

The first part of *Having It All* is devoted to work, and, as expected, Brown's advice on this subject is excellent. However unremittingly tacky her own professional attainments, they do represent a substantial achievement, and much of her information about how she pulled this off is transferable to other ends.

In speaking sensibly on this subject to a readership of women, Brown is a voice in the wilderness. Career advice for men has tended (at least, until recently) to stress hard work, initiative, and careful planning. It has more or less accepted hardship and hazard as "dues"—legitimate and necessary steps in the rise to the top. Women's career books, on the other hand, have tended to stress defense—against certain kinds of labor which to do, their authors believe, is to be exploited; and against any manifest recognition that one is a woman, because such recognition is surely a prelude to exploitation.

Helen Brown is unusual among women's career counselors in assuming that an office is a reasonable working environment—tough, but reasonable. She does not offer the ordinary women's career advice of defend, defend, defend, but the career advice traditionally offered to and by men. She does not believe that menial office labor is a trap; rather, she insists on the inevitability and utility of delayed gratification. She even suggests volunteering for extra menial work—"those denigrated 'personal chores!' "—as a demonstration of good faith. She dispenses with the theory that the cards are stacked. She urges her readers to be hard on themselves.

More sensibly still, she does not fear admitting gender to office life. Brown devotes a great deal of space to the simple getting along with people that is a prerequisite for the production and exchange of work. She understands that the personal—and the interpersonal—are fundamental to the professional. Hence, she is willing to consider the inevitable sexual aspect of office interactions in terms more complicated than those of simple power and abuse.

With commendable realism, she urges women to work within their femininity—to use it—rather than to take on the impossible and disagreeable task of evading it or rendering it irrelevant. She is absolutely comfortable with the sexual undertones of office interactions between men and women, and enthusiastically endorses a woman's use of charm to get out of those interactions whatever it is she wants. Her theory is that employees aren't in danger of anything they don't deserve, but that niceness greases the wheels, because people are still people, even at work. "The sexual you is part of the *whole* you, and doesn't snap off—God, we *hope* not, anyway!—between nine and six."

This brings Helen Brown to what must be the most clear-headed assessment of the business of "sexual harassment" yet written. In a section called "Sexual harassment isn't what it's cracked up to be," she advances the idea that "man-woman awareness" in offices is at least unavoidable, probably useful, and, at best, enjoyable. She writes: "Of the millions of naughty suggestions made by millions of male employers to their 'defenseless' female employees yearly, I'd say half cheered the girls *up,* half brought the girls *down,* but probably nothing bad came out of *most* of them. . . . I think sexual tension and electricity between men and women in an office can *help* get the job done. Trying to please somebody you're nutty about can be productive."

A huge part of *Having It All,* though, is not advice about careers; it is advice about grooming, and discussion about what beauty means to women, and it is here that Helen Brown reveals her uneasy reasons for taking up the pen.

At first the candor of Brown's discussion packs an illicit thrill. *Having It All* goes on for pages about the cataclysmic importance to a woman of whether she is beautiful; about the hours that she, Helen Brown, has spent in crying over her own ordinary appearance; about her frequent suspicion that looks are all that matter in life; about her inability to trust beautiful women. She ruthlessly destroys the series of defenses most women have constructed for their own, "different" good looks—no, Brown tells you, the truth is that you just haven't got it and you never will. At the end she tosses in a couple of caveats about how it is brains that really matter, and how sweetness works, too—the stuff women tell themselves, all the time—but they don't really have any greater effect, in this chapter, than they do in real life. She writes:

This very morning I looked in the three-way mirror and observed this unsymmetrical face—not ugly or repelling, just totally *undistinguished,* and, what with the aging, I said to myself, My God, I've got to be *nicer* to people, got to endear myself to them with love pouring out of every *pore* of me to make up for this *face*! I've got to be Mother Teresa, Eleanor Roosevelt, Helen Keller, Scarlett O'Hara's *mother* and why, Lord, didn't I start *sooner?*

Endearing herself "to people," though, is not really what she means. As the discussion continues one thing becomes absolutely clear: beauty is important to Brown and to other women, she believes, because women perceive that it attracts men.

This, then, being the truth about men and women, Brown declares vanity to be OK. In fact, she believes, it even demonstrates a sort of fine spirit; to lavish money, time, and attention on your appearance is to refuse to take lying down the looks you were delivered. It is to enter actively and positively into the game of attraction that she boldly assumes us all to be playing.

On the strength of this logic, Brown launches into page after page of instruction in the business of dressing up. The instruction is on the whole superb, the writing is lively, and the frankness about its ultimate purpose is exciting, but eventually—as Brown goes on and on—one becomes aware of disquieting excess. For no matter how exciting it is to hear someone say that vanity is OK, vanity in truth is still a vice and it doesn't make you happy to indulge it too far.

The healthy woman sets limits to this vice in herself. For a while she will permit herself to become absorbed by her appearance, but then will tire of it; even if the job remains imperfect, she will feel it improper and unnecessary to continue. Helen Brown, however, does not quit when it stops being fun. For her, grooming is not simply a diversion, it is a grim and essential struggle, which she pursues—with her characteristic discipline—unto and beyond even the point of pain.

Her obsession with beauty is clearest—and its profound significance for her begins to surface—in her discussion of exercise. Brown claims to have exercised with extraordinary rigor and discipline every day since she "discovered" it 13 years ago, "missing only two days (to have a D-and-C in the hospital, but I exercised the day I went in and the day I got home and the day my mother died) in that entire time." She insists that her routine is unremittingly unpleasant. Yet she is "an addict," she explains, because it has gotten to be "a test of will. . . . you against failure, against defeat, even against death. . . . Am I getting too intense? You get to feeling that as long as you exercise *every* day, life cannot ever really do you in; you are no longer vulnerable, but like breathing, if you *stopped,* you might die! Yes, I *am* intense!"

Shortly thereafter she retreats from this point, explaining that she exercises not because she fears death, but because she fears aging, and that she fears aging because it means the loss of sex—"of femininity, of attraction between me and a man."

Yet to Brown, sex is meaningful precisely because it is the furthest extreme from death. She describes it as power. "Kings and lesser men," she writes, "have been toppled by this power of ours, but you and I don't want to destroy anybody, we just want to enjoy a man's being totally hooked on us." It is this that Helen Brown cannot bear to lose. It is the ebbing away of this most fundamentally reassuring of all capabilities that terrifies her into huffing and puffing, and submitting herself to plastic surgery, and "starving" herself to 105 pounds—all in the name of "staying female."

So desperate is she for the kind of affirmation that sex gives her that she allows it to override both her reason and her moral sensibilities—no merely sensual need would make such a slave of an otherwise deliberate woman. Her treatment of adultery is here revealing and pathetic. Brown makes it plain that she knows exactly how wrong and destructive extramarital affairs are. In the very course of her advice on the logistics of carrying one out, she indicates her awareness of both the instincts and the arguments that such behavior violates. A few pages later, she eloquently describes how she would feel if she discovered her husband to be cheating on her, and then explains to single women that they should consider married men to be at their disposal. "When you're single," she writes, "it's important to have heterosexual male companionship. You must *connect* with men. . . . You should not go without *sex* too long. . . . [Married men] are *there* during a drought. You can 'use' them selectively."

She makes no effort to rationalize this staring moral contradiction (in fact, she confronts it almost ostentatiously). She is simply helpless before the fear of erosion that overtakes her without the constant reinforcement of sex. This is the offensive and disturbing aspect of *Having It All.*

It is disturbing, but not surprising, for this is a woman whose ambition has fixed exclusively on the world of the present. Brown has no children. She herself avows that her work is not enduring; in one anecdote, she explains that *Cosmopolitan's* virtue is in its consistency, rather than in the contribution of memorable writings. Helen Brown, in short, has absolutely no stake in the future. Why shouldn't she fear mortality?

But consider the poignance of her position now. She is 59 years old, and exercise isn't going to do it forever. She's about ready to confront her first full face-lift. In the photos released upon the publication of *Having It All,* she already looks a bit freakish—a no-longer-young woman in girl's clothing. After a lifetime of triumphing over seemingly impossible obstacles—59 years of successfully buying time—she is soon to be confronted with something against which no discipline in the world will prevail.

Which comes back, perhaps, to the reason for *Having It All.*

Brown devotes her last chapter to broad reflections on life and happiness, and it is a serious effort. Her voice, here, is that of an older woman passing along her accumulated wisdom to a generation of girls for whom she feels affection and concern, and the voice sounds sincere. Helen Brown would have us understand that this book is a thoughtful and generous work, and I believe that it is.

It makes sense, after all, for her to make such an effort now. What else can an intelligent woman in her position do, as the passage of time forces itself upon her awareness? She can't make herself love children, if in fact she does not love children, and she can't make herself trust in the transcendent, if in fact she does not so trust, but she can try to write something real, and that is what she has done. In the end, *Having It All* is a touching piece of work, and deserves to be taken account of, when her life is reckoned up.

Gay Times and Diseases

(1984)

PATRICK J. BUCHANAN AND J. GORDON MUIR

Gay Rights is no longer a debatable issue within the Democratic Party
—Ann Lewis,
Political Director, DNC.

Well, Ann, perhaps. But when the Democratic Convention opens with fifty thousand Sodomites marching down Castro Street under the command of Sister Boom Boom—the transvestite who wears a nun's habit and rolled up 23,000 votes for city supervisor—the Democrats observing from home may consider it a "debatable issue" indeed.

Gay Rights promises to become for the eighties what busing and abortion were to the seventies, the social issue that sunders the Democratic coalition. Mondale, Hart, and Jackson have all signed on to the non-negotiable demand of the movement: that "sexual preference" be written into the Civil Rights Act of 1964 to designate another category, homosexuals, against whom it will henceforth be a federal crime to discriminate. Can the Democrats have reflected seriously upon the ramifications of this latest pandering to a militant special interest?

Currently, gays and Lesbians are routinely severed from the armed services. The military has always considered such severances essential to good order, discipline, and morale. But if Gay Rights are written into federal law, not only will homosexuals in the service come out of the closet; they will have to be admitted to West Point and Annapolis, the Air Force Academy and VMI.

Basic training of 18-year-old Marine recruits will include sensitivity training on the proper respect to be accorded the "alternative life style" of their gay comrades in the barracks. Landlords who refuse to rent apartments or beach houses to homosexual couples will be subject to federal prosecution. So, too, will high schools, grammar schools, nursery schools, and day-care centers that recoil at hiring homosexual teachers, counselors, or custodians.

Already, political collisions are occurring. Mayor Ed Koch was forced to terminate $4 million in program grants when the Salvation Army refused to sign a pledge not to discriminate against gays in hiring for its day-care centers. The Catholic Archdiocese sided with the Salvation Army. In New Orleans, Archbishop Phillip Hannon warned the city council a gay rights ordinance would be met with a diocesan-led campaign for repeal. The council backed down. In affluent, trendy Montgomery County, Maryland, a gay rights ordinance goes on the ballot this fall because 25,000 voters signed a Christian Fundamentalist preacher's petition demanding a referendum on repeal.

Increasingly, traditionalist religious communities and the Gay Rights activists are seeing each other as social and political antagonists. A microcosm of this conflict is the annual Gay Pride march in Manhattan, where the strategic objective of the marching homosexuals has become capture of the cathedral steps of St. Patrick's, and their conversion into a "reviewing stand" for the parade.

The bizarre details of these parades are usually censored in the national press. Last year, there were men marching naked except for public pouches and floats proclaiming "Dykes and Tykes." A giant banner was unfurled on the cathedral steps proclaiming, "Intolerance and Ignorance Taught Here." The mockery of Christ, the Virgin Mary, and the late Cardinal Cooke has been commonplace. Two years ago, the featured float was a garbage can on wheels with a huge crucifix inside it.

On the flip side, however, Paul Moore, Episcopal Bishop of New York, has written the *New York Times* that gays "make an enormous contribution to the commercial, artistic, and religious life of our city."

Then there is the issue of children. Gay activists vehemently deny there is a greater incidence of child abuse among homosexuals than heterosexuals. But the presence in Gay Pride marches of NAMBLA—the North American Man/Boy Love Association, which lobbies for repeal of laws prohibiting sex with children—is hardly reassuring. Declares NAMBLA militant Charles Snively of Boston: "[We at NAMBLA] attack a presupposition . . . that parents have a hereditary right to their children, that parents have a right to their children that we do not have." At a 1975 conference of the Campaign for Homosexual Equality in Britain, the question was put to a thousand gays as to how many would find child sex attractive. One-third responded in the affirmative, according to the *Daily Telegraph*.

To most Americans, however, a tolerant people, the prevalent attitude seems to be: So long as they don't bother us, leave them be. What now threatens this attitude of benign neglect is the alarming and deepening health crisis inside the homosexual community—especially in cities like New York and San Francisco, the Sodom and Gomorrah of the Sexual Revolution.

AIDS, acquired immune deficiency syndrome, the killer disease that has claimed 4600 victims—40 percent of whom are already dead—is but the tip of an immense iceberg. Within the homosexual community, there are today incubating pandemic, rare, and exotic diseases with a time-bomb potential of exploding into the general population. Without descending into clinical detail, some concept of the "gay life style" needs to be understood. Its essence is random, repeated, anonymous sex—runaway promiscuity. The chapel of this new faith has been the bath house.

According to Dr. Kinsey, the *average* homosexual has 1000 sex partners in a lifetime. *Village Voice* put the figure at 1600. One activist has said that 10,000 sex partners in the lifetime of a "very active" homosexual would not be extraordinary. (Frank Sinatra was once quoted as saying that had he romanced half as many women as gossip-mongers contended, he would be speaking from a jar at the Harvard Medical School.) Many gays visit these bath houses two and three times a week, where ten contacts a night are not uncommon. A study a decade ago found that more than half the active gay males (lesbians have more enduring relationships) engaged in group sex at least once a month.

As a consequence of this jack-rabbitry, young men living the gay life in America's large cities are infecting and re-infecting one another with a variety of diseases that suggests that the proper term to describe their behavior is suicidal. By the precise way in which they define themselves, they are killing themselves.

That realization is hitting the Gay Community. A year ago, a co-author of this article was denounced as a "homophobe" by Governor Cuomo and Mayor Koch for suggesting that Gotham's bath houses be shut down as a health hazard during Gay Pride Week. Early this year, San Francisco homosexuals themselves took the lead in demanding a municipal decree outlawing sex in the city's baths. As one gay writer told the *Washington Post:* "You can take away AIDS and you're still looking at a community that happens to be a diseased community. I'm sorry. The bulk of your venereal diseases now reside within the gay community. The bulk of enteric (intestinal) diseases is now within the gay community."

When it comes to health, declares the *Medical Tribune,* the gay life is "no bed of roses." It never was—notwithstanding the mendacious propaganda of gay activists to paint homosexuality as a natural and healthy alternative. Laboring under this self-generated delusion, hundreds of thousands of young men have been indulging themselves in what *Newsweek* termed a "carefree sexual adventure, a headlong gambol on the far side of the human libido." Well, the adventure is ending—and it is revealed for what it always was: an egregious assault upon the ecology of the human body. Call it nature's retribution, God's will, the wages of sin, paying the piper, ecological kickback, whatever phraseology you prefer. The facts demonstrate that promiscuous homosexual conduct is utterly destructive of human health.

This is not to disavow sympathy for those horribly caught up in the most highly publicized consequence of the homosexual life style—AIDS. There are few sadder or more pathetic human tragedies than the stories of young men trying to cope with the sudden crushing agony of discovering that they have this inexorably fatal disease. An element of that tragedy is that the victims were lied to—consistently. As one 28-year-old AIDS victim from New York City told *Newsweek:* "The belief that was handed to me was that sex was liberating and more sex was more liberating." Nobody told that young man, now under a sentence of death, that his life style and his body were on a fatal collision course.

The AIDS epidemic has been the single most prominent factor in blowing apart the "natural alternative" myth about homosexuality—a myth that should have been dispelled before the first AIDS case came to light. But organized medicine has been timid to the point of cowardice in speaking openly about the health consequences of homosexual practice. Why? Quite simple. Warning people about the health hazards of promiscuous eating or drinking is sound advice. Warning people about the health hazards of promiscuous or unnatural sexual activity is not advice. It is "moralizing." And moralizing is wrong!

As a consequence of this "conspiracy of silence" in the medical community—one physician's phrase—tens of thousands of young men joyously embarked upon their pleasure cruises, ignorant of the fate awaiting them at journey's end—while the science pages of the fashionable press were given over to learned discussion of the medical consequences of exhaled cigarette smoke upon the nonsmoking passengers of United Airlines.

The real story is that there are several epidemics running loose, not all of them permanently confined to the gay community. They have been largely or solely caused, and perpetuated, by the growing urban population of active gays whose modal form of sexual behavior is impersonal, repeated, random, and anonymous sex. (The typical AIDS victim admits to five different sex encounters monthly.)

How did gays get led into this mess? Again, very simple: They followed leaders who spouted slogans and clichés about "rights." They took intellectual comfort from harebrained psychologists who peddled nonsense in the guise of learning. When George Will, in a 1977 *Newsweek* column, suggested that homosexuality was "an injury to healthy functioning," gay leaders John O'Leary and Bruce Voeller screamed "outrage" at this "unsupported and totally false statement." Shortly thereafter, gay history professor Martin Duberman, challenging the view that homosexuality was abnormal, wrote in *Skeptic* that "almost all the recent scientific literature . . . points to exactly the opposite conclusion." (Duberman did not indicate what scientific literature he had been reading.)

Some of the most profound rot on the subject was penned back in 1975 in *Psychology Today* by San Francisco psychologist Mark Freedman (a founding member of the Association of Gay Psychologists):

. . . homosexuality in some cases can lead to better-than-average functioning and to a fuller realization of certain fundamental values.

Gay people . . . commonly decide to have sex for the sake of sex . . . The prospective partners don't have to feign love or any other emotion . . . Moreover, gay men are more comfortable engaging in group sex than nongay men, and group sex in my opinion offers pleasures that are impossible for couples.

Gay people constitute a large and varied group and they are capable of providing new kinds of personal fulfillment and social vitality.

With this sort of science-fiction in vogue, gay liberation became clamorous. The movement demanded all manner of reform: That sex education courses in public schools taught by gays portray homosexuality as a valid, healthy life style. That gay love stories be available in libraries and schools.

One goal the gay movement sought desperately was removal of the term "homosexuality" as a category of mental disorder from the diagnostic manual of the American Psychiatric Association. This they achieved. The APA had probably never before seen such pressure, but that is a story in itself. The APA capitulated. In an attempt at explanation the APA said, "no doubt homosexual activist groups will claim that psychiatry has at last recognized that homosexuality is as 'normal' as heterosexuality. They will be wrong. In removing homosexuality *per se* from the nomenclature we are only recognizing that by itself homosexuality does not meet the criteria for being considered a psychiatric disorder." *Time* magazine called the APA's action "an awkward compromise by a confused and defensive profession." That the APA was confused and defensive should be no surprise. So was almost everyone else.

Despite intense pressure to recognize homosexuality (and its model sex practices) as normal human behavior, a few in the medical profession refused to capitulate. In a letter to *Patient Care*, Prof. James Kurfees of the University of Louisville School of Medicine declared himself "appalled" at the way "this deviant sexual behavior is now dignified with more and more pseudoscience. Most of the homosexuals I have known have been pretty miserable, unhappy misfits." A 1982 report by the American Medical Association's council on scientific affairs stated that "Any person, of whatever sexual preference, who shows a dominant pattern of frequent sexual activity with many partners who are and will remain strangers, presents evidence of shallow, narcissistic, impersonal, often compulsively driven genital- rather than person-oriented sex and is almost always regarded as pathological."

A recent signed editorial in the *Southern Medical Journal* refers to the homosexual disease epidemics as a "kickback." Quoting from the book *Homosexuality and the Law: From Condemnation to Celebration,* the author notes that "The law on homosexuality is changing rapidly. It is moving from condemnation to legitimation and next . . . to sponsorship." Even now, he points out, we have such things as "Gay Pride Month, with notable politicians lending their support to gays by marching with them down public thoroughfares." The author proceeds to ask the key question:

If we act as empirical scientists, can we not see the implications of the data before us? If homosexuality, or even just male homosexuality, is "OK," then why the high prevalence of associated complications both in general and especially with regard to AIDS? Might not these "complications" be "consequences"? Might it be that our society's approval of homosexuality is an error and that the unsubtle words of wisdom of the Bible are frightfully correct?

The writer adds that "from an empirical medical perspective alone, current scientific observation seems to require the conclusion that homosexuality is a pathological condition . . . certain cause and effect data are convincing—so convincing that health care providers, in this age of unbridled enthusiasm for preventive medicine, would do well to seek reversal treatment for their homosexual patients just as vigorously as they would for alcoholics or heavy cigarette smokers, for what may not be treated might well be avoided." (Although life-style changes for homosexuals appear to be difficult, there is good evidence they are not impossible.)

Back in 1977, a fourfold to tenfold increase in GBS-type diseases was noted in the San Francisco area. Since then the situation has deteriorated. The incidence of shigellosis and hepatitis A in men 20 to 29 years of age is now six to ten times that of men or women in any other age group. Amebiasis and/or giardiasis are estimated to affect between 10,000 and 50,000 men in New York City. The facts are beginning to bear out the contention of one leading British expert, writing in the *British Journal of Venereal Diseases* in 1982, that the common mouth-anal contact of active homosexuals carries "the almost inevitable risk of transfer of bowel pathogens."

A 1979 study of gay men in New York City turned up an infection rate of 39 percent for amebiasis or giardiasis (that was using only a single fecal specimen; three are usually required to be sure of not missing the diagnosis).

Back in 1974 shigellosis began to turn up as a common homosexual infection, first in San Francisco and later in New York, London, and elsewhere. In 1976 physicians at the New York hospital found that 57 percent of cases of shigellosis, not related to foreign travel, were in homosexuals, who made up only 2.5 percent of the patients.

Hepatitis A is also common in homosexuals. Among gay men attending a venereal disease clinic in Seattle there was evidence of previous hepatitis A infection in 30 percent. The yearly attack rate was about 22 percent.

A public health debacle is here in the making. The *New England Journal of Medicine* reported in 1980 that in San Francisco *an average of 10 percent of persons reported as having amebiasis, giardiasis, or shigellosis were employed as food handlers.* Between 60 percent and 70 percent of these persons were homosexuals.

Clearly, homosexuals no more belong in the food-handling business than they do in the blood banks. As Dr. Selma Dritz of the San Francisco Department of Public Health wrote in the *Western Journal of Medicine* in 1982, "special precautions are required to protect the public from [carriers] who work as food handlers, bartenders, attendants in medical care facilities, and as teachers and aides in day-care centers for infants and young children." Common sense suggests that sexually active gays have no business in any of these occupations.

Finally, gonorrhea is also rampant in the homosexual community. In one large survey of U.S. gays, 40 percent reported known infection with gonorrhea. Common homosexual varieties of this disease (oral and rectal) are also more difficult to detect and treat. Antibiotic-resistant gonococci are now making an appearance; the pharmaceutical industry is only about one drug ahead of these strains, and there is no guarantee it will remain so.

Syphilis, an old disease that was in decline, is also making a comeback. In the same gay survey, 13.5 percent reported a previous infection with syphilis. Among gays attending saunas in Amsterdam there was evidence of old or recent syphilis in 34 percent; only half the men were aware of their infection.

It is self-evident that gay sexual practices are an assault upon the ecology of the human body, that the gay communities of America's cities are polluted with disease. With respect to AIDS, there exists a potential for disaster.

The general public has been grossly deceived about the gravity of this homosexually engendered public health menace. Hollywood and the media under the tutelage of the Gay Media Task Force have done their part, portraying gays in programs like "Dynasty" as all-American types with boy-next-door good looks. Of the movie *Partners,* Richard Schickel wrote: "Like all the other pictures, in what looks like a trend . . . it shows homosexuality neutrally, as just another fact one is likely to encounter." Of the movie *Making Love,* he added, "the people who made this picture are determined to prove that 'nice boys' do, that homosexuals can be as well-adjusted and as middle-class as anyone else."

According to *TV Guide,* we can expect to see many more "almost commonplace" gay characters. " 'We're very pleased,' says Chris Uszler, chairperson of the Alliance for Gay Artists . . . 'there are [going to be] more of what we call "happens-to-be-gay" characters.' "

Perhaps so, Chris. Still, one is reminded of the observation of the nineteenth-century historian J.A. Froude: "One lesson, and one lesson only, history may be said to repeat with distinctness [and that is] that the world is built somehow on moral foundations."

Why We Have Families

(1985)

WILLIAM TUCKER

The 1980s are shaping up as the "Decade of the Family." It is finally beginning to dawn on Americans that many of the things that have gone wrong with this country stem from the disintegration of the nuclear family.

The statistics are astounding. "By 1990 half of all American families may be headed by only one adult," announced *Newsweek* in a cover story entitled "The Single Parent." More than 25 percent of all children are now being raised in "single-parent homes"—up from 12.5 percent in 1970. In over 90 percent of all cases, this parent is the mother.

Single-parent homes quickly veer toward poverty. A staggering 54 percent of all single-parent families are below the poverty line, compared to 18 percent of two-parent families. Over 60 percent of black children are now living in single-parent homes, and 70 percent of these are officially classified as "poor."

Faced with this overwhelming evidence that something remarkable is happening, the really important competition has already begun—the race to define the problem.

As usual, liberals are first out of the starting gate, riding high on a horse called "The Feminization of Poverty." They have taken their usual early lead.

According to their interpretation, family breakups mainly victimize women. Since women are the victims, then the feminist agenda must be the solution. Raise women's salaries, legislate "comparable worth," eliminate "sex discrimination," and these truncated families of women-and-their-children will be able to take their rightful place in society.

I was up at Harvard last April when Senator Daniel Patrick Moynihan presented his own somewhat similar analysis in a widely reported lecture series on the "Crisis in the Family." Senator Moynihan is an odd source for such ideas. His classic 1965 report, "The Negro Family: A Cause for National Action," which traced increasing black poverty to female-headed households, is more relevant today than it was twenty years ago. Unfortunately, Moynihan received so much criticism for being a "racist" that he now shies away from the issue.

Senator Moynihan's present interpretation is that *children* are the "new poor." "In the 1930s, everyone feared getting old because it meant falling into poverty," he said. "But government intervention, through social security, solved the problem. Today we face a situation where *children* are becoming an

176

impoverished group," he argued. The solution—unfortunately—is increased welfare payments to female-headed households.

Moynihan casually brushed aside Charles Murray's argument that welfare is actually aggravating black poverty. "He hasn't been able to prove his case to me," Moynihan said grandly. Therefore the perverse incentives in the welfare system can be casually dismissed.

What was remarkable about Moynihan's performance—and about the entire liberal approach to the problem—is its incredibly shallow perception of the family as a human institution. Through the entire three days at Harvard, Moynihan made only one reference to the origins of the nuclear family. This was a vague suggestion that the nuclear family emerged "somewhere around the seventeenth or eighteenth century in Europe." Although I'm sure Senator Moynihan doesn't realize it, this notion is taken straight out of Friedrich Engels's portrait of the family as an "oppressive institution" invented by capitalism. The implication, of course, is that since we are now headed into a post-industrial welfare state, we can safely lay the nuclear family aside in favor of single-parent homes, "group" families, and whatever other kinds of "alternative" institutions catch people's fancies.

Even more remarkable is that all this ill-formed discussion is taking place at the precise moment when anthropologists have been revising evolutionary theory to put the nuclear family at the center of human culture. Not only is the nuclear family now believed to be as old as mankind itself. It also appears that the family may have been the primary social invention that turned us into human beings in the first place.

Since 1979, the anthropological view of the human family has changed rapidly. In that year, Owen Lovejoy, an associate of Donald Johansen (discoverer of the "Lucy" skeleton), proposed that the nuclear family was the first evolutionary step that lifted us above the apes and put us on the road to becoming human beings. The theory has since been elaborated in many ways, but the major premise still stands and most anthropologists now agree with it.

Thrilling confirmation of Lovejoy's thesis came in 1981 when anthropologist Mary Leakey discovered the "first human footprints" in a fossil lava bed in East Africa. Made more than 3.5 million years ago, they clearly indicate two creatures about four-and-a-half feet tall, walking upright.

What is most astonishing is the "family constellation" that can be inferred from the discovery. The fossil impressions show two different-sized creatures— probably a male and female—walking side by side. Mary Leakey thinks they were holding hands.

But there is also a third set of footprints, made by a smaller creature. They are within the larger footprints. It appears that a young child followed one of the adults across the newly fallen lava ash the same way a boy would follow his father's footsteps across a field of freshly fallen snow.

The nuclear family was not invented in Europe in the eighteenth century, nor in Europe of the eighth century, nor even Ancient Egypt of the eighteenth century B.C. When the first diminutive human-like creatures walked on the planet 3.5 million years ago, they had already formed the nuclear family.

"The crisis in the family" is very much an American phenomenon. It is not occurring to the same degree in any other country.

There are really two things going on. First, divorce, for many reasons, has become easier. This has produced single-parent homes across the entire population. But something else is happening as well. Among American blacks in particular, families are no longer *forming.* Women are simply having children without bothering to acquire husbands—a practice that is the rule in nature, but has been almost unknown in human cultures.

How have we entered what can accurately be called "an evolutionary retrogression"? To answer this, we should review what biologists and anthropologists have discovered in the past ten years about why the human family formed in the first place. And we can start by asking a simple question that doesn't seem to require an answer: "Why do we have mothers?"

About ten years ago, biologists developed the concept of the "selfish gene." This theory essentially confirms Samuel Butler's aphorism, "A chicken is just the egg's way of making another egg." According to selfish-gene theory, the *gene* is the fundamental unit of evolution, with every living creature operating under an imperative to "spread its genes." One of the most immediate payoffs of selfish-gene theory has been an explanation of "motherhood."

Both male and female reproductive cells—the sperm and egg—carry half an offspring. As carriers of genetic material they are identical. Where they differ is in their *post*-conception reproductive strategy. "Sperm strategy" is built around the tactic of producing many offspring and hoping that a few will survive. "Egg strategy" is built around producing a few offspring and taking good care of them to ensure their survival.

Thus, there is a certain inherent promiscuity built into male reproductive strategy. The male's advantage lies in spreading as many sperm cells as possible as widely as possible. Eggs, on the other hand, are usually fewer and larger. They often come packaged with nurturing material for post-conception survival. Egg strategy is based on using resources wisely.

Once an egg has been fertilized, both male and female have an interest in seeing that it survives. But the job can often be handled tolerably well by only one parent. How is it decided which parent does the "mothering"? Selfish gene theory has provided an answer. It may not be very pretty, but it is a good thing to have in mind while designing social policies.

The answer appears to lie in the "first chance to abandon." After coitus, each parent knows that if he or she abandons the fertilized egg, the other parent will still be there to take care of it. Thus, the abandoning parent will have the opportunity to go out and mate with other partners, and increase his or her chance of "spreading its genes."

The parent who is abandoned, on the other hand, has a more difficult choice. If he or she now abandons the fertilized eggs, no one will be there to protect them. The abandoned parent may be able to go out and find other mating partners, but it will only face the same dilemma as before. Therefore, once the first parent has abandoned, the second parent's best bet is to stay and nurture the fertilized egg to viability.

This is how "motherhood" comes into being. Of course, individual animals don't go through this reasoning process; such behavior has been selected through evolutionary history until it has become "instinctive."

In almost all species, the male deposits its sperm in such a way that the female is left "holding the egg." The female may carry the egg, or lay it, or nurture it within her body. In any case, the female is almost always left with the "last chance to abandon," while the male can be long gone. Thus, in the great majority of species, the female becomes the "mother."

There are a few exceptions, however, and they very nicely prove the rule. With many fish, for example, males care for the young. This is because, when fish mate, the female first releases her eggs into the water. Only then can the male fertilize them. By the time he is finished, the *female* can be long gone. Therefore, the male is left "holding the egg" and must assume the task of nurturing the young.

The pattern of female motherhood has become particularly well established among mammals, where females carry the fertilized eggs within their bodies over a long period of time. Moreover, because this extended period of gestation is more time-consuming, females have an incentive to nurture their young following birth as well. Mammals have extended post-natal "motherhood" far beyond that of most other animals. Chimp mothers, for example, nurture their babies for five years.

Thus, nearly all mammals form "families," but they are very different from the human family. Mammalian families almost always involve only the mother and her children. Males will often collect "harems" or "prides," but only to have a group of fertile females available for reproductivity. In many species, males and females live entirely apart, coming together only briefly during the mating season.

The mammalian family of mother-and-her-children became so common as to be almost a universal "law of nature." Yet once it became firmly established, evolution suddenly took another unexpected turn. It created the human family—the mother, her children, and that peculiar human invention, the "father."

To understand the implications of this unexpected turn in human evolution, we should take a look at those animals that form "pair bonds" between mating males and females. Birds are the best example.

The female is almost always left nurturing the young. But what if the job proves too difficult? What if it involves sitting on a nest for three months, for example, without the opportunity to hunt for food? The female cannot do it all herself. Nor can she expect to enlist other females—they have their own responsibilities. Her best bet is to persuade a male to help her. Which male? The one that fertilized her egg is the obvious candidate. How does she persuade him to help? The answer lies in one word—"courtship."

Since females usually have far fewer eggs than males have sperm, the female must be more selective in her mating habits. As a result, "female coyness" is very common in nature. "A man chases a woman until she catches him" is the way we express it, and this is quite correct. In nearly all species, males do the pursuing until the female makes her choice.

In many species, this behavioral pattern has evolved into courtship rituals. In courtship, the female makes the male go through a certain performance—a dance, a display of feathers, a nest-building enterprise—before making up her mind.

This ritual has two important consequences. First, it gives the female some information on which to base her decision. Does the male have beautiful plumage? Is he physically up to par? Is he capable of building a good nest? Second, it prolongs the mating procedure so that by the time it is over, the male no longer has the opportunity to seek other female partners. In courtship, the male's options become much more limited. All his eggs are now in one basket. Without the opportunity for promiscuity, he now has as much stake as the female in nurturing the offspring. Instead of being "irresponsible" (from the female's point of view), he now has a strong incentive to stay on as well. This is how "mated pairs" are created.

Take as an example the emperor penguin. Mating among these birds takes place in the dead of the Antarctic winter, with temperatures often reaching 50-below-zero and winds at 100 miles an hour. The entire population pairs off in courtship rituals that take four to five weeks, leaving little room for illicit liaisons. After the female lays her egg, the couple takes turns sitting on it for two months, barely moving. They do not eat through the entire three-month ordeal, and may lose half their body weight. Nevertheless, the eggs hatch and the next generation arrives.

As mammals evolved, however, "nesting," which restricted both male and female, was no longer necessary. The female began incubating the egg inside her body. The male no longer had to stick around to protect his investment, and as a result, the need to form a "two-parent family" diminished. Few mammalian species form mating pairs. Almost none ever did, in fact, until human beings came along.

In terms of mating behavior, we have evolved remarkably over an astonishingly short period of time. Consider, for example, our closest cousins, the chimpanzees.

Chimps live in gregarious tribes of loosely associated males and females. The strongest bonds are those between mothers and their children, although males also form strong "friendships" among themselves. Mating is entirely promiscuous. When a female chimp goes into heat she advertises it by developing bright red buttocks. Males seek her out, and she will mate with all of them. In her book, *In the Shadow of Man,* ethologist Jane Goodall described the mating periods of "Flo," a very popular old female, who would attract males from miles around. Chimp copulation lasts only about 30 seconds, and Flo would often have a half-dozen males lined up, patiently waiting their turn.

This behavior makes sense for both males and females. As usual, males have a wide opportunity to spread their genes with minimal effort. For females, however, there is also an advantage. Living in gregarious social groups, chimp mothers have to deal with a large number of males every day. If paternity is uncertain, they can count on at least tacit protection from all the males. If they favored any particular male, however, they might face jealousy from other males, who might even harm their children. In other species, adult males often kill offspring that are not their own.

It is virtually certain that our evolutionary ancestors observed mating patterns similar to those of chimps today. Yet our mating rituals—our very biology—have changed completely. How and why did it happen?

In 1979, Dr. Lovejoy proposed that it had to do with the *spacing* of children. He pointed out that female chimps spend five years raising one offspring before they go into heat again. This is a huge investment of time. If males started helping females take care of their children, Lovejoy argued, the female could go into heat again sooner, spacing children only a year or two apart—exactly the pace at which humans reproduce today. Thus, the formation of the nuclear family would have given proto-humans an ever-so-slight evolutionary advantage—particularly in the harsh Pliocene environment in which we originally evolved.

Just how this family formation tied in with the emergence of other human characteristics is still a matter of intense debate. Did we start walking upright to bring vegetation back to a central place, as Lovejoy and others suggest? Or was it to catch small game or to defend ourselves while scavenging for meat on the African savannahs? No one is yet certain. But Lovejoy's major premise is now widely accepted—the formation of the nuclear family and two-parent child-rearing was a crucial step that occurred *at the beginning* of our evolutionary history.

The most persuasive evidence has come from human biology itself. As Edward O. Wilson, the founder of sociobiology, puts it, we are very "sexy" creatures. When compared to that of other animals, human sexuality has evolved to the point where we could almost be called "sexual connoisseurs."

Most notable is the human female's year-round sexual receptivity. All other mammalian females "go into heat," becoming sexually active only at very specific times of the year. They usually advertise this blatantly with smells or visual signals, such as the female chimpanzee's bright red buttocks. The human female, on the other hand, is sexually available all year round. Her fertile periods are so little advertised that a woman herself often does not know when she is ovulating. Thus human sexual activity is constant.

There are many other aspects to our well-developed sex lives. The male penis, for example, is about four times as large as the gorilla penis, even though gorillas have three times our body weight. Pubic hair is designed to set off the sexual organs. There is no known purpose for the enlarged female breast except to prove an attraction to the male—most mammals nurse their young very well with only a nipple.

The obvious purpose of these evolutionary developments seems to have been to bind the male and female together permanently through an active, year-round sex life. Human sexuality is evolutionary millennia away from the quick, 30-second copulations of our chimp and gorilla cousins. For us, sex is a leisurely, friendly, intimate activity.

Jane Goodall took note of these differences in the 1950s when she observed older male and female chimps grow affectionate and pair off for a few days after mating periods. They seemed to enjoy each other's company, she said, but there could be no sexual bond between them. The female, newly pregnant, would not be sexually receptive for another five years. Without the possibility of ongoing physical intimacy, these chimp couples soon drifted apart.

In 1983, anthropologist Helen Fisher pulled this information together in a book called *The Sex Contract.* She argued that the "sex bond" has been the key to human evolution.

Our upright posture, she noted, narrowed the female pelvis. This made childbirth more difficult. In most mammals, the gestation period is directly related to adult body weight. The bigger the animal, the longer it carries its young. Human beings, however, are slightly off the scale. As a result, we are all born a bit premature. This makes human children even more helpless, and thus creates another reinforcement of the two-parent family.

Fisher also noted that our diet seems to be formed around the male-female bond. Chimps are 95 percent vegetarian, the males hunting small animals only occasionally. Human societies, however, generally have a diet of about 30 percent meat. Moreover, there is a division of labor. In almost all primitive human societies males hunt while females gather vegetables and roots. The most effective way to pursue this mixed diet, Fisher pointed out, would be for a pair-bonded male-and-female couple to share their meat and vegetables. This became still another strand woven into the web of the pair-bonded nuclear family.

But what was the key behavior mechanism that triggered family formation? Writing from a mildly feminist viewpoint, Fisher suggested "the human female's increased capacity for sexual enjoyment." The female orgasm is unknown to other species, she pointed out, and females can theoretically exhaust several males in non-stop sexual encounters. It was this increased sexual capacity, argued Fisher, that tied a single male to his female partner, and bound him to child-rearing.

This is an attractive theory, but it has a serious flaw. Human females do indeed have an increased capacity for sexual activity, but that does not necessarily create a pair-bond. If only one woman possessed it, she could use it to attract and hold onto a male of her choice. But once every woman has it, we are back where we started. Males still retain an evolutionary advantage in promiscuity, while females have to worry about getting pregnant. The permanent sexual availability of every female does not automatically create a male-female bond. It only increases the opportunities for male philandering.

"What does a woman want?" was a question that puzzled Freud. The answer turns out to be very complicated. While it is true that human females have evolved into highly sexed creatures, with a capacity for sexual enjoyment greater than that of other mammals, this isn't the end of the story. Their evolution has only left them more vulnerable to the inherently more promiscuous males.

In short, once the human female developed this capacity for year-round sexual enjoyment, she had to turn around and repress it again, in order to attend to the age-old concern of binding the male to the task of raising children.

The evolutionary task assigned to the human female is indeed one of the most complex in nature. Human females obviously have a highly developed sexuality, yet most cultures have been built around courtship, chastity, and the "myth" of the female's lower sexual capacity. In almost every culture, women withhold sex in order to obtain marriage. This pattern predominated in our own culture up until less than twenty-five years ago. (When I was in college in the 1960s, I knew men who would sleep with every girl they met until they ran into one who refused them. Then they would marry that one.)

Yet these patterns have now been changed radically, if not entirely shattered. What has happened to undermine them? And what has it meant for family formation?

The most obvious new element is the sexual revolution. Birth control and abortion have erased the need for females to act coyly and to refrain from premarital sex in order to avoid getting pregnant.

A recent study among blue-collar families in Chicago, for example, shows that premarital sex is actually quite common. Couples often live together for more than a year without getting married. At some point, however, they "make a mistake" and the woman gets pregnant. At this point, they "have to" get married. To the researchers, it seems obvious that this "mistake" is actually a mutual consent between the couple that they are willing to make a long-term commitment. The possibility of abortion, however, has considerably disrupted this folk custom.

Like it or not, the new sexual freedom is now a technical possibility. Still, the sexual revolution is probably overrated as a cause of family breakups. Whatever havoc it may have caused originally is now largely over. Social custom is adjusting. Of probably much more lasting impact have been long-term changes in the divorce laws.

Traditional divorce laws were built around the principle that the *father* got custody of the children. Our immediate reaction may be to say this was determined by "male chauvinism." In fact the underlying principles were much different.

Consider again the biological impulses of males and females. The fundamental inclination of male sexuality leads to abandoning children and going on to produce others. The inclination is intensified in human males who can reproduce often well beyond the age of 50. It is always easier for a man to pick up his stakes and start a new family.

Female biology, on the other hand, argues for keeping the children. Women usually feel they have made a larger biological investment in their offspring. There is more physical pain involved, and it is much more difficult for a woman to begin reproducing anew after 40.

Thus, traditional divorce laws—awarding custody of children to the father—worked against the biological interests of both men and women, but in favor of the family and a family-oriented society. If men wanted to divorce, they couldn't just dance off care-free. They had to take the children with them. On the other hand, if women wanted to divorce, they couldn't just "take the children and run." They had to give up their children in the process. By working against the biological impulses of both men and women, paternal custody made divorce much more painful for both parties.

We, of course, have quickly and effortlessly dismantled this convention. Since the 1920s we have "liberated" ourselves by shifting the system to work in favor of both *individual* men and women, but *against* stable families. Women now routinely get custody of the children in most cases.

As a result, it is the easiest thing in the world for men to run off and leave the responsibility of child-rearing to the mother. Alimony payments once restricted this freedom, but lax enforcement and "no-fault" divorce have weakened the deterrent. It is also the easiest thing in the world for a woman to walk out on her husband (or ask him to leave), knowing that the courts will award her custody. As for the long-term social costs, everyone else pays the bill.

The male tendency to wander is well documented in history. What has been less recognized, however, has been the female desire to have children without going through the trouble of securing a husband. Women do not automatically desire to share their children. Jane Goodall noted that chimp mothers are very possessive and usually reluctant to allow their children to play with friendly males, even when the children themselves obviously desire it.

In truth, the family is really a carefully constructed compromise. The female exchanges sexual availability for male companionship. The male is assured of paternity by the promise of female chastity (as the saying goes, only women really know when they are raising their own children). The female gives up her claim to be the sole creator of life in order to secure male cooperation.

Yet this delicately created social institution cannot suffer too much disruption—particularly the kind of social mayhem that we have created over the past twenty-five years. The evidence of this can be seen in what has happened to the American black family.

The breakup of the family among blacks is a phenomenon that is almost unique. This is often overlooked in statistics that lump together black and white single-parent homes. Although 25 percent of the nation's families are now headed by single women, fully one-third of these are concentrated in the 12 percent of the population that is black.

Divorce rates among whites have soared in recent years. What is rarely observed, however, is that black divorce rates were always about double the white rate, and have *remained* almost twice as high as white rates have soared. Over half of black marriages now result in divorce—and this doesn't include the shifting common-law marriages that have become characteristic of lower-class black culture.

More important, however, is the rate at which blacks are completely failing to form families. Although 17 percent of white children are in single-parent homes, all but 2 percent of these are the result of divorce or death of a parent. But 28 percent of black single-parent homes are headed by a mother who has *never* married. One-half of all black females now have a baby before they turn 20, and one-quarter have two. A small percentage of these teenage mothers are married.

Marvin Harris, perhaps the country's most widely published popular anthropologist, examined the disintegration of the black family in his 1981 book, *America Now.* Not surprisingly, he traced the disintegration of black families to America's ill-conceived "family allowance"—Aid to Families with Dependent Children (AFDC).

The AFDC grant, Harris pointed out, serves as a kind of dowry—a "nest egg" a woman inherits when she becomes pregnant. "In a world without stability or assets," he wrote, "AFDC [becomes] a vital resource that puts women and motherhood at the center of things. Inner-city men respect women who have this resource; they vie with each other for their favors. And by having children with them the men establish a claim on the shelter which women control."

As Harris pointed out, the welfare matriarchy has not entailed a *complete* disintegration of the black family. Instead, it only shifted its center of gravity to a new female-dominated structure built around a woman who has a string of children with various men. For a woman, this can be a very positive strategy. She no longer has to share all her children with a single father. The family becomes "matrilocal" and "matrilinear." "At sixteen [welfare daughters] can get pregnant and apply for AFDC on their own, adding their own child's stipend to the family's income and perpetuating the female-centered dynasty of their mothers and grandmothers."

In addition, the various paternities give welfare mothers a wide net of potential economic support. "As . . . shown in [one] study of a black Midwestern ghetto neighborhood, AFDC women have a surprisingly large circle of relatives based on ties built up by their sequential liaisons," wrote Harris. "These kinship ties give AFDC women additional security and influence and people to turn to in case of emergencies."

What AFDC has accomplished, then, is to free lower-class women from the age-old female problem of having to find a husband before she can have children. It has also freed black men of the age-old problem of having to take on the responsibility of a family in order to produce offspring.

And so, as Marvin Harris concluded: "Despite all the crafty scheming that has gone into the design of AFDC, the program has succeeded best in achieving exactly what it was designed to prevent: the formation of mother-centered families living on the dole."

The first thing to be recognized about the disintegration of the family, then, is that it is bound to create poverty. The great contribution of the nuclear family has been its efficiency in yoking men and women together to the task of raising children. Family disintegration undoes the original compromise on which the evolution of our species has been built. Thus, to say that people are becoming "impoverished" because they have broken up their families (or are failing to form them) is about as profound as saying that people have trouble picking things up after they have cut off their thumbs.

What can be done to stem the tide of family disintegration? Changing the divorce laws to favor paternal custody is a first priority. As long as both men and women can run off from their responsibilities without sacrificing anything, high divorce rates will continue. As for the failure in family formation— particularly among blacks—the welfare system is the obvious target. It cannot be said often enough that reforming welfare would be the single most positive way to begin lifting black Americans out of poverty.

Although the family has been with us since the beginning of human evolution, it remains a relatively fragile biological institution. The desires of individual men and women do not "naturally" work in its favor. Without cultural reinforcement—or with wrong-headed social intervention—our biological drives can quickly carry us back to the earlier mother-and-her-children mammalian family. The pain we feel in witnessing this retrogression is only a measure of the degree to which we have become human.

The About Men Men

(1986)

ANDREW FERGUSON

Late last year, the Playboy organization announced that it had hired its first male bunnies. They'll work at a new Playboy club in New York City. Jeff Rector, one of the thirty-five novice bunnies chosen from nearly 1500 aspirants, said this transformation in his life process was "an awesome responsibility. We represent all of mankind, of manhood." The sad truth is that Mr. Rector is quite close to being correct. Consider these other developments:

• The League of Women Voters has announced that its new executive director is one Grant Thompson, a biological male.

• Senator Joseph Biden, whom my fellow Democrats often point to as the model of the new Democratic leader, rising up and striding boldly forth from the ashes of the Mondale-Ferraro campaign, speaks often of his heroes. Martin Luther King and the Kennedys are among them, he says, for the rather simple reason that "they made me feel good about myself."

• After ending a "relationship" with a former secretary, Dave Durenberger, a Republican senator from Minnesota, recently left his wife and moved into an all-male retreat—actually a large colonial mansion—in Arlington, Virginia. Senator Durenberger was giving enough of himself as a person to share the news in front-page stories in the *Washington Post* and the *Minneapolis Star and Tribune*. He blamed what had heretofore been his personal troubles on the fact that "I didn't love myself well enough." Although "I'm a married person—I believe in the sanctity of marriage and the whole business," the Senator didn't know when he'd go back to his wife. "I'm not at that point yet," he shyly told his millions of readers. "The good news is that I'm not at the point so many people get to at the beginning of one of these things when they say it isn't even worth doing."

I could go on, but my point should be clear: no matter what they tell you, these are tough times for the old-fashioned American male. Alan Alda may have gone into semi-retirement, but the flowers he planted in the 1970s continue to bloom. For all the dedicated trampling of Chuck Norris and Rocky, Rambo and Reagan, the brightly colored blossoms sprout thickly around our ankles, entangling ever more of our number, causing them to tumble softly into the comfy poppy field of the New Age man, where self-absorption equals sensitivity and

187

compulsive confession is mistaken for candor. The signs are everywhere—even in America's newspaper of record, the *New York Times.*

More specifically, I'm referring to the *Times* Sunday magazine, and its "About Men" column. Tucked neatly between four-color, bled-to-the-edge ads for Waterford crystal and clothes designed by the rugged Ralph Lauren, "About Men" has for several years now been a soapbox for the sort of man who is forever given to the minute, infinitely loving examination of his favorite subject: himself. I can scarcely believe that when the *Times* editors launched the column—presumably as a companion to the equally horrific "Hers" column that appears each Monday—they realized they were opening Pandora's trunk. Since then every freelancer in the country has lunged forward, eager to spill his guts. An avalanche of confession has poured in over the transom. But whatever their original intention, the editors apparently decided, as an "About Men" man might put it, to feel the flow and go with that.

The typical "About Men" contributor is not hard to define: he is between the ages of 25 and 45; he is successful in his work; he is vaguely uneasy; he is divorced, with kids who teach him more about life than he ever dreamed possible; and he is extremely eager to talk—so long as the monologue doesn't stray too far from his favorite subject. Of course, there are exceptions to this profile of the self-possessed chatterbox. The occasional World War II vet, reflecting on the disappearance of civility, or the former Golden Gloves champ, remembering his blue-collar father's pride, can turn out columns that are witty and even affecting. But far more often "About Men" is about newspaper column as public therapy, where the patient rises from the couch and struts and preens.

The result is a series of amazing documents, a gushy diary produced by many different hands. Reading "About Men," you can imagine the manuscripts as they arrive at the *Times* office, adorned with loopy *l*'s and *i*'s dotted with enormous circles, a cute caricature of a snuggly bunny rabbit crouched in the corner of the page, a smiley face below the signature at the bottom. Gushy diaries are no longer the private preserve of insecure school girls; today they are written by wealthy men and published in magazines. David L. Dworkin, the president of Neiman-Marcus, recollects a littoral stroll with his daughter, whom he likes because she has given "tremendous validity to my life." The girl is only twelve and shouldn't be blamed for not knowing any better, but she makes the huge mistake of asking Dad whether he's happy. If you ask a guy like Mr. Dworkin a question like that, you'd better sit back and get ready for the long haul. It was, he writes, "a question I have never forgotten." Eight hundred words later, he's telling us that "there are nights—many nights—when I am awakened by disturbing thoughts that do not seem to retire with the rest of my mind/body functions. Nightmares of a sort. Images of a world not right. The future perhaps. . . . They make me ask, in the face of a life dedicated to achievement, 'Is this all there is?'" Like most "About Men" columns when they hit their confessional stride, what Mr. Dworkin's lacks in originality it makes up in obviousness.

Then there is Wayne Kalyn, the managing editor of *World Tennis* magazine. Mr. Kalyn tells us how his wife left him (she needed "time and space";

he lumbered into the bedroom and cried); he then tells us how he went to his wife's apartment to surprise her with flowers and was himself surprised to discover her with another man. Instead of "being noble enough to have respected my wife's right to determine the direction of her life," Mr. Kalyn got steamed. He was a brute. He has gone to "About Men" to ask forgiveness from himself. It is granted.

You would think that confessions such as these would be better told to a bartender in the wee hours, when most of the other customers have stumbled home. Or maybe given man to man—say, to a best friend. Unfortunately, as Professor Michael McGill, author of the indispensable *McGill Report on Male Intimacy,* makes clear in his contribution to "About Men," this is no longer possible. He has discovered that men make crummy best friends because we "use interaction with one another to prove ourselves, following conventional rules of commerce and competition, ever aware that if we get too close, confide too much, it may be used against us." Quite a problem! He has hit on a solution. "Women," he writes, "use interaction as a way to improve relationships." Ergo, get yourself a woman for a best friend. Professor McGill himself has Sharon. "Sharon and I are intimate but sexually innocent; our interest in each other is relational, not romantic." That innocence comes as a great relief, he tells us, to his wife Janet, although from time to time she still suspects that Professor McGill plans, in fact, someday to jump Sharon's bones. "I have some more explaining to do," he says.

Professor McGill's situation, by the way, is an "About Men" anomaly, in that he has charged headlong into the New Age while his wife is the one who has lagged behind. More often the reverse is true; the writer is the dolt, and his wife/ex-wife/daughter/homosexual son has to drag him down the bumpy road to wisdom. These journeys are the stuff "About Men" is made of. John Dunne, for instance, says his daughter Nicole allowed him "to return to my childhood, to see things through her eyes, to giggle and be as silly as I wanted to be." And in a mild variation on this theme, the literary critic Benjamin DeMott records that he was taught how truly to enjoy an apple by a horse named Terence. (The details are numerous and, for our purposes here, insignificant.)

It is, then, a central contention of most "About Men" pieces that men aren't what they used to be—they are softer and gentler, more contemplative and refined. The column in that sense is self-evidential. Left a bit foggier is the question of whether this is a good thing; as an ethical matter, "About Men" writers strive to be nonjudgmental. But sooner or later they tip their hand. Many of the pieces have a tendentious, even exhortatory, flavor. Dr. Zick Rubin, a professor of social psychology at Brandeis University, worries that American men are too quantitative, and celebrates the fact that in his son's Little League games no score is kept ("The important thing . . . is the playing and the building of skills, not the winning"). Nevertheless, he scowls: "One can always find a father or two on the sidelines who is surreptitiously but scrupulously recording every run that scampers across the plate." Dr. Rubin shudders at the kind of example this must set for the kids.

"My sons may be better off in a country in which 'Manhood' will mean little more than, say, the name for an after-shave lotion," says Leonard Kriegel, who is moreover aware of "the price exacted" in our national life for the idea that a man should be "tough, resilient, independent, able to take it." Owen Edwards realizes that "medals are atavistic, mere archaic mementoes impressive to those who need to believe in a man's worth. Without the weight of tradition and the reflex of retrograde machismo, a chest full of medals is nothing more than a résumé in 3-D and Technicolor." After lamenting that fewer and fewer Italian men hold hands in public, Roger Youman sadly takes note of "the terrifying problems of a planet whose political leaders . . . seem to believe that their first priority is to prove their manhood. Nevertheless, at a time when the survival of the human race may depend on the willingness of men to walk hand in hand metaphorically, I see evidence that they are drawing apart physically. I take that as an ominous sign."

But this is just fretfulness on Mr. Youman's part. "About Men" writers are always seeing ominous signs, even when it is clear that the battle is won—even when, *pace* Eastwood and Stallone, most men have already defected to their side. Every Sunday my papergirl delivers fresh evidence, in the form of the *Times* magazine, that this is so.

Why then the fretfulness? Perhaps it's because of the insatiable nature, the remorselessness, of the Master the "About Men" men—and, in truth, all men—struggle to serve. This morning I saw a religious talk show on television. The host, a mild, extremely solicitous man, was interviewing a woman theologian. After a couple of minutes she castigated him for using the masculine pronoun when he referred to God. In abject apology he twisted his mouth into a grotesque grin and began talking very fast. He had not long ago enrolled in a seminar on "the female component of the divine," he recalled, and he was the only man there. "Talk about process and getting in touch with your own prejudices!" he said, but the woman theologian merely forced a thin smile and said nothing. In the silence that followed the host ran his fingers around his collar, squirmed a bit in his chair, and cleared his throat, ready to try again—ready to say whatever was necessary.

John Maynard Keynes:
Hopes Betrayed, 1883–1920
by Robert Skidelsky

(1986)

COLIN WELCH

Sir Roy Harrod's *Life* of Keynes was published in 1951. It omitted all reference to Keynes's homosexuality. Why was that? In his fascinating introduction to his own fascinating life of Keynes, Robert Skidelsky adduces a number of reasons, credible but not to him or to anyone else wholly satisfying or convincing. A distinguished Keynesian economist himself, Harrod admired, even venerated his friend Keynes. But this was not enough to endear or even render tolerable to him his hero's active homosexuality, his loose ethics, derived from the epicurean Cambridge philosopher G. E. Moore, or the ambiguous Cambridge secret society, the Apostles, and the epicene Bloomsbury set, of both of which Keynes was a committed aficionado. Faced with the disagreeable, Harrod hastened past, eyes averted, nose held. His Keynes is accordingly a Tadzio-less Aschenbach, a Portnoy with no complaint.

Much of Keynes's individuality had to be suppressed, and this, according to Keynes himself, for long periods of his life the most important part. Keynes said, though Harrod does not quote him, that of his prime objects in life before 1914, when he was already over 30 and a prize fellow of King's (an honor he would characteristically have liked to celebrate by raping an undergraduate [male] in the dons' combination room, "just to make them see things a little more in their true light"—though many King's dons can have needed no such instruction), love (homosexual) came a long way first. Homosexuality was not for him, as it was for Harrod, an unfortunate but irrelevant aberration, but rather a vital part of "the good life" as he saw it. Nor was it in any way sublimated or repressed. The statistics of sexual encounters he kept in his diary made James Strachey "gasp," his conversation struck Lytton Strachey as "inordinately filthy." To disgust Lytton Strachey, high priest of "the higher sodomy" (their own phrase), was no mean feat.

Harrod did not suppress the influence on Keynes of Moore, in whose philosophy Beatrice Webb saw nothing "except a metaphysical justification for doing what you like and what other people disapprove of." But he diminishes it, in Mr. Skidelsky's view, to "yet another of those adolescent stages through which his hero passed on the road to maturity." Yet at the age of 55, on the eve of World War II, Keynes, while gently criticizing certain aspects of the Moorite creed, reaffirmed that he found it "nearer the truth than any other that

I know . . . nothing to be ashamed of," still "my religion under the surface
. . . I remain and always will remain an immoralist." A long, long adolescence,
this!

As for the Apostles' Society, Harrod implied that it had ceased to exist (it
still meets thirty-five years later) and announced that it was "time to desist from
prying into the affairs of that august body." An "august body," indeed, in which
Keynes himself inspected "beauties" (male) for potential membership and
which nourished the spies Burgess and Blunt as well as other scaly figures. Time
perhaps to *start* prying rather than to desist!

Even the normally shrewd Mr. Skidelsky takes a relaxed view of the Apostles: "It was widely if implausibly suggested that the Society had fostered, or
by its secrecy in some way facilitated, [the spies'] treacherous activities." This
suggestion seems to me in no way implausible. The Society's prevailing ethos
was defiantly expressed by Keynes himself: "We repudiated entirely customary
morals, conventions and traditional wisdom. We were . . . in the strict sense of
the term, immoralists. The consequences of being found out had . . . to be
considered, for what they were worth. But we recognized no moral obligation
on us, no inner sanction, to conform or to obey. Before heaven [!] we claimed
to be our own judge in our own case." It is a dull mind indeed which cannot
see in these arrogant and unedifying sentiments every sort of treason, treachery,
and disloyalty sanctioned, as also in E. M. Forster's famous Bloomsburian *mot:*
"If I had to choose between betraying my country or betraying my friend, I
hope I should have the guts to betray my country." As if one's country did not
contain many friends!

With a certain sly exultation, unless I misjudge him, Mr. Skidelsky finds that
"the most striking thing about the Apostles is their quintessential Britishness,"
a remark he justifies by conventional references to the exclusiveness of English
upper-class society and its distaste for commerce and industry, to the barbarities
of English public school education, to the stifling moralism of English family life,
and to the English capacity to keep its upper-class males in a state of petrified
adolescence. If there is or was, as I ruefully concede, some truth in all this, it
serves not to excuse the Apostles but to spread the guilt far wider, through a
whole decadent intelligentsia, clerisy, and ruling class.

Mr. Skidelsky sympathizes with other difficulties facing Harrod—the problem, for instance, of "the widow and the friends," as Virginia Woolf called it.
Keynes's actual widow, the delightful ballerina Lydia Lopokova, gave little
trouble. But there were other relations, notably Keynes's brother Geoffrey,
who understandably wanted to destroy all Keynes's letters to Lytton Strachey.
Harrod, though he did not use them, honorably prevented this epistolary vandalism. Then there were Keynes's Bloomsbury friends and fellow economists,
many in command of sources, all to be consulted, all demanding the suppression
of this or that, never the same thing: all had different axes to grind. Harrod was
reduced to a *crise de nerfs;* the strain brought him to "the end of his tether."

But Harrod also suppressed much off his own bat—Keynes's application,
for instance, to be a conscientious objector to military service in World War I.
This application seems quite superfluous—a bad case of belt *and* braces—since
he was at the Treasury in a reserved occupation. But he may have half-intended

to resign from the Treasury, rather than go on working for "a Government I despise for ends I think criminal"—another sentiment omitted by Harrod. Other letters are cleaned up by Harrod, including one which lightheartedly expresses Keynes's longing to "swindle the investing public."

One of Harrod's purposes in cleaning up Keynes's act was to sell Keynes's reflections on "demand management" and permanent boom, highly salutary as Harrod thought them, to the all-important Americans. These innocents were supposed then to take as dim a view of homosexuality and draft-dodging as Keynes normally took of Americans, whom he treated with an arrogant rudeness which is still embarrassing. With Melchior, his German opposite number at the Paris peace talks in 1919, Keynes fell "in a sort of way . . . in love." I can think of no American who inspired even such modified raptures.

Another justification for Harrod's reticence lies in the tormenting dilemma: Are the private life, personal opinions, whims, and antics of a great "scientist" relevant to any account or evaluation of his public works, scientific hypotheses, and discoveries? Keynesian economists, disciples, and groupies have naturally denied that they are and have manfully struggled to insulate "life" from "thought." Prof. Maurice Preston has written: "It is obvious philosophical nonsense to suggest that there is a connection" between Keynes's sexuality and his economics; "the logical validity of a theory and its empirical relevance are independent of its progenitor. What help is knowledge of the lives of Newton and Einstein in predicting the movement of the planets?"

The life-thought connection is perfectly apparent to Mr. Skidelsky, himself no enemy to "funny-money" theories: indeed, he thinks Keynesian economics "robust" enough to survive revelations about Keynes's private life. Well they may survive, but less to my mind because of whatever is robust in them than because of what is slippery, evasive, delusorily beguiling, and calculated to fulfill many wish-dreams. The life-thought connection, long apparent to me and others, must have been in the mind of the great Schumpeter when he wrote in 1952 about Keynes: "He was childless, and his philosophy of life was essentially a short-run philosophy. So he turned resolutely to the only 'parameter of action' that seemed left to him, both as an Englishman and *the sort of Englishman he was* [Mr. Skidelsky's italics]—monetary management." Schumpeter refers elsewhere to Keynes's "childless vision," exemplified in his famous dictum, "In the long run we are all dead"—not a sentiment which would occur readily to a father or grandfather, well aware that after he is dead his offspring will normally be living, and deserve his forethought now.

Economics is not in fact an exact science—least of all did Keynes think it so, with his healthy mistrust of mathematical economics. It is not susceptible to scientific experiment or proof. It has to deal with too many variables, indeed, with the whole of human life seen from a certain angle. In that life millions of wills are free, and the *ceteris paribus* condition, the bane of all economic prediction, endures no longer than a mayfly. Somebody dubbed economics "the science of choice." Professor James Buchanan objected: Where there is genuine choice there can be no science.

Into a field in such flux, economists can reasonably import and apply their own noneconomic value judgments and prejudices, their views of what constitutes a good society: more free or less so, more or less equal, orientated to present opulence or future, more harshly motivated or more lazily content, richer or happier, and so on. This being so, we can reasonably take an interest in what an economist's values really are and how they are connected to his "scientific" activities. Keynes was always hostile to thrift, which he regarded as economically and socially harmful, and savings, exemplifying for him an age-old Puritan fallacy; consumption was for him the source of economic growth; he flirted long with Malthusian population theories about "excessive fecundity," for him the cause of revolutions and other evils. True, false, or neither, are not such views and interests natural to a man of Keynes's values and personal predispositions or, to put it more crudely, as Keynes did, natural to a man who found the Arabs of Tunis "wonderful, very beautiful and the first race of buggers I've ever seen," as if their very existence did not demolish his enraptured misapprehension!

To say that Mr. Skidelsky has corrected many misconceptions about Keynes is perfectly true, but a totally inadequate tribute to his achievement. This is not a nitpicking commentary on other people's errors but an artistic triumph, a virtual resurrection, a living portrait of a remarkable man, seen for the first time as a complete whole and alas, thus seen, revealing himself as in some respects woefully incomplete. But not in all respects.

Mr. Skidelsky repeatedly reminds us of how far above his values Keynes continuously rose. Indeed, says Mr. Skidelsky, "many economists have had higher ethical ideals; none have achieved so much practical good." A bit thick this, in a field once graced by Adam Smith—Shakespeare, say, to Keynes's Shaw or Noel Coward. Yet Keynes's loyalty to free trade, his tireless work to create arrangements and institutions favorable to it, did produce for us thirty years of unequalled prosperity, only now in jeopardy. For this new age of the Antonines he deserves our abiding gratitude.

Wherever four economists were gathered together, it was said, there would be five conflicting opinions, two of them advanced by Mr. Keynes. He was infinitely various, fruitfully self-contradictory, often self-correcting. For whatever poisons or quack remedies he recommended, he usually supplied his own antidotes. Dubbed "the father of inflation," for instance, no one of his generation wrote more eloquently or harshly about it and its dire consequences. It was widely rumored that at the end of his life, he was gravely disturbed by some of the possible consequences of his theories, rightly or wrongly interpreted and applied. Never mind, he is reported to have said, there will be time for me to put all that right. But there wasn't. In the short run, alas, he was dead. Wiser are those who think always of the long run, and bear in mind that it may start tomorrow!

IV

Communism
and Fellow Travelers

Leonid, We Hardly Knew Ye

(1978)

J.D. LOFTON

This headline-making book represents a major contribution to Soviet-American understanding. It was prepared as a direct result of an approach by Simon and Schuster to the Soviet Union and covers Mr. Brezhnev's life in full detail. In it, Mr. Brezhnev's personal views on major international questions— détente, disarmament, co-existence—and his meetings with various Western leaders, including American Presidents, France's Giscard d'Estaing, and such Socialist leaders as Fidel Castro, are given in detail. Pages From His Life *is perhaps the first fully-rounded portrait of the Soviet leader and is a work of extraordinary importance, scope and depth. It is a book of rare and genuine excitement.*

—Text of a full-page Simon and Schuster ad
in the *New York Times Book Review,* April 30, 1978.

Let's be honest, open, candid, and above board and and, as Lowell Weicker frequently says, let's put all the cards on the table face up: This book isn't for everybody.

So, who is it for? An excellent question which I would prefer to answer this way. It having slipped your mind, have you ever turned to a friend or loved one and asked: "Do you remember the date that the tabloid newspaper of the Dzerzhinsky steel mill in Kamenskoye, the Ukraine, ran the story about old Leonid being among the top four engineer graduates at the Arsenichev Metallurgical Institute?"

Have you ever wondered if, during the 1930s when Leonid worked in the Dzerzhinsky steel mill as "a good fitter and an even better gas purification machine operator," he was also "a good mixer and sought the company of people his own age, especially those who were bold, energetic, and eager and considered the building of the new world something close to their hearts"?

Have you ever been in a heated debate about Leonid's life and found yourself stumped and humiliated when your opponent put his nose against yours asking, as a sneer rippled across his upper lip: "Okay, wise-guy, if you're so smart, can you tell me when Brezhnev was elected First Secretary of the Zaporozhye Regional Party Committee, when he was elected First Secretary of the Dnepropetrovsk Regional Party Committee, and when he was elected First and then Second Secretary of the Central Committee of the Communist Party of Kazakhstan?"?

If your answer to all these questions is "yes," then this book is for you. This book is also for Muhammad Ali, who recently returned from a ten-day trip to the USSR to inform us that in Russia: "There's no big shots. Everybody's plain and simple. Even Mr. Brezhnev [who is] as cute as ever"; there are "100 nationalities living in peace"; "[I saw] only one policeman. I didn't see no guns. No crime. No prostitutes. Not one homosexual. No hitchhikers, not one beggar [and no] bad, bad poverty"; and "I never felt so free from being robbed." Ali says it is a "lie" that there is no freedom of religion in the Soviet Union because he saw houses of worship for Moslems, Jews, and Catholics.

Unfortunately, Ali's glowing account of life in the Soviet Union was somewhat marred by the fact that on the very day he held his New York press conference, back in Moscow Vladimir Slepak was being sentenced to five years internal exile for the heinous crime of having hung a sign from his apartment balcony reading: "Let us join our son in Israel." And, a few days later, also in Moscow, a young Soviet citizen, undoubtedly elated over being no more plain and simple than Mr. Brezhnev, demonstrated his exuberance by axing to death a couple of elderly Swedish tourists. And, a few days after this, eight Pentacostalists, protesting the lack of freedom to practice their religion in the USSR, sat-in at the U.S. Embassy in Moscow saying they would not leave until they were allowed to emigrate.

But, what the hey, Champ, these are nits that I'm picking. I mean, you were there and know what you saw, right?

Oh, I almost forgot. The answers to the above questions are:

February 2, 1935; yes; August 30, 1946; November of 1947; August of 1955; and February of 1954.

What I like most about this book is its simplicity. It is, as Leonid tells us in his special introduction, a modest, low-key account—a story of how "only Soviet power enabled me, the son of a worker, to rise to the leadership of a glorious many-millions-strong party and of history's first socialist state." Local boy makes good. This book is a story of your average, run-of-the-mill, man-of-the-people who is a combination of Socrates, Desiderius Erasmus, Christ, Florence Nightingale, St. Francis of Assisi, Alexander the Great, and Albert Schweitzer, all rolled into one hell of a nice guy, if I may paraphrase.

Now, to be sure, there are going to be some criticisms of this book. Already the negative nabobs are beginning to natter. For example, a Mr. Adam B. Ulam, a so-called expert on Russia who teaches at Harvard, complains in the *New Republic* that this book doesn't contain "much light stuff." He writes of Mr. Brezhnev: "Perhaps deferring to their subject's modesty, the authors have refrained from describing those special skills and qualities which must have enabled him to get where he is." Questioning Leonid's version of his own upward mobility, Ulam observes: "Here we have a young graduate of an engineering school rising rapidly in the party hierarchy in the Ukraine in the late 1930s. How come? And why in 1950 should the Moldavian Communist Party select a Russian working in the Ukraine as its First Secretary? Well, the authors don't believe in dwelling on unhappy episodes of the past, and carry this restraint to the point of never mentioning the name of J.V. Stalin, or of alluding to the purges of the 1930s and 1940s. The reader is thus denied the full appreciation of how clever, as well as lucky, Brezhnev must have been: at a time when people in the party hierarchy were being liquidated right and left, he not only survived, but prospered."

Picky, picky, picky. First of all, the statement that Stalin is never mentioned in this book is a flat lie. Right there on page 53, in black and white, is this passage relating to Mr. Brezhnev's military record: "At this critical time Brezhnev was a frequent visitor on the Little Land. Marshall Georgi Zhukov, who came to the Novorossiisk area with a special assignment from the Supreme Commander in Chief, Stalin, regretted that he had missed seeing Brezhnev at the Army Field Administration." Quote, unquote. Can you read, professor! What word do you see in the middle of this passage? See it: S-T-A-L-I-N! STALIN! I must say that such incredible distortion of what's in this book makes one wonder if you really read it. I guess we'll really never know though, will we?

Now, to the more general thrust of your comments, Mr. Russian Expert. The plain fact of the matter is that whether you or I like it or not, the whole so-called purge thing has been done to death, as has Mr. Brezhnev's alleged role in doing Mr. Stalin's dirty work. Of course the USSR Academy of Sciences authors put no "light stuff" in this book. Of course they refused to indulge in the name-game or the numbers-game as regards this purge business. But so what? We all know about this stuff already.

In his 1974 book, *Brezhnev: The Masks of Power,* former *Newsweek* reporter John Dornberg describes Brezhnev's role in the Ukraine as follows:

It was Brezhnev's responsibility to stimulate "ideological vigilance" against all manner of saboteurs, spies and enemies of the people who represented a wide spectrum of nemesis. . . . Brezhnev also had to justify the terror and purges. . . . Brezhnev was charged with organizing mass meetings, rallies, "spontaneous" demonstrations, parades, and celebrations to whip up popular enthusiasm for Stalin and the regime. . . .

Between 1945 and 1950 an estimated 500,000 of the republic's original 3,000,000 population were executed, sentenced to prison camps or deported. . . . In July, 1950, Leonid Brezhnev was sent to Kishinev to complete the task. It was no job for the pusillanimous . . . the information that is available leads Western observers and the few emigrants from the republic to the consensus that Brezhnev's reign was draconian and represents one of the darkest periods of his career.

In conclusion, Dornberg says:

It is a fact that the Brezhnev era has been characterized by persistent re-Stalinization for which Brezhnev himself must take major responsibility. . . . History will also record Brezhnev's greatest transgression: placing the ghost of Stalin in the niche left by Khrushchev's fall. . . . Culturally, intellectually, and in terms of human freedom, the USSR has regressed under Brezhnev's rule. . . . Under Khrushchev the labor camp gates opened and the prisons emptied. . . . But under him [Brezhnev], a tentative thaw has turned into a new freeze. The prisons have begun to fill again and the camp gates are once more being slammed shut on desperate thousands whose only crime has been to speak their own minds. Brezhnev has but one prescription for the Soviet Union's malaise: more vigilance against foreign influences and more ideological discipline. The Soviet Union he will leave behind will be an infinitely sadder country than the one he found upon becoming its ruler.

See what I mean, professor? All this is extremely old hat. What the USSR Academy of Sciences is trying to do in this book is give us some hitherto unrevealed insights into Brezhnev the man. The following examples are chosen at random:

—We learn of Brezhnev's finely-tuned perceptiveness, how in 1915 at the age of nine, during several strikes at the Kamenskoye steel mill, "he sensed the determination of the workers and their exultation when they managed to wrest concessions from the mill-owners."

—We learn of Brezhnev the fun-person with a razor-sharp sense of humor, a man who worked hard as director of the Metallurgical Workers' Faculty but still "found time to join in singing and dancing" among "the people." During World War II, to go to the area known as Little Land was a journey of extreme peril, yet Brezhnev went there often and even found time to joke: "One day as Brezhnev was inspecting the landing places, which were constantly being shelled by the enemy, he noted how fearlessly the sailors were keeping them going and said to the soldiers: 'The sailors merit your respect, for without these heroes you would not have held that bridgehead.' And he added with a smile [and undoubtedly impeccable timing—J.L.]: 'True, they give us infantrymen a bath now and then, but that is not their fault.' "

—Speaking of World War II, this book is full of never-before-told tales of Brezhnev's personal courage which, quite frankly, makes one wonder why the rest of the Red Army was really necessary. In April of 1943, during heavy fighting on the Little Land, Brezhnev uttered a "winged phrase" which passed from mouth to mouth among the soldiers. The phrase? "You can kill a Soviet man, but you cannot defeat him!" Ranking right along side this immortal utterance is another Brezhnev rallying cry, made to a unit of Kazakhs, Azerbaijanians, Ukrainians, and Russians: "This land will be a memorial to friendship among peoples, as indeed the whole war we are now fighting will be."

A man who displayed constant concern for the officers and their men, for all his subordinates, Brezhnev often forgot to take care of himself. Once, after machine-gunning a group of entrenched Nazis, Brezhnev was forced to hit the ground in a hail of return fire. This caused a Colonel Volkovich to exclaim to him: "You have no right to be here. What are you doing?"

"The same as you, Colonel," said Brezhnev.

"Please, go away. This is no place for you." To which Brezhnev replied: "My place is where the situation requires the earliest fulfillment of the combat task. Don't get excited, Colonel. Let's smoke these Nazis out of these damned barracks together."

In his smart-assed review of *Brezhnev: Pages From His Life,* Peter Osnos, a former Moscow reporter for the *Washington Post,* has the audacity to say that this "may well be the least revealing book about a personality of such importance ever published by an American book company. . . . [It] is pure boilerplate—the sort of stuff cranked out by party publicists before their first morning tea break." To you, Mr. Osnos, I say: hogwash!

No revelations? What, pray tell, do you call it when this book officially characterizes as progress the fact that the income of farmers in Moldavia actually declined under Brezhnev's rule in the early 1950s? What am I talking about? Well, it's all right there on pages 109–112.

In October of 1950, soon after Brezhnev was elected to the leading post in the Moldavian Communist Party, the sixth plenary meeting of the Central Committee was held, at which Brezhnev "put forward proposals for further measures to strengthen the republic's collective farms politically, organizationally, and economically." An "interesting" table in one of the displays in the Museum of History of the Moldavian Communist Party contains the following figures: In 1949 there were 375,000 collective farmers who made 110 million rubles in cash and kind for their work; by 1951 there were 3,388,000 collective farmers who earned 567 million rubles. Thus, in 1949 the average collective farmer was paid less than 300 rubles a year, but in 1951 under Brezhnev's reign, when the Moldavian countryside "took a big stride along the road of socialist reorganization," the average collective farmer was earning less than 200 rubles a year. This achievement in agriculture in the republic, we are told, "vividly demonstrated the vitality of the collective-farm system and the advantages of large-scale socialist agriculture, which made the use of machinery and intensive diversified farming possible."

Okay, Mr. Osnos, you're probably saying that this is a big book and you missed this one revelation. But, if you're saying this, you're wrong—w-r-o-n-g. There are many, many other revelations in this book about which I would be extremely surprised to hear you say honestly: "Oh, I already knew that." For example, did you really know that "a characteristic feature of Soviet reality is that there is no unemployment in the Soviet Union. The last of the unemployed got a job back in the early 1930s. Since then the Soviet people have completely forgotten the labor exchange and what it means to be dismissed. They have a confidence in the future and know that the right to work recorded in the Constitution is a reality"?

Were you truly aware, Mr. Osnos, that "as a result of the complete triumph of the socialist social relations, the Soviet state, which arose as a dictatorship of the proletariat, has developed into a state of the whole people"?

Did you know that Brezhnev himself emphasizes that "Communists have no privileges save the one privilege of giving more of themselves than others to the common cause and of fighting and working better than others for its triumph. Communists have no special rights, save the one right of always being in the forefront, of being where things are the hardest"?

Were you fully conscious of the fact, Mr. Osnos, that Brezhnev believes "the Soviet Union stands firmly for non-interference in the internal affairs of all states, for respect of their sovereign rights and of the inviolability of their territory"?

And can you say, Mr. Osnos, that you knew that in the late 1930s, when he was Secretary of the Dneprodzerzhinsk Regional Party Committee, Brezhnev "inquired into everything, even the smallest details, including how many amateur art circles there were at the palaces of culture and clubs. However busy he was, he would ask the charwoman at the Regional Committee about the health of her grandson, inquire of an official of the Regional Committee about the news from his son in the armed forces, or congratulate a girl from the typists' pool on her marriage"?

And last, but certainly not least, Mr. Osnos, there are Brezhnev's moving and intimately personal views on détente. Before reading his book, could you say, without qualification, that you were already fully cognizant of the fact that he believes "the edifice of détente cannot be allowed to collapse under the onslaught of the protagonists of the cold war and the arms race. . . . Détente means readiness to settle differences and disputes not by force, not by threats and saber rattling, but by peaceful means, at the negotiating table. Détente means definite trust and the ability to reckon with one another's legitimate interests"?

This may all be boiler-plate to you, Mr. Osnos. But there is also another phrase that might be used more accurately to describe these heretofore unrevealed revelations. Perhaps you've heard the American expression: telling-it-like-it-is.

Footnote: I hate to end on a sour note, but I do have a small complaint about this book. In my copy of *Brezhnev: Pages From His Life* pages 161–192 were repeated whereas pages 193–224 were missing altogether.

Chambers' Music
and Alger Hiss

(1979)

HUGH KENNER

The headline read, HISS ASSEMBLING CASE FOR RETRIAL, VINDICA-
TION. The story was big and bylined ("By Mark Bowden, Staff Reporter").
It had a socko one-sentence lead:

"Alger Hiss may be on the verge of the longest awaited, best deserved last
laugh in American history."

It went on:

"His brilliant diplomatic and legal career was ruined more than 25 years
ago with perjury convictions and a cloud of cloak and dagger communism.
Today the native Baltimorean believes he will win a new trial by spring."

So what else is new? This was new: As you'd guess from its native-son
angle, the story appeared, yes, in a Baltimore paper: but not in the Baltimore
paper that comes to mind. It ran on page one of the October 25, 1976 Baltimore
News-American: the *Hearst* paper.

The *Sun,* yes, the Baltimore *Sun* will wobble all round the ideological
compass. But when the true-blue unproofread *News-American* fixes its gaze on
a convicted perjurer whom only the statute of limitations shielded from an
indictment for pro-Communist espionage, and perceives him on the verge of the
"best deserved last laugh in American history," then the sun in the sky, you'd
be inclined to say, has taken to rising in the northwest. As it regularly does,
when the press and Alger Hiss are in critical proximity.

Mark Bowden, Staff Reporter, questioned nothing that Alger told him.

" 'Those microfilms didn't amount to anything,' he explained. 'You know
what was on them? One was blank. The others were films of pages inside a
common U.S. Navy manual that had been available for years on public library
shelves. After Nixon had his day with them before the cameras, they were
never introduced as evidence during the trial. They weren't evidence of anything.

" 'But the microfilms worked against me. It didn't matter what was on
them. Microfilm is spooky. It sounds like spy stuff, with cameras stuck in belt
buckles and watches. The microfilm made Americans think I was a spy, and, I
think, ultimately influenced the grand jury and the trial jury.' "

Yes, yes, there was a lightstruck microfilm roll. And there were two rolls of Navy documents, some of them unclassified (but not from "a common manual"), in which no one ever claimed Alger Hiss had a hand; so naturally "they were never introduced as evidence during the trial."

What Hiss didn't mention to Mr. Bowden was the existence of two more strips of microfilm that did get introduced at the trial. They contained, among other things, State Department documents with Alger Hiss's initials, and how Whittaker Chambers could have obtained them for photographing, if not from Alger Hiss, has been a theme for much improvisation which Mr. Bowden was kindly spared.

A crack "Staff Reporter," which means he writes down what people say to him, Mr. Bowden in the best traditions of the free press wrote down what Mr. Hiss told him, and was not even made wary when Hiss flaunted his expertise at playing journalists—"If you want a good topical angle for a story you might be interested in knowing. . . ." That gambit should have set off inner alarms but didn't.

No, the readers of the *News-American* were allowed to suppose that brilliant Baltimorean Hiss was framed by squalid non-Baltimorean Nixon (Boo). In the long (32-inch) story Nixon is named eight times, Whittaker Chambers ("the confessed spy-ring courier") twice. " 'Just think of all the people Nixon ruined,' " Alger Hiss exhorts, and Bowden dutifully paraphrases: "He believes Nixon prejudiced the nation against him 'for purely opportunistic reasons.' " Very possibly. But the Hiss nemesis, as reporter Bowden never got around to considering, was Whittaker Chambers, not Nixon: the implacable testimony of Chambers, those damning documents. Nixon in 1976 was merely a better blue herring even than he is now.

The clipping, admittedly, is no longer current. I linger on it because it's stuck in my mind for three years, so admirably does it epitomize the skills by which Alger Hiss has contrived to gain credibility as the American Dreyfus: pilloried, railroaded to Lewisburg for 44 months, latterly toiling as a (for gosh sakes) stationery salesman—*are* there stationery salesmen?—while he expects vindication momentarily. One of his techniques is to keep a heavy thumb on the Nixon button. Another is to feed reporters information he can feel sure they won't check. This is easy because when he went to jail in 1951 today's most vigorous reporters were unborn or toddling. It was easier still before April 1978, since when whoever wants to can check out the facts in a single heavily-documented book, Allen Weinstein's *Perjury.*

Never mind that though belief in a-new-trial-by-spring was reported by the *News-American* in 1976, spring '77 didn't after all come up daisies, nor did spring '78 or spring '79; nor will, we may safely predict, spring '80 or '81 or '82 (by which time Alger Hiss will be an octogenarian). A new trial is not the point. The point is the gullibility of the world's Mark Bowdens, who get the word to some 200,000 readers per story that Alger Hiss was Framed.

Sometimes you will hear that he was framed by Chambers, "a self-confessed perjurer." This is quaint, because Chambers' only substantiated perjury occurred early in the case. He was still shielding Hiss from the worst, and *denied* under oath that Hiss was guilty of espionage! So if Chambers was a perjurer that day, Hiss was a spy. But never mind. Hiss is the American Boy, and the case against him is tainted. He keeps denying everything, doesn't he?

Whittaker Chambers understood why. "Alger Hiss," he wrote to William F. Buckley, Jr., late in 1954, "is one of the greatest assets that the Communist Party could possess. What is vindication for him? It is the moment when one of the most respectable old ladies (gentlemen) in Hartford (Conn.) says to another of the most respectable old ladies (gentlemen): 'Really, I don't see how Alger Hiss could brazen it out that way unless he were really innocent.' Multiply Hartford by every other American community. For the CP, that is victory. . . . And all that Alger has to do for this victory is to persist in his denials."(1)

Chambers, as everyone knows, had been a member of the Communist underground, circa 1932–1938. On August 3, 1948, he let it be known that Alger Hiss, previously a State Department luminary and by then President of the Carnegie Endowment for International Peace, had been one also. Fifty-five days later Alger Hiss sued for slander. Another nine weeks, and Chambers had produced typed copies of papers, and microfilms of more papers, purloined from the State Department late in the 1930s. He had squirreled them away, he said, while planning his dangerous break with the Party. He said furthermore that he had them, and had passed similar things to the Russians, thanks to his source at State: Alger Hiss. On December 15, 1948, a grand jury indicted Alger Hiss on two counts of perjury: having spoken falsely, first in denying that he had passed those papers to Chambers in February–March 1938, second in denying that he "did in fact see and converse with the said Mr. Chambers" in the months in question at all. On July 7, 1949, a hung jury was dismissed. On January 21, 1950, a second jury found Alger Hiss guilty on both counts. He was sentenced to five years and served 44 months.

So ran the bare scenario, and to cinema-guided tastes it has everything wrong with it. Would *you* let Peter Lorre bring down Robert Redford? Alger Hiss was a graduate of Johns Hopkins ('26) and of Harvard Law ('29), moreover had clerked for Oliver Wendell Holmes, Jr., whereas Chambers dropped out of Columbia and had bad teeth: not matters for the ladies (gentlemen) of Hartford to overlook. Chambers' credibility, by 1948, had little going for it. He was a *Time* hack. Before that he had been by his own admission a CP functionary: not a gallant Communist either, like an English poet, nor a tart screw-you Communist like you know, whatshername, nor even a devoted faceless spearcarrier, but the wrong sort of Communist, with a taste for theatrics, pseudonyms, History, microfilms even; and in the newsreels (remember newsreels?) he had little shifty eyes; and he had reneged on the Party too, and how could you trust him after that? One respects people who stick by their convictions; yes, even when the arsenic of their convictions is destined for your soup.

The Communist Party too had its concern for images. The late Louis Zukofsky, as sharp a skeptical intelligence as I've known, was a Chambers classmate; his elegy for Whittaker's brother Ricky (dead by suicide, 1926) bespeaks affection:

(1) *Odyssey of a Friend: Whittaker Chambers' Letters to William F. Buckley Jr., 1954–1961,* pp. 87–88.

At eventide, cool hour
Your dead mouth singing,

 Ricky,

Automobiles speed
Past the cemetery,

No meter turns.
Sleep,

With an open gas range
Beneath for a pillow. . . .(2)

It's a cool transcension of the many turgid poems Chambers wrote on the same theme. And Zukofsky enjoyed telling how Chambers (about 1926?) recruited him for the Party. To the all-important meeting Zukofsky went, tie in place and by custom trousers neatly creased, and Ma Bloor herself rejected him because he looked insuperably bourgeois ("And my father pressed pants all his life!").

Then a student of no special prospects, Zukofsky was indeed an implausible passer-out of pamphlets. Chambers, though, pudgy, in slacks and open-necked shirt, was a different proposition; he had been accepted on sight. Ma Bloor's son Harold Ware organized the Washington underground in which Chambers was to meet Alger Hiss, and for Hiss, who by Chambers' account went direct to the underground without passing through the open Party, pressed pants and fedora were no disqualification at all: in fact indispensable cover. They still help render implausible the suggestion that he was ever anything as scruffy as a spy: perhaps, at most, a member of a left-wing Study Group.

For in that disorienting decade, 1925–1935, when everybody on the hard Left seemed to go by a false name—Chambers at various times was "Bob," "Charles Adams," "David Breen," "Lloyd Cantwell," "Arthur Dwyer," "Hugh Jones," "Karl," "John Kelly," "Harold Phillips," "Charles Whittaker," perhaps "George Crosley"—in that time of roles and show trials, the very mainspring of Party activity was the proposition that things are never as they seem. Communism is almost exclusively concerned with images (though its guns and bombs are real and go off). The Capitalist System survives because people believe the official theory of its workings; let them once discard Adam Smith's cover story, though, and it will collapse. All evaluations, all alliances, are provisional, instrumental; there was a Hitler-Stalin pact before the Hitler-Stalin war.

Amid public realities which according to his creed are wholly unreal, the Communist is always on stage. If in the open Party, he is impersonating one of the prescribed ways of being a Communist: a theoretician, a strike-leader, a marcher, a Friend of the Soviet Union, a shrewd son of toil. If in the underground, he is impersonating a lawyer, a newspaperman, a screenwriter, an English professor—trades in which he is fully credentialled; we may even say that he *is* what he impersonates, that the Communism with which he burns is the off-hours role. This is bottomless. And the Hiss-Chambers case resembles an Ames Box, carefully arranged so that if you look through the peephole you

(2) Louis Zukofsky, "*A*", p. 9 (written 1928).

see normal things—a parlor, a Ford car, a typewriter, the bourgeois bric-a-brac of a Washington lawyer in the 1930s, and two dolls, one decent, upright, one shifty, vengeful. It is only when the lid is taken off the box that you can see the scatter of elements out of which that illusion was contrived, their wrenched perspective a tax to the perceptions, their variousness a burden to the memory, their disarray an affront to normal experience, which, whether in arranging cues into 3-D space or threading a story line through happenings, is guided by economy and by experience with the usual.

The mere evidence which compelled the second jury to believe Chambers rather than Hiss dismays by its miscellaneousness, its profuseness, its frequent triviality. Making it cohere was the prosecuting attorneys' job, and in *Perjury* Allen Weinstein achieves an even more conclusive coherence, chiefly because he's dug up so much more that we need no longer suspect a controlled selection.

The logic is ultimately simple: It depends on connecting Alger Hiss with those documents Chambers produced. These included (1) ten microfilmed pages which Hiss had handled (he initialled them) and to which Chambers' other source at State, a man named Wadleigh, would not have had access; (2) typed copies of State Department messages, to the extent of 65 pages, the typing of which matched the output of a Woodstock, serial #N230099, which the Hisses had owned and used in the 1930s.

So *prima facie,* the most probable link between State and Chambers is Hiss. But life is not always linear, and if you're encumbered by few enough facts it's easy to doodle alternative topologies. There were two typewriters, one skillfully faked. Alger and Priscilla had parted with the Woodstock before the State papers were copied (and when was that?). Chambers (or someone) snuck into their house and used the machine, or spirited it away and used it. . . . Making a tight prosecution case meant nailing down hundreds of such wearisome details. Conducting a defense meant making the details difficult to establish (it was all ten years ago), meanwhile developing a motive for a monstrous trouble-making Chambers.

Tracing it all out has taken Allen Weinstein, a crisp and economical writer, some 325,000 words, including whole pages summarizing tergiversations about typewriters. It was that kind of case. (His researchers show, by the way, what was never evident from the public record, that while the FBI and defense gumshoes were both hunting the Woodstock, Alger Hiss and his brother Donald knew where it was and lied persistently.)

Having read *Perjury* through twice I can see no reason to dissent from Sidney Hook's verdict, that thanks to Weinstein's expert labors the guilt of Alger Hiss "can no longer be contested on any reasonable grounds."(3)

There are only two ways to discount Weinstein. One is to decline to read him, for fear of having a symbolic allegiance disturbed; Hook remarks that "there is no arguing with symbolic allegiances." The other is to pick nits in the manner of the *Nation,* hoping simple folk will conclude that Weinstein falsified, elided, tampered, or that for all his digging he didn't dig deep enough. (Or perhaps he's an FBI stooge?)

(3) Sidney Hook, "The Case of Alger Hiss," *Encounter,* August 1978, p. 55.

To summarize. Hiss was not framed by Nixon, whose role in the case was ambiguous throughout. (When the "pumpkin papers" burst upon the scene he was a safe distance away, in Panama, just in case there was a backfire.) He was certainly not framed by the FBI, whose director, every time we catch him dictating a memo, sounds like a Commissioner of the Keystone Kops (when he first heard that Weinstein was interested in the case—in 1969—his immediate response was to open a file on Weinstein!). He didn't go to prison on the word of Whittaker Chambers. He was entrapped by numerous and carefully established and inexorable facts.

Which being said, we may safely regret that *Perjury* isn't perfect. Allen Weinstein is not Dostoyevsky, and when his narrative is over we may feel that we know everything except who the protagonists *were.*

That the Hiss of this intricate narrative should remain schematic, as contrived as an Agatha Christie least-likely-suspect, a jointed paper doll we've watched gesticulate, is unsurprising; the scenario after all establishes that Alger Hiss has been perjuring himself for 31 years and living a lie for at least 45. If there's a real Alger Hiss down under that cope of fanatical self-discipline, it's safe to guess that the Alger Hiss who files briefs and grants interviews lost touch with him long ago.

Whittaker Chambers is more interesting and more puzzling, and though his own long confessional narrative, *Witness,* offered to bare all as long ago as 1952, tracts of the merely factual remain pointlessly mysterious.

Take the question of the Russian language. At about 16, he tells us in *Witness* (p. 146), he memorized from a book, at his mother's urging, "two or three thousand Russian words," but remained innocent of any grammar. At age 31 (*Witness,* pp. 301–2) he was still, he says, incapable of reading anything in secret Russian messages save the salutation, *Dorogoi droog*—Dear Friend. Nor (*Witness,* p. 306) could he follow a Russian conversation. At age 58, the Hiss case long behind him, he enrolled in the University of Western Maryland College ("I do not wish to die an ignoramus"[4]) in part to study elementary Russian.

Dr. Weinstein tells all this differently, saying "occasionally he even feigned ignorance of Russian, a language in which he was fluent" (p. 116). Weinstein certifies the fluency on the word of unspecified "close friends" (p. 602), and even informs us (p. 602) of the present whereabouts of "the introductory Russian primer used by Chambers to learn the language early in the 1930s." He doesn't mention the 1959 classes in Maryland.

Who were the "close friends," we may wonder; rather, what were their standards of fluency? (To an ignoramus you could sound fluent in French if you merely said rapidly, *"Avec la plume de ma tante, le chat etait assis sur la natte."*) More: Since Weinstein has read (and cites) *Odyssey of a Friend,* what does he make of its disclosure of those Russian classes at a rural Maryland college, two years before Chambers' death? Was Chambers really never good at Russian at all, though he picked up other languages easily? Was the lifelong player of roles assuming yet another role, the world-weary man become as a little child, humbly

(4) *Odyssey of a Friend,* p. 260.

attending classes with adolescents? Was he perhaps going through the motions of opsimathic study to establish (contrary to fact) that in his Party days he'd been ignorant of Communism's mother tongue? If so, why on earth?

Why, for that matter, did he always deny having been in Russia, where he and his wife Esther went on fraudulent passports in early 1933? Postcards in their handwriting with Moscow cancellations survive (*Perjury,* pp. 115–16, 602). He was presumably there for top-level indoctrination. Yet the pages of *Witness* which conduct us so circumstantially through the preparation of a secret agent are silent on this trip, and on p. 352 Chambers even remarks flatly, "I have never been in Russia." Why? Was he minimizing Esther's complicity in his secret life?

Though Weinstein is aware of these and other contradictions, he does nothing with them beyond noting their existence. For which bless him; we've had in this case and others enough psychohistory, something normally confected out of an Identi-Kit on the model of Freud's analysis of Moses. They nag, though; they nag at me not because I sniff sinister ramifications, but because their existence makes the latter-day Chambers who's projected in *Witness* and in the letters to Buckley—the weary sojourner in an ultimate Siberia of the psyche, a Last Man whose last luxury is bleak and utter candor—appear to be but one more fabrication, a last role in the long sequence of roles that began as early as 1919, when Jay Vivian Chambers began to use his mother Laha Whittaker's family name. "Whittaker Chambers" was merely the most enduring of his aliases.

> My brother lies in the cold earth,
> A cold rain is overhead.
> My brother lies in the cold earth,
> A sheet of ice is over his head.

> The cold earth holds him round;
> A sheet of ice is over his face.
> My brother has no more
> The cold rain to face.

That was "written in the Sand Hill graveyard," he tells us, "the first winter of my brother's death."(5) The second quatrain would be doggerel had it not the first to modulate away from. By rhythm and repetition, a 25-year-old is exorcising a corpse he nearly feels is alive. By rhythm and repetition, in sentences of mounting complexity, he exorcised all his adult life what he calls rather often History. (There are pages in *Witness* on which the word "history" occurs a dozen times.) "History hit us with a freight train," is a phrase from his last letter to Buckley.

Readers have not been wanting who detected a false, a passé, note in Chambers rhetoric. Conor Cruise O'Brien observed Chambers writing in *Cold Friday* that the depth of the special Russian feeling for Byzantium was "perhaps suggested by the fact that Tsargrad alone, among the names of foreign cities, is declined through all nine of the inflections of the Russian noun." O'Brien

(5) Epigraph to Chapter 2 of *Witness* (p. 89).

leaped: The Russian noun has only *six* inflections, and the mistake was revealing. For "the pressure to distort is a rhetorical pressure. 'All nine of the inflections of the Russian noun' gives just the reverberation Chambers needed at this point in his boomy incantation."

O'Brien leaped too fast, and William Buckley roasted him on a slow spit: There are indeed nine forms of the noun Tsargrad.(6) Still, O'Brien in his shallowness was on to something: Chambers' need to resolve his cadences, in a prose propelled less by the wish to impart information than by the need to give it shape. To turn terrible actualities into music was an insistent pressure, an hourly need. That, we may speculate, was what Communist theory did for him: It shaped actualities of want and warfare into a dissonant music you could dance to. It was a long, agonizing, increasingly dangerous dance, and by 1938 the harsh music had lost all enchantment. In 1949, between the two Hiss trials, a newsman asked him, "What do you think you are doing?"

"At his question I turned to look out at the mists that were rising from the bottom below the house, filling the valley. I answered slowly: 'I am a man who, reluctantly, grudgingly, step by step, is destroying himself that this country and the faith by which it lives may continue to exist.' " (*Witness,* p. 715).

With a sharp ear for cadences you can catch overtones of the Gettysburg Address. In breaking with Communism, he had defined a new role and formulated its rhythm. That, if I gauge him aright, was central: a rhythm: one that could accommodate his shorter themes, overarch his longer ones, and permit what he cherished, the harmonization of his mishaps and History. Man, the symbol-using creature, makes shift to make himself at home in the world by the way he talks about it and in no other way; moreover, the most efficacious stratum of language, the one that effects the orienting adjustments between his experience and his sense of himself, is not semantic but rhythmic. Everyone's habits with language have a characterizing cadence, what we recognize when we recognize a "style." Its gestures mime his sense of how the world goes, how *he* goes.

Chambers' taste, especially in paragraph endings, was for the resolved cadence, to an extent perverse in the twentieth century. (His way of signalling an irony is to leave them unresolved.) A rhythm surrendered to is a self-definition. There were facts, presumably, such as knowledge of Russian, which the rhythm would not accommodate. The principle at work here is mysterious but demonstrable; it is related to the fact that every poet's rhythm excludes certain images. Hence, in the edifice of written words Chambers constructed so carefully, those odd little blurs and lapses. He possibly could not have explained to himself why they were necessary. They don't affect the substance of his testimony.

Alger Hiss lives yet, to a rhythm of his own. It is the rhythm of the sewing-machine, busily piecing and stitching; the parts glinting, the motor humming, the needle hopping, the pieces of material lapped and fed: no thread in the bobbin, none in the needle.

(6) William F. Buckley, Jr., *The Jeweler's Eye,* pp. 203–210. A polemic to study for its pacing.

Malcolm Cowley Forgets

(1980)

KENNETH S. LYNN

Almost 50 years ago, Malcolm Cowley remarked in regard to *Exile's Return,* his forthcoming memoir of the 1920s, that "There is always the temptation, in writing about your own past, to interpret the facts discreetly with the purpose of showing what a wholly likeable fellow you were." In *The Dream of the Golden Mountains,* his recently published memoir of the 1930s, Cowley has succumbed to that temptation even more blatantly than he did in *Exile's Return.* Supposedly, the book is based on the articles and reviews he regularly contributed to the *New Republic* during the Depression years, but the image of himself he presents to us in *The Golden Mountains* is rather different from the man of the *New Republic* pieces. Although Cowley finally foreswore his political fellow traveling in 1940, he still has not acquired an adequate respect for historical truth. Just as he once ignored the patent falsity of the defendants' confessions at the Moscow purge trials in order to argue that the trials had been eminently just, so in *The Golden Mountains* he has not hesitated to consign unpleasant facts about what he said and did in the thirties to an Orwellian memory hole. Cowley is now in his eighties, and he has posterity very much in mind. If he has his way, history will not remember him as the man whom Eugene Lyons described in *The Red Decade* (1941) as "the Number One literary executioner for Stalin in America."

What the author of *The Golden Mountains* wants us to find most likeable about him is his honesty. One man is always representative of an age, he says of himself in the preface, "when he gives honest testimony about what he has felt and observed." On page 82, he recalls the nature of his literary ambitions in the thirties—"I wanted to write honestly." On page 228, he reminds us that in *Exile's Return* "I had taken the risk of speaking candidly about my own life." But Cowley's campaign to persuade us of his honesty is not merely carried out by bald assertion. Through the details he chooses to emphasize about his personality, he also seeks to convince us that he is a man to be trusted. "And that author, that observer who is trying to be candid about himself," Cowley writes, "what sort of person was he in 1930?" From a Harvard man who had spent most of the 1920s in Europe, we might expect an answer emphasizing his cosmopolitanism. But, as Benjamin Franklin discovered long ago, a cosmopolite

211

can often enhance his credibility by pretending to be a rustic, and this lesson has apparently not been lost on the author of *The Golden Mountains*. Without qualification, Cowley insists that

he was still a country boy after spending most of his life in cities; he had a farmer's blunt hands. . . . He never forgot that he came of people without pretensions, not quite members of the respectable middle class. He was slow of speech and had a farmer's large silences, though he was not slow-witted; people were fooled sometimes.

Along with his trustworthiness, Cowley would have us admire his benignity. Other historians have stressed the combativeness of American intellectual life in the early 1930s, but Cowley remembers the battles of those days as "good fun," and he plunged into them, he says, with the exhilaration of a college halfback diving into a scrimmage. Only gradually did he realize that "real blows were being exchanged by others." Did this realization then cause Cowley himself to turn nasty? *The Golden Mountains* offers no evidence that it did. Thus Cowley repeatedly praises John Dos Passos and Edmund Wilson without ever once suggesting that his earlier opinions of these writers had sometimes been less than complimentary. And while he freely admits that William Phillips, Philip Rahv, James T. Farrell, and other leftists sometimes "bludgeoned or shillelaghed me," as he ruefully says about Farrell's attacks, we get only the faintest sense of why they were so angry at him, and no sense at all that he ever replied to them in kind. In the confrontation he cites with Phillips and Rahv, for instance, Cowley asserts that, in the face of their comments, "not many [of which] were eulogistic," he was simply "amused and polite."

Yet while Cowley does not want us to fail to notice the contrast he alleges between his own manner and that of his critics, the principal business of his memoir is not to snipe at ancient adversaries. Indeed, more often than not Cowley is at pains to evade the issue of sectarian differences on the Left. Thus in his discussion of the Communist-front League of American Writers, the impression is created that anti-fascist intellectuals were indiscriminately welcomed into the organization and that no one was ever excluded or condemned for criticizing the Communist Party or the USSR, whereas the reverse was true. For the overriding purpose of *The Golden Mountains* is to rehabilitate the myth that the 1930s was an era of revolutionary brotherhood. What Cowley wants us to remember above all else about the thirties is that it was a time when hundreds of writers were caught up in a dream of a new social order—a dream of the golden mountains. "Our right fists raised in the Red Front salute," says Cowley, we marched forward toward "a classless society." The Soviet Union had "shown us the way."

The vision of a marching band of brothers so dominates Cowley's book that vitally important individuals frequently get lost in the shuffles, including, not least, the author. Repeatedly, the narrative "I" gives way to "we," or "they," or "the writers," or "the members," or "the delegates." And as the decade progresses and the bickering of the brotherhood intensifies to the point where it can no longer be ignored, Cowley is still apt to speak of anonymous groupings rather than of specific people.

As for the Russian purges, . . . there would never be unanimity about them, except in respect to the general uneasiness they created among left-wing intellectuals. Even those who believed that the defendants were guilty of the crimes to which they confessed couldn't help feeling that the evidence revealed a disheartening state of affairs in Russia. As one trial followed another, more and more persons rejected the confessions, and soon they would also reject the Communist Party. But there was no unanimity even among the rejecters.

This passage does not even make clear where Cowley himself stood on the issue of the purges, but it does make clear why the author of an ostensibly personal book should have found it convenient to speak as often as he does in an impersonal vein. What better way, after all, for Cowley to avoid taking responsibility for certain positions he once held than to hide himself in a crowd?

Readers who are eager to meet the historical Malcolm Cowley will have to turn from *The Golden Mountains* to the relevant volumes of the *New Republic*. But readers who are concerned with the more interesting question of how a man goes about creating a historical myth about himself will want to read memoir and magazine in conjunction. The first of the many discrepancies between the two involves an obscure writer named Ralph Borsodi. On page 6 of *The Golden Mountains,* Cowley genially recalls him as one of the many visitors who came to the offices of the *New Republic* in the early years of the Depression to describe their schemes for remaking America. Borsodi's idea was to resettle millions of urban families on five-acre subsistence homesteads. The difficulty with the project, Cowley observes with wry good humor, is that it required capital, a part-time job in the city, and a cooperative wife like Mrs. Borsodi.

When we turn to Cowley's assessment of Borsodi in the *New Republic,* we find a different point of view. The writer's crackpot scheme did not strike Cowley as at all funny, it infuriated him. With the sort of rhetorical overkill which at the end of the thirties would belatedly prompt Edmund Wilson to castigate him for practicing "Stalinist character assassination of the most reckless and libelous sort," Cowley tore into the harmless crank as "a dangerous messiah." The reason for his fury was that as a back-to-the-land enthusiast Borsodi regarded the Soviet Union's titanic effort to industrialize as a terrible mistake. "He speaks with contempt and hatred," said Cowley, his voice quivering with contempt and hatred, "of everything done in Russia."

But of all the false impressions about himself that Cowley creates in *The Golden Mountains,* the most audacious is the proposition that he was fully committed to the Communist cause for only a few years. By 1935, he asserts, he had developed "doubts about what the party was doing in America and in Russia too." His *New Republic* pieces, however, demonstrate a continuing and unqualified adoration of Stalin. On April 24, 1935, for instance, Cowley drew a sneering contrast between the socialist H.G. Wells's Utopian fixation on the "golden future" and the Soviet dictator's awesomely impressive concentration on the "iron present." (If as a memoirist Cowley had been more true to the man he used to be, he would not have employed a golden metaphor in the title of his book; inasmuch as his imagination in the thirties was actually enthralled by a baser metal.)

One week later, the *New Republic*'s literary editor celebrated May Day with a review of the Communist Anna Louise Strong's *I Change Worlds.* With glowing approval, Cowley recapitulated Miss Strong's account of a high-level conference held in Moscow on the problem of what to do about the *Moscow News,* a somewhat unsuccessful illustrated weekly for American engineers and tourists, of which Miss Strong was the managing editor. Among those present at the conference was Stalin. "Stalin did not frown or pound his fist on the table," wrote Cowley, paraphrasing Miss Strong,

he gave no commands; he scarcely made suggestions. He merely listened, asked people what they wanted, what they thought, but his questions went straight to the heart of things. Suddenly all the difficulties had vanished. It was decided to transform the *Moscow News* into a bigger and livelier paper. . . . These were not Stalin's orders. The decisions seemed to come from everybody and to express a common will. . . . [Thus was Miss Strong] given a sudden and lasting insight into the whole Soviet system of administration. . . . A system like this—which Miss Strong describes more intelligently than any other writer on Russia—seems tyrannical to people on the outside, whereas, to those millions who help to formulate policies, it seems the most democratic system that ever existed.

On September 11, 1935, Cowley dismissed George Kitchin's *Prisoner of the OGPU* as one of the myriad anti-Soviet books currently being published because "Messrs. Hitler, Hearst and their allies" are "frantic" that Western labor movements will take heart from the Soviet experiment. "Liars are paid by them at the best space rates. Old manuscripts are taken out of trunks, dusted off, peppered with atrocities and published as the latest news from Moscow." The real news, according to Cowley, was that "Yes, thank you, our Russian neighbors are doing quite well." With some of their major industrial and agricultural problems at last out of the way, the Soviet leaders were now "turning their attention to minor products—flower beds, jazz bands, joy, light wines and the secret ballot."

Cowley's whitewash of legal murder in Moscow appeared on April 7, 1937, in a review of *The Case of the Anti-Soviet Trotskyite Center,* issued by the USSR's Commissariat of Justice. That the defendants had displayed a Dostoevskian eagerness to confess to the most outlandish crimes was an idea without merit, in Cowley's opinion. "The behavior of the prisoners on the witness stand . . . was certainly that of guilty men lacking popular support and ashamed of the deeds that had brought them there." Far from being Dostoevskian, their behavior was "normal under the circumstances." It was only "their actions before arrest that belong in a Dostoevsky novel." The confessions, Cowley reiterated, were "undoubtedly sincere." As for the indictment, the major part of it was "proved beyond much possibility of doubting it." A year later, in a review of another volume of stenographic evidence about another trial, Cowley again was impressed by the "enormous accumulation of evidence" against the defendants, and again was contemptuous of the forced-confession theory. "There were no Tibetan drugs, no subtle Chinese tortures." The real question, he opined, "is not why the conspirators pleaded guilty, but why they conspired."

During the remaining months of 1938, Cowley demonstrated his unwavering devotion to Stalinism with a defense of the political censorship of literature and a scathing critique of the anti-Stalinist *Partisan Review* which its editors quite rightly termed "a malicious and politically motivated attack." Throughout 1939, Cowley still kept the faith, despite the announcement of the Nazi-Soviet Pact. Thus in October of that year he described Stalin's embrace of Hitler not as the final betrayal of a revolution but as the "experiment" of a realist. The most shameful exhibition, however, of what Cowley was prepared to do for Stalin in 1939 was his participation in the literary execution of John Dos Passos.

When the second volume of *U.S.A.* was published in 1932, Cowley had praised the book as "a landmark in American fiction"; Dos Passos' writing, he said had "conviction, power, and a sense of depth, of striking through surfaces to the real forces beneath them." The reviewer also had warm words for the third volume of the trilogy when it appeared in 1936. On February 9, 1938, Cowley again took space in the *New Republic* to express his admiration for *U.S.A.* Sixteen months later, however, he and a number of other reviewers came down on Dos Passos' latest book, *Adventures of a Young Man,* like the knife blades of a rank of guillotines. As James T. Farrell shortly thereafter pointed out in an indignant essay in the *American Mercury,* Dos Passos had been judged on political, not literary, grounds. Having become disillusioned with the Communist Party's cynical manipulation of causes and issues, Dos Passos had written a novel to say farewell to the Left. *Adventures of a Young Man* had both the strengths and the weaknesses of all of Dos Passos' social fiction. While its characters were half-baked, the narrative had power and conviction and it struck through surfaces to the real forces beneath them. But because the book was much too strongly anti-Communist for prevailing Popular-Front tastes, it was condemned as a weak and inferior work. Cowley and company's reception of the novel, said Farrell, "reads like a warning to writers not to stray off the reservation of the Stalinist-controlled League of American Writers."

The thirties, in W.H. Auden's phrase, was "a low dishonest decade." One of the representative men of that era was the literary editor of the *New Republic,* but unlike Whittaker Chambers and other erstwhile servants of tyranny, he has not sought to redeem himself by coming clean about his former activities. *The Golden Mountains* is a cover-up. To the multiple dishonesties of Cowley's career we must also add the leading reviews of this book, all of which have praised it for precisely the quality it most conspicuously lacks. In the *New Republic,* R.W.B. Lewis spoke of the "cogency" of the memoir. In the *New York Times,* Alfred Kazin saluted the author as an "honest writer." In the *Washington Post,* Daniel Aaron asserted that "among the memorialists of the 1930s, Malcolm Cowley is one of the most reliable and informative." Moreover, Aaron adds, Cowley has "never confused literary standards with political loyalties." The memorist's "easy idiomatic prose," says Aaron, "perfectly conveys his air of speculative detachment."

What in the world could have possessed these reviewers to make such irresponsible statements? The case of R.W.B. Lewis can be quickly dismissed. He simply does not know what he is talking about. The dishonesty of his review of Cowley's book consists of a pretension to an expertise about American literary life in the 1930s that he does not possess. The cases of Kazin and Aaron, however, are more complicated. There can be no doubt that both men are familiar with every piece of journalism that Cowley ever published. They were certainly in a position, therefore, to detect the disingenuousness of *The Golden Mountains.*

But in order to expose Cowley, Kazin would have been obliged to acknowledge certain unflattering truths about his own reviewing in the thirties, and, as Kazin's autobiographies amply demonstrate, he has no taste for self-criticism. In Kazin's books, Hell is other people, never himself. He has savagely caricatured the chairman of the Amherst College English Department, for instance, in which Kazin taught for some years; but if Kazin knows that he himself sometimes failed as a teacher, he has not shared the knowledge with his readers. Praising Cowley's cover-up as the work of an honest writer was the act of a writer who has a cover-up of his own to maintain.

Aaron's comments about *The Golden Mountains* are, in my opinion, a reflection of a personal need to go on ingratiating himself with the aging lions of the American Left. Twenty years ago, Aaron interviewed or corresponded with almost all of them in the process of writing a large book called *Writers on the Left,* and he apparently was so awed by the experience that he has never been able to criticize them. In a severely disapproving review of *Writers on the Left,* William Phillips of the *Partisan Review* called attention to Aaron's failure to offer any sort of critical evaluation of the people he had written about. "Aaron's seeming lack of bias actually produces a biased view of the 30s," Phillips pointed out, "the bias coming from the assumption that something called the 'record' is identical with the history." Clearly troubled by Phillips' review, Aaron published a long and defensive essay a few years later in which he announced that his attitude toward critical scholarship was the same as that of the ancient lady who owns the Aspern Papers in Henry James' story: "The truth is God's, it isn't man's; we had better leave it alone. Who can judge of it?—who can say?" If Malcolm Cowley says he has tried to write about the 1930s as candidly as he could, what right does a mere reviewer have to say that he has not?

Solzhenitsyn Reconsidered II

(1980)

DELBA WINTHROP

The recently published book, *Solzhenitsyn at Harvard,* is at once too much and too little. It consists of a translation of Solzhenitsyn's June, 1978 Harvard Commencement address ("A World Split Apart"), a dozen early reactions and responses to the address, and several further reflections. Many of the early pieces exhibit unreasoned outrage, and most of the later ones are displays of academic expertise. From the array we learn more about the foibles and follies of liberal intellectuals than we do about Solzhenitsyn.

To treat one speech as if it revealed the heart and mind of a man is always a questionable endeavor. In Solzhenitsyn's case, however, we have some license to make the attempt, for he has informed us in his writings that his every action is deliberate. He does not speak with haste or waste. When he cannot choose his audience, he can still choose what to say to it. The Commencement speech, we may assume, was altogether his choice.* He undoubtedly chose to examine the fundamental principles of liberalism at Harvard because Harvard is the symbol and bastion of liberalism's noblest aspirations. That it remains so was eloquently reaffirmed by Harvard's President Derek Bok that same day. The contributors to *Solzhenitsyn at Harvard,* even the ones without Harvard pedigrees, are all respected representatives of that tradition. To the extent that they have failed to appreciate or to understand Solzhenitsyn's argument they lend credence to his thesis: Liberalism cannot sustain liberalism's noblest aspirations, and liberalism is consequently not enough.

Most of the contributors implicitly dismiss James Reston's contention that the speech is "the wanderings of a mind split apart," but they acknowledge that "A World Split Apart" is complex and in need of explication. One might shed some light on it by means of textual exegesis, but of the contributors only Charles Kesler has attempted this (and acquitted himself quite well indeed). Or one might have recourse to what is known of Solzhenitsyn's deeds and to his other writings. Only Ronald Berman, the literary scholar and editor of this volume, and Harold Berman, the expert on Soviet law, have used Solzhenitsyn's

---

*Solzhenitsyn has not publicly rued his choice, but he has recently acknowledged a misjudgment: He thought Americans desired and appreciated criticism. (In fact, they savor criticism only from the Left.) See Solzhenitsyn's "The Courage to See" in the Fall 1980 issue of *Foreign Affairs.*

other works in their arguments. Or, finally, one might rely, as have most, on one's expert knowledge of the Soviet and Russian dissident traditions from which Solzhenitsyn has emerged.

Of Solzhenitsyn's deeds little is known other than what he has told us in *Gulag, The Oak and the Calf,* and rare interviews. We do know in addition that he is a member of the Russian Orthodox Church, and we have no right to doubt his piety. He is said to take pains with the religious education of his children (as did many of our parents). He has made his home in exile in the United States, and we cannot suppose that he did so because Vermont is the only place in the non-Communist world that resembles Mother Russia. He has felt sufficiently endangered to have built a large unattractive fence around his property, and he went to a Cavendish town meeting to apologize for the fact. Combining Soviet-bred fears and American ways once again, Solzhenitsyn has improved upon Samizdat with the Xerox machine he keeps in his living room. Rumor has it that he knows more English than he allows, but Solzhenitsyn is not given to spending time "chatting at filling stations." Rather, he leads a life of isolation no serious scholar or writer could fault except out of envy. A man in his sixties with a sober awareness of human mortality and a burning desire to complete his life's work, Solzhenitsyn spends his days writing.

Since these details are at best sketchy and, in any case, do not account for the content and tone of the Harvard speech, more satisfying explanations must be sought. Unfortunately, the most common ones seem the least justified.

Solzhenitsyn is referred to by most commentators as a "prophet." Since prophecy is less in vogue with the intellectual establishment than with the Moral Majority, the appellation is not meant as a compliment. The epithet, in any case, is unwarranted. To my knowledge Solzhenitsyn has never proclaimed himself to be a prophet, and the language of neither the Commencement speech nor his other writings can fairly be termed prophetic. Solzhenitsyn has no more pretensions than any social scientist who makes predictions on the basis of his data and thus speaks "Truth." In fact he has fewer pretensions, for all he does is to state the choices open to us and account for their being our choices. His analysis of the West is strikingly similar to that of the enduring darling of American social scientists, Alexis de Tocqueville. In his memoir Solzhenitsyn does say that his life has a "higher and hidden meaning" of which he has to be reminded by "the Supreme Reason which no mere mortal can at first understand." By this he seems to mean that events in his life forced him to infer some purpose to it. His life's purpose, he has come to understand, is to speak and act with political intent, for example, to do his best to ensure that justice is aided with the publication of *Gulag.* Justice can be done only when the truth is known, and Solzhenitsyn's not yet completed multi-volume history of the Russian Revolution is meant to bring to light truths that are "universal, and even timeless." Ronald Berman argues that Solzhenitsyn's true greatness as a writer lies in his ability to understand and depict human life in its political context; "his ideas of culture and politics . . . are the work itself." What is required of us to hear the Harvard speech is not an openness to prophecy, but a willingness to consider that many truths about our politics and culture are indeed bitter.

If Solzhenitsyn is not a prophet in the usual sense, then surely he is a theocrat? But common opinion notwithstanding, Solzhenitsyn is not a theocrat. True, he has contended that the only alternative to Communism for the Russian people at this time is Orthodoxy. Yet he has never urged the Soviet leaders to do more than tolerate *all* religions (as do we). When he elaborates on his hopes for the spiritual regeneration of the Russian people he speaks of the school, not the Church. None of the heroes of his novels and stories are religious, or at least their virtue does not presuppose piety. Nor has Solzhenitsyn promoted organized religion, much less theocracy, in the West. He has said, "Religion should make an appropriate contribution to the spiritual life of the nation" (whatever "appropriate" means). He laments the fact that we have lost the "concept of a Supreme Complete Entity which used to restrain our passions and our irresponsibility." But on its face this statement no more evokes worship of the Christian Trinity than intellectual appreciation of the Platonic Good, the Aristotelian *nous,* or the Parmenidean One. Solzhenitsyn speaks not of a personal god to whom we necessarily owe obedience, but of an intelligible principle of order. He uses the words "spirit" and "spiritual" in as many senses as we do—not only as the locus of religiosity, but as intellect, as the animation of a people or an individual, and as that which leads us to suspect that there is more to a human being than a body with material needs and physical pleasures. And for all his insistence that our world find a place for the principle of soul, he could not reject more emphatically a religion that contravenes nature by contemning the body's needs and desires altogether. As Kesler suggests, the deepest meaning of "a world split apart" is a world in which the natural unity of body and soul is denied and the needs of one or the other neglected. Kesler also leads us to recall that only the Classical world (which Solzhenitsyn neither praises nor criticizes here, but of which he shows an appreciation in his writings) strove for such wholeness.

Michael Novak, who welcomes the Commencement speech as "the most important religious document of our time," can do so only because he interprets Solzhenitsyn's lament for the loss of "the concept of a Supreme Complete Entity" as a demand for the return to religion and a "theocentric" society. He also believes that Solzhenitsyn agrees that it is possible to ground the political institutions of a "liberal, pluralistic, constitutional democracy" on various religions which grow, that is, converge on the basis of their common principle of truth-seeking. Unfortunately, Novak's cheerful characterization of Solzhenitsyn's position requires Solzhenitsyn to have lost the understanding of what a revealed religion is. Each religion begins with its own non-negotiable truth, and none needs to seek what it already has. In contrast, the philosopher Sidney Hook holds that in his concern with a Supreme Complete Entity Solzhenitsyn is "profoundly, demonstrably, and tragically wrong." Rather than demonstrate Solzhenitsyn's error, however, Hook asserts (without demonstration and contrary to all experience) that mankind can agree to unite in the defense of freedom and morality without any agreement about "God, immortality, or any other transcendental dogma."

If Solzhenitsyn's critics cannot have him as a theocrat, they would at least have him as a partisan of autocracy or authoritarianism. But here too their assertions lack a firm foundation. Solzhenitsyn's explicit recognition of the obvious fact that some authoritarian regimes are better or worse than others cannot be construed as a recommendation of either variety. Solzhenitsyn has said that a non-Communist authoritarian regime would be best for Russia now because in her thousand-year history Russia has had only eight months experience with constitutional government. (Why do those who cannot abide Solzhenitsyn's defense of the Vietnam war, because they regard the war as an attempt to impose our ways on another people, not extend their cultural and political relativism to Russia?) The authoritarianism he recommends for Russia is, moreover, a curious one, for it would be ruled by law and incorporate the principle of separation of powers. So far is Solzhenitsyn from urging the West to adopt authoritarian ways that he criticizes the American press for subverting our representative institutions while it wields power irresponsibly. Elsewhere Solzhenitsyn has voiced a more fundamental objection to Western constitutional democracies: Western constitutional democracy invariably means party government, and party government is rule on behalf of a part or in its interest. The only consensus is that somebody's interests be served. A statesman is not required and is hardly permitted to think about the common good. Perhaps Solzhenitsyn did not offer this objection in the Commencement speech because he wished his audience to think about the most urgent common good for the sake of which all liberals can unite—the survival of the West and thereby of humanity.

It is also said of Solzhenitsyn that his "rantings" can be disregarded because he does not know the West; either he is unfamiliar with it or his own cultural bias blinds or blurs his vision. But as George Will, Kesler, and Ronald Berman suggest, the real issue is whether Solzhenitsyn knows Western ideas, particularly those on which modern Western politics are grounded. We do not know what Solzhenitsyn has read. Before World War II and Gulag he had been trained in mathematics and physics, but surely none of the contributors to this book believe that all human beings stop reading and thinking once they have their diplomas in hand. In any case, what Solzhenitsyn has read about the West is not decisive, for if (as the old saying goes) "truth is one," the same truth can be discovered anew in any time and place.

To assert that Solzhenitsyn is a latter-day Slavophile, implying that this is all we need to know to understand Solzhenitsyn and his speech, is at best a diversion. The issue is whether Solzhenitsyn is right or wrong, not who has taught him to pose the questions he raises. If the finding of similarities and tracing of influences is to be at all fruitful one must have a firm grasp of what it is one is about to reduce to its antecedents. Ronald Berman can cite as many Western sources as Richard Pipes can cite Slavophiles. Who is the winner? The danger in being content with tracing influences is apparent in Harold Berman's otherwise intelligent and interesting essay. In finding Solzhenitsyn's criticism of Western legalism rooted in Slavophile objections that laws tend to be all letter and no spirit, Berman overlooks a crucial fact of Western legal history. In the seventeenth and eighteenth centuries the very principle of law in Western civilization underwent a radical change. The principle "what the law does not command, it forbids" became "what the law does not forbid, it permits." Laws that were to "command all the virtues" were replaced by mere "hedges." The issues involved in this change are at the core of what is, according to Will, "the most ancient and honorable theme of Western political philosophy." William McNeill is only mildly and briefly upset by the whole issue of perspective and cultural relativity because he thinks Solzhenitsyn's central proposition is that a nation needs "a unifying ideal or myth"—not a universal truth—to sustain its will. McNeill expects us to be saved by a nihilistic assertion of Western will in the name of nothing more than a myth.

Solzhenitsyn holds that the precariousness of the West's existence is due to a mistake at its very root: the "rationalistic humanism or humanistic autonomy" that became the basis of its political and social doctrine. The principle of modern Western politics, he says, is "that governments are meant to serve man and that man lives in order to be free and pursue happiness." Thus Solzhenitsyn understands liberalism better than liberals do, for just such a principle was articulated by Thomas Hobbes, proponent of modern liberal politics whom Solzhenitsyn has recently attacked in *Foreign Affairs* magazine. According to Hobbes, man is naturally free. Unhindered, human bodies would move not toward "a Supreme Complete Entity," but toward the various objects of their desires, the continual attainment of which might be called happiness. But in such a condition of perfect freedom, life would be so intolerable that men would consent to government and laws to limit their natural freedom. Government serves man by securing peace and preservation. Laws, when good, are as few and as limited in scope as possible out of respect for the presumption of natural liberty. The morality of modern liberalism is nothing more than obedience to the laws that make peace possible. However minimal these laws might be, modern politics does not require—nay, forbids—individual appeal to any higher moral or religious principles.

Because Hobbes' doctrine is grounded on a universal fact of human nature, it should be universally applicable. And Hobbes insists that it is true as well as salutary. All opinions compatible with the metaphysical dogma of this "humanistic autonomy," that the first principle is the individual human body, are tolerable. Religion can therefore be tolerated in a modern polity only when the faithful no longer take religion and its possible truth seriously.

The most obvious political defect of liberalism, as Hobbes and his critics anticipated, is that it cannot sustain military courage. If the preservation of one's own body is one's greatest (and most justified) concern, how could it ever be reasonable to risk one's life for any person or principle? Although Hobbes' doctrine does not require a petty materialism in everyday life (one is still free to indulge the "lust of the mind" for knowledge), the common desire for material well-being is likely to be ubiquitous. Liberalism is transformed into the welfare-statism or socialism and finally the nihilism of liberal intellectuals only when they try to elevate the vulgar passions for equality and material well-being to principle. Having lost any measure of man but his state of preservation, they become incapable of making a reasoned distinction between noble and base aspirations.*

---

*That Solzhenitsyn believes our most fundamental danger to be intellectual, not military, has been made perfectly clear in his two recent statements in *Foreign Affairs,* as well as by the fact that

Solzhenitsyn advises us, his friends, that "no one on earth has any other way left but—upward." He does not urge a return to either the Middle Ages or the early optimism of the Enlightenment. We cannot defend liberalism without an awareness of its weaknesses as well as its strengths. Liberalism's claim to be universally true and beneficial is belied in a world split apart. To think about the profundity of liberalism's difficulties is to have begun our ascent. Solzhenitsyn's demeanor, which offends most of the contributors to *Solzhenitsyn at Harvard* and even its publishers, complements his argument, for he personifies a quality which is antithetical to the spirits of both Christianity and liberalism, but is the peak of Classical virtue; *megalopsychia*—greatness of soul, or pride.

---

he chose as his forum a scholarly journal. A political science that has become contemptuous of universal doctrines is blind to the nature of Marxist regimes as well as liberal ones. Our scholars leave Western statesmen dumb before those who still wish to see and hear what Solzhenitsyn calls "a proud, principled and open defense of freedom."

The Worldly Ways
of John Kenneth Galbraith

(1981)

SIDNEY HOOK

Like other autobiographies of contemporary figures, J.K. Galbraith's *A Life in Our Times* may be approached on various levels and from various points of view. As a story it is a fascinating account of the ascent of a Canadian farm boy to dizzying political heights in the United States where he became a spokesman and at times a critic of the Establishment. To be sure, those he supported, with the exception of JFK's fluke victory, lost, despite not because of his counsel. But it is hardly disputable that if Stevenson, McGovern, or Edward Kennedy had ascended to the presidency, Galbraith would have been an important power in the nation. His views on foreign policy, had they prevailed in the past, would have had momentous consequences. He is still wedded to those views and the chief moral of his tale is an apologia and defense of them. They are of primary concern to me and should be to all Americans regardless of their differences on domestic economic issues.

On these economic issues I am closer to Galbraith than most of his critics. I am still an unreconstructed advocate of the welfare state who believes its waywardness and abuses can be corrected. Nonetheless, to me the basic issue of our time is not capitalism *or* socialism in any of their variants and combinations but the defense of the open society against totalitarianism.

As a commentary on our political history since the thirties, Galbraith's book is absorbing, in places highly amusing, and fiercely partisan. Galbraith never forgets a slight nor a compliment. In many ways he confirms Auden's rueful comment on my "Ethics of Controversy": To abide by them ruins the aesthetics of controversy. But some of his malicious comments are sparked not by memory of conflict but only of friendly disagreement. Thus his characterization of Bernard Baruch as a "name dropper" seems unfair. Baruch personally knew the persons in high places whose names he mentions at least as well as Galbraith knew those whose names in far greater number stud his pages. And to imply that Baruch's friendly telephone calls before the appearance of his *Autobiography* was to insure a favorable review is hardly justified. It makes one wonder why Galbraith goes out of his way to praise, and sometimes to withhold expected criticism of, some of his colleagues. Those who stood in the way of his promotion or hold economic views at variance with his, get it in the neck without a convincing exposure or refutation of their positions. This is no great fault in a work of journalism—and Galbraith is indisputably a brilliant journalist—but rather a drawback in the serious analysis of ideas and policies. And Galbraith's great public conceit is that he is a profound and original thinker.

As a journalist one of Galbraith's important contributions to the gaiety of the nation is the exhumation of optimistic predictions and assurances of bigwigs on the eve of disaster. This is a valuable and much neglected public service particularly with reference to the records of economists and military men who have profited from what Galbraith calls "our system of upward failure"— reward and promotion despite their miserable batting averages. He takes pains, in order to claim an intellectual humility he does not feel, to document some minor errors of economic and electoral prediction of his own. But on some matters of momentous significance like his celebration of the economic success of the Chinese Communist economy, then in the throes of the Cultural Revolution, he suffers a lapse of memory. Like so many other memoirists whom he reproves, Galbraith has his own historical dustbin.

There is an interesting passage in the volume that possibly accounts for this. "After a lifetime in public service* self-censorship becomes not only automatic but a permanent part of one's personality. Only in the most infrequent cases can there be escape for autobiography or memoir. And what passes thus for candor is only a minor loosening of the chains . . ."

One senses this absence of candor in the account of his switch in 1960 from Stevenson to Kennedy at a time when Stevenson's prospects of winning the presidency were excellent without the necessity of Cook County electoral larceny. I still remember Agnes Meyer's blazing fury at Galbraith's "opportunism" and "betrayal" in attaching himself to the Kennedy clan whose reputation for liberalism at the time was not high, and what she said about the hardly more contained indignation of Eleanor Roosevelt, and the deep hurt rather than anger of Stevenson himself. Although Galbraith was aware of this feeling among Stevenson supporters, he shrugs it off without really explaining why as a *liberal* he switched. His appetite for power whetted by his experience during the war years had grown in the period he was out of government service to a point where it overcame his fidelity to liberal principle. He rationalized this to himself and others by saying that Stevenson was a "born loser."

Even more mysterious in such a highly principled man and one who rather smugly proclaims his inveterate tendency to be "compulsively against any self-satisfied elite," and "to oppose and infuriate" the well-heeled, is his undeviating loyalty to the Kennedys. J. F. Kennedy in his campaign speeches irresponsibly attacked the Eisenhower administration for not actively supporting the Cuban freedom fighters—which was tantamount to a call for invasion. After his election he approved the ill-advised and ineptly planned Bay of Pigs imbroglio— mistakes that could only have been retrieved by American air support, cancelled after Kennedy's failure of nerve. Galbraith tells us now that he vehemently opposed all these moves except the last. But he did not go public with his opposition or resign in protest as he should have done.

---

*I have substituted the word "service" for "office" because Galbraith tells us that he had come to think of himself as part of the permanent government of the United States.

His memory fails him when he writes about Robert Kennedy to whom he would have undoubtedly transferred his allegiance from Eugene McCarthy at the 1968 convention had Kennedy not been assassinated. He is silent about Robert Kennedy's role in Joseph McCarthy's rampage, and his wire-taps when Attorney General on Martin Luther King and others.

Most puzzling of all is Galbraith's undeviating support of the hero of Chappaquiddick whom he regards after George McGovern as possibly "my closest friend in politics." This is indeed passing strange for such a stern moralist for whom Nixon's character, despite Galbraith's enthusiasm for his policy of détente and the opening towards China, unfit him for any public office, even that of a lowly dogcatcher. Nixon was certainly foolish beyond words and his political villainies, albeit flowing from an excess of personal loyalty to subordinates and political partisanship, are reprehensible. But if character is relevant to politics what act of Nixon's begins to compare in infamy, moral cowardice, and deception with that of Edward Kennedy's? And as for cover-ups, what act of Nixon's was as degrading as the bribe to the parents of the victim of Chappaquiddick to forbid an autopsy whose findings might have raised the question of whether what occurred, that is, the delay in getting help and reporting what happened, was purely an accident? Conscious decision by Galbraith not unconscious censorship operates here, not only in the failure to make even passing mention of the incident but in not informing the reader what advice, if any, Galbraith gave at the time.

All this is relatively minor save as an illustration of how the double standard in morals and politics pervades Galbraith's memoir. Much more significant to the serious reader is the theme song that runs through the book with respect to the mischievous role American concern with Communism has had on our foreign policy. It is this topical theme which deserves closer attention.

Galbraith is convinced that the bane of American foreign policy since the end of World War II has been its obsessive anti-Communism. It threatens to end the world in a nuclear holocaust. American statesmen have been rendered both foolish and bellicose out of fear of being considered "soft" on Communism by those who are rhetorically "hard." Communism constitutes no danger *in* the United States nor *to* the United States. All the Communist powers want are safe borders. Integral to the debilitating syndrome of the anti-Communist complex that has gripped American statesmen from the onset of the cold war is that the Communist movement is a monolithic world organization driven by an unchanging ideology which has inspired its zealots everywhere to engage in conspiratorial practices. The result is that we have done more harm to ourselves than to our reputed enemies. Although the original architects of this disastrous policy are long dead, Galbraith is convinced that their spirits have poisoned the minds of the current inhabitants of the White House and his advisors. (Party loyalty prevents him from seeing that a better case can be made for finding the roots of the current attitude in Truman's belated policy of containment than in the actions of Eisenhower and Dulles.)

It is this bitter attack on current and past American foreign policy with respect to the Soviet Union and Communism that is likely to have the greatest influence on uninformed readers. It varies little from the position of those like former Secretary of State Vance and his advisors, Marshal Shulman et al., who believe that the Soviet Union, far from being a threat to the United States, feels threatened and insecure by its "failures" in Europe, Asia, and Africa, and that the invasion of Afghanistan is a sign of Soviet "weakness." Galbraith does not yet go as far as George Kennan who has abandoned advocacy of the policy of containment for Bertrand Russell's position—"Rather Red, than Dead"—if an arms agreement cannot be negotiated. There are suggestions, however, towards the close of the book, that this may soon be Galbraith's view, too. Were he consistent, it would be because on his theory of convergence, as we shall see, technology not ideology determines our future under any system, and the technological imperatives of Communism and capitalism as industrial systems are the same.

Before addressing myself to this criticism of American foreign policy, I should like to challenge two assumptions that invariably attend Galbraith's exposition of it. The first, relatively minor, is his attempt to preempt the designation of "liberal" for his position in which he is abetted by some stupid conservatives. The only sense of the term "liberal" that would justify such presumption is one that defines liberalism as the belief that there are no enemies to human freedom on "the Left"—often a euphemistic expression for Communism. This kind of liberalism is always anti-Fascist but more often *anti* anti-Communist than anti-Communist.

The foreign policy Galbraith and his confrères are attacking is the foreign policy more strongly advocated by the liberal, organized labor movement in the United States (the AFL-CIO) than by any group of plutocratic monopolists and/or free marketeers on the scene. Yet Galbraith mistakenly attributes the chief opposition to the Communist movement to big business which notoriously has been more interested in trade with Communist Countries than have the trade unions. It is the same foreign policy defended by men like Adolf Berle, Paul Douglas, Reinhold Niebuhr, and scores of others whose liberal credentials are as long standing and every whit as authentic as Galbraith's. To be sure, this has no bearing on the validity of the policy but it is sufficient to expose—nothing can apparently limit—the patronizing arrogance of the assumption that where Galbraith stands, even in his call for quota systems and reverse discrimination, the liberal flag waves.

More serious is the factual error that United States foreign policy, of which I have often been a critic for reasons quite different from those of Galbraith, has taken as axiomatic the monolithic character of the international Communist movement. Even under Truman, despite the fact that Tito's Yugoslavia was ideologically the most intransigent and aggressive of the Communist states, the United States was quick to offer economic and military assistance to Belgrade after the Tito-Stalin rift. The development of polycentrism was a slow process in the Communist world, and the United States was not unduly tardy in recognizing it. It may be true that Kim Il Sung decided on his own to invade South Korea after Acheson had gratuitously declared it outside the confines of the American national interest. But once the invasion was launched, North Korea could not have continued to wage the war against the U.S. and UN resistance without the active collaboration of the Soviet Union and Communist China. The worldwide campaign against the United States that circulated the monstrous lie that the U.S. was waging germ warfare in Korea was initiated and orchestrated by the Kremlin.

And now that the United States has decided to play the China card in a very modest opening in order to restrain the current expansionist tendency of the Soviet Union, Galbraith and other appeasers deplore the move as a dangerous provocation even as they continue to indict American policy for its "mindless" assumption that the world Communist movement is monolithic. Actually, there is a good precedent in United States policy for helping, in the national interest and the ultimate cause of freedom, one form of totalitarianism resist another, about which we hear little from human rights absolutists, namely, United States military and economic aid to the Kremlin after Hitler double-crossed his erst-while ally and invaded the Soviet Union on June 22, 1941. Such aid, under existing law, would not have been possible then.

Of course it is fatuous to contrast "hard" and "soft" attitudes towards Communism. Nor do I recall any policy being accepted or rejected by leading American statesmen in these terms despite Galbraith's assertion that their use was systematic. All American political figures, including Henry Wallace and George McGovern, have been *against* Communism. But that is not enough to develop "intelligent" and avoid "unintelligent" policies resisting it. "Intelligent" and "unintelligent" are the only appropriate epithets to apply in consider-ing alternatives of policy, not "hard" or "soft." Although knowledge of Com-munist theory and practice is certainly no guarantee of wisdom here, that is, of developing an intelligent policy, ignorance of Communist theory and practice almost invariably results in unintelligent policies, policies, for example, that assume that since Communists are just as human as we are, their foreign policy is therefore motivated by the same considerations as those of other non-Communist states, or that since they are Russians, their foreign policy must therefore be a continuation of czarist foreign policy. Granting that Communists behave like human beings, and that they behave like Russians, too (or Chinese, as the case may be), the question is: Do they behave like Communists? Those who are ignorant of the theory and practice of Communism cannot answer this question. Note that even if one believes that the rulers of the Soviet Union behave like Communists, this does not mean that they behave *only* as Commu-nists or *always* as Communists. Ideology is not everything. But it certainly is not nothing as the history of our century shows.

Although I found it difficult to believe, I have reluctantly concluded, on the strength of this book and some others of his writings, that Galbraith really is innocent of knowledge of the theory and practice of Communism. For him Communism is purely an economic system in which private property in the instruments of social production has been abolished. On this view, the only individuals who are obsessively hostile to it are those who mainly live on profit, rent, and interest, and who sense in the intrusion of government into economic life the ultimate take-over of the system of collectivism. Galbraith has no notion of what the dictatorship of the proletariat means in Communist theory and practice, of the dictatorship of the party as the necessary and only means of carrying it out, and of the theory and practice of democratic centralism which insures the dictatorship of the Political Committee of the Communist Party to oversee and enforce the political, cultural, social, and intellectual orthodoxy of the members of the Communist Party and of the entire population over whom they rule. In short, Communism as a system of totalitarianism is beyond his ken. One may doubt whether totalitarianism as an "ideal type" in Weber's sense exists anywhere in the world. Neither does democracy. But the existing differences in one type or another, and the possibility that under certain historical conditions one may be transformed into the other, do not preclude the proper use of the designation.

My reasons for concluding that Galbraith lacks understanding of the nature of Communism are varied. Before detailing them I must confess that the conclusion is a blow to my vanity. In 1952 as one of the organizers of Stevenson's campaign, Galbraith asked me through Arthur Schlesinger, Jr. (the suggestion, I was told, originated with John Macdonald, a former colleague of Galbraith's at *Fortune*) to write two speeches on Communism for Stevenson. Not only were they not used, they were apparently unread (perhaps they were lost in the mail).

The most striking of Galbraith's assessments of a Communist society is to be found in his book *China Passage* published after his visit to mainland China in 1972. It is odd that although large chunks of his other volumes are reproduced or summarized in this memoir there is no reference to the book in its pages or a revaluation of its judgments in the perspective of later years. Galbraith was in China while "the cultural revolution" was still raging, when its economy was crippled, its universities paralyzed, and the manifold terrors of the Chinese Gulag Archipelago pervasive in most areas. Nonetheless he reported to the world that China's economic system is "highly effective," that it "functions easily and well," with a performance rivaling Japan's. (The true state of affairs, economic as well as political in China at that time, or at any time, could have easily been learned by talking to recent refugees in Hong Kong— especially those who fled to avoid religious persecution and who had no political axe to grind.) Feasting on the elaborate, exotic *haute cuisine* in a succession of banquets the Chinese lay on for distinguished visitors—just like those the Kremlin provided for visiting Western dignitaries during the famine of the early thirties—Galbraith does not in so many words say that the general population are as well but implies that it was well fed—despite the suspicious absence, noted by one of his companions, of any cats or dogs. To Galbraith's credit he forbears mentioning the absence of flies in China. But neither does he note anywhere the absence of freedom except in a Pickwickian sense. He has a peripheral consciousness of some oppression but it is the easy and satisfactory functioning of the economy that impresses him most. "Dissidents are brought firmly into line in China but one suspects with great politeness." And why does he suspect this? Because his Chinese hosts invariably smiled at him. He actually writes that the Chinese "command with a smile." No one was ever a more willing and self-deluded victim of skillful Chinese Potemkins. He has an appreciative eye for the aesthetic delights of the countryside but seems blind in both eyes to the totalitarian character of every social landscape. He prefers not to stress the drab unisex uniforms of Chinese adults in order to point up the brightly attired five-year-olds. He remains silent about the educational and cultural significance of these children pirouetting and celebrating with Mao's little Red Book in their tiny hands.

His final pronouncement: "For the Chinese, the system works . . . It is the Chinese future." We may not like it nor the French. The Chinese do. It is a pity Galbraith does not tell us how he knows that the Chinese like it. When did they choose it? The only choice the Chinese have had since the Communists took over was when the Chinese prisoners of war, after the Korean conflict, were given an opportunity to return home or go elsewhere. Despite the bullying of their Indian interviewers, the great majority chose the bitter bread of exile. When the Communist Chinese officials lifted the bamboo curtain for a few days, they hurriedly dropped it lest Southern China be depopulated.

Galbraith's insensitiveness to the totalitarian character of Communism is a corollary of his theory of convergence according to which the society and culture of the future are determined by the technological imperatives of large-scale industrial organization. He denies therefore that there is much sense in defining the world conflict as one between capitalism and Communism as economic systems or especially between democracy and totalitarianism. All the palaver about free enterprise is so much hokum or what Thurman Arnold, who long ago recognized Galbraith's economic genius loyally reciprocated by Galbraith, called "folk lore." And as for Marxism-Leninism, and all its variants, that is so much theology whose chilling language imperialists and militarists, and their academic hirelings, often cite out of context to increase appropriations. Denounce totalitarianism as one pleases. It cannot survive, according to Galbraith, where we have large industrial organization "that sustains technology, and the nature of the planning that technology requires." Celebrate democracy as one pleases, the same technological imperatives "impose a measure of discipline . . . of subordination of the individual to the organization which is very much less than the individualism that has been properly identified with the Western economy." We can now understand how anachronistic free trade unionism is in the new industrial state! Galbraith sees no threat to his abiding liberalism in the convergent tendencies of industrial societies which result in oligarchies both in Communist and capitalist societies. "Ideology is not the relevant force." In 1966 to make this simplistic technological determinism more palatable he predicted that the Soviet Union "will necessarily [sic!] introduce greater political and cultural freedom" (New York Times, December 18, 1966). Why this did not occur in the new industrial states of Germany and Japan he does not explain. Actually, political and cultural conditions in the Soviet Union since Galbraith made this prediction have worsened but he still clings to his simplistic technological determinism that would have shared Howard Scott, the father of the technology movement. On his theory, why should the Soviet Union become like the West rather than the West become like the Soviet Union since ideology is irrelevant and technology is decisive? Anyone who believes, as Galbraith does, the proposition that "technical specialization cannot be reconciled with intellectual regimentation," to use one of his favorite expressions, is capable of believing anything. The proposition is demonstrably false— historically, psychologically, and politically. Technology makes certain ideal uses possible, it does not determine them. He obviously has not pondered the moral of the Nobel Peace Foundation. Galbraith falls below the level of a sophisticated Marxism in failing to realize that human ideals, which are always at the heart of an ideology broadly conceived, cannot be reduced to economic or technological equations of the first or any degree.

A cognate failure to grasp the animating ideals of Communism as a movement grasping for power by any means is evidenced in his discussion of the Vietnam war. Here, too, there is a hard and fast treatment of the facts. The theme is too complex for exhaustive or even adequate analysis here. Suffice it to say that the initial error of the United States was not to bring pressure on France, as it did on the Netherlands with respect to Indonesia, to live up to de Gaulle's war-time pledge to give Vietnam independence. It was imprudent to get involved in an area so distant but it is false that the United States was seeking to impose its own way of life on a foreign nation. It was Adlai Stevenson who stated the true issue on the day of his death. "My hope in Vietnam is that resistance there may establish the fact that changes in Asia are not to be precipitated by outside force. That was the point of the Korean War. This is the point of the conflict in Vietnam." It was the same point that led the United States government to condemn and therefore reverse the war of England, France, and Israel against Egypt a decade earlier. This was during the very week in which the Soviet Union invaded Hungary to suppress with ruthless bloodshed the indigenous political development of a government formed, according to the words of George Lukács at the time, "to represent every shade and stratum of the Hungarian people that wants peace and socialism."

Once the United States became involved, given the ineptness of the military, the hostility of the media which turned the defeat of the Viet Cong Tet offensive into a psychological and political victory, and the political constraints on military operations, the real question was how to get out of Vietnam without inviting horrible excesses on a population unwilling to accept Communist despotism, and whom we encouraged to resist. Another major mistake to which Galbraith contributed was to conspire against Diem who might have come to terms with the North before our massive involvement. Galbraith himself defended not complete withdrawal but a system of enclaves in South Vietnam, which would have resulted in a series of Dien Bien Phus but which might have provided for a short time a sanctuary "for those who have joined our enterprise in Vietnam." But there is something macabre in his self-vindicating remark: "My warning of the boat people was better than I guessed." Were his concern with the myriad of victims of a Communist takeover more than a face-saving piety, he would have at least supported the Accords Kissinger worked out with the North Vietnamese, protested the congressional cutoff of arms to the South Vietnamese to defend themselves, and urged some counteraction when with blatant cynicism the North Vietnamese violated the Accords we had pressured Thieu into accepting.

Galbraith never asks himself why the Communists feel free to violate their agreements whether at Yalta, Potsdam, or Helsinki. Distrust of agreements with Communist powers and insistence upon safeguards that are verifiable (which require mutual site inspections) he tends to regard as a kind of paranoia. Of course, Galbraith would be the first to oppose Soviet aggression if there were any evidence of it that trenches on our vital interests. The changes in global power reflected in the changes in the map of the world since the end of World War II do not constitute persuasive evidence to him. They show Communist influence in areas far removed from where our national interests lie.

I am put in mind of a conversation I had with Charles Beard whose attitude towards Japanese and Nazi aggression was somewhat similar to that of Galbraith's towards Soviet Communism. Beard's eminence as a historian and his reputation as a master craftsman among his colleagues far exceeds Galbraith's standing among professional economists. When I visited Beard late in 1940 in the company of Herbert Solow he scoffed at the idea that Hitler was out to conquer Europe, no less the world. As for the defense of freedom, Beard told me: "I am prepared to fight Hitler in defense of freedom in the streets of New Canaan." I am convinced that if George Kennan does not win him over and he continues to resist the lunacy of unilateral disarmament, Galbraith, too, would fight for human freedom in Cambridge, Massachusetts, or Townsend, Vermont.

It is both in large matters and small that Galbraith reveals his innocence of Communism as an ideology and as a movement. He is scornful of the necessity of a security program in the apparent belief that membership in the Communist Party is hardly different from membership in any other political party. When he mentions Communists who have served in government, or those suspected of Communist connections, here as in his other writings, they are portrayed as victims persecuted because of their views, victims of a witchhunt. The one exception is Lauchlin Currie, of whom Galbraith strangely says nothing at all. He is tolerant of what he calls "enlightened malfeasance" in destroying official files on possible security risks. One does not have to endorse every silly decision of uninformed security boards, who disregarded or could not distinguish the difference between Norman Thomas Socialists and Communists, or countenance McCarthy's demagogic antics to accept as a premise, to which even Roger Baldwin subscribed, than anyone who owes a superior allegiance to a foreign government is unqualified to serve his own in any sensitive post. Some might say any post. To be sure, because the American Communist Party pledged allegiance to the Stalinist regime to a point where its leaders publicly acknowledged that in the case of conflict between the United States and the USSR they would side with the latter, it did not follow that every individual member would carry out instructions to betray his country. But there is no way of telling in advance who will and who will not. It is notoriously true that the most dedicated Soviet agents are drawn from the nationals of satellite Communist Parties, a proposition that only a fool would simply convert into the statement that all members of the Communist Party are Soviet agents. But the fact that some may be cannot be dismissed. Like so many others, Galbraith seems unaware that a security program is designed not to detect or apprehend those guilty of malfeasance, a task beyond its powers and irrelevant to its task, but to prevent the likelihood of such malfeasance by identifying and excluding security risks. It goes without saying that he ignores—elsewhere he scoffs at—the possible usefulness and effectiveness of intelligence agencies and espionage in our modern world. He probably has not heard of Richard Sorge whose report to Stalin that the Japanese warlords had decided to strike at the United States and not at

Russia—something Stalin carefully concealed from the United States while accepting its aid—enabled Stalin to transfer the Siberian regiments in time to save Moscow from the Nazi assault. There is a monument to Sorge in Moscow and he has been immortalized like Lenin and Stalin on postage stamps. The Kremlin knows better than Galbraith how useful its agents can be.

Galbraith's *A Life in Our Times* concludes with a plea for nuclear arms control about which no person of intelligence need be persuaded. The fear-and-tear-jerk rhetoric on its behalf is unnecessary. To this cause Galbraith pledges the rest of his life. It is to be hoped that he will devote his thought to its many intricate problems, especially to the difficulties of reliable inspection without which arms control may prove a sham. In an open society there is sure to be a public-spirited citizen who will blow the whistle in the ever vigilant press at the slightest transgression. In closed societies any attempt to do so would invite summary execution.

It is also to be hoped that in his discussion of the subject Galbraith will avoid the elementary confusion between *cause* and *ground* that mars almost every mention he makes of defense and defense appropriations as well as taxes. He has a lamentable tendency to impute motives of self-interest to those with whom he disagrees about defense appropriations and taxes without adequate assessment of their argument. There are many *causes* for a person's beliefs but in considering their validity only the *grounds* are relevant. A person's belief in vegetarianism may be caused by his aversion to killing, a weak stomach at the sight or thought of blood, or an allergy to meat. But if he argues that the imposition of unnecessary suffering on sentient creatures is morally wrong and that mankind can survive without the necessity of consuming the flesh of slaughtered creatures, the causes of his beliefs are irrelevant to the logical force of his position. Galbraith tends to believe that those who argue for greater military appropriations or tax policies of which he disapproves do so out of self-interest. That may or may not be so, and in many cases it certainly is not so, but that has no bearing on the truth or falsity of their position. I have no doubt that some who urge higher defense appropriations have stock in defense industries but if there has been an absolute and relative decline of American defense power with respect to the Soviet Union, they may be right. I know very well why some physicians are opposed to socialized medicine, but anyone who favors it must be prepared to meet their arguments against it. Naturally, knowledge of the causes of their belief will impel one to look hard and carefully at their arguments and evidence.

I had looked forward to reading Galbraith's memoir of his busy political life for revelations that are not on the public record. They are not to be found. His pages tell more about himself than about others but still not enough. His style is lively and entertaining. One can forgive his apparent arrogance since it is an obvious protective device against the suspected judgment of economists of the first rank. My disappointment may be due to the fact that my expectations were so high. Although he is rather boastful of his size and achievements, at second glance there is not as much to him as meets the eye.

Prague Winter

(1983)

JOSEF ŠKVORECKÝ

Suppose an aircraft designer talks the Boeing Company into financing an airplane which, according to its creator, is guaranteed to be faster, safer, and more comfortable than any ever built. In the course of a century the company goes on to build several dozen prototypes, but they all prove slower and more uncomfortable than the previous models, and able to return to Mother Earth only by means of crash-landings. Yet the company continues to turn them out. Certainly, the originator of such an insanity would be recognized as a genius; not perhaps of aircraft design, but of conmanship.

This year marks the 100th anniversary of the death of Karl Marx. The ultimate result of his dialectics seems to be Poland, where the workers' party has been replaced by an alliance of army and special units of stormtroopers, where class justice has been superseded by martial law, and where the folksy party leader has given way to a ramrod general who looks like a South American junta boss envisioned by Costa-Gavras. As predicted, the state has withered away: first into the country-wide jail of martial law, then into the universal barracks of military discipline imposed on the industrial work force, with everybody drafted for an indeterminate length of time.

The past 25 years or so have witnessed other crash-landings of Marxism, and the story is becoming a bore. Consequently, the year 1968 does not ring many bells, and *The Writing on the Wall* will go unnoticed by most Americans. In the distant days when I still attempted to explain things to left-leaning North American acquaintances I invariably asked: "If you are interested in Communism because you think it would be good for this country, why try to find out how it works in Albania, Angola, Mozambique, or in some other safely unverifiable region of the Earth? Wouldn't it be more logical to study what it does to old Western cultures, as for instance that of the Czechs and Slovaks?"

What it does to such cultures is touched upon in *The Writing on the Wall*. The gory events of the fifties do not find their way into the 35-odd pieces in this volume. This is not a book about Communism's past but about its future. That's why it will move only such readers who, in this land of soft bodies and pampered souls, still believe that to oppress the mind is as reprehensible as to oppress the body.

A remarkable story by Eda Kriseová, "Our Small Town," illustrates the

233

impact of Marxist social engineering on a society where problems of literacy were solved in the previous century. Its female intellectual narrator quietly observes the daily habits of contemporary villagers who spend their free time gorging themselves on smoked pork and drudging on the building sites of private retreats. No music, either folk song or symphony, resounds against the strangely barren landscape. Only the smell of wieners seeps through an atmosphere of devastating senselessness. A metaphor, of course, for what the Czech Party ideologues have come to call *reálný socialismus.* This recent addition to the Marxist lexicon cannot be translated as "real socialism"; English lacks the decidedly pejorative connotations "reálný" has acquired in Czech, and "real" in English may also mean "true." But *reálný socialismus* can mean a deadpan general or toneless country gluttons, depending on the state of the local economy. But never a workers' council or a blooming contemporary culture.

"Really? And what about those wonderful concerts in the Renaissance Rudolfinum Hall in Prague? What about the lavish Shakespearean productions?" say my left-leaning acquaintances, fresh from a trip to Prague of half-Didion duration. "And although we, unfortunately, cannot read Czech, we are told that not everything in the bookstores there is trash."

Well, all dictators love fiddlers, but suspect penpushers, except those who are safely dead. There is a crucial difference between the creative and performing arts when it comes to their manageability and propaganda value. And as for "not-so-trashy" books . . .

Let's imagine a young Mark Twain who lives in the Old South in the days of slavery but under conditions of literary censorship as strict as those in today's Czechoslovakia. This hypothetical Sam Clemens is as obsessed by literary fame as any budding writer anywhere anytime. He gets the idea for *Huck Finn.* But he faces a dilemma. If he builds his novel around the central issue of Southern society, i.e., slavery, the book will be seized by the censors, and its author, quite possibly, by the police. Yet the call of the printer's ink is irresistible. So young Clemens does a little focus-shifting—away from the immorality of taking a man's freedom to, let's say, offenses against proper Southern table manners—and his "sivilized" *Huck Finn* is soon on the market. It is a funny, entertaining, well-written book. It's just that something is missing from the story.

In a feuilleton by Vlastimil Třešňák, a man badly in need of money sells a few drawings to an art shop. In better days, an artist-friend had given him those pictures. The manager displays the new acquisitions in his shop window. The police soon arrive, equipped with a secret list of undesirable artists. The uninformed manager is reprimanded, the drawings are confiscated. The police ask for the address of the seller, who is then apprehended and accused of trafficking in anti-state art.

Nothing much, is it? Just a little unpleasantness. Multiply it by ten million, and chances are you will begin to sense the quality of daily life under *Realsozialismus.* But chances also are you won't. If, like Mr. Doctorow, you don't see much difference between Auschwitz and Disneyland, how could you see the dissimilarity between New York and Prague?

One aspect of this daily life is a special kind of schizophrenia. In Pavel Kohout's story "Trouble," two secret policemen, by means of electronic bugs, tape the goings-on in the private apartment of a dissident writer. What is going on is perfectly normal: the writer has breakfast with his wife, they are seized by a sudden lust and make love on the floor; the man then goes to the toilet and has a bowel movement (at this point, one of the policemen discreetly turns down the volume). Then the woman says goodbye, the writer retires to his room. For the rest of the policemen's shift he pounds on his typewriter.

What goes on between the two policemen is also perfectly normal: the younger complains about his unfaithful wife, the older gives him advice about how to deal with females in general, and with fickle ones in particular.

In short, everything in the story is perfectly normal. In that kind of society. Some of the pieces are more ominous. When Ludvík Vaculík leaves home to attend the funeral of Professor Patočka, a 70-year-old philosopher who died during a twelve-hour police interrogation, he is picked up and driven to the police precinct, where he is kept until the funeral is safely over. In the meantime, on a track adjoining the cemetery, a group of motorcycle racers begins intensive training, and the priest's funeral oration is drowned out by the unmuffled exhausts. A police helicopter hovers a few feet above the open grave. This is not an attempt to emulate Kafka; it is not even a story. Just a piece of reportage.

These little clashes with real-socialist power accumulate, and eventually become nauseating. But there is little blood in these stories. Only the soul bleeds occasionally. More horrifying things happen to bodies elsewhere. In countries where the Marxist-Leninists got their first chance at blood-letting only recently; not way back in the fifties, as in Czechoslovakia. Prague, these days, is simply uninteresting. Newsunworthy.

Or is it? This city of ancient Western culture, driven over by the Marxist steam roller? All right, so far the stories I have quoted have been about intellectuals who, if American experience is any indication, have a tendency to grumble. What about ordinary folks who are believed to be better off—perhaps because the Western liberal presumes such types can live by bread alone—than they were in the old days of the Thomas Baťa Shoe Company? In Ivan Klíma's story "A Christmas Conspiracy," a former writer, now working at odd jobs and occasionally finding a "front" for his TV plays, gets a temporary job selling Christmas carp for a grocery store. The job becomes his initiation into socialist entrepreneurship. A shopgirl, regularly employed by the grocery, tells him about a number of tricks based mostly on mixing cheap stuff with more expensive stuff, which brings the store a nice profit. The profit is split up among all the employees who work as a team. Or rather, a gang: penalties for betraying the collective are forbidding.

But such shares in the fruit of fraudulence are small change. The girl has a more grandiose dream. She tells the writer about gas stations where one can "pull in ten thousand a month if it's a halfway decent pump." There is just one hitch: the franchise costs, in bribes, at least 25,000 crowns. The girl is so obsessed by the vision of the riches-bringing pump that she drags the writer into a big crate in the storage room and offers to sleep with him if he'll promise to become a partner in the bribing scheme. "Mr. Ivan . . . your friend told me about you, that you write for the TV and make a nice bundle . . . Mr. Ivan, for a man like you twenty thousand means nothing. I've already saved up the rest, I know about a great pump, in six months it would be paid off and from then on it would be all gravy . . . in two years we'll save up enough for a house . . . we'll take trips to the seashore, won't that be great?''

Yes, ordinary folks definitely are better off under *Realsozialismus.* To the amazed former writer, who compares them to himself and his fellow dissidents, officially described as "antisocialist conspirators," their lively community appears as a "world full of real conspirators . . . an all-penetrating conspiracy of people who saw the futility of all ideals and the murderous ambiguity of human illusions . . . a determined fraternity of true materialists who knew that you could count only those things that can be counted, that money can buy anything and anyone—except Death (which they don't worry about) and except a few isolated fools whom they clap into prison, kick out of the country or shove into cellars to stoke furnaces and indulge their idle cogitations."

This perhaps is more useful reading for the Western left-leaning man than news items about poetry workshops, recently organized for the Nicaraguan police force. We had them, too, thirty years ago. This is a story about the future of the future, and how it works.

The final metaphor for the metamorphosis of the working class and their leaders in *Realsozialismus* is Vaculík's feuilleton "First of May." This is a traditional socialist holiday in Europe, commemorating the victims of the Haymarket Riots in Chicago. In Czech literature, its mood was first captured in a feuilleton by the poet and journalist Jan Neruda (a nineteenth-century Czech liberal whose surname was misappropriated by the twentieth-century Chilean Stalinist Ricardo Reyes). Apparently one is not permitted to quote from Neruda's account in today's Czechoslovakia. It contains allusions to the Prussian invasion of the country in 1866, and a surrealistically associating reader might be reminded of something the Soviets did in 1968. Neruda writes about the silence of the marching workers and about the dedicated speeches of their leaders. In Vaculík's description of the same day's celebration three quarters of a century later, a worker, waiting for the commencement of the march, calls to a busy functionary: "Mr. Organizer, mark me present!" The difference between what Neruda saw many years ago and what Vaculík witnessed in 1975 stands revealed; defamiliarized, if you wish. Yes, indeed. You have to be marked "present," if you happen to have a daughter, and she wants to go to high school.

Eventually, Dr. Gustáv Husák, the Czech president, is about to make a speech, when all of a sudden the public address system fails. No sound comes out of the amplifiers, and so the crowd resumes talking "quite loudly" about what interests it most; mainly soccer. In the feuilleton of the past, the workers listened silently and attentively to their leaders. In the feuilleton of the future's future, the leader performs the pantomime of a TV announcer rendered mute, and the workers, not giving a damn about him, twaddle about trivialities.

I am not particularly fond of literary symbols, but some are simply a natural outgrowth of reality.

The Writing on the Wall is a book of ruins, of hopes "grotesquely betrayed, ideals caricatured" (Joseph Conrad). Only readers who once lived among those ruins are likely to pick it from a bookshelf. This, I suspect, is the fate of most such works published in the United States. Aimed at readers who will never know of their existence, they end up in libraries of people who do not need their message. They know it by heart. They remember what happened in 1968.

Yes, the Democratic Convention; that too. But it was also the year of the Prague Spring, of the glorious temporary insanity that befell the Czechoslovak Communist Party. Quite a few unread volumes describe and analyze the events, idealize or defame their protagonists. To me (I was there) this *annus mirabilis* remains something of an enigma. Was it naivete that led the Dubcekists—all of them, for years, dedicated Marxist-Leninists, in many cases with a shady Stalinist past—to create a situation that could not but become explosive, and eventually unmanageable? Were they serious about their promises? Did they indeed intend to hold free elections, convinced, as some of them said, that the people, out of gratitude to the Communist Party for giving political freedom back to them, would return it to power? But how grateful can you be to a thief, who, for unclear reasons, returns your stolen property? And can you trust him in the future?

Such naiveté in people as politically hardened as the Dubčekists seems incredible. In my own simplified view, it all started in the early sixties, after official revelations of Stalinist "excesses" began spilling out. Smacking so patently of the Gestapo rather than of noble revolutionary violence, these confessed horrors shook the idealists among the comrades: the former young activists and hotheads who had been blinded by uncritical acceptance of an unexamined ideal. I remember them after these revelations, talking excitedly into the wee hours over empty bottles of slivovitz, swearing, blaspheming, weeping, even apologizing to some of their victims. At least a portion of such carryings-on could have been genuine.

In 1963, Alexander Dubček, a bona fide working-class boy, signed one of the most horrifying documents on the unspeakable crimes of the fifties, the report of the Kolder Commission "investigating the violations of socialist justice." The one which describes innovative methods of Marxist penology, such as keeping prisoners' hands in tight rubber gloves until fingers begin to rot away, or a spectacular variation of age-old hunger-torture which leads half-crazed prisoners to offer their eyes for medical research in return for a piece of bread, or to eat their own excrement. He was also familiar with the content of the later Piller Report which cited the recommendation of the Ministry of Justice that the passing of death sentences be slowed because their accumulation in brief spans of time affects the sanity of the executioner. All this, mind you, in an official Party document, available—in the Czech—also in the West. Not some John Birch Society pamphlet.

So, as I see it, in the beginning was this eye opener. Then came Ludvík Vaculík's famous speech at the Writers' Congress in 1967, contrasting optimistic visions of socialist reality with actual achievements. It followed in the wake of a long internal Party struggle between those who were not shocked—the convinced Stalinists and the cynical opportunists—and those who were. The struggle was fierce and outspoken. Although Communism creates an elitist society and there is no democracy for the citizen, there is something called "inner Party democracy" (a Leninist heritage). It enables high Party functionaries to indulge in frank discussions behind closed doors. Naturally, for the public stage, they are required to change back into parrots, no matter how openly they quarreled *in camera*.

But the shocked ones got used to this private-club democracy, and slowly, with the Stalinist guard weakening and the opportunists changing sides, some of it spilled over, first to the cultural weeklies, eventually to general periodicals. The public was puzzled, then amused, finally excited. The Stalinist president Antonín Novotný along with his cohorts and censors tried to curb the flow. Savage battles were fought over such grave ideological issues as the nakedness of the protagonist in Miloš Forman's *Loves of a Blonde,* about the resemblance to Lenin of the leading actor in Jan Němec's *Report on the Party and the Guests,* or about the wasting of food in Věra Chytilová's *The Daisies.*

So far so good. Unfortunately, the process created new illusions. The shocked ones, having once succumbed to the illusion of a just dictatorship, now began to see themselves as the natural leaders of a democratic movement; in fact, as pioneers of some kind of democracy. In the heat of battle, it slipped their minds that other leaders had once been duly elected, and then—often with their help—silenced, forced into exile, or even liquidated. They forgot also that the majority of the public had never subscribed to Communism. In the end, they labored under the illusion that, far from just being leaders of a Party faction, they were spokesmen for the entire people, loved and esteemed by the masses. In actual fact, the common people supported them only because they knew— having learned the hard way—that in a totalitarian state decisive change can come only from above.

On this there was tacit agreement between the public and the proponents of reform. Where they differed was in the forgetfulness of the self-hypnotized Party liberals, and the good historic memory of most of their subjects. The rest was almost all a bad miscalculation by politicos who, despite their many years of speaking in the name of the masses, knew nothing about the real and often vengeful spirit of the democratic crowd. They expected, for instance, that the enforced discipline of Stalinism would continue even after the total abolition of censorship (another bit of lunacy from a CP gone mad). But the lure of uncensored freedom proved too tempting. Ivan Sviták, now a professor of philosophy at California State University, drew attention to the case of Jan Masaryk, the half-American son of Thomas Garrigue Masaryk, who although he owned a revolver and a wide assortment of sleeping pills, was said to have committed suicide by jumping out of a third-floor window. A nurse revealed that the priest Father Toufar, arrested after a cross had miraculously moved in his village church at Čihošť, died on the operating table from numerous internal injuries suffered during police interrogation. A criminologist showed me, without commentary, police photographs of a hanging judge from the fifties who had just hanged himself from a tree, his legs bent stiffly at the knees. An old butler of a former non-Communist politician fell into a well and perished. The director of my publishing house, the one-time secretary of the Stalinist president Klement Gottwald, died in Prague after a prolonged visit to Moscow, of a heart attack during a stroll in the park: his body was never seen by anyone, not even his widow. Just a sealed coffin in the crematorium. The commander of the

Czechoslovak armored forces put a bullet through his head. The Communist reform movement was quickly assuming the characteristics of a cheap thriller.

And people literally got drunk on freedom. Political prisoners organized themselves into a vociferous Club. Non-Communists started the KAN, a club of non-Party activists. Those window-dressing parties listed in the *Encyclopaedia Britannica* as proofs of pluralism in Communist Czechoslovakia made efforts to come to real life. Father Plojhar, the quisling priest (and worthy ancestor of Nicaragua's pro-Sandinista divines) who for twenty years had been chairman of the Catholic People's Party, had to resign in disgrace.

By then, completely flabbergasted by the incredible *commedia,* I saw with absolute certainty how this experiment would end. I just thought it would be with a bang, not with a whimper. Like the *Zauberlehrling* in Goethe's poem, the reformists had brought to life the dangerous spirit of democracy, and now they were unable to get rid of its logical consequences. For too long they had been used to shouting meaningless slogans, which no one had ever taken seriously. But this time people did take their words seriously, and so did the Soviet Union.

For a brief time after the armored ambush the public supported the Party leadership as their acknowledged leaders; perhaps even loved some, above all the kindly, innocent-looking, and so obviously suffering Mr. Dubček. Emotions naturally swelled under the impact of Soviet violence, cruelty, cynicism, primitivism, and murder. The fact that close to one hundred people died in Prague alone during street fighting (including, allegedly, the black actor from my film *End of a Priest*) is often overlooked; Czech resistance was not entirely passive. A general strike saved Dubček's life. Instead of treating him like Imre Nagy, the Kremlin masters returned him to office—to office, mind you, not to power. Then, with the help of a Fifth Column, an anti-Semitic pressure group of old Stalinist stormtroopers called the Jodas Men (*Jodasovci),* and also of the surviving Stalinists in Dubček's Central Committee, and of the opportunists on all levels of the Party apparatus led by Dr. Gustáv Husák, the Soviets began to undermine the reformists' position. The popular emotions reached their peak after the self-immolation of Jan Palach, a non-Communist Charles University student,* and then, in true Czech style, after two consecutive victories of the Czechoslovak ice hockey team over the Soviet *kommanda* during the 1969 World Championships. Crowds shouting ultra anti-Soviet slogans filled Wenceslas Square, drivers honked their horns. A victorious pandemonium: the joy of a small nation over the justice of games, where an ant-sized David can beat a brontosaurus of a Goliath. Then somebody smashed the shop-windows of the Soviet airline Aeroflot.

The Soviet commander responded with an ultimatum: either the Dubček government prove to be in control, or he will move his forces stationed twenty miles east of Prague to the capital. Proof was provided by the ever-ready Dr. Husák, who replaced Dubček as Party chairman. Dubček resigned, lingered on

---

*One detail about this pathetic youngster was rarely mentioned even when Palach himself still was: he spent the first part of the summer of 1968, before the Soviets stepped in, in a student camp in the USSR where he apparently ran into trouble with the camp's authorities when he tried to organize a protest against the mismanagement of the place. The second part of the same summer he worked for a private farmer in France. No trouble there.

as the chairman of the National Assembly, a powerless club of yes men, then as ambassador to Turkey, then as a clerk in a forestry office in Bratislava, eventually as old-age pensioner. His supporters from among the shocked emigrated or submerged. Some ended up in jail, others as professors at American universities.

The people, disgusted, frustrated, oppressed more than ever before, came mostly to the conclusion that the entire Prague Spring was just another case of one set of Commie rascals fighting another set, and since non-Communists will never again have a say in anything, anyone in his right mind should not concern himself with these gang-wars, but instead give all his energies to the building of private retreats of well-furnished apartments, well-stocked wine cellars, and well-chosen country cottages. Eventually—quite soon, in fact—only a tiny group, which in time proclaimed the Charter 77 document, was still willing to combat the plague, not just abuse it over a glass of beer. The group had the sympathies of most people; some even sent anonymous donations. But most also regarded its members as dare-devil idealists; yes, even as characters who are not quite right in the head. In a perverted way, Soviet psychiatry is accurate: civil disobedience in the Soviet empire is indeed a symptom of mental abnormality.

But there is a hitch here; a subtle demagogic trick; a shift in meaning. The demands of the dissidents are perfectly legal: respect for the Constitution which guarantees personal liberty and all the human rights specified in the UN Charter and reaffirmed by the Helsinki Agreement which was signed by the Czechoslovak government. But to make such demands in a Soviet colony exposes the demander and his family to untold miseries, to the dangers of socialist prisons, even of death. So whereas the dissidents ask for things that, in terms of the Constitution and of valid laws, must be considered *legally* normal, the *act* of demanding them is *psychologically* abnormal. It is in conflict with the instinct for self-preservation. Soviet psychiatrists, naturally, never ask the interesting question: namely, what, indeed, makes such actions abnormal? Bertolt Brecht knew the answer when, in *Galileo Galilei,* he has one character exclaim: "Unhappy is the country that needs heroes!" And he was being hypocritical when he got mad at Orson Welles for telling him the play was anti-Stalinist.

Of course, every citizen of Czechoslovakia is aware of the answer, too. He knows that he owes his relative safety and relative prosperity to his civil obedience. Which, in the context of all totalitarian dictatorships, translates as cowardice.

Few people who feel like cowards will relish the power that makes them feel that way. Judging by the manuscript novels smuggled to me from Prague, the vast and truly silent majority is now past even hating Communism. I am not speaking about the works of known dissidents, but of authors who are university students, members in good standing of the Communist youth, "progressive non-party citizens": in short not the third- but the second-class citizens. On the outside, these "conformists," the "grey zone" of real-socialist society, have become "normalized," as the Party lingo has it; that is, they have conformed to the post-1968 political climate. They express their thoughts and feelings only in intimate circles of the most trusted friends, otherwise they follow the nauseating rituals of "socialist progressivity."

But occasionally the accumulated frustration spills over into the clandestinely penned pages, delivered then by courageous emissaries to distant Canada. The feelings about Communism captured there are much more critical—to use a polite word—than those one can find in books by such dissidents as those represented in *The Writing on the Wall.* The dissidents (they themselves don't like this label, since it's not they but rather the government that dissents from the Constitution) either continue to consider themselves democratic socialists, or, understandably, are somewhat inhibited by the fact that they are not and cannot be—their literary styles are easily recognizable—anonymous. Out of frustration and disgust, some have become apolitical. But the non-normalized voices of the "normalized" are anonymous, and they therefore speak without solicitude, without the hard-to-overcome consideration for one's political past (they have none), and without illusions. They are *jenseits von Kommunismus und Kapitalismus.* They don't even *hate* Marxism-Leninism. All they feel for it is boundless contempt.

A Refined Irving Howe

(1983)

ARNOLD BEICHMAN

You don't have to be a sadist to enjoy Irving Howe's "autobiography" but it helps. Not being (I think) sadistic, I can't say that reading Howe, the memoirist, was a particularly pleasant experience, as pleasant, say, as reading his literary celebrations. The book reveals a New York intellectual, now in his early sixties, wriggling, twisting, ducking and dodging any possible accusation that, because he is critical of Communism, he might be mistaken for a—CONSERVATIVE; that somebody out there on the Left might accuse him of being a secret believer in democratic capitalism rather than "socialism." (The reason for the inverted commas is that since Howe says he is no longer a Marxist, the "socialism" in which he still believes is little more than a sympathy for justice, brotherhood, peace, and other laudable virtues.)

For example, he praises the *Federalist Papers* because their stress "on the need for countervailing powers in a democratic society represented an important truth"—but ever fearful of the accusation of being a you-know-what, Howe quickly adds that this important truth was "not rendered any less so by Madison's conservative opinions."

For heaven's sakes—Madison, an ally of Thomas Jefferson against Hamilton! It's 1787, just after Madison and his compatriots have won a revolution against colonialism, have invented a style and form of government without precedent in history; when they have created, in Seymour Martin Lipset's phrase, the first new nation; Madison, a towering intellectual force in the building of America, the product of Locke and James Harrington—and Howe feels duty-bound to impose his view of conservatism, via Charles A. Beard's fictions, no doubt, on James Madison, turning him into a sort of eighteenth-century American Lord North. Really!

Howe describes the late Dwight Macdonald's long defunct magazine, *Politics,* as "a stopping place for independent leftists who were bored with Marxist sects yet refused Cold War conservatism." Was there no Cold War liberalism? Were Americans for Democratic Action being Cold War conservatives when they supported the Truman Doctrine against the USSR? Was Arthur Schlesinger, Jr. a Cold War conservative when he wrote powerful articles against Soviet foreign policy? And as for Macdonald himself, anyone who saw him operating as I did as an opponent of the Stalinist "Waldorf" peace conference in 1949 would quite properly call Macdonald a Cold War something. Macdonald eventually lapsed from this state of grace but not before serving a tour of duty as an editorial associate of *Encounter* magazine.

And then there is the sly Lionel Trilling, a man who exhibited "subtly conservative moods" and whose "critique provided a rationale for an increasingly relaxed and conservatized liberalism"; Trilling the conspirator who "embarked on an oblique campaign to transform the dominant liberalism into something more quizzical and less combative than it had previously been." Trilling's work "had come to serve as a high-toned justification for the increasingly accommodating moods of American intellectuals." Accommodating to what—to the essential anti-Communism and anti-Stalinism of the postwar world, the Taft-Hartley Law, the Marshall Plan, midcult? As for Richard Hofstadter, the peerless American historian, he had, for Howe, "veered too far toward a conservative brand of liberalism." Everybody is marching to the wrong drummer except Howe, onetime Trotskyite, Marxist, isolationist, now preaching something he calls "radical humanism," a "maybe" Socialist. Isn't it possible that Hofstadter and Trilling were right then and, in the light of contemporary history, are still right?

There is worse yet. Howe wants his anti-Communism to be aesthetically uplifting. So we have the silly business that in the 1950s "among once-radical intellectuals there now prevailed a coarse version of anti-Communism often ready to justify whatever the United States might do." (I wonder whether he would have called George Orwell's pro-U.S. anti-Communism "coarse.") And there are "Jewish trade unionists, 'old Socialists' as they still like to call themselves, worthy people who have done worthy things but are now locked into a single passion: a coarse [sic], monolithic anti-Communism."

These old Socialists, writes Howe, "keep talking about 'the Commies' and something about that phrase strikes me as marking a collapse of standards, a vulgarity of mind that will soon prompt some of them into alliances with the Far Right." And I suppose, in keeping with Howe's aesthetic sensitivities, we should never have referred to them as "the Nazis" but rather as National Socialists to avoid vulgarity of mind and collapse of standards.

The aesthetics problem for Howe knows no end. Early in his book, he writes that "there is something unattractive about a right-wing Social Democrat who has found his bureaucratic niche and makes a safe politics out of anti-Communism . . ." But just when you think he's going to fall into the morass of anti-anti-Communism, Howe makes a quick leap into the safety net by adding, ". . . correct as that anti-Communism may be."

Supposing, then, that the right-wing Social Democrat hasn't found his "bureaucratic niche" and still makes "a safe politics out of anti-Communism," is he still unattractive? And what kind of "bureaucratic niche" is Howe talking about—something like that of the late David Dubinsky who certainly made a "politics" out of anti-Communism, or George Meany? The "right-wing Social Democrat," says Howe, is to be reprobated because "he has lost that larger sympathy for the oppressed, that responsiveness to new modes of rebellion that a Socialist ought to have." Such prose from a man who can write clearly and even brilliantly when he wants to is simply unacceptable. What "new modes of rebellion" is Howe talking about? Castroism? Baader-Meinhof? Or is the phrase nothing more than Howe's trying, at his tiresome worst, to show where he really stands: no conservative he.

It is particularly distasteful to watch Howe engaging, to use his language, in "a masquerade of innocence" and even "posturings of rectitude" about his own past while seriously maligning the record of Sidney Hook, one of the bravest of American intellectuals in our century.

Howe tells us that in 1941 he became editor (actually managing editor on the masthead) of a Trotskyite journal, *Labor Action,* at the tender age of 21. Now the Trotskyites whether of the Cannon or the later Schachtman sect, were Leninists, just like their opponents, the official Stalinist Communists. As Leninists, they believed in the same ghastly ideology and tactics as the Stalinists, except that their prophet was Leon Trotsky, not Stalin. But like the Stalinists, they vilified Socialists and Social Democrats alike as betrayers of the so-called revolutionary working class.

Howe writes that his "main intellectual journey, difficult enough, consisted of a break from an earlier, orthodox, anti-Stalinist Marxism." Such a break, however, was meaningless unless it subsumed opposition to an anti-Leninist Marxism as well. After all, it was just as totalitarian to be a Leninist Marxist, which is what Trotskyism was all about, as to be a Stalinist Marxist. As a Communist schismatic, Howe and his Schachtmanite brigadiers had to prove to their erstwhile allies, the Cannonites, that they were Leninists as true, pure, and orthodox as those from whom they had split.

Little of this is mentioned by Howe, who tosses off a euphemistic phrase that his faction "moved to what Marxists called a position of 'critical support' of the [Second World] war, though we didn't make this explicit."

Nothing could be further from the truth than to say that Howe's faction gave even "critical support" of the American effort in World War II, let alone made that support explicit. I have examined some of the copies of *Labor Action* from the period that Howe was managing editor. A week before Pearl Harbor, the Trotskyite weekly published its "Program Against the War." The Socialist Workers Party, it said, was "against both imperialist camps," meaning isolated Britain and Nazi Germany. It was "for the Third Camp of World Labor and the colonial peoples."* "Not a man, not a cent for Wall Street's War," the paper trumpeted. Jay Lovestone, expelled secretary of the Communist Party, USA, who was supporting the war, was described caustically as "a pure and simple war mongering bourgeois liberal." In an article dated December 8, 1941, the editors referred to "a war fought solely and completely for profits."

Most shocking was the post-Pearl Harbor issue which Howe edited. "All the solemn assurances that peace would be preserved," read the front-page

---

*Forty years later, Howe was still peddling the "Third Camp" idea, this time for Vietnam. In an article, jointly authored with Michael Walzer (*New Republic,* August 18, 1979), he defended his neutralist position by saying that "Some of us . . . hoped for the emergence of a Vietnamese 'third force' capable of rallying the people in a progressive direction by enacting land reforms and defending civil liberties." As in 1941, so in 1979—the Great Copout, even though you know that "a victory for a Communist or a Communist-dominated movement [in Vietnam] means another totalitarian dictatorship suppressing human freedom." (Howe's letter, *New York Review of Books,* December 28, 1965.)

manifesto, "all the pledges that the United States would not enter the war have been flouted and discarded by the very statesmen who made them. . . . This noble hatred of tyranny has been cunningly exploited by the imperialist statesmen of the so-called democracies for the purpose of whipping up a pro-war sentiment among the masses of the people."

Since Howe now writes that his Trotskyite sect gave "critical support" to the war, let me remind him of just what the paper he edited wrote in its issue of December 15, 1941: The Socialist Workers Party, "as the uncompromising foe of capitalism and capitalist war, cannot and does not give any political support to the government and the war . . . this is not a war for national defense; it is a war of imperialist rivalry." And such language was not temporary nor were the ideas behind the rhetoric. In 1942, there were stories headlined "The bitter struggle for Singapore/Involves Vast Imperialist Stakes"; an editorial sloganeered, "Make the rich pay for their war." In March 1942, for example, Howe's paper still described the war as "a struggle for world mastery between two imperialist camps" and still claimed to be upholding "the banner of Lenin and Trotsky."

Under Howe's own name there appeared a story May 4, 1942 with the page-one headline "Exposing the Merchants of Death/Their Profits Born in Blood" and a paragraph that "this is the picture of the capitalist world gone mad—profits, profits above all. Everything else is just so much hogwash designed to trick the unwary into surrendering their lives for these profits."

This is " 'critical support' of the war, though we didn't make this explicit"? For shame. Now look at what he writes about Sidney Hook.

Howe says that Hook, "once a leading Marxist," saw "merit" in the "infamous Smith Act." While Hook, according to Howe, was not for the passage of the law, Hook "had doubts about the wisdom of repealing it." This statement is palpably unfair. Hook opposed the Smith Act and especially its use by the Roosevelt Administration against the Trotskyites. Recognizing the Smith Act's dangers to civil liberties, Hook proposed amending the law to prevent possible abuses in its application. The amendments would have made the act congruent with the "clear and present danger" criterion imposed by Supreme Court Justices Holmes and Brandeis. If Howe has any doubts about Hook's position, I recommend he read Hook's book, *Heresy Yes, Conspiracy No* (1952), Chapter 5.

Howe also accuses Hook of taking a blanket position against the employment of professed Communists as teachers through the device of "declaring categorical bans." In actual fact, Hook was criticized in a *New Leader* article by Arthur Lovejoy, the eminent co-founder of the American Association of University Professors for *not* urging a categorical ban on Communist teachers. In his recent book, *A Better World,* Professor William L. O'Neill says that Howe, among others, was "imputing views to [Hook] that he did not hold."

What then can we say about Howe? He has made serious misstatements of Sidney Hook's politico-cultural positions and unjust criticisms of Hofstadter and Trilling among others. He has glossed over (to put it mildly) his own political past. Are these the casual judgments of a memoirist trying to compose grand, sweeping intellectual, rather than factually exact, history? Or is the pattern of this autobiography, with its emphasis on "socialism" and its omnipresent mistrust of "conservatism" and "anti-Communism," a pattern which reflects a writer's desire somehow to make peace with his past and present without jeopardizing his intellectual future? Is it the strategy of the Great Copout?

"To quit a movement," says Howe, "in which one has invested one's strongest feelings can be terribly painful—at least as painful as leaving home or starting a divorce." It is especially difficult to quit when one is editing a magazine like *Dissent* which seeks miracles—a new radicalism, a new humanism, a new ethic, a new socialism, a new social change, a New Everything based on a New Utopia—and when all around you are to be found ghastly Communist or socialist dictatorships, whether in Africa or Asia, the Caribbean or Eastern Europe, and nothing—but nothing—brings certainty, let alone hope, for tomorrow.

It is really time—and it's late in the day—for Howe to realize that the enemy is not Sidney Hook, or Irving Kristol,† and to stop pretending that there is such a thing as benevolent Trotskyism; or that by a process of self-mystification one can create out of nothing a Third Force, a Third Camp and thereby avoid having to make nasty political choices.

The enemy is neither the White House nor democratic capitalism. The enemy is the head of the Soviet secret police who, in changing jobs, has taken over half a world and brought George Orwell's frightening prophecies into a reality earlier than had been expected.

In short, it is time for Irving Howe to dissent from *Dissent* and to seek his fulfillment, not in rewriting history or dreaming up new strategies for old politico-cultural frauds, but to free himself from a faith which, in his "intellectual autobiography," has driven him to forget his chosen vocation as scholar.

---

†Howe writes about ". . . the conservative ideologue Irving Kristol, whom I confess to having recruited to the City College Trotskyite youth group in 1938 . . ." but forgets to mention that he was instrumental in expelling Kristol from this same group because Kristol pressed for a reading list which would go beyond Marxist-Leninist propaganda tracts.

Traveling the Afghan Archipelago

(1984)

MATTHEW STEVENSON

Pakistan's capital, Islamabad, is a patch of tranquillity on the Asian mainland. Twelve miles from Rawalpindi, the fading British way station between Kabul and Delhi, it appears at the end of a four-lane parkway, rather the way Washington, D.C., surfaces on the ride in from Dulles International Airport. Islamabad is a new city in the fashion of Brasilia and Canberra, capitals that have sprung fully formed from an architect's drafting table. Before, it was a town, at best, surrounded by cool mountains and an expansive prairie. Now it is Islam's first suburb, a grid of neatly laid-out bureaucracies and vacant lots reminiscent of an industrial park near Houston. So few people actually live there that one can't help wondering if, when the American embassy was sacked in 1979, the demonstrators were bused in for the performance.

Wanting to find out more about the refugees from the war in Afghanistan, I arrived in Islamabad shortly before midnight on a cool evening late last summer. The train from Lahore goes only as far as Rawalpindi; a taxi brought me the rest of the way. The choice of hotels—between the Islamabad Hotel and the Holiday Inn—seemed a tidy symbol of modern-day Pakistan's dichotomies. I chose the Islamabad, as it was nearer the ministry of public affairs, and the following day went next door to a small cluster of shops where, over a drug store, I found the department that handles press credentials for anyone wanting to visit the refugees.

The office was a replica of so many on the subcontinent. Officials in traditional Pakistani cotton suits sat behind tired wooden desks. Paper the consistency of newsprint was stacked everywhere. Only the strategic use of paperweights kept it from scattering in the jetstream created by the ceiling fans. True to form, I was greeted warmly and served lukewarm tea with milk. After an hour of polite conversation—interrupted by numerous phone calls and document signings—it was arranged for me to visit some of the refugee camps in Peshawar, the provincial capital of the Northwest Frontier Province.

First, however, I was scheduled to meet General Said Azhar, the high commissioner for Afghan refugees, whose office in Islamabad is literally on the edge of town. General Azhar, a sturdy man in his late fifties, welcomed me in what had been the living room in a ranch-style house. On the walls, in military fashion, were a number of maps, all seemingly charting Pakistan's proximity to danger. Several showed the region: Iran and Afghanistan to the west; the Soviet Union and China to the north; India to the east. Another showed the archipelago of the nearly 350 refugee camps along the border with Afghanistan, yet another volcanic chain of islands forced to the surface by Soviet cruelty.

The general summarized the refugee situation for me. In 1973, after Sardar Daoud overthrew the monarchy of Mohammed Zahir Shah, a few hundred opponents of the new Afghan regime trickled across the border into Pakistan. But the flow was insignificant until April 1978, when Muhammad Taraki staged a successful coup. The Daoud family was eliminated and in the general upheaval more than 100,000 refugees fled Afghanistan. That September Taraki himself was swept away in yet another coup and replaced by his prime minister, Hafizullah Amin. Again the refugees took to the mountainous trails that lead into Pakistan. At the same time violent opposition to the Moscow-supported Amin threatened to topple his frail government. It was at this point, in December 1979, that the Soviet Union intervened, anxious to protect a potential client and buffer state. In the turmoil, Amin died mysteriously, and Babrak Karmal, then Afghanistan's ambassador to Czechoslovakia, was brought in to run a puppet government. The resistance now began in earnest; so did the flight of the Afghans.

Since the Russian invasion, more than three million Afghans have actually registered in Pakistan as refugees. Who knows how many more have crossed the border and ignored the bureaucracy? Many Afghans are nomadic by tradition, and persist in their habit of migrating in summer from the mountains to the valleys, and back again in winter, despite the fighting. Now, however, Pakistan is a long stop on these wanderings, a safe harbor from the war. In the spring of 1980 the number of refugee immigrants reached a high point of 130,000 a month. At the beginning, General Ahzar's agencies and colleagues provided emergency shelter, food, and clothing. Tents were supplied wherever the Afghans camped, producing the network of tent villages that is now, more or less, a permanent home for these uprooted Afghans. The state within a state stretches from the red deserts of Baluchistan in the south to an area in the mountains near the ancient kingdom of Swat.

In 1983 the cost of maintaining the refugees came to $441 million, or about $12 for each refugee. Pakistan paid just under half of this, no mere gesture for a country as poor as any in the Third World. The United States committed itself to donating $8 million, 170,000 blankets, used clothing, and 240 International Harvester trucks. Other nations gave tea, medical supplies, food, tents, and other relief supplies. But considering that the Afghan dislocation constitutes the greatest population dispersal in the world since 1947, such assistance barely meets the needs of most refugees. When each Afghan registers as a refugee in Pakistan, he is entitled to cash, food, and other assistance totaling 150 rupees a month—not much, with the Pakistan rupee worth about nine American cents. Worse, for all concerned, is that the longer the war continues, the more the status of the refugees appears to be permanent.

Said Azhar has visited all the 350 or so encampments under his jurisdiction. He made arrangements for me to see several near Peshawar the following day and then dropped me off at my hotel on his way home. On the way, we passed the ribbed-iron and marble skeleton of the unfinished parliament. If Islamabad is a model city, this will be the model capitol; and if function follows form, Pakistan will soon resemble Gladstone's England.

The next day began in the rain. I met my driver, Omar, in the hotel lobby at six A.M., and we set off through a cloudburst for Peshawar, seventy-five miles to the west. The road was mostly two lanes, with an occasional aspiration to expressway status. The trucks and buses on the highway looked like advertisements for Islam. Each was decorated with colorful stencils and chrome embroidery, giving their front ends the silhouette of a mosque. Some of the stenciling showed landscapes. One, I noticed, was the vivid detail of an armored vehicle shooting down a Russian plane. Others had portraits of departed war heroes. It made the journey to the frontier a festive occasion.

At first impression, Peshawar seems to have been built for the purpose of buying and selling guns. Signs advertising "Guns" and "Ammo" are everywhere, making the place look like one's idea of Cheyenne during the era of the six-shooter. But this is indeed a frontier city—be it that of internal Pakistani squabbling or the Cold War.

Peshawar's importance lies in its location. Kabul, the capital of Afghanistan, is through the Khyber Pass to the west, and, until the war started, a narrow-gauge train took passengers as far as the mountain town of Landi Kotal near the border. Peshawar is also the strategic intersection between Islamabad and the sometimes rebellious province of Baluchistan. And from Peshawar one can take the only road north to Chitral, the northwest corner of Pakistan, close not only to Afghanistan but also to the Soviet Union, China, and India. Little wonder that the military government in Islamabad has kept its defense establishment in Peshawar. In any conflict larger than the present one in Afghanistan it would take on the significance of El Alamein.

While I was there, I heard someone refer to Peshawar as "a page from *Homage to Catalonia*," an allusion to the factionally divided Barcelona that George Orwell described in his memoir of the Spanish Civil War. Peshawar is indeed headquarters for the principal factions of the resistance in Afghanistan, though in the beginning, despite their common cause, these groups barely spoke. Now they have coalesced into two tenuous wartime alliances, "the group of seven" and "the group of three." Still, the struggle among the groups is almost as fanatical as the struggle with the Soviets.

Long before it became the shadow capital of free Afghanistan, Peshawar was notorious for sheltering undergrounds. In the days of the British empire it was a favorite of intelligence agents slipping in and out of Afghanistan, which the empire never managed to subdue in the course of three wars. And though the names of the clandestine rivals have changed, the city still feels one part Kipling and one part Le Carré. The Soviet mission in Peshawar has lately taken to verifying Russian casualties in Afghanistan by buying back the dogtags that have been stripped from killed Russian soldiers and returned to the city as booty.

Nevertheless, the principal commodity traded between Russian intelligence and the divided Afghans is disinformation. It is in the Soviets' interests to keep the resistance divided—fratricidal, if possible. And it's easy to feed the bad blood with rumors and an occasional killing. Nor could there be a better cover for both sides than a city of bazaars and narrow, cobbled streets through which intrigue passes as quietly as small boys with bare feet.

At Dabgri Building, yet another dim municipal office with paper-strewn desks and languid ceiling fans, I met Mr. Affridi, the local press attaché. He was about forty and, although not in uniform, looked like a major on assignment. He introduced Mr. Nawaz, who was to accompany me to the camps, and then talked about the negotiations on Afghanistan in Geneva.

"You know," he said, "there is a proverb that says the Russians never withdraw."

A number of proposals have been put forward in Geneva to end the fighting in Afghanistan. One suggestion even has the exiled king returning to Afghanistan from Rome. But what prevents any kind of settlement being reached is that neither the resistance nor the Soviet Union has any incentive to end the fighting. The Afghans may be fragmented, but they are at least agreed on fighting until the Russians leave—even if that isn't for another hundred years. The way the Russians see it, withdrawal would result in the overthrow of Babrak Karma's government and perhaps the establishment of a fundamentalist Islamic regime hostile to Moscow. As Mr. Affridi remarked, "The only thing that would change their mind on this would be heavy losses, heavier than those they are now suffering." But casualties on both sides are difficult to estimate. The resistance is reported to have suffered 100,000 casualties. The Soviets may have lost 10,000 to 15,000 men killed, but neither side is especially concerned with body counts; nor, I might add, with taking prisoners.

Before I could actually visit the camps, I needed yet another signature on my papers—this one from the district commissioner for Afghan refugees. The otherwise nondescript two-story building that housed his office was distinguished by a milling crowd of Afghan men near the front door and in the lobby. They wore pajama-like cotton suits and full beards and were remarkable for the intensity of their expressions, with eyes that seemed eternally fixed on distant enemy encampments. These were *mujahidin,* or holy warriors, on leave from the fighting, and they appeared uncomfortable away from the front lines, without their guns.

Waiting in the district commissioner's office, I leafed through the *Jihad Days,* an English-language magazine of the resistance produced on faded newsprint. It contained profiles of soldiers killed fighting the Russians. One, Dr. Man Nasrat, was described as having "girded up his loins as soon as the Red coup of communists gained victory." In a desperate last stand, according to the magazine, he killed thirty-five Russians before "the soul of this heroic man and of this brilliant beacon went loft high to the creator of the world . . ." There was another article entitled "A liberation gained through muskets and axes," a fairly accurate summary of both the weaponry of the resistance and its determination.

Nasir Bagh, which means "green garden," is the first piece of flatland down from the hills of the Khyber Pass. The encampment's eastern boundary is an irrigation canal, edged by graceful hanging trees—no doubt the first water found by refugees filing out of the mountains; the rest of the settlement spreads out over an arid, almost lunar landscape whose hardpacked sandy soil is divided by culverts from the storms that sweep the plain. The drab olive-green military tents recall the fate of refugees all over the world, except that this lot seems even more tenuous than most.

It is misleading to call the "refugee tent villages"—their bureaucratic description—camps. No barbed wire or guards surround the Afghans, who are free to come and go as they please. It's easier to think of them as entire villages that have migrated across the border. Tribal discipline and rituals have remained intact.

Mr. Nawaz and I were greeted by an elderly Afghan. He was over six feet tall, with a stringy white beard and the long, precise gait of someone who has spent a lifetime climbing through mountain passes. Now he is a village elder, looking after the women and children while the men are away fighting the Russians.

Walking through the encampment was like touring an adobe village in the American southwest. As a supplement to the original emergency-supply tents, which keep one neither warm in winter nor cool in summer, the Afghans have put up their traditional houses from blocks of dried mud.

Children followed us everywhere. First they would peek from behind a mud wall; then, with urging from our guide, join the tour. Not one begged for food or money, even though it was clear they could use both. All posed solemnly for the camera whenever asked.

Amid the monotony of mundane routine—school for the children, hauling water for the women—life in the refugee villages is reduced to a never-ending series of expectations: waiting for the Russians to leave; waiting for the men to return from the fighting; waiting for the supplies of food to arrive.

As I left Nasir Bagh along the absurdly stately irrigation road, the villages seemed transplants not just from Afghanistan, but from the Middle Ages. Only the few jeeps of the relief agencies interfered with a landscape that would have been familiar to anyone living 500 years ago. Since then foreign invaders have come and gone with the regularity of supernatural tides, but the Afghans have always held on, somehow.

That afternoon, I found Louis Dupree, the author of several books about Afghanistan, and his wife eating lunch and packing for departure to the U.S. in their room at Dean's Hotel.

Dupree is a short, vigorous man in his late fifties. During the Second World War he jumped into the Philippines with an American airborne division. He got a doctorate at Harvard and has taught and lived in Afghanistan whenever possible ever since. Just before the last coup and the Russian invasion he was jailed for a week in Kabul as an "undesirable" and then deported. He is now in Pakistan working on a book about the Afghan refugees. Needless to say, Dupree is no supporter of the Karmal government; nor, for that matter, of U.S. indifference to the Afghan cause.

He described the fighting in Afghanistan as a cross between the Spanish Civil War and the resistance against the Nazis in Yugoslavia. "The one difference here," he said, "is that the Western world hasn't been drawn to the cause of the Afghans as it was to the Republicans in Spain. The tactics the Russians are using are worse than anything used by Franco, only nobody seems to care."

One problem is how to supply guns to a badly divided resistance, whose armies tend to be tribal and rarely larger than 4,000 men. In any event, of the estimated 100,000 *mujahidin,* only about 30,000 have rifles. For the rest, it's the way *Jihad Days* described it: a holy war fought with muskets and axes.

Russian broadcasts would have it believed that the West, especially the United States, is funneling substantial arms to the resistance. But Jere Van Dyk, the author of *In Afghanistan: An American Odyssey,* described the military assistance as "rifles and sleeping bags." Before he was assassinated, President Anwar Sadat said that the United States was purchasing some of Egypt's surplus of Russian arms for shipment to the Afghans. Yet the reluctance of the West is in supplying the *mujahidin* with the weaponry—notably heat-seeking "Red-eye" missiles—that will knock out Soviet helicopters. The problem, Louis Dupree said with exasperation, is one of accountability. "No one wants to be responsible for aiding the Afghans and killing Russians, however indirectly. It's fine to go all out in Latin America. But the Russian army is here. And the Afghans feel bitter. They think, and rightly so, that they are fighting the West's fight against communism and the Soviets. But then they don't see any help."

Those neighboring countries that also live in the Soviet Union's shadow are no less afraid of antagonizing the Russians. Pakistan has been careful not to appear as a participant in the struggle. Aiding the refugees is all very well, but the regime of President Zia ul-Haq fears that the war would spread if Pakistan openly supported the Afghan cause. China is reluctant to help the resistance for the same reason.

"What I would like to see," Dupree told me, "is the U.S. and other Western governments guaranteeing the territorial integrity of Pakistan. Not the regime, but the country. Since the end of World War II, we've been backing regimes, not countries. This would be different. Announce that you will defend Pakistan. That would free up a lot of aid for the resistance. Tell them that a Russian footprint in Pakistan is the same as a Russian footprint in Washington, D.C. We should be one of the policemen of the world; not the only policeman. That's when we get into trouble."

So far, however, the extent of the American commitment to the Afghans has been to use their suffering to score moralistic points against the Soviets. President Carter canceled American participation in the Moscow Olympic games after the Russian invasion, but didn't do much else. This summer both Secretary of State Shultz and Defense Secretary Weinberger—on separate occasions—flew by helicopter to the Khyber Pass to address the *mujahidin.* Secretary Shultz told them: "Fellow fighters of freedom, we are with you." Secretary Weinberger said: "I want you to know that you are not alone." Each then flew off to other appointments, leaving the Afghans still facing the Soviets with their muskets and axes.

There is yet another reaction to the resistance in Afghanistan, one that sees it as "a self-sustaining revolt," which means: As long as the Afghans, with nineteenth-century guns and a few bombs, can keep bleeding the Soviet army white in mountainous combat, why should the West do anything to disturb things? Louis Dupree stands in the doorway to his room at Dean's and says, rapidly: "I find that notion obscene."

Late that afternoon, before leaving Peshawar, I went to a house on the outskirts, hoping to find Abdul Haq, one of the leaders in the resistance. The guards near the front door of the two-story house said he was in, and the one with a machine gun slung across his chest showed me to a small office toward the back. Inside was a couch, a few chairs, and an empty desk. A few minutes later in came Abdul Haq, a bearded man in his late twenties. He looked remarkably like Fidel Castro but had none of the Cuban's stridency. Haq spoke English effortlessly and said he had been in Peshawar for two weeks. He was here to visit his wife and family. Soon he would be going back to the fighting where he commanded 4,000 men in the Kabul region. In the war's most crucial theater, he led possibly the largest single body of Afghan troops.

He grew up in Nangarhar, a province along the border with Pakistan. His father worked as a civil servant; his mother raised the family of eight children. One of the influences in his upbringing was clearly the code of *Pushtunwali,* the ethos of a major tribe in eastern and southern Afghanistan, which serves as a guide for all Afghans. According to *The Struggle for Afghanistan,* an excellent book about the war by Richard and Nancy Newell: "It is simple but demanding. Group survival is its primary imperative. It demands vengeance against injury or insult to one's kin, chivalry and hospitality toward the helpless and unarmed strangers, bravery in battle, and openness and integrity in individual behavior." In accordance with this, the Haq family has divided the responsibility for the struggle. Several brothers are working abroad—in Saudi Arabia and West Germany—to earn money. Several other siblings live in the camps, taking care of the elderly and the children. The rest, led by Abdul, are fighting the Russians.

As a commander in the Kabul sector, he organizes everything from guerrilla raids to major offensives—or at least what can be mounted with the weaponry available.

"In the beginning," he said, "we were using the tactics that had defeated the British in the last century. Now we are learning, changing. We have no teachers. We learn from experience." The warrior-poet is one of the ideals of Afghan society. Louis Dupree told me that a lot of poetry was coming out of Afghanistan these days—much of it dreary—and that, like it or not, many men were happy to be back in the traditional role of fighting an oppressor. Abdul Haq struck me neither as a warrior nor as a poet. He was fighting because his country had been overrun. What choice did he have? He spoke of his experience in combat, but expressed none of the awe of the Soviet army currently in vogue in the West. Russian soldiers, he explained, are "very stupid."

He went on to say: "They have two kinds of soldiers. One, the draftees, who don't want to be in Afghanistan. They're scared of everything. Second, the regular army. They have all the latest equipment. Tanks. Helicopters. Everything. But they can't do anything for themselves. We know the land: every stream, every hill. They know nothing. When we attack, they have to wait for orders as to what to do next. But then we are gone." He described how the Russians would march arrogantly into a battle behind all the latest machinery, but would be left vulnerable as soon as they were in hand-to-hand fighting.

"Without their officers, the soldiers are lost," he said. "The Russian army is trained to fight against governments. They are trained for tank battles in the desert. But they are no good against the *mujahidin.* This is our home."

Despite such brave words, the war remains a stand-off. The Russians control the cities and the major supply routes. Nearly half their troops are in or near Kabul, maintaining the Karmal government that is reportedly despised by a majority of the Afghans. In Kabul and Herat and Kandahar, the principal Afghan cities, there are few men between the ages of eighteen and forty-five to be seen on the streets. The Soviets have taken to door-to-door sweeps to bolster "enlistments" for the Afghan army, which averages about 30,000 men. The Russians might just as well be recruiting for the *mujahidin,* since there is a steady underground flow of troops out of the Afghan army to the resistance. The defectors take with them guns and ammunition, and as a consequence the Russian army is the greatest source of weaponry for the Afghan resistance.

With the support of the rural population—or what's left of it—the resistance can move freely through large portions of the country, especially in the mountains. They receive food and shelter from local residents, and try to fight the Soviets in isolated guerrilla actions. Abdul Haq likes to say: "We started on the mountaintops. Then we came down the mountain. Now we are in the valleys and the towns. Next we want Kabul."

The Soviet response has been to concentrate large amounts of firepower against villagers and encampments. Helicopters, unchallenged by ground-to-air missiles, can move Russian troops anywhere for a surprise, concentrated attack, often backed up by artillery and air support. The idea is to discourage the villagers from aiding the *mujahidin,* but the effect has only been to lengthen the historical roster of massacres.

For the Afghans the decisive battle of the war is Kabul, but the action there remains fragmented, if brutal. Abdul Haq said that office workers in the Russian-occupied capital often join the resistance on their nightly raids. But these actions are far from the divisional-size attacks that would dislodge the Russians. And as long as the Soviet government is willing to tolerate high casualties, the war will continue as a vicious stalemate.

If you ask Abdul Haq why the Soviets decided to invade his country, his answer contains none of the qualification that a similar question might prompt at a symposium in the West.

"They took Afghanistan to drive a wedge into the subcontinent. Look at a map," he says, with a trace of irritation. The map, in fact, shows Afghanistan at the crossroads of Asia, midway between India and the Middle East. Control of the country puts the Soviet Union within striking range of the Iranian oil fields and Baluchistan, which might like to be rid of both Pakistan and Iran. Afghanistan is also rich in minerals, which the Soviets are already exploiting. Their invasion, which has tapped deposits of iron, chrome, copper, and possibly uranium, can produce a balance of trade surplus—mineral profits less military costs—even if things stay exactly the way they are now.

To Abdul Haq, the war is simply a matter of geopolitics, but one of surprisingly little interest to the Western allies. Because of his flawless English, Haq is occasionally pulled from the front lines and sent to Paris or Washington to state the Afghan cause. Last year, on a trip to the United States, a cousin actually took him to Disney World: There can hardly be a greater metaphor for the gap between the resistance and the West than the image of a commander from the Kabul region taking a trip around the Magic Kingdom.

In the West, he notes, there has been some outrage at the Soviet use of poison gas against the Afghans. But the greater problem for the villagers, he says, is the cluster bombs that the Russians scatter about. These small, black fragmented objects look to the children almost like candy or little toys, and more than one child has paid with a limb or a life for his curiosity.

As we talked, the room slowly filled up with *mujahidin* until they were crowding the door. They were there to listen to and watch their leader. Who knew—maybe this would be the conversation that would secure substantial Western aid? Abdul Haq finished by talking about supplies for the refugees. Air conditioners, destined for the Afghan hospitals, were winding up in the houses of relief workers, he said. His tone was that of a man with many burdens and none of the breaks. We walked outside, and each Afghan came forward to shake my hand. It took some time. Each looked me directly in the eye; their firm expressions were those of the old men at the tent village. Abdul Haq walked me to the car. He said he was sorry that we could not talk further. Perhaps someday we would meet again? I wished him well and said goodbye. And every time I read of Afghan casualties in the newspaper, I think of the eyes that watched my car move down the narrow lane and turn onto the highway.

America's Crack-Up

(1984)

VLADIMIR BUKOVSKY

Exactly one hundred years before I was born, the great Russian writer Nikolai Gogol prophetically described Russia as a troika rushing headlong for no apparent reason or purpose, just for the joy of fast driving:

O troika, thou bird of a troika! Who was it that first thought thee up? It must have been a resourceful nation that gave thee birth in a land that brooks no nonsense, but has spread its plains, smoothly, evenly, over half of the world; and now go, count its milestones until everything is blurred before your eyes.

And no elaborate job either is this contraption of a vehicle. No iron screws hold it together. An ax and a chisel—that was all a smart Yaroslav peasant needed to make it and fit it in a jiffy. The driver wears no German top boots: he is all beard and mittens, and he sits on—the Devil alone knows what it is he sits on. But the moment he has half-risen in his seat, has swung his whip and struck up a song, off shoot the horses like a whirlwind. . . .

. . . And thou, Russia, art not thou, too, rushing headlong like the fastest troika that is not to be outdistanced? The road smokes under thee, the bridges rumble, everything falls back and is left behind. Lost in amazement at this, God's own miracle, stands the onlooker. Is this not a flash of lightning sent down from heaven? What is the meaning of this awe-inspiring onrush? What is the mysterious force that is contained in these steeds? O ye steeds, steeds—what steeds they are! Do whirlwinds dwell in your manes? Is every fibre of yours endowed with a quick, eager ear of its own? The moment you hear the familiar song above your heads, you strain your mighty chests of bronze, all as one, all at the same instant, and barely touching the earth with your hoofs, you become transformed into straight lines flying through the air, and the troika dashes along, all inspired by God. Russia, whither art thou speeding? Answer me! . . . She gives no answer. The jingle bells pour forth their wonderful peal, the air, torn to shreds, thunders and turns to wind. Everything on earth is flying past, and the other nations and states, eyeing her askance, make way for her and draw aside.

The contemporaries of Gogol were at a loss at how to interpret such a strange prophecy. The Russia of their time was a fabulously immobile country; no apparent rush was in evidence, or even hinted at. But now, a century and a half later, we have no difficulty identifying even the smallest details of the picture.

Who is so blind nowadays who cannot recognize this contraption of a vehicle called "developed socialism," put together by a smart peasant in the hurry of a five-year plan out of odd bits and pieces procured from foreign lands? The Devil alone knows how the driver manages to hold on when the horses dash along, and why the unwieldy carriage does not fall apart at the first bump.

And the steeds, those steeds . . . what steeds they are! I could write a whole poem about what these steeds think when they hear above their heads the all too familiar songs of proletarian solidarity and fraternal assistance, of eternal duty and the bright future. Their only hope is that the driver will somehow tumble down and break his neck as, all as one, they strain their mighty chests.

Still, the problem remains. No one knows where the carriage is going. She gives no answer, but continues her awe-inspiring onrush through Asia, Africa, and Central America. And the other nations and states, at their wits' end after trying everything from containment to détente, still make way for her and draw aside.

Unfortunately, I wasn't able to find in American literature of the nineteenth century anything equally prophetic and graphic to symbolize modern America. Perhaps I didn't search hard enough, but neither Mark Twain's steamboat on the Mississippi nor the great white whale of Melville could satisfy me.

But just as I was fishing for an appropriate passage in the old books, I happened to look down to the street—and there he was, our symbol in flesh and blood. Speeding recklessly along on roller skates was a middle-aged Californian (about 45 years old, I'd say, judging by his grayish beard) in defiantly red swimming trunks, mouth chewing gum and steadily making bubbles, ears plugged safely by Walkman earphones. His eyes seemed to be the only part of his body not entirely pleased with their occupation. They expressed total amazement, as if repeating that favorite American phrase: "What's going on here?" I imagine this amazement would disappear if our friend could watch TV at the same time.

As outraged as some Americans might be by this image of their country, the resemblance is too striking to deny. This great nation of pioneers and gold prospectors, this land of opportunity and tough competition has become effeminated by a few decades of peace, prosperity, and Social Security. It has become obsessed with the pursuit of pleasure, comfort, and entertainment, as if being happy were a constitutional obligation. Irrespective of their age, Americans are supposed to be "kids," and the ultimate objective of their lives is to have "fun."

The world may be going to pieces, but the best-selling books in America are about diet, health, sports, and sex. And to hell with the world, so long as "our boys" are not being killed somewhere, or not involved in anything troublesome.

Like all egocentrics, Americans feel that the world exists only in their perception and, therefore, the less they know about external troubles the less they themselves are troubled. This is not just ignorance, but a deliberately cultivated mental block. External problems appear in the minds of Americans only when their government becomes involved in them. Is it any wonder that these same problems are always looked upon as being *caused* by the American government?

Like all children, Americans are blissfully irresponsible and demanding, but at the same time very generous. Quite consistent with this attitude is the popular notion of foreign policy as some sort of charity: If everything at home is in good shape, why not go and help some poor people abroad? Nothing more sophisticated than a relief convoy or a few billion dollars—perhaps an arms sale in the extreme case of a highly sentimental issue.

In truth, the American people don't mind foreign policy so long as it doesn't require any effort or sacrifice on their part. They don't mind having the CIA so long as it doesn't do anything. They don't even mind having some sort of army—after all, other nations have armies too for some odd reason—but also on the condition that it not be used anywhere, and, above all, that no one get hurt. In short, Americans view foreign relations as something primarily ceremonial and formal—like the Queen's visit to California, or an extra holiday in Paris when the rate of exchange is very favorable for the dollar.

Not surprisingly, those who manage now and then to tear themselves away from the TV screens and earphones are divided into two unequal groups: the "liberals" and the "conservatives." I use these terms as they are used in the U.S., although I've never been able to understand them. As my friend, Russian poet Naum Korzhavin, once observed: "I am a liberal too, but I am a severe liberal."

This term "liberal" in the American context does not mean anything definite, or anything similar to traditional European liberalism. In fact, it's nothing but an extreme mental aberration best described by the Russian saying: that it is like a dog in reverse because it barks at its own folks and wags its tail in front of a stranger.

Another peculiarity of American liberals is that they never know what they want, but they want it very badly. They are always well organized, well financed, and on some campaign or other. They are a minority, but a very noisy one, and forever on the offensive, no matter what the cause.

It would definitely be a mistake to call these people "left-wingers," at least in the European sense of the word. The European left is ideological, philosophical—and one can have an intelligent argument with them. They may agree or disagree, but they are willing to change their views under the pressure of arguments and events, and they will remain friends with you despite the disagreement. In short, they have certain principles and ideas, and they formulate and develop their views according to what they have learned. For example, even the Communists in Europe now reject the so-called "Soviet model of socialism" and have no illusions about the aggressive nature of the Soviet system. Italian and Spanish Communists have even gone so far as to acknowledge the need for the NATO alliance. If nothing else, they need it to protect their own "model of socialism" from the Soviet dictate.

When watching American TV or looking through American newspapers, on the other hand, I sometimes get the feeling that American liberals haven't changed in thirty years. What else could I conclude after watching Professor Kennan show American viewers photographs of happy Soviet children, mothers, and babies as proof of peaceful Soviet intentions? I certainly hope that Americans stand in no particular need of persuasion by Mr. Kennan that the Soviet people have neither horns nor tails, but I really am surprised that American liberals have not learned to distinguish the Soviet people from the Soviet system.

At least Europeans, even those on the left, remember that the Nazis could enjoy Bach and Mozart and could also be good husbands and loving fathers and at the same time could exterminate Jews in the gas chambers. At least they, in Europe, are clever enough to listen to the stories of thousands of political refugees coming in wave after wave from the Soviet Union, Hungary, Czechoslovakia, Poland, Vietnam, Cambodia, Ethiopia . . .

Not so in America. A few months ago PBS produced a remarkable film called "Russians Are Here" which used every trick possible to distort the truth about refugees from the Soviet Union—presenting them as misfits, drunks, and, above all, as people who "regret" their decision to emigrate, who don't know what to do with the freedom America has given them, and who even "miss the KGB" (the very words used in the film by a narrator). The producers must have spent many weeks trying to locate the most bizarre characters out of some 200,000 recent emigrants; they must have spent miles of film to be able to cut the appropriate passages out of lengthy interviews; and they miraculously managed to avoid a single case of success—all of it just to prove to the American people that the "Russians" (as they persistently call the Soviet Jews recently arrived in this country) are generally happy with the regime back home, do not deserve anything better, and, therefore, should be of no real concern to the American public when news comes of more repression in the USSR. This outrageous forgery was made with public money and shown repeatedly all over the country despite vehement protests from the refugee communities. Just try to make a similar movie about Hispanics or about emigrants from, say, Chile, and the press will crucify you for instigating national hatred and for persecuting a national minority. You may even be sued in court for millions—all of it by the very same liberals.

No, your liberals will never learn. They are here to teach us about ourselves, not to learn.

What is most remarkable about liberals is that their persistently wrong judgment never affects their credibility. Regardless of what happens they remain untouchable, free of moral responsibility, a shining example to us all. Did they not assure us in the past that the Vietcong had nothing to do with the Communists—that they were just "nationalists" fighting for the independence of their motherland? For decades liberals have been shouting at the top of their voices that their critics are "too simplistic." Yet did they not assure us that the PLO was just a patriotic organization with no Soviet connections? Did they not scream that Americans were the aggressors and should withdraw from Southeast Asia without fear of the "domino effect"? Today they advise us that Central American guerrillas aren't like all the others and that there will be no "domino effect" in Central America, no new Communist strongholds and bases, no totalitarian oppression of Central American nations.

These very same people once assured us that Castro is a "true revolutionary," that Angola is not a Communist state, and that Cuban troops in Angola are just "stabilizing the situation." They assured Carter that Sandinistas are not Communists and, as such, deserve American support. They persuaded Carter that the Shah must leave Iran and that there would be no revolution. Millions have died and lost their homelands because of their relentless moralizing and bad judgment, but our liberals don't give a damn about these nations. And they are never responsible for all the rivers of blood and mountains of corpses produced by their progressive protégés around the world.

But what about the majority, the conservatives? Unfortunately, they are still a silent majority. Whereas liberals always want something very badly, traditional conservatives want nothing from this world at all, only that it remain as it is. They may grumble about the liberals' frenzied activism; they may complain to each other about liberal bias in the media. But just try to get them to organize, to get them into the streets, or even to vote for a conservative candidate on a rainy day!

For example, we all know how dangerous the so-called "nuclear freeze," "non-first-use," and other numerous peace campaigns aimed at disarming the United States could become. We also understand, I hope, that given the fabulous naiveté of our 45-year-old baby on roller skates, the peace movement requires only a modicum of financial support to make its campaign a pivotal political factor. All it needs is a well-planned rock concert to endorse any suicidal political idea. Indeed, on March 25 the *New York Times* published an article by Kathleen Teltsch entitled "Philanthropies Focus Concern on Arms Race," which spoke of the open commitment of the biggest American foundations to make "the prevention of nuclear war to be to the 80s what civil rights was to the 60s." Since these words belong to Mr. William Dietel, president of the Rockefeller Brothers Fund, one imagines that the millions designated by the Carnegie, Ford, MacArthur, George Gund, and other foundations are not going to be spent promoting the idea of a stronger defense policy. We can be warned in advance, then, that a huge effort is under way to brainwash the American public into accepting unrestrained Soviet blackmail.

And do conservatives plan to counter this effort of massive public opinion manipulation? Do they reach for their check books and try to match this gigantic liberal fund-raising, dollar for dollar? Do they mobilize activist groups across the country, in every town and on every campus? Do they plan lectures, workshops, petition drives, rallies, exhibitions, festivals, media events? Of course not. A few years from now they will sit around and grumble, blaming the liberal media, popular ignorance, Soviet agents—everyone but themselves.

The problem with conservatives is their belief that the truth is self-evident and does not need to be marketed, advertised, or otherwise promoted. The mere word "propaganda" makes them shudder, just as the word "nuclear" leaves the liberals furious. Unfortunately, neither nuclear power nor ideological warfare is about to go away.

The twentieth century, with its industrial revolution and technological progress, has changed the face of human society irrevocably. It has provided us with the means of mass destruction, and so placed a far greater responsibility on everyone. On a more mundane level, it has provided comfort and security, thereby making us soft and vulnerable by playing on our conformist tendencies. But, most importantly, it has created means of mass communication, mass media, and thus mass culture and mass psychology.

As a result, we all are close neighbors now, irrespective of geographic location. It takes only about 15 minutes for a missile to reach the opposite side of the globe. It takes only a fraction of a second for news to reach the same destination. Strictly speaking, there is no longer any such thing as purely internal affairs.

What is so often overlooked is that political tools have also changed. We live in an era of ideological wars, with mass ideologies, mass propaganda, and mass movements as their indispensable instruments. Sovereignty and national borders, war and diplomacy, peace and stability—all these notions of the nineteenth century have become obsolete. The nuclear weapon is not a weapon in the strictly military sense of the word, but a huge psychological factor in the ongoing ideological war. War is no longer simply military confrontation between nations, but anything from popular unrest to terrorism and guerrilla movements. And the battlefield of modern war does not confine itself to the borders of nations, but it exists in people's minds, whether in Indiana or Siberia. And what are peace and stability in this context? They have lost all meaning. Stability of what? Of a concentration camp, or of Fifth Avenue? And what do we mean by peace? A continuation of the "class struggle" and of "liberation," the triumph of Islam, the capitulation of democracy?

The trouble is that Americans in general and conservatives in particular stubbornly refuse to accept the political consequences of technological progress, that very progress to which their country has contributed more than any other nation. They simply refuse to enter the twentieth century politically.

The Communists were the first to grasp these new realities and to utilize the opportunities they offer. They have mastered the art of ideological war to the point of perfection. Their ultimate goal may be absurd, their concept of history may be ridiculous, their methods unscrupulous and cruel, but they fit perfectly into the twentieth-century socio-political environment, much as an epidemic of plague befitted the Middle Ages.

Say what you will about Comrade Lenin, but he was a tactical genius, and the first to think up this contraption of a vehicle which continues to rumble across the world. Sixty years after his death, the Soviet Union remains the same ideological state serving the purposes of the world revolution as he had conceived it. Never mind that no one nowadays believes in Communist ideology. In their everyday life the Soviet people perceive it as a nuisance, or as a source of the numerous jokes shared equally by the people and their rulers. But at the end of the day, the Communist party is still in firm control of every aspect of Soviet life, and Communist ideology is never challenged within the Party.

What was once a utopia, a dream, became a structure, an institution, and an everyday job for millions of people. They might hate it wholeheartedly, but there is no other choice: Either be a part of the system, or be locked up until death comes to your rescue. And the famous troika still rushes onward, its horses cursing the driver, its driver cursing the horses, and together all cursing the damned foreigners who so obligingly give way and draw aside.

The difference between professionals and amateurs is usually defined in terms of payment. Professionals, it is said, are those who are paid for their work, while amateurs do it for fun. In my view this definition is misleading. People in the State Department or in the CIA are also paid, but are they professionals? Let me give you a better definition: Professionals hate their job, but they do it well; amateurs enjoy what they are doing, but they do it badly.

A friend of mine once overheard the following conversation while riding on the Moscow underground, a conversation between a lieutenant and a captain, quite ordinary guys going home to their wives and kids after a long day at the office.

"You know," said the lieutenant, "I still can't get over the unfair treatment you received. Just think of it, you worked on that damned Ethiopia for three years, and just when things started moving they replaced you with that fool with the high connections. And now that the people you found, prepared, and promoted in Ethiopia have came to power in their 'glorious revolution,' this fool gets promoted to major. But you are still a captain. What dirty play."

Tomorrow, our deeply offended captain may defect to the West and come to New York. He will display a remarkable knowledge of the advantages of democracy upon arrival—no need to educate him about the great American liberties. He knew about them all along, even while masterminding a bloody revolution in Ethiopia, even while professionally subverting those very liberties. But as long as he is still in the Soviet Union, he will do his job very well. He is probably doing it as a matter of duty right now in El Salvador. He hates what he does, but he does it well.

Yes, the Soviet system is a gigantic professional machinery of subversion which has entrapped 275 million people. Of course, the Soviet system is not perfect, it makes its share of mistakes, but who is here to exploit them? Soviet policy is planned some twenty years in advance with considerable precision, and to be successful the U.S. response must be equally precise and well planned. But what in fact do we have? A bunch of very nice amateurs, a sloppy system of policy-making comprised of chaotic and sporadic reactions to yesterday's events. No long-term concept, no policy, just reactions when the trouble becomes too apparent.

This is not to say that the United States lacks gifted people, or that they never produce good ideas. Zero Option, the withdrawal from UNESCO, the threat to exile the United Nations to Moscow—these were brilliant ideas. But they have to be developed into a principle, a concept, to become effective.

To begin with, no one in the vast U.S. foreign policy apparatus knows what the U.S. wants from the Soviets. Nor has anybody ever tried to formulate this question. Once I raised this matter with several friends working within different branches of the American government, and all of them came up with different answers. Some said it would be just fine if the Soviets left us alone, others said they'd like to see the Soviets lose their grip on Eastern Europe, or show some respect for the human rights of their people. But no one ever tried to establish how any of this might be remotely possible.

What is more, there seems to be total disagreement on what the Soviets want from us. Are they really frightened and paranoic, as some continue to insist, or are they still pursuing Lenin's plan of world revolution? Or, perhaps, something else? Just a few thousand miles from us is a political system that has enslaved several hundred million people for half a century, that backs every enemy we might have, that can destroy the globe five times over, and still we know not what they want from us or we from them.

Meanwhile, numerous negotiations are conducted and agreements signed without any clear understanding of either side's objectives. It's not even known whether the terminology used in these agreements has the same meaning for both sides. And no sooner are they signed than, lo and behold, they are violated by the Soviets. So, does the U.S. then declare these agreements null and void? Of course not. Instead, it rushes to the negotiating tables to start all over again. Why?

In the absence of any defining concept, American foreign policy vis-à-vis the Soviet Union has become governed by a few "golden rules" created out of fear, impotence, and frustration.

The most "golden" of these rules and definitely the most absurd is "keep talking." Can anyone prove that to "keep talking" is better than to "quit talking"? Are there any facts to support this rule? Did anyone ever try not to "keep talking"? Of course not. Unfortunately, this "rule" is not simply a matter of innocent stupidity, for it implies, first of all, that the organic differences between democratic and totalitarian societies can be resolved by a negotiated settlement. This misleading notion misrepresents the East-West conflict as a sort of tragic misunderstanding that can be cleared up only if we "engage in constructive dialogue," "try to understand each other," "sit down and talk," or perform some other rite of liberal nonsense calculated to lay the blame on the West for not trying to "understand" the poor Soviets.

On the other hand, the "keep talking" rule deprives the West of much-needed flexibility and initiative in choosing when to talk and when not to, and on what conditions and for what purpose, while leaving the Soviets under no obligation to "keep talking." As a result, American policy is left hostage to Soviet interests and dependent on Soviet "approval." The success of American policy is therefore judged by the number of "agreements" concluded between the two sides, by the number of "talks," "dialogues," and concessions made to—and not by—the Soviets. At the same time, such criteria confuse the notion of what "normal" relations between the East and West are. If American policy serves Soviet interests and the Soviets condescend to a "dialogue," relations are said to be "normalizing."

Underlying this strange "rule" is an understandable fear: It is too scary not to keep talking. Just as a frightened child lost in the woods starts talking loudly to himself to dispel the dark shadows, Americans believe that talking to the Soviets will dispel the threat of war.

But to add insult to injury, a second "golden rule" comes into play as soon as "talks" start: "Better something than nothing." Perhaps this would be a good rule to follow in a democracy, or when dealing with another democratic country. But when dealing with the likes of the Soviets, this is a sure way to get mugged: They'll take what they want from you in exchange for "something" neither you nor they care about. The Americans will celebrate this as an achievement: After all, they will have obtained "something" from the Soviets, and something is surely better than nothing.

One small problem: Even this "something" is not likely to be delivered by the Soviets, not that international relations will suffer. For as soon as their cheating becomes obvious the next "golden rule" takes over: "We-should-not-demand-too-much-from-the-Russians," "We-should-not-press-them-into-a-corner." In practical terms, this means that we should not demand anything, even what was promised by them under an international agreement. Meanwhile, our side should of course continue to deliver: We are civilized people, aren't we, and cannot imitate Soviet behavior, can we?

Thus, even if the Soviets manage to get themselves into a truly tough corner, when they make a really serious mistake and the moment comes to force them to retreat, to make them give back whatever they have previously grabbed, American "professionals" cry out, all as one: "Leave them a Golden Bridge," "Let them save face." And everyone rushes to save face for the Soviets more eagerly than the Soviets have ever tried to. Can anyone recall a single case where the Soviets actually took advantage of such a ready-made "Golden Bridge" or showed any interest in "saving face" and retreating? Why should they? The U.S. will always come up with a good excuse for their behavior, and it will never try to exploit their most obvious mistakes. With enemies like this who needs friends?

So, the vicious circle is now complete: We have talked at the wrong moment; we have signed a bad agreement; we have refused to call our opponents to task for obvious violations of this bad agreement; we have even covered up their violations; and we still have no inkling of what must be done to stop that crazy troika which threatens to knock down everything in its way. What next?

"Keep talking."

Games Anti-Nukes Play

The Government Accountability Project's assault
on nuclear energy
(1985)

RAEL JEAN ISAAC

On December 22, 1983, ABC's "20/20" featured an expose of alleged "bizarre activities" at the Palo Verde nuclear plant being constructed in the Arizona desert. According to "Secrets of the Desert," as the segment was called, the Bechtel Corporation, prime contractor for the plant, was engaged in secret massive dumping of new or barely used tools in a giant landfill on a scale so large that it could go at least part way toward explaining the project's huge cost overruns. Several earnest-sounding former employees came before the camera to contend that they had themselves been involved in regular evening burials of electric tools, portovans, acetylene hose, hard hats, welding gloves, boots, wrenches, tape measures, saws—some of them still in crates. ABC's reporter, Tom Jarriel, held up large whirring tools in each hand to illustrate the useful character of the machinery Bechtel had entombed in the shifting Arizona sands.

What was the motive for Bechtel's peculiar management decision? In explanation, "20/20" offered the theory that the tools were supplied by a company Bechtel owned. Bechtel buried them unused or barely-used so as to be able to buy more tools from its subsidiary company, thus increasing profits.

On the program, one of the workers declared, "We know what size the pits are and where they are." The state attorney general vowed to Jarriel that he would find some way to dig up the desert dump site, but lamented the absence of any funds at his command to do so. After the program, the Bechtel Corporation, stung by the dreadful publicity, paid $300,000 for the attorney general's office to dig up the sites pinpointed by its accusers. In December 1984 the attorney general's office issued its report, which said that apart from a few broken hammers and pieces of wire, it had found nothing at all. Despite the wide publicity accorded the original charges, the revelation that the charges were without substance was confined to such journals as *Highway and Heavy Construction.* While "20/20" could not totally ignore the conclusion of its own story, it used the fruitless search for buried tools as a means to put the knife into Bechtel once again. On March 7, 1985, in the context of yet another attack on the Palo Verde plant, this time focusing on "rate shock," "20/20" complained loftily that the ratepayer had to pay for such controversies, which "drive up the cost of the already over-budgeted project."

ABC may have extricated itself with admirable agility, but what had led it

265

to broadcast the report in the first place? The source of ABC's story, it seems certain,[1] was the Government Accountability Project (GAP), at the time part of the Institute for Policy Studies, the Washington, D.C. based "think-tank" which for two decades has served as the intellectual hub of radical activism in the United States. (Like other successful IPS projects, it has now formally "spun off" from the mother organization, although its headquarters remain in the IPS building.) GAP has become the most successful anti-nuclear organization in the country, stopping at least one multi-billion dollar project cold (Cincinnati's Zimmer plant), playing a role in stopping Consumers Power's Midland facility in Michigan, and running up many millions of dollars in costs for other plants whose operations it has delayed by a variety of means.

GAP's *modus operandi* in the tale of buried tools was a variation on its normal procedure. It was typical in that GAP worked together with a local anti-nuclear group (in this case, the Palo Verde Intervention Fund), that it relied upon "whistleblowers," usually former workers at the targeted plant, and that it went directly to the media with their stories. Normally, however, GAP "stores" allegations until a plant is almost complete—sometimes awaiting the plant's license from the Nuclear Regulatory Commission to operate at low, or even full power—before it charges the plant is unsafe and should not be permitted to operate. (In the case of Palo Verde, the timing coincided with hearings scheduled by the Arizona public utility commission on the utility's request for emergency rate relief.)

Whatever the details of GAP's approach in the particular case, the group owes its success to its masterful playing of an anti-nuclear "game." GAP has devised the rules, and it has made the media, the Nuclear Regulatory Commission, the courts, and the utilities play by them. GAP established the pattern of its game in 1980 when it first entered the anti-nuclear energy arena to stop Cincinnati Gas and Electric's Zimmer plant, which was then 97-percent complete. GAP's chief whistleblower in this case was Thomas Applegate, a private detective who had been hired by the utility to check rumors of time-card cheating by workers at the plant and who claimed that, in the course of his investigation, he had discovered dangerously bad work at the plant, above all faulty welds.

GAP went to the media with its charges, triggering an NRC investigation. While no one ever proved there were faulty welds at Zimmer, GAP had stumbled onto something. It turned out the utility had neglected its paperwork, and was helpless to prove that the welds, or other work, were good. In the end, pounded by the media, excoriated by politicians leaping on a popular band-

---

[1] I say "seems certain" because ABC refuses to confirm that GAP was its source. Pressed by Reed Irvine of Accuracy in Media, George Watson, vice-president of ABC News, would say only that GAP had been "among [their] sources." I tried to elicit information on the origin of the story from the "20/20" segment's producer, Kathy McManus, who said she was unable to speak without permission of Mauri Perl of the ABC public relations department. Miss Perl would not give the necessary permission. The circumstantial evidence, however, is overwhelming. The Palo Verde Intervention Fund's press conference in December 1983 first publicly airing the charges could not have triggered ABC's interest because ABC had already filmed its interviews with local whistleblowers months earlier. GAP had acted as counsel for the Palo Verde Intervention Fund, a tiny group, and so it seems obvious that GAP used its media connections to bring "20/20" to Palo Verde.

wagon, placed under a stop-work order by the NRC, and facing huge costs to tear down large parts of the plant so as to start the paperwork all over again, Cincinnati Gas and Electric in 1984 abandoned its plant, announcing it would convert it to coal. Paul Sieck, a business executive active in Energy Ratepayers United, a group that fruitlessly did battle against GAP, says that Zimmer had become such an emotional public issue the utility had no choice: It simply saw no light at the end of the tunnel. Ironically, once the decision was made to abandon the plant, an independent study commissioned by the Ohio Public Utilities Commission, while highly critical of what it called Cincinnati Gas and Electric's "substantial mismanagement," concluded that the plant had in fact been well-built overall but had "become the victim of an elusive unknown percentage of unacceptable work which cannot be identified."

GAP had developed a game-plan so successful it saw no reason to alter it: Go in with accusations of defective welds and inadequate paperwork, known in the trade as "quality assurance," and demand the NRC issue a stop-work order until a full investigation of all safety-related issues could be completed. GAP could hope, with good reason, that the millions in interest the utility would be forced to pay at this last minute stage of construction would force it to abandon the plant before such a study could even be undertaken. In the wake of Zimmer, GAP was flooded with requests from anti-nuclear groups from around the country, and it selected eleven plants that looked particularly promising.[2] To be sure, the game has never gone quite as smoothly again, if only because the other plants GAP targeted did not suffer from such overwhelming paperwork failures. In the case of Zimmer, an NRC official estimated that 4 million documents were missing. While this is indeed a tribute to bad paper work, it is also an indication of the paper quagmire into which those who construct plants are pushed by NRC regulations and of the propitious conditions under which GAP works.

In any event, the media never failed to rise to the bait, and the NRC dutifully launched last minute investigations in plant after plant, even though the allegations of GAP whistleblowers were repeatedly found to be inaccurate or of no consequence for safety. What GAP achieved in most cases was significant delay that drove up costs to consumers, and creation of a climate of fear and distrust of nuclear power among the public to be served by the plant.

Whistleblowers, the key to GAP's game, were solicited, with the cooperation of local anti-nuclear groups, through everything from printed appeals to plant workers to visits to their local hangouts. When despite such efforts insufficient workers came forward, GAP accused the utility of intimidating workers and demanded the NRC "break down" the plant's "omniscient image." At Duke Power's Catawba plant in North Carolina, for example, where GAP teamed up with the local Palmetto Alliance to stop the plant, GAP announced that its "previous experience" with Zimmer and Midland had given it "a good idea of what to look for and what we will find at Catawba." Although GAP

[2] Apart from Zimmer, the main GAP targets have been Callaway in Missouri, Catawba in North Carolina, Comanche Peak in Texas, Diablo Canyon and San Onofre in California, LaSalle and Braidwood in Illinois, Midland in Michigan, Palo Verde in Arizona, Three Mile Island in Pennsylvania, and Waterford in Louisiana.

managed to wring three separate investigations from the NRC, it suffered from an embarrassing paucity of whistleblowers, and Catawba was ultimately licensed earlier this year.

What motivates GAP's whistleblowers? Jay Harrison, whom the NRC's Office of Special Cases assigned to investigate many of GAP's 190 allegations against Midland, summed up his experience: "You get some real strange people making charges for various reasons. . . . When you go to interview them they are incoherent or vague for whatever reason." Harrison found there were people who were disgruntled, who had vendettas, who were getting even for having lost their jobs. Sometimes allegations were the by-product of tensions, typical of all the plants, between workers and safety inspectors, who often faced verbal abuse for refusing to approve work.

Whatever the motivation, GAP after a while even had "traveling allegers," workers who discovered hazards at more than one plant. E. Earl Kent had been employed by Bechtel at the Midland plant for three months. He came forward with GAP's favorite charge of defective welds. It turned out Kent had been fired after twice failing the certification exam for his job as welding inspector. Moreover, it appeared that Kent had earlier worked for Litton industries, building ships for the Navy. After being fired in 1971, Kent sent a 26-page telegram to President Nixon, claiming the ships being designed and built would create "a bunch of widows and orphans." The Navy set up a board of inquiry, which found the charges without merit. (One senior welding engineer remarked that Kent wanted tungsten steel around the turbine exhaust so thick and heavy it would have sunk the ship.) All the ships challenged by Kent remain in safe operation today.

Undaunted, after Midland Kent turned up on the West Coast at another GAP-targeted plant, San Onofre, to allege thousands of defective welds. At a cost of $200,000 these charges were duly investigated by the NRC with the assistance of Southern California Edison and Bechtel, and found to be without merit. GAP lashed out at the investigators, announced that Kent's credentials were "impeccable," and declared the NRC would be held accountable for his "shabby treatment." There was even an effort to bring Kent to testify at Catawba, although he had never been there, to back up the testimony of one Howard Nunn, fired for excessive unexcused absences, who had announced: "I'm concerned [Catawba] is permeated with laminated, stinking rotten pipe."

In playing its game, GAP is greatly helped by an even bigger player: the Nuclear Regulatory Commission. As one disgusted Commonwealth Edison of Illinois official put it, the NRC's licensing process "in no way lends itself to the objective of licensing nuclear power plants. Rather it seems to be designed to offer opponents every opportunity to interfere with licensing."

The NRC's rules provide that allegations against a plant can be brought forward in any form or forum (for example, the rules specifically mention phone, letter, newsmedia reports, offices, business meetings, even social functions), at any time, by anyone. There is no cut-off point, which permits GAP to store up its allegations—and, in the case of California's Diablo Canyon, to unload thousands of them on the unfortunate NRC commissioners at one time. There is no requirement that the allegations have any relation to safety or that they be backed up by proof, and there is no penalty for false charges, although investigating them can consume vast quantities of taxpayer dollars and, because the cost of delay is so high, increase the cost of the plant by millions of dollars.

In a single eight-month period (from November 1983 to June 1984) the NRC calculated that it devoted 18,000 staff hours to examining GAP allegations at Diablo Canyon alone. Of course, no issue is ever resolved to GAP's satisfaction. During an NRC meeting on the plant, one commissioner observed: "You know, collectively we have spent several years and probably a billion dollars dealing with the seismic issue." Yet most of GAP's last minute allegations were based on the "seismic issue." One of GAP's attorneys, Tom Devine, cheerfully dismissed the NRC's efforts: "We don't know any better now whether Diablo Canyon can withstand an earthquake than we did in 1981." Perhaps the ultimate effrontery came from Mothers for Peace, the anti-nuclear group that invited GAP to Diablo Canyon. A leader of the group, which over the years had thrown up every possible roadblock to completion of the plant, from mass demonstrations to legal challenges, complained to the NRC: "That plant is fourteen years old. The whole plant is old. It's an obsolete plant."

And yet, were it not for the bottomless credulity of the media, it is doubtful that GAP's game would work. Local media are crucial in arousing the public and politicians, forcing the NRC to bend over backwards in its dealings with GAP. While typically the media invite the utility to respond to GAP's charges, the utility, which has no prior knowledge of the charges, is afraid to call them groundless without a detailed internal investigation; GAP wins the battle, because in being unable to deny the charges immediately, the utility has given them credibility. GAP is equally successful with national media. For example, ABC, in addition to the Palo Verde fairy tale, earlier this year featured GAP's charges against Texas's Comanche Peak in a three-hour anti-nuclear documentary entitled "The Fire Unleashed," whose segment on nuclear energy must go down as one of the silliest performances in television history. A national television audience was soberly treated to a collection of old wives' tales about staggering cats, deformed dandelions, under-producing ducks, waves of heat, hair turning white overnight—all the result of Three Mile Island, whose clean-up GAP successfully delayed by a full year.

Ultimately GAP's game rests on the pretense that we all share the same goal, namely the safe operation of nuclear power plants. Thus in a 1983 statement submitted to the NRC, GAP was careful to insist that "the Project [GAP] is not an 'anti-nuclear' organization"; its purpose was rather "to prevent health and safety dangers, corruption, fraud and other abuses." When Energy Ratepayers United, the citizens' group that tried to save Zimmer, sent letters-to-the-editor trying to expose GAP's real purposes, Louis Clark, GAP's executive director, took the trouble to write to the group's leader, Robert Acomb, denying the charges. In his letter of April 16, 1983, Clark said that the purposes of Energy Ratepayers United and GAP were the same: "At least I have been given to understand that you want the Zimmer Nuclear Power Station to operate safely. . . . The Government Accountability Project has no hidden agendas." A bare two weeks later, however, GAP prepared a memorandum for its own use analyzing a Supreme Court decision permitting the state of California to rule out nuclear plants on economic but not on safety grounds; the decision, the GAP memo said, could be used "creatively," so as "to impose a statutory ban on construction and probably on operation," since economic impact studies could be demanded even after a plant was on line. At that point, according to the memo, GAP could demand that the utility prove its ability to compensate all claimants in the event of an accident, and to pay for all possible future repairs. In the event of an accident or even "major unanticipated repairs" the notion of "psychological trauma" could be introduced. For, said the memo, the economic consequences could be "devastating if a significant percentage of the population tried to leave due to fear that the facility will reopen."

The hypocrisy can get wearing. When the anti-nuclear groups have their annual get-togethers under the aegis of Ralph Nader's Critical Mass, they let their hair down. Robert Hager, a member of the law team that represented the estate of Karen Silkwood, told the assembled activists in 1983: "Let's face it. We don't want safe plants—we want the ones being planned to be blocked and the ones operating to be shut down."

The media never question GAP's public persona. In the hundreds of stories on GAP's activities that I read in local papers near GAP-targeted plants, not one described GAP as an anti-nuclear group. It was an "environmental watchdog group," a "government watchdog group," a "national public interest organization." Even specifically business-oriented segments of the national press are no more probing. The *Wall Street Journal* has referred to GAP as "a private watchdog group" and *Business Week* describes it as a "public interest group."

Under these conditions the NRC for the most part is helpless to do anything but play the fly to GAP's spider. Occasionally the commissioners flap their wings in protest. When in October 1984 GAP, two days before the NRC's final hearing on granting a full power license to Union Electric Company's Callaway plant, came up with forty-eight new allegations, two of the commissioners lost patience. One of them declared, "I simply find it difficult to believe that many of these [allegations] were not known for some period of time," and added that GAP's effort to toss all the charges on the table at the last minute "just isn't going to work." And in a rare show of unanimity, all five commissioners promptly voted to license Callaway.

But for the most part the NRC has meekly played GAP's game. Even when presented with opportunities for bringing GAP to heel, the NRC has been afraid to act. In 1982, Consumers Power received permission from the Atomic Safety and Licensing Board to subpoena GAP affidavits alleging serious safety problems at its Midland plant. When GAP claimed it was concerned about keeping the identities of its whistleblowers secret, Consumers Power said the identities of GAP's sources could be deleted from the affidavits—the utility wanted only the substance of the charges so that it could correct any problems that might exist. But the last thing GAP wanted, of course, was for the utility to investigate the allegations; when GAP was ready to demand a stop-work order, the utility might be able to refute the charges or say the problems had already been addressed. GAP refused to honor the subpoenas, and it was then up to the NRC to request court enforcement. The NRC put off making any decision until the end of June 1984. By then the issue was moot: A week earlier

Consumers Power had thrown in the towel, postponing the project indefinitely.

Allowing utilities to know what allegations are pending against them is not the only means to stop GAP's game: A more courageous NRC could change the rules. Whistleblowers could be required to provide evidence for their charges. There could be a cut-off point after which charges could no longer be submitted. Above all, there could be penalties for false allegations. Intervenors like GAP and the local anti-nuclear groups it works with might have to post a bond which would be forfeited if the allegations proved untrue. (In courts of law, those who are found to bring a case frivolously can be forced to bear its costs.) Ironically, the Government Accountability Project's ability to operate rests on the fact that it is accountable to no one and nothing.

The NRC does little to impede GAP's game because of fear, and the NRC has good reason to be intimidated. For it would be taking on not only GAP and its formidable parent, the Institute for Policy Studies, but the entire complex of organizations seeking to eliminate nuclear power. GAP has taken on the task of administering the last blows to a nuclear power industry already on the ropes, thanks to the earlier efforts of organizations such as Ralph Nader's Critical Mass, the Union of Concerned Scientists, Physicians for Social Responsibility, and the Mobilization for Survival. If the NRC dared to take on GAP, the weight of the entire anti-nuclear complex would be thrown into the lists, with the media as its propagandist.

As it is, the NRC reaps no gratitude from GAP for its forbearance. GAP community organizer Billie Garde appeared on ABC's "The Fire Unleashed" to say of the NRC: "The agency is ideologically corrupt. They believe that the public is the enemy and it is their job to help the industry figure out a way to break the law and survive." Nor does GAP allow an NRC decision to go against it without a fight. When an NRC investigation of GAP allegations at the San Onofre plant in California failed to come up with the result GAP desired, it demanded—and got—an NRC investigation of the original NRC investigation. When that too exonerated the plant, GAP, along with the local anti-nuclear Orange County Alliance for Survival, staged a press conference in March 1985 demanding an investigation of the investigation of the investigation!

And when the NRC, after years of delay, finally issued operating permits for both units of Diablo Canyon (one at full power), GAP went to court. The U.S. Appeals Court for the District of Columbia ruled that the issues GAP raised were the province of a federal court in California, and at this writing GAP has readied its mandamus action for filing in that state. Simultaneously GAP has turned to Congress. Last June Massachusetts Congressman Edward Markey, chairman of the Subcommittee on Energy Conservation and Power (and author of *Nuclear Peril,* which calls for the elimination of nuclear energy), blasted the NRC in words that directly echoed Billie Garde's on "The Fire Unleashed." The NRC, admonished Markey, should "stop looking at the public as 'the enemy,' " and he demanded a written statement within 30 days explaining why hearings on the earthquake issue should not be held now. Through Congress it appeared GAP might well succeed in reopening the seismic issue after even the NRC had done with it.

There are in fact signs that GAP may be shifting its tactics to make the NRC its primary target. Both in its current effort to prevent restart of the undamaged TMI reactor and to block the licensing of Commonwealth Edison of Illinois's Braidwood plant, GAP has dispensed with worker allegations to focus instead on charges that the NRC has failed to follow its own rules. For the courts this might seem a more clear-cut issue than deciding disputed safety claims—and could be equally effective in stopping nuclear plants.

GAP has been playing behind the scenes for quite a while. It began as IPS's Project on Official Illegality, which helped whistleblowers from national security agencies, like Daniel Ellsberg of Pentagon Papers fame (IPS had the Pentagon Papers a year before they were published by the *New York Times*), Victor Marchetti (of the CIA) and Robert Wall (of the FBI). The Project on Official Illegality served to assemble sensitive information and leak it to the press. In 1976 it was expanded beyond the national security and intelligence agencies to include other branches of government and renamed the Government Accountability Project. This gave it greater legitimacy. (Congress, with only ten dissenting votes, passed a whistleblower protection act partly based on model legislation drafted by GAP.) GAP now described itself as a "public interest group to help restore confidence in the federal system" and handed out brochures to government employees in colors of red, white, and blue, with an American flag on the cover, inviting them to contact GAP with stories of waste and abuse in their agencies.

When GAP turned its attention to nuclear power in 1980, it thus had experience in presenting a mask of "working to make the system function better." Those early red, white, and blue brochures had their counterpart in the appeals sent out by alleger Richard Parks on behalf of GAP to workers at the Callaway plant. (Park's earlier allegations, focusing specially on a polar crane designed for use in removing the reactor vessel head at the damaged Three Mile Island plant, held up work there for a full year—the crane was ultimately used and worked fine.) Parks explained to workers that "we are the line of defense to protect the general population" and urged them to come to GAP with their "concerns," assuring them that "our intention is not to stop the nuclear plants."

In respect to energy, the goals of GAP can be inferred from the sketch of an ideal energy system that IPS provides in its proposal for an Encyclopedia for Social Reconstruction, a long-favored IPS project.

The energy will be produced and disseminated through small scale technology. . . . We simply would have got rid of most of the extra high voltage wires strung around the country; closed up the coal mines, oil and gas fields; taken down oil refineries and much of the petrochemical establishment.

Nuclear energy, in other words, is only the initial target, selected because of the ease of arousing public fear, and the broader goal is to eliminate *all* centralized energy. This in turn is seen by IPS as fundamental to the total reshaping of society in accordance with the sixties movement philosophy it espouses. IPS leaders have called since 1971 for "dismantling" what they refer to as the "national-security state." IPS co-founder Marcus Raskin specifically called for the dismantling of America's "Colonies," including "the Violence Colony" (our military and police), "the Channeling Colony" (our educational system), and "the Plantation Colony" (our economic system). Cut energy and you cut the jugular of our way of life.

Given GAP's origin and goals, it is ironic that its funding comes from foundations representing some of the major beneficiaries of the economic system IPS seeks to "dismantle." Yet GAP's funders include one of the largest U.S. foundations, the J. Roderick MacArthur Foundation, as well as the Mary Reynolds Babcock Foundation (Mrs. Babcock was the daughter of R.J. Reynolds of tobacco fame), and a member of the Rockefeller family, whose identity is not revealed by GAP, which has disclosed only that it is a younger member of the family who earmarked a $20,000 contribution specifically for "nuclear investigations."

It is possible, although not likely, that simple stupidity is the explanation for these donations to GAP. But there is no question that much of GAP's money comes from foundations in no way averse to GAP's goals. For example, the Youth Project, which gave GAP $35,000 in 1984,[3] serves as a funnel to transfer money, much of it from corporate foundations (these, to be sure, in most cases have no conception of the nature of the Youth Project), to radical grass-roots groups. The Playboy Foundation, another donor, has liberally supported IPS, the more radical "peace" groups, and remarkably, women's liberation groups. Another donor is the Funding Exchange, which channels money from nine of the most radical funds in the United States, their money coming from young people whose wealth in turn derives from such fortunes as DuPont, Gulf and Western, IBM, Pillsbury, and General Motors. These funds are quite explicit about their goals. Haymarket People's Fund, one of the nine, announces in its annual report that the fund is "dedicated to eliminating rich people" and to remaking "a sexist and racist system that puts profits for a few people before the needs of the majority." There can also be little doubt that GAP can be straightforward in its dealings with the Fund for Constitutional Government (the single largest donor to GAP), which receives most of its funds from Stewart Mott, a perennial funder of radical causes whose wealth derives from his father's part in building General Motors.

Unfortunately, it looks as if the achievements of GAP and its sister antinuclear organizations—halting nuclear energy development and blowing billions of dollars of investment in abandoned plants—may be invisible to those who will pay the price. In February 1985 *Forbes* magazine, self-styled "capitalist tool," published a 17-page analysis of the decline and fall of nuclear energy by executive editor James Cook. His thesis is that nuclear energy had been destroyed not by its enemies but by its friends. Indeed neither the activities nor even the names of "the enemies" are mentioned in the article. One would never know there was such an organization as GAP or the Clamshell Alliance or Critical Mass or even the Union of Concerned Scientists. Cook divides the blame among the federal government and the NRC, equipment manufacturers, contractors and subcontractors, utility executives, and state regulatory commissions. Cook's analysis was then echoed by *National Review* several months later.

[3]All the figures are for 1984, but normally the pattern of donations to IPS and its spinoffs is fairly stable from year to year.

If even conservative magazines dismiss the role of anti-nuclear activists as inconsequential, there is every prospect that GAP and the others will enjoy the ultimate triumph of seeing the blame for the consequences of their actions fall upon their victims.

Yet Cook's own analysis should have led him directly to the anti-nuclear intervenors. He zeroes in on cost overruns as the culprit, and points to the indifference of the NRC to the economic cost of the regulations it imposed. (Although Three Mile Island had a handful of causes, most of them to do with deficiencies in the control room, the NRC imposed 2,000 new regulations resulting in an additional 6,000 required steps to comply with the guidelines.) Cook notes that in some cases utilities had to tear apart nearly completed plants to conform to the changes. He blames contractors and subcontractors for failing "to question the cost-effectiveness of the NRC's dictates." Yet surely the NRC's behavior cannot be explained without reference to the vociferous demands of the anti-nuclear groups which have been so successful in intimidating it. The costly retrofits that in some instances may have actually *reduced* plant safety,[4] the often absurd paperwork demands, the delays to examine frivolous allegations were attempts to satisfy the anti-nuclear activists as they rode high in the wake of Three Mile Island. All this is not to say that there have not been management failures or a few companies that have managed to surmount all obstacles, like Duke Power, which Cook singles out as the best of the utilities. (Of course, this did not stop GAP from doing its best to prevent completion of Duke's Catawba plant.) But for the cause of the problems one must look to the intervenors, not management or the NRC, which have merely responded to their challenge in totally inadequate fashion.

At the end of his article, Cook obliquely gives the activists their due. Comparing the surge in nuclear plant construction abroad with the U.S. debacle, Cook notes that like the U.S. France has a two-stage regulatory process, but permits no public participation once the project gets underway. Canada goes France one better and permits no public participation at all. Cook writes that "prohibition may be half the battle. . . . In the end the problem may boil down simply to this: Can a technology as rigorous and demanding and for all that as useful as nuclear power find a place in a society as open as the U.S.?" Cook's contention about management failures in the U.S. is ultimately beside the point. Nuclear energy abroad has been successful because plants are built in half the time it takes in the United States. Much of the technology is U.S. technology; the plants built many years ago in the United States provide inexpensive and dependable energy. If GAP had been let loose while these were being built, who can doubt but that it would have found "allegers" and paperwork deficiencies with which to have demanded stop-work orders? It strains credulity to

---

[4]In March 1985 James R. Tourtellotte, appointed by the NRC to be chairman of its Regulatory Reform Task Force, delivered a devastating and, in view of his position as an NRC executive, distinctly courageous report. He concluded that the "backfitting" demands of the NRC, which have "cost consumers billions," inflicted "paralyzing delays into the administrative process," and "made nuclear plants more difficult to operate and maintain," may also in some cases "have reduced rather than enhanced public health and safety."

believe that all over the world, management has the secret of building U.S.-designed plants, while U.S. managers alone lack competence.

While the focus here has been on the Government Accountability Project, it is simply the most effective of the many groups who play similar games. For instance, the Center for Defense Information, an "expert" source for both the media and liberal congressmen, describes itself in a full page newspaper ad soliciting memberships and contributions as an organization that works to "support a strong, but not excessive, military posture." In fact it has opposed all major new weapons systems since its inception in 1972, releases data that obfuscate Soviet superiority in any weapons area, even conventional forces, and works to incite pacifist and neutralist sentiment in Europe. The Center for National Security Studies (which targets our intelligence agencies), the Center for International Policy (which targets our alliances), and the Center for Constitutional Rights are only a few of the most skillful game-players. The Center for Constitutional Rights recently conducted a series of "war crimes trials" of the United States in cities around the country and submitted to the United Nations an "indictment" charging the U.S. with "conspiracy" to unleash nuclear war "against the peoples of the world."

Despite such activities, these groups maintain their credibility with the media as "public interest" organizations. When, in 1985, the Institute for Policy Studies published a handbook disclosing nuclear weapons sites around the country (based, according to its authors, IPS fellows William Arkin and Richard Fieldhouse, on information obtained through the Freedom of Information Act and "leaks"), ABC's "20/20" did a respectful segment on the publication, with Arkin explaining the most "interesting" findings (e.g., the high number of sites in New York State). ABC did not question why IPS had put out such a publication—that IPS was dedicated to the public's "right to know" was simply assumed. Nor did the ABC interviewer inquire of Arkin as to the extent to which "leaks" had been used, whether the "leaks" had involved secret documents, and the propriety of publishing information thus obtained. It is true the IPS volume also contained information on Soviet nuclear sites. But there were only 18 pages on this subject in the appendix as against 82 pages on U.S. sites, and the material on the Soviet Union came from published Western sources, while much of the information on the U.S. had not hitherto been published. Thanks to publicity such as that provided by "20/20," IPS could look forward to excellent sales of its book, being called upon by Congress as a source of expert advice, many more articles on the *New York Times* op-ed page, and continued foundation grants.

GAP stands out not because it alone has mastered this game, but because it can boast that rarely have so few wreaked so much damage upon so many. GAP's 1984 budget was a mere $180,000, its staff three poorly paid lawyers and a community organizer (a fifth staff worker was added in 1985). Yet merely investigating one relatively minor GAP charge at Consumers' Midland plant cost the NRC $800,000, and overall GAP has cost the nuclear industry (and ultimately the consumer) many billions of dollars. This does not include the much larger damage to the economy that will result from shortages of electricity in the years ahead. For the impact of intervenors has not been solely on nuclear plants. Utilities are reluctant to invest in building *any* new capacity: While it has been eight years since the last nuclear plant was ordered, in the last three years only one coal plant has been ordered. Yet demand for electricity has been growing steadily, and merely replacing existing aging plants makes new capital investment essential. Essential or not, Frederick Mielke, chairman of the board of Pacific Gas and Electric, remarked in February 1985: "No prudent investor will risk the capital needed to build coal or nuclear-fueled plants in California." By their actions, it is clear that utility executives around the country share his sentiments.

Execution Day in Zhengzhou

(1986)

LIU FONG DA, WITH JOHN CREGER

Since Mao's death in 1976, Deng Xiaoping's relatively moderate policies of steady modernization, relaxed state control over production, and individual initiative have brought China to the point of entering into widespread exchanges, including trade, with the West. Enthusiastic about China's opening, Westerners often mistake the reports of increased economic freedom inside China for signs of incipient democracy.

But we Chinese know that there are many faces to what is happening in China under Deng Xiaoping. In the fall of 1983, as a teacher from a university in another part of China, I led a group of graduate students in fieldwork outside Zhengzhou, the capital of Henan Province, on the Yellow River plain in north central China. For almost three thousand years, from perhaps 1500 B.C. to A.D. 1200, the city was the center of China's cultural and political life. Today, under socialism, the area around Zhengzhou is mainly agricultural, producing much of the nation's wheat and some of its corn. One morning while on this field expedition, my students and I witnessed an event, carried out at Deng's order, which shows a face China rarely turns to the West.

The morning of September 23, 1983 was clear and warm in North China. It was what we call there a golden autumn. The sky was deep blue and the warm air hung with the sweet smell of cut wheat. Fields of the light brown wheat stubble stretched in from the countryside to the outskirts of Zhengzhou. My students and I had not gone to the field as usual that day, but had stayed in our dormitory on the city's main street to analyze soil samples for my students' thesis work. Around 10:30 one of the students came up to my room where we were working to ask permission to go to a parade which he had just heard was about to begin. Curious, I gave permission and we all went down to the street.

As visitors in Zhengzhou, we had heard nothing before about a parade. No announcements had been posted or printed in the newspapers. No official holiday had been declared. But I could see by the number of expectant people pouring onto the streets that for some time the peasants and workers, the cadres and students and small children of Zhengzhou had known: an execution day was coming.

Of course no one knew who or how many were to be killed, or for what crimes. Unless it is deemed politically necessary to publicize them, executions

277

in China are kept secret and carried out under tight security. This time, though, the news must have come quietly down from the city's highest cadres and through Party branches to schools, factories, shops, and hospitals. So, I saw, the Party means to instruct the people with a show. It means to give them lucky eyes . . .

In a city of two million it seemed all work and school had come to a stop. I estimated later that close to half the city's population—almost a million people—must have left their jobs and classrooms. People crowded into every available place—along the sidewalks, on steps, jammed in doorways. Faces pressed at each small window of the five-story red and yellow brick buildings. Soldiers and policemen stood along the streets at intervals to keep the way clear.

A shout went up the four-lane main street: "It's coming!" At once everyone froze still and silent. People stood on tiptoe and small children sat on shoulders.

First it was the sound of motorcycle engines. Then fifteen or sixteen armed policemen on two- and three-wheelers came slowly into sight. The only sound above the low-throttled engines was the crackle of a police radio.

The main attraction followed immediately: Forty-five flatbed trucks, one after another, rolled by at no more than five m.p.h. Since the police department had very few of its own, the trucks had been borrowed from factories, all different makes and colors. At the front of each truck bed, just behind the cab, stood a condemned man bound with heavy rope. The rope ran in an "X" across his chest and around to his back, holding in place a tall narrow sign. On the top half of each sign was an accusation: "Thief," "Murderer," "Rapist." On the bottom half was the accused's name, marked through with a large red "X." The prisoners seemed to be wearing their own tattered clothes. Each was flanked by two policemen.

When we have seen something special, we Chinese say that our eyes have been lucky. The thought crossed my mind that the parade was moving so slowly to give the people lucky eyes. Parading criminals this way is a practice going back deep into Chinese feudalism. For two thousand years we have been conditioned to feel we are fortunate to see such things.

The forty-five carried themselves in various ways. Some were standing with heads down. Others carried their heads upright, defiantly. Others wept openly, seeming full of remorse at their crimes, or perhaps despairing of clearing their names. As the trucks rolled past, some of the condemned turned their heads from side to side, staring wide-eyed—as if the whole scene were unreal and they were already on the way to the West Heaven of the common people's traditions.

I thought of the many modern Chinese movies and novels that continually show scenes of Guomindang (Nationalist) and Japanese executions of Communists during the Party's thirty-year struggle for power, in which a hundred thousand Communists died. Before being executed, the heroes are asked if they have anything to say. Invariably they shout out, "Long live Chairman Mao!" or "Long live the Communist Party! Long live Marxism!" And just before dying they break into the Internationale.

But this day in Zhengzhou, if any of the forty-five had something to say to the people, no one heard it. Another, more slender rope was draped around each condemned man's neck. If he had begun to shout or struggle, we all knew one of the two policemen standing beside him would have pulled on the choking rope. If he continued, the other policeman had a small dagger. Driven in the back and left undisturbed, the dagger would let no blood escape. The two policemen could then hold the body up all the way through the parade and execution. For the performance must go on. The people must receive some education.

Behind the trucks came about twenty-five small black cars, carrying fifty or sixty party or police cadres. Very slowly the parade wound through the main streets of Zhengzhou, attracting followers at every turn. By the time it reached the outskirts of the city, perhaps a hundred thousand of the million onlookers in the city were actively following. The streets were strewn with trash, everyone was stumbling and streaming with sweat and out of breath, but still they followed the forty-five trucks. Some rode bicycles. Most, like me, alternately ran and walked. We knew the most dramatic act was coming.

Three miles outside the city a dry creekbed widens out in a cornfield. The widening is maybe two hundred by four hundred yards. Yellow banks from three- to six-feet high form a huge natural amphitheater. Corn the height of a man grows on the banks, up to their edges. And below, a fine green grass covers the creekbed. The horde following the parade swept onto the site, flattening the corn on the banks. I followed along in the crowds, wondering, Why are we trampling food to watch people killed?

The lower end of the widening is bounded by a highway, the same height as the banks. The parade vehicles sat in formation on the road, stopping all other traffic. A ramp, in the right corner, led from the road down to the creekbed. A loose ring of policemen in white jackets and blue pants stood around the edges of the creekbed to keep the people from spilling from the banks down into the grass.

Out in the center was a row of wooden stakes with circular signs numbered one to forty-five. About six feet in front of each stake a hole had been dug, roughly a foot in diameter and six-inches deep. The cadres got out of their cars, walked down the ramp, and stood in a group, looking over the preparations. The accused already had been brought down from the truckbeds and were being kept in waiting beside the trucks.

Three red flares suddenly shot high into the sky from the road somewhere behind the prisoners. Each escorted by two white- and blue-uniformed policemen, the accused were now marched rapidly down the ramp, the signs still tied behind them. Some had lost the use of their legs from fear. These the policemen dragged to their places.

The moment the forty-fifth reached his place, three green flares launched into the air. Before they fell out of sight, from seemingly nowhere a line of forty-five green-uniformed policemen carrying rifles filed quickly into the creekbed. They took positions behind each prisoner.

Several seconds after the last policeman reached his place, three yellow flares went up. The two escorting policemen in blue and white caught each man behind the knees, forcing him to a kneeling position, and then separated to each side. In unison, the green-uniformed policemen stepped forward and put rifle barrels within ten inches of the backs of the accused's heads.

The forty-five shots rang out in one voice.

Together, the bodies jerked forward and splayed out in different ways on the grass, bloody pieces landing to both sides of the holes, and some actually in the holes. The ring of policemen below the banks held the staring crowd back. A hundred and thirty-five policemen—two escorts and one executioner for each prisoner—made a single line, marched quickly back to the trucks, and were driven away. Their job was finished.

Down the ramp came fifteen or sixteen white-gloved policemen with clipboards and pistols. Stopping at every body they jotted quick notes on the clipboards. A few of the bodies, not having been hit squarely, still lay twitching or quivering. These were shot again.

The cadres stood briefly at the bottom of the ramp discussing something. Then they looked at their watches, walked up to their cars, and drove back to the city. The white-gloved policemen with the clipboards filed into two of the remaining trucks. I glanced at my watch. It was twelve noon.

The only officials remaining were the twenty or thirty policemen who now were ringing the bodies. Suddenly, as the cadres' cars went out of sight down the highway, the people surged down from the banks and closed in, shouting. The front rows broke through the police line to where the bodies lay, and stopped short in horror as they got near enough to make out details. But the pressure behind them was too great; many were pushed ahead and forced to trample the bodies. Some fell sprawling over them. One man beside me was pushed out of his shoes. Kids screamed at the sight of blood and pieces of skull. Some blood got on my shoes. To protect the bodies, a policeman pulled out one of the numbered stakes, scooped up some brains on the circular sign, and held the people at bay with it. They reared back ten or fifteen feet in a circle around him.

An hour or so later, along with most of the crowd, I left. But I heard that at midnight, under a bright moon, several thousand people remained staring at the bodies, and that through the night others continued coming.

Most of the executed's families did not come to claim the bodies, although they would have had to pay just the minimal "bullet fee" to take possession. It wasn't only that the bodies were badly mutilated. It was necessary to draw a clear line between an executed relative and oneself. Claiming the body would demonstrate that one still had some sympathy with a criminal. So the bodies remained displayed until the third day, when they were taken somewhere and disposed of.

The following day everywhere in the city the city court posted announcements, with pictures of the executed's mutilated upper bodies. They described the criminals, their backgrounds, and their various crimes. Nowhere was there any discussion of the justice of the sentences. No mitigating circumstances of any kind were mentioned. There had been no trials; no one really knew what kind of people had been killed.

But the people knew there were Party activists circulating among them dressed as peasants, listening for inappropriate opinions. So they gathered in front of the announcements and chattered about the misfortune of the executed's families. Many of them had had lucky eyes. But no questioning showed in their faces . . .

This one performance was finished. Across China that September and October there were many shows. This one in Zhengzhou ran twice again. And China has thirty provincial capitals. Shanghai sent a hundred and one purported criminals on to West Heaven; Wuhan, sixty-eight; Peking, maybe seventy-nine. Inside China many have guessed at the number killed during that golden autumn of 1983. Some put it at 80,000. Some at 150,000. But this is only guesswork.

The number almost certainly runs well into six figures. During those two months every provincial capital and county seat in China produced such shows. China has two thousand counties. If every county executed only five, the tally would come to 10,000. If ten, 20,000. And if the play was produced three times, how many?

I don't know.

One man, though, knows. He ordered all the fresh clipboard reports sent to his office. Like all Chinese, Deng Xiaoping is very proud of five thousand years of civilization. And government of, by, and for the people is no more a part of Deng's policies than it is part of China's historical legacy.

This too is a face of what is happening in China.

Yellow Rain over Laos

(1982)

NICHOLAS ROTHWELL

Slowly, a cloud of yellow rain began to fall from the sky. It was a fine morning in May 1978, and the small village of Bang Non Po in Central Laos was about to be eradicated.

The assistant chief of the village of Hmong tribesmen, Yong Mang Yang, had heard the drone of an aircraft minutes before but had scarcely looked up from his work. He heard no explosions as the MIG-21 fighter circling above him dropped four brown rice-sacks from its belly, then turned and headed northwards. The bags split, releasing another cloud of yellow fumes. In the windless spring morning, the cloud dropped silently toward the houses of the village.

Minutes later, Yong Mang Yang saw his people beginning to die. There were only a few families in the village, and 14 of their members died in the gas attacks. Almost all the rest fell severely ill. Moments after the yellow rain touched them, the women and children began vomiting and blacking out, followed seconds later by the men.

Yong Mang Yang could smell nothing, and he could not breathe through his nose, which ran and itched. He staggered through the cloud, feeling as if sand were in his eyes, crying tears of blood, realizing he was blinded. Minutes after the rain cleared, he himself began vomiting, his stomach ached, and he felt a crushing sensation in his chest. Gradually, his skin turned reddish and small black spots formed all over his body.

Bang Non Po was attacked by the yellow rain four times within the next year. Scores of other villages in the rough hill-country in Central Laos, inhabited by Hmong tribesmen, were also attacked by Pathet Lao government planes releasing clouds of toxic, bright-colored gas. After the last attack, which was the most severe, Yong Mang Yang, as assistant village chief, composed a letter to the area hospital at Bon Don requesting emergency help. Days later, a messenger reported that a medical team would be sent to the village to "check into the matter."

Several weeks afterwards, a six-man Lao medical team arrived and diagnosed the villagers' illness as "fever" rather than the after-effects of chemical warfare. The Pathet Lao district leader, Taseng Mai Chank, told Yong Mang

Yang what to do. "If you are attacked again," he said, "shoot the plane down for proof."

Although such evidence has for the most part been studiously ignored, the campaign of poison gas attacks carried out against the Hmong people in the central hill-country of Laos between 1977 and 1979 is well documented. Some of the information comes from interviews conducted in the Ben Vinay refugee camp in northern Thailand. Yong Mang Yang's story is one of 40 separate accounts of gassings told over the past three years to refugee workers and State Department personnel, and later made public.

But in addition to these interviews, there is another set of findings which is not as widely known. Based on interviews with Laotian government defectors and various other sources, it was compiled into an amorphous body of U.S. intelligence assessments and included in some drafts of a State Department report on chemical warfare in Southeast Asia,* and apparently also in materials made available to the House subcommittee which in late 1979 began hearings on the matter.

Although all the major powers have had nerve gas stockpiles since before World War II, chemical warfare has hardly ever been used before. To understand how such a blatant breach of international law was permitted to continue in the face of overwhelming evidence—the scarred and pitted bodies of refugees—one must begin with the history of the Hmong.

Laos has been a battlefield for 30 years. Once part of French Indochina, then an independent kingdom, it was overrun during the 1960s by the Communist Pathet Lao guerrillas, who gradually wrested control of the country from Western-backed forces. As a vital part of the Ho Chi Minh Trail supply line for the Vietnam war, Laos was inevitably part of the sphere of influence of Vietnam—a "sideshow" in Indochina if ever there was one. During the sixties, the United States mobilized several clandestine groups to fight the Pathet Lao and the North Vietnamese. The most famous of these was the CIA's "secret army" of Hmong tribesmen, led by the charismatic General Vang Pao. The fall of Laos to Communist forces in 1975 did not end their struggle, if only because they knew their past resistance had marked them for reprisals.

Vang Pao, now resettled to a farm in Montana, claims the first gas attacks against the Hmong villages began in early 1976. Whatever the case, systematic campaigns were not mounted until the next year when Pathet Lao soldiers began to encounter organized military attacks by Vang Pao's men.

When first reports of the Pathet Lao campaign came out, they were discounted as tall stories—the evidence, after all, came from a "biased source," the Hmong, who were tainted by their association with Vang Pao. As reports became more frequent in the late seventies, events in Laos were overshadowed by the tragedy of Cambodia. The few American State Department employees, Australian relief workers, and Western correspondents in Thailand who first heard of the gassings found their efforts to alert the public scarcely encouraged

*These internal documents do not disclose the organization that conducted the studies. They simply state that "the U.S. government has received a report."

by the Carter Administration's desire to improve relations with Hanoi. In addition, anything having to do with the after-effects of the clandestine role played by U.S. intelligence during the Vietnam conflict rankled the guilt-laden Carter foreign policy. So did concern that closer study of the Hmong tragedy itself might point to the use of discarded U.S. weapons and supplies in the gassings. Finally, during the Carter years U.S. policy-makers, including the Congress, were reluctant to pursue growing evidence of Soviet complicity in the gassings.

Thus, even though samples of the poison gases were obtained, and exact dates, places, and even a long roll of the names of the Hmong victims established, it has taken Western leaders a full three years to admit openly that the Laotian government has lived up to its promise to "exterminate the Hmong" and that it has done so with Vietnamese—and Soviet—support.

Regular gassings had been underway for two years when the U.S. House of Representatives Subcommittee on Asian and Pacific Affairs held a hearing in December 1979 on the "Use of Chemical Agents in Southeast Asia Since the Vietnam War." Ironically, one purpose of this inquiry was to establish beyond any doubt that American herbicides left behind in Vietnam at the end of the war, such as Agent Orange, were not being used in the attacks on the Hmong. "I hope we will be able to put to rest any fear that those lethal agents used in Laos are captured American stocks left over from the war," said Rep. Lester Wolff (D-NY) at the outset of the hearings.

Rep. James Leach (R-Iowa) said he had been given "persuasive corroborating evidence" that the poisons came from the Soviet Union. "Our intelligence agency," Leach added, however, "has determined for national security reasons that this information should not be made public." One reason for this reluctance may be that the evidence implicates captured U.S. weaponry in the gassings. But more importantly, the information also details Soviet involvement in the gassings.

Most of the critical information given to the House subcommittee members came to U.S. intelligence from two Laotian defectors, both pilots who had flown on the gassing missions (many of the investigators in the State Department and U.S. Army Medical Corps who worked with the refugees in Thailand had no knowledge of any of this information). The pilots provided chapter and verse on the entire operation, including how it was run by the Vietnamese and Soviets.

The first narrative is the story of a Laotian People's Liberation Army Pilot, who began flying chemical warfare operations against Hmong resistance strongholds in 1976. The missions, "specifically intended to dispense toxic chemical agents on Hmong villagers" in the vicinity of Phou Bia—one of the hide-outs of Vang Pao's secret anti-Communist army—began in April or May 1976. They were flown in Soviet-built Ilyushin L-19 "Ravens" or in converted T-41 Cessnas, as part of a coordinated operation between the Laotian army and the People's Army of Vietnam.

The first sign that a special campaign was to be mounted came when two Laotian helicopters were flown from the Phonsavan airfield in Xieng Khouang province to Long Tieng on a series of missions that transported rockets back to

Phonsavan for storage. The entire operation was mounted within the hills of Central Laos. The backbone of the country is a series of steep ridges and valleys, covered in jungle. The area is impassable to conventional troops. It was these hills, the territory of the Hmong, that the Laotian army had decided to target. Their bases were strategically located within striking range, and any resistance soldiers trying to flee to Thailand would have to cross enemy lines at least once in a month-long trek.

Between June and August of 1976, the Laotian air force Ravens mounted several attacks on Vang Pao's troops in the same area, concentrating on the redoubt of Bouamlong. Rocket attacks were made, but the crews responsible for loading rockets on the attack aircraft were told that the special ammunition moved to Phonsavan should not be used—even though Phonsavan was much nearer the target zone of Bouamlong than was Long Tieng, where the aircraft rearmed. These conventional attacks on Bouamlong went on for three months, until the dry season began. Then, the special rockets were brought from Phonsavan to a depot near the Ban Xon airfield and were fitted onto special external arms racks on the L-19s.

The pilot claims he flew some missions using American-manufactured warheads which came in two parts, with the tip and canister separated for storage and then joined together before being loaded onto the aircraft racks. But all the special rockets loaded at Ban Xon were already joined. Part of the pilot's routine pre-flight check called for him to examine the tip portion of the new rockets. Most of these, he saw, were loose at the point where tip and canister joined, unlike ordinary explosive-type rockets.

In late 1976, in preparation for airstrikes against two Hmong strongholds—the villages of Phou Bia and Kasy—Laotian pilots began to fly reconnaissance missions. Piloting a Cessna, the Laotians would take two or three Vietnamese army staff officers at a time on detailed overflights of Hmong villages. Then the first attacks began.

Initially, only Laotian officers accompanied the pilots on the airstrikes, but a fortnight into the campaign, Vietnamese officers began riding in the rear seats of the L-19s and alternating missions with the Laotians. All the Vietnamese spoke excellent Lao, and would go over situation maps of the target areas with pilots before the mission, just as the Laotian commanders did.

The pilots knew nothing about the targets until they were told what to attack at the pre-flight briefings. A different Vietnamese officer was assigned to each strike. They never communicated with Laotian ground officers during the flight. Before every mission that carried the special rockets, the L-19 pilots were warned by Laotian commanders to fly at above normal altitudes when firing the rockets; otherwise, the operation could prove hazardous to the crew. The pilot could see the rockets which he was firing at the Hmong were little more than smoke dispensers. Unlike ordinary ground-burst explosive shells, they detonated in the air, some producing a mixture of white and blue smoke, some red and yellow.

Before each mission, the pilots were given a pep talk by their commander. They were told the purpose of firing the rockets was to "cause the Hmong people to die out completely." This type of operation would "wipe out" the reactionary Hmong people.

The pilots were also warned to keep the smoke rocket missions secret. During the two years that the pilot flew these missions, he learned from the Laotian People's Liberation Army officers who flew with him that there were two types of rockets. The first kind, the smoke rockets, could only be fired at targets away from combined Laotian and Vietnamese troops. But the second kind, conventional close-support rockets, could be fired near friendly troop positions. The L-19 raids at first carried five conventional rockets and three smoke rockets. But later only four rockets, normally all smoke ones, were carried.

At the end of every strike in which smoke rockets had been used, the pilot was returned to a "rest house" at Phonsavan where an army doctor and nurse would give him a physical examination. By 1978—the year when the most serious effects from the gassings are reported—the pilot was being given a very thorough physical check by the doctor, and being "closely watched" by the nurse.

Gradually, an elite corps of pilots who flew the L-19s on the special missions formed. They were allowed privileges unheard of in the Laotian army. In addition to the standard pilot's salary of 12,500 kip monthly, they received a bonus of 3,700 kip daily as additional "flight pay," and free meals at Phonsavan. This special treatment continued until late 1978, when a squadron of MIG-21 fighters supplied by the Soviet and Vietnamese air forces took over the attacks on Phou Bia.

Coincidentally, U.S. intelligence sources also received some of the most detailed information of the whole campaign from Hmong refugees who were driven into Thailand by the same series of repeated attacks during 1978. This makes it possible to piece together just what effect the raids carried out by the L-19s had on the "enemy tribesmen" below.

Hmong from the same central highlands of Laos described a bewildering variety of different-colored clouds of gas, all producing deadly symptoms. One Lao National Forces officer claimed he had seen Soviet observers inspecting a village after a chemical attack on July 15. Repeated attacks on Phou Bia and the nearby center of Phu Kong Klao were reported. Other refugees said small aircraft had fired rockets at their villages. These had released a yellow powder that contaminated water supplies and produced "harmful gases." Whoever drank the water began to vomit, their eyes turned red, and they died within the hour.

Phu Kong Klao had been hit repeatedly, with the last chemical attack of 1978 occurring in October. L-19s had fired rockets which released green or red smoke that caused unconsciousness, vomiting, and bleeding from the mouth and the nose. The gas was dangerous for a week unless washed away by rain. Those badly affected died within 24 hours. Refugees said 1,200 people had been killed by the gas in this area alone.

The eyewitnesses of attacks on Phou Bia said propelled aircraft—probably the L-19s—had dropped two or four rockets from external racks on several passes over the village. The rockets had released a green cloud that caused headaches, dizziness, vomiting of blood, and death shortly afterward. There was also a "yellow gas" which was even more rapidly acting than the green one.

Other sources described earlier attacks in the Phou Bia region. A pair of Hmong children reported two aircraft dropped a green gas which killed their parents within 20 minutes, although there were no visible signs of injuries and "they appeared to be asleep." Another attack, said to have killed 1,000 villagers, involved green, red, and yellow gas drops. Those exposed to the gases began to vomit, ran about, lost their balance, and died within ten minutes. Reports were even received of accidental attacks on friendly villages by aircraft with Vietnamese markings, which dropped chemicals that led to the death of 300 Hmong, mostly children, who had sided with and even sheltered the government troops.

A report from the second Laotian pilot, who had defected after serving in the Lao People's Democratic Republic Air Force, confirmed many of these details. He provided information about the gas attacks carried out against the Hmong of Phou Bia, and said chemicals had been dispensed from light aircraft by Lao People's Liberation Army units in a concerted campaign in May 1978.

From his account, the secret American report of the gas operation was compiled. It read in part:

The LPLA unit responsible for the chemical warfare rockets is a special LPDR Air Force unit to which is attached a Soviet expert. In Vientiane there are three persons, led by a Socialist Republic of Vietnam expert, who are responsible for putting the chemicals into the heads of U.S. manufactured jackets.

At Phonsavan, Xieng Khouang province, there are two persons responsible for this activity along with four Soviet experts. In Savannakhet province, there are two other persons responsible for Southern Laos.

In spite of all the compelling and detailed evidence that systematic poison gas attacks on the Hmong people were taking place, the House subcommittee concluded that evidence of Soviet involvement in the gassings was "circumstantial."

It was not until September 1981, when the Reagan Administration produced chemical analysis of foliage affected by the spray of "yellow rain," that U.S. officials even suggested the poisons had been supplied by the Soviet Union. Documents on which the foregoing account is based, however, show that American intelligence knew more than three years ago that Soviet personnel were managing the gassings.

The Soviet Union rejects allegations that it prepared the poisons used to kill the Hmong tribesmen and says the United States is trying to blame Moscow for what it did itself in Vietnam. "The world public knows the extent of American chemical warfare during the U.S. intervention in Indochina," announced a Novosti Press Agency statement released last fall to rebut the new American allegations. The official news agency Tass asserted that the United States is only repeating these charges to prepare Americans for a limited nuclear war in which it will use its own chemical weapons. In late November, a five-man UN medical team investigating reports of chemical warfare in Southeast Asia and Afghanistan reported that it "found itself unable to reach a final conclusion as to whether or not chemical warfare agents had been used." The team was headed by Viacheslav Ustinov, the UN Under Secretary General for Political and Security Council Affairs and former head of the Soviet Ministry of Foreign Affairs "Third African Department."

The Soviet reluctance to admit to any role in the gassings is understandable. Less understandable, however, is the implicit sympathy it received from unexpected quarters: Even as the subcommittee held its hearing on December 12, 1979, U.S. diplomats were presenting the Soviets with the detailed reports of their evidence that the Lao government was gassing the Hmong. This was done at the request of the Congress, since the Soviet Union, "as the principal sponsor of Hanoi, particularly in the military sphere, had special responsibility to join with the United States in seeking permanently to outlaw the use of chemical agents in warfare."

Such actions led American diplomats in Thailand, who had been directly exposed to the horror of the refugees' stories, to decide that only firm evidence—in the form of samples of the poison gas itself—would convince public opinion. This step led to a quest for hard evidence, such as trees and clothing charred or partly destroyed by the unknown gas. Odd samples had already been brought over the border by Hmong refugees, but were in such poor condition they could not be chemically analyzed.

The yellow rain in fact turned out to be not one, but many different chemical agents. A rainbow of toxic gases had colored the skies above Laos. As discussed above, Soviet and Vietnamese supervisors had been seen, according to refugees, checking the effects of the poisons. For two years attempts to isolate known chemical poisons on the foliage collected proved fruitless. Because the clouds had been described as "yellow rain" the experts tested for mustard gas, soman, and other nerve gases. Eventually, a journalist, Mr. Sterling Seagrave,* pointed out that the reported symptoms of the yellow rain sprayed in Cambodia, Laos, and Afghanistan coincided with those caused by a class of chemicals known as mycotoxins.

A specific poisonous mycotoxin group, trichothecene, derived from the grain mould, *fungus fusarium,* has been frequently reported as a naturally occurring poison in the Soviet Union. The trichothecene mould isolated on foliage sprayed by the poison gas could not occur naturally in Southeast Asia, and could not grow naturally anywhere in such heavy concentrations. This was the "compelling but preliminary" evidence presented on September 14 by United States Secretary of State Alexander Haig.

But was it less "circumstantial" than the information given American intelligence three years before—in the middle of the gassing campaign—which was kept secret for want of proof while thousands of Hmong continued to suffer and die? The information was gathered in late 1978. The large-scale gassings went on in Laos until at least May 1979, while American diplomats asked Soviet officials to "use their influence" to stop the attacks, even though the intelligence community had intimated to Congress that Soviet experts were running the campaign.

*Seagrave's findings have since been detailed in his book, *Yellow Rain.*

The Hmong made perfect targets. Their villages were small and isolated. Their reports of the attacks tended to be exaggerated. Their regard for detail did not match the needs of Western officials looking for "hard evidence." It was next to impossible to draw up an accurate picture of the military operations being conducted against them.

The last surge of attacks in Laos began in June 1979—the same month that Jimmy Carter and Leonid Brezhnev embraced each other, signed the Salt II treaty in Vienna, and pledged themselves to fight for world peace.

The Real Bulgaria

(1987)

ARCH PUDDINGTON

One of the ugliest—and most obscure—chapters in the history of Communist Eastern Europe is currently being played out in Bulgaria. In the name of a "unitary, socialist nation," the party leadership has undertaken nothing less than the cultural extermination of the country's largest national minority, the Turks, who make up roughly ten percent of Bulgaria's nine million people. Although several hundred Turks at minimum have died in this "Bulgarization" campaign, physical elimination is not the regime's goal.

Instead, in Bulgaria we are witnessing one of the purest examples of what black radicals in the United States once referred to as "cultural genocide." Although the term has grown out of favor in the U.S., and rightly so, cultural genocide is an accurate description of the Bulgarian authorities' intentions. Speaking Turkish, dressing in traditional Turkish clothing, practicing Turkish (or in some cases Moslem) customs, and most importantly, maintaining a Turkish name—all have been declared illegal, and the decrees are rigorously enforced, to the point where men have been murdered for refusing to have their names changed from Turkish to Bulgarian. The whole affair has been conducted with a crude, Stalinist competence reminiscent most recently of the Polish military's awe-inspiring efficiency during the imposition of martial law. As for the regime's explanations of policies which are, to say the least, uncharacteristic of Communist regimes in the era of Gorbachevian "liberalism," they can only be described as typical products of the tried-and-true Big Lie technique. As Interior Minister Dimitar Stoyanov announced: "There are no Turks in Bulgaria. The issue is closed."

If indeed the issue is closed it is largely due to the outside world's having done little beyond raising the occasional discreet eyebrow during the period when the worst atrocities were being committed. Here, the absence of sustained press attention has been crucial, a situation for which the media cannot entirely be blamed. The authorities have effectively sealed off those areas with large concentrations of ethnic Turks. Very occasionally, groups of Western reporters have been given brief, and carefully chaperoned, tours of villages where Bulgarization was implemented. Otherwise, the sources of information have been limited to diplomatic circles in Sofia or Washington, or to Bulgarian Turks who have fled abroad. Under such conditions, television coverage has been ruled out and the volume of newspaper attention unimpressive. In an excellent report on the persecution of the Bulgarian Turks, the human rights organization Helsinki Watch published a bibliography which listed nine articles from the American press for the year 1985, when most of the violence associated with the Bulgarization drive occurred.

The Turks' plight was further obscured by the lack of an internal democratic opposition of the kind which endures, with varying degrees of influence, in Poland, East Germany, Hungary, and Czechoslovakia. In Poland, where the underground press gives detailed accounts of every act of official misconduct, the successful cover-up of state repression is practically impossible. Bulgaria, by contrast, has no tradition of underground or *samizdat* literature, something which is even more pronounced among the Turkish minority, which is made up largely of laborers and agricultural workers.

Thus the burden of defending the political and cultural rights of Bulgaria's Turkish minority has largely fallen to the government in Ankara. Yet Turkey's attempts at the United Nations and other forums to raise the question of Bulgaria's racial policies have met with minimal success. Turkey, unfortunately, has its own image problem in Europe and the United States, somewhat unjustified to be sure, but a reality nonetheless. Another presumed interested party, the Moslem world, has not ignored the unpleasant situation of Islamic Bulgarians. But Moslem countries have addressed the Bulgarian question with uncharacteristic politeness. There have been no harsh accusations, no tantrums at the U.N., no threats of retaliation. The few inquiries that have been made at the U.N. have been ignored by the Bulgarians, who refused to permit an Islamic Conference delegation to conduct a fact-finding mission. On this occasion, at least, the restraint of the Islamic countries is regrettable. Given the Soviet Union's keen interest in cultivating improved relations with Saudi Arabia and other Arab nations, a noisy protest directed at Sofia might conceivably convince an embarrassed Kremlin to take a more active interest in the internal policies of its smaller, and traditionally obedient, neighbor.

At the heart of the forced assimilation drive is the demand that traditional Turkish names be abandoned for Bulgarian ones. The universal adoption of Bulgarian names has been a party objective for some time. During the 1970s, Turks were pressured to accept Bulgarian names during the periodic issuance of internal identity cards. But few Turks took this option, and the amount of coercion was relatively mild, especially in light of what was to follow.

Beginning in January 1985, a new, much more determined, and often violent effort was launched to compel the Turks to adopt Bulgarian names. The campaign was planned in military fashion, with the secrecy and swiftness of execution which that implies. Halil Ibishev, an ethnic Turk who served ten years in Bulgaria's rubber stamp parliament, believes that the decision on forced assimilation was made by the Politburo several years before its implementation. Yet neither he nor other ethnic Turks within the party were aware of the leadership's plans until the Bulgarization offensive actually got under way.

The tactics of the campaign were relatively simple. Brigades of soldiers and police would arrive, unannounced, at a village or town. All points of entry and exit would be barricaded, and telephone links with the outside world severed.

All Turks would then be assembled in the main square, where they would be informed of the new policies. There would be lists of Bulgarian names, and Turks would be given the opportunity to make their own selection. Those who refused usually would be assigned new names; Ibishev's name was changed from Halil Ahmedov Ibishev to Lubomir Alekseev Avdjiev. Those who resisted would be beaten or taken away to special prison camps; Turks who put up stronger opposition were sometimes shot. Amnesty International has placed the number killed at between 300 and 1,500. If even the lowest estimate is accurate, it would place Bulgarization among the bloodiest episodes in postwar Eastern Europe that did not involve foreign troops. The first three months of Bulgarization claimed more victims than did the 1953 uprising in East Germany, the 1968 Soviet invasion of Czechoslovakia, or the imposition of martial law in Poland.

In case anyone was overlooked in the initial dragnet, the authorities had in reserve other, more bureaucratic methods to ensure compliance. Birth certificates would no longer be issued unless the child had a Bulgarian name, and marriages could not be registered if either party had failed to have its name Bulgarized. The state could also punish dissenters with economic sanctions: those who maintained a Turkish name could not be paid by state enterprises or receive a pension.

Among the more absurd consequences of the name change was its effect on family members who lived in different parts of the country. The authorities demanded that all names be Bulgarized: first, middle, and family. However, ethnic Turks living in different villages or regions were not allowed to communicate with one another. As a result, a family consisting of a father and three grown sons—all living in different villages—might be assigned four different family names. Moreover, according to Ibishev, the authorities extended the name change policy to the dead as well as the living by assigning new names to deceased relatives of ethnic Turks (and even to living relatives who had emigrated to Turkey).

The authorities also banned the speaking of Turkish in public, a rule enforced by the deployment of massive numbers of police in villages which had previously required a single constable to keep the peace. A *Chicago Tribune* reporter who was permitted to spend a few hours in an ethnic Turkish town one year after the climax of the Bulgarization offensive wrote of "grim faced men in leather jackets . . . spaced every few yards" whose "sole task was to listen for anyone speaking Turkish."

Another target was the ritual practice of circumcision. At the time the name change was prosecuted, the authorities conducted examinations of all male children of ethnic Turks to determine who had and had not been circumcised. From that time hence, circumcision was banned, and those children who had not been circumcised were reexamined every few months to ensure that the edict had been obeyed. Failure to comply could result in a fine or imprisonment for the child's father, for the person who carried out the circumcision, and for anyone who had helped to arrange the ritual. Typically, the whole disgraceful policy had to be given an ideological rationale. Thus an article, published in

Nova Svetlina and entitled "Circumcision—Form of Spiritual and Physical Disunity of the People," proclaimed:

The practice of circumcision is an anti-social and anti-state deed on the part of the parents and the person performing the circumcision. This is a hostile, anti-Bulgarian and anti-social act, whose perpetrators must be punished according to the full strictness of our country's laws. Marx and Engels, the founders of scientific atheism, pointed out that religious customs, rites and traditions are a "great bother and a force of inertia throughout history; however, it is a passive force and therefore must die." This applies with a special force to the barbarous Islamic rite of circumcision . . . [which] is a crucial unit in the arsenal of imperialism's ideological diversion, aimed at differentiating and disuniting our country's working people, and alienating a part of them from the Socialist Motherland.

As added insult to Bulgarian Moslems, the party periodically trots out leading Islamic clerics to acclaim government actions and denounce the critics, particularly those from abroad. While the conditions facing religious leaders in Communist societies are never easy, it nevertheless would appear that the hierarchy of Bulgarian Islam has been more than usually pliant in accepting the regime's policies. An attitude of cooperation might be understandable if it helped to advance the status of the religion. Instead, recent years have brought a steady deterioration of Islam in Bulgaria. Mosques have been closed, on the curious ground that they contained violations of the housing code, and religious schools have been shut down, leading to a serious shortage of imams. The Koran is not being published, and its importation is banned. Nor is the situation likely to improve. Among the steps taken as part of forced assimilation were the elimination of separate Turkish cemeteries, complete with the smashing of tombstones, and the prohibition of Moslem funeral rites.

The party has not only cited God's representatives as sanction for its policies, it has claimed the support of history as well. Since Bulgarization was launched, several "archaeological studies," based on a putative examination of human skulls unearthed in Turkish regions of the country, have concluded that the original inhabitants of these regions were not Ottoman Turks, but something called "proto-Bulgarians." This research is frequently cited by party spokesmen to bolster the argument that Turks never existed as a distinct ethnic group in Bulgaria, and that Bulgarization thus represents nothing more than a return to one's historical roots.

A key question is whether Bulgarization is a uniquely Communist phenomenon or a natural outgrowth of the fractionalized racial history of the Balkan peninsula. Those who prefer the latter explanation can point to countless instances of national and religious strife throughout Balkan history, especially in those areas once controlled by the Ottoman Empire. In 1876 Turkish irregular forces slaughtered thousands of Bulgarian peasants in reprisal for Bulgarian efforts to achieve independence. Today, the most persuasive justification for forced assimilation *within Bulgaria* is the argument that Bulgarians are only doing to the Turks what the Turks once did to Bulgarians.

In fact, however, relations between Bulgarians and ethnic Turks have been relatively free of tension since Bulgaria won its freedom from the Ottoman Empire in 1878. The Turkish minority fared much better during pre-Communist times, perhaps because the Turks, mostly land-hungry peasants, were not perceived as an economic threat by ethnic Bulgarians. Whatever the reason, the Turks were generally left alone by successive Bulgarian governments. Emigration to Turkey was not restricted; interestingly, emigration levels were not high until the Communist takeover. A further testimony to Bulgaria's tolerance was the country's eschewal of the strident anti-Semitism that marked other European countries in the interwar years, and its refusal to cooperate with German demands for delivery of Jews to the death camps.

But something changed with the coming of Communism. Initially, to be sure, the party went out of its way to win the support of the Turks through promises of autonomy and cultural liberties. The first problems arose over collectivization, not cultural rights. Collectivization was unpopular among the Turks, as among all peasant groups, and for a brief time in 1950 Bulgarian authorities were aggressively encouraging Turkish emigration (some accused Bulgaria of deporting them outright) in order to make land available for a massive collectivization project with which the government was enamored.

Over the years a number of the concessions made in the name of cultural distinctiveness—Turkish language newspapers, special schools—were gradually withdrawn. Yet it could not be said that the Turks suffered any more than the rest of the Bulgarian people; no one, after all, enjoyed cultural freedom in Communist Bulgaria.

There was, however, a distinct shift in attitude during the 1970s. An anti-Turkish bias could be detected in the official media, with Turkish cultural and religious practices disdained as archaic and reactionary. Gerrymandering was used to limit the political representation of the ethnic Turks in governmental bodies. A modest start was made in a program to resettle Turks in non-Turkish regions. Perhaps most ominously, statistical surveys began omitting tallies for the Turkish subgroup; the 1965 census was the last to list figures for Turks and other minority groups.

Yet right up until the final offensive against Turkish distinctiveness, Bulgaria's external propaganda continued to brag about the rights and freedoms enjoyed by its national minorities, the Turks most of all. Indeed, the regime's claims to racial fairness created some embarrassing moments once the assimilation drive got underway. For example, a Bulgarian report submitted to the United Nations Committee on the Elimination of Racial Discrimination just a few months before the name change campaign was launched made frequent reference to the cultural rights guaranteed minority nationalities, most prominently the Turks. Subsequently, the authorities submitted a hastily revised report—with all mention of the Turks expunged.

Whatever the role of Communism as an ideology in Bulgaria's anti-Turk policies, it is clear that the totalitarian structure of the state was essential to the successful prosecution of forced assimilation. It took but three months to impose Bulgarian names on all ethnic Turks, with scarcely a murmur of protest from outside the country's borders. The absence of competing political parties and, probably more important for a Muslim minority, a truly independent clergy, left the Turks without effective leadership, and the authorities made sure that no indigenous leaders would emerge by placing potential dissenters in preventive detention at the beginning of the assimilation drive. The state's monopoly on economic power rendered strikes or boycotts futile. Oddly enough, much of what was accomplished by force could have been achieved through bureaucratic methods, the state holding total control over jobs, pensions, travel, marriage, and other basic rights of the sort we take for granted. Indeed, perhaps the most telling evidence of the absence of the rule of law is the refusal of the party leaders to publish the various secret decrees on forced assimilation. Officially, it seems, nothing unusual has happened in Bulgaria.

This still leaves open the question of the motives for a policy that appears to clash sharply with the current drive of other Soviet bloc nations for acceptance as normal members of the international community. The most common theory stresses Bulgarian apprehensions over a Turkish-Moslem population bomb. Right now, population growth for ethnic Bulgarians is hovering near zero, a trend shared by European nationalities throughout the Communist world (Poland excepted). Through a strange combination of crash industrialization, urbanization, improved education, easy access to abortion, and an extreme shortage of decent housing, Soviet-style Communism has unwittingly fulfilled much of the agenda of the population control movement, and without the draconian controls imposed by the Chinese. But these dramatic changes have been largely limited to Europeans; in the Soviet Union, the various Asian nationalities continue to reproduce at relatively high levels. This is also the situation in Bulgaria, where the Turks and other Moslem groups enjoy markedly higher reproduction rates than ethnic Bulgarians.

The prospect of a shift in the population balance holds a number of implications for the party leadership, none of them pleasant. One possibility is an eventual Turkish demand for some form of national autonomy, say, a separate Turkish republic within a larger Bulgarian confederation. Another possible concern is a surge in Moslem fundamentalism. Yet here the Bulgarians appear to have been as successful as the Soviets in smothering nascent fervor for Islam, and there is no evidence that the country's Moslem inhabitants are vulnerable to the siren call of religious fanaticism.

There remains the question of Communist ideology. Although Lenin and other Bolshevik icons can be cited to support just about any position on the nationalities question, as a utopian theory Communism is generally hostile to national distinctiveness. More to the point, as a practical matter national differences complicate the task of political and social control.

Through the years, Communist regimes have used a variety of techniques to encourage the full assimilation of minority groups. Periods of repression have alternated with periods of tolerance. Under certain conditions, Communist regimes have demonstrated a breathtakingly cynical willingness to exploit national differences when it suited their purposes; the Soviets, for example, concocted an entire ethnic group, the Moldavians, to justify the seizure of territory from Romania after World War II.

Ultimately, Communists believed that national differences would inevitably evaporate, overwhelmed by the combined power of socialism, secularism, and industrialization. This of course has not happened, in Bulgaria or any other Communist society. Despite decades of pressure against their culture and religion, the Turks obstinately resisted full integration in Communist Bulgaria; even today, party officials acknowledge that many Turks cannot speak Bulgarian fluently. The party leadership may well have concluded that full assimilation would never be realized unless the prevailing policies of moderate coercion were replaced by outright terror. The short-term costs—a moderate degree of internal disorder and a few words of opprobrium from the free world—will have been more than offset if in a generation or so the very fact that a Turkish nationality ever existed will have slipped down the memory hole. One can even imagine that the Bulgarization drive was undertaken with a genuine sense of ideological mission—no previous Communist government, after all, has "solved" its nationality problem by simply decreeing the nonexistence of an entire people.

V

America
and the World

Sideswipe: Kissinger, Shawcross and the Responsibility for Cambodia

(1981)

PETER W. RODMAN

At the end of 1979 **The American Spectator** *awarded its Worst Book of the Year award to William Shawcross for his epic bowl of applesauce,* Sideshow: Kissinger, Nixon and the Destruction of Cambodia. *We accorded the book high marks for Shawcross's masterful juggling of documents and for his assiduity in propounding themes at once illogical and moronic. Unfortunately, Mr. Shawcross failed to show up at our award ceremony—a practice that has become all too common with our laureates—but he was injudicious enough to challenge me to reveal examples of his legerdemain.*

Now I have asked Peter Rodman, formerly of the National Security Council Staff and currently Henry Kissinger's research assistant on the Kissinger memoirs, to illuminate the Shawcross method of cooking up history. It has been a demanding task. Through the Freedom of Information Act, Shawcross gained access to thousands of documents relating to America's foreign policy in Southeast Asia. Rodman is one of the few scholars who actually bothered to check Shawcross's work. What Rodman has discovered is that Shawcross is even slipperier than I reported in our February 1980 issue.

I suppose I could have kept this matter private—a mundane scandal known but to Rodman, Tyrrell, Shawcross, and Shawcross's favorite cleric. A private communiqué to the great artist would have fulfilled my Christian obligations, had the preposterous theme of the Shawcross book not come to be accepted by the Left as one of recent American history's Great Truths, namely: that the United States is responsible for the Cambodian holocaust. Left-wingers are repeating it fervently in the universities and other realms of the intelligentsia. In time it will assume the sacrosanct quality of so many other left-wing lies: the innocence of Alger Hiss, the Great Red Scare of the 1950s, the American responsibility for the origins of the Cold War.

These are some of the lies that the left-wing brethren live by. And of course the brethren are very fine at spreading them. A few weeks ago during Senate hearings on the confirmation of Alexander Haig, some senators intoned the Shawcross thesis as though it had just been passed on to them by Herodotus in a vision.

It is the responsibility of any intelligent journal of opinion to keep the record straight even from the credulity of senators. The Left has been successfully disfiguring history for years. In the following piece, Rodman shows one of the ways the surgery is accomplished. Incidentally, Rodman's scholarship appears all the more exquisite when one considers the lofty laudations Shawcross has received for his "scholarship." This piece might not stop the Left from spreading its mumbo jumbo on Cambodia, but it will make the Left's job more difficult, at least among the literate.

—RET

In April 1975, the Communist Khmer Rouge took power in Cambodia, emptied Phnom Penh of its entire population, and embarked on a nationwide campaign of terror and destruction that claimed the lives of somewhere between one million and three million Cambodians—out of a total population of seven million.

Four years later, British journalist William Shawcross produced a book entitled *Sideshow: Kissinger, Nixon and the Destruction of Cambodia.* As its subtitle suggests, it attempts to prove *American* responsibility for the horrors wrought by the Khmer Rouge. Shawcross argues in essence that American bombing in 1969 "destabilized" the neutral government of Prince Norodom Sihanouk; that the U.S.-South Vietnamese incursion of 1970 triggered the bloody war in Cambodia that engulfed the country; and that America's prolongation of the conflict for five years paved the way for the victory of the Khmer Rouge and accounted for their genocidal brutality after they took power.

The Shawcross book was widely praised for its impressive documentation, even by some who did not entirely swallow its conclusions. The book advertises itself as based on "thousands of pages of classified U.S. Government documents" obtained under the Freedom of Information Act (FOIA). Without the time or inclination to verify his evidence, reviewers seemed mesmerized by invocation of the Freedom of Information Act, as if it were a voodoo incantation that paralyzed all critical faculties. I have had the opportunity to examine a duplicate set of the government files that Shawcross obtained under the FOIA. It was an experience full of surprises. Close scrutiny of the materials shows that the evidentiary basis of the book is so seriously flawed as to discredit his whole enterprise. He had no White House documents, since they are exempt from the FOIA, yet he presumes to pass judgment above all on White House decisions. His vaunted research turns out to be slipshod, distorted by bias, and in some cases bordering on the fraudulent. It is a compendium of errors, sleight of hand, and egregious selectivity; he has suppressed entirely a mountain of evidence in his possession that contradicted his principal points.

The chronicle of Shawcross's errors is in itself a brief history of Cambodia's tragedy.

Beginning in about 1965, North Vietnam established a string of military bases on the territory of neutral Cambodia, along the border, just opposite South Vietnam. From these sanctuaries North Vietnamese forces launched forays into South Vietnam, attacking South Vietnamese and American troops and escaping back across the border into Cambodia where self-imposed restraints prevented our pursuit or retaliation.

The Nixon administration in early 1969 lifted some of these restraints. At a time when major American troop withdrawals were being planned, the North Vietnamese shelled a number of cities in South Vietnam, in flagrant breach of the pledge that had been the quid pro quo for President Johnson's halt to the bombing of North Vietnam. No one in the Nixon administration was eager to resume the bombing of the North; a less explosive form of retaliation seemed warranted. President Nixon undertook the bombing of the Cambodian sanctuaries in the knowledge that 1) Prince Norodom Sihanouk, Cambodia's neutralist leader, did not object to American military action against the North Vietnamese bases, and that 2) the risk of harm to Cambodian civilians was minimal.

Shawcross struggles without success to prove that both these propositions were false.

Chester Bowles: The Missing Quotation

Sihanouk was powerless to prevent North Vietnam's expropriation of Cambodian territory for prosecution of the Vietnam war. The Prince went considerably beyond acquiescence, however; he allowed the Communists to ship war materiel to the port of Sihanoukville and then to transport it by a leisurely truck route to the sanctuaries along the border. Even Shawcross describes this (p. 64), and anyone wanting an authoritative account of the active help Sihanouk gave to the North Vietnamese will find it in Sihanouk's recent memoirs.* This would seem to say something about how "neutral" Cambodia was under Sihanouk.

In fairness to the agile Prince, however, in the late 1960s he began to feel put-upon by the heavy-handed North Vietnamese and tried to square accounts by telling American officials that he would not object at all if the United States attacked the Vietnamese Communist bases and drove them out of Cambodia. He said this to various visitors, one of the most important being Ambassador Chester Bowles, who on January 10, 1968, met with the Prince in Phnom Penh on a mission for President Johnson.

Sihanouk's conversation with Bowles has become controversial. The Nixon administration cited it when the Cambodian bombing became a *cause célèbre* in 1973. Shawcross devotes a great deal of effort to the Bowles mission, attempting to discredit, evade, deny, or dismiss the administration's contention. The reason for this exertion is obvious: If Sihanouk invited us to attack the North Vietnamese bases, then we were defending Cambodia's neutrality, not violating it, and the bombing of Cambodia appears in an entirely different light.

Shawcross pronounces the claim "questionable" (p. 28). For three and a half lengthy pages he walks us through the Bowles mission (pp. 68–71), citing Bowles's State Department briefing papers, Bowles's escort officer's summary report, and Bowles's cables to Washington. Never does Shawcross quote a word of what Sihanouk said to Bowles on the subject. He apologizes that his documentation is incomplete and therefore not "conclusive evidence"; "whether Sihanouk actually told Bowles that the United States was free to bomb the sanctuaries cannot be definitely determined from the sanitized State Department papers," he writes. Nevertheless, Shawcross is confident enough to inform his readers that his documents "suggest that it is not so."

A look at the documents is illuminating. While Shawcross may not have had a verbatim transcript, he had an explicit summary of what Sihanouk said. The State Department escort officer's report of the Bowles mission, which Shawcross received under the Freedom of Information Act, contained evidence that could not be more conclusive, which Shawcross chose to conceal from his readers:

*See Carl Gershman's "Cambodia and the Prince" in the September 1980 *American Spectator*.

Then, in one of his amazing reversals [the report read], the Prince said he would not object if the U.S. engaged in "hot pursuit" in unpopulated areas. He could not say this publicly or officially, but if the U.S. followed this course it would help him solve his own problem. Of course, if the U.S. engaged VC/NVA [Vietcong/North Vietnamese Army] forces on Cambodian territory, both sides would be guilty of violating Cambodian soil, but the VC/NVA would be "more guilty" (sic). If we pursued VC forces into remote areas where the population would be unaffected he would "shut his eyes."

The same thing could have been found in Chester Bowles' memoir *Promises to Keep*, published in 1971:

Later, in a quiet private visit, Sihanouk volunteered that he would not object to the United States' engaging in "hot pursuit" in unpopulated areas of Cambodia. He pointed out that while he could not say this publicly or officially, if the United States followed this course, it might even help him to solve his problem.

Bowles was skeptical, but Sihanouk's position never deviated from this. After the B-52 bombing started in 1969 and was reported in the American press, Sihanouk responded in similar terms publicly: He complained if Cambodians were hurt but did not object if we attacked the Vietnamese Communists who were illegally occupying a portion of his country. Sihanouk drew closer to the United States. In July 1969, four months after the bombing started, he invited President Nixon to pay a visit to Phnom Penh and promised a warm reception. He began to write and speak more openly against the North Vietnamese. This avid observer and barometer of the balance of power now saw the United States as a potent counterweight to the hated North Vietnamese, restoring his country's freedom of action and enhancing—yes, enhancing—its neutrality.

Shawcross's treatment of the Bowles mission is a sham. Kissinger has published part of Sihanouk's verbatim remarks in his memoirs but it adds little to what was already available. In a lecture at Harvard in March 1980, Sihanouk admitted what he said to Bowles. Stephen Young, Assistant Dean of Harvard Law School, heard Sihanouk's lecture and called it "an incredibly significant admission." For "that means that, in the debate that has riven our country for 10 years, Henry Kissinger is right and William Shawcross is all wrong."

What the Chiefs' Memorandum Really Said

Nixon ordered the B-52 bombing of certain North Vietnamese sanctuaries on the Pentagon's assurance, secondly, that attacking them posed minimal danger of Cambodian civilian casualties. The Joint Chiefs of Staff examined 15 North Vietnamese base areas in Cambodia with the explicit mandate, *inter alia*, to consider the risk of harm to civilians. General Earle Wheeler forwarded the results to Secretary of Defense Melvin Laird on April 9, 1969, in a lengthy memorandum with numerous appendices and maps. Only the base areas in which the danger to civilians was found to be "minimal" were recommended for targeting.

This exercise might suggest to an impartial observer that the United States took extraordinary pains to avoid civilian casualties. But not to Shawcross. He quotes from the memorandum in the most selective fashion (*Sideshow*, pp.

28–29) to imply a callous disregard for human life—exactly the opposite of the memorandum's obvious meaning. Shawcross accomplishes this by quoting at length only from the caveats that the memorandum's draftsmen included for the sake of honesty: that all estimates of likely civilian casualties were "tenuous at best," that "some Cambodian casualties" would likely be sustained in certain kinds of military operations, and that the "surprise effect" of attacks could tend to increase the danger, "as could the probable lack of protective shelters around Cambodian homes to the extent that exists in South Vietnam."

On reading the Chiefs' memorandum carefully one finds, first of all, that these acknowledged risks to civilians applied to combined air and ground operations against the sanctuaries, not to aerial attacks on specific military targets ordered by Nixon. What is more, Shawcross acknowledges only in passing what the memorandum emphasized over and over again: that civilian casualties would be "minimal," for the simple and obvious reason that the North Vietnamese did not allow any Cambodians anywhere near their military dispositions. The point was made repeatedly, in passages that Shawcross found inconvenient to call to the reader's attention. For example:

a. There is very little mixing of the VC/NVA Forces with the Cambodian populace. Conversely, Cambodians rarely go into areas under de facto control of the VC/NVA.

b. Cambodian villages and populated areas are readily identifiable and can be essentially avoided in conducting preplanned operations into the base areas.

c. Very few permanent structures exist in the base areas outside the Cambodian villages. Virtually all those that do exist are enemy-occupied. (JCSM-207–69, 9 April 1969, Appendix E, p. 27)

[T]he enemy's military forces in Cambodia habitually occupy areas close to the SVN [South Vietnam] border and away from significant Cambodian presence. (Cover memorandum p. 2)

Extreme care would be taken to attack only known enemy bases in Cambodia, thus minimizing the risk of engagement with Cambodian forces or of causing Cambodian casualties. (Appendix B, p. 8)

The canard that we callously assumed the risk of massive harm to civilians should finally be laid to rest by Prince Sihanouk's recent memoirs. Before the March 1970 coup that overthrew him, Sihanouk writes, the North Vietnamese sanctuaries were "limited to a few outlying and uninhabited sectors along the Cambodia-Vietnam borderline."

There is more to this April 9, 1969 memorandum. It sets out in detail the strategic importance of the enemy sanctuaries and the danger that they presented. Indeed, it is one of the most impressive statements ever made of the case *for* attacking them. For example:

An appropriate time to undertake operations to destroy an enemy force is subsequent to a contact in which the enemy has been defeated and is withdrawing. It is at this point that the enemy force is most disorganized and vulnerable. The option of conducting pursuit operations has essentially been withheld from COMUSMACV [the U.S. Command] because the best place to conduct such operations is against his rallying and collection points in Cambodia.

Authority to conduct pursuit operations to limited depths in Cambodia could result in destruction of enemy units involved as effective fighting forces, and could require the enemy not only to provide filler replacements to regenerate such units but also to provide new cadre leadership. Pursuit operations also could result in capture or destruction of munitions and supplies in the sanctuaries to which enemy forces are withdrawing. Possibly most important of all, however, is the fact that once US/RVNAF [U.S./South Vietnamese] pursuit operations have been undertaken, the enemy would be forced to adjust to the possibility of future pursuit operations, and would not be able to operate in border areas with confidence that sanctuary was available nearby. Reestablishment of bases deeper in Cambodia would be very difficult for the enemy, due to increased visibility and the likelihood of confrontation with the Cambodian populace and forces, the International Control Commission, and the foreign press. . . . It is estimated that, as the enemy reaches his full deployment for the current offensive, and his operations begin to run their course, an opportunity will be presented in the III Corps area to strike a strategic blow of major proportions. If successfully exploited, this blow could change the whole balance of forces in Vietnam, severely curtail enemy capability in the vital III Corps area, and shorten the war. (Appendix C, pp. 23–24)

Shawcross preferred not to call this strategic analysis to his readers' attention.

Base Area 704: The Wrong Box

From the Joint Chiefs' memorandum of April 9, 1969, the White House selected as targets only six base areas minimally populated by civilians. The target areas were given the codenames BREAKFAST, LUNCH, DINNER, SUPPER, SNACK, and DESSERT; the overall program was given the name MENU.

With only six base areas, one might have thought that Shawcross would get it right. But he did not. To his embarrassment, a glaring error was discovered during the taping of David Frost's interview with Henry Kissinger in October 1979. Frost hurled at Kissinger the accusation that the White House ordered hundreds of B-52 attacks against a North Vietnamese base area in Cambodia that the Joint Chiefs of Staff had specifically recommended *against* attacking because it was heavily populated by Cambodians. Frost based the accusation on the following passage in *Sideshow:*

Three of the fifteen sanctuaries—base areas 704, 354 and 707, which had "sizeable concentrations of Cambodian civilian or military population" in or around them—were not recommended for attack at all. . . . The Chiefs' warning seems to have made no difference. Base Area 704 appeared on the White House's Menu as Supper. In the course of events, 247 B-52 missions were flown against it. (p. 29)

The only problem with this is that Base Area 704, because of its sizeable number of civilian inhabitants, was *never* a target of the B-52 bombing. The target area code-named SUPPER, against which 247 B-52 missions were flown, was Base Area 740 in eastern Cambodia—minimally populated by civilians and about 200 miles away from Base Area 704 which is in southern Cambodia along the Mekong River. Shawcross's assertion that Base Area 704 was attacked by B-52s is totally wrong. The map on page 27 of his book labeling Base Area 704 as target area SUPPER is also wrong.

Shawcross has admitted the error. The map and the relevant pages in his book were redone in subsequent editions. David Frost, informed of the error by Kissinger, was sufficiently embarrassed to request that the taped segment be deleted from the NBC program broadcast on October 11, 1979. It was deleted. But Shawcross was unapologetic. In a letter to Nigel Ryan of NBC News on October 10, 1979, Shawcross acknowledged that his book was wrong—and then offered an explanation as false as the original error. Shawcross excused his mistake on the ground that he had relied on a Defense Department White Paper submitted to the Senate Armed Services Committee in September 1973. This Defense Department statement indeed listed Base Area 704 as one of the six base areas targeted in the MENU program, apparently by a typographical error. What Shawcross failed to mention to NBC News is that he had two documents in his possession making clear that Base Area 740, not 704, was one of the six targets of the B-52 bombing program. A memorandum for Secretary Laird from General Wheeler dated November 20, 1969, recommended "additional" B-52 strikes against Base Area 740 in the MENU series. A similar memorandum of November 25, 1969, again listed Base Area 740 as a MENU target. The first memorandum was published in the Senate Armed Services Committee hearings of 1973 (pp. 151–153), to which *Sideshow* refers frequently; the second memorandum was released to Shawcross in 1977 under the Freedom of Information Act.

A meticulous scholar would have noticed the discrepancy between the 1973 White Paper with the typographical error and the contemporaneous 1969 documents listing Base Area 740 as a MENU target. Had Shawcross noticed the discrepancy he might have guessed that the contemporaneous documents were more authoritative than the after-the-fact summary of 1973. Or he could have checked with the Defense Department, as he did in October 1979, six months after the publication of his book and only after Kissinger pointed out the error. Shawcross did neither. The erroneous figure "proving" American barbarity was too tempting to admit of noticing discrepancies.

It is interesting to read what else the 1969 documents contain. According to the JCS memorandum of November 25, 1969, Base Area 740 contained enemy troop concentrations; anti-aircraft, field artillery, rocket, and mortar positions; eleven North Vietnamese base camps and bivouac areas; two storage areas; road and trail networks including six bridges; as well as numerous bunkers, trenches, and defensive positions—none closer than one and one-half kilometers to any civilian habitation. None of this is mentioned in *Sideshow*.

"Destabilizing" Sihanouk: The Elusive Evidence

Sihanouk was deposed as Cambodian Chief of State on March 18, 1970, by his own government and National Assembly. This set off a chain of events that ultimately engulfed Cambodia in ten years of bloody conflict.

It is an article of faith in anti-American demonology that the United States had a hand in the coup. (In fact, the United States was taken by surprise.) Shawcross naturally pursues this line of enquiry, only to admit in the end that he can find "no direct link" between the U.S. government and the coup plotters (*Sideshow*, p. 112). He would earn credit for his honesty were it not for two paragraphs of thick insinuation that the United States had plenty of motive and its denials must always be suspect, as if only bad luck can account for his failure to unearth the "direct link."

Shawcross then resorts to a more complicated line of argument to establish American responsibility. Most observers ascribe the coup to Cambodian popular resentment at the continuing North Vietnamese occupation of Cambodian territory tolerated by Sihanouk. Shawcross's thesis is that American B-52 bombings of remote sanctuary areas in 1969–1970 forced the North Vietnamese and Viet Cong troops to push their supply bases "deeper into the country" and "spread the fighting out from the border areas," thereby disrupting Cambodian politics and "destabilizing" Sihanouk's rule. (*Sideshow*, pp. 35, 95, 113–114)

It is difficult for anyone at this point to reconstruct North Vietnamese movements under the American bombings. Undoubtedly they moved to evade the precisely targeted attacks. The crucial questions are where, and to what extent, and with what traceable consequences. Shawcross's documentary evidence is so weak and so tendentiously handled that it casts serious doubt on whether his thesis holds any water at all.

The first document cited by Shawcross is General Wheeler's memorandum of November 20, 1969, to Secretary Laird, which we saw earlier. Shawcross cites it as evidence for the following:

. . . in Cambodia, as the Chiefs reported, it [the bombing] forced them to "disperse over a greater area than before." The raids spread the fighting out from the border areas. . . . (*Sideshow*, p. 95)

General Wheeler's memorandum, however, turns out not to refer to "spreading the fighting" at all. It refers rather to the enemy's dispersal of *supplies* "over a greater area than before." And far from endorsing Shawcross's claim that they moved "deeper into Cambodia" into conflicts with Cambodian authorities, the passage describes the North Vietnamese as dispersing supplies, and secondarily personnel, into more *isolated* areas on the immediate periphery of the main base areas, or in between the various base areas, which were strung out along the Vietnamese border. The passage cited by Shawcross actually reads:

Supplies have been dispersed over a greater area than before; and supplies have been moved into densely covered, unstruck areas. This tends to be confirmed by the increased activity noted since mid-October approximately mid-way between Base Areas 350 and 351. . . . However, even with his increased dispersal of personnel and supplies, the enemy continues to use portions of his old areas. (Wheeler memorandum, 20 November 1969, quoted in the 1973 Senate hearings, p. 152)

Thus the source cited by Shawcross is not only irrelevant to his main point but in direct contradiction to it. His use of the document is either deceptive or notably inept.

But there is more. Shawcross then invents a phony quotation from General Creighton Abrams:

To escape the bombardment [Shawcross writes], the Vietnamese Communists had begun to move deeper into Cambodia—"thus," as Abrams later acknowledged to the Senate, "bringing them into increasing conflict with the Cambodian authorities." . . . The effect was inevitable. . . . Sihanouk's balance of right against left became more precarious. The bombing was destabilizing him. (*Sideshow*, p. 113)

It turns out that the quoted words attributed to General Abrams in testimony to the Senate Armed Services Committee were spoken in reality by Senator Stuart Symington. In a book so fawned over for its scholarship, this is remarkable sleight of hand. Senator Symington put forward the proposition that U.S. bombings and ground probes from South Vietnam must have induced the North Vietnamese "to expand their areas of control or operations, thus bringing them into increasing conflict with the Cambodian authorities." Abrams indeed "acknowledged" this in the vaguest terms ("Yes, I think that is a fair statement"). Unfortunately we do not have General Abrams's own analysis because Senator Symington moved to a different subject. Nor is it likely that the Army Chief of Staff would tell a powerful senator on the Armed Services Committee that he was full of baloney. And neither General Abrams nor Senator Symington even touched upon the two central steps in Shawcross's argument: that the bombing drove the Vietnamese and the war "deeper into Cambodia" and was responsible for undermining Sihanouk's government. The Abrams/Symington exchange, even if quoted honestly, does not establish the crucial points.

The claim of North Vietnamese "spreading in Cambodia" is repeated in another passage shortly thereafter. This time Shawcross invokes an article published in Sihanouk's monthly journal *Le Sangkum* in October 1969 written by Sihanouk's Prime Minister and Defense Minister, Marshal Lon Nol:

. . . their spread [Shawcross writes] was due [in Lon Nol's words] to flooding and to "the operational pressure exerted by their adversary," that is, to clearing operations by American and South Vietnamese troops. (*Sideshow*, p. 114)

Lon Nol was writing of incidents of conflict between the North Vietnamese and Cambodian troops, thus confirming what General Abrams "acknowledged" to Senator Symington. But rather remarkable in this article, seven months after the beginning of the MENU bombing, is the absence of any reference to North Vietnamese "spreading" and, indeed, the complete absence of any mention of the U.S. bombing. Lon Nol is describing a totally different cause and a totally different effect. He writes of the increase in numbers *(accroissement)* of Vietnamese Communist forces *in* their base areas—not the spreading *out* of these bases. And he blames not the enemy's flight from American bombing in Cambodia but the enemy's withdrawal *(repli)* from South Vietnam, made necessary (as Shawcross notes) by American and South Vietnamese clearing operations *in South Vietnam.* Seven months after the bombing began, if Shawcross is to be believed, the Cambodian government should have complained of the American bombing as the cause of disruption and "destabilization" that Shawcross is so eager to prove. Yet Sihanouk and Lon Nol saw the menace elsewhere; they placed the condemnation precisely where it belonged. The article was entitled: "The Implantations of Viet Cong and North Vietnamese Along Our Frontier."

Shawcross has been backtracking lately, writing in a recent *Harper's* that the movement of North Vietnamese "deeper into the country" may not have been very extensive but that "a few miles deeper" was enough to disrupt Cambodia's political equilibrium. Considering how much of the weight of Shawcross's entire argument rests on this complicated syllogism, it is striking how weak is the evidentiary basis for it. (Even the map on page 27 of *Sideshow* showing the Communist base areas in the 1969–70 period offers no indication of any change in their location or extent over those two years.) Prince Sihanouk is rather more honest, telling the Cambodia Affairs Institute in Washington ten years after his overthrow: "If I lost my *Fauteuil presidentiel* and my Chamcar Mon Palace in Phnom Penh to Marshal Lon Nol who occupied them for five years, it was because I tremendously helped the Viet Cong and the North Vietnamese."

North Vietnamese Assault on Cambodia: The Missing Month of April

Like Sherlock Holmes' dog that didn't bark, the most striking distortion in *Sideshow* is an epic event in Cambodian history that is simply omitted from the book.

The new Cambodian government, even before it stripped Sihanouk of his powers, formally asked the North Vietnamese and Viet Cong in mid-March 1970 to vacate their Cambodian sanctuaries. The North Vietnamese responded with the humanitarianism for which they are renowned: They invaded the rest of Cambodia. Sweeping out of their bases along the border, they attacked and overran Cambodian military outposts, Cambodian towns, Cambodian roads, and Cambodian river communications all over the eastern half of the country, linking their scattered sanctuaries into one massive continuous base area aimed at South Vietnam and advancing westward on Phnom Penh, surrounding and menacing the capital with the evident intention of intimidating the new government into passivity, surrender, or collapse.

It was this wholesale North Vietnamese assault on eastern Cambodia, beginning in late March 1970, that plunged Cambodia into the Indochina war for the first time. To be sure, the remote sanctuaries along the border had been the subject of North Vietnamese occupation and American counterattacks; there had been occasional local incidents between North Vietnamese and Cambodian authorities. But Cambodia had never been at war; the Cambodian armed forces had never before been belligerents in full-scale hostilities. The North Vietnamese changed all that. It was after a month of these assaults that the United States and South Vietnam launched the so-called Cambodian incursion on April 30 to block the North Vietnamese and to protect American and South Vietnamese lives against the vast new North Vietnamese military base ballooning over all of eastern Cambodia.

The reader turns eagerly to *Sideshow* to see what this brilliantly comprehensive investigative reporter has to say on the subject of this North Vietnamese invasion. Nothing. Absolutely nothing. There is but one disingenuous descriptive sentence, ascribing only defensive motives to the North Vietnamese:

[T]he North Vietnamese moved westward into Cambodia with the apparent intention of securing their lines of communication. (*Sideshow*, p. 130)

There are one or two oblique references elsewhere in *Sideshow* that would indeed require Sherlock Holmes to piece them together and deduce that something was going on. It is not that Shawcross lacked information. Under the Freedom of Information Act, he had, for example, an important cable of April 21, 1970, in which Acting Chairman of the Joint Chiefs General William Westmoreland informed General Abrams in Saigon of the fact that Phnom Penh was surrounded and threatened:

As you are certainly aware, there is highest level concern here with respect to the situation in Cambodia. This concern has been heightened by the following:
a. It appears that the success of NVA and VC troops to date have encouraged them to expand what may have been limited objectives initially to a current drive to isolate Phnom Penh.
b. Most lines of communication leading into Phnom Penh from the north, east, and south have been interdicted by enemy forces and the security of Phnom Penh and the Cambodian Government appears to be seriously threatened. (JCS 05495, 21 April 1970)

The North Vietnamese were systematically interdicting all the major roads and waterways that led into Phnom Penh, cutting off the highways particularly to the north, east, and south of the city and blocking traffic on the Mekong River that was the city's lifeline. This North Vietnamese assault would seem to have little to do with "securing their lines of communication," as *Sideshow* fatuously claims, but a great deal to do with strangling the lines of communication of the Cambodian capital.

None of this is to be found in *Sideshow*. Shawcross prefers to regard the U.S.-South Vietnamese incursion as gratuitous and unprovoked, explained by the psychic aberrations of the Nixon administration: "the White House's truculence," Nixon's eagerness for "restoring his slighted authority" after domestic setbacks, "negligent and emotional decision making," and other ad hominem imputations of pathological aggression (pp. 130ff). The whole month of April is practically missing from the book—except for minor *American* actions after mid-April, without reference to the North Vietnamese attacks to which they were a response.

When Kissinger described these North Vietnamese attacks in his book and the David Frost interview, Shawcross took evasive action. His first response was to claim that Kissinger's account of the North Vietnamese assault was an afterthought: "[A]t the time of the [U.S.-South Vietnamese] invasion, neither Nixon nor Kissinger mentioned these moves or used them to justify American actions," *Newsweek* reported him as claiming. Yet no one could possibly read the Nixon administration's public statements of the time—April 30, June 3, June 30, 1970; February 25, 1971—and not find that the North Vietnamese invasion of eastern Cambodia was *the* reason for the allied military operations of April 30, 1970. Shawcross later retreated to the narrower assertion that "many" of the individual clashes listed in Kissinger's book "have never been mentioned before, neither in Nixon's announcement of the invasion, nor anywhere else." This is ridiculous. The *New York Times* reported the rapid advance of the North Vietnamese invasion of Cambodia throughout the period and published a map on April 18, 1970, showing them already in control of a third of the country.

If Kissinger's is indeed the most detailed and comprehensive description of the events of 1970—which it is—how this is a criticism of the Kissinger book is not obvious.

Shawcross's other tack has been to claim that Hanoi's *intention* in devouring eastern Cambodia in March-April 1970 "has never been proven" and has always been in dispute. The assertions that Hanoi really sought to topple the Cambodian regime, Shawcross now says, "have no basis in reality." This is first of all false and second of all a curious line of argument. Presumably it is possible to invade a country, occupy a third of it, lay siege to its capital, and yet claim sufficient ambiguity about one's motives to render any countermeasures not only unwarranted but immoral. The only account in *Sideshow,* remember, is that the North Vietnamese moved westward to "secur[e] their lines of communication."

What is the evidence? Shawcross certainly had enough documentation to show that the American government at the highest levels had good reason to believe the worst about North Vietnamese intentions. Witness Westmoreland's message of April 21, 1970, that Phnom Penh was surrounded, quoted above, not to mention all of Sihanouk's public statements including his March 23, 1970, five-point declaration calling for the overthrow of the Lon Nol government, and the declarations of solidarity from the North Vietnamese, Viet Cong, and Pathet Lao. On the ground, the North Vietnamese efforts to establish (and dominate) the insurgency aroused the resentment of, among others, the Khmer Rouge (the Cambodian Communists, who came to power in their own right five years later). The "Black Book" issued by the Khmer Rouge (Pol Pot) regime in September 1978 recounts:

After the coup d'etat, of March 18th 1970, the [North] Vietnamese organized their nationals living in Kampuchea, they armed them and used them as particularly ferocious instruments of oppression against the people of Kampuchea. . . . [The North Vietnamese] secretly organized a shadow national administration in Kampuchea, particularly in the north-east zone. . . . [They] organized a secret shadow army in Kampuchea. . . .

This was published seven months before *Sideshow* appeared but Shawcross does not refer to it.

Among North Vietnamese documents captured by the allies in the post-April 30 sweep through the sanctuaries were guide-books for the organizing (by the North Vietnamese) of the Sihanouk-proclaimed "National United Front of Cambodia" (FUNK) at the hamlet and village level to take power after the overthrow of the Lon Nol government; directives pledging support by North Vietnamese cadre and armed forces for the FUNK; soldiers' notebooks detailing North Vietnamese activity in forming and training guerrilla units; military staff notebooks on the formation of Cambodian units led by North Vietnamese cadre and of signal battalions, and so on. This is public knowledge.

Even *Sideshow* contains a damaging admission by Shawcross that "a government dominated by Hanoi" was the probable outcome if the United States did nothing (p. 165). Nor have any of Shawcross's emotional rebuttals to the Kissinger book even addressed one of its most important revelations: that in secret talks with North Vietnamese negotiator Le Duc Tho on April 4, 1970, Kissinger proposed joint diplomatic steps to guarantee the neutralization of Cambodia. Le Duc Tho contemptuously dismissed the offer and insisted on the overthrow of the new Cambodian government.

It was the North Vietnamese assault of March-April 1970 that plunged Cambodia into war, whatever *Sideshow*'s evasions. In 1979, four years after the Khmer Rouge victory, the North Vietnamese invaded Cambodia again, demonstrating that the heirs of Ho Chi Minh never had the slightest intention of tolerating a truly independent Cambodia, even an independent *Communist* Cambodia.

The Strangulation of the Cambodian Army

The Cambodian Army resisted the assault of the North Vietnamese and Khmer Rouge for five years, succumbing finally in April 1975. Their struggle was prey to a host of difficulties: poor organization and logistics; lack of training and the technical know-how to maintain and use equipment; petty corruption; and the progressive, Congressionally mandated withdrawal of American military support—from the 1970 ban on U.S. advisers, to the 1973 halt of U.S. air operations, to the 1975 strangulation of military supplies. Pentagon accounts document this well, and Shawcross under the FOIA had access to two of the best: the end-of-tour reports of two American officers who headed the Military Equipment Delivery Team in Cambodia (MEDTC), Major General John Cleland and his successor, Brigadier General William W. Palmer.

These accounts are quite moving, but Shawcross suppresses their principal points and turns the documents totally on their head. By quoting selectively he develops a tendentious thesis of his own to explain Cambodia's failure. He dismisses the generals' own analysis (without informing his readers of its contents) in a crude ad hominem attack:

These reports must be read with caution, since each man was anxious to promote his own career in the Army despite the Cambodian debacle. Each, therefore, was concerned to attach all blame to the Cambodians and refused to analyze carefully the effect of his own work in Phnom Penh. (*Sideshow*, p. 312)

Shawcross second-guesses the American strategy and blames Generals Cleland and Palmer for the disaster that befell the Khmer National Armed Forces (FANK):

Cleland explained the rationale—and, unconsciously, its serious implications—in his end-of-tour report: "The FANK depend on firepower to win. Seldom has FANK outmaneuvered the enemy—he has outgunned him." But his own actions made this inevitable; instead of improving the intrinsic fighting quality of Lon Nol's troops, Cleland created a fatal new dependency in them. By mid-1974 fully 87 percent of all American military aid was being spent on ammunition. If the Congress began to cut back aid or if the Khmer Rouge closed all lines of communication, then the government's troops would be deprived of "the quickfix" (to use another Cleland expression) which the Americans had thrust upon them. Both these things did happen and each contributed toward making the fall of the regime inevitable. (*Sideshow*, p. 313)

Shawcross's military critique is utterly disingenuous. Generals Palmer and Cleland stress an obvious and totally different point: that Congressional restrictions made any other strategy impossible. The ban on U.S. advisers meant that there was no possibility of "improving the intrinsic fighting quality of Lon Nol's troops," as Shawcross professes to recommend; escalating legislative prohibitions deprived the Cambodians of what assets they had. Shawcross is not really recommending an alternative approach to assistance; his argument is that no assistance should have been given the Cambodians in the first place. He faults the Congress, indeed, but only for the degree to which it acceded to administration requests at all. (*Sideshow*, p. 350)

General Palmer's end-of-tour report, for example, makes poignantly clear how even the minimum objective of achieving a military stalemate (for purposes of negotiation) was rendered impossible because the Cambodian Army's few advantages over the enemy were eroded by the progressive reduction of American aid. It is a powerful account that Shawcross understandably did not want his readers to see:

(1) *Congressional Restrictions*

In January 1971, the Cooper-Church Amendment specifically prohibited "advisors" in Cambodia. The Symington-Case Amendment of February 1972 prescribed that the total number of U.S. personnel in Cambodia should not exceed 200. In view of the U.S. Vietnam experience, the intent of these restrictions is understandable. However, their cumulative effect was to severely limit any MEDTC ability to ensure that millions of dollars in MAP [Military Assistance Program] funds were being well spent. FANK was provided modern equipment but was denied the overall training, technical know-how, and military professionalism desperately needed to modernize it in the areas of tactical leadership, staff planning and coordination, personnel and financial management or logistics operations. Proper management and effective use of the equipment provided was apparently to be learned by a trial and error, do-it-yourself process which time would not permit.

Lacking any authority to provide in-country advice or U.S. training, any improvement in FANK leadership was predicated on almost non-existent Khmer initiatives since American officers were too restricted to assist. (Palmer Report, 30 April 1975, Part One, IV/B (1))

(2) *Reliance on Firepower*

FANK was originally conceived as a "light infantry force" designed to fight "Khmer Insurgents." When it became apparent that the "insurgents" were rapidly evolving into main force units in their own right, the U.S. objective of keeping FANK alive and the GKR [Government of the Khmer Republic] viable was assured through the quick-fix of massive U.S. airpower. With the U.S. bombing halt in August 1973, the Khmer Army artillery and tactical air inventories were augmented because this solution provided less expensive and politically more palatable sources of firepower to offset the leadership and manpower deficiencies in the Khmer Armed Forces. As that firepower was increasingly denied to them because of escalating munitions costs and reduced funding, the only remaining option appeared to be manpower.

However the Army's inability even to maintain the strength of its intervention brigades, let alone achieve significant growth, soon became self-evident. Moreover, serious leadership and training deficiencies, combined with the absence of any U.S.

advisory or training effort, obviated major changes in the Khmer force structure, battle tactics or doctrinal reliance on firepower, even if sufficient time had been available.

In sum, the U.S. taught the Khmer Armed Forces to survive through firepower. FANK was equipped with the means to employ it in large amounts. Outside sources of firepower were withdrawn so that they relied solely on their own firepower assets. Firepower and the logistics to support it became the two most important advantages FANK had over the KC [Khmer Communists], and by 1974 it was too late to change that orientation to any extent in the short term. Therefore, as escalating prices drove munitions costs progressively higher, increasing rather than decreasing levels of MAP funding were necessary to promote successful achievement of U.S. objectives in Cambodia. (Part One, IV/B (2))

Feeling Sorry for the Khmer Rouge

Shawcross at least acknowledges the genocidal brutality of the Khmer Rouge after they took power, in contrast to other prophets of the Left who still consider the charges to be imperialist propaganda. But Shawcross nevertheless excuses the atrocities by another line of argument: that they were all America's fault. Apologetics nonetheless. His book is not subtitled "The Khmer Rouge and the Destruction of Cambodia," but "Kissinger, Nixon and the Destruction of Cambodia."

The viciousness of the Khmer Rouge he attributes to a paroxysm of vengeance, a seizure of "Manichean fear" induced by the severe "punishment" inflicted upon them in the years of their struggle—that is to say, by American and Cambodian efforts to resist them. This is one of the central theses of his book, and for it he offers no documentation whatsoever:

All wars are designed to arouse anger, and almost all soldiers are taught to hate and to dehumanize their enemy. Veterans of the combat zone are often possessed of a mad rage to destroy, and to avenge their fallen comrades. It does not always happen, however, that victorious armies have endured such punishment as was inflicted upon the Khmer Rouge. Nor does it always happen that such an immature and tiny force comes to power after its country's social order has been obliterated, and the nation faces the danger of takeover by a former ally, its ancient enemy. In Cambodia that did take place. In the last eight years, degree, law, moderation had been forsworn. The war and the causes for which it was fought had brought desolation while nurturing and then giving power to a little group of zealots sustained by Manichean fear. (*Sideshow,* p. 389)

It is enough to make one feel sorry for the poor Khmer Rouge. How perfectly natural that they would up and murder three million of their own people! This is, of course, ridiculous. Most soldiers in combat have "endured . . . punishment" but none before have murdered a third of the population of their country after the war was over.

American bombing had ended twenty months before they came to power. The evacuation of Phnom Penh was planned months before. The savagery was systematic—forced dispersal of whole populations; destruction of traditional social structures, organized religion, and even the family; forced collectivization of agriculture; liquidation of the middle class and civil service; police terror—

and it was all standard Khmer Rouge practice in all the areas they controlled in Cambodia from as early as 1971. The genocide was premeditated, motivated by ideology, and the work of political fanatics. And the definitive evidence for this is found in Shawcross's own sources.

One of the best is *Cambodia: Year Zero* by François Ponchaud, a French Jesuit who lived through the early horrific phases of the Khmer Rouge victory. Ponchaud is a friend of Shawcross and no defender of American policy; nevertheless his book shows a clarity about Khmer Rouge motivations that Shawcross seems to have deliberately avoided. Shawcross cites Ponchaud extensively but never the passages stressing the ideological premeditation of Khmer Rouge policies dating back at least to 1972. Ponchaud writes, for example (emphases added):

[A]ccusing foreigners cannot acquit the present leaders of Kampuchea; *their inflexible ideology had led them to invent a radically new kind of man in a radically new society.* A fascinating revolution for all who aspire to a new social order. A terrifying one for all who have any respect for human beings. (p. xvi)

So we must look elsewhere for an explanation of the deportation from Phnom Penh. The official reasons certainly had something to do with the decision to clear the city, but they do not seem sufficient. *The deeper reason was an ideological one,* as we later saw clearly when we learned that the provincial towns, villages, and even isolated farms in the countryside had also been emptied of their inhabitants.

The evacuation of Phnom Penh follows traditional Khmer revolutionary practice: ever since 1972 the guerrilla fighters had been sending all the inhabitants of the villages and towns they occupied into the forest to live, often burning their homes so they would have nothing to come back for. A massive, total operation such as this reflects a new concept of society, in which there is no place even for the idea of a city. The towns of Cambodia had grown up around marketplaces; Phnom Penh itself owed its expansion to French colonialism, Chinese commerce, and the bureaucracy of the monarchy, followed by that of the republic. All this had to be swept away and an egalitarian rural society put in its place. (p. 21)

On April 17, 1975, a society collapsed; another is now being born from the fierce drive of a revolution which is incontestably the most radical ever to take place in so short a time. *It is a perfect example of the application of an ideology pushed to the furthest limit of its internal logic.* (p. 192)

Shawcross had another important source as well: a U.S. government study by Foreign Service Officer Kenneth M. Quinn. From interviews with refugees fleeing Cambodia in 1973 and 1974, Quinn pieced together a detailed description of Khmer Rouge totalitarian practices and shows that they began in some areas in late 1971. Shawcross cites some of Quinn's account (pp. 321–322) but leaves the impression that it all dates from 1974. Another source, a Cambodian intellectual, is quoted at length in reference to the 1972–73 period, but all the quotes describe Khmer Rouge organizational structure and political indoctrination, including their "respect for 'the ways of the people.' " (pp. 251–255)

The distortion is calculated. American bombing reached its peak in the spring of 1973. The evidence of Father Ponchaud and Kenneth Quinn that the Khmer Rouge were totalitarian thugs in 1971 and 1972 contradicts the thesis that Shawcross struggles mightily but in vain to prove: that it was American bombing that turned the Khmer Rouge into butchers.

Sideshow is filled with countless other errors and distortions. On one page he asserts that "no Communist offensive had been launched" when the secret bombing began in 1969; yet the preceding page had quoted from a North Vietnamese document hailing the Communist spring offensive of 1969 because it killed more Americans than the Tet offensive of 1968 (pp. 109–111). His tendentious account of the role of the U.S. Embassy in the bombing procedures of 1973 (pp. 272–277) relies on a Senate Foreign Relations Committee staff report that is itself wildly erroneous. His chapters on alleged "missed opportunities" to negotiate a settlement are undercut by the mountain of evidence that the North Vietnamese and later the Khmer Rouge rejected all American and Cambodian overtures to compromise.*

As a work of history the book is worthless. It is an elegant polemic in which scrupulous regard for evidence has been swept aside by political bias and emotional compulsion. Its elaborate documentation is impressive only if one has not seen the original documents. To understand it, one must leave historiography and explore the realm of psychiatry.

The antiwar movement's temptation to gloat at the long-predicted collapse of the "corrupt" anti-Communist regimes of Indochina was quickly stilled by the tales of holocaust that emerged from Cambodia. (The "boat people" of Vietnam and the poison-gas campaign to exterminate the Hmong in Laos came a bit later.) For antiwar critics had assured us beforehand that the collapse of the Lon Nol government would end the killing and be a blessing for the Cambodian people. "What future possibility could be more terrible than the reality of what is happening to Cambodia now?" asked Anthony Lewis on March 17, 1975, urging a cutoff of American aid. Abandoning the Cambodian government was "for the good of the suffering Cambodians themselves," the *Los Angeles Times* assured us on April 11. "Indochina Without Americans: For Most, a Better Life," was the headline of a piece in the *New York Times* on April 13, datelined Phnom Penh. Its author, Sydney Schanberg, had comforted us a month before with a report that the Khmer Rouge would be more moderate after victory and that fears of a bloodbath were unfounded. These predictions turned out to be horribly wrong. The people of Cambodia paid the price. But there were no recriminations in America. The administration was stuck with a failed policy, and its opponents were understandably sheepish at the results of an outcome they had long urged.

Then along came Shawcross. Vietnam critics could now "resist all attempts to make them feel guilty for the stand they took against the war," as Stanley Hoffmann urged them in an enthusiastic review. Shawcross was a godsend. How psychologically comforting to have in hand a convoluted theory and purported evidence that *American* government decisions were the propelling

*The "Black Book" published by the Pol Pot regime in September 1978 reveals the reason: The Khmer Rouge resisted all pressures for a cease-fire in 1972–73 because "if the Kampuchean revolution had accepted a cease-fire it would have collapsed." Later they rejected a compromise because they smelled victory. This will not be found in *Sideshow*.

force behind the horrible events after all. How politically convenient to be able
to focus responsibility on a Republican administration for the most gruesome
outcome of a failed military commitment begun under two liberal Democratic
Presidents.

But it was too convenient to be true. The book's evidentiary basis is shoddy
and deceitful. By no stretch of moral logic can the crimes of mass murderers
be ascribed to those who struggled to prevent their coming into power. One
hopes that no craven sophistry will ever induce free peoples to accept the
doctrine that Shawcross embodies: that resistance to totalitarianism is immoral.
So whatever the book's value as psychotherapy, as a history of Cambodia it is
a joke. And as political apologetics it is obscene.

Why the Rescue Failed

(1980)

STUART L. KOEHL & STEPHEN P. GLICK

When ignorance has gotten ten men killed where it should have cost but two, is it not responsible for the blood of the other eight?

—Napoleon

Some time during the second week of April, President Carter, after nearly six months of "diplomatic appeals," reversed his position opposing the use of force to achieve the release of the American hostages in Iran. On April 23 he launched Operation Eagle Claw, a mission to rescue the American captives by a *coup de main* at the American Embassy in Teheran.

Awakening Friday morning, most Americans were horrified to discover that a secret rescue attempt had been aborted in the Iranian desert, that mechanical failures had caused the cancellation, and that eight American servicemen were dead in an aircraft collision. Official White House and Department of Defense statements claimed that the mission was successful up to the point where it was cancelled, that a series of unfortunate events beyond human control were responsible for the failure. And most Americans came to believe that bad luck foiled a gallant attempt to save our fellow countrymen from a barbaric captivity.

But is this the truth? Or is the failure of Eagle Claw attributable to conscious actions taken on the part of American political and military leaders? Is Eagle Claw merely an isolated incident, or is it indicative of greater flaws and potentially catastrophic failures in the American military? To understand the true significance of the mission, one must view it as a military operation and judge it on strictly military terms. This in turn requires an understanding of the mission plan, the actual events, and the general principles governing this sort of commando operation.

Had Mars favored American arms that week in April, we would have awakened on the twenty-sixth cheering the release of our compatriots and the heroes who saved them. No doubt the Pentagon would have been quick to release the details of this miraculous feat, revealing the following operational plan:

American agents, probably from the Southwest Asia Special Forces Group (Green Berets), would infiltrate Iran several days prior to the rescue attempt and assume positions to support the main force when it arrived. The rescue

317

mission itself would be undertaken by volunteers from the Department of Defense's special anti-terrorist unit, a multi-service force established in 1977 under Project Blue Light. The unit assembled for the raid would be code-named Delta Force. On Wednesday evening, April 23, they would fly from Egyptian airfields near Luxor aboard C-130 Hercules transport aircraft to an abandoned airstrip near Tabas, in the Iranian desert, with a short layover in Oman to rest the aircrew. Along with Delta Force the planes would bring additional aviation fuel and refueling gear, and electronic equipment to jam Iranian radar and radio communications. At this airstrip, code-named Desert One, these planes would be joined by eight RH-53 minesweeping helicopters from the carrier Nimitz, in the Gulf of Oman. (The helicopters' minesweeping apparatus would have been replaced with equipment more appropriate for Eagle Claw, such as armament and night vision devices.) The helicopters would remain at Desert One all day Thursday, resting the men and refueling the helicopters.

On Thursday evening, Delta Force would board the helicopters and fly to a second landing zone in the remote mountains near Darmavand, about 50 miles northeast of Teheran. There they would meet some of the Green Beret infiltrators, who would have acquired trucks from friendly Iranian sources in order to take Delta Force and its guides to a warehouse on the outskirts of Teheran. Here, final intelligence reports would be digested and assault plans confirmed. Then Delta Force would divide, a small contingent moving to the Foreign Ministry building, where three senior American diplomats are "guests" of the Iranian government, and the bulk of Delta Force proceeding to the American Embassy compound, where they would storm the Embassy proper by means of nonlethal chemical agents which would incapacitate the terrorists before they could harm their captives.

Having freed the captives, Delta Force would signal the helicopters, already en route from Darmavand, to land in the Embassy parking lot and soccer field. The small contingent having rejoined the bulk of Delta Force, all the American troops and the ex-prisoners would embark and fly to a third landing zone northwest of Teheran, where they would rendezvous with the C-130s from Desert One, destroy the helicopters, and leave Iran. All movements prior to the helicopter landings at the Embassy would take place in darkness, men and equipment hiding camouflaged by day, so that, there having been another layover at Darmavand on Friday, the raiders would not actually leave Iran until Saturday morning.

Throughout the raid, an E-3 AWACS aircraft would maintain command and control, monitoring Iranian airspace and maintaining direct communications between the carrier task force, Washington, and the mission commander. Presumably, the AWACS would coordinate air support over Teheran from the time Delta Force assaulted the Embassy until it left Iranian airspace.

Of course, what happened was something much different from this. On the way to Desert One, one RH-53 suffered a possible rotor failure, landed, and was abandoned in the desert. Another helicopter suffered an electrical failure, which disabled its gyrocompass and navigation equipment and fored it to return to the Nimitz. The remaining six helicopters and six C-130s arrived at Desert One.

On Thursday, a busload of Iranian civilians driving down the road running through Desert One were stopped and detained. On Thursday evening it was discovered that one of the remaining helicopters was unserviceable due to a hydraulic system failure. Repairing the helicopter was impossible: All of the spare parts were aboard the helicopter which had returned to the Nimitz. Because the operation's planners had decided that six RH-53s were the minimum required to ensure the mission's success, a rambling discussion about the advisability of continuing the mission now began between the mission commander, Colonel Charles Beckwith, and the White House and Pentagon.

At this point a tanker truck towing a jeep blundered into Desert One. Soldiers stopped it at a roadblock, but the driver ran to the jeep and took off across country. Under orders to avoid killing Iranian civilians, the soldiers failed to stop the jeep. Feeling that security was now compromised, somebody—whether Col. Beckwith, higher military authorities, or the President himself—ordered the mission scrubbed. The evacuation of Desert One began at a frenzied pace. The helicopters were to have been topped off and flown out of Iran, but while crossing the landing zone to refuel, a taxiing RH-53 struck a stationary Hercules: Both aircraft exploded, killing eight men and seriously wounding five. Beckwith now dropped everything, got his men on the remaining C-130s, and took off, leaving behind the bodies of eight American servicemen, a small library of secret documents, five intact helicopters, and America's military reputation. Ironically, the men in the tanker truck were smugglers; they never reported the Americans to the Iranian government.

The Carter administration and the Pentagon have both tried to excuse this fiasco by referring its failures to "equipment failure," but the conception and execution of the mission were so deficient and amateurish that it was probably doomed to failure from the start, especially when judged by the rules of warfare generally and of commando warfare in particular.

It is axiomatic that in war only the simple succeeds, but the mission plan for Eagle Claw was complex, maximizing the chances for confusion and mishaps. It called for the coordination of two foreign governments (Egypt and Oman), Green Beret advance teams, Iranian collaborators, Delta Force, and the Nimitz Task Force; for the seizure and maintenance of three landing zones, the staging of a major refueling operation, and an approach drive to the Embassy of some 60 miles in borrowed trucks; and it called for a force of six large transport planes, eight helicopters, and more than a hundred men to remain inside a hostile country for more than 72 hours. This last part of the plan obviously violates one of the cardinal rules of commando operations: fast in and fast out.

And other rules were broken as well. For instance, it would have been impossible to retain secrecy or surprise for the duration of the mission, at least as the mission was planned. Of course, in any commando raid, surprise is of the essence. Operating far behind enemy lines, commandos are outnumbered and outgunned and must rely on surprise—open-mouthed, dumbfounded incredulity—to paralyze the enemy, if only temporarily. But given the nature of Eagle Claw, somewhere along the way Delta Force would inevitably have given the game away. The incidents of the bus and the tanker truck at Desert One are example enough, especially considering the President's injunction to avoid killing Iranians.

A less hypothetical error was in the selection of the men and equipment to be used in the raid. The choice of helicopters, for instance, was crucial to the failure of the mission. The RH-53 Sea Stallion was never meant to undertake long, nape-of-the-earth flights over land. It is not a combat assault helicopter: It lacks power, armor, and armament. And given these generic inadequacies, of course, it did not help that the RH-53s used in the event itself had been poorly maintained: Of the 110 flight hours needed to keep the RH-53s fully operational between January and April, only 25 had been flown.

The proper helicopter for the mission would have been the CH-53Es used by the Marine Corps. These are the combat assault cousins of the RH-53. Unlike the RH-53, they have armor, heavy armament, aerial refueling capability, and fully redundant systems. Having three engines instead of two, they are more powerful than the RH-53, which fact would have obviated the need to remove the sand filters from the RH-53s in order to achieve more power. More important, because they may be refueled in the air, the CH-53Es need not have landed in the desert, which in turn suggests the possibility of a direct flight to Teheran from the Nimitz.

Unfortunately, the men picked for the mission were as ill-suited as the equipment. The forces established under Project Blue Light were not intended, or trained, for commando operations. Rather, they were to be a unique anti-terrorist squad to be used in hostage situations in the United States, or abroad when the local government was at least tacitly supporting the American position. All of their training presupposed that they would have some control of the area surrounding a terrorist redoubt. Before the preparation for Eagle Claw, they had never trained for the sort of long-range clandestine activities they were called upon to perform.

In addition, the training laid out by the planners was inadequate and unrealistic, considering the mission's requirements. Helicopter training flights were made only in clear weather. Their pilots were not made familiar with low-level blind flying. Moreover, Delta Force never trained on a full-scale mock-up of the Embassy compound (practice assaults were made at the Fort Bragg brig). Had Delta Force arrived at the compound in the dead of night, they might well have gotten lost inside it. Certainly they would not have been able to negotiate the interior of the Embassy itself. If nowhere else, the poor training of the men manifested itself in the fact that personal effects were found on the bodies of the dead. Taking wallets, credit cards, and personal letters into a mission suggests a lack of serious intent and a thorough ignorance of the rules of warfare.

Aside from the simplicity, equipment, and men appropriate to a commando raid, Eagle Claw lacked flexibility or contingency planning. Apparently, no one considered the effects of bad weather, or the possibility of running into the kind of sandstorm which contributed to the first two helicopter failures. And the lack of a contingency plan for a rapid evacuation of the landing zone in the event of detection only increased the chances of something like a collision happening, a condition which the lack of proper air traffic control did nothing to mitigate.

Certainly no contingency plans were made to continue the mission if a portion of the force failed to arrive at its objective, and contingency plans of this sort are essential to commando operations.

Perhaps most important, the leadership of Col. Beckwith during the mission was something less than inspiring. Beckwith failed to maintain proper security at Desert One, which allowed the smugglers' jeep to escape. He obviously did not maintain adequate control over the evacuation. And he did not exhibit the independence and resolution which a commando leader must have. When the sixth helicopter was discovered non-operational, he consulted his superiors rather than making the final decision himself. Apparently he also allowed himself to be overruled by his superiors after the jeep incident; as field commander, the decision to scrub or go forward with the mission was his and his alone. After the collision he gave way to panic and immediately evacuated the landing zone, in effect allowing himself to be stampeded out of Iran by fear of a handful of untrained militiamen in Tabas. He could have, and should have, extinguished the fires, collected the dead, and destroyed the helicopters and secret documents before staging a deliberate withdrawal.

In retrospect, it was perhaps for the best that Eagle Claw failed when it did. At some later point, the mission's inevitable cumulative errors might well have resulted in the death or capture of the entire force.

Were the bungling and ineptness of Eagle Claw an anomaly, the raid would have no more significance than any other isolated incident of military stupidity. Instead, it is indicative of a decline in American military competence first noticed by some observers during the Vietnam war. This trend towards ineffectuality is marked by a decline in the standards of training for the enlisted men, and by the absolute corruption of the officer corps, not in pecuniary terms but in the more insidious abrogation of its military function.

The American officer corps today values careers more than operations. It values efficiency more than effectiveness. It is over-controlled and over-centralized. It lacks initiative. American officers today are no longer students of war. Rather, they are students of managerial techniques. They abhor combat because it is messy and screws up organizational charts. They have lost contact with and refuse to acknowledge the nature of war, which is killing the enemy.

All of which was illustrated by Eagle Claw. A militarily unsound plan was approved by high-ranking officers who wished to please the President and the Secretary of Defense rather than see American arms succeed. The mission was not conceived with the primary aim of freeing the captives. It was planned to conform with President Carter's desires that there be no combat. For this reason it was incredibly convoluted and impossible.

The mission was also planned to serve the ideals of "managerial competence" at the expense of military effectiveness. In the interests of efficiency, for instance, all the helicopter repair kits were prepacked and palletized, so that all the spare parts taken on the mission were on one helicopter—which, as we pointed out earlier, had to turn back. (The effective method would have been to split up the parts among all the helicopters, with lots of redundancy.) And the chain of command was a bureaucrat's dream. Thanks to the miracle of modern telecommunications, which allows generals and even presidents to lead a battalion in combat without getting within 10,000 miles of the front, the operation's field commander, on whose daring and on-the-scene judgments the operation's success depends, apparently felt compelled to check back constantly with "higher authorities" before departing from the operation's plan.

Most important of all, the tendencies so well typified by the failures of Eagle Claw affect American military operations in pervasive and dangerous ways. The American officer corps, for example, recognizes its deficiencies, at least at the subconscious level, and lacks any operational self-confidence. Compare the cautious and tentative fumbling surrounding this raid with the energy and daring of the Russian *coup de main* in Kabul. A plan made by confident men would have been bold, risky, and successful. Using the proper machines, they would have flown to Teheran directly and swooped out of the night, gone before they were noticed. Much of the timidity of American foreign policy can be traced to a lack of confidence in our military forces to carry out the missions assigned to them, while much of Soviet boldness is a result of their new operational confidence.

This is an alarming development. Very often a nation's military reputation will outlive its prowess. The illusion of competence survives until the first severe test. Thus the Prussians were destroyed at Jena-Auerstädt in 1806, and the French in 1940. Like a tree rotten from within, an army can appear strong until the first winter storm blows it over. Sometimes, though, a nation is fortunate enough to have the truth revealed in less catastrophic fashion. In the early 1950s the Israeli Army cleaned out its deadwood after a series of small but humiliating failures. By 1956 it was the most effective force in the region. Eagle Claw has given us a unique opportunity.

If the United States is to survive the military challenges of the next decade, it will require more than just a larger military budget; it will need a complete overhaul of our military system, a massive reform. Officers must become soldiers again, and men must be trained to fight effectively. America requires an armed force of formidable competence if it is to stand up to the dynamic, aggressive, and self-confident Red Army.

Rather than hiding or forgetting our failure in the Iranian desert, we must take steps to root out its causes and correct our deficiencies. Our time is short, and if we do not begin now we might never have the chance. If the failure of the rescue attempt was a blow to our pride, it was a signal of opportunity to our enemies.

Hiding from
the Nuclear Age

(1980)

STEPHEN ROSEN

For the last 15 years American thinking about nuclear war has been dominated by an idea that by now seems as natural as it is simple. War will be deterred by the existence of a stable nuclear balance. But what if deterrence fails? The strategic theories of the 1960s were suitable for the 1960s, and the emphasis on deterrence was proper when the chance of war was small. But an examination of the development of American strategic thought reveals that an emphasis on what ought to be done if nuclear war did break out was often thought necessary. Since World War II, the major groups involved in American strategic planning, the scientists, the military, and, later, the civilian strategic analysts, have traditionally displayed a striking sobriety when real danger was in the air. With the United States today no longer in a dominant strategic position, it is necessary to restore realism to American strategic planning.

At the outset of the Cold War, the American scientific community would have preferred that problems caused by the emergence of nuclear weapons be resolved through international agreements regulating the use of atomic power. Yet when efforts towards this end quickly proved impractical, the scientists did *not* immediately turn to assured destruction, the doctrine with which they would later become closely associated. This is surprising. Military theorists such as Bernard Brodie had already articulated the essential elements of assured destruction and the doctrine is one with obvious allure to the scientific mind.

The idea of a mutual hostage relation among nuclear powers is simple and logical, far more so than the messy, inelegant theories that had emerged from conventional military operations. Unlike the unpredictability of conventional wars, assured destruction promised a simple war. Assuming that the enemy had also adopted assured destruction, war would be based on attacks against undefended civilian targets and would involve no clash of opposing armed forces. Cities would simply stand still while attempts were made to destroy them. In addition, because of their familiarity with missile and aircraft engineering and with the physical effects of nuclear explosions, assured destruction would give the scientists a distinct advantage over the generals in any political struggle for influence in the area of strategic policy. Assured destruction thus meant that military competence would become, all at once, superfluous.

In the area of international politics, assured destruction offered the scientists the realization of their dream of world peace through world harmony. It seemed to eliminate the need for arms races, for once both nuclear powers obtained enough second-strike weapons, they would stop producing additional weapons. At the same time, a fear of mutual annihilation would create a common interest between the United States and the Soviet Union. By forcing the two superpowers to overcome their differences, assured destruction thus contained strong incentives for the creation of a peaceful world order.

For all these reasons, it might be expected that the scientific community would have embraced assured destruction with open arms. Instead, for the 12 years beginning with 1948, the scientists advocated a policy diametrically opposed to assured destruction—they called for the adoption of defensive systems, whose chief purpose would be to minimize the destruction that a nuclear war would cause the United States.

In 1952, the dean of American nuclear scientists, J. Robert Oppenheimer, and many of his collegues participated in a conference called the Lincoln Summer Study. The conference discussed the state of American air defenses and concluded that the American nuclear force structure had become grossly distorted by its emphasis on offensive strategy. After speaking with some of the participants, Stewart Alsop reported that "the experts believe" that the Soviet offensive forces were becoming increasingly more dangerous, and that the remedy lay in "very early warning devices, ground-to-air guided missiles," and an emergency engineering project that would construct these defenses at a cost of up to "$25 billion in a two-to-three year period." The defensive orientation of the scientific community was underlined further during the Atomic Energy Commission's 1954 investigation of Oppenheimer. Suspicious of Oppenheimer for a variety of reasons, the investigators also wanted to know if Oppenheimer had "espoused what might be described as a Maginot line type of defense?" In response to this hostile question, a flock of professors from Harvard, MIT, Cal Tech, and Columbia testified in Oppenheimer's behalf that his call for greater defensive measures was perfectly sensible. Isadore Rabi of Columbia, who later went on to edit the anti-militarist *Bulletin of the Atomic Scientists,* summed up the position of his colleagues:

. . . I think Dr. Oppenheimer and I agreed. It is threefold. One, we think that to protect the lives of Americans is worth anybody's while. Two, that one is in a stronger position in a war if one is fighting from a protected citadel, rather than just being open. . . . Thirdly, and it is more political, that the existence of such a defense would make us less liable to intimidation and blackmail.

Today, conservative critics of the assured destruction doctrine argue that the doctrine may fail if the Soviet Union decides not to leave itself open to attack as we do, and concentrates rather on winning the military contest. Rabi was making a similar point 25 years ago when he testified that the threat to retaliate

is a psychological weapon, a deterrent. But the other fellow may not be the same as you, and you have to have some kind of defense before he does you irreparable damage, and, furthermore, your plans may not go as you expect. They may miscarry. Unless you have a defense, you are not getting another chance.

These and similar statements by other scientists testifying before the Agency are remarkable primarily because they came in many cases from men who by 1967 would be opposing an anti-ballistic missile defense of the United States. This shift in attitude is explained in part by the scientists' eventual disillusionment with their earlier experiences. The Air Force interpreted their advocacy of strategic defense as an attack on the Strategic Air Command, and so responded with its own criticisms of the scientists' "Maginot Line" mentality. More important, by the late sixties the scientists were arguing that technological progress had rendered unfeasible their earlier vision of the United States as an impenetrable, protected citadel.

To be sure, technology had changed, but not necessarily to the point where defense was no longer worth pursuing. Although ICBMs were far more difficult to defend against than bombers, the radar, missiles, and computers used in defense systems had also improved dramatically. As imperfect as our actual anti-bomber and proposed anti-missile defenses might have been, both would have reduced the extent to which the United States would have been open to blackmail and intimidation, as Rabi pointed out.

Unfortunately, what had changed most during these intervening years was just this perception of the probability of blackmail and intimidation. So long as the Korean War, the Soviet-American dispute over Germany, and the memories of Stalin's diplomacy contributed to the feeling that a direct Soviet-American conflict was possible, the scientists regarded strategic defenses as attractive. But as the danger of war began to recede, the scientists became preoccupied with the disadvantages of strategic defenses. On the practical side, they stressed costs; we would be forever having to improve and increase these strategic defenses in response to the Soviet Union's continual development of its offensive forces. On the psychological level the scientists feared that because strategic defenses made war seem less apocalyptic, statesmen would be more willing to risk war. Moreover, the scientists feared that strategic defenses would be destabilizing, encouraging the enemy to attack before the strategic defenses were implemented. The scientists, then, advocated strategic defenses in the early 1950s when the danger of war was great and opposed them in the late 1960s when the danger of war was small. Why?

An explanation for this puzzling intellectual shift suggests itself. The presence of danger concentrates the mind. Its absence removes the immediate need to make realistic plans for survival, leaving one free to pursue those objectives that had been set aside when tensions were at their peak.* By the time of the post-Khrushchev thaw, the scientific community was fully content to pursue its natural preferences by openly advocating assured destruction.

For its part, the military community responded to the birth of the nuclear age by demobilizing. In 1946 and 1947 the Air Force possessed perhaps two

---

*In a similar fashion, the strong advocate of arms control, Paul Warnke, defended the anti-Chinese anti-ballistic missile (ABM) system in 1967 when the Peking government seemed to be in the hands of hostile fanatics and the danger of war, however slight, seemed real. He, too, used the argument that an ABM would reduce our vulnerability to nuclear attack and intimidation, and he, too, washed his hands of the whole idea once relations with Peking improved and the danger of war receded.

dozen Nagasaki-type atomic bombs, but these were kept unassembled in stock-piles. It would have required a 24-man crew two days to assemble one bomb, but there were no such crews available after the men of the Manhattan Project had dispersed. Thus, the Air Force's military strategy remained essentially unchanged from World War II. To counter any Soviet advance into West Europe, the Air Force would attempt to destroy Soviet war production, particularly its oil-refining capacity. This would eventually weaken the Red Army, but it would be defeated only by allied armies fighting it on the ground. This doctrine was not illogical given the weaknesses of our atomic forces and the history of the war against Hitler. The equivalent of at least 500 Nagasaki bombs had been dropped on Germany, most of them in the last 12 months of the war, and still the Wehrmacht had fought to the end. The U.S. Air Force had 29 atomic bombs to drop on a country 30 times as large as Germany. It was an air-power doctrine with strictly military objectives, although it was recognized that the destruction of Soviet oil refineries would inevitably be accompanied by the deaths of hundreds of thousands of civilians.

There was, however, an obvious discrepancy between the plans of the Air Force and the political need of the United States to protect West Europe without turning the entire continent into a battlefield. By 1948 the Berlin crisis forced the military to rethink the problem of safeguarding Germany without destroying it. The hour found its man in Curtis LeMay, who advocated the expansion of the American nuclear arsenal for the purpose of "nation killing." We would conduct a campaign lasting about one month to destroy the 70 largest urban-industrial centers in the Soviet Union, which would, by itself, end the war. This was not a doctrine of deterrence, but of military victory. Nonetheless, its blood-thirstiness set off a ferocious debate within the armed services. Rear Admiral Daniel Gallery denounced the strategy as clearly unacceptable: "For a civilized society like the United States, the broad purpose of a war cannot simply be the destruction and annihilation of the enemy." The strategy of annihilation "is a strategy of desperation and weakness. I believe we should abandon the idea of destroying enemy cities one after the other until he gives up and find some better way of gaining our objective."

This argument was in some measure the reaction of an Admiral to a war without a Navy. But it was also the reaction of a soldier to a strategy designed to kill as many enemy non-combatants as possible. Moreover, Gallery's conclusions were supported by an inter-service committee chaired by an Air Force General, Hubert Harmon. This committee unanimously agreed that, as long as our conventional defenses remained weak, it would be necessary to plan for an attack on Soviet cities, but that such attacks would disgust the world, and would become terribly dangerous once the Soviet Union had the means to retaliate.

Contributing to the fierceness of this debate was the simple fact that there were not enough nuclear weapons to go around. Not until 1951 were there as many as 400 atomic bombs in the U.S. arsenal, which was still inadequate for use against both military and urban targets. The age of nuclear plenty that quickly followed silenced but did not resolve the debate over what kind of targets to attack. Although money has continued to be available for routine development and modernization, which has allowed the services to acquire more and more warheads, in the absence of a well-defined doctrine, this has been an incremental process without a clear logic. As a result, the military has never formulated a clear rationale to help justify the acquisition of weapons powerful and accurate enough to attack the primary military targets inside the Soviet Union, the Soviet ICBM silos. Instead, the armed forces have until comparatively recently acquiesced in the doctrine of assured destruction.

This acquiescence is explained largely by the difficulty the military has had in coming to terms with its mission in a nuclear age. From its viewpoint, additional money for strategic forces has always meant less money for aircraft carriers, tanks, and manned aircraft. Soldiers, sailors, and pilots are more likely to be motivated by the prospect of combat than by the idea of cruising in a hidden submarine or sitting in a missile silo command post. The military thus has been content with a strategy that limits its strategic nuclear obligations, but which releases monies for conventional wars against Soviet soldiers. In addition, the American military has never taken to defensive strategies. If the alternative to assured destruction is a strategy of shelters, urban evacuation, and ballistic missile defenses, all designed to minimize American civilian casualties, then the military prefers to retain an offensive posture.

The early 1960s was a period of crisis, and, as in previous crises, the heightened tension that marked the first Kennedy years resulted in realistic strategic thinking. The question raised by Kennedy during the Berlin crisis of 1961 was the same as the question raised by the scientists during the crises of the 1950s. How can we protect the American people? Once again, it seemed necessary to think about what would happen if deterrence failed and war ensued. When Kennedy, in July 1961, called for a rapid expansion of the American civil defense program, he was advocating the only means available for increasing the safety of Americans. Given the relatively small size of the Soviet nuclear strike force, this shelter program would have been extremely useful. As more and more American missiles became operational, we obtained a nuclear superiority that made it possible to consider a strategy of striking at Soviet missile installations, instead of Soviet cities, and so reduce the number of casualties on both sides. This was in fact the policy set forth by McNamara in his speech at Ann Arbor, Michigan, in 1962. But having begun, like the scientists, by calling for programs that would reduce civilian suffering, the Kennedy administration quickly backed away and adopted the principles of assured destruction. After the Cuban missile crisis, the beginnings of detente together with the growing superiority of America's nuclear arsenal made war seem quite distant.

For his part, McNamara, while dedicated to the security of the nation, was also determined to establish strict and rational civilian control over the American military. Not surprisingly, this desire for rational controls found its strategy in assured destruction, which under McNamara reached fruition and has continued to dominate our strategic policies to the present time.

Students of bureaucratic politics have long noted that it is easiest to bend an organization to one's will if it is possible to set out clear criteria by which the performance of the organization can be measured. It is difficult to apply such criteria to a peace-time army, since the only real criterion of military success is victory on the battlefield. Assured destruction, however, offered an opportunity to lay down straightforward measures of success in a nuclear war. If we could "deliver" payloads of a few thousand tons to a finite list of fixed Soviet locations under a certain set of conditions, we could rest easy. No more money would need to be spent on these weapons, no matter what the generals said. With this doctrine, strategic success became almost as simple to define as success in delivering milk, and civilian control, in this area at least, was enormously facilitated. It is not surprising that McNamara quickly dropped the idea of "counter-force" targeting against Soviet strategic forces. An enemy could hide, move, defend, or increase his military assets, and we would have to increase our forces to deal with these problems. Nuclear war would then become as complicated as conventional war. Thus, the criteria of being able to destroy one-third of the Soviet population and two-thirds of its industry were sufficient for McNamara to justify a 10 percent cut in the Navy Polaris fleet, and to halt Minuteman deployment at 1000.

The problem today, unfortunately, is that our present strategy was made in happier circumstances than we now enjoy and lacks that fixed concern with national survival which now is more important. During the 1960s, strategic analysts busied themselves inventing scenarios for the initiation of nuclear war. The most plausible ones assumed the outbreak of an anti-Soviet rebellion in East Germany, followed by a West German invasion of East Germany, American intervention, and general war. This ignored the fact that there had already been massive riots in East Germany in 1953 during which we had done what might have been predicted—exactly nothing. Now, it is easy to imagine a Soviet-American war for control of the Persian Gulf. We cannot permit Soviet control of this part of the world. The Soviets may well believe that we have neither the strength nor the resolve to resist them. Yet, if they do march into Iran, and we do respond, what will happen if we do unexpectedly well, and the Soviet Union is faced with a massive military defeat right on its own border? What will happen if we do so poorly that we must contemplate the destruction of our expeditionary force? Either side may decide that the threat to use—or actual use of—nuclear weapons is preferable to the alternative.

In view of this new danger we must consider, as others have done during earlier crises, how best to protect ourselves. To do this, we will have to overcome our fear of "instability," an idea that for the last 15 years has paralyzed any movement toward strategic defenses. We have convinced ourselves that the USSR-U.S. relation is "stable" if we are able to kill each other's civilians, but that war will result if we try to reduce the amount of damage civilians would have to endure in a war. As we begin defensive programs, the Soviet Union, it is supposed, will perceive a threat to its ability to strike at American civilians and missiles, and thus will decide to go to war to prevent any further erosion of its position.

Only someone who has immersed himself in the arcana of strategic theory to the exclusion of everything else could begin to believe this. It is implausible that the Soviet Union would start a nuclear war that would cause the deaths of millions of Soviet citizens only because we had begun serious planning for the evacuation of our cities—planning which could save the lives of tens of millions of Americans. The Soviet Union itself has already completed extensive plans to evacuate its cities in a crisis. At no time did we feel in the least bit compelled to start a war before these plans were completed. In a crisis, the evacuation of American cities would certainly prompt the evacuation of Soviet cities, if this had not already occurred, but not a strike that would leave the Soviet Union in ruins.

As its long history suggests, civil defense has never been provocative. American civil defense efforts during the Berlin crisis of 1961, the Chinese civil defense effort in the wake of the 1969 border clashes with the Soviet Union, and the sharp increase in the Soviet civil defense program in the early 1970s induced no threats or attacks. Yet these programs, in theory, were "destabilizing." Nuclear war, however, even if one is superior and protected, is a frightening prospect, and it is not likely to be touched off by anything short of impending military or political catastrophe.

To a surprising degree, there is agreement, shared by the liberal employees of the United States Arms Control and Disarmament Agency (ACDA) and the conservative analysts of the Committee on the Present Danger, that civil defense programs based on urban evacuation can be very effective in saving civilian lives. ACDA has estimated that 10 to 15 percent of the Soviet population would be killed by an American attack if the Soviet cities had been evacuated. T.K. Jones of the Committee on the Present Danger has estimated a death rate of about 5 percent. Given the uncertainties associated with such estimates, it would be foolish to take a dogmatic position in defense of either figure. The difference between 5 and 15 percent dead is quite large; in the case of the Soviet Union, it is the difference between 13 and 40 million dead. Although both figures represent catastrophic damage, they are closer to the fatalities suffered by the Soviet Union in World War II than they are to the total destruction of civilization that we usually believe will result from a nuclear war.

The other major method by which American lives might be protected is through the use of ballistic missile defenses (BMD) to shoot down enemy warheads. Proposals to do this have created an enormous amount of controversy, largely on two grounds. First, the familiar complaint that BMD would be destabilizing and would make war more likely; second, that it could be easily overwhelmed by the attacker. Here, again, we find that there is historical evidence that suggests that the importance of "stability" has been exaggerated. Both the United States and the Soviet Union began work on operational anti-missile defenses in the 1960s. This caused neither war nor an increase in tensions, though, of course, Soviet construction did create pressure in Congress for a matching American system. Even if greatly more effective than its predecessor, BMD in the 1980s will not provoke war any more than anti-missile defenses did in the 1960s. No BMD system under consideration will be accurate enough to prevent extraordinary destruction in the event of nuclear war— although BMD could help to preserve our national existence. Again, the idea that a government would go to war just because its enemy had begun work on its defenses is completely fanciful. A government so ready to risk destruction would have gone to war long ago.

We should not find it alarming that governments *are* likely to begin work on their defenses when they see their enemy doing so. If we can protect our population as well as or perhaps better than the enemy, why should we be unhappy that we can kill "only" five instead of fifty million Soviet citizens? Our thinking on this subject has been so twisted by the ideas of "stability" and assured destruction that it has become necessary to remind ourselves of the obvious: We have absolutely no interest, as such, in killing Russian civilians. Simple morality as well as reasons of state demand that we try to minimize the number of civilian casualties in any war we fight. As our ability to defend ourselves increases, our need to hold innocent Russians hostage decreases. Soviet BMD systems are no threat to us as long as we can protect ourselves at least as well. If both sides deploy defenses, there is likely to be a competition between the two, but it will be a contest to see who can save the most lives on its own side. On the surface, at least, this seems to be a competition a good deal more benign than the present competition in destructive power.

It is by no means clear, however, whether we can do anything to protect ourselves with missile defenses. If the Soviet Union can simply add more offensive warheads more cheaply than we can shoot them down, the defense will be playing a losing game. This is a complex technical question, but some figures are suggestive. In 1969, the largest Soviet missile, the SS-9, cost around $30 million, according to the congressional testimony of American Defense Department experts. The latest Soviet heavy missile, the SS-18, is far more sophisticated than the SS-9. Assume it also costs $30 million. If each SS-18 carries ten warheads, one additional warhead will cost an average of $4 million. In 1969, the American anti-missile interceptors cost approximately half that amount. These interceptors, however, needed radars and computers to guide them. The radars alone cost over $100 million each, and were relatively vulnerable to enemy attack. Had *we* started building extra radars to make sure enough would stay in operation, it would have run into billions of extra dollars. If the need for radars and computers could be removed, however, the cost of the defense would drop radically. For the last ten years, the Army has been working on just this problem, and with some success. By utilizing interceptors that use methods and hardware analagous to those now used in conventional "smart" weapons, the need for ground-based radars and computers is greatly reduced, if not eliminated. No revolutionary technology is involved, only sensors and miniature computers derived from those used in existing air-to-air missiles costing $100,000. The methods that make it possible to shoot down a multi-million dollar aircraft with a missile costing thousands of dollars are also applicable to anti-ballistic missile defense.

It will, of course, be possible for the attacker to fool, blind, or destroy some of these new homing interceptors. The battle between offense and defense will become a complicated military problem, instead of remaining a simple problem of delivery. Yet the possibility of substantially reducing American civilian casualties, in conjunction with civil defense, does exist. A doctrine designed to reduce the number of American dead would deal with the existing danger of a war caused by miscalculation, and would reduce the extent to which the United States would be sensitive to Soviet nuclear diplomacy. This doctrine would emphasize defenses because it would recognize that an American offensive build-up that would enable us to strike at Soviet missile silos would inevitably be countered by the development of Soviet mobile missiles. Unconcerned with the need to make their mobile missiles compatible with an arms-control agreement, the Soviet Union could rapidly and relatively cheaply deploy missiles that we could not find and so could not destroy. A doctrine of damage limitation would evaluate the success of strategic programs by counting the number of American lives saved, rather than of Soviets killed. It would acknowledge that strikes at enemy civilian targets are, as Admiral Gallery noted long ago, a desperate measure, and the need to carry out these strikes should be minimized.

It is a curious fact that our fundamental military doctrine for the last 15 years has rested on the threat to commit suicide. Sober reflection reveals that such a doctrine was irresponsible, unnecessary, but convenient. We have escaped the consequences of our irresponsibility, first, because we were strong and the world was peaceful, but also, because we were lucky and the Soviet Union cautious. It would be an error of the highest order for us to allow the foreign policy and even the existence of the United States to continue to depend on the caution of the Soviet Union. We live in bad times, and our doctrine must come to terms with them.

Catatonic Canada

(1981)

JOHN MUGGERIDGE

A recent article in the *New York Times* worries about Americans not taking enough interest in Canada's constitutional crisis.

Oddly enough we have the same problem up here: apathy. Questions such as whether or not the new constitution should have an entrenched bill of rights may excite the fancy of cabinet ministers and academics, but what they inspire in most Canadians is a mounting desire to switch channels. This is not to say that we lack interest in our collective future. We have lost hope in it. We tune out the media profs who tell us that they have found a way out of the impasse over offshore mineral rights, and the Ottawa-desk men who explain to us the importance of preserving French in Medicine Hat, Alberta, not because we are too lazy or too unlettered to follow their line of reasoning, but because we have come to the conclusion that it leads to a dead end. Nations need more than clever lawyers and well-informed journalists to keep them going. They need credible ideologies. Canada's has died, and no amount of redistributing power among its various levels of government can bring it to life again. We have been demythologized.

It happened in the last 25 years. When I first came here in the late fifties Canadians knew very well who they were supposed to be. They were British. The national flag contained a Union Jack; the armed forces wore British-style uniforms; grade-school children learned by heart the names of the Royal Family, and being a British subject automatically entitled you to vote in Canadian elections.

But nowhere was there a more obvious old-country glint than in the eyes of fifties intellectuals. In books with such titles as *Dominion of the North, The Kingdom of Canada,* and *The North Atlantic Triangle* they placed Canada's past firmly in an imperial perspective. Their thesis was that Canada had attained nationhood not by breaking with the British Empire but by imitating it. Canada, they argued, was a UK on the St. Lawrence; its founding fathers were the Loyalists who fought for George III during the American Revolution and later fled north to escape the horrors of republicanism. Thanks to them a new British North America arose beside the ashes of the old one, "the very image and transcript," as its first governor boasted, "of the British Monarchy." The law calling this frontier Albion into existence provided for an Established Church and a hereditary peerage. Fifties historians regarded it as having been deservedly entitled "The Canada Act."

Being British, however, did not mean being committed to political reaction. Even the Loyalists, as the late W. L. Morton, author of *The Kingdom of Canada,* claims, were Tories only by force of circumstance. He calls them "unreconstructed North Americans" and asserts that they favored representative institutions every bit as strongly as did the signers of the Declaration of Independence. Where they differed with Jefferson's party was over the question of legitimacy. To them rebellion in the name of popular sovereignty was unjustifiable; they wanted to go on living in a North American way, but under British institutions. So they moved to Canada.

And in Morton's view they could not have hit on a wiser destination. Morton not only documented the Loyalist Tradition; he belonged to it. Like the Loyalists, he took for granted the inherent benevolence of the British system of government. At Westminster the struggle for freedom was over; ignorance, stupidity, even wickedness might triumph there for a season, but never permanently. However deeply England slept, one day she would wake up again; 1984 was a physical impossibility. As Morton saw it, what the Loyalists opted for in choosing to stay British was ideological stability. In rejecting the overtures and later resisting the armies of the Continental Congress they had escaped the whole sterile argument over whether a particular course of legislative action enhanced or violated certain enumerated rights. At Ottawa the only right worth bothering about was the right to govern. Canadians, enjoying as they did what their imperial birth certificate, the British North America Act of 1867, calls "a constitution similar in principle to that of the United Kingdom," could assign to their Queen "by and with the Advice of the Senate and the House of Commons" exclusive power to "make laws for the Peace, Order and good Government of Canada" without so much as raising a civil libertarian eyebrow. Under the British dispensation, Morton felt, Queens and Parliaments knew their business; authority, far from being the enemy of freedom, was its precondition.

It was all a question of escaping the written-constitution syndrome. Morton points out that the Crown is Canada's equivalent of "We, the People . . ." For Canadians, in other words, the authority to govern comes from the authority which governs. We are prosecuted by Crown Attorneys, investigated by Royal Commissions; we funnel our political grievances through Her Majesty's Loyal Opposition. Who shall guard the guardians? Why, the guardians themselves, of course, in the name of the British parliamentary system. The great advantage which scholars such as Morton saw in this arrangement was its flexibility. The United States, said Northrop Frye, is trapped in an eighteenth-century trance. Canada, being British, can move with the times; precedent for political change comes not from the interpretations which ivory-towered judges place on 200-year-old documents, but from the latest development in cabinet procedure at Westminister. Through Canada's connection with Britain she had access to what Chester Martin, a constitutional historian from the Morton era, called "a teeming laboratory of constructive statesmanship."

But what the Mortons and Martins liked best about the Anglo-Canadian system was the way in which it facilitated government action. Canadians can get things done "Britishly." A cabinet decree issued while we were still at peace in August 1939, invoking a law passed by the federal parliament in 1914, empowered Ottawa to control the price of automobiles throughout the Second World War; another such executive order, this time issued without reference to previous legislation, sent 15,000 Canadians into combat in France when the specific conditions under which they had enlisted included a government undertaking that they would not be sent overseas. It is no surprise that John Kenneth Galbraith cut his academic teeth in Canada. The Canadian intellectual world is a statist's paradise. In the land of the ordered free even taboos come under parliamentary jurisdiction. We literally legislate morality; a 1968 Liberal Party majority at Ottawa, with what then Justice Minister Pierre Trudeau, for want of a better title, called "The Omnibus Bill," amended the Canadian Criminal Code to allow legal abortion, homosexuality, and gambling.

Neo-Loyalists such as Morton never tired of contrasting the efficiency of constitutional monarchy with the cumbersomeness of the American congressional system, and their favorite example of this difference was the history of the West. Above the 49th Parallel Indians were pacified, whiskey traders put down, railways chartered, and administrative structures set up *before* the arrival of settlement; below it the settlers had to contend by themselves with wilderness living, as well as with their own anarchic natures. In Canada's West order came out of the barrel of a Mountie's revolver; in America's it depended on lynch mobs and vigilantes. Having ended Custer's Last Stand, the Sioux Chief, Sitting Bull, moved to Canada where, still anointed with war paint, he tamely submitted while Major James Walsh of the North West Mounted Police rode into his camp with six companions to procure the return of stolen horses. According to the Anglophile school of western mythologists, Sitting Bull and his compatriots put themselves peacefully under Ottawa's jurisdiction because they knew in their hearts that the Great White Squaw in whose name Ottawa did business meant well.

And so did French Canadians. It was a leading fifties assumption that they too liked the Union Jack better than the Stars and Stripes. During the War of 1812, as every schoolboy once knew, they even fought for it, Quebec Militia having stood shoulder to shoulder with Redcoats at the Battle of Chateauguay in 1813, less than sixty years after they had been ranged against each other on the Plains of Abraham outside Quebec. Nor was this closing of ranks by the conquered with their conquerors a result simply of blind obedience. Fifties historiography insisted that the coming of British rule to the St. Lawrence Valley created a true community of interests among its inhabitants. Canadianism began here. Loyalists and Quebeckers might look back on different pasts; they might speak different languages and practice different religions, but *ideologically* they were on the same wavelength; both were social conservatives; both equated revolution with treason; both were what Arthur Lower, another Morton contemporary, called Canadians in the making. What Lower saw the British Empire providing them with was a medium through which to express their likemindedness. French Catholics joined English Protestants in giving it their allegiance because a government committed to hierarchy and kingship suited them better than one dedicated to liberty and equality. They felt more at home in the Province of Quebec than they would have done in the State of Louisiana. The last cannon shot in defense of British rule in North America, to borrow a quotation much favored by first-year history lecturers and givers of papers at national unity conferences twenty years ago, was indeed destined to be fired by a French Canadian.

History, moreover, or at least history as it was written by the above-mentioned lecturers and paper-givers, proved that French Canadians could not have deployed their artillery more sensibly. British Canada gave them what, in the nature of things, the United States could not: an officially recognized collective existence. Their Frenchness and Catholicity are guaranteed by imperial statute. Thomas Jefferson might rail all he liked at George III for "abolishing the free system of English laws in a neighbouring province," but the inhabitants of the neighboring province in question blessed that king for having done so, even naming their sons after him. The Quebec Act of 1774, for which Jefferson had such harsh words, was their cultural *Magna Carta.* It emancipated Canadian Catholics over half a century before a similar happy fate befell their coreligionists in Britain. Thanks, moreover, to the precedent it established, provincial governments in Canada to this day have exclusive jurisdiction over property, civil rights, and education. Federally ordered school busing is a Canadian impossibility, and so is the issuing of federal injunctions against school prayer. Some years back Quebec's provincial legislature legally placed a crucifix behind the Speaker's chair, and more recently the highest court in Canada has upheld the legality of a Quebec law closing all but French-speaking public schools to the children of immigrants from foreign countries as well as from other Canadian provinces. No wonder *Te Deums* were sung, so argued Lower and his contemporaries, in Quebec churches on the occasion of Nelson's victory at Trafalgar.

But according to Last-Cannon-Shot theorists British rule in North America did more than just provide Canadians with a focus for national loyalty; it refined them. In the pre-Third-World fifties (ah, blessed thought!) it was still possible to talk with a straight face about Britain's civilizing mission, and no faces were straighter than those of Canadian academics. The most influential among them having got their doctorates either in Britain or from Britons, they took for granted that Anglo-centricity was an intellectual virtue. The British Community of Nations was their own ideological turf, one international grouping into which the United States could not follow them, and they used to like nothing better than to make scholarly pilgrimages to the Institute of Commonwealth Studies at Duke University in North Carolina, where they would discourse on Britain's role as a Third Force or talk portentously about the need to heal the rift among English-speaking peoples caused by the American Revolution.

Oxford was their Athens. Americans, to use the title of a 1968 book contributed to *en masse* by Canadian pundits, were the New Romans—powerful, practical in a limited sort of way, but unpolished, possessing know-how but lacking *savoir faire.* Their ambassadors misspelled proper names; their Aid Programs sent tractors to lands ploughable only by water buffalo and installed electric-razor outlets in facilities designed for use only by Sikhs. Such lapses were the penalty for having turned their backs on Europe. By staying British,

Canada had stayed enlightened. The New Romans themselves admitted as much by making their annual push northwards to our Stratford Shakespearean Festival, listening clandestinely to the Voice of Britain in America as heard through the Canadian Broadcasting Corporation, and enrolling in droves at such institutions of higher learning as Massey College, Toronto, where gowns are worn and port circulates in the best Oxford manner.

Being British meant above all being able to see the wider implication of things. Marshall McLuhan with his vision of a global village was typically Canadian; so was Lester B. Pearson, who studied at St. John's College, Oxford, began his public career in the Canadian High Commissioner's Office in London, and later won a Nobel Peace Prize for his work at the United Nations in defusing the Suez Crisis of 1956. Cosmopolitanism came naturally to Canadians. At graduate school one of the first things we learned to show a proper scholarly condescension toward was Turner's Frontier Thesis. Poor old Frederick Jackson! He tried to explain North American history solely in terms of North America, arguing that the Frontier, not Europe, had shaped the American psyche. Hadn't he heard of Canada, where the very last thing the average pioneer wanted was frontier democracy? Didn't he know that Canadians, far from shunning old-world loyalties, positively revel in them, so much so, in fact, that Northrop Frye calls us a garrison society?

There was no point, however, in blaming Turner for his terrible simplifications. He suffered the misfortune of coming from an isolationist tradition. Born a hundred miles further north, he would have had access to a world culture; he might even have got accepted at St. John's; at least he would never have been foolish enough to conclude that history is a North American affair. As a Canadian he would have had a mind that necessarily moved along international lines. The victory of Loyalism, so fifties mythology asserted, not only gave Canadians a separate existence in North America; it kept them in touch with the world at large.

Thus spake Anglo-Canadian liberals of the last generation. They took their inspiration from Oxford and Westminster. Whether true or false, their picture of Canada as a manifestation of British world culture in North America was at least a coherent one. It served as the basis for a workable national mythology.

Then came the debunking sixties. Canadians spent the decade in an orgy of throwing out British models. First to go were the Royal Canadian Navy and the Royal Canadian Air Force. In 1964 they were amalgamated with the army, ordered into green commissionaire-style uniforms, and given the all-purpose label, the Canadian Armed Forces. A year later, after a few months of acrimonious debate, the Union Jack went, being replaced by a red, white, and not-blue maple-leaf flag. In what was one of the last loyalist stirrings in Canada, an irate Conservative opponent of the new flag asked why, after we had been following a cross since the Crusades, we should now have to turn around and follow a leaf, but no one took up his challenge. Then, one day the government quietly dropped "Dominion" from its vocabulary (despite the fact that the British North American Act expressly designates us "One Dominion under the name of Canada"); July 1st became Canada Day, and we were left in Orwellian doubt as to whether there ever had been a Dominion Day. By 1978, what with prime ministers beginning to replace the Queen on banknotes and miniature Canadian flags beside the words "Canada Post Postes Canada" appearing on mail boxes, the de-Britishing of Canada had reached the point where as acute and well-briefed an observer as William Safire could describe us as "a parliamentary republic."

Like all liturgical revolutions Canada's developed a momentum of its own. Fading images quickly lose their credibility, and as the pace of change quickened, so did the need for it come to seem more obvious. In 1953, one of Canada's most influential journalists wrote an essay called "The Real Meaning of the Crown" in which he argued that the British system is ideally suited to a politically and culturally divided society such as Canada. Twenty years later Canada's largest newspaper, the *Toronto Star,* described the Queen as a foreign ruler and wondered how much longer Canadians, a majority of whom now came from countries outside the British Isles, would go on accepting her as their head of state. Thenceforth it was pro-monarchists who were out of the intellectual mainstream. When in the late sixties and early seventies, for example, John Diefenbaker began rightly pointing out that the Trudeau policy of transferring royal prerogatives from the Queen to her trans-Atlantic stand-in, the Governor-General, was closet republicanism, the media depicted him as a man with a royalist obsession. Today the task of publicly defending the real meaning of the Crown has largely devolved on the Canadian League of Monarchists, a doughty band of old believers centered in Montreal who publish a newsletter, keep a media watch, and are Her Majesty's best gift to talk-show moderators and letters-column editors.

Meanwhile, a new un-British version of Canadian history is in the making. Out of the seminar-room window have gone *Dominion of the North, The Kingdom of Canada,* and *North Atlantic Triangle.* The old arguments that Canada is a beneficiary of British rule no longer hold water. Britain, it now appears, was no better than any other imperialist power; what chiefly distinguished her was the slickness of her propaganda, peace, order, and good government being simply a cover-up for colonial exploitation. The revised standard edition of Canadian history is nowhere more clearly reflected than in the two volumes of Robin Martin's 1972 history of British Columbia, *The Rush For Spoils* and *Pillars of Profit.* Martin has government and big business join hands in looting the natural resources and destroying the indigenous culture of unoffending pre-industrial North America. The book's ideological tone is set by a quotation from Rousseau's *Discourse on the Origins of Inequality* used as a heading for the first chapter: "The Poets tell us it was gold and silver, but for the philosophers it was iron and corn which first civilized man and ruined humanity." To Morton's generation Rousseau was anathema, equality a false American god, and the uniqueness of the British system consisted in its capacity both to civilize man *and* to save humanity.

Inevitably the new history recasts empire-builders as imperialists. A 1973 study of Canada's national police force called characteristically *An Unauthorized History of the R.C.M.P.* (it has quickly found its way to the shelves of every university and college library in the country) refers to the erstwhile heroes of the Canadian West as "instruments of racist . . . and class oppression." The

Mounties, it argues, were "A crucial part in the conscious scheme by which powerful economic and political interests destroyed the economy and way of life of entire peoples and wrested a vast territory from its inhabitants for a pittance." The degree to which the unauthorized has become the authorized may be gauged not just from the rising popularity in Canadian Studies circles of such platitudinous prairie Marxism, but from the fact that the Mounties themselves are currently under investigation for wrongdoing. It used to be popularly claimed that a Mountie always gets his man; now what he always seems to get is his innocent victim of police brutality. Major Walsh has been publicly stripped of his buttons.

Like the West, Quebec too has been moved by the new national mythologists from being a beneficiary to being a victim of British rule. Until around 1960 the ideological Children of Light in Quebec were federalists; the Anglo-Canadian system was looked upon not only as a guarantee of Quebec's collective rights, but also as a countervailing force to nativist extremism; separatists in those Britannic days were billed as Catholic reactionaries, and in the late thirties the *Canadian Forum, L'Osservatore Romano* of enlightened Canadianism, actually berated Ottawa for not calling out the army to protect innocent Montrealers from priest-led separatist demonstrators. Then came the Quiet Revolution of the 1960s; Catholic power in Quebec committed suicide, and separatism by going Marxist went respectable. CBC documentaries about "Quebec on the March" were no longer complete without footage of Roman Catholic statuary being reduced to rubble, or be-jeaned students burning Union Jacks, while a chapter on "The Decolonizing of Quebec" became required writing for college history text authors.

But the most remarkable expression of the changed attitude among Canadian intellectuals towards separatism was their response to the FLQ crisis of October 1970. Sympathy for FLQ aims if not for their methods is a theme that runs through the literature generated by that crisis. It is the Ottawa authorities who are perceived to have overreacted. Whether or not Trudeau did exercise more than minimum force—when, political kidnapping and murder having taken place, he called out the army and invoked the War Measures Act—cannot be known for certain until all the facts come out. Certainly, however, his action was popular with Canadian voters, particularly voters who, since October 1970, have steadily supported his party, and even intellectuals, despite all their talk of bleeding hearts and bleeding country, were as much pro-separatist as they were anti-interventionist. By contrast, Tommy Douglas, a leader of the federal left-wing opposition, complained that the government had used "a sledgehammer to crush a peanut." Douglas, had he been speaking 30 years earlier about right-wing nationalists, would have used a different metaphor. He would have been like his predecessors at the *Canadian Forum,* pro-British and anti-separatist. Canada in the interim had gone from being a nation of enlightened counter-revolutionaries to being a colony of oppressed subject peoples. FLQ terrorists were simply over-enthusiastic patriots.

And finally, even the Britishness of the Stratford Festival has come under attack. When in the middle fifties Sir Tyrone Guthrie and his merrie troupe of Old Vickers were brought over at public expense to put on Shakespeare in a small Ontario railway town that happened to be called Stratford, the consensus was that it was the best thing that had happened to Canadian culture since Rhodes scholarships. No longer. In 1980, for the first time in the Festival's history, public criticism was leveled against the Board of Governors for appointing a British director. The argument was that a home-grown director could do as good a job, if not a better one. In 1980 choosing a Brit had come to symptomize the worst sort of colonialmindedness. The Actors' Union threatened strike action, and in the end Ottawa got into the act by refusing to grant the old-country candidate a visa on the grounds that the Board had failed to make an adequate search for a Canadian. Talk about crushing peanuts with sledgehammers. The Board had no option but to cave in. They have now appointed a non-British Canadian and next year, no doubt, we can look forward to a production of *Hamlet* in parkas.

So has the idea of Canada been divorced from that of Britain. Perhaps it was inevitable. With the Suez Crisis of 1956, Canadians, like the rest of the world, could see that Britain as an international power no longer mattered. On dune and headland sank the fire; we watched it happening. Nationalism is above all an ideology of hope; nationalists must have some reason for believing that their dreams will come true, or else they must change their dreams. For a few years after 1956 the pilgrimages to Duke continued, and John Diefenbaker went on shaking his jowls in favor of the Commonwealth, but even he was realist enough in 1958 to sign the North American Air Defense Agreement. Like the rest of us he knew that it was time for Canadians to start following a non-British star, even though as things now stand it is extremely unlikely that the last guided missile in defense of United States rule in North America will be launched by a Canadian.

Why, then, has this necessary adaptation to a changing global reality proved so disastrous? Because it has been presided over by doctrinaire leftists such as Trudeau and Levesque who have succeeded in identifying their particular brand of statism with Canada's emerging nationhood. To be a good Quebecker you used to have to go to Mass on Sundays; today you must believe in the virtue of government-run auto insurance. To be a good Canadian it used to be necessary to salute the Union Jack; today one has to pay comparable homage to Petro-Canada, and even Joe Clark's Conservative administration did not dare to tamper with the state-owned oil company. As for advancing the valid claim that the sort of public-sector empire-building that Ottawa and Quebec City are currently going in for is a prime cause of inflation: in today's intellectual climate it would be tantamount to treason. Enemies of the Left are *per se* enemies of the new Canada. The fact that leftism is by all accounts the most discredited of world ideologies sufficiently explains the current mood of disillusionment with constitutional reform.

The sad fact is that Canadian neo-Conservatives have no Ronald Reagan to vote for, and no prospect of finding one. In Trudeau's Canada, where the only Britishism to survive is a predisposition in favor of government intervention, we are resident aliens.

Where the Majority Rules:
A UN Diary

(1981)

WALTER BERNS

Early June: I am asked whether I would be willing to serve as the American "expert" in a United Nations Seminar on the Relations that exist between Human Rights, Peace, and Development. (Actually, my caller begins by asking whether I would be willing to kill two weeks in New York in early August.) The Seminar, he explains, is one of those UN functions whose establishment the United States votes against but, when outvoted, it feels obliged to attend, the principle being that a no-vote is better than no vote. I protest that I hope to be in Maine in August and, in any case, in August I would prefer to be anywhere other than New York; he replies that I should look upon this as a form of national service. Besides, he adds, since the appointment would be made by the UN Commission on Human Rights, I would receive the UN per diem allowance which is somewhat more generous than the American (even though the money comes from the same source, us). Warming up to his task, he leads me to believe that if I stay at a modest hotel—he must have had in mind the YMCA—I might break even. Well, with one thing or another, it proves to be an offer I cannot refuse.

June 22: Today I receive from Geneva a formal notice of my appointment. The Director of the UN's Division of Human Rights writes that participants in the seminar are expected to contribute working papers "approximately ten quarto-sized, double-spaced typewritten pages in length," which papers will be translated, reproduced, and distributed "in advance of the Seminar, if possible."

July 1: A packet arrives from Geneva containing three working papers: one from the Soviet participant (44 pages) detailing the life-long human rights work of Mr. Brezhnev; one from the Indian (55 pages); and one from the Norwegian (85 pages). The Norwegian is not a participant, although he will participate; he is a "consultant" employed by the Seminar; reading his paper, I wonder if consultants are reimbursed on a per page rather than on a per diem basis. All three papers indicate that there has been a marked improvement in the "overall global human rights situation" in recent years; proof of this is to be found in the number of UN declarations on the subject.

July 15: I finish a ten quarto-sized (actually a ten 8½ × 11 sized) page double-spaced typewritten paper and send it off to Geneva. In it, among other things, I point out that I don't think the "overall global human rights situation" is actually so hotsy-totsy. "Billions of the world's peoples," I write, "are being governed without their consent, millions are being systematically and deliberately annihilated, hundreds of thousands are crowding fearfully into the flimsiest of vessels and fleeing the lands of their births, millions more see their homelands suddenly and viciously occupied by an army launched by a neighboring state, while, across a continent, another people trembles at the prospect of being invaded—because they had committed the horrendous mistake of forming a free trade union!—by troops launched by that same friendly neighbor, and so on." Where, I ask, is the evidence of an improved human rights situation? "Iran? El Salvador?"

August 3: I arrive at the U.S. Mission to the United Nations (otherwise known as USUN), am assigned an office and an "alternate participant," who is a foreign service officer and a UN veteran; he will act as a kind of shepherd for me. When leaving the Mission to cross the street for the opening session, we run into one of our UN ambassadors, a friend from Washington, who gives me an idea of the importance generally attached to the Seminar by greeting me with the words, "What in the hell are you doing here?" It is a blistering day, so it is a relief to leave USUN, where Jimmy Carter's thermostat rules are still in effect, for the General Assembly Building, where the temperature is kept at a comfortable 72 degrees. My shepherd introduces me to a number of my fellow participants who prove to be not "experts" at all but members of their various countries' UN missions; in fact, the only other country that appointed an "expert" is the Soviet Union, which named its "Director of the Institute of State and Law of the Academy of Sciences." He is accompanied by a short chap with dark glasses who, I presume, is the KGB agent. Since under the prevailing alphabetical seating rules we are placed next to the Soviet delegation, the four of us are soon engaged in an exchange of pleasantries. The same cannot be said of the situation with our neighbors on our right, the PLO, with whom, my shepherd informs me, we do not speak and *must* not be photographed. The PLO, along with SWAPO, the African National Congress, and the Pan African Congress, is present as an observer, one of the "Liberation Movements" recognized by the UN. My shepherd, who has an eye for such details, notices that the alphabetical rules have been violated in the seating of the observers; a quiet word with some UN functionary leads to a rearrangement of the plastic name cards and a reshuffling of the observing delegations. We end up with the African National Congress on our right.

The first order of business and, as it turns out, the morning's only business, is the election of the Seminar's officers, all of whom are elected unanimously. The chairman (or, as the Australian participant, a woman, will insist on saying, the chairperson) is from Sri Lanka, the rapporteur is a charming lawyer from Sierra Leone, and there are three vice-chairmen: one from the Soviet bloc (Bulgaria), one from the Third World (Cuba, formally nominated by Mexico), and one from the WEOG (the Western European and others group). By some alchemy that I do not understand, we decide that WEOG's vice-chairman must be the participant from Finland; unfortunately, due to the air controllers' strike, he has not yet arrived. Belgium, speaking on behalf of the WEOG, asks the chair if the election of the third vice-chairman can be delayed pending his arrival.

None of this matters so nobody objects. We adjourn for lunch, which I take with a USUN friend in the UN cafeteria where prices seem to have been set in the late 1950s and, perhaps in an effort to refute Milton Friedman, not changed since. We reconvene 30 minutes late—every session begins at least 30 minutes late—and spend the afternoon adopting the agenda and deciding, despite the wishes of Kenya who prefers that we be divided into three discussion groups, to do our business in plenary sessions. As France points out, most delegations consist of only two members and some of only one, and neither two nor one is divisible by three. A very sensible observation, but what the decision will mean is that there will be nothing resembling discussion, merely one speech after another.

August 4: The WEOG vice-chairman is elected unanimously. The chairman delivers his opening lecture and sets the tone of the Seminar by saying that it is "cynical to speak of civil rights to a poor and hungry man." The rapporteur follows by reciting a long list of UN declarations on human rights, peace, and development, and contradicts the chairman, whether knowingly or not I don't know, by saying that "people living in freedom are likely to work harder and thereby contribute to development." Cyprus is next; after congratulating each of the officers on his election to an important post in this important Seminar, he drones on until 12:10. Since no one else indicated a desire to speak, we adjourn until 3 P.M. During lunch I am informed by a USUN friend that it costs $400 to publish one page of an official UN document. This includes the cost of translation and distribution; it also represents more than twice the annual per capita income of some countries. We reconvene shortly after 3:30 and spend a few hours listening to India, the USSR, France, and the Norwegian consultant congratulate the officers on their election and speak of the interrelation of human rights, peace, and development. Everyone speaks of a right to development, so I raise my hand, which, when noted by the secretary, will earn me a place on the list of speakers. In due course, I speak my piece: Development is not a right but a necessity. To say that the 780 million people living in absolute poverty have a right to development suggests that they are poor because they are not developed (which is true), and that they are not developed because someone—guess who—is denying them this right. And to say (as every other speaker does) that the human right to develop is a right possessed by collectivities as well as individuals is merely to invite the governments of those collectivities to violate individual rights. For example, a government might decide that agricultural development can best take place through collectivization and then seize all private farms. This is likely to be resisted by the dispossessed farmers, who will then be dealt with harshly, in fact, they will be killed. And why not? The right to develop includes a right to the means of development as well as the right to decide on which means are appropriate or necessary. Thus, in this case, the UN would be sanctioning the elimination of the farmers. (A half hour later the "distinguished participant from the USSR" will take exception to my remarks, but I will lean over and say, innocently, that I didn't mention the Soviet Union or even utter the word "kulaks.") The Norwegian consultant says he is for human rights and peace and development, urges us to "embrace all three and to rise above them," and says there must be a "comprehensive redistribution" of income, which, of course, is what this seminar is really about.

August 5: Morocco identifies Israel as the world's chief villain. Bulgaria tells us that the "great October Revolution opened up a new epoch for human rights," and that individual rights cannot be separated from collective human rights. He concludes by calling on "some countries" to transfer wealth to the poor. Cuba, who, after Algeria, will prove to be the nastiest participant, says there is no possibility of tension between individual and collective rights; Prime Minister Castro solved this problem when he said the UN must recognize the rights of mankind. He spends the next 15 minutes denouncing me. In my working paper, I had criticized the idea that human rights can be declared into existence by the UN; what the UN can give, I wrote, the UN can take away (which it now proposes to do with freedom of the press). In any case, it is simply foolish to suggest that one can discover his human rights by telephoning the UN Secretariat. (Dial a human right?) Cuba's answer to this is that, unlike 1945, the UN now represents the majority of the world's people, so it can say what human rights are—and the United States better get used to it. Syria denounces Israel, and we adjourn for lunch. Resuming at 3:40, Czechoslovakia, in the person of a rather attractive young woman, gives its version of the Soviet line, but gives it in English. Ireland, in an eloquent speech, reminds us that this is supposed to be a seminar of experts, and that "we don't come here with instructions in our pockets"; this is followed by a series of speeches—by Algeria, Belgium, Senegal, Kenya, Australia, and then the World Council of Churches which has no instructions because it has no government to issue them. The day ends with a passionate speech by the PLO; it appears that "almost all the miseries in the world, during the past 200 years, have been caused by capitalism."

August 6: The chairman tells us that "fruitful discussion has taken place." In the afternoon, Senegal, the World Council of Churches, and the USSR call for disarmament.

August 7: I put in an appearance at the appointed hour merely to see if anyone else is present; the only person in the chamber is the representative of the African National Congress. He is reading the *New York Times.* In the course of the day, Romania, Morocco, Egypt, Finland, Ireland, Australia ("Thank you, Mr. Chairperson"), Costa Rica, and Kenya deplore the arms race. Kenya also thanks the USSR for the most appropriate gift ever given to the UN and the world; it seems that some years ago, the Soviets installed a piece of sculpture in the UN garden depicting the beating of a sword into a plowshare. Cuba follows with a vituperative speech calling upon the United States to beat *its* sword into a plowshare. We adjourn one hour and fifteen minutes early, being told by the chairman that it has been an arduous week. That evening my wife calls me from Mount Desert Island to say that Maine is very pleasant.

I spend the weekend writing my objections to the Seminar's report, which, of course, I have not yet seen because it is not yet written.

August 10: The week begins (37 minutes late) with a long speech by the Soviet Union calling upon the UN to ban production of the neutron bomb (which, over the weekend, the United States said it was *going to* produce and deploy), and calling upon the United States to ratify SALT II. He also says the UN should establish the new International Economic Order (a code term for massive redistribution of wealth from us to the developing nations), adopt the resolutions on mass communications (a code term for restrictions on the freedom of the press), and promote research on the relations between human rights and peace; the results of this research are to be given to students. (I note that in addressing the participants he always says "gentlemen," which must make Australia squirm.) Nigeria recommends that we denounce colonialism, neo-colonialism (and I remind him of quasi-colonialism), imperialism, and racism. China, in its first utterance of the Seminar, adds hegemonism to the list. Cuba calls for a "massive transfer of resources to the developing countries and complete forgiveness of debts accumulated in the past." This strikes most seminarians as a good idea. The World Jewish Congress speaks on behalf of Israel. We adjourn an hour-and-a-half before the scheduled 6 P.M. closing.

August 11: The Indian participant sweeps in, clad in still another dazzling sari. This reminds me of the story in the *Times* today; it seems that in India, which, of course, has signed the UN convention on women's rights, women can still be bought and sold on the open market. I resist the temptation to ask India about this. During the morning session we listen to many speeches, including one from the Bahai International Community. The Soviet Union leans over to ask, "Vat's Bahai?" I tell him it's a religious organization and he smiles condescendingly. In the afternoon, I point out that everyone present, even the Soviet Union, is for human rights, although Marx himself had nothing but contempt for the very idea of rights; that it is foolish to think that we can agree on a report because we have incompatible ideas on what these rights are. Some of us, I point out, say human rights are those natural rights delineated by the political philosophers of the seventeenth and eighteenth centuries, and those that are reasonably derived from them; others say that a human right is any desired good— development, for example—that the UN transforms into a right; still others define as a human right whatever their own governments are prepared to grant, such as free dental care (or as Clifford Orwin and Thomas Pangle put it mischievously in a recent paper, free *bad* dental care). As for what the peoples of the world think about human rights, I suggest we look at the countries people escape from, or try to escape from, and the countries they escape to, or try to escape to. This right to emigrate, I say, is derived from the fundamental natural right not to be governed without one's consent. If this right is secured, the civil rights (the right to speak, to vote governments out of office, to acquire, possess, and pass on to one's heirs the property one earns by the sweat of one's brow or the acuity of one's brain, and to associate in free trade unions, etcetera) are likely to be secured. The truth of this was demonstrated in America by an egregious denial of rights: I refer, of course, to the failure to afford black Americans the opportunity to vote for or against the Constitution in 1787–8. The consequence was a denial of their right to be part of the constitutional majorities that governed the country, and it is not surprising that, until after the Civil War, they did not enjoy civil rights. That is why we in the liberal democracies attach so much importance to this right to be governed only with consent.

In fact, of course, we all know that human rights properly understood are best secured in liberal democracies, and that liberal democracies are the most developed; as for peace, it is worth pointing out that there has never been a war between two liberal democracies. This ought to form the basis of our report on the relation of human rights, peace, and development; better that than a listing of demands which we call rights and which, as Ambassador Kirkpatrick said recently [and she picked it up from that Orwin and Pangle paper], may be likened to letters to Santa Claus. I have news for the participants of this Seminar: There ain't no Santa Claus. And if the report is going to contain a condemnation of Israel, honesty requires us to point out that Jordan has killed more Palestinians, that Syria has killed more Palestinians, than has the state of Israel. Finally, although I cannot speak for the government of the United States, I think the record shows that it stands ready to assist any country that demonstrates its willingness to use assistance in a way calculated to foster development. Bulgaria, Australia, India, and Cuba deplore my letters to Santa Claus allusion. Cuba points out (unnecessarily, I think) that property rights are "out of fashion" at the UN. As for this immigration business, he asks, what is it in fact? "A brains drain." The United States only takes the doctors and scientists educated in the poor countries. As for freedom of the press, why has the American press paid no attention to this Seminar? (I could have told him, because they're all in Maine.)

At 5:26, the PLO begins a violent speech and suddenly the Seminar becomes interesting. He makes a deprecatory reference to the Camp David accords, and Egypt bangs on the table and shouts, *"Pointe d'ordre! Pointe d'ordre!"* She insists that Camp David is not on the agenda. It seems, however, that points of order are not allowed in a seminar, but, then, what we are engaged in cannot fairly be described as a seminar. The chairman seems to be aware of this because he asks the PLO to confine his remarks to agenda items, and Egypt settles back in her chair. I decide that this is fun, so when the PLO, without referring to Camp David, launches a tirade against Israel, I pull out the plastic name card— "the United States of America"—and begin pounding on the table. Israel, I say, is not on the agenda. This produces some consternation among the participants because most of them are of the opinion that Israel (along with South Africa and American wealth) *is* the agenda. Still, I am sustained by the chair. But this has no effect on the PLO who, of course, has only one speech in his repertory, and when he continues his denunciation of Israel, I again bang with the name card. Under what conditions, I ask, are observers permitted to speak? At the pleasure of the official participants, I am told. Well, if it comes to a vote, I am sure to lose, so I, too, settle back in my chair. When the tirade resumes, I gather up my papers and walk out, which, I confess, gives me some pleasure: The United States walks out (even though, of course, as an independent "expert" I am not representing the United States). Back in the USUN, I report all this to my shepherd (who, wisely, no longer bothers to accompany me to these sessions); he says I must be late to the next day's session to make it clear that my departure was not required by the need to attend to one of nature's functions. I point out that it is not easy to be late; one has to be later, and that is not readily accomplished. It is decided that he will take my place for the first hour tomorrow, which has the further advantage of allowing me to be absent when the Soviet Union replies to my speech.

August 12: I arrive at noon and am told by my shepherd that the time was given over entirely to the USSR's reply to me. On the table there is a set of draft recommendations, fifty-odd in number and largely repetitive, since it is largely a compilation of recommendations made by the various participants. France makes the reasonable suggestion that there should be a drafting committee, but Nigeria says there is no time for that. We adjourn to confer privately on the question of whether there is time for a drafting committee. When reconvened, various participants argue over who possesses the collective right to development: Algeria insists it is the states, Australia prefers communities, Cuba agrees with Algeria but nevertheless fancies the term "peoples." Aware that we are not making progress and that time is running out, we agree that the rapporteur should return in the afternoon with a two- or three-page draft of recommendations, which, surprisingly, he manages to do. So, being pressed for time, we reconvene at 3:25, only 25 minutes late, and begin consideration, item by item, of the recommendations. It appears that UN seminars are expected to achieve consensus on their recommendations, which affords me opportunities to toss a few monkey wrenches. I cannot agree with any resolution, I say, that speaks of the right to development. Rights, I say, have corresponding duties; for example, in the United States we have a right to speak freely, and the government has the duty to protect speakers; in the Soviet Union they have a right to work, and the government has the duty to provide jobs, at which point the Soviet Union interrupts to say that Soviet citizens have the right to free speech, too. I say that is nice, then ask (pretending not to know the answer), who has the duty that corresponds to a country's right to development? Ireland asks more or less the same question concerning the so-called right to peace. France asks what the fifth resolution means. I offer the following new resolution: "This Seminar appeals to the General Assembly to devise procedures by which it may be ascertained whether the peoples of all countries enjoy their fundamental human right of being governed only with their consent." The USSR objects to this. On behalf of the PLO, Algeria argues vigorously in favor of the resolution calling upon the UN to guarantee the Palestinian people their rights; I offer an amendment adding, "the people of Israel, the people of Afghanistan, and the people of Cambodia." This proves to be a formidable monkey wrench, and haggling continues until 6:15 when the chair announces that the various interpreters (some twenty in number: French into English, into Chinese, into Spanish, into Russian; Russian into . . .) insist on their right to go home.

August 13: We spend the day haggling, much to the annoyance of the Soviet Union, who wants to get on. I ask why the Soviet Union is so anxious; after all, Soviet delegates are renowned for their ability to outlast, or outsit, the delegates of other countries. "Iron-bottom Molotov" was a term of grudging respect in the United States, I add. He is not amused. By the end of the day, we have approved—i.e., gained consensus on—one innocuous resolution.

August 14 (last day): We WEOG's have our customary pre-session meeting to discuss strategy. As usual, the expression most frequently heard is, "We can live with that." That speaks volumes, because it reflects the fact that the West is engaged in a holding operation here, and that the initiative, and the power, here as in the UN generally, is in the hands of others. Australia is becoming annoyed with me and, truth to tell, I with her. The morning session is devoted entirely to consideration of the following Algerian resolution:

The Seminar recognizes that racism as a state ideology violently negates the basic humanity of its victims. Apartheid, racism, and racial discrimination, colonialism, neo-colonialism, foreign domination and occupation [the Namibia situation], aggression, and threats against national sovereignty and territorial integrity, and the denial to self-determination of a people are flagrant breaches of human rights, deny the political and social conditions for development, and constitute a threat to international peace. Collaboration with states that have racism as a complement to state ideology endangers peace and international security. The fight of oppressed peoples for self-determination is an inalienable right.

That's quite a mouthful, but I indicate my support, provided the following words are added: "The right of a people not to be governed without its consent is also an inalienable right." Algeria makes the reasonable point that my addition is not germane to the subject of her resolution. Cuba, in what he would have me believe is the spirit of conciliation, says I should introduce this as a separate resolution. I say I am quite willing to do this if the two resolutions can be voted on as a package. Cuba and Algeria refuse this, and I refuse to withdraw my amendment unless, as a separate resolution, it is voted on along with the Algerian resolution. Cuba becomes angry, saying that there is no reason why we cannot vote on, first, the Algerian, then the American resolution. Since it is now after one o'clock, the chairman adjourns us, whereupon the Soviet Union says to me, "I agree with you. Package deal, yes?" I thank him for his support and he makes a beeline for the Cuban participant. One minute later the Cuban comes to me, a broad smile on his handsome face. "O.K.," he says in halting English, "a package." I apologize for my inability to speak Spanish and we shake hands. When, after lunch, the package is formally proposed, France offers what I see as an insignificant amendment, saying that, at least in the French version, there is a troubling phrase that he cannot accept. Algeria refuses to accept the French changes and the package deal collapses.

We then turn to another resolution championed by Algeria:

This Seminar appeals to the U.N. member states to implement U.N. resolutions and decisions concerning the inalienable rights of the Palestinian people to freely determine their political status and exercise their human rights as a prerequisite to achieving peace and development.

I offer the following amendment: After the words, "Palestinian people," add, "the people of Israel, the people of Afghanistan, and the people of Cambodia." To put it mildly, no consensus is reached on this, and the wrangling becomes somewhat nasty. The Soviet Union cannot understand me, he says; Professor Berns is surely not like the American people he has encountered during his very pleasant visit to New York; they are cooperative, friendly. "And Professor Berns? He's not democratic. He's preventing us from doing our business. He talks about democracy. O.K. Why doesn't he go along with the majority?" Algeria pipes up, claiming I have not kept a promise I made to her, and proceeds to lecture me on morality. (At this point I half expect to see a blind man grope his way into the chamber and start lecturing me on the colors of the rainbow.) Australia joins in the attack, then Morocco. I haven't felt so uncomfortable in a parliamentary situation since the Cornell faculty meetings of 1969; still, I don't budge. Instead, I remind the participants of what it means to have a right, and that I intend to exercise my right to withhold my consent. They have a corresponding duty to allow me to exercise it. Kenya proposes a recess during which some of us might get together privately. The chairman agrees, and a half dozen of us repair to the adjoining small conference room. Here I am persuaded by Morocco that my amendment is not really germane to the Algerian. O.K., I say, I'll withdraw it and replace it with this one: Add, "and the right of Israel to live in peace within secure and recognized boundaries." This, I point out, is germane; this is the language of UN resolution 242. . . . Of course, this is unacceptable. Senegal complains that no one else supports my amendment, but Ireland immediately says he supports it. Morocco then recalls a precedent; it seems that at least one previous UN seminar presented its recommendations in two categories, one for recommendations on which there was consensus, and the other for recommendations on which there was no consensus. We troop back to the main chamber where a new quarrel erupts: Cuba argues that my resolutions don't even belong in the second category because no one else supports them, or almost no one else supports them. He suggests a third category for my resolutions but, because there is no precedent for this, and because I threaten to object to all recommendations (even the innocuous ones), I eventually win. In this context, I insist that the chair determine how many participants support my resolution concerning Israel's right to live in peace within "secure and recognized boundaries." There is some confusion and hesitation, but eventually the following raise their hands: Ireland, France, Australia, Portugal, and Belgium. Conspicuously not raising their hands are Cyprus, Egypt, India, Mexico, Finland, and, of course, all the Soviet bloc and Third World countries—this in a Seminar that will adopt resolutions on the sovereign rights of nations, etc. . . .

Eventually, we adopt our two categories of recommendations: consensus (innocuous) and nonconsensus (contentious). But it is now 7:45, and the interpreters have agreed to remain only until 8:30, and we have not yet adopted our report. (Our recommendations constitute only chapter four of a four-chapter report.) The chairman suggests we begin immediately to consider the draft submitted by the rapporteur, and that we do so page by page. But the draft numbers some 150 pages, being a compilation of all the various points made during our two weeks. I suggest that we will never finish if we adopt this procedure, that he should merely ask whether there are any objections. (Since we were given the draft only today, I doubt that anyone has had time to read it all; I know that I got through only 30 pages of chapter one.) Australia objects to the uniform use of the masculine pronoun, etc., and suggests that it be redrafted, but when the rapporteur winces, Australia says she is content that her objections be noted somewhere. Most of us sigh in relief. Whereupon Algeria objects to paragraph 39 of chapter one, which reads as follows: "The view was therefore expressed that it would be preferable to speak of development as a necessity rather than a right. . . ." Yes, she says, that view was expressed, but only by one participant. Here (and elsewhere) it should be indicated that the view was expressed only by one country. (So saying, she glares at me.) Cuba, Senegal, the Soviet Union, et al., rally to her support. I say, I have no objection to these changes being made, but insist that this be done in every case. That is, we must ascertain the number of participants who agree with each view expressed. The chairman shouts that that would take us another two weeks and it is now almost 8:30. "Distinguished participants, we *must* adopt our report. . . . It would be unprecedented for a seminar not to adopt a report, unprecedented!" (Who, I wonder, will ever read it?) Some thirty minutes are consumed by this dispute; finally, the chairman says he will assume that there are no objections to the draft report as written, and before anyone can open his mouth, he bangs his gavel saying, "the report is adopted." It is, in fact, now a few minutes before 9 P.M., but, so far as I can learn by twisting my dial, the interpreters are still with us. This is fortunate because the chairman must make a closing speech. He thanks us, we thank him—and the rapporteur, and the secretary, and the vice-chairman, and the various members of the Secretariat who have been so helpful, and the documents' custodian.

With that we adjourn. As we gather up our papers, Ireland, who is a charming and eloquent man, asks me for my impressions. I say that if asked I shall recommend that the United States reduce its contribution to the UN. (We now pick up 25 percent of the tab, and more.) He says he was afraid I would say that, but for us to do that will mean the end of the United Nations. I reply that that might not be the tragedy he implies, but he thinks it will be the prelude to World War III. He then chastises the United States for its attitude: "In one sense, you don't take the UN seriously. For example, you are constantly changing your personnel, and as a result you don't establish the relationships that might permit you to work effectively here." We shake hands; in fact, there is a general round of handshaking, and I even receive a friendly slap on the back from Bulgaria. I run for a cab—I am of course late for a dinner engagement—and as I am being driven uptown I reflect that most of the participants will soon be meeting and working together again—in fact, unlike me, they do represent their countries, most of them on the UN's Third Committee (which deals with human rights)—and most of them will regularly vote against the United States. As Cuba said, they are the majority.

August 15: I go to my USUN office and begin discarding part of the mountain of paper that has accumulated on my desk (and to which, I confess, I contributed a few foothills). Then, as I promised, I go up to the eleventh floor to chat with one of our ambassadors. When I report what Ireland had said about our attitude toward the UN, he says Ireland may be right. And the ambassador may be right, but I wonder what difference it would make if our UN representatives served longer and succeeded in establishing closer relations with other delegations.

I suspect this Seminar was typical of UN meetings, especially of meetings on human rights, and it was surely not convened with the view that we might learn something from each other. It was not conducted with that purpose in mind. One can argue, as I did, that to know what human rights are requires that we understand what it means to be human, and what it is that distinguishes humans from other classes of beings, but all this falls on deaf ears. Jefferson and Tom Paine, following the political philosophers, could speak of the rights of man and were prepared to explain how these rights were related to and derived from man's nature; but UN seminarians are impatient with such talk. What they want is a UN declaration saying that the "South" has rights and the "North" (which means the United States) has duties, and it matters not a fig to them that, when challenged, they cannot present a rational argument on behalf of their demand. They have the votes.

Privately, some of them will concede that human rights have been best secured in the liberal democracies, but such concessions are quickly overwhelmed by their resentments toward their "former colonial masters." Privately, some of them will acknowledge that the Soviet Union is acting with gross hypocrisy, but the Soviet Union and its bloc supplies them with votes. A U.S. mission made of scores of Eleanor Roosevelts and Adlai Stevensons, all serving for life, would not, I sadly conclude, change this situation one whit.

Kissinger II: Henry Kissinger and *Years of Upheaval*

(1982)

H. J. KAPLAN

Early this summer when the battle for Stanley was drawing to a close and the Israelis were tightening their noose around Beirut and the Russians belatedly beginning to growl, I had visions of Henry Kissinger rocketing around the globe again, from Moscow to Peking to Cairo. *Years of Upheaval,* the second volume of his memoirs, reminds us that diplomacy in the old-fashioned sense can still play a significant role, even in an age of implacable ideologies. Conflict keeps creating new facts, but even after apparently decisive military action, these are variously perceived, ambiguous, impermanent. Everything depends on whether and how they can be put together, the kind of task that our once and future Metternich, if his memoirs are to be believed, had a genius for solving.

I do believe them. One of Kissinger's critics, unconsciously mimicking the tone and style of his text, remarks that no statesman ever writes memoirs to denigrate his own role. This is a truism, with a sniff of Harvard about it, but the self-serving purpose is hardly achieved if the events are twisted, the reasoning specious, the style (*the man himself,* as Buffon observed) inauthentic. We now have two-thirds of the Gospel according to Henry, and while there is still no sign that anyone has organized a church it is obvious that the News he brings is from On High, the reasoning is compelling, and the style does honor to our culture.

This is the man who once, in an interview with an Italian journalist, described himself as a loner in terms that people thought rather ridiculous at the time, but the fact is that Kissinger was and remains *sui generis.* His memoirs read sometimes like a work of literature, bathed in an atmosphere of historical fiction, with occasional longueurs but carefully plotted and filled with suspense. Only, the world in question is the one we share, the world of current events. The hero is neither an artistic sensibility like Jean Christophe nor a "delicate child of life" like Hans Castorp nor even Lanny Budd. He is Henry Kissinger, a man from nowhere, who appears at a time of great national travail, almost by accident, without authority other than that conferred by his competence and wit, to wield enormous power and conduct our foreign affairs. Of course he had a brilliant staff and the paraphernalia of a superpower (armies, fleets, alliances) behind him; and a little help from his friends—Nixon, Ford, et al.—but the fact remains that he made history almost singlehandedly, in a manner entirely his own.

As I clear my throat and prepare to make solemn noises about this extraordinary performance, I find that the noises I had in mind have been largely preempted by Norman Podhoretz, editor of *Commentary,* and Stanley Hoffmann, a distinguished professor at Harvard. These two gentlemen, who rarely agree on public issues, nonetheless agree that whatever one may think of Kissinger's record he has written an extraordinary book. Podhoretz has a problem with the word "great," being repelled (he tells us) by the fashionable inflation of language; and Hoffmann seems less moved than bemused by his erstwhile colleague's achievement, as if astounded that so ugly a duckling could have evolved into a swan. But their judgment is univocal and clear and appropriately touched with awe: A masterwork has entered the American canon. Podhoretz, with his customary brilliance and passion, "reconsiders" Kissinger in the June 1982 issue of *Commentary;* and Hoffmann goes and does likewise in the *New York Review of Books* for April 29, only occasionally showing the strain of his determination to give the devil his due.

These are serious, thoughtful, and (each in its way) successful attempts to get "at" the second panel of Kissinger's huge triptych, 1,283 pages of narrative, documents, and reflection on his service as secretary of state during the truncated second administration of Richard Nixon. To be sure, they take issue (again, each in his way) with the author's views: on détente, on the Middle East, on Vietnam, on arms control. They not only doubt the solidity of the "structure of peace" which Kissinger presents as his grand design, but regretfully pronounce it a failure. But both point to the felicity of his portraits, the aptness of his language, his ingenuity as a negotiator—all of which, as pure *story,* informs, fascinates, and delights the reader. No author could wish for a more perceptive reaction to his work.

But what about the statesman? A friend of mine who is well acquainted with Kissinger insists that he is not primarily a writer; that he would rather be Bismarck than Goethe; and that if you reject his policy you do not console him by admiring his prose. This strikes me as improbable, but if one takes the trouble to be Kissinger why should one excellence exclude the other? What he might wish for, in any case, if he is as insatiable as one surmises from the boundless energy and the lust for power displayed in these pages—and what we all might wish for him and for our country—is not merely agreement and praise but a closer attention to what he is saying. There is little evidence, aside from the two instances I have mentioned, that the appearance of *Years of Upheaval* has changed the terms or raised the level of the ongoing foreign policy debate among us. Months have passed since publication (on March 25), and though the event was attended by the usual hoopla, I suspect that the book has been more widely touted and bought than read, and that its significance will take many more months, indeed years, to sink in.

In the current atmosphere, this should not surprise us. For one thing, the inside story of Watergate, to which Kissinger adds a bit of pathos, has lost its morbid fascination. For another, today's world is (like yesterday's) too much with us, the background noise is hardly conducive to reflection, and Kissinger's account of his experience raises so many complex issues that people tend to be overwhelmed by it. They "skim" the book or put it aside for a more propitious time, and meanwhile the events so carefully recorded and interpreted recede at a rate approaching the speed of light and Kissinger's monument takes its place—already!—with the memoirs of Churchill, Eisenhower, and De Gaulle in that undifferentiated limbo we call the Past.

Although many of Kissinger's personae have disappeared from the scene, if not from this life—Nixon, Mao, Chou, Sadat, Heath, Golda Meir, and a host of others—the issues raised in *Years of Upheaval* are very much with us. Kissinger is not the sort of memorialist who merely tells us what happened. He is telling us, directly or by implication, what he thinks we should do.

Volume II, which is no less inordinate in size and ambition than *White House Years,* begins on a note of triumph in August 1973, with the author sitting on the steps of the President's pool at the western White House ("The President of the United States floated on his back in the water") and hearing that he is about to be appointed to the highest post this country can offer a foreign-born citizen.* But in this volume the mood has changed. The exhilaration of the mover and shaker is still there, the frank appetite for power and the apparently self-mocking humor with which he doubles as poet and philosopher. Occasionally, as in volume I, he steps back from his story to declare a principle or sketch a portrait; one could make a little anthology of his aphorisms and bravura pieces. In this volume, however, Watergate is constantly looming, at first in the background and then front and center, so that everything is chastened and darkened by the gathering catastrophe that hangs over Nixon and ends by striking him down. The final scenes will send him back to California, presumably to float in that pool again, but this time as a political corpse.

It is worth noting that Kissinger has gone out of his way to create this symmetry. The events narrated in *Years of Upheaval* actually begin in January 1973, with Nixon's second inauguration, not in August of that year. We are deliberately led to juxtapose two images—the President floating on his back in the water and the President returning in defeat to the western White House, to float, as it were, face down. In the interim a few little things have happened: visits to Hanoi and Peking, the fall of Allende, meetings with Brezhnev, war in the Middle East, the famous shuttles, the energy crisis, rapprochement with Sadat, trouble with the Europeans—and our hero has been at the center of them all. Incredibly, Nixon seems to have clung to the idea that the ceaseless activity of his secretary of state would help to save him. The last pages, including that eerie evening with Nixon in the White House on the night before his resignation, have a Hamlet-like quality. The President is thinking about his place in history. He seems to be asking Horatio to absent himself from felicity and write his story. So, for one last moment, it is Nixon who has become the hero again. But now, as his helicopter disappears over the horizon, Fortinbras, alias Gerald Ford, observed by the same implacably indispensable eye, "strides firmly toward the White House, his arm around his wife's shoulder." *In his beginning is my end.*

*It should be recalled that upon being named secretary of state, Kissinger continued to serve as national security adviser until November 1975.

"Engulfed in anguish" but "feeling an immense relief," Kissinger—who has also acquired a wife in volume II—prepares to stride firmly into volume III. "Somehow we have preserved a vital foreign policy in the debacle," our author says, and he prays that "fate would be kind to this good man [i.e., Ford] and that his heart would be stout and that America under his leadership would find again its faith."

All irony aside, this is artfully done, composed and written with a sensibility and skill that set it apart from even the more distinguished memoirs of our time and make us reach far back for parallels—to Theophrastus, for example, or La Bruyère, although Kissinger's portraits are not of "types" but of flesh-and-blood leaders. Or to Saint-Simon, for the narrative verve and color, except that Kissinger was no envious onlooker, curdled with scorn and spite, writing his memoirs because he had been denied the employment he deserved. There is a quality in Kissinger's writing that betrays the outsider, nonetheless, the refugee from Fürth, Germany, who can never forget that he is an intellectual, a scholar, not really a typical American man of action, as if the whole situation were some cosmic joke. But the fact remains that the "vital foreign policy" preserved in the Nixon debacle was his own, and we approach volume III in the expectation that he will be allowed to carry it forward, despite the congressional watchdogs who have tasted blood and will now be baying in pursuit.

What, then, was this "vital foreign policy," and why do Podhoretz and Hoffmann pronounce it a failure? The word seems a bit flat. *Failure?* For the reader who emerges blinking from this prodigiously detailed account of a performance without precedent in diplomatic history, the judgment has a summary—almost comical—ring to it. To paraphrase the master himself: What, in the name of God, is strategic failure? The opening to China, long a gleam in the eye of American Presidents (and an idea that had even occurred, believe it or not, to John Foster Dulles) was finally accomplished, while preserving the freedom and integrity of Taiwan. The Yom Kippur war was concluded without damage to the essential interests of Israel, while preparing the ground for Camp David and helping Sadat free his country from dependence on the Soviets. The war in Vietnam was terminated at last and if the aftermath was cruel (as indeed it was and is) it is at least arguable that Congress, by refusing to allow the President to enforce the terms of the agreement negotiated between Kissinger and Le Duc Tho, was responsible for turning the possibility of an honorable exit into a disgraceful rout.

Meanwhile, relations with the Russians, now solemnly baptized (and ballyhooed for internal political reasons) as détente, proceeded in their normal adversarial fashion, only occasionally lightened by Kissinger's sardonic chumminess with Anatol and Andrei and Leonid. Each side won a few and lost a few; no great breakthrough, no "structure of peace" was achieved by agreement; none could be, by any imaginable policy under the circumstances; and nothing notable was lost except—and here is the crux of my difference with Podhoretz and Hoffmann—that which in the nature of things could not be saved. Because the Soviets were willing and able to increase their military spending by some 40 percent throughout the decade, and we were not; because the Europeans and the Japanese were excessively inclined toward accommodation; because OPEC had bared its teeth and the Iranian debacle was approaching—it is also arguable that the world was a more dangerous place for our country when Kissinger left office than when he was sworn in, and that the Nixon-Kissinger foreign policy can and should be faulted on a number of counts, e.g., the neglect or mishandling of international economic arrangements, our European relations, Iran. But does it really follow from this proposition that Kissinger, as his Harvard colleague ends by suggesting, was a "dogmatist" who fell prey to "dubious self-vindication" and to "a kind of cosmic pomposity"; that he was mistaken in fancying himself a "strategist and conceptual thinker"; that he was guilty of displaying "far greater compassion for the petty mischief-makers of Watergate than for the victims of Pinochet"; and finally that "it would be a service to posterity—one that would not have to be paid by anyone's blood or tears"—if he took up another line of work?

Hoffmann's perfidious advice to Kissinger—to become a writer of biographies and so to "indulge his taste for great men"—puts me in mind of a dimly remembered passage in Saint-Simon that recounts the long and laborious journey of a provincial nobleman to Versailles, where he hoped to dazzle the court with his brilliance and play a great role. He scales mountains, fords rivers, endures interminable roads and horrid discomforts, then prepares himself with elaborate care for his presentation at court—to which Saint-Simon (who has described all this in detail and with delectation) devotes exactly two words: *Il déplut.* A marvelous bit, written long after the event about someone who (if memory serves) makes no further claim on our remembrance. But there is something preposterous about applying a similar treatment to the events related in Kissinger's memoirs, as if so many and many-sided actions, so diversely inspired, undertaken under such ambiguous circumstances, could all be summed up in one cruel thrust: *He flopped.*

Let me hasten to repeat (on pain of being guilty of doing unto Kissinger's critics what they would do unto him) that both Hoffmann and Podhoretz render full and fair homage to the literary qualities of this book: the psychological penetration of the portraits, the brief essays on national problems, the obiter dicta on tactics and the sustained vivacity of the style; and both are generous in their praise of the negotiator who put the pieces together with Sadat, Assad, Brezhnev, and the Israelis after the October War, and worked out the Shanghai communiqué with Mao and Chou Enlai. But none of these operational achievements can alter the judgment of these two intellectuals that the ideas which Kissinger brought to the conduct of foreign policy were mistaken; that his performance was *conceptually* flawed.

Hoffmann cites with apparent approval Kissinger's "spirited defense of détente" (mainly against criticism from the Right) but ends by complaining that a strategy of confrontation *and* negotiation was too complex for the American public to follow, and that such an interpretation and practice of détente "was bound to force the Russians to ask themselves whether there was enough in it to make it worth their while." Besides, by excluding the Russians from the Middle East, Kissinger "contributed to the decline of détente," and this helps to explain why the Russians "tried a few years later to turn the tables on their rivals in Africa and on the periphery of the Middle East." This sounds like *Le*

Monde, and the ineffable balancing act of French neutralism: If the Soviets engage in imperialist adventures in Angola and Afghanistan, American policy is not precisely to blame but not without responsibility either. Negatives proliferate in this view of the world, and so do dichotomies: Kissinger is too confrontational *and* too devious to conceive of a genuine accommodation.

If this gets us into a bit of a muddle, it preserves our options and is intellectually painless. Hoffmann also reproaches Kissinger for failing to understand "the extent to which a state's external performance and strength depend on domestic cohesion and consensus." This, not Watergate, is why Kissinger overestimated his ability to manage an orderly retreat from Vietnam—a not implausible hypothesis, to revert to the style of *Le Monde* again, although Kissinger's frequent references to Watergate would suggest that he was not unaware of it. But for Hoffmann it also explains why Kissinger "reduces liberals to caricature" and "favors rightwing regimes." In the view of a neo-Kantian liberal, domestic consensus always depends on the prevalence of "progressive" policies and ideas. Whatever elections and opinion polls may say to the contrary, legitimacy in this view derives from "being on the side of history," which means in the hills or jungles or wherever the language of the Left is spoken. History has been cruel to this notion, as our good professor must know, but for decent liberal people it remains an article of faith. So Hoffmann can say—of a man who was demonstrably the most popular secretary of state in living memory, and surely the most prestigious on Capitol Hill since George C. Marshall—that "his concept of power was often too crude to be accepted at home."

Too crude—or too complex? Hoffmann seems to want to have it both ways. But it doesn't matter. Add what Hoffmann calls Kissinger's ruthlessness, his personal ambition, and his resort to fantasy (a polite word for prevarication—specifically with respect to the alleged plan to enlist Chou and Sihanouk to save Cambodia from the Khmer Rouge) and what it all comes down to is that Kissinger failed because he was not a nice guy. In power, he behaved and thought like a man of power, not like a progressive professor of political science.

So much for what one might call Kissinger's Hoffmann problem. The foreign policy elite of which Stanley Hoffmann is at once a spokesman and a critic is the milieu from which Kissinger sprang—an academic arm of the awesome Eastern establishment that Richard Nixon presumably was attempting to disarm and co-opt when he appointed him in the first place. In *White House Years* we learned how Kissinger was not only allowed but encouraged to set up his famous "back channels" to undercut the Department of State and reduce the titular secretary, Rogers, to a figurehead; to handle the press, which he did with consummate skill to the greater glory of the White House and, of course, himself; to staff the national security office with the people he needed even if they were exotics (Democrats, left-wingers, and god-only-knew-what) who would never have been tolerated in the proximity of the Chief had Kissinger's large shadow not screened them from view; and finally—the purpose of it all—to end the Vietnam war and undertake a series of spectacular initiatives: détente, the opening to China, the approach to Sadat, the Nixon Doctrine, which were to constitute the Nixon legacy, a "structure of peace." The establishment, whose thunder was thus to be stolen, suspected Nixon of betrayal from the moment he entered the White House; and for its "progressive" wing, as Hoffmann shows, these suspicions were amply confirmed.

Although Kissinger only occasionally pauses for polemics with bureaucratic adversaries like James Schlesinger or with senators like Jackson, he is visibly sensitive to the criticism of his peers, and not merely because it complicated his task with Congress and the press. It must have weighed on his mind because he keeps complaining of being caught in the middle between the Left, who insisted on viewing foreign policy as "a branch of psychiatry," and the *theological* Right. The latter were not, as one might suppose, premature moral majoritarians or any other element of the non-establishment Right. They were the sophisticated hardliners, from Paul Nitze to Lane Kirkland, for whom détente was a vast mistake.

Exactly who should be included in this category is not clear; people move in and out of it on different issues. But a major culprit is surely Norman Podhoretz, whom Kissinger takes the trouble to chide in a footnote as a critic who moved from one (anti-Vietnam) extreme to another, and whose current aberration is to insist that détente is impossible in the nature of things, that economic exchanges and arms control negotiations can only redound to the advantage of the Soviets, that American policy must maintain an attitude of unremitting hostility and confrontation in order to mobilize an American people historically "reluctant to support large standing armies, let alone to use them in combat" and "in the absence of some higher meaning . . . to be overwhelmed by the ever-present isolationist temptation." This is the view that Podhoretz expounded brilliantly in *The Future Danger,* and now repeats in his "reconsideration" of Kissinger:

[B]y representing the Soviet Union as a competing superpower with whom we could negotiate peaceful and stable accommodations—instead of a Communist state hostile in its very nature to us and trying to extend its rule and its political culture over a wider and wider area of the world—the Nixon, Ford and Carter administrations robbed the Soviet-American conflict of the moral and political dimensions for the sake of which sacrifices could be intelligibly demanded by the government and willingly made by the people.

In other words, détente breeds illusion and illusion disarms us, witness the current outburst of unilateralist sentiment in Europe and the growth of antinuclear hysteria in the United States. Furthermore, Podhoretz argues, Kissinger not only created illusions but fell victim to them himself. He was so skillful a negotiator he forgot that some things were simply not negotiable and that given the nature of the adversary the very idea of accommodation was a trap. This was just as true in Vietnam and in the Middle East, wherever, in fact, our policy ignored "the terrible dangers of contriving a negotiated settlement between a party that wants peace and a party that, although it may at certain moments pretend otherwise, wants only victory." So the famous structure of peace was nothing but a mirage. It was, Podhoretz maintains, "based on a misconception of what was possible in the real world."

This strikes me as reductive, much as the idea of détente or almost any other strategic orientation becomes reductive when removed from context and looked at abstractly, as a proposition. Coming as it does after a graceful and sensitive appreciation of Kissinger's achievement as a writer, Podhoretz's sudden plunge into what he calls the "real world" (which is in fact the world of language and logic) astounds us by its rigor. For a moment we are almost persuaded that reality *is* the propositions we devise to represent it. But only for a moment. Which of the parties in the Middle East wants peace and which wants only victory? The answer may actually be both, or now one and now the other; in any case, the law of the excluded middle need not apply. The real world is not a series of statements, however cogent, but (as the philosopher said) *everything that is the case.* Whether one agrees or not—and I do not—with Podhoretz's (and Hoffmann's) dismissive view of Kissinger's talent for "conceptualizing," the essential political question remains: What did he do?

It may be that the very concept of détente misled the American people. But how much does it really weigh in the balance against the fact that every major crisis we have lived through since World War II—Berlin, Korea, the Cuban missiles, Vietnam, the "red alert" during the October War—involved the Russians on the adversary side? Kissinger uses the term détente quite loosely in *Years of Upheaval,* so that it becomes synonymous with practically all Soviet-American relations. The tactics may not always have been effective but the principle remained precisely what it had been during the coldest days of the Cold War: containment—with the hope (and what American secretary of state has not expressed it?) that someday this too shall pass.

One might have wished in these memoirs for more attention to the ideological battle; welcomed, for example, a proposal for promoting democratic ideas and practices, such as the one Ronald Reagan presented before the British Parliament early this summer. It may also be true that Kissinger and Nixon aroused exaggerated hopes in the ability of regional surrogates such as Iran to help defend our interests in the Near East and elsewhere, instead of relying exclusively on American military power, assuming Congress would ever have allowed them to do so. But surely it is unfair to blame them and the so-called doctrine of détente for the unprecedented military buildup the Russians undertook during the 1970s. How would Podhoretz have proposed to stop it?

More could have been done, I suppose, to induce the American people to match it. When the alarm was finally sounded there was no unwillingness to accept the necessary sacrifices, only a great confusion about what precisely needed to be done. But that is another story. I am suggesting not that the record is unflawed, but that in retrospect it stands up quite well. To call it an utter failure begs the obvious rejoinder: compared to what? It is not my present purpose to engage in long post-mortems to determine whether Kissinger's tactics were right or wrong, successful or not, in Cambodia, in the Middle East, in the opening to China, on arms control, but simply to point out that in not one of these most visible events was our action misdirected or vitiated by illusions about our adversaries or, for that matter, about any of the other "concepts" that Podhoretz (or Hoffmann) would offer to guide our foreign policy.

I find it impossible to quarrel with the Podhoretz catechism. What he says about the nature of the Soviet state, about the American national character, about the intentions of Jews and Arabs in the Middle East, about the purposes and prospects of our "de facto alliance with China," and so on, generally strikes me as pertinent and true. Most, if not all, of these theses could be aptly illustrated by aphorisms or vignettes from *Years of Upheaval*. But the guidance they offer is necessarily limited. Could any set of general concepts, even if spelled out in greater detail than Podhoretz does, give access to a world more "real" than the one so vividly pictured in these memoirs?

In such a world, profound insight, e.g., into the nature of the enemy, may or may not be as relevant in the short run as some passing circumstance, e.g., the enemy's food supply, or an election at home. The policymaker, in any case, must "stay loose," as our popular language puts it—but this is easier said than done. Without abandoning or betraying his convictions or forgetting what we have learned from the past he must remain aware that the future is open and that—if he is a Kissinger—his book remains to be written.

The Reagan Doctrine

(1985)

GREGORY A. FOSSEDAL

Nuclear weapons kill people. They should be limited and, ideally, completely dismantled. Satellites and other systems that defend people against those weapons should not be limited. Indeed, they should be encouraged: It will be easier to limit offensive arms if such defenses are allowed.

This, in a nutshell, is the U.S. arms control position that emerged from the furious parlaying at and around Geneva. In the face of Soviet attempts to use negotiations to kill our "Star Wars" defense program, Ronald Reagan and his spokesmen—Caspar Weinberger, Robert McFarlane, George Shultz, and Kenneth Adelman—made it clear before, during, and after the talks that Star Wars is no mere bargaining chip. Rather, strategic defenses are the foundation of a whole new structure for arms control talks between the U.S. and the Soviet Union.

This new Reagan Doctrine was conveyed time and again in the weeks surrounding Geneva. In a major speech on Star Wars before Christmas, Caspar Weinberger stated emphatically that Star Wars will not be traded away. He also gave several reasons why the American left and the Soviets should welcome a gradual build-up of defenses and a gradual build-down of offenses as a step toward disarmament. Asked about Weinberger's speech, Reagan reiterated that he does not intend to trade Star Wars away. Pressed by reporters to explain if this would eliminate any "linkage" at Geneva, Reagan publicly announced his instruction to Shultz that he should inform the Russians we will not trade away Star Wars to get an agreement on offensive arms. Rather, he said, we will talk about limiting or eliminating almost any offensive system, but only under an umbrella of defensive protection. Shultz effectively did this in refusing Gromyko's demand that the U.S. freeze its Star Wars program while talks on offensive weapons continue.

All the signs that this was the official U.S. position were somehow missed in what must have been a million words of sometimes perceptive, often inane commentary by Western journalists. The press insisted on jumping for joy when the U.S. and Soviets agreed to talk about space weapons. Some even praised Reagan for cleverly using Star Wars as a ploy to get the Soviets back to the table. Yet at a press conference the evening after the talks closed, President Reagan emphasized, as he had for Margaret Thatcher just before Geneva, that our aim at the talks would be to explain that the encouragement of defenses will promote progress on eliminating nuclear weapons, not hinder it.

Ironically, by treating the mere opening of talks on Star Wars as a major victory for arms control, the press unwittingly implied that the legitimacy of such weapons is no longer in doubt. Where does that leave the 1972 treaty on anti-ballistic missiles, which outlawed strategic defenses? As Morton Kondracke astutely pointed out, the real meaning of Geneva is that the ABM treaty, in effect, will have to be renegotiated. This will have no bearing on whether Star Wars will proceed, but rather on the larger issue of whether the limits on defenses established twelve years ago will ever apply again.

How could so many commentators and pundits miss such a radical change of arms control course? Part of the answer lies in simple fatuity. Television and even newspaper journalists were so busy reading entrails—Did the inflection in Shultz's voice change from the first meeting? Was Gromyko smiling, or didn't he like the shrimp cocktail?—that they had no time to listen to what Reagan and his deputies were saying.

What is fortunately beginning to sink in is that Star Wars is not some hopeless boondoggle. If it were, we would not be seeing such a panicky determination on the part of the Soviets to kill it. Indeed, the Soviet Union's frenzied effort to stop Star Wars has convinced many conventional wisdomers—Henry Kissinger, Zbigniew Brzezinski, and Charles Krauthammer—that it may be useful in providing the Soviets with a great incentive to bargain, constituting a "chip" in the old arms control sense.

But the bargaining chip argument ends the moment the chip is traded away. And if Star Wars really is so effective, why squander it? This is the essence of the Reagan Doctrine, which sees that defenses are one thing that should not be traded for "progress" on other fronts. Rather, both sides should vigorously pursue Star Wars and other related ideas because the protection of defense-oriented systems will make it easier to negotiate both arms control and, ultimately, disarmament.

This proposition sounds radical only to those mesmerized by the countervailing logic of Mutual Assured Destruction, on which the ABM treaty was based. The idea of "defense-protected build-down" was in fact first stated by the Soviet Union. In a long-since forgotten speech to the U.N. General Assembly in 1962, Andrei Gromyko set forth the case for what is now the Reagan Doctrine:

Policy-making officials in the United States, the United Kingdom, and other Western countries can be heard saying that the best guarantee against a new war is the "balance of fear." Means of destruction and annihilation have become so powerful, argue the proponents of this view, that no state will run the risk of starting a nuclear war since it will inevitably sustain a retaliatory nuclear blow. . . . But to base the policy of states on a feeling of universal fear would be tantamount to keeping the world in a permanent state of feverish tension and eve-of-war hysteria.

Instead, Gromyko and the Soviets argued for a swift program of nuclear disarmament. In case the West should suspect the Soviets of cheating on such an agreement, Gromyko proposed that both sides be allowed to build defenses against nuclear weapons, providing "a cover" against such trickery. Now, in 1962, the Soviets had rather more to gain than the U.S. from nuclear disarmament. The U.S. enjoyed a substantial strategic advantage, as the Soviets would soon learn during the Cuban missile crisis. We relied on nuclear weapons to back up the conventional defense of Europe. Nevertheless, John F. Kennedy was intrigued by Gromyko's draft disarmament treaty, and rightly so. Kennedy was also receiving reports on a "Star Wars" program of his own—Project Defender, a proposed space-based defense against Soviet missiles under study since the Eisenhower Administration. Kennedy saw that Gromyko's disarmament offer when combined with a Project Defender program might enable his administration to free the world from the nuclear threat, at the cost only of a slightly larger budget for the United States and Europe.

But JFK's interest in strategic defense, and the Gromyko treaty, never had a chance to come to fruition. First the Cuban missile crisis, and then Lee Harvey Oswald, deferred any serious discussion of these ideas. In the aftermath of JFK's death, Robert McNamara emerged as the chief creator of strategic doctrine in the Johnson Administration. And McNamara was seized by the logic of Mutual Assured Destruction, believing that in a few years, when the Soviets achieved offensive parity, the futility of MAD would make disarmament inevitable.

The Soviets, for their part, went along reluctantly. By the late 1960s, however, they became aware of how the MAD strategy was eroding America's will. Suddenly, it seemed possible that the Americans really would not pursue strategic defense. It was even possible for the Soviets to envision and plan for a first strike of their own. With the signing of the ABM treaty in 1972, the Soviets codified the MAD doctrine that has made their buildup of nuclear weapons so effective.

The Reagan Doctrine enjoys even better technologies for defense than President Kennedy had in 1962. But it is based on principles similar to those outlined by Gromyko at the U.N.

In the first place, strategic defenses constitute a kind of "automatic arms control," as Reagan science adviser George Keyworth put it. An 80-percent-effective defense constitutes a reduction of an opponent's destructive capacity just as surely as an arms control treaty requiring an opponent to dismantle 80 percent of his force. Of course, that still leaves each side with thousands of warheads. But then, so did the Salt II treaty. According to MAD proponents, defenses must be "perfect" to have any utility, whereas pieces of paper need only represent a "first step" in the right direction. The Reagan Doctrine, as expounded by Keyworth and Weinberger, simply undoes that old double standard, and says that defenses should be evaluated on the same scale as treaties: In other words, are they moving us in the right direction?

Even more important, however, is the incentive effect set up by such defenses, no matter how imperfect they may be. The presence of U.S. Star Wars systems greatly argues for smaller Soviet expenditures on strategic missiles. Just as an 80 percent tax on widgets will tend to channel investment capital into products other than widgets, so too an 80 percent "tax" on Soviet missiles will lead the Soviets away from the massive buildup of missiles that they have undertaken since the 1960s.

Naturally the Soviets will do what they can to thwart such a system with various countermeasures, a number of which have been suggested by domestic critics of Star Wars. On the other hand, the United States will try to thwart those countermeasures and, over time, can expect to improve its defenses to catch more and more offensive weapons. And there are no cheap counters to the multilayer defense envisioned by Star Wars proponents. Overall, the rationale for building offensive weapons cannot be as strong in a world where defense is allowed, and this holds true whether the defenses under discussion are 1 percent effective, 50 percent effective, or 99.999 percent effective.

Furthermore, strategic defense can greatly ease what might be called the greatest sticking point of arms control today: verification. In the first place, a U.S. (Soviet) strategic defense reduces the advantages to the Soviets (the U.S.) from cheating. Facing an 80-percent effective defense, the Soviets might add 1,000 new warheads to their offensive force, but they would gain only 200 deliverable warheads for their effort.

Knowing this, moreover, the United States would have less to fear from Soviet cheating. Once our defenses are in place, the cost of responding to a Soviet offensive buildup is not building more offenses of our own, or even building a whole new defense. Rather, we would only need to add a few interceptors on the margin to an already existing defense. Thus, if the Soviets add 1,000 (very expensive) nuclear missiles, we need only add 1,000 or 2,000 (very inexpensive) non-nuclear interceptors in space or on the ground.

What good are all these incentives, however, if the world is still left armed to the teeth with offensive weapons, against which there is no final and perfect defense? The Brookings Institution provides the answer, saying that while leak-proof defense may not be feasible,

other missions, for less-than-perfect defenses, are technically achievable and might be very useful. And missile-delivered nuclear weapons might indeed be rendered "impotent and obsolete," to use President Reagan's phrase in his speech March 1983 in the following sense: defenses might someday be possible for which each missile warhead added by the offense could be offset by defensive improvements of comparable or lesser cost. This would make marginal increases in missile forces unattractive to the offense, and ballistic missiles would be "obsolete" . . .

Indeed, unlike the SALT treaties, such dynamics do not at all depend on U.S.-Soviet cooperation to limit arms. Defense-protected build-down thus not only would enhance the prospects for signed, formal treaties, but would function as a kind of "arms control without agreements," as Kenneth Adelman has argued in *Foreign Affairs.*

By contrast, it is hard to imagine any arms control treaty without defense achieving anything useful. Gary Hart, writing in the bulletin of the Arms Control Association last year, suggested that nothing short of "demand-style, on-site inspection" would suffice. But the Soviets will not agree to that.

If they did, even "on-site" inspection would not cover the very kinds of weapons that both superpowers are now concentrating on building. As Geraldine Ferraro admitted this fall on "Nightline," a "comprehensive, verifiable nuclear freeze" is an oxymoron, since the better part of U.S. and Soviet forces are sufficiently small and mobile—sub-launched and bomber-launched cruise missiles, small intercontinental and theater missiles, and the like—as to be undetectable. One general illustrated the problem well not long ago when he took a group of journalists into his office and walked into a closet—emerging with several true-to-scale cruise missiles. "How do you verify these?" he asked the reporters. Silence.

One of the more persuasive arguments against Mr. Reagan's Star Wars plan and its concomitant arms control strategy is that a U.S. defense would deal a severe blow to the East-West balance of power. Star Wars truly would cancel out years of Soviet investment in ICBMs, about 90 percent of the Soviet force. And combined with better air defenses against Soviet bombers and better anti-sub techniques and civil defense, U.S. defenses could arguably leave Moscow vulnerable to a first strike. In a world in which the Soviets still have substantial forces, such "destabilization" is not a negligible consideration.

But this merely illustrates a final advantage of the Reagan Doctrine, one that should be particularly compelling for those on the left. Precisely because Star Wars would greatly enhance U.S. power, it would leave the U.S. in a position to make unilateral gestures toward the Soviets. After all, one thousand survivable missiles are of much greater deterrent value than five thousand vulnerable ones. Suppose the United States deploys an 80-percent effective defense that the Soviets cannot match, either with a defense of their own or with an equivalent offensive buildup. As that system is completed, the United States could unilaterally tear up half, or more, of its offensive missile force—and still be in a much more secure position vis-à-vis the Soviets.

It would be even better, however, if the Soviets moved to deploy similar systems. In that case, each side would have greatly "built down" the destructive capacity of the other. Deterrence, far from being undermined, would still exist. But it would exist at a much lower level of destruction, and with much greater uncertainties about the success of any attack.[1]

[1]In an article in the January 21 *New Republic,* Charles Krauthammer examines what would happen if in fact the U.S. and the Soviet Union both established "elaborate, say 99-percent effective defenses" while continuing to beef up the accuracy and quantity of their missiles. Though his article is otherwise brilliant, Krauthammer makes several conceptual errors which lead him to conclude such a situation would be undesirable.

On a technical level, he describes such defenses as "highly vulnerable." This is not true if they are designed correctly; a defensive satellite that can shoot down ICBMs can also shoot down anti-satellite weapons aimed at the satellite itself. What really will be vulnerable are U.S. early-warning and other satellites if we do not build a Star Wars defense. More important, though, any attack on a multilayer spaceborne defense would take between several hours and several weeks to complete. Thus if our strategic defense is under attack, we will have ample warning to put our offensive systems on alert, making a Soviet first strike unachievable—even if our offensive force is much smaller than today.

Furthermore, Krauthammer argues that such a defense "might break down." Well, individual components might. And this might render a defense only 80-percent, or 70-percent, effective. But this, far from weakening deterrence, strengthens it. An attacking country must assume an opponent's defenses will work at peak effectiveness. He must also make a modest estimate of how effective his own defenses would be. You do not launch a nuclear war, after all, without any margin of conceptual safety. Thus the inherent imperfection of defense is an asset, not a liability, deterring a nuclear attack both because your opponent's defense might work really well and because your own might not. In the nuclear age, it is offense, not defense, that must be "perfect."

Indeed, most broadly, Krauthammer confuses deterrence with MAD, a special case of deter-

For some reason, the left never makes this argument. No liberal of note has argued in favor of Mr. Reagan's Star Wars program provided it be accompanied by offensive reductions. More typical has been the response of such leading Democrats as John Glenn who have spoken out against Star Wars while voting in favor of the MX. Those who do support the President's program in some way, such as Messrs. Krauthammer and Brzezinski, do so only to the extent that strategic defense is viewed not as a way of protecting people, but only as a defense of offensive missile silos.

Why only a silo defense? Even imperfect defenses might save millions of lives in the event of war. They might prevent an all-out war in the event of an accidental launch, or a strike by a small nuclear power. Imperfect defenses also form a bridge to more perfect technologies in the future, even as cavemen found uses for the wheel several thousand years before the invention of the internal combustion engine. Does not an 80-percent effective defense constitute 80 percent of a 100-percent effective defense?

As both William F. Buckley and Irving Kristol have observed, one of the more interesting facets of the Star Wars debate is the virulent, monolithic determination of the American left to believe that there is no chance of defending America. What most surprises, according to Buckley, is that so many prefer not even to hope for such a development.

As I see it, the problem with the arms control movement is just that: It is an arms control movement, not a disarmament movement. The two, after all, are not the same. Indeed, such groups as the Harvard Nuclear Study Project have been at great pains to argue that disarmament is an unrealistic objective, that the world must "learn to live with nuclear weapons." To do this, the Harvard group argues, we must discard the pipe dreams of defense and of disarmament, and seek as our objective a world in which the U.S. and the Soviet Union agree to freeze their strategic arsenal at some agreed-on, stable level. In other words, we must have *as our goal* perpetual nuclear stalemate. By this thinking, MAD is not a stopgap policy or a second-best means of keeping the peace until defense or disarmament is possible. It is an end in itself.

Such nonsense led Jonathan Schell, in his second book, *The Abolition,* to break ranks with the mainstream arms control movement. After all, Schell asked, can we expect to "live" with such arsenals forever without eventually using them? The hope that that situation will never produce a war is no hope at all. For making this common-sense point, Schell's major thesis was roundly rejected by Paul Warnke, Jimmy Carter's arms negotiator and probably the dean of the MAD-is-good school. Writing in the *New York Times Book Review,* Mr. Warnke called the idea of total disarmament "incompatible" with arms control, indeed "alarming."

---

rence. Like many, he actually uses the terms as if they were interchangeable. Under MAD, it is the threat to obliterate an opponent that deters, and the more certain an opponent is of your capability and intentions, the better. Deterrence, on the other hand, can exist at any level of destruction. All that counts is that your opponent calculate that he has more to lose by attacking than he is likely to gain. Any move away from the threat of total destruction is "destabilizing" and threatens MAD, but it need not threaten deterrence.

Most rank-and-file freeze supporters would side with Mr. Schell. So, too, do a growing number of politicians on the left and right. Both hardliner Rep. Jim Courter and dovish Rep. Les Aspin have expressed an interest in proceeding with Star Wars while paring offensive systems that Star Wars would make unnecessary. And so, ironically, does Mr. Reagan, who persistently points to complete nuclear disarmament and not mere "arms control" as the goal of negotiations. Why, then, do Warnke, Robert McNamara, Dean Rusk, and the rest of the arms control establishment so doggedly insist that MAD is the supreme objective?

In one sense, they cling to MAD because it keeps them in business. Just as the poverty worker has a kind of interest in the continuation of poverty, the arms negotiator has an interest in the continuation of MAD. If the world is somehow made substantially safer from nuclear weapons, Warnke and McNamara suddenly become much less important people. This is not to say that these men oppose such ambitious solutions as defense and disarmament out of a sinister desire to maintain their own standing. But it is only natural to regard what you've been doing the last twenty years of your life as important.

But if we clearly state that the goal of arms talks and weapons deployments is to make nuclear weapons "obsolete," then it becomes clear that most of what has been exalted as "arms control" since the 1960s has been essentially a vain set of squabbles over relatively secondary objectives. This is so not because men such as Paul Warnke and Henry Kissinger are dupes, but because they have been laboring under a framework that cannot produce success. We might even say that arms control, by repeatedly focusing on short-term gimmicks and objectives and debates, has actually distracted the world from the only real solutions to the nuclear threat. We have argued and niggled over this many nuclear missiles or that many ABM interceptors, seeking after limits on systems that cannot be verified or can be verified but are not worth limiting—all without getting any closer to the real objective. We haggle over the next step without even asking whether it is a step in the right direction.

One party has a compelling interest in all this: the Soviet Union. After all, the supreme argument of arms controllers is that the Soviets and the United States have a mutual interest in limiting nuclear arms. But do they? In a chilling column in the *New York Times,* Harvard's Nick Eberstadt challenged that assertion, asking readers to "imagine what the world would be like" if the U.S. and the Soviets were suddenly able to abolish nuclear weapons. Would the Soviets remain a serious international power? Would Moscow be able to compel Poland, East Germany, and Hungary to remain in the empire? Would Americans or most Europeans much care what the Soviet position was on any issue? Would the Chinese be content to engage in mere border skirmishes, or would they advance on the historically successful conquerer's road to Moscow—from the East? In short, would the Soviets be anything but a second-rate power?

In a vague, inchoate way the American left understands this, which more than anything else accounts for its deep psychological resistance to anything other than the prospect of continual arms negotiations with the Soviet Union. Nuclear weapons, Phil Nicolaides once observed, are like a bright light, to which the West reacts like a frightened animal in the dark—frozen with fear, unable to move while the Soviet Union points the paralyzing lamp in its face. The connection is so deeply imbedded it no longer even has to be stated: The *New York Times* doesn't say we can't aid the freedom fighters in Nicaragua because it might lead to a nuclear war; it simply calls the policy "dangerous" and "provocative," and our imagination supplies the rest.

Of course the one thing worse for the Soviets than a world in which both superpowers are free of the threat of nuclear annihilation is a world in which only the United States is. That is why Moscow will, eventually, be willing to go along with a U.S. Star Wars program as the basis for genuine arms control. It has no choice. With Star Wars, Mr. Reagan, like Bernhard Goetz, can now take the law into his own hands.

For what Star Wars promises is to inch us, ever so tenuously, toward a world without nuclear weapons, and that is why the Soviets, who have no interest in such a world, will fight it more bitterly than they have fought any American defense program in history. And yet, provided it is clearly and persistently explained, the Reagan Doctrine is well armed to resist any attack that can be launched against it.

The scientific argument against Star Wars will be repeated ad nauseam. But it will prove increasingly impotent, in part because such Star Wars advocates as George Keyworth, Daniel O. Graham, and Robert Jastrow have done a good job of swatting down the arguments of Carl Sagan, Ashton Carter, and other MAD enthusiasts, which have little to do with strategic defense. The Union of Concerned Scientists, for example, begins its 100-page plus attack on Star Wars with the straightforward statement that it seeks to evaluate only a "total" ballistic missile defense. It goes on to assert that to be leak-proof, such a defense must catch all missiles in the "boost phase," i.e., within minutes of firing. A criterion of this sort makes it easy to argue that strategic defense is unworkable. Indeed, the scientific critique of Star Wars is just another variant of the MAD argument that defenses must be "perfect" to have utility.*

A more serious stumbling block to Star Wars has to do with the long lead time envisioned by the Administration. Even with its dramatically improved explanation of the program in recent months, the Reagan team plans to spend $25-to-$50 billion on research and development alone, stretching the first deployment until well in the 1990s. Will Star Wars still be popular eight years from now, when the American people find they have spent $50 billion and are not an inch closer to actual defense?

Robert Jastrow argues the program can survive even such momentous delays; Daniel Graham thinks not. History, and common sense, alas, are with Graham's assessment that the present mega-year program will not survive the yearly budget assault of Congress. If a fifteen-year, business-as-usual procure-

---

*In recent articles, the UCS and other Star Wars critics have attempted to portray this case for less-than-perfect defense as a kind of fall-back position. There is no merit to such charges. In a *Wall Street Journal* article the day after Mr. Reagan's 1983 speech, Gen. Graham and I straightforwardly conceded that there is "no such thing as a perfect defense." We went on to explain there is also no "perfect" defense against the crossbow—a weapon which is nevertheless obsolete because defensive technologies against it are good enough to make crossbows a bad investment for the military planner, just as nuclear weapons will someday become a bad investment if defenses against them are allowed.

ment cycle governs Star Wars as it has the MX and B-1 bomber, the program could be doomed, and perhaps rightly so: By the time the Pentagon (with the usual kibbitzing from Congress) has over-designed and over-built today's emerging defensive technologies, the systems that result may well not be worth building.

Happily, the Administration has of late been inching towards the Graham model, though without giving its feisty author any credit. In recent congressional testimony, Fred Iklé, a top Weinberger aide, argued that "interim" Star Wars systems could be deployed much sooner on the road to future, more hi-tech layers. Even George Shultz said in January that the Administration might consider a deployment scheme to begin "by 1989."

The final threat to the Reagan arms control doctrine, of course, is arms control itself. Patrick Buchanan framed the problem with characteristic concision in a recent telephone conversation: "What if the Soviets offer to trade away 2,000 missile warheads if we don't build Star Wars? Can Reagan resist an offer like that?"

The correct answer to such an offer is not hard to discern. Mr. Reagan simply tells the Soviets, "Thank you for the offer, but we're not giving up Star Wars. Tell you what: We'll go ahead with that program, and *we'll* tear up the 2,000 warheads." It is not clear, however, whether Mr. Reagan would be prepared to give this answer. Yet, there are good reasons to think that when push comes to shove, he will stick with strategic defense.

The chief reason is Mr. Reagan himself. He knows history will not much value him for signing yet another meaningless treaty with the Evil Empire. But the President who defended America, who ushered in the beginning of the end of the nuclear age—such a President would rank with Churchill, FDR, and Abraham Lincoln. That is the company Mr. Reagan is shooting for, if he can steer his Star Wars program through the coming months of fury.

Prime Time Terror

(1985)

MICAH MORRISON

The contour of the story is, of course, still familiar: the hijacking of TWA Flight 847 by Shiite terrorists, the demand that Israel release 700 of their comrades, the threats to kill the hostages, the quick deterioration in relations between Washington and Jerusalem and the subsequent patchup job. The images, too, are probably still fresh: the pictures of the Boeing 727 stranded on the runway at Beirut International; the faces of weary, frightened Americans speaking to reporters, choosing their words carefully, surrounded by grinning thugs; the Shiite warlord, "Justice Minister" Nabih Berri, leering uneasily into the cameras; and all those talking heads on our television sets, spewing out an endless stream of "expert" advice. But some significant details of the story are perhaps already fading from memory, some of the specifics may already have been forgotten. There are things we should remember.

Specifically, we should remember Robert Dean Stethem, 23, of Maryland. He was six feet tall; he had dark hair and a dark mustache, a strong young man who enjoyed his work as a Navy diver. He was wearing a blue Hawaiian shirt and light blue cotton trousers on the last day of his life. "They dragged him out of his seat, tied his hands and then beat him up," sixteen-year-old Ruth Henderson told reporters in Algiers and London. "I watched as they kicked him in the head, then they kicked him in the face and kneecaps and kept kicking him until they had broken all his ribs. Then they tried to knock him out with the butt of a pistol—they kept hitting him over the head but he was very strong and they couldn't knock him out." At the end, they stuck a pistol behind Robert Dean Stethem's right ear and blew him into oblivion. His body was dumped on the tarmac at Beirut.

Specifically, we should remember the removal of those, as the media rather delicately put it, "with Jewish-sounding names." It was "the most terrible moment" of the ordeal, said one of the women from Flight 847. It reminded her of the selections at Auschwitz. "They were looking for Jews or Israelis," another passenger said. After the passports had been collected, "I heard them calling those passengers one by one: 'You, come here! You come here!' . . . They pushed them off the plane." One of those selected turned to his fellow passengers as the terrorists led him away. "Don't forget us," he said.

Specifically, we should remember the way a small band of professional

369

killers brought the government of the United States of America to its knees for a few days, temporarily drove a wedge between Washington and its firmest Mideast ally, and turned an all-too-willing world media into the bootlicking lackey of international terrorism. It is important to keep these things in mind, not to let them fade into the amnesic haze brought on by next week's horrors, the next hijacking or bombing or famine or massacre or war. There are lessons to be absorbed from the murder of Robert Dean Stethem and from the echo of Nazism implicit in the selection of the "Jews," lessons to be learned about the nature of Mideast conflicts, about the use and abuse (and non-use) of American power, including the technological power of the communications industry, and about our options for the future.

Without question, the hijackers of Flight 847 were professionals. These were not the teenage suicide commandos who drive truck bombs into army posts and embassies, knowing they will go straight to the Gates of Paradise for their glorious acts of martyrdom. (In fact, recent reports from the area indicate that many of the car bombers are aligned with secular, pro-Syrian terror groups. The popular view in southern Lebanon has long been that the young kamikazes are more fired up on drugs than religious fervor when they make their last drive, and that pledges of substantial Syrian-provided financial reward to their families are a strong factor in convincing them to commit suicide.) In many ways Flight 847 represents a perfect case of air piracy: Athens Airport was used because of its lax security and proximity to Beirut; the plane was kept moving to thwart any quick, early rescue attempt; fresh men were brought in to relieve the hijackers; women and children and the elderly were removed from the plane— holding these types of hostages has very negative PR value; a young man was murdered, just to show that the boys meant business; and then the hostages were scattered through a tightly guarded area, effectively ending any chance for a rescue. The hijackers made all the right moves.

In contrast, the Americans seemed to be making all the wrong moves during the first critical hours and days of the crisis. On the operational level, Washington's Delta Force counter-terror outfit simply wasn't close enough to the action. If it were stationed in the Mediterranean region it could, theoretically at least, have mounted a lightning strike against the plane when it first touched down in Algeria. Unless the terror war moves to North Carolina, there's not much sense in stationing Delta Force at Fort Bragg.

But it was at the diplomatic level that the Americans seemed to exceed all natural bounds of incompetence, while in Jerusalem bewildered Israeli officials tried to make sense of U.S. intentions. A small part of the snarl was due to plain bad luck: The most trusted and informed American in Israel, U.S. Ambassador Sam Lewis, had just wound up a lengthy tour of duty, leaving matters in the hands of his relatively inexperienced second-in-command. Yet the base treatment of Israel can hardly be laid at the doorstep of the American Embassy in Tel Aviv—it was Washington that for the first ten days of the crisis led Jerusalem through a crossfire of mixed signals and ambiguous statements. Anger and confusion—was this any way for an ally to act?—began to mount.

"The United States does not know what to do with itself," wrote the center-right daily *Yediot Aharonot* on June 18, four days after the hijack. "It is deterred by Algeria, which blocked U.S. access to the plane; it fears the hijackers' leader, a minister in the Gemayel government; and it is wary of an operation against the hijackers. . . . The U.S. is pinning all its hopes on little Israel to rescue her. If the United States took some action and asked us for assistance—that would be one thing. But to shirk all responsibility and to quiver through and through in hiding while uttering a silent prayer to Israel to bear the entire burden of rescuing the Americans—this is going too far. . . . This approach will ultimately hurt America more than Israel."

Less than a week into the affair, the view from Jerusalem, expressed in numerous "background" comments and journalistic fulminations, was that the White House was tacitly encouraging the American media to put "unofficial" pressure on Israel to release the 700 prisoners. The Israeli media began to run stories about the negative impact of the hostage crisis on U.S. public opinion regarding the Jewish state. Jerusalem tried to calm the situation by instructing its diplomats in the U.S. to turn down all interview requests for the time being.

Israelis were, by and large, dismayed by the American double-dealing. "A cat and mouse game is being played between the United States and Israel," Gideon Samet wrote in the prestigious and, by Israeli standards, rather stuffy center-left *Ha'aretz* newspaper. "The American government has avoided requesting the release of the Shiite prisoners in order not to look as though it's capitulating to terrorism. Israel, justifiably, is awaiting a formal, high-level request before making a decision. This is a situation without precedent in the close friendship between Israel and the U.S. It stems from the special circumstances surrounding the hijacking, but there is also a confluence of frustration between two countries which, over the course of several years, have lost their capacity for deterrence. Having been burned in the past, they're reluctant to take action now."

The commentator pinned the Israeli loss of a "capacity to operate" on the results of the Lebanon war, which he compared to an "enormous rescue operation" in which the army was sent in to "free an entire country from the hands of PLO hijackers." Heavy casualties were sustained in that three-year operation and Israel today is a country traumatized by its still-fresh wounds. America's weakness, in the *Ha'aretz* writer's view, an opinion echoed elsewhere in Israel during the crisis, stems from the Iranian hostage debacle. "The American hostages in Tehran who returned the day President Reagan was sworn in (they were freed in exchange for the release of Iranian deposits in American banks) returned as a symbol of the government's failure to rescue them through different means. America's military pride had already been trampled in the Iranian desert in an embarrassing operation. Since then, Washington has been wracked by the nightmare of weakness in its battle against terror. . . . Conservative American experts and past government leaders (Kissinger, as usual) expressed their belief that the U.S. will overcome its weakness and will do 'something' . . . but that is just wishful thinking about restoring America's capacity to use its strength."

The "official" Israeli response to American waffling came in some characteristically blunt comments by Defense Minister Yitzhak Rabin in an interview with ABC. Rabin was prime minister during the dramatic rescue of the Air

France passengers at Entebbe. In a long and distinguished career in the Israeli army and government, Entebbe is said to be the event Rabin is most proud of—and it was his pride and reputation as one of the tough heroes of Entebbe that was severely battered when, less than a month before the TWA hijacking, he released more than a thousand convicted terrorists in exchange for three soldiers held by a splinter faction of the PLO. Rabin was hurt by the storm of criticism over the swap. The old soldier wasn't about to be lured into appearing weak again.

"Look," he testily replied to the questioner, "let's not play games. . . . If there is a request on the part of the United States [for the release of the Shiites as part of a deal to free the TWA hostages] please come out and say it. . . . The problem is an American problem. The hostages are Americans. They were caught on board an airline which carries the United States flag. The United States government has to make up its mind: What do they want to do? It's first and foremost their decision. I've never tried to avoid responsibility. I've never shrugged off my shoulders the need to make a decision as a prime minister and now as a defense minister, facing terror acts against Israelis. I expect the United States to do the same."

The Israeli press reported that Rabin's remarks "astonished" Secretary Shultz and "angered" President Reagan, but the substance if not the style of delivery was welcomed in Jerusalem. After all, the tactlessness of Rabin's statements did not detract from their truth: The hostages were Americans and they were flying under the protection of the U.S. flag. Once again, America was appearing paralyzed by indecision, and to make matters worse it was slipping into a cowardly and half-hearted attempt to shift some of the responsibility.

Whether as a result of the Rabin flare-up or not, within a few days—by Day 10 of the crisis—officials of the two countries finally got their act together. Letters of mutual support were exchanged, and Israeli officials kindly floated the suggestion that the American wavering was due to the confusion of "mid-level personnel." The left-wing *Al Hamishmar* newspaper reported that the "current trend" in Jerusalem was toward "maximal coordination" with Washington. The crisis was winding to a close. Thirty-one Shiites were released from the Israeli jail at Atlit—government spokesmen insisted that the release had nothing to do with the terrorists' demands, a transparent piece of nonsense—and within a week the Savior From Damascus would step in and the hostages would be winging their way home.

Viewed in relation to the Washington-Jerusalem diplomatic axis, the TWA episode demonstrated the need for better emergency communication channels and procedures. A temporary news blackout and high-level consultations early in the game could have prevented many of the problems that arose between the allies. Viewed, however, in relation to the terrorists and their unwitting accomplices, a news blackout was the last thing they wanted. Jimmy Dell Palmer, the hostage with the bad heart released midway through the crisis, laid his finger right on the pulse of terrorism when he told a radio reporter in London that "the Shiites have achieved their goal. They wanted publicity. They got it."

Boy, did they get it. The world media, and particularly the U.S. television media, transformed little Nabih Berri and the Shiites into major players on the international stage, proving again to terrorists and potential terrorists every-where that the disgraceful rapaciousness of ratings-hungry television executives and sycophantic TV reporters will guarantee that, at minimum, the messages of terrorism's often sick and twisted causes will gain worldwide attention if a dramatic incident is arranged, media access furnished, and sufficient "color" provided. "You should not be surprised that Americans are still thought of as innocents abroad," an Israeli security official who served in Lebanon told me. "Look at the behavior of your television crews. They run around searching for a story. They hand out more money than many poor Arabs get from a year's work. Suddenly every illiterate Shiite carrying an assault rifle is appearing on the news all over the world. Of course the terrorists are going to prolong the crisis—they are absolutely delighted by all the publicity."

So the world media, allied with Shiite terror, provided a public relations platform that beamed messages to the Western world. Yet the TWA hijacking served another important purpose, directed toward the Arab, not the Western, world. For weeks prior to the hijacking, Berri's Amal militia and its allies had been slaughtering Palestinians in the refugee camps around Beirut. The Shiites want to prevent the return of the hated PLO to a position of power in Lebanon. (Oddly enough—or not really so odd when you consider the menacing under-currents of the Mideast—preventing a PLO return is also a goal shared by Syria and Israel.) The fighting around the camps triggered an angry reaction in many parts of the Arab world, including efforts to convene an Arab League summit to condemn Amal. Kuwaiti newspapers, in a view coinciding with the opinions of some experts in Israel, charged outright that Amal commissioned the hijack-ing to divert attention from its massacre of Palestinians in the camps. Berri pulled a neat switch here. He not only deflected attention away from the camps, but also gave the media a "good guy" image to play off the nasties holding the plane. Berri was portrayed as a sort of white-hatted Lebanese cowboy riding to the rescue of unfortunate Americans held hostage by mysterious extremists. This total lie was swallowed by many people, although anything more than a cursory glance at a few facts available early in the affair would have indicated something of the degree of Amal's involvement. There was, for example, the hijackers' original demand that four suspected terrorists held in Spain and Greece be released immediately. All four men are or were known members of Amal. There was also the report from several sources identifying the two hijackers as former bodyguards of—guess who?—none other than the minister of justice himself, Nabih Berri.

Some things in Lebanon never change. Whether it was Berri's Amal or one of the dozens of sicko groups operating out of the slums of Beirut that actually pulled off the hijacking, it's clear that Berri cynically manipulated the situation and then, when the hostages departed for Damascus, went back to the pressing business at hand—slaughtering the Palestinians.

Ironically, one of the biggest Arab killers of them all, Hafez Assad of Syria, won much American praise for his "constructive and helpful" role in freeing the hostages. Although there are conflicting opinions about whether Syria had a hand in initiating the hijacking, it certainly could have stopped it sooner. Shiite and other terrorists train in "Terror Academies" in the Syrian-held Lebanese

Bekaa Valley, and although the schools are controlled and funded by Iranians working out of the Iranian embassy in Damascus, the area is completely under the thumb of Syrian Intelligence. Nothing moves in or out without Syrian approval. Praising Assad for help in the fight against terrorism is like praising a rabid dog for keeping cats out of the neighborhood. This is the man who ordered the assassination of Lebanese President Amin Gemayel's brother and Druse leader Walid Jumblat's father when they got in his way, who ordered the murder of at least ten thousand citizens in the Syrian city of Hama when the Moslem Brotherhood began to chafe under his dictatorial and corrupt rule, who has imprisoned and tortured untold thousands of Syrians, and who—in an event little noticed during the TWA affair—welcomed an Iranian delegation that had just signed a pact with Libya pledging to terrorize "moderate" Arab countries, annihilate Israel, and strike at U.S. interests in the Arab world.

Indeed, warning signs of a new terrorist offensive are appearing all over Lebanon. "Various terrorist groups are organizing in preparation for future action on a broad scale," cautioned the respected and well-informed military commentator Ze'ev Schiff in *Ha'aretz*. Schiff reports that the Syrians have arranged meetings for the Iranians with extremist Shiite and Palestinian groups in Lebanon, that links between pro-Syrian Palestinians and Shiites are becoming stronger, and that Yasir Arafat is desperately trying to get his al-Fatah men back into the country. The Iranians, writes Schiff, "are investing funds in extremist groups among both the Shiites and the Palestinians, with the motto that all Moslems must organize for the great war against Israel." Arafat, for his part, and despite all the sound and fury about diplomatic initiatives, cannot allow his control of a dwindling PLO to be further diminished by the dramatic terror acts of others—to remain a player among Arab warlords, Arafat must keep his terror options open. Thus the April 20 attempts to land more than twenty al-Fatah terrorists on an Israeli beach. The Israeli navy intercepted the ship and sank it. Prisoners captured in the operation told of being personally briefed by Abu Jihad, one of Arafat's top aides, who ordered them to kill as many people as possible. On other Mideast terror fronts, the underground war between Syria and Jordan and their respective surrogates seems to be heating up, with bombings and assassinations in the Arab world and Europe; car bombings and ambushes continue to plague the Israelis in their narrow security zone on the Israel-Lebanon border; on the Golan Heights, several sabotage incidents have been attributed to a hostile Druse organization; and in Egypt there are numerous reports of a new upsurge in Islamic fundamentalism.

What can be done about threats like this, about terrorism that emanates from no one central source? Tying a yellow ribbon around the old oak tree is not part of the solution; indeed it may be part of the problem in that it sends the wrong message to terrorists. It signals a naive, spineless America, an America that dwells in an atmosphere of appeasement, helpless when confronted by the hooded face of an unknown enemy.

The answer lies in action, intelligent and forceful action. If the United States is serious about stopping terrorism it should go past the rhetoric of a "war on terror" and actually, legally, make a formal declaration of war. In a war you pay the tragic price today with the certainty that tomorrow will be better. How much danger would we face now if the United States and Israel had mounted a commando raid on the TWA jet on the second day of the hijacking, with the simultaneous bombing of selected targets in Beirut, the terror training camps in the Bekaa Valley, the Iranian embassy in Damascus, and terror bases in Libya and South Yemen? A sophisticated, superbly coordinated show of massive force would put a very clear message across: Strike at us once and we will go to the ends of the earth to destroy you.

In a war you impose censorship, which in this case would deny the enemy propaganda outlets. In this respect the media barons in the U.S. might be shamed into borrowing a page from the Israeli book and forming an editors' committee that would exercise voluntary censorship. How much terrorism would there be if the major media institutions agreed to give terrorist incidents only, say, a one-minute spot against a black background on the nightly news, and agreed to bury the story back on page five in a somber, black-bordered box?

It would help, too, if America stationed its counter-terror troops where they are needed. The logical place is Israel. The country has the most experience in dealing with terrorism, it is technologically advanced and strategically located. Much was said in the closing days of the hostage crisis about the special relationship between the United States and Israel, but terrorism drove a wedge between the two allies once and it could do so again. Next time—and there most certainly will be a next time—we must be ready to strike hard and fast. Terrorism has already declared war on democracy, and in this most unusual of wars the democratic nations are going to have to use some pretty tough tactics to fight back. We have no choice. Our future depends on it.

Sailing from Byzantium

(1986)

RICHARD BROOKHISER

Istanbul, like Rome, is an imperial city. Unlike Rome, the transitions between the phases of its past have been swift and violent, with little continuity between them. Modern Istanbul has been for sixty years the chief city of a secular, nationalistic republic, kept in order by a business-like military. Ottoman Constantinople was, for four hundred years before that, the hub of an oriental empire that started out crass and competent, and ended merely crass. The Constantinople of the Byzantines—or the Romans, as they styled themselves to the very end—lasted longest of all. It is also the most interesting today.

The emperor Constantine made the city capital of half his empire in 330 A.D. A Turkish army took it in 1453. The interval of time between the two—eleven centuries—is almost incomprehensible, as a measure of social duration. Buildings may survive that long, or bristle cone pines—not human institutions. In the modern world, only the papacy and the god-emperor of Japan have had a better run for their money.

At its greatest extent, in the sixth century, the Byzantine Empire stretched from Spain to Egypt. Five hundred years later, it still covered an immense rectangle with corners in Syria, Sicily, Croatia, and the Crimean peninsula. A long succession of enemies tried to whittle it away. Some—the Persians and the pagan Bulgarians—were beaten. Others—Arabs, Normans—took their bits and pieces before they were finally stopped. Catholic western Europe, in the form of the Fourth Crusade, sacked the city and gave the empire its death blow. (The Pope, to his credit, excommunicated the crusaders when he found out what they had been up to.) Moslem Turks disposed of the husk.

Surprisingly little remains in the city the Byzantines built. An aqueduct straddles one of Istanbul's main north-south roads, swirling with little Turkish Fiats and aged DeSoto limousine taxis. There are the walls of the emperor Theodosius, which were manned and maintained until the end of the nineteenth century, when developments in naval gunnery made them obsolete. There is a small park whose outline preserves the course of the chariot track of the Hippodrome, and which contains two characteristically imperial monuments—plunder from somewhere else: an Egyptian obelisk, and a broken trophy stand from the oracle of Delphi. (The park also has an iron gazebo, Victorian and absurd, a present from Kaiser Wilhelm II.) Here and there are columns, mostly toppled, and churches, turned into uninteresting mosques. Two churches, once mosques, have been turned again, into museums.

The church of St. Savior in Chora (still known to cab-drivers as Kariye Jami, or Kariye Mosque) lies in sight of the Theodosian walls. When it was erected, in the sixth century, it was in the countryside, like St. Martin-in-the-Fields in London, though the city soon swept around it. After eight hundred years, it was touched by a genius. Between the Crusaders' sack in 1204 and the final Turkish siege, the Byzantine empire shrank to a mini-state, about the size and importance of Belgium. But in that period of political impotence, it experienced a cultural renaissance. The glory of St. Savior dates from that midwinter spring.

The patron of the work was a statesman and dilettante, Theodore Methochides. There is a mosaic of him in the church today, wearing a bright, bulbous turban (in their final eclipse, the Byzantines adopted Turkish fashions). He offers a model of the church, the size of a big toy, to the Virgin. Methochides fell from power in a court intrigue, and ended his days as a monk in the church he covered with splendor (it would be interesting to know whether the mosaic of himself was a source of joy or pain).

The mosaics that cover the outer rooms of the main church are mostly intact. The Turks did not whitewash them, as they usually did, but only covered them with wooden partitions. In a small church with a low ceiling, they make a sumptuous and intimate feast. The most striking thing, to Western eyes, is the absence of a Passion. There is a fine death of the Virgin, which must have elicited the same emotions of pity and terror. But the Byzantine Christ, at least as St. Savior depicts him, is a young middle-aged man in the fullness of his vigor, with stern eyes and brows—a dispenser of justice, not a sufferer of injustice.

But the prize of the church, even more than its mosaics, are the frescos of the side chapel. Under the dome at the end stands a row of church fathers, dressed in robes of black and white checks and stripes, stark as Mondrians. Over them is one of the great resurrections. The ground is strewn with a litter of locks—the broken bonds of death. Adam and Eve, who brought death into the world, come to life first—Adam a noble, ruined old man, Eve a failed Mary in red. Between them strides Christ the resurrector, hauling them from their tombs with a firm, irresistible grip. They seem surprised, maybe still half asleep. He is a picture of power, love, and impatience. When this vision becomes too hypnotizing, you may retreat outside, where the Turkish Automobile Club has planted trees and painted the neighborhood.

St. Savior is small and perfect. Hagia Sophia, the Church of the Holy Wisdom, is huge and perfect. It was the cathedral of Constantinople, dedicated on Christmas Day, in the year 538, at the height of Byzantine power. When Justinian the Great, who had commissioned it, first saw it, he is supposed to have exclaimed, "Solomon, Solomon, I have beaten you at last." It is surely the most impressive non-Gothic church building in the world. The Gothic succeeds by the use of light and darkness, by the seeming defiance of gravity and the suggestion of vast spaces. Hagia Sophia is vast—75 yards from floor to dome—but almost doesn't seem so. Its classical shapes—right angles and circles—are so perfectly proportioned and arranged, it can be grasped in one overwhelming glance.

If you want to study a big building gone wrong, you can walk across a little park to the Blue Mosque. By its position and its appearance—in the skyline, the two domes look almost identical—it invites comparison with Hagia Sophia. There's no contest. There must be beautiful mosques in the world, but this isn't one of them. Huge, obvious pillars cut the space. It is an adequate building, nothing more, with all the emotional force of a granary or an airplane hangar.

It is easy to examine the proportions of Hagia Sophia, since they are almost all that remains. A few mosaics here and there, including one large Virgin— nothing else. The building is desecrated, a shell. The crusaders dragged its icons in the mud. The Turks destroyed what was left. Their additions are as unsightly as their obliterations. The walls are now hung with Koranic inscriptions on huge medallions. Arabic calligraphy can be a beautiful thing when it is hand-sized. Blown up fifty times, it looks like Coke billboards.

It was a strange civilization. We think of it, when we think of it at all, as a parallel Middle Ages—an eastern version of what was going on in western Europe. But it was a Middle Ages without barbarians and their vernaculars, without chivalry and feudalism; without Aristotle and Aquinas, or Guelphs and Ghibellines, or the wars of England and France and their nationalistic heroes— King Harry, Joan of Arc. In short, no Middle Ages at all. It was an unimaginable afterlife of the Roman Empire, Christian and Levantine, which held off its barbarians until the fifteenth century.

When the Sultan finally breached Theodosius's walls, after a 52-day siege, a remnant of the Byzantines fled to Hagia Sophia in the hope of a delivering angel. Turkish soldiers came instead, to lead them into slavery. Sly Gibbon described the scene, and for once, forgot to smile.

In the space of an hour, the male captives were bound with cords, the females with their veils and girdles. The senators were linked with their slaves; the prelates with the porters of the church; and young men of a plebian class with noble maids whose faces had been invisible to the sun and their nearest kindred. In this common captivity the ranks of society were confounded; the ties of nature were cut asunder; and the inexorable soldier was careless of the father's groans, the tears of the mother, and the lamentations of the children.

This is one of the uses of Byzantine civilization: as a lesson in history's finality. Historical consciousness, which is a modern invention, has persuaded us to think of history as an enormous buffet, whose courses are always available. But this is an illusion. We can, by tremendous efforts of study and empathy, think our way back to parts of the past. But we cannot truly share its life unless something of the era we seek to retrieve still lives in us—unless, in a sense, it is still a part of our present. But extinctions, when they come, are final. History is a thorough killer. Byzantium is a way the West didn't go. It was a cousin, but it left no descendants, in us, or anyone. We are in some ways more remote from the world of Theodore Methochides than from that of Caesar or Socrates or Isaiah. Byzantium is our easiest access to real strangeness.

Which makes it particularly relevant in the years after 1984. George Orwell's book, whose title has finally obsolesced, was also about extinction. Its hero saw himself as the last representative of pre-totalitarian culture; Big Brother's victory, when it came, was total and final. It is a commonplace of Orwell scholarship that the idea of *1984* was not original. He borrowed the shape of its world from another book, James Burnham's *The Managerial Revolution.* Burnham, writing in 1941, as an analyst, not an artist, predicted the emergence of three antagonistic world empires, engaged in constant warfare, despite the fact that their social systems would all be essentially similar. This state of things, Burnham warned, was already upon us. "The managerial revolution is not just around the corner. . . . The corner of the managerial revolution was turned some while ago." *1984,* if anything, made Burnham's world-picture grimmer, for it depicted the totalitarian era as eternal. "The proletarians," Orwell's grand inquisitor explains, "will never revolt, not in a thousand years or a million. They cannot. . . . The rule of the Party is forever."

The irony of Orwell's Burnham borrowings is, of course, that when he had considered *The Managerial Revolution* in his own persona, as a socialist journalist and reviewing hack, he had scorned it for its gloomy determinism. "Fortunately," Orwell wrote, "the 'managers' are not so invincible. . . . The huge, everlasting slave empire of which Burnham appears to dream will not be established, or, if established, will not endure, because slavery is no longer a stable basis for human society." Hopeful words, written a few months before he began work on *1984.*

The discrepancy is not simply a bookish quarrel, or a matter of literary biography. It comes up constantly in our foreign policy debates. How we deal with the Soviet Union depends, in part, on what is at stake. If the Soviet system is mellowing, or converging with ours; if our "values" are eternal things, like geometric theorems, or the spectrum of colors, which will persist whatever happens to the United States of America, or to "Western civilization"; we may temper our behavior accordingly.

So which is it? What would be the result of a world, responding to the Soviet magnetic field (or the Third World's, or some combination of both)? Endless night, or passing cloud? Constantinople suggests something in between.

A Byzantine resurrected in twentieth-century America would notice several current ideas at least formally similar to his own: concepts of law and the state; or Christianity. But the substance and practice of modern beliefs would be as strange to him as his are to us. In place of autocracy and Roman law, he would have to rummage among such notions as democracy, socialism, and natural rights. Instead of a Universal Patriarch and a Priest-Emperor, Peer of the Apostles, he would confront Jerry Falwell, Bishop Moore, and John Cardinal O'Connor.

So with us, after our demise. Orwell the journalist was right. No empire, not even a slave-empire, is immortal. The impulse to human freedom would revive, in some form or other. America is not, as Lincoln claimed, the last, best hope of earth. But Orwell the artist, and Burnham, were also right. Liberty, as we know it, would be extinguished, and the form in which it revived, unrecognizable. History, and men, never return to exactly the same spot. America is the last, best hope of the earth we know.

Outside the entrance to Hagia Sophia is a teahouse in a shaded garden, stacked with architectural rubble. There, for a quarter or so, you may sit among the shafts and capitals, and think of these, and other matters.

VI
Conservatives

The Alternative Interviews An American Gothic:
William F. Buckley, Jr.

(1968)

R. EMMETT TYRRELL, JR.

William F. Buckley, Jr. is a columnist, editor, politician, yachtsman, and—most allur- ing—he is an American Gothic. Striving for a very private ideal ever since age six, when he wrote George V exhorting him to retire British war debts, Buckley has gracefully raged through America beneath a banner of conservatism derided by the left, disdained by the right and confused by the modern muddled middle. In truth he is an eminently cultivated gentleman prancing about a culturally immature nation—but, one suspects, he has fun.

He claims that his journal of opinion, National Review, *". . . is committed to stand athwart history yelling 'Stop!' " Yet New York's voguish liberals endure him, for as his roommate from Yale, Thomas Guinzburg, of Viking Press says "he feels pain."*

I flew to New York on 31 March and interviewed Buckley in his offices at National Review *on 2 April accompanied by our characteristically shaggy literary editor, Stojan Tesich. Though* National Review's *offices are confusedly shelved on three cramped stories of a building somewhat more prehistoric than Maxwell Hall, the receptionist looked impatiently at Tesich, attired in leather jacket, paisley tie and huaraches. Fearing she was about to inform us that "deliveries are made at the rear" I hastened to tell her I was from Monroe County, Indiana, and Tesich serves merely as my guide and bearer. Thus recognized, she directed me to Buckley's upstairs office. With utmost caution I mounted the stairs, for only one year before I had, in reply to a fund-raising letter, sent him a personal check for $250,000. As I approached his office Buckley burst from a door, chest forward, eyes twinkling, teeth glinting, and hand outstretched, all I could imagine was that a resurrected Robert Taft stood behind me. But we were alone, the greeting was meant for us, and had not Tesich, as we entered Buckley's office, mistaken a drawing of Buckley's wife for Jacqueline Kennedy, I would have remained uncomfortably bereft of aplomb all afternoon.*

As Buckley's desk was a Himalayan range of books, manuscripts, magazines, and memos, we held our interview at a long table across from it. Surrounded by pictures of sailing sloops and dwarfed by a huge bulletin board adorned with insults he could not quite throw away, Buckley comfortably intwined himself around and over three chairs and graciously replied to the following questions:

TYRRELL: Mr. Buckley, you are considered the father of the New Right. What is the New Right, and are you happy with the develop- ment of the New Right?

383

BUCKLEY: Ahhhh. Yes. Yes I am. I think that the New Right is con-
solidating a criticism of Liberalism—a consolidation that progresses in part because of the intellectual penetration of the
New Right, but in part also because history is catching up with
orthodox Liberalism. So I am very much happy with the progress that has been made. You say what is the New Right? Well,
it seems to me it is a lot of things. It is anti-utopian, for
instance. It is a recognition of the limitations of the public
sector. It is a recognition of the necessity to protect the individual in a highly centrifugalized and technological society.
It's other things too, but those are what it's famous for.

TYRRELL: Do you think it manifests itself most efficiently in Intercollegi-
ate Studies Institute (ISI), Young Americans for Freedom
(YAF), and certain Young Republican organizations?

BUCKLEY: At the student level, yes. At the post-student level it's manifested by the work of critics—academic and journalistic—of the
Liberal Establishment.

TYRRELL: On the campuses is the right wing advancing effectively?

BUCKLEY: Ahh. When you say effectively, you've got to say, "Compared
to what?" I think that it's been effective in the sense of defending defensible positions and not being associated with the
kook right. I suppose, here and there, such associations have
continued or have taken place, but by and large, they haven't.
When people think of YAF or ISI they don't think of the John
Birch Society, for instance, and that much is healthy. They
haven't been as effective dramatically as the New Left has, in
part because the New Left was able to operate with the leverage of the Vietnam War which was not available to the New
Right. And for that reason *theatrically* the New Left has been
much more in evidence than the New Right.

TESICH: Wouldn't the Negro question be also kind of a theatrical
element that the New Left could use?

BUCKLEY: I think that was so a few years ago, but it is definitely not so
in the last couple of years, because the New Left—unless you
talk now about the kook left, the total separatists and so on—
haven't really known what to say about the Negro question.
"We did everything they told us to do and paradise wasn't
ushered in" so that they've been, or haven't you noticed,
rather constipated in discussing the Negro question since,
roughly speaking, Watts.

TYRRELL: Mr. Buckley, how can the New Right effectively improve
proselytizing its philosophy on campuses?

BUCKLEY: I think that it is largely a matter of tone. I think that what one
has to avoid is purely abjurgative polemics—mere recapitula-
tions of received conservative truths. What, I think, one has
to do is to be *interesting.* The trouble with a lot of conservatives
is that they're boring, and it is important, I think, that when

one edits, let's say a college paper, to edit the college paper so that it will be read with interest by at least *that part* of the college community that reads *that kind* of thing. Too many right wing college papers, I think, tend to fill their magazines with articles on price controls by a remote professor of economics somewhere, without any journalistic flair. I think that journalistic flair ought to focus on the events of a particular college rather than to try always to speak *sub specie communalis.*

TYRRELL: The New Left often giddily attests to having similar goals with the New Right, and suggests the New Right work concomitantly with the New Left. Are the goals similar and should young conservatives work with the New Left?

BUCKLEY: I think that they are programmatically similar in some respects. But I think that what Lenin used to call the sin of opportunism is something one needs to watch out for. He distinguished between opportunism and sectarianism. Sectarianism is when you don't want to work with anybody because he isn't *exactly* (sibilantly) like you. It's sort of Platonic activations of one's own maturity. Whereas the sin of the error of opportunism is that, let's say, if everyone else is in favor of socialized medicine—be he Stalinist or Marxist or whatever—and you're in favor of public medicine, then you make common cause with him. The big common unions of the 'thirties, the common fronts of the 'thirties, were distinctively errors in opportunism. Now take for instance the New Left's opposition to the draft, which coincides also to the opposition to the draft on the New Right. I tend to feel that most of the people on the New Left who oppose the draft, oppose the draft simply as a useful way of opposing the Vietnam War. And that under the circumstances I find myself, and some of my colleagues disagree with me, declining to join some of those abolish the draft committees, even though I do believe in abolishing the draft. So I think that accidental congruities between the positions of the New Left and the New Right tend to be more accidental than genuine philosophical congruities. One exception to this I suppose is what seems to be a *genuine* fear on the part of members of the New Left of big government, something which is rather new and very refreshing.

TYRRELL: As the founders of emetic journalism, *The Alternative* would like to know how you founded conservative journalism in America. How did you go about founding *National Review*?

BUCKLEY: Well, it was an incredibly hard thing to launch. We figured we needed about $400,000 to $450,000. You'd need more than that now, by the way—quite a lot—and it turned out to be extremely difficult to raise, extremely difficult to raise. And it's extraordinary to say this in light of the fact that there didn't then exist a really conservative journal of opinion, at least one that was in any sense journalistically inclined. But what we did was set up a stock company and go out and sell stock and debentures and eventually sold about $350,000 worth. And finally launched it. We've always had deficits—large deficits—which I think is true of every journal of opinion in America, even those subsidized by the CIA. And what we do is make up that deficit by an annual fund appeal which so far has kept us afloat. Our deficits range from $125,000 to $250,000 a year, and are made up by three or four thousand people sending in checks. So it can be done. As you probably know, the principal difficulty of the journals of opinion is not so much that they don't have a substantial circulation. 100,000 is a substantial circulation and with any such circulation in England, for instance, you can make money. *The Economist* is a very prosperous journal, so is the *New Statesman,* and *Nation,* with considerably less circulation. But what you have is an enormous discrepancy between the cost of publication and the cost of subscription. The *New Republic* in 1932 was available to its readers for six bucks, now a 300% increase in the cost of living since then—and it's available for eight bucks. But the reason it doesn't sell for more than eight dollars is because *Life* magazine and *Look,* and so on, are available for eight dollars and they set up a competitive paradigm against which you can't survive for psychological reasons unless you keep your price as low as their price level. If we could charge $18 a year we'd be a prosperous journal of opinion. But we can't do that and keep the marginal subscribers, and it's the marginal subscribers that are of course the ones you want.

TYRRELL: What of your style? Did you establish one specific style? We feel your magazine is written elegantly and with wit. How do you establish a style?

BUCKLEY: I think that people should write in the way that comes naturally to them. Somebody, reviewing a book on Goethe, wrote in *National Review:* "Sometimes upon reading Goethe I have the paralyzing suspicion that he is trying to be funny." And there's nothing worse than people who can't be funny trying to be funny, or people who can't be serious, trying to be serious. So that it isn't simply a matter of whiplashing people into trying to write in a particular style as it is *selecting* people who can write naturally in a real style. The Editors of *National Review* always have their own laws of which one of mine is don't try to write like Murray Kempton unless you can. And *National Review* therefore does attempt to look at politics as something which has a ridiculous dimension. And if you keep your eyes trained to the ridiculous dimension of politics, you can, I think, be instructive in discussing politics. There are a lot of people who don't like me by the way. A lot of people feel that if you see anything amusing in politics, it's like laughing in church. There are x number of readers we don't have because they can't stand what they consider to be our insouciance.

TESICH: Wouldn't you feel that exaggeration has to be one technique, and that by exaggeration you can point to things you can't point to in any other way?

BUCKLEY: Oh, sure, I couldn't agree with you more and incidentally it's definitely in the American tradition—the tall tale. It's part of the American way of saying things.

TYRRELL: Is it true that originally you intended *National Review* to be a journal of conflicting and diverse ideas?

BUCKLEY: Well, within a certain framework, and we do publish different views of lots of thing—McNamara, marijuana and so on, and so forth. But it was always projected as a conservatively oriented periodical.

TYRRELL: What of the future of *National Review*?

BUCKLEY: The only people who could discontinue it are its supporters, but our circulation is higher now that it ever has been.

TYRRELL: What of the *American Mercury*? The *American Mercury* was a leading journal under H.L. Mencken. In the early 'fifties you worked with it. It's become quite a pile of junk since you left it, is this so?

BUCKLEY: Yeah, quite a while ago. I worked with the *American Mercury* for about three months, three very hectic months under William Bradford Huey. He went broke, and sold it to a mad man called, what was his name? He was sort of an obsessed anti-Semite and so on and so forth but he—I quit when Huey sold it. But he agreed to stay on as editor, it being understood that he would have plenary editorial powers which he continued to exercise up until a point where he was fired and somebody else was brought in who also continued to have plenary powers, but then he was fired about 1955. And then it went into straight anti-Semitism and it became completely junky. Now it's owned by some fundamentalist out in Texas.

TYRRELL: Had the character of Mencken lingered at all?

BUCKLEY: It was there sort of as a memory. There had been several intervening editors—Henry Hazlitt, Eugene Lyons, and Lawrence Spivac. So although Mencken was alive when I worked on the *Mercury,* it was after he had had his near-fatal strokes.

TYRRELL: How do you estimate Mencken? Do you think there is a place for his type of thought today?

BUCKLEY: Well, I think that the trouble with Mencken was that he tended to *theologize* skepticism. It became almost a religion with him. Lesser toward the end, but for a while one had the feeling that he debunked for the sake of debunking, but the only things he really cared about were Beethoven and beer.

TYRRELL
AND TESICH: (indignantly) We care quite a lot about those things.

BUCKLEY: Oh, I agree with you! I care about them too! But that's why I think that Mencken—other than his dictionary, the *American Language,* which was a formidable academic and scholarly achievement really ends up not speaking to this generation at all. Other than, that is, as a great, rollicking, wonderful polemicist. I don't think anybody reads Mencken to find out what he said so much as to enjoy how he said it.

TYRRELL: Well, at least Mencken needled people into thinking and reviewing their opinions. Here I see an analogy with *National Review.* Do you feel Mencken's old *Mercury* has a similarity with *National Review*? Don't you try to get people to reflect by needling them?

BUCKLEY: Well, yes. Yes, sure. However, it seems to me that there is this stylistic difference—at least between what *National Review* hopes it is and what we understood Mencken to be. Mainly that we know about the quality of reverence and feel it strongly and feel that the holy things should be treated venerably, whereas, of course there was practically no area at all that was immune to the raillery of Mencken—specifically religion, which should be an excellent example.

But skepticism as an epistemological instrument is something that of course was preached by Socrates. But Socrates himself was highly venerable toward the venerable things, and that I think is an important distinction.

TYRRELL: Are you still having difficulty getting people to debate you on *Firing Line*?

BUCKLEY: No. We don't have trouble getting people on *Firing Line;* we have trouble getting some people on *Firing Line*—Wayne Morse, the Kennedys, Fulbright. Those are the only ones I can think of who have said "no." Oh, whatchamacallit said "no"— Kenneth Tynan, but most others have said "yes."

TYRRELL: What is your estimate of Kennedy?

BUCKLEY: Complicated. I don't think he's qualified to be President, not only because of what he thinks, but because of himself. I think that Kennedy is *terribly* gullible. This is a curious criticism which is not often made of him. I think he is *terribly* gullible. He is the kind of person who, although he can be very hardboiled in dealing with, let's say Mayor Daley, can be swept off his feet by Sukarno. That, I think, is undesirable.

TYRRELL: The increasing liberalism of the Church disturbs the editors of *The Alternative*—especially George Nathan who resides in Gethsemani, Kentucky. We are apprehensive of the flabby lack of restraint on the part of young clergy and the growing influence of situational morality. Do these things concern you?

BUCKLEY: What I worry about and what I assume you worry about is the spirit of accomodation. I think that the Church is most attractive and most alluring when it resists the times. As to the plight of youthful clergy, the blame is not with the young clergy, it is with the older clergy—their teachers.

TYRRELL: America supposedly trembles with the seismographic rumblings of all sorts of crises. *The Alternative* ignores most of these crises, much as we ignore Modern Republicanism. America just could not have that many crises. Aside from Bobby Kennedy's procreant powers, what is the greatest crisis in America?

BUCKLEY: *Self-doubt,* and it is a world problem. It is the feeling that there is nothing worth defending.

A Conversation
With Irving Kristol

(1969)

R. EMMETT TYRRELL, JR.

Irving Kristol, co-editor of **The Public Interest** *with Daniel Patrick Moynihan, is one of those stalwart Liberals who answers the call to truth even when it entails disturbing the fustian of the Realm. Recently he has, through his persuasive prose, impaled more than a few of the Republic's leading quacks. In* **Foreign Affairs** *he transfixed a whole genre of charlatans by defining the intellectual as "a man who speaks with general authority about a subject on which he has no particular competence." Combining effrontery with obscenity he maculated the pages of* **The New Republic** *with a thoughtful essay endorsing Hubert Humphrey's candidacy and but a few months later uttered the unmentionable: to wit, the country is moving to the right and the universities are a blight on education in America. The stars had fallen from the heavens, even Irving Howe expressed concern. Had Irving Kristol thrown in with the Albigensians?*

We doubt it. Mr. Kristol still seeks the dilation of opportunity and a more bearable life for all. He is still a Liberal. But he is also a man possessing the intelligence and audacity to look for answers beyond the encumbrances of stylish ideology. It is not he but "the intellectuals" who have changed, making anti-intellectualism the sought after epithet of thinking men.

The Alternative *greatly admires Mr. Kristol. We assume his life has its unpleasant moments such as when, in his kindness, he grants interviews to people like our editor, Mr. Tyrrell. But things could always be worse, we could have sent Nathan.*

TYRRELL: Before the 1968 election, you said you saw the future of American politics as being "considerably less liberal than in past decades." Do you still have this view and is Nixon the fulfillment of your vision? Or will things go farther to the right?

KRISTOL: Yes, I still have that view, though I wasn't thinking specifically of Nixon or of this administration when I made that prediction. I was looking much further ahead. Basically, what I was trying to say was that any kind of militance—especially extralegal activity—on the part of the left in this country will certainly give rise to a corresponding reaction on the part of the public at large and the governmental authorities. In short I think it likely that even liberal administrations of the future are likely to be far less liberal than they have been in the past.

TYRRELL: Do you think a Wallace type has a chance of getting elected in 1972?

KRISTOL: No, certainly not in 1972. I see no prospect of that whatsoever.

TYRRELL: You have remarked on the emergence of an "unreasonable revolution of Utopian expectations on the part of a significant minority." Has that minority yet emerged and who constitutes it? How will it exist in the future?

KRISTOL: I was thinking, of course, primarily of students and some faculty on the campuses. These are people, who not only have had no political experience—one really couldn't expect them to have had political experience—but who have a singular unwillingness and uninterest in learning from past political experience and therefore have no sense of the limits of politics. They have no sense of the time that is needed to make constructive social change. They have no sense of the way in which human purposes go awry. These people demand instant improvement and of course you never do get instant improvement in real life. What was your other question?

TYRRELL: Who are they exactly? SDS? (Students for Democratic Society)

KRISTOL: Well, not only SDS, although of course SDS is one of the groups. But I think you have a much larger group, of students and faculty both, who have an insistence that this country change in a radical way very, very quickly. Unfortunately they seem to have no method for changing the people who live in this country overnight in a very radical and quick way, and therefore I regard their plans as Utopian.

TYRRELL: Do you think it has to change radically?

KRISTOL: I don't know whether it has to or not; I don't think anyone really knows. Much of their dissatisfaction is mysterious to me. Some of their dissatisfaction I understand. This is not the most beautiful of all societies and this is not even the most civilized of all societies. On the other hand, it is what it is as a result of several hundred years of history. The people who live in it are what they are as a result of these hundreds of years of history. The notion that you can change things overnight strikes me as utterly fantastic.

TYRRELL: How are they going to exist in the future? Are Wallace types going to repress them?

KRISTOL: Oh, I'm not really worried about the Wallace type. I mean I don't see any specter of Neo-fascism on the American horizon. What I do see, however, is that if they insist on being militant and resorting to extralegal activities, they will probably be put down, not by Wallace, but even by a liberal administration.

TYRRELL: You have stated that the church and the family have neglected transmitting moral authority and traditions. How has America, as you said, "progressively diminished the moral authority of all existing institutions?" Through the inclination of relativism?

KRISTOL: Well, that's one part of it, yes. Let's put it in its simplest terms. We did it because that's what we set out to do. The modern spirit of critical inquiry as it developed, not only within the universities, but within the world of letters and within the world of journalism over the past eighty years, had as its purpose precisely that: the diminishing of the authority of existing institutions, and most especially of the family and of the schools and of the churches. If you go back to Jane Addams, who was a very sweet woman, and read her works you will find that she very expressedly declared that one of her purposes was to diminish the authority of the family and replace it by the authority of the social work profession and the state and so on. So that I don't think this was entirely an accident—though, I do think a great many people didn't realize what was happening. But there was a theory behind this, and the theory was that if you diminish these traditional authorities, a latent and hitherto repressed creativity and goodness and sweetness would flow from human beings. These people were Utopian (not particularly radical people, like John Dewey, Jane Addams, the entire progressive movement in academic studies the "new realism" in law, the "new history") and of course they contributed to the prevalence of relativism as a philosophy. They really did feel that these authorities could be dispensed with, that if you got rid of them, human beings would live much fuller and happier and more contented lives without the benefits of external authority, that a sense of free community could flow from their innermost souls. It was a very attractive vision which is one of the reasons it had so much success. So that it's a historical process (partly of course it's a sociological process, I've not mentioned that; the fact that certain economic developments have made the family, as an economic unit, weaker than it once was). But basically I really do think this was a program of, one might almost say, the modern world, since very few people opposed it. It was the program of modern liberalism and even of much of modern conservatism. And no one expected it to have such cataclysmic consequences.

TYRRELL: Has it had unfortunate consequences?

KRISTOL: Obviously, yes. You know, John Dewey was against censorship and for freedom, but John Dewey, were he alive today, would be absolutely horrified at the things that are being done in the name of free creativity. This is not what he had in mind.

TYRRELL: In a recent *New York Times* article you said the church and family left it to schools to transmit values. Now the schools are neglecting this. Why is this undesirable? Aren't our traditional values rather corrupt? Isn't western civilization about to fall apart from exhaustion?

KRISTOL: Oh, I don't know what that means. Civilizations have a way of not falling apart all that easily. Are our values corrupt? In a way they are. I don't know that they're more corrupt than the values of other civilizations, though I might even concede that in some senses they are. On the other hand, these are the values that regulate the way we live together. And even if they may be false in certain important respects, they simply can't be shoved aside; people cannot live in a vacuum. False values are better than none. And until these values are amended and improved, we'll have to cope with them as best we can.

TYRRELL: Do you agree with Frank Meyer when he says western civilization is superior to all other civilizations because it stresses the primacy of the individual? No other civilization places so much importance on the individual.

KRISTOL: Yes, I would agree with that. On the other hand, it has paid a price for this. And everyone is now becoming aware of the price, that western individualism does create tremendous strains upon the individual, and does produce tremendous strains within the community, and is corrosive of many of the things that even Frank Meyer would cherish. It is very hard to be for tradition, for instance, and at the same time to celebrate the unqualified virtues of individualism. On the whole I'm in sympathy with—I mean, as I say, being a product of western civilization—I'm irrevocably more individualist than, for instance, any Buddhist is likely to be. On the other hand, this civilization has created problems for itself.

TYRRELL: You once drew a distinction between the hippie and the new left. Do you still make that distinction or do you see a convergence in certain situations?

KRISTOL: I honestly don't know. I mean they're obviously converging in some respects. The appearance of—I think they call themselves the Yippies—would seem to indicate that some people feel an amalgamation or a merger is possible. And in the abstract, there is no reason why it shouldn't take place. I think there is one obstacle to a full-scale merger, which is that the new left, if it ever is really going to do anything politically, has to create a disciplined organization out of people who are "high" half the time, who don't come to meetings on time, who are not responsible for the execution of small assignments and so on.

TYRRELL: You mentioned, in the New York *Times,* that you felt the hippie was interested in moral ends. Can you explain that?

KRISTOL: Well, let me say this in favor of the hippies and even of the new left. They have done what our academic political thinkers have singularly failed to do over the past eighty or ninety years. That is, they have challenged the values and the ends of bourgeois society. Not just pointing to its imperfections, but saying "Is this the kind of society we want to have?" And "Is this the kind of life we want to live?" Now these are the traditional problems of political philosophy. But they have not been discussed by political philosophers in any serious way within this century. Political philosophy has taken a completely different turn.

TYRRELL: Well, I'm reading a book by Richard Weaver right now. He certainly seems to be interested in the quality of life one leads.

KRISTOL: Yes, but Richard Weaver is a sport. He's an exception. Hardly anyone in philosophy courses at a university reads Richard Weaver, except in a few places. He's not regarded as an important American philosopher.

TYRRELL: Why?

KRISTOL: Well, because his whole approach to philosophy deals with problems that modern philosophy has abandoned. Modern philosophy is overwhelmingly analytical. It does not feel that it has any authority even to discuss the ends of man, the ends of society. It feels it has nothing to say about that. All it can do is criticize the way in which other people discuss the ends of society. Similarly political theory and political philosophy say they have no competence to discuss the ends of political society. All they can do is discuss the mechanisms whereby people reach whatever ends they assign to themselves. I therefore think it is true that a good deal of modern academic thinking, especially in the humanities and those social sciences which are closest to the humanities, I do think that these disciplines are not "relevant," as the younger people say. These disciplines do not respond to the basic questions which any sensitive and intelligent young person wants to see discussed—not only wants to see discussed, but wants to discuss and explore for himself. And so I have a certain sympathy with the hippies and the new left because I do think that for the first time in many decades they are posing before this society some philosophical questions—real fundamental questions, which the academics have been avoiding very diligently now for quite a few decades.

TYRRELL: Well, this anticipates a later question of mine. It seems to me that the young right has been asking these questions also, though they are not so darlingized for their utterances. Is there a convergence here of the left and the right, the young left and the young right?

KRISTOL: I think there's a convergence of youth, yes. The young people of this country today are bored with a lot of the sterile academicism. Now mind you, I must be careful about this. So often when young people denounce their studies as "irrelevant," very often that is simply an exercise in anti-intellectualism—that is, they don't want to read Plato because he is very hard, and he lived a long time ago, and the meaning of what he said is not instantly obvious. And I certainly don't want to pander to any such sentiments. On the other hand, there's also no doubt that students, especially in the humanities, and especially in the so-called softer social sciences—areas which traditionally used to deal with the basic issues of human existence, human society and human life—find that these disciplines have abandoned that field. And the result is that the field has been invaded by all sorts of quackeries, all sorts of amateur philosophies. I think that, in this respect, young people both of left and of right have a very legitimate complaint.

TYRRELL: You don't feel affluence plays that great a role?

KRISTOL: I think affluence does play a role, but in certain special ways. I don't think what you call affluence has corrupted the soul of the average American because the average American just isn't that affluent. After all, when a man's annual income moves from $6000 to $8000, this does not permit him to live like a lord or a king. And the difference is not of an order that is likely to greatly affect his moral values. When we talk in the mass, these are the kinds of changes we are talking about; that is, the movement towards affluence among the mass of Americans has been relatively small as far as its affects on daily living is concerned. Instead of living in an apartment you live in a house. But the house, after all, is not a lavish thing—I mean, most Americans live in quite modest houses. And, as I say, moving from $6000 a year to $8000 a year or from $7000 a year to $10,000 a year (which is almost a 50% increase) does not transform a person's values. But where affluence has played a role, a very important role, is among young people. It is the young people in our society today who are far, far more affluent than young people ever were. And affluent not only in the sense that they have more pocket money, but that they have control over resources. For instance, the whole transformation of the mass media that we have been witnessing in the past ten years or fifteen years is to a very large extent a response to the affluence of young people. These people are consumers. The record industry sells its products to young people; television orients itself more and more to young spenders. The affluence of young people has, I think, had a tremendous effect upon our entire culture, much more so than the affluence of the average American, or even of the rich American.

TYRRELL: George Nathan says it is unhealthy for a state to suffer liberalism's domination of education, communication and national policy. The proper role of the liberal is to snipe at the society from the periphery as he does.

KRISTOL: I don't agree with that. But then, you see Nathan like Mencken—

TYRRELL: No, this is a different Nathan.

KRISTOL: Oh, this is not George Jean Nathan? Which Nathan is this?

TYRRELL: This is one who writes for *The Alternative.*

KRISTOL: I've never heard of him. I'm sorry, should I have?

TYRRELL: No, no, no.

KRISTOL: Oh, I'm sorry. I thought you meant George Jean Nathan. God. No, well, we'll wipe that out. This traditional notion of what a liberal should do strikes me as wrong. Indeed it is the traditional notion of what a liberal has done and most liberals unfortunately have done that. I don't think it's very helpful for society to have its best brains deciding beforehand that all they're going to do is sit on the sidelines and throw rocks. I really see no justification for such a proposal. If a single individual, for personal reasons, feels that he must sit on the sidelines and throw rocks, all right. But to urge this and prescribe this for a large body of people strikes me as absurd. I feel, for instance, that that kind of liberalism itself has been a corrupter of modern values.

TYRRELL: Are you disturbed by the growth of the new left, and if so what aspect of it?

KRISTOL: Yes, of course I'm disturbed by the growth of the new left. Mainly I'm disturbed by two things. First, its rather mindless commitment to confrontation and violence. I think this is going to be self-defeating for them and is going to create a great deal of damage to all of us. I'm also alarmed at what I can only call the intellectual infantilism of the new left. Obviously, it is not surprising that some young people should be radical. And I personally have no objections to a young man wanting to become a radical if he feels the need for radical change. But I don't think anyone, young or old, has the right to be mindless. I think they must analyze the causes of the condition they seek to cure and the consequences of the cures they recommend. And what alarms me about the new left is that it is the politics of expressionism. Everyone is far more interested in the kind of posture he strikes than in a program that would have some effect upon society.

TYRRELL: Is the new left really that new? Where did it come from?

KRISTOL: Well, what is new about the new left is its identification of a political mythology with a generational mythology. The major difference between the new left and the old left is that the new left is a left of young people. The old left had young people in it, but it was an adult movement—led by adults, defined by adults, organized by adults, with a program written by adults. What really is new about the new left is not any particular ideology—the fact is that it is somewhat more anarchist and less bolshevik, that doesn't matter, we've had anarchist movements in the past. What is distinctive about the new left is that it is a generational movement as well as a political movement.

TYRRELL: But it's led by older people like Marcuse. Marcuse almost programs it, it seems, and Paul Goodman and Mailer . . .

KRISTOL: It has its gurus, obviously, older gurus—any movement will. But I think it is true that the generational quality of this movement is just as important as its political beliefs.

TYRRELL: Is it more sophisticated than the old left?

KRISTOL: No, I think it's less sophisticated than the old left, precisely because it is a movement of young people.

TYRRELL: Is it more open, as Howard Zinn says?

KRISTOL: Yes and no. It's more open in the sense that it has no fixed, carefully thought through ideology. It's less open in that it doesn't think seriously about ideological issues at all.

Defending Liberalism

(1974)

HARVEY C. MANSFIELD, JR.

Lyndon Johnson's death on the day before the peace settlement in Vietnam was announced gave Richard Nixon the opportunity, while making the announcement, of vindicating Johnson against his critics. It was a chance befitting the course of events, for Nixon's policy has rescued Johnson's, and with it Johnson's supporters, the liberal Democrats whom he inherited. Now they need not abase themselves before radical critics of the war or before liberal defectors who claimed to be "right from the first." Those who had the wisdom or dignity to go "all the way with LBJ"—in many cases further than LBJ himself went—can now return to being liberals as distinguished from radicals or radical-liberals. But they must do so with the appalling recognition that Richard Nixon made it possible. This obligation is not cancelled by Watergate; it is only made more painful.

Why do liberals have so much trouble defending themselves? Liberalism as an "ism" implies a body of doctrine, a more or less consistent whole more or less closed to doctrines inconsistent with itself. But it is evident that liberalism, if it is a whole, is a whole that is afraid to be a whole—and therefore has difficulty in rousing partisans to its defense. To defend oneself it is necessary to recognize the enemy, and thus to have defined oneself against the enemy. Liberals, however, are tolerant, and to show their tolerance they favor a large and various society in which all groups, even enemies, are encouraged to take an interest. Liberal society is a society of interest groups, with the consequence that there is no interest group for liberalism. Even the American Civil Liberties Union, which might seem to be such a group, defends not liberals but the enemies of liberalism, in the spirit (though not the letter) of the maxim attributed to Voltaire that "I disapprove of what you say, but will defend to the death your right to say it." To a degree, this lack of spirit on the part of liberals is merely silly complacency, but to a greater degree, it reveals the nature of liberalism as originally propounded.

Let us turn from the "liberalism" of today's partisan rhetoric, which is opposed to "conservatism," and "radicalism" to the liberalism of America's founders which comprises all three positions or parts of them. The best explanation of that liberalism is to be found in the papers of *The Federalist,* and in No.

10 (written by James Madison) we find clear and authoritative thoughts on liberal society as a whole and partisanship within it. *The* problem of a free society, according to *Federalist* No. 10, is the control of faction, for in the free society produced by a popular government, the question immediately arises of what to do about those citizens who abuse freedom to the detriment of others or of society as a whole. When combined, such citizens are defined by the author as a faction, which is a number of citizens, whether a minority or a majority, actuated by passion or interest against the rights of others or "the permanent and aggregate interests of the community." Two methods of cure are proposed for factions: removing the causes and controlling the effects. Of the first cure, there are again two methods: abolishing liberty, which is immediately dismissed as a remedy worse than the disease, and "giving to every citizen the same opinions, the same passions, and the same interests." This method of curing factions is also rejected, but with reasoning that reveals the fundamental difficulty liberalism has in defending itself.

Madison argues simply and cogently: "As long as the reason of man continues fallible, and he is at liberty to exercise it, different opinions will be formed. As long as the connection subsists between his reason and his self-love, his opinions and his passions will have a reciprocal influence on each other; and the former will be objects to which the latter will attach themselves." To this he adds "the diversity in the faculties of men, from which the rights of property originate" as an insuperable obstacle to uniform interests. Protection of these faculties is the first object of government, and since diverse faculties produce different degrees and kinds of property—and property influences opinions—society will be divided into different interests and parties. "The latent causes of faction are thus sown in the nature of man," Madison concludes. These causes, to repeat, are self-love and diverse faculties, and they come together in property. Although men zealously dispute over different opinions on religion or government, or attach themselves to ambitious or exciting men, "the most common and durable source of factions" has been property in its different degrees and kinds.

Because of human nature, then, society has no sameness of opinion, passion, or interest; and *liberal* society is managed by a government whose principles and practices recognize and respect the character and strength of human nature. "Modern legislation"—for the necessity of bowing to human nature so understood has only recently been discovered—"involves the spirit of party and faction in the necessary and ordinary operations of government." *Federalist* No. 10 goes on to show how government can control the effects of faction, especially majority faction. Majority faction is more difficult to control in a popular government than minority faction, because majority faction looks like the republican principle of majority rule, whereas minority faction must work against the genius of republican government. Majority faction may be controlled by delegating government to representatives and by extending the sphere of society to "take in a greater variety of parties and interests."

A majority faction, Madison says, must be obstructed by *preventing* the existence of the same passion or interest in the majority, which is the purpose of delegating government to "fit characters" meeting apart from the majority;

and majority faction can be *prevented* from concerting together in the extended sphere of a large republic taking in a variety of parties and interests. Thus we see that the sameness which was said to be impossible to produce without destroying liberty must indeed be prevented from coming into existence and operation, in order to secure liberty. In a large republic it is less probable that a majority will have "a common motive to invade the rights of other citizens," but this is because citizens are less likely to have a common motive at all. Or, they have a similar motive, each working at the interest, especially the property interest, which will best prevent the creation of a *common* motive. Apparently, the latent cure for faction, as well as the latent causes, is sown in the nature of man.

From this argument it becomes evident that liberalism has a reasonable fear of being or becoming a whole. Liberal society not only thrives on variety, but requires it for survival; and its sameness is distributive rather than collective. As we saw, Madison defined the whole endangered by faction as "the permanent and aggregate interests of the community." Yet it remains true that liberalism must defend itself as a whole, and hence collectively. Self-interest or group interests, being divided from each other, cannot supply either the motive or the instrument of self-defense, since self-defense is not effectual except when all defend themselves together and spiritedly. Adding interests to make an "aggregate" is successful when the purpose is to add to one's interests, but when under attack, one may leave the aggregate rather than defend it. Now it is to liberals so circumstanced, divided in interest and united only in tolerance, feeling guilty when defending themselves against nonliberals and feeling uneasy when they do not, that radicalism makes its appeal. Radicalism offers a view of liberal society as a whole which may be grasped and then defended as the true liberalism against the confused so-called liberals. Radicalism will supply both the whole and the partisanship that liberalism needs.

Radicalism supplies an understanding of the whole to liberalism by its analysis of liberal society as a whole, epitomized in the phrase of Herbert Marcuse, "repressive tolerance." Among liberals, the phrase has currency as the name of a conservative policy mistakenly followed by some liberals today, for which a policy of greater permissiveness could readily be substituted. But that is not what Marcuse meant, and that is not what radicalism asks or requires of liberals. "Repressive tolerance" exposes to liberals the unheard-of fact that in a liberal society liberals somehow come out on top. they do not rule the society but they administer it, using permissive tolerance as the means of dissipating nonliberal opposition. For nonliberals are first allowed the opportunity of purging their partisan humors and then offered the temptation of developing an interest in public talk and private gain. This administered tolerance lacks the ceremony of a formal embrace and the warmth of an informal hug, but to call it "repressive" would seem to be an act of aggression following from downright revulsion. But such is not the case; there is admiration in the phrase. Tolerance need not be rejected because it can be made militant—that is, subversive and liberating. Liberal tolerance once had organized religion for its enemy, and liberal philosophers like Milton and Locke made it clear that liberal tolerance was not for the intolerant, not for the clerics who would not tolerate liberalism.

Thus "repressive tolerance," despite its cloying hospitality and its bland disclaimers today, had a partisan bite when first brought forth. *Ecraser l'infame!* said the same Voltaire who is quoted otherwise by the ACLU. Radicalism has attempted to recover this original aggressiveness for itself and for the purpose or with the effect of attracting liberals, not with blandishments but with a shocking reminder to make them believe that contemporary radicals are the original liberals revived. Liberals can feel their own community and learn to assert it in self-defense by recalling that liberalism was a revolutionary doctrine, and by turning from the system of liberty now established to liberalism in its phase of liberation. Despite their accusations against liberals, radicals present themselves as friendly to liberals, or rather the more consistent (because original) liberals. They do this, to be sure, not by direct appeal to liberal philosophers and statesmen, but with the apparently liberal doctrine of the liberated self. Inspired with this doctrine, the liberal can know himself and defend himself against the enemies of the radicals. But are these *his* enemies? The answer depends on whether "the liberated self" is indeed a liberal or a wholesome doctrine.

To profess the "liberated self," radicals do not make a frontal attack on liberal politics, or on the American Constitution. They do advocate "power to the people," claiming that under liberalism the people suffer from a sense of powerlessness. But this complaint sounds very different from Madison's political concern for factions adverse to the rights of others and to the interests of the community. Evidently, it represents or constitutes the expression of the un-liberated self in the act of liberating itself. For according to radicalism, tolerance is possible altogether without limitations on the activities of the self. "Repressive tolerance" having the purpose or effect of keeping liberal society liberal is no longer necessary, and the liberal pretension of allowing men to live as they like can now be realized.

The reason why tolerance can now be unlimited and become liberating is that the "struggle for existence" no longer need continue. It is this struggle, according to radicalism, which turns men against each other and forces men to calculate means of overcoming other men and to conspire in secret against them. Since society—liberal capitalist society, it will be admitted—now produces an abundance sufficient to make "the struggle for existence" seem a dramatic phrase for a forgotten condition, the necessity of struggle has been eliminated, and the excuse for repression has been made obsolete. The competitive struggle still carried on in this fat society has lost any connection to need, and men go through the paces of enterprise and employment pretending that their lives depend on success, while knowing that they do not. Only unnecessary repression maintains these silly and harmful habits based on self-delusion and self-repression. It is now possible for reason to cease its calculating, conspiratorial promotion of self-interest and come out into the open. Society can be ruled by reason, as was the hope of liberal tolerance; but contrary to the fears of liberals, reason can rule society without politics. Not only does reason not rule in the guise of a ruling opinion supposedly unreasonable; this would be, or run the risk of becoming, the majority faction that Madison sought to avoid. But also, the indirect administration of various interests by involving "the spirit of party and faction in the necessary and ordinary operations of government" can be foregone. The activities of the self can become "expression," an outward release of energy over the fallen constraints of embarrassment, respect, and awe. Liberal tolerance itself is raised to the radical extremes of excitation, provocation, and shock. Precisely because we can be confident that reason can rule society without government, we need no longer stop or even hesitate at the supposed boundaries of unreason. Precisely because no justification exists for self-defense against rivals and enemies, we can loose our anger at the restraints, justifiably called "repression," which remain. Free society is overdue, and we can begin to live it now. We can be liberated from the administered system of liberty by acting as if we were already liberated. A difference does exist between hard and soft radicals as to the necessity of a transition, the former asserting that the experience of alienation builds militancy, and the latter wondering why not now? But the possibility of "now" unites them with the belief that, in principle at least, the future can be seized and lived in the present. On the way to being liberated *is* liberation.

As compared to *Federalist* No. 10, then, radicalism sees no problem in the connection between reason and self-love. Its premise is that selfishness is caused by the struggle for existence. This struggle forces men apart by making them aware of their separate bodies and responsive to separate and competing needs. But when each belly is satisfied, the self is apparently liberated from concern with its own separate body and becomes capable of acting as if it shared a common body with other members of the class, the society, or mankind. Individual pleasures remain, including the pleasures of separate bodies interacting, but they are a matter of choice among delights because no individual pleasure subtracts from another, either for oneself or for others. Chance made us with separate bodies only so that we could have fun rubbing them against each other.

Liberalism is not against fun, but it does not hold this opinion. Clearly the danger of faction refers to the struggle for superfluities. Different property interests arise from diverse faculties as applied to self-love, not from a scramble to supply one's needs. "Self-love" seems to be a name for ambition understood generally as one's competitive sense or spirit of self-defense. It is associated with an appetite but it cannot be satisfied with any goods but those which are by their nature scarce, such as honors. Even if each body were satisfied in its separate appetites, it is implied, a man with self-love would be angry if his separateness were not recognized with appropriate distinctions of respect and prestige. The psychology of *The Federalist* is of course much less visible than its politics—the reverse of radicalism—but it seems to propose that the angry passions of self-love be contained with the principle of self-interest. Self-interest allows for the differences demanded by men's self-love, and so does not presume that the satisfied self is ready to amalgamate with others in a common body; but at the same time it turns ambition to the bourgeois desire for property, away from the pseudoaristocratic love of victory and command.

To encourage the desire for property allows something to ambition, but different degrees and kinds of property translate success into terms in which one man's victory is not so clearly another man's defeat as in politics. Self-interest is thus more open to persuasion on behalf of "the permanent and aggregate interests of the community" than is political ambition, because unlike ambition, self-interest can be calculated as if men shared a common body (as we have seen): what is good for me can be good for you. In the persuasion of interests, reason is the instrument and free speech its guaranteed right. This is not to say that liberalism supports free speech for the sole purpose of uniting men in societies by persuading them to their self-interest; it also has the nobler purpose of uniting mankind by inspiring the advance of science. So reason promotes the interest of society and that of mankind in the separate vocations of politicians on the one hand, and scientists and intellectuals on the other. Yet these kinds of vocations are connected by their interest in a whole, and the American founders followed both.

In the liberal system, self-love is calculated as self-interest, and reason stands for the interest of the whole. The business of liberal politicians is to connect them. To do this they must be acquainted with both the low and the high in human nature and must have a sense of how the one can be raised and the other lowered to make (so far as possible) a community of free men. This means that in making the connection between self-love and reason they must never forget the difference. For self-love is as adamant in its defensiveness as reason is unbending and high-minded. Under liberal constitutionalism, therefore, political institutions have the double function of stating differences and bringing about agreement. When those institutions work well, they bring about agreement by consent and through persuasion; but they begin with the need to gain consent from men who have the right to withhold it. The resulting agreement is typically by majority vote rather than unanimous, and by a coalition that mixes interest and principle rather than by either interest or principle alone. Agreement so attained gives liberal society its own sense of being a whole while recognizing, tolerating, or even purging its partisan humors. Such an agreement holds better than a mere aggregate of interests because it is tested by opposition while it is made, and men stick to positions they have defined in partisan dispute. Liberal politics solves the problem of reason and self-love, when it does, by solving it again and again, not once and for all. Liberal institutions are an aid to this continuing solution, no doubt an indispensable aid, but they do not guarantee a solution merely by being instituted. On the contrary, they work by recreating and then resolving the problem for whose solution they were originally instituted. If liberal institutions could guarantee a solution, men would be such that liberal institutions would not be needed.

This remark returns us to contemporary radicalism because we are reminded of its indifference to liberal political institutions and of its hostility to the difficult process of gaining consent. What is the difference between liberal self-interest and radical self-expression? We see immediately that the notion of self-expression combines free speech and self-interest not by connecting them but by equating them: self-expression is the free expression of one's self-interest. But to make free speech and self-interest identical, it is necessary to change them. Since the liberated self does not respect the necessary separateness of human beings in their separate bodies, its self-interest is appetite only, with no recognition of human defensiveness and anger. The consequence is not the redirection of ambition to property and the taming of anger by appetite, as with liberalism, but the redirection of anger. Radicals take umbrage not at those individuals with whom they may compete, but at the system of competition as a whole. They are angry at anger, and therefore more angry than the angry— because those who compete in the "rat-race" of liberal society cannot win merely by getting angry, but those who believe they care nothing for success have no reason to restrain their anger. Indeed they understand their anger as reason, and therefore free speech not as persuasion but as giving vent to indignation. For radicals self-interest is all appetite in theory, and in practice all anger; free speech is all reason in theory, and in practice all anger. In both cases the practice is the consequence of the theory.

Self-expression is now becoming accepted in the practice of liberal society; partly by the process of administered tolerance that radicals describe, partly by simple inattention from the liberals. Recently the Supreme Court has accepted in some degree the self-expression of burning the flag or a draft card as instances of "free speech," although burning is not speaking and the purpose was not to persuade but to "demonstrate" and to "protest." It is as if the right of free speech were the right to be angry in public. The right of conscience is also used as the right to make a public spectacle by radicals who would have a hard job defining "conscience" as anything more than angry opinion. But the most expressive demonstrativeness has been saved for the matter of sex. Sex is an appetite, but an uncalculated appetite, hence available for use by anger (also uncalculated) as in obscenity, for example. In some demonstrations radicals have used obscenity as a kind of gesture in defiance of liberal society. Still, angry self-expression about sex is most visible today in the so-called movement (not interest group) of women's liberation.

Speaking about women's liberation is not easy because it is natural to take the part of one's own gender. Indeed, to expect this is the beginning of wisdom on the subject, as opposed to that vestigial gentlemanliness which opens doors for angry women and acquiesces in everything they demand. This movement is based on the opinion that no feeling or activity is essentially feminine; those feelings and activities which have been considered feminine up to now have merely been imposed on women. There is a feminine body but not a feminine self, because the self (as we have seen) has the power of overcoming the separateness of bodies, including the sexual distinction. The self, indeed, would best reveal its power when it liberates itself from the weakness of female body—a weakness that must have some basis in fact if all the oppression hitherto has been male rather than female.

Women's liberation is liberation *by* women, but also *from* womanhood. It is an assertion, but of what? It cannot assert the rights of the womanhood from which it is trying to escape, and to claim the rights of manliness would be joining the class of oppressors and admitting that they were right. It must be that manliness is not essentially male, as indicated in the asserted fact that independence in the very crude sense of capacity for sexual satisfaction by oneself is possible for a woman as well as a man. The self-expression of women's liberation is an assertion of manliness liberated from the male body, and to demonstrate one's liberation from both female and male, it would be necessary to engage (not indulge: it would be a duty) in sexual activity, precisely where men and women have been imprisoned most in their sexual roles. At this point of culmination, women's liberation borrows not only from adolescent masculinity but also, surreptitiously and with outward signs of abhorrence, from the movement of sexual liberation, to get unisex and polymorphous perversity.

Still, doubts linger. Who will mind the home? asked Aristotle of a similar proposal (for a different purpose) made by a friend of his. And does not unisex bear a resemblance to masculine sex, after all, in its selfishness as well as in its independence? Men mistreat women when they consider women "sexual objects" in the sense of means to another's pleasure, but men achieve what tenderness and fidelity they are capable of when they consider women as sexual objects in the sense of ends to whose happiness one may be devoted. Thus unisex is not even masculine sex in the better sense. It is the expression of power without object, not appetite at all, but a generalized anger in defense of an impossible, imhuman common body.

Old-fashioned feminism promoted the feminine, instead of denying it. Liberalism gave a courtly welcome to feminism, and with reason, because feminism was based on the sexual distinction and recognized the separateness of human beings. With less reason, liberals now give nervous hospitality to the varieties of radical self-expression. To be sure, liberal hospitality in the system of administered tolerance tends to transform expression into speech and interest. Obscenity takes the verbal form of pornography so that it can have "redeeming social value," and women's liberation is placated with quotas. But the system of administered tolerance does not work by itself in any context of opinions or with any cast of characters. Contrary to the radical analysis, liberal society requires successful politics in which competent politicians act imaginatively and speak skillfully to produce a ruling majority. Liberals today are not likely to take this requirement for granted, for they sense quite correctly that their leaders have been outgeneraled by Richard Nixon.

To support able politicians, certain fundamental opinions hostile to the radical doctrine of self-expression are also required. As we have seen, politics is recognized as important only if the connection between reason and self-love is understood as a problem for men. With this understanding, which does not have to be sophisticated in most, a liberal citizen will found his opinions on the separateness of human beings, and accept that there are others outside himself who have rights and to whom he has duties. He will regard the making of a whole community not as a matter of course, but as requiring care in construction and preservation. If he is reflective, he—or she—will wonder why the separateness of human beings is unchangeable and what this implies about the power of human beings.

The radical doctrine of self-expression, implying the facile, though destructive, creation of a common body of human beings, stands in plain opposition to these opinions. That doctrine is drawn from Marx and Nietzsche, Marx supplying its wish to make man whole again and Nietzsche furnishing the partisan bite of willful mastery. I have not attempted to examine the doctrine here, but only to show some of its consequences and its hostility to liberalism. On the way we have seen that liberalism does after all have an understanding of itself as a whole in the work of liberal politics. As for partisan spirit, one may suggest a moderate, retrospective anger at the angry, as it is rather late for a liberal backlash against their radical enemies.

Operation Death-Wish

(1977)

MALCOLM MUGGERIDGE

At the beginning of the seventies I wrote an article entitled "The Decade of the Great Liberal Death-Wish." It appeared in *Esquire* magazine, then edited by Harold Hayes, and attracted a certain amount of attention, being reprinted in various periodicals, including, surprisingly, the Soviet magazine, *Literaturnaya Gazeta,* along with an explanatory, and by no means wholly critical, commentary. The theme is one that has haunted me ever since, as a young journalist in Moscow in the early thirties, I observed the truly extraordinary antics there of visiting intelligentsia from Western Europe and the United States. Almost all of them displayed a credulity about the regime, and about what they heard from its professional apologists, that would have shaken an African witch doctor. Notable examples were Bernard Shaw, the Webbs, André Gide, Lincoln Steffens, Julian Huxley, Henri Barbusse, and Harold Laski. The performance of visiting clergymen was particularly striking; there was nothing, it seemed, they liked better than being shown round the anti-God museums, and, though mostly ardent pacifists at home, they heard with delight the roar of Soviet war planes overhead and the rattle of Soviet tanks across the Red Square. I had been brought up to regard these western intelligentsia as the chosen elite, the Samurai of our time, and there they were adulating to an extravagant degree the most ruthless and comprehensive dictatorship the world has yet seen. What was I to make of it? If the Pope had suddenly issued an encyclical in favor of wife-swapping, or Dr. Spock had come out strongly for birching in schools, I could not have been more surprised and shocked.

I brooded long on this strange phenomenon, constantly expecting that some new instance of Soviet perfidy and resort to terrorism would produce a change of heart in the regime's liberal admirers. For instance, the Purges, when all the old Bolsheviks, the men who had made the Revolution, the USSR's founding fathers, were first humiliated publicly and then executed, on Stalin's orders. Again, the Nazi-Soviet Pact, the betrayal over the occupation of Eastern and Central Europe after the 1939–45 war, the suppression of the Hungarian, East German, and Polish risings, and the invasion of Czechoslovakia by the Red Army, not to mention Khrushchev's denunciation of Stalin at the twentieth Party Congress, and the subsequent posthumous dethronement of the most adulated and wiliest of all the Soviet leaders. In each case, after some momen-

406

tary disconcertment and protest, the old spirit of acquiescence and adulation resumed its sway; as the late A.T. Cholerton, the most brilliant and perceptive British correspondent ever to be stationed in the USSR, put it, the vomit returned to the dog. Finally, I was forced to conclude that this attitude of western liberals to the Soviet regime was not so much a delusion as an addiction, signifying in them a death-wish, a built-in passion to destroy everything and everyone they purported to hold dear, with a view to ultimately abolishing themselves.

The same point is made with superb artistry and insight by Dostoevsky in his novel *The Devils* (in its first English translation, by Constance Garnett, called *The Possessed;* itself a sort of liberal gloss, demonic possession being commonly regarded as less pernicious than actual diabolism), which portrays a group of quasi-revolutionaries and the havoc they make with no other purpose than to create disorder and stir up violence. Their leader, Peter Verkhovensky, gives them the order-of-the-day: "A generation or two of debauchery, followed by a little drop of nice fresh blood, and then the turmoil will begin." It is only necessary to look round the world today to realize how thoroughly this program has been carried out, and how infallibly the predicted turmoil has come about and is continuing. Dostoevsky, too, brilliantly shows how the nihilism of Peter Verkhovensky derives directly from the sentimental liberalism of his father, Stepan Trofimovich Verkhovensky—a superbly drawn farcical character; as it might be, a male impersonation of Mrs. Eleanor Roosevelt. It would seem to be the case that liberal genes automatically breed revolutionary ideologues and activists. After all, Donald Maclean, who operated as a Soviet spy in the British Foreign Office, and then defected to the USSR, is the son of an eminent liberal politician; while Labour Party firebrands like Michael Foot and Tony Benn were sired and reared in sentimental liberalism, and the *Guardian,* an emanation of the liberal mind if ever there was one, has long been a favorite shop-window for Marxist and other revolutionary bric-a-brac.

In my *Esquire* article I attempted to trace something of the part the great liberal death-wish is playing in the decline and impending fall of what we continue to call western civilization. As the decade of the seventies draws to a close, the forces of demolition can be seen to be advancing at an accelerating rate on all fronts; in view of their liberal orientation, ostensibly representing progress rather than regress, compassion rather than brutal necessity, liberation rather than oppression, freedom rather than servitude. Thus, a process of what amounts to creeping revolution is seen as a mighty leap forward in the quest for a kingdom of heaven on earth, and Christendom's setting sun is taken to be a new dawn breaking. I venture to quote the concluding words of my article:

As the astronauts soar into the vast eternities of space, on earth the garbage piles higher; as the groves of academe extend their domain, their alumni's arms reach lower; as the phallic cult spreads, so does impotence. In great wealth, great poverty; in health, sickness; in numbers, deception. Gorging, left hungry; sedated, left restless; telling all, hiding all; in flesh united, forever separate. So we press on along the valley of abundance that leads to the wasteland of satiety, passing on our way through the gardens of fantasy; seeking happiness ever more ardently, and finding despair ever more surely.

It would seem to me abundantly clear that the feature of our time that will strike posterity most forcefully will be precisely this bizarre working out of a death-wish in terms of utopianism. They will note that the more money spent on schools and colleges, the more illiteracy increased; the higher the hopes placed in education as a civilizing and enlightening influence, the more evident was the reversion to barbarism, as exemplified in hooliganism of one sort or another—baby and wife-battering, vandalism, muggings, rape, and the like. More ostensibly humane attitudes to crime and criminals resulted in sharp increases year by year in crimes of violence, especially by juveniles of both sexes; as easier procedures for divorce led to the break-up of ever more marriages and homes, and the legalization of abortion to a positive holocaust of unborn babies—in England over a million in three years, which is more deaths than in the 1914–18 war.

Will it not, then, appear as though, woven into the history of our time, was a principle of *reductio ad absurdum,* whereby the liberal mind, pursuing its utopian fantasies, managed to frustrate the very purposes to which it was ostensibly dedicated? What, for instance, could more effectively discredit the liberal notion of substituting the conference table for traditional diplomacy and the battlefield than, first, the League of Nations, and then its successor, the United Nations—two towers of Babel whose deliberations have created even more confusion than already existed, and whose directives have succeeded in multiplying confrontations and intensified conflicts in a world given over to strife? Again, who has more effectively exposed the absurdities, contradictions, and inherent weaknesses of capitalism than its sometime reputed savior, John Maynard Keynes? Or who the fatuities and monstrosities of Communism more relentlessly than its foremost twentieth-century exponent, Joseph Stalin? Has not the very word "welfare" come to stink to high heaven in light of the consequences of its elevation into a way of life, as writing the pursuit of happiness into the American Declaration of Independence has vilified the very notion of being happy, luring many pursuers of happiness into cul-de-sacs like drug-addiction, and sending them aimlessly about the world, bearded, tousled, and hopeless?

These are all symptoms, however; the basic cause, I have come to believe, of the phenomenon of the great liberal death-wish is simply that western man has grown weary of the struggle to be free. He has come to find the burden of the freedom he inherited from the past centuries of Christendom insupportable; his freedom is too much for him, and he wants to shed it. As Leslie Fiedler has put it: There is "a weariness in the West which undercuts the struggle between socialism and capitalism, democracy and autocracy; a weariness with humanism itself which underlines all the movements of our world, a weariness with the striving to be men."* In other words, the liberal mind, it would appear, is possessed with a passion to abolish freedom in the name of freedom. Prometheus who stole the fire of the gods to make himself free was punished by being bound to a rock, and each day having his entrails gouged out by ravening birds of prey; western man seeking to shed his freedom has arranged his own punish-

*Quoted by Duncan Williams in *Trousered Apes* from Fiedler's *Waiting for the End.*

ment, binding himself to a rock, and daily feeding on his own entrails and calling it liberation. In the great scene in *The Brothers Karamazov* when the Grand Inquisitor and the returned Christ confront one another in Seville, the Grand Inquisitor speaks for all liberal minds when he explains to the returned Christ that He cannot be permitted to stay because, if He did, He would once again, as He had before, offer mankind His dreadful gift of freedom. It has taken the Inquisition, the Grand Inquisitor explains, much toil and trouble to undo the disastrous consequences of this misguided offer, and they just can't risk having all the work to do again, which is what Christ's continuing presence in Seville would necessarily involve.

Subsequently, there came a time when the Inquisition no longer sufficed to achieve the Grand Inquisitor's purpose, and it was of this need for a substitute that the great liberal death-wish was born. Where the Inquisition disposed only of crude instruments like the thumbscrew and the rack to enforce orthodoxy, and the fear of excommunication to sustain it, other more subtle means of persuasion have been developed, reaching in the twentieth century a high degree of effectiveness. For instance, the ingenious device has been adopted of preaching anarchy to promote servitude, of acclaiming eros to spread impotence, of announcing the imminent withering away of the State—Hobbes' Great Leviathan—to extend and enhance its power, thereby preparing the way for authoritarian government of one sort or another, it matters little, in Grand Inquisitor terms, under whose auspices and what the precise ideology may be.

To produce the maximum effect with such devices, however, a *voice* was needed; a Pied Piper to lead the way to the rainbow's end, where, instead of a crock of gold, there turns out to be a Gulag Archipelago. Now the voice has been found, coming out of a microphone; the Pied Piper in living color beckons us on from a television screen, and lo! the media have taken over from the Grand Inquisitor. In the media the great liberal death-wish realizes its perfect fulfillment; in the TV gurus, charismatic, verbose, sincere, its perfect spokesmen. With a little help from makeup, lighting, and an autocue, who better equipped than they to denounce an unjust war and bring it to an ignominious and disastrous end, to unseat a President and jeopardize the institution of the Presidency, to unmask the CIA and dismantle the whole intelligence setup of which it is an integral part? Imagine subversive conspirators operating underground, well provided with money and weapons, well entrenched altogether— could they have hoped to do a thousandth part as well as this Operation Death-Wish, mounted and carried out, not by alien enemies or domestic traitors, but by the pampered, favorite sons of the very institutions and interests whose downfall they promote? Jericho's walls were brought down by a trumpet-blast from without its gates; the trumpet-blast which brings our walls tumbling down sounds from within. Our western civilization is the first in all history to breed and indoctrinate its own destroyers, educating at the public expense the barbarians who will overthrow it, brainwashing its citizens to expect and even welcome its downfall; silencing all warning voices, scorning the faith that might yet avert catastrophe. In short, involving the many in the death-wish of the few.

When I was working in Moscow all those years ago I had an extraordinarily strong conviction, amounting to a kind of mystical certainty, that what was happening there was, in essentials, bound to come to pass everywhere else. This did not signify a triumphant proletarian revolution sweeping through the world in accordance with the Marxist prophesies. Nor did it mean the acceptance elsewhere of the ideology and system of government in the USSR as then existing; still less, the final realization of the Slavophile dreams of conquest that the Soviet regime under Stalin took over from its Tzarist predecessor. Rather, it meant that I was seeing in Moscow the shape of things to come, in the sense that western man was fated to fall into a collectivist way of life such as existed in the USSR as a result of the Russian Revolution; and this quite irrespective of whatever might happen to him historically, however inimical to such an outcome might be the principles he ostensibly adhered to, and however furiously and valiantly he might struggle in an opposite direction.

Moscow in 1932, that is to say, was a preview of the life-style of the future—collectivized in every sense of the word, with an imposed comprehensive orthodoxy relentlessly enforced. As in a vision, I saw in London, in Paris, in New York, in all the cities of the West, the same sort of crowds drifting along the same streets as I had seen in Moscow, Leningrad, and Kiev; looking in the same sort of way into shop-windows and newspapers, echoing the same sort of slogans masquerading as thoughts and opinions, crowding onto the same sort of buses and trains, and infesting the same sort of beaches, parks of culture and rest, and places of entertainment—Broadway, Piccadilly, the Champs Élysées scarcely distinguishable from the Nevsky Prospect, the Arbaat, the Red Square.

The role of the great liberal death-wish in bringing about this collectivist consummation will be, I am confident, seen historically as decisive. Here, a comparison may be made with the troubled former inmate of a criminal insane asylum released on parole who finds himself longing nostalgically for the peace, the seclusion, the silence of a padded cell; for the key turning in the lock which not only shut him in, but also shut everyone and everything else out; for the harsh commands of the jailor and the inflexible prison rules against which there was no appeal. As the plain van comes to fetch him, screaming to be free, he yearns for confinement. Similarly, the liberal mind, screaming for democracy, yearns for a one-party authoritarian state, in darkest Africa if not yet in twilight Britain. As I write these words, Mr. Andrew Young, the United States Ambassador to the United Nations, and Dr. Owen, the British Foreign Secretary, are away on their African travels with a view to furthering the setting up in the Union of South Africa and Rhodesia of black majority rule based on universal suffrage and parliamentary democracy—a system of government not to be found anywhere on the African continent, least of all in the former British colonies or in the recently *soi disant* liberated Portuguese ones. Messrs. Young's and Owen's journeyings irresistibly recall those of Don Quixote and Sancho Panza, likewise directed towards liberating the enslaved and delivering the oppressed. Nor would it surprise me if they met with similar adventures to those which befell the Knight and his Squire. I am thinking particularly of the occasion when they set free a chain of galley slaves who, the moment they were liberated, set themselves to hurling stones at their liberators.

The great liberal death-wish, then, may be seen as a kind of do-it-yourself collectivization kit enabling us to enslave ourselves rather than be enslaved;

sleepwalking into our own Gulag, incarcerating ourselves in our own high-rise prisons, murdering our own innocents before they are born and planning our own families out of existence, making ourselves sick by swallowing our own drugs and impotent by wallowing in our own porn, reducing ourselves to penury by printing ever more of our own currency, poisoning ourselves with our own pollution, and believing our own lies fed to us by our own media. Romantics believe that the outcome will be a great, glorious nuclear bang, a fireworks display in our own corner of the stratosphere, and then curtains. Realists, on the other hand, foresee the coming to pass of a socio-biological Garden of Eden to which Adam and Eve have been readmitted by spewing up the apple giving them knowledge of good and evil, attaining thereby a second innocence with no real choices to be made; only the inexorable working out of a predetermined genetic destiny. I know, however, that in either case, whether the nuclear fireworks or the socio-biological bliss, in some remote forgotten place a naked savage, all unaware of such apocalyptic developments, will feel impelled to daub a stone with colored mud and prostrate himself before it in an act of worship, somehow aware in his dim brain and simple heart that he exists only as a participant in the purposes of a Godhead requiring to be worshipped and adored. And in that act, yet another chapter will begin in the unfolding drama of our human destiny, with time reaching up to eternity and eternity stooping down to time, making Now Always and Always Now. Once more the Word will become flesh, and dwell among us full of grace and truth.

Airborne: A Sentimental Journey
by William F. Buckley, Jr.

(1977)

DAVID NIVEN

When the Editor of *The Alternative* invited me to review William F. Buckley, Jr.'s book *Airborne* I was first flattered, then appalled.

The flattery is easy to diagnose; the reason for my unease, more complicated because it is two-fold. First, the Editor correctly describes his publication as. . . . "a monthly intellectual review." Also anyone with the price of a Newsletter, a Book, or a Television set knows that William F. Buckley, Jr. is . . . an intellectual, but the Reviewer Designate of Buckley's latest work has private information that there lurks in his own closet a skeleton of alarming proportions—David Niven is a semi-educated half-wit.

Second, D.N. is a close friend of W.F.B., so this review is rightly suspect on both counts.

One mitigating thought, however. I was sent, between the ages of six and seventeen, to English boarding schools during their most ferocious period. The prefects (older boys in authority) were allowed to administer the cane to other boys. The number of strokes was ordained by the Headmaster who gleefully dealt with the more hardened criminals among us himself. Occasionally therefore it would transpire that friend would have to chastise friend; but to show there was no favoritism, a strict code of honor existed and friend laid mightily into friend if not with zeal at least with a certain sense of "fair play."

I have tried hard to be overly critical of Buckley's book and I have come up empty—I loved it!

His political writings frequently send me scurrying to the Oxford Dictionary for clarification of certain words but, apart from a glorious (and I suspect homemade) "Buckley verb" that appears on an early page in connection with the cleaning of some dirty glass—"to repristinate"—I sailed through the book with the greatest joy and no intellectual inferiority complex.

This is a book written by a kindly, acutely observant adventure-loving man for *all* of us, a book about an adventure upon which he had long promised himself he would one day embark—to sail a small (30 ton, 54 foot at the waterline) schooner from Miami, Florida to the Mediterranean sea, 4,400 miles across the Atlantic Ocean.

When Buckley sometime in the winter of 1974 told me that he was definitely planning to make this trip the following summer, I put out no feelers as to whether there might be a place for me among his crew. To tell the truth, I held certain reservations about the success of the enterprise. A few months previously he and his wife Pat had paid us a visit at our home on Cap Ferrat. Alongside our house lay my two unreliable and very small sailing boats. Buckley luckily dismissed my catamaran as a bad risk becuase a vicious "Mistral" was blowing. But he insisted on putting to sea in the other, a top-heavy, over-canvassed 20-foot cabin "cruiser" with far too light a centerboard and a rudder that was apt to leave its appointed sockets and flap about uselessly in an emergency.

"Let's go take a look at *Sarina,*" said Buckley pointing to Löel Guinness' sparkling, burnished beauty built by Krupp in the late twenties. Riding at anchor across the bay, she was full of guests and a 24-man crew, her great schooner bow sniffing disdainfully at the rising wind, her huge yellow funnel slanting aft, and the white Ensign of the Royal Navy (and members of the Royal Yacht Squadron) flapping proudly from her stern.

Foxie, my little boat, had lately been redecorated by our two small daughters and was covered with a riot of color, large stick-on flowers of every sort, animals of all shapes and sizes, and several Ban the Bomb emblems. We approached *Sarina* at a great rate with our sail scraping the water and about half an inch of freeboard to spare before the Mediterranean boiled in and sank us. As I prepared to jump, because it seemed to me that Buckley at the helm was about to dismast *Foxie* on *Sarina*'s anchor chain, I noted the expression on his face—total calm, the sort of incandescent peace that fakirs display when sitting bareassed on nails.

Buckley conceived a spectacular maneuver which would bring *Foxie* head to wind and alongside the great yacht's highly polished gangway, but something went badly wrong and he produced instead a "Chinese gybe"—a dreadful happening when the end of the sail becomes wrapped around the top of the mast; we also hit *Sarina* hard amidships. She withstood this onslaught and shook us off as a Great Dane might dismiss a Yorkshire Terrier, but the "thud" caused a steward in a white jacket who was serving luncheon to appear at the rail far above our heads and to flap at us vaguely with a napkin . . . "P--s Off!" he commanded in his native tongue. As *Foxie* fell away and scraped along the spotless white side of *Sarina,* leaving a colorful deposit of daffodils, goldenrod, zebras, and horned toads, Truman Capote's round bespectacled countenance appeared beside the steward. "Come *Quick!*" he hissed over his shoulder. "Bill Buckley's come to call!"

Buckley remained admirably calm and issued sensible instructions to me for rectifying our strange appearance and effecting a dignified retreat while at the same time ignoring the pointed remarks that now rained down upon us from Mr. and Mrs. Löel Guinness, Mr. and Mrs. William S. Paley, and others. The incident came sharply to mind when he told me during the winter that he was planning to navigate across the Atlantic. The great joy of *Airborne* is that it is not a straight narrative of the actual crossing. It prepares the reader for all sorts of possibilities because as the voyage progresses Buckley recounts with warmth and high humor several *Foxie*-type shambles during his cruising and racing life that occurred prior to embarking on "THE BIG ONE."

With his deep, almost mystical love of the sea and his abiding respect for it, Buckley has produced a heart-warming, moving, and often hilarious mix of happenings, flashbacks, and excitements skillfully spiced with his own notes made during the voyage and the "journals" kept by several members of his crew—all easy to digest by the landlubber who has no need nor wish to know the difference between a gollywobbler and a Fisherman.

There are masterful portraits of his crew which included his son, his sister-in-law, and three close friends, one of whom was replaced for urgent business reasons on arrival in Bermuda by a large young man who comes aboard, promptly gets seasick, and is not mentioned or apparently seen again until he bobs up in somebody's journal 1,800 miles further East asking between brandies ashore in the Azores for the quickest way to get to London. Splendid descriptions abound of the near disasters which seem rather ominously to have dogged the author's seafaring days since the age of thirteen when he capsized his first 17-foot boat and saved the life of a friend clinging to the hull by undertaking a long hazardous swim from the middle of a cold Connecticut lake; and then in quick succession when he failed to throw a life preserver to his sister who fell overboard off Martha's Vineyard.

Two months before his first Bermuda Race his 40-foot racer *The Panic* mysteriously sank at her moorings during the night, and she almost repeated the performance a year later in the middle of the Chesapeake. During the Vineyard Race Buckley blew the navigation and the same craft ended up on the rocks, and in another race, with his wife aboard, *The Panic* was later dismasted off Block Island.

Soon after Buckley found *Cyrano* his chosen conveyance for "THE BIG ONE," she "several times ran aground in Bahamian waters" and then, while she was on charter to a friend for a dinner cruise on the Hudson, a cable snapped upon which a nonswimmer was sitting, with tragic results. Only one month before her great Transatlantic effort, *Cyrano,* on charter once more, was the silent witness of another disaster when the charterer's wife, a certified diver, was found dead on the ocean floor forty feet below.

Buckley is a confirmed optimist but he is also a realist and his precautions against possible mid-Atlantic emergencies, (sinking in two minutes, or in five and over) make fascinating reading. So too does the understanding he displays of his wife's apprehensions about the whole undertaking and of her anguish at the realization that she is saying goodbye to the three most precious things in her life—her only son, her only sister, and her husband.

Obviously "THE BIG ONE" was a success or this book would never have been written, but as a movie actor I despise film critics who in a few sentences presume to tell a story which has taken others months of hard work and preparation to bring to the screen, so I will simply recommend *Airborne* wholeheartedly as being well worth the price of admission: in fact it is cheap at the price.

Everything that could go wrong or break down during this production did so, but Buckley led his troops to final victory, with great panache (though he does not say so himself) relying almost entirely on a salt-soaked sextant, and occasional glimpses of the sun, the moon, and the swinging stars. Don't forget the supporting cast, though: they all came through nobly, and son Christopher is already a literary force to be reckoned with . . . A lovely "TRIP" and you can smell the sea.

Norman's Conquests

(1979)

ROGER STARR

For almost 20 years, Norman Podhoretz has been editing *Commentary,* making of it a magazine to which few readers can feel indifferent. He is a man renowned for his enemies, and yet he has attracted to the pages of *Commentary* over the period of his stewardship almost every member of the intellectual community of the country. Indexed end to end they would make a list so replete with incompatible personalities, warring ideologies, and uncongenial sensibilities that it seems impossible they could have been gathered together by a single editor of principle. Yet it is the principles in Mr. Podhoretz that they alternately hate and admire. They came in response to his vision of *Commentary* over the two decades. In his new book, *Breaking Ranks,* the editor himself tells the story of the 20 years, bringing to them a unity that underlies the two major changes in editorial emphasis that broke the ranks.

At the time of each major change, one at the beginning of the 1960s, the other about ten years later, Podhoretz turned the magazine away from the line of march of the majority of the intellectual community. Disturbed in 1960 by the shallow values of a euphoric America, he plunged off toward the left, bringing to *Commentary*'s pages writers like Paul Goodman and Norman O. Brown who were seeking a radical transformation of the dominant notion that America had solved its social problems and was firmly establishing an era of international peace based on anti-Communism, economic strength, and the new sensitivity of its political Camelot to the ideas of intellectuals.

Within ten years, he broke ranks again, this time running in the opposite direction, the intellectual community having in the interim swung away from the substantially pro-American view of the world to a countervailing notion that America not only could not do anything right, but could scarcely do anything that was not criminal. Today, he tells the reader, he grudgingly accepts being called a "neoconservative," but he refuses to interpret this in the economic sense in which it is usually meant. He believes that he has been consistent while the intellectual community itself has been faithful only to its own taste for power. He believes he has, on both occasions of breaking ranks, resisted the then dominant trend in the intellectual community, the trend that posed the greatest threat to the very intellectual values the members of that community believe themselves to treasure.

In the 1960s, he saw the paramount danger in the acceptance of anti-Communism as the fixed base of international relations, and in the loss of the spirit of adventure in the institutions of a society that seemed blandly to have stuffed its social problems in a drawer marked "solved." Ten years later, he regards as most dangerous those intellectuals whose reaction to the blandness of Camelot was too uncritical, and who have deliberately stripped their own radicalism of responsibility, threatening the very continuity of political discourse.

This new book, thus, is the story of Mr. Podhoretz' own movements in phase with his view of the changing tempers of his time. Since his life was spent in the company of the writers, academics, and editors who formed the core of the intellectual community, the book is a chronicle of New York intellectual life, with some attention to outlying suburbs like Washington, Cambridge, and, for a time, Berkeley. When Mr. Podhoretz emerged from Columbia College after World War II, the intellectual community included writers, mostly with left-wing backgrounds, who lacked significant connections with the large institutions of their time. Their reputations (with some exceptions, including Lionel Trilling and Edmund Wilson) depended on their essays in magazines of high culture and low circulation. Today, the author notes, the intellectual world has broadened; some members hold responsible posts in government; serious academics have become public figures; and now the magazines that vent their views include the nation's most widely read.

Mr. Podhoretz discusses the effect (and causes) of this change on American life, and concludes that for a contemporary man of affairs, association with a literary lion is an authentication of success, much as Theodore Roosevelt authenticated his success by shooting elephants. But the Roosevelt way, though bad for the elephants, was less dangerous for the country. Intellectuals, with a clear tendency to line up along either the port or starboard rail of the ship of state, can cause immense, sudden, and destabilizing shifts of weight and direction. They can actually menace its seaworthiness. It is, obviously, conceivable that an author who concentrates on the activities of intellectuals exaggerates the weight of their opinions. But Mr. Podhoretz makes a good case (though, as will be noted, not a scholarly one). And if he were to wait in making it for his catastrophic predictions to be proved by the event, he might well be unable to write about the matter at all.

To those who would appraise *Breaking Ranks* by the formal tests of academic social history, it must fail on every count. Its precise textual references are few. Its tracing of the links between Paul Goodman and the hard-rock culture simply does not exist. Its substantiating footnotes are few, and depend largely on Mr. Podhoretz' own memory, unrecorded in any library of oral history. But the book is a personal memoir and its values far outweigh its academic laches. It is illuminated by conviction and the unmatched personal recollection of events lived with passion. It pits loyalty to friends, like Hannah Arendt, against loyalty to ideas on which the same friends profoundly disagree. The author is serious about his work. He makes few cheap points for which the temptation—given the kind of points others have made against him—must have been formidable.

In the years since he first broke ranks, Podhoretz has been vilified as a racist, a fascist, and, equally wounding, "mean-spirited." He has been caricatured, with incongruous and imprecise details, in fiction. And, ironically, although his 1967 book *Making It* brought a flood of invective against his allegedly careerist ambitions, he points out that the effect of its candor in some New York literary circles was to hang a silent leper's bell around his neck.

Nevertheless, it is only in the case of Jason Epstein, who serves at every stage of the Podhoretz narrative as the face on the far end of the seesaw, that the author yields to the urge to repeat bits of undergraduate history that might, with a special surge of restraint, have better been left out. But the reader who does not know Epstein will accept the total characterization as easily as Anthony Powell's readers accept Widmerpool.

Podhoretz brings to *Breaking Ranks* talents that might be summed up in a child's catalogue of the Animal Kingdom. The author has the memory of an elephant, the eye of a hawk, the nose of a beagle, the suspicions of an owl, and the drive of a beaver. He also has demonstrated a quality known to horsemen: "early foot." He was quick off the mark to be published, fresh out of college, in *Partisan Review* and *Commentary,* among little magazines, and the *New Yorker,* among big ones. He took over the editorship of *Commentary* when he was 30, and reshaped it, as noted, culturally leftward and out from a somewhat more intense focus on Jewish matters.

The move to the left alienated many of the magazine's readers who were then interested in cultural affairs ("Why are you writing so much about Viet-Nam?" Dwight MacDonald asked Podhoretz when Kennedy's involvement was just beginning. "No one's interested.") But, of course, interest mounted, not only in Vietnam, but in the Berkeley Free Speech Movement and the birth of a new force in American politics, Students for a Democratic Society. *Commentary* leaned toward them, but Mr. Podhoretz detected the seeds of immense destructiveness in movements whose leaders, ostensibly educated, felt they had to dismiss intelligence as a regressive force in human behavior. He was as put off by their urgent self-righteousness as by the smugness of the Camelot period a few years earlier. By the end of the 1960s, he was questioning his own turn to the left. As the magazine became concerned with the excesses of the "counter-culture," the problems of integration, and the post-Vietnam foreign policy challenge, many of those who had opposed his move to the left now opposed what they read as a swing to the right.

An author who confesses to changing his mind must raise in the minds of his readers the question of whether he suffers from intellectual or moral instability, or whether, as he claims, everyone else does. Though Podhoretz does not directly set forth his own views of the nature of a good society, the narrative itself makes them clear. It is obvious that Podhoretz holds three positions about which current controversy rages, and his obstinate clinging to these positions accounts for his willingness to oppose current vogue, and for the anger levelled against him by so many others in the intellectual community. His crucial positions are in the sectors of success and egalitarianism; race and ethnicity in a pluralistic society; intellectuals and revolutionary change.

Podhoretz won his first stripes of public disapproval with his earlier book,

Making It, in which he called the "enjoyment of success" the "dirty little secret" of his age. By success, Podhoretz meant not only the approbation of one's intellectual peers, which few are embarrassed to savor, but also the acceptance of oneself as a figure of importance by the popular culture. Success, and its enjoyment, also mean relishing the attributes of success in a culture: in ours, money, personal mobility, association with the highly-placed in other hierarchies of the general culture. He claimed not only that intellectuals enjoy these stigmata of success, but that the desire for them is a valuable motivating force even in stimulating intellectual activity. This enraged his colleagues, who feared that the allegation would menace their claim of freedom from such streaks of common clay as the desire for power, prestige, influence, and adulation. But Podhoretz' view of success and its importance bore even more heavily on the arguments of the egalitarians who are now insisting that society has scarcely begun to achieve equality when it offers all citizens equality before the law.

The new view would require society to assure each citizen that he will attain equal material standards, equal responsibility, equal authority, with all other citizens. Clearly a world that guarantees equality of result removes from human experience the feeling of success even as it removes the possibility of failure. Podhoretz consistently speaks for the responsibility of society to avoid handicapping people so heavily that they cannot fulfill the potential of their talents, but, equally, to stop society from assigning its own handicaps in order to make human competition come out even. If he broke ranks to the left because America was neglecting the cultural impediments of the early sixties, he has broken back again in the seventies, to stand against those who would impose their own "socially desirable" handicaps in the pursuit of equality of result.

In the sector of inter-communal relations, it is fair to say that, with one immense exception, American society has managed them far better than, say, Ireland, Nigeria, and Belgium. Race is another story. On this subject, Podhoretz has managed to offend as many as on the subject of success. In the early sixties, he published an essay of his own in *Commentary* that frankly, and to some eyes brutally, dealt with the then widely-held notion that the race problem was to be solved by integration of blacks and whites. For Podhoretz, government had a substantial and significant role to play in the abolition of all legislation that required the separation of the races, and an obligation to provide, as Bayard Rustin later wrote in *Commentary,* the economic assistance with which black Americans might overcome the immense handicaps they had suffered under slavery and imposed segregation. But he dared to say that the immense cultural differences that separated blacks from whites (and tended to separate other ethnic groups in America) made integration unlikely without actual miscegenation. Governmental power, supreme in the area of law, powerful in the economic realm, has relatively little power in the elimination of the gross misunderstandings and misperceptions that accompany ethnic differences.

Podhoretz' sense of the depth of those differences, coupled with his insistence on the inability of government to ensure equality of result, places him in square opposition to the large number of intellectuals who believe that preferential action by government can establish equality among blacks and whites, and that such action is justified. They find Podhoretz' contrary view anti-black and racist. But Podhoretz' position is not based on a view of race; it is based on a view of government and communal relations. The preferential action that Podhoretz resists is the action that would assign numerical quotas to any communal or ethnic group in the population, or that would offer members of one group the opportunity to qualify for credentials or employment with a standard lower than that of other groups. The Podhoretz line would not exclude the taking into account of individual factors, including hardship, in the appraisal of candidates who fall within a reasonable range of the standard, and it would encourage heavy investment in special educational and training programs. But it draws a heavy line against the establishment of systematic preferences, or rights ascribed to specific categories of people, on the grounds, among others, that such acts are incompatible with the most felicitous of American principles.

Finally, Podhoretz has made clear over the years that he distinguishes between the radical, which may be necessary and is often beneficial, and the revolutionary, which he regards as the pet, unexamined idea of the intellectual community. Nowhere does he support the notion that the ascendancy to power of a new class, or the alteration of the political system to change in a fundamental sense the economic relationships between producers and consumers, will avoid any of the problems society now faces. In great part, Podhoretz says, he reached his disenchantment with intellectual revolutionaries because of their readiness to abandon rational process of thought and to tolerate youthful gibberish about the significance of changes in consciousness. Basic to Podhoretz' social values is the insistence on free discussion, and the retention of faith in the effectiveness of intellectual analysis, a faith which many in the intellectual world were prepared to drop under the press of fashion.

Podhoretz buttresses this last allegation with a long list of the offenses of anti-intellectual intellectuals during and since the Vietnam war. This is not an indictment of criticism; criticism is the primary function of an intellectual, but it loses its effectiveness, and raises questions about the good faith and basic value system of the critic, when it becomes hyperbolic, inaccurate, and vilifying, as in the use of "Amerika" during the Vietnam era, when the country was being compared with Nazi Germany by some who should have been aware of the imprecisions of the comparison (their being free to make it, for one).

Podhoretz himself was an early, indeed a premature, opponent of American military participation in Vietnam. As the war continued, however, he became increasingly disturbed by his fellow opponents. Too many found in it the occasion for spiteful misreadings of American intentions. They romanticized the monolithic brutalities of the North Vietnam government. And later, having distorted the significance of the Vietnam experience, they hampered the conduct of foreign policy by the world's few remaining non-totalitarian states.

Somewhat too young to have participated in the Stalinist-anti-Stalinist intellectual civil war of the 1930s, but old enough to have applied its lessons to the revival of intellectual revolutionary interest during Vietnam, Podhoretz disclaims the usefulness of revolution and, in so doing, offends that whole section of the intellectual community that, while not itself advocating revolution, seems to believe it has purified its soul when it foresees the inevitability of a revolutionary future and argues that such a radical change will somehow make things "better."

So the three basic Podhoretz positions—that a good society must offer, not equal results, but the possibility of personal satisfaction that we call "success"; that communal and ethnic friction cannot be resolved by the allocation of roles or tampering with standards; and that revolutionary enthusiasm is devoid of intellectual seriousness—account for much of the present antagonism to Podhoretz by his critics. To these ideas might be added a fourth factor of which one cannot speak without a measure of embarrassment: Podhoretz is in the deepest sense a patriot, an almost crippling infirmity for a modern intellectual. He genuinely loves America, not only for broad principles to which he believes it has generally clung, but because he continues to be absorbed by the concrete details of life here; they bring out the beagle in him. This weakness—added to his vision of social responsibility—stirs his critics as nothing in his style, presentation, or frankness would. While they complain about the author's methods, they would not give his message credence if it were brought down from Sinai by Marx, Freud, and Einstein, fully annotated. It is the message they deplore, not the medium.

Why Are There
Neoconservatives?

A Symposium
(1979)

Sniffing the intellectual winds of our glorious era, and poring piously over the learned reflections on neoconservatism, we grow apprehensive. It seems to us that the eminences of polite thought are up to something. Their reports on the neoconservatives' doings strike us as generally dissembling attempts at damage control and intimidation. That is to say, they want to portray neoconservatism as a very narrowly based operation, intellectually limited, and not to be touched by any young intellectual desirous of advancement in the realm of higher cerebration.

There is always a danger that the intellectual history of an era will be written by ideologues, and the more evidence gainsaying their prejudices the better. With this in mind, we asked some of our younger writers to contribute to a symposium on neoconservatism, addressing themselves to the following questions:

(A) What makes you neoconservative or at least not liberal in the way that term is being used today? (B) Where have you stood in the past? (C) What issues—political, cultural, or economic—most disturb you today?

Their responses are here presented in alphabetical order. —*Ed.*

Elliott Abrams

A bit of autobiography: Not only was I in general terms a "liberal" in my youth, but I was in fact a certified, card-carrying liberal and served as National Chairman of the campus division of ADA. I am (I believe) the only chairman of national or campus ADA ever *not* to be reelected to a standard second term, this punishment having been the only one available for my crime of supporting Hubert Humphrey over Eugene McCarthy in 1968.

What had happened was simple: In college I came across, in order, Edward Banfield, the *Public Interest* (which he gave as assigned reading), Samuel Huntington, Henry Kissinger, and Nathan Glazer. Eventually, all this had an impact. What they had in common was, at least, an unwillingness to accept the prevailing liberal pieties—which we may summarize for present purposes as "Always and everywhere, public housing is good and military power is bad"—and a willingness to criticize, indeed to satirize, these pieties when logic or experience proved them inadequate.

What is it that separates neoconservatives from today's liberals? (Today's liberals have abandoned the liberal tradition of leaders such as Harry Truman,

Lyndon Johnson, Humphrey, and Henry Jackson. Instead, liberalism today is a philosophy embodied by such men as George McGovern and Andrew Young. Today's "liberals" thus have less right to that term, of course, than do neoconservatives, and are instead better described as New Leftists. But over these matters CBS, not *The American Spectator,* reigns.) The key difference, in my view, is that neoconservatives are concerned with the lives of *individuals,* while liberals are more concerned with the condition of *society.* Most probably, behind this difference lies a deeper, if unarticulated, disagreement on the perfectibility of man in society. Grant that all injustice, poverty, disease, and war are the products of inadequate social arrangements, and there follows a reasonable desire to rearrange. As there is but one means of rearranging social patterns, the state, liberals tend more and more to be statists.

Grant that injustice, poverty, disease, and war are in part simply endemic to the human condition, and in part the result of ignorant or mistaken or evil acts by individuals, and a very different result emerges. Where liberals see "problems," neoconservatives see "conditions." Neoconservatives are less sanguine about the range of achievable goals, and lean to the view that the achievement of many of these lies in our hearts and not in our state. Thus neoconservatives greatly value the role of mediating structures which teach the individual virtue—structures such as the family, religion, and social traditions. They are, on "social issues," rather conservative. And believing that the growth of state power will solve few of our society's problems, while limiting our liberty and creating new and unintended, unforeseen problems, neoconservatives strongly oppose the growth of the state.

This picture is overdrawn, for neoconservatives do see some crucial roles for the state. Liberals and those who are now neoconservatives joined in supporting social security, collective-bargaining laws, voting-rights guarantees, and much other social legislation. It is this that separates neoconservatives from conservatives: this support for a minimum of social provision, distributed usually through the state. Where liberals and neoconservatives parted company was at the point liberals moved from basic social provision to wholesale income redistribution. This fits the liberals' vision of egalitarianism, but has no place in the neoconservatives' view.

This analysis has the virtue of absorbing all of today's political battles. Behind such issues as inflation, taxes, and government spending, or quotas, race, and "social justice," lies the issue of statism. The underlying question is what the state can successfully, or ought to, undertake: to make society over, or to make it somewhat less rough, the better to guarantee social peace and individual liberty?

And what of foreign policy? As liberals today are statists, they have weak defenses—in their public rhetoric and in their private thoughts—against the socialist ideology of our nation's chief enemies. Witness, for example, the fact that the State Department's annual volume on "human rights" in countries receiving American aid includes comments on medical care in those countries. The "semantic infiltration" of which Senator Moynihan has eloquently spoken is easy for our enemies if one starts with their view of the role of the state. And it follows that liberals will see extreme statist societies as less awful than will neoconservatives, and will see our own as less a uniquely valuable place with special lessons to teach. Of course, those who had special experience with Communism—the Mensheviks and their intellectual successors, or labor leaders with long lives and long memories—had a special understanding of its horrors. But as these influences wane over time, liberalism becomes simply the mildest form of statism, whose more authentic exemplars may be seen outside our borders. An active American foreign policy will seem to liberals all too often to oppose "benevolent" statist regimes in the Third World—where the lines between "liberal" statism, socialism, Marxism, and plain old despotism seem blurry to many liberals. And so such a policy will be opposed. Instead, liberals are willing to focus on those regimes' goal—the use of state power to achieve "social justice"—as indeed they should, this goal being the liberals' own. For the neoconservative, this very goal is, as it were, a red flag. Instead, neoconservatives are inclined to see American interests as threatened by a statist world, and "socialist" regimes as but another form of limitation on individual liberty.

All this has the result we see around us: Andrew Young's foreign policy is the purest essence of the liberal view, as Moynihan's is the soul of the neoconservative view. To close on a note of optimism: Who can doubt with which man our countrymen stand?

Tom Bethell

"Genes," or something similar, must cause ideology. Maybe I should add the usual complication—early upbringing. The strange thing about political ideology is the way in which apparently quite unrelated issues group themselves together coherently in the perceiver's mind. In my case it was as though I woke up one day quite unexpectedly and involuntarily believing that (a) the economy should be deregulated, (b) we should take a tougher stand with the Soviets, (c) affirmative action is abhorrent, and (d) higher education is to a large extent a waste of time.

Why should these things go together?—and they do tend to. I think that "nature" or psychological makeup must ultimately be invoked. It is flattering to believe that the implications of the issues themselves (which one is uniquely intelligent enough to perceive) dictate ideology, but I doubt it. On the basis of exposure to roughly comparable information, plenty of other people are "liberal" on all the foregoing issues.

Before 1973 or thereabouts, I was not interested in political matters. I was vaguely liberal, but only in the sense of not wanting to be accused of harboring unfashionable attitudes. This fear of seeming unenlightened has been a major element of liberal support over the years. In fact, it comes very close to defining liberalism as that term is currently understood. The current ideological debate derives primarily from confusion as to what are now the "correct" positions.

In addition, I became an American citizen in November 1974. What a time! Now I'm beginning to think that I booked passage on the Titanic. (You feel an obligation to attract the captain's attention under such circumstances, but the bridge seems to be deserted and the navigator has lost his charts.) My pessimistic perception is that the powers are moving back East after hundreds of years of westerly motion. I feel more optimism about the future of the Soviet Union than I do about the future of America.

The encouragement of individual creativity, which has been America's great contribution to the twentieth century, is now under assault by a burgeoning class of homegrown statists. They aspire to the impudent, demoralizing ideal of "equality," whose tedious premise is that life is about nothing more important than the relationships among people. (Anyone who embraces equality as an ideal is in danger of serving a self-imposed lifetime sentence of resentment and jealousy.)

The most important change in attitude which conservatives must try to bring about is to persuade the all-important college-educated young (who do not know much but want to be in fashion intellectually) that the government now is not the solution to problems but the exacerbator of them (and often the cause of them). The Depression, World War II, and the civil rights movement in turn persuaded intellectuals that to be "liberal" meant to be on the side of more government. This is really a contradiction in terms and it is high time for the old meaning of "liberal" to reassert itself.

In particular, the most serious danger facing the country is the determined thrust against the market economy. Such an attack was formerly, and more candidly, conducted in the name of nationalization. Today, a more devious strategy is being employed—one of incremental politicization: regulation, "environmentalism," and the like. The important point to bear in mind is that a market economy is the principal obstacle blocking the ambitions of the political class. To the extent that markets persist, we have little need of government and all its works. But when markets are destroyed—as recently happened, but fortunately only briefly, with the energy market—then we are all quite abruptly at the mercy of the statists-in-power, with their doctrines of "fairness," with their set-asides and allocations, with their five-year plans, rations for the proles, and commissaries for the commissars. Make no mistake about it, an increasing number of people in America would like such a system because they have made the rational calculation that they would profit by it. They wouldn't have to compete anymore with the upthrusting tackies in doubleknits called the middle class.

The great strength of capitalism is that it generates widespread and rapid upward mobility—economic and thence social. But this necessitates an equal and opposite downward movement. It is our tattered, downwardly mobile former elites who are primarily interested in arresting a system that confers such precarious and transitory benefits. In a static, politicized economy, many of our beleaguered preppies would sink no further. It is these people who are the true enemies of liberal society.

I realize it is just as paradoxical for a conservative to say all this as it is for a liberal to believe in state control. But wasn't it Irving Kristol, or perhaps Daniel P. Moynihan, who said that the new conservatives didn't go to Harvard or Yale but to City College? He was right, whoever he was.

Naomi Decter

I am a neoconservative born and bred.

Born, because there is an element in the Jewish gene pool that sometimes transmits the acceptance of life for what it is: a difficult, often painful and frightening, but always profoundly satisfying venture.

Bred, because I was raised on the notion that one is wholly responsible for one's own life; that is to say, that all behavior has moral significance, every action has consequences to be lived with, and the source of the former as well as the response to the latter lie entirely within.

Politically I am a neoconservative only insofar as I apply those standards to everything, including politics, and always seem to come up on the neocon side. If a political position is inimical to the idea of individual will and responsibility, I am against it. If that position is supported by people who place the blame for every ill and the burden of remedy exclusively on some vague, all-encompassing vision like "society" or "culture," I oppose it all the more heartily.

If I had grown up at a different time in a different place, I might have been tempted to reject heredity and training, if only briefly, in the name of youthful rebellion. But living, as I always have, at the very heart of the "liberal" ethos, I had ample opportunity to observe the effects of its denial of responsibility. Nothing could have been less tempting.

For one thing, it created a repressive atmosphere most unpleasant to live with. The mere suggestion, for example (made in rash disregard for consequences in the middle of my tenth grade "Urban Sociology" class), that an impoverished childhood, or even ancestral slavery, need not condemn one to a life of illiteracy and violence was enough to evoke the passionate enmity of students and teachers alike. Fascist and racist were epithets too good for such as I. The terror was clear beneath the rage, as was its source: If those poor little black children up in Harlem, who had nothing but lead paint to eat for supper, could be asked to be responsible citizens, what might not be demanded of *us,* who dined often on steak and Brie, and most of whose ancestors had escaped slavery in the time of the Pharaohs?

Not much, in fact, was demanded; and ultimately, not much could be demanded. For, miserable as these people made me, they made themselves more than miserable. They were filled with bitterness: toward their parents, who had toilet-trained them too early or too late; toward their teachers, who had wasted their time with "irrelevancies"; toward society, which had crippled them by wrapping them in blue blankets or pink blankets. Consumed by the idea that they were meant to be "happy," and that if they were not, someone, somewhere, had failed them, they never had a moment's satisfaction in life.

And, as we grew, I watched them dropping like flies around me, always in retreat: from the university to the carpenter's bench; from the marriage bed to the sex-therapy clinic; from the employment agency to the welfare office.

I take it as a sign that my day has come that my contempt for them has turned to compassion.

Christopher De Muth

I have a cute answer for people who ask about my politics. It is that I came out of Harvard College a liberal, so I went to work for the federal government—where I looked around and realized I was really a conservative. So I left for law school and went to work in private industry—where I looked around and realized I was really a socialist. So I returned to Harvard.

This gets me off the hook at Brattle Street cocktail parties, but the punch line is only a joke, and in any event I don't believe in dramatic ideological tergiversations. Remember how the "Up With People" singers used to testify what rotten, delinquent kids they had been before being saved by Moral Rearmament? Once I asked one of them what kinds of trouble he had been in before joining the group, and he told me that he had served himself first at the dinner table, almost never took out the trash, and often left his bed unmade for *days* on end. Of course, there are famous stories of intellectuals who started out as Trotskyites and ended up writing for conservative journals or at the Libertarian Party, but one suspects they were never the truest believers among their young comrades, and the political movement virtually never goes in the opposite, leftward direction.

As for myself, I certainly counted myself a liberal during college days. I worked in civil-rights activities in Chicago and New York City, and in my senior year impulsively blew my savings and grades to go to Martin Luther King's funeral. I tried to get a job working for Senator Paul Douglas' re-election campaign in Illinois. I put in obligatory appearances at antiwar rallies. I also chased girls, cut classes, and didn't make my bed.

Looking back, however, I realize that I was not a *good* liberal even then. When I didn't get the job working for Senator Douglas I went to work for his opponent, Charles Percy, a close neighbor and not exactly Philip Crane, but nevertheless a *Republican.* Soon I was reading *The Ripon Forum* and sometime after that even began glancing at *National Review.* (This last step became respectable after I asked a professor what books I should read to learn about urban politics and, to my amazement, he recommended William F. Buckley's *The Unmaking of A Mayor.*) The professors who caught my fancy were Edward C. Banfield and James Q. Wilson and Daniel P. Moynihan—for their civility and seriousness before I came to appreciate their scholarship in any depth; the crowd-pleasers on the faculty seemed glib and supercilious in comparison. I also harbored doubts about the antiwar leaders—already the Big Men On Campus in 1968 (my senior year) and acting like it—and concerning the war itself I was always more confused than adamant.

So, while it would be nice to think that the evolution of my views was a conscious thing, brought about by keen observation and deep reflection, perhaps it was just a matter of growing up, and perhaps I have been a man of "conservative disposition" (Michael Oakeshott's term) from the start. A clue from the examples above is that in first instances I have always been attracted (or repelled) by the characters of specific individuals rather than by the abstract merits of specific policies. But is the drift of a man's political views as he matures simply a function of his turn of mind? Unfocused sentimentalizing about the human situation, which is the proximate flaw of modern liberalism, is also the natural impulse of those who are just beginning to learn about the world; the enormous difficulties of human organization and cooperation, the imperative presence of the market, and the advisability of keeping your powder dry are lessons learned only at the hands of experience—and how can anyone *avoid* learning them? Anyone who has worked inside a government bureaucracy must know how hard it is to coordinate the activities of a group of people to achieve a preconceived objective. But isn't the lesson equally apparent to anyone working in a business organization, or, for heaven's sake, to anyone who has simply gotten married and tried to manage the affairs of a small family? Winston Churchill and Irving Kristol are right in saying that, in politics, liberalism is the natural tendency of the young and conservatism is the natural tendency of the adult.

One could say that the lessons of personal life are indeed ineluctable, and that "liberalism" in the modern sense is simply the political expression of modern man's fear of middle age, of his clinging to his adolescence, kidding himself about life's possibilities. I think there is some truth in this, but as an argument it smacks of technique, like the way the *New York Times* used to treat conservatism matter-of-factly as a known type of social pathology. Another answer is that in the current state of democracy there are no true liberals anymore, just as there are no true conservatives—just politicians with different constituencies, dictating appeals to different sets of general ideas according to the contingencies of the moment. Farm-state politicians anguish over Hunger in America, just as oil-state politicians anguish over The Future of the Free Enterprise System. This, however, is not so much an answer as a reformulation of the question, since it does not say why a particular set of ideas should be thought to have wide political appeal.

I do think that people are too quick to let the distant lessons of political events overrule the immediate lessons of their personal lives. Perhaps this is because people fail to realize that rhetoric and symbolic behavior play an enormously greater role in politics than they can ever play in private life, and that for this reason there are few "lessons" of a practical nature to be learned from any singular political success or failure. Consider the civil-rights movement of the 1960s. The movement's goals were so morally right, they were met with such vehement resistance, and then they succeeded so spectacularly, that the movement is bound to remain the crucial domestic political experience of my generation. But we seem to have learned from it the wrong lesson—a bad habit, really—of reflexively relying on extensions of federal power whenever any aspect of the nation's life seems to leave room for improvement. I have come to appreciate the substantive merits of Barry Goldwater's arguments against the Civil Rights Act of 1964. It was, however, manifestly a time to lay these substantive merits aside, in part to maintain a proper appreciation for them later on. Surely things would have gone better for us in the past 15 years had Senator Goldwater voted resoundingly for the Civil Rights Act, so as to command attention as he explained the transcendency of the circumstances requiring its extraordinary provisions. Instead, the Act somehow became an indistinguishable, irresistible political precedent.

But my generation does have a few things going for it insofar as clear thinking is concerned. At least we were spared the wrong lessons from the twenties, from the Depression and the New Deal, and from the labor organization movement. We are the first to come to maturity in an America where black citizens are not subject to institutional public humiliations. The Vietnam war has, if anything, left us too introspective, and too morose about political action. And we are faced with a rather dour set of objective circumstances, such as the Soviet Union's dominance of the world's military and political affairs, chronic inflation, and the prospect that the social security system will break down before we have worked our way up to the payout window. At the same time, the liberal agenda of "unmet needs" is by now virtually exhausted. (About the only thing left is the proposal to require everyone to buy a health insurance contract, and the list seems not to be expanding in advance of actual legislation; no one today is calling for government-issued work uniforms, for instance.) Perhaps for these reasons the usual positions of the generations seem now to be strangely reversed: At least within the opinion-making elites, those under 40 appear to be considerably more conservative than those over 50. In business and in government, in the prestige academic departments of economics, government, and law, in medicine, architecture, journalism, and religion, we seem for the moment to be in a world of old swingers and young fogies.

Charles Horner

The student of international affairs will ponder the relationship between the growing influence of American "neoconservatism" on the position of the United States in the world and the conduct of American foreign policy generally. The neoconservative critique of American domestic policy, gaining force from failed experiments in "Great Society" programs, extends into foreign policy as well, but not yet as forcefully. For, in the realm of foreign relations, there need be no necessary connection between approaches to domestic problems on the one hand and conceptions of our international predicaments on the other. Thus, there are those whose views on domestic affairs are of the traditional "Left," but who nonetheless recognize the requirement for a stalwart national defense and a firm and consistent foreign policy. And there are those on the "Right," supporters of the free market, who believe—quite mistakenly— that the workings of trade and commerce, on an unregulated basis, can moderate Soviet international and internal behavior. But when the export of American grain and technology is separated from larger strategic considerations, we are left with little but self-congratulation about our own "efficiency." So there is a curious paradox: One can be quite right on economics and exasperatingly wrong about strategy; one can be wrong about economics, yet possess profound insights into the nature of our contest with our totalitarian enemies.

It is true that, in the main, one can divine an individual's views about foreign relations from his views on domestic affairs. But since that seems not always to be the case, I prefer a distinction Norman Podhoretz has drawn between a "pro-America party" and an "anti-America party." This, I believe, is a more fundamental cleavage than that between "conservatives" and "liberals" as such. The "pro-America party" takes proper pride in the achievements of the United States and maintains that the United States is a force for good in the world. It believes, accordingly, that the enhancement of American influence in the world promotes and protects civilization. There is, within the "pro-America party," a range of views on domestic social organization, recognizable differences between a "Left" and a "Right." But all are united in their opposition to totalitarianism, and all understand the role that national power and assertiveness must play in resisting it.

By contrast, there is an "anti-America party." It believes that the United States is a failed, or at least seriously flawed, society. It believes that the American system is destructive of civilized values. It holds that the United States is a force for evil in the world and that, accordingly, the power of the United States should be diminished, not enhanced. It sees no real conflict with the totalitarians that is not of the United States' own making. Here, too, one finds a range of views, mostly of the "Left" to be sure, but extending also to the extreme "Right," with its historic isolationism, even its penchant for conspiracy theories which regard both Communism and "high" capitalism as parts of the same apparatus. Such "rightists" can be as much in favor of the idyllic life of some lost pre-industrial era as the anti-industrial "progressives" who seek withdrawal from the "corrupting" influences of modern society. "Statists" can worship totalitarianism, but not all "anti-statists" understand how to resist it.

In an era when the raw military power and the intellectual legitimacy of totalitarian societies are clearly increasing, the defense of America and what America represents comes to override other issues. It may now be a time for stark choices; it may yet prove more important to minimize the influence of the "anti-America party" over foreign policy than to weaken the grip of the "regulators" on our domestic life. Or, put more constructively, we must consider how some portions of "Left" opinion in domestic matters may be enlisted in the "pro-America" coalition on foreign affairs. Not easy, but possible.

There was once a powerful consensus directing the role of the United States in world affairs; it needs urgently to be reestablished. At one level, we can understand that the application of proper economic policy can accelerate productivity, restore economic vitality, reestablish national and international confidence in the American system. But this, by itself, will not guarantee our survival in a world grown increasingly hostile and belligerent toward the United States and what it represents.

Surely, we reject the Maoist notion that "political power grows out of the barrel of a gun." But we should also reject the notion that the sensible and healthy patriotism our situation requires will grow out of microeconomic theory alone.

Roger Kaplan

There are plenty of matters to be concerned about these days, but there always are plenty of matters to be concerned about. The mistake is to think that a great and complex society can solve its problems; it lives with them as best it can, and, if it is successful, maintains a political system in which private citizens can solve their own problems without stepping on other people's feet.

In a sense, therefore, my major concern is for the center to hold. It probably has to be said again—and, in fact, it is a good sign that it is said often—that "Left" and "Right" (in opposition to "Center") are words that the seating arrangements in the French National Assembly gave to the lexicon of politics, and they aren't very good words for a constitutional democracy to use; they are words that came out of the experiences of the first totalitarian democracy.

We resisted the French vice, which the Napoleonic armies carried throughout Europe, for a long time, as did the British of course. (When you think about it, the French resisted it pretty well too, following their initial catastrophic inoculation. Periodically it comes back to them and they get feverish and sweat it out, but they have for the most part let conservative governments rule.) But French or French-inspired ideas played an important role in the radicalization of the post-World War II generation. It's unfortunate that 1776 isn't considered a more significant date than 1789.

Political radicalization may be over for a time, though the linking of Hiroshima and Harrisburg by the nuclear know-nothings is a sign that the illiberal forces are regrouping around the slogans of isolationism (unilateral disarmament) and a kind of hostility to progress from which only the most wealthy strata of our society can benefit. But much of the harm is done. The political delusions of the sixties did something to the character of my generation. I don't mean to sound pompous or sanctimonious. The fact is that it means something when people your own age not only don't want children, but manifestly don't like them. I can't help asking myself what these people are living for. I can't help thinking that the lofty ideas of our adolescence were corrupt to the marrow.

But I hate to generalize. Some of these ideas were perfectly sound, perfectly respectable. A lot of people used them selfishly though. If they really were interested in civil rights, they wouldn't support the parody of civil rights which affirmative action now resembles. Incidentally, the same sometimes holds for those who did not go against the political system, or who made their peace with it in the course of this decade.

The conflict now has to do with the individual. The great modern enterprise is freedom. The question is how you balance the desire for individual freedom with the needs of society and the demands of tradition. How is the authority of tradition to exercise itself?

Much of the generation of the sixties' quarrel had to do with this. Civil rights had to do with a very important idea, the sanctity of the individual (and, therefore, his political rights). Much of the opposition to the war in Vietnam had to do with young people's sense that they would die for nothing of great value to them. The proof of this is that, despite the efforts of the Communists, opposition began to melt away very quickly as soon as the draft ended. (But by then opposition was concentrated in the political class, which prevented us from providing the Vietnamese with the means of defending themselves.)

Not to want to die for the freedom of Vietnam may or may not have been a thoughtful position. But the way a lot of people these days behave toward children leads one to suspect that this position was not arrived at very thoughtfully. We might have decided regretfully that Vietnam was not the place to make a stand for freedom, preparatory to defending it on our own shores. A lot of good people honestly came to that conclusion. But in many cases it was: *I* don't have time to go fight in Vietnam. Now it's: *I* don't have time for children, et cetera. It would seem that society is failing to convince a lot of people that they owe it anything.

As far as our experience in Vietnam is concerned, the lesson is that our policy there was no good. Intervening was right, but we intervened in the wrong way. The intellectuals were mistaken, both those who came up with the "limited-war" theories and those who tried to explain the war politically. The military men and others who counseled an attack upon the source of the problem, they were right. The proof of this is that when President Nixon mined Haiphong harbor, he got his peace treaty.

On the other hand—and the military men did not try to conceal this, quite the contrary—the risks of attacking the problem at the source in 1963 or 1965 or 1967 were very real. In those years, such an attack might have brought in the Chinese. It might have led to a mending of the Sino-Soviet split. Given the support we could expect from our European allies, that might have been too much. We'll never know, but we can't be sure that, given those risks, the prudent policy was not to avoid carrying the war north, Korea-style.

What followed was that President Johnson made an enormous, an appalling, mistake. Of the two options—pull out and cut your losses, or attack the North—he chose neither. He should have chosen one or the other and gone to the country, but he didn't. He should have said, We'll give our allies help, but no men. If they can't hack it, too bad, we'll draw the line someplace else; and explained why this was not a good place to make a stand with American bodies. Or he should have said: We inherited this line from the French. It was stupid of them, and we may not like it, but it is ours now and we've got to hold it. And to hold it we are going to carry the war beyond the 17th parallel, occupy Hanoi, blockade the ports, clean out Laos and Cambodia, and God help us if the Chinese come in. It will cost a lot and we will pay for it with additional taxes, but if you don't like it you can vote for my opponents in 1966 and against me in 1968.

Instead, he chose Rolling Thunder, pacification, counterinsurgency. He believed that if he could protect the South (which he did, at great cost to us and to the South Vietnamese), the Communists would tire. The Communists did not tire. They could do only one thing well, and that was make war, and they never tired of it. They still haven't tired of it. They are still making war. Often in defending the war, President Johnson and his supporters appealed to the memory of Munich. Quite so; but it is curious, if they remembered that Munich could not stop a totalitarian power, that they did not remember how a totalitarian power thrives on war, lives only for war, will never tire of war, certainly not sooner than a democracy. We're paying for that now.

Rachel Mark

In my eyes, the world is entirely a personal place; the creatures who inhabit it are its movers, and by the small creations of their imaginations, their spirits, their wills, they form its history. I measure everything by this fragmentary vision. You ask why I am a neoconservative; given that my bent is personal rather than political, I take the liberty of answering with a story.

The story's protagonist is Lilly-Maria. She is not a creature of my imagination; I have known her for many years. I give her that name in a polite effort to protect her, though I wager that if she were to glance at this in one rare moment of lucidity, she would know herself immediately. In every other detail my story is faithful to the truth.

Lilly and I went through elementary school together. It was a New York City public school whose great distinction was its service to "gifted" children. And if ever a child fit the bill, the irrepressible Lilly was it. There was no stanching the flow of her in those years: She wrote stories, poems, even plays, which, under her own direction, were staged frequently by her friends in Upper West Side living rooms to the delight of assembled parents. Her Halloween costumes were the most amusing and ingenious, always. The rest of us were the Queen of Sheba, Delilah, Cleopatra, Isabella. Lilly was Rasputin, in tatters.

I remember all of this about her now, and yet I remember also taking it perfectly for granted that she should be like this. It did not occur to me that Lilly was extraordinary, though I daresay she took the breath out of the adults who knew her. Her own parents were a mystery then, and it was only much later, when she and I had been reacquainted after a hiatus of four years, that I saw how she had taken the breath out of *them*.

Our reunion took place after her parents had undergone the transformation to sweet liberality that intellectual and worldly success brings. Her father, having completed the obligatory stint at a western "think tank," and having established himself as the regnant authority in a complex area of foreign affairs, was a much sought-after graduate professor at a great university in New York. He had so far surmounted life's obstacles as to have escaped whatever distinctive stamp of feature God had given him, and he bore a close resemblance to his tweed jacket and his dun bow-tie. His child, secured against any threat of vulgar difficulty, was free to flourish in the most benign circumstances. His wife was a pliant and agreeable university female.

Lilly was thus sent, as I was, to the city's most fashionable private school. It was, in the mid-60s, a place renowned for the rich variety of experience it afforded the world's most promising people, the children of New York's eminent intellectuals. (The climate of the school has changed somewhat since then, though on Parents' Day it is, I am sure, awash with the rich and famous.)

I had seen Lilly-Maria last when we were 11; she was familiar still, but four years had wrought some remarkable changes. The most palpable were the studied slovenliness of her appearance and the dullness of her once-inextinguishable eyes. Now we were 15, and we were ferociously sophisticated (she far more than I, owing to her greater appetite for knowledge). She appeared suddenly quite extraordinary to me, and I was full of wonder at her.

She had contrived, while still out west, to have her name legally changed. She had dropped the Lilly, and insisted upon being called Maria. (I was compliant, but could never, and even now cannot, bring myself to *think* of her as anything but Lilly.) Her mother and father, she told me, had approved wholeheartedly of this decision, acknowledging that she had the right to do as she wished, agreeing that she knew better than they what was best for her. This was freedom, I thought, and I envied her. It was not the sort of suggestion one made in my household.

It emerged that she had experimented with drugs; and that, upon announcing this fact to her parents, she had received their permission to continue these experiments, so long as she would carry them on in the privacy, and safety, of her own home. This was rather an infringement of her rights, she felt, and she disregarded the restriction.

She confided, most intriguingly, that she had already done "it"—our conspiratorial and embarrassed language—with the approval of her mother, who had shared her gynecologist's table and signed a form authorizing the doctor to supply Lilly with birth control pills (they were so much more reliable, not to mention convenient, than anything else). When Lilly's pregnancy occurred, in the summer of her fifteenth year, her mother attended to the abortion, referring to it later as "Maria's own private little biology lesson." And Lilly-Maria went on weekending with her series of lovers at the family cottage by the sea, together with her parents.

In this generous atmosphere she grew: Every stamp of her foot elicited a smiling, and ever more understanding, response. What I found most bewildering at the time was the contemptuous, teasing hatred she felt for her parents. She complained of her suffocation, of her inability to "relate" to them, of their stuffy, authoritarian, interfering ways. They gave her stomach aches. I was unable, in my extreme innocence, to comprehend that every word she uttered meant its very opposite, and so I argued heatedly in their defense. What amazes me now is that Lilly managed to remain intact for as long as she did. She had actually dragged herself a full four years through college—America's most prestigious—before she fell unmendably to pieces.

I have heard from her intermittently in the years since her breakdown. She calls me to account for sudden disappearances: She has undergone treatment for migraine headaches; she has had polyps removed from her vocal chords; she has been in for a bit of a rest. This last is the closest she has ever come to telling me the truth. I suppose she is ashamed to say she has lost control, though the fact announces itself in every conversation. The last time she called me it was to ask, in lowered voice, if I didn't think the weather had been particularly frightening lately.

I didn't think it was the weather. Something frightening has always lived in the air around Lilly. It extinguished her; it made a neoconservative of me.

Adam Meyerson

I opposed the Vietnam war. I favor the Equal Rights Amendment. I don't believe there's any such animal as a "new class." I have reservations about nuclear power, and think there's a good case to be made for affirmative action. I don't much care whether Alger Hiss was guilty. I want to save the whales. And I'm proud to be a neoconservative.

Neoconservatives are liberals with a sense of tragedy. We wish it were possible to live without defense budgets, but realize that it is not. We'd like to campaign for comprehensive national health insurance, but are afraid that its costs would interfere with the achievement of other humanitarian ends. We wish we could call out clearly for the downfall of corrupt despots, but we fear, for example, that what may follow the Shah or Somoza will be even worse.

And neoconservatives are conservatives with a liberal attachment to the common man. We think that, for all its many, many injustices, the United States has given more freedom and more opportunities both for self-rule and for economic advancement to more people over a longer period of time than has any other political system in the history of the world. So we think that our institutional traditions and constitutional heritage should be modified only with the greatest caution and deliberation. We cling to the market economy because, even though it is often heartless in the short run, we feel that over the long run it lets more people make more decisions about what's most important for themselves than any other form of economic organization we know of. If we oppose many social welfare programs, it's often because we think they rob their supposed beneficiaries of their dignity and place them in a debilitating culture of dependency. And if we're more suspicious of the environmentalists than we ought to be, it's because we feel they are denying to the mass of citizens privileges that the exclusive few already enjoy.

Neoconservative objections to specific government programs are more often pragmatic than ideological. We don't quarrel, for example, with the idea of economic regulation by the state; we argue that much existing regulation in the United States is strangling private resourcefulness, is unjustifiably serving particular economic interests, and is just plain stupid. We don't object to the idea of the welfare state, and think it's worked rather well in such countries as Sweden and West Germany. But in the United States, we feel that many social security programs have been breaking up families, contributing to unemployment, and, by reducing capital investment, making life more difficult for our grandchildren.

Nevertheless we do object, on ideological grounds, to the growth of government in general. We fear that too many decisions are being politicized—not only in business but also in medicine and now the arts. We worry that all the wrong incentives are at work, that economic rewards are increasingly flowing to those who are best at building political coalitions and amassing political power rather than to those who most efficiently provide goods and services that people want. And, being democrats, we object to the manner of politicization; we think that social policy decisions should be made principally by legislatures, not by courts or administrative agencies.

Neoconservatives fret. We worry about the military buildup of the Soviet Union, a buildup which we cannot explain without inferring belligerent and aggressive intentions, and which we see as the greatest threat today to life, liberty, and the pursuit of happiness. In our own country, we worry about the decline of self-restraint, hard work, private charity, and other old-fashioned virtues that may be necessary both for economic advancement and for the survival of liberal democracy.

But neoconservatives also have a sense of progress, and are happy to live in the late twentieth century. Sometimes we are accused of being indifferent to the suffering of the poor, but it does not please us that poverty, disease, and starvation have afflicted most of our brethren throughout most of our history. What excites us about modern times is that the lives of ordinary people in most countries are improving so rapidly—that so many are living so much longer, in such better health, and with so many more opportunities. The population explosion heartens more than it frightens us; it means that fewer parents see fewer of their babies dying. We welcome more than we fear advances in technology, even though we recognize that they often require careful safeguards. We are proud to belong to a species that has landed on the moon.

Neoconservatism, or, if you prefer, paleoliberalism. Our ideas are as old as Adam Smith and Edmund Burke. Our heroes come from musty civics books—Lincoln and Washington, Jefferson and Madison. But our faces are fresh and our spirits are bold.

Stephen Miller

My political education began in the spring of 1962, when I decided that I wanted to become an intellectual. A first-year graduate student in English at Yale, I suddenly discovered a world elsewhere, the world of strange and horrible events that Hannah Arendt describes in *The Origins of Totalitarianism,* a book that I had just read. As a result, the world of English studies, with its *Seven Types of Ambiguity* and *Anatomy of Criticism* (two bibles for graduate students in English) no longer compelled my attention. Having been introduced to modern political history, I found it hard to keep up with the daily regimen of literary criticism—with the 20-odd essays, say, on the meaning of Andrew Marvell's "The Nymph Complaining For the Death of Her Fawn." Spending most of my time reading modern novels and literary-political journals, I came to the conclusion that intellectuals and not English professors knew how to go about understanding what had happened in the twentieth century. The writings of intellectuals may be difficult, I said to myself, but at least they did not label everything ironic, ambiguous, symbolic, or whatever other terms graduate students in English used to display their ingenuity as readers. In any case, Albert Camus and George Orwell, my two heroes, had not become intellectuals by earning a doctorate in English.

But becoming an intellectual, I decided, not only meant learning about politics; it also meant moving to New York. That May I impulsively quit Yale, found a job in New York, and settled into an apartment on the Upper West Side of Manhattan, an area that supposedly was the haunt of intellectuals. And I began to read Marx and Freud, for both writers were continually quoted in the journals that I faithfully read.

I soon learned, however, that I was behind the times. According to my two roommates (acquaintances from Yale), who were much further along the path to becoming intellectuals than I was, the writer one should read was Herbert Marcuse, who had managed to synthesize Marx and Freud. Even more important than Marcuse was Theodor Adorno, the presiding genius of the Frankfurt School. One of my roommates spent the whole summer translating Adorno. Adorno, he said, understood the pernicious effect of capitalism on culture.

But I was not up to Adorno. He had not yet been translated into English, and my German was simply not strong enough. Towards the end of the summer I bought two of his books and spent three days trying to translate two pages of one of his seminal essays. I gave up. Marcuse would have to do instead, and for the next three years I was a devout Marcuse-ite, convinced that Marcuse was right about the "repressive tolerance" of capitalist America. And when I returned to graduate school in the spring of 1965, enrolling at Rutgers to take a degree in comparative literature, I wrote a long paper on Marcuse's latest book, *One-Dimensional Man*.

Yet there was something in me that resisted Marcuse—resisted, in general, the world of intellectuals. Intellectuals were masters of understanding who could speak clearly and logically, throwing ideas around with ease. I lacked such talents. Despite my desire to be an intellectual, the world of ideas confused, irritated, and bored me. Philosophy—especially German philosophy—was beyond me. For I was an aesthete, I said to myself, not an intellectual, and I prided myself on my ability to appreciate Matisse, Klee, Stravinsky, Bartok, Yeats, Stevens. In my heart I preferred the nuances of art to the complexities of political theory. Nevertheless, I remained faithful to Marcuse, perhaps because I sensed that he too was an aesthete and that his criticism of capitalism was based on his distaste for the vulgarities of mass culture. I sensed that he too walked through shopping centers holding his nose high and inwardly jeering at the American consumer, who had such bad taste.

My faith in Marcuse was shattered not by a particular book or a particular professor but by my wife, a Hungarian émigré whom I married in 1967. She was scornful of my airy contempt for capitalism—scornful because she knew that I had not the faintest idea of what life was like in societies that pledged allegiance to Marx. Perhaps because I felt a need to resist her strong anti-Marxism, I began to read more political theory and modern history to see if I could find arguments to refute her. Yet the more I read, the more I realized that Marcuse's equation of Soviet Communism with American capitalism was absurd. The two regimes had little in common, and Marcuse's attempt to unmask the so-called "formal" freedoms that existed in the United States was a denial of the obvious fact that Americans possessed liberty whereas Russians did not. The important distinction, I decided, was not between capitalism and socialism but between freedom and tyranny.

Thus I made my break with the Marxist tradition—a tradition, I felt, that did not pay sufficient attention to political freedom. (I had long since lost interest in Freud, whom I have come to regard as the most overrated thinker of the twentieth century.) But I did not abjure socialism. Surely, I argued with my wife, there could be a democratic socialism, but she didn't agree. Nevertheless, I found myself gravitating towards *Dissent* magazine, whose editor, Irving Howe, strongly opposed totalitarianism and espoused the values of a democratic socialism that owed more to writers such as Ruskin, Tawney, and Orwell than it did to Marx. In the early seventies my first two articles on politics were published in *Dissent*.

By the early seventies, moreover, I became more determined to become a man who could understand things rather than only appreciate things. I no longer kept up with the latest work in art, music, poetry, and fiction. For several years I read only history, political theory, and science. The result was a growing disenchantment with the tradition of democratic socialism—not because I thought men like Howe constituted a threat to liberal democracy but, rather, because their ideas seemed muddled, impractical, and contradictory. On the one hand, democratic socialists attacked bureaucracy; on the other hand, they continued to regard governmental intervention as the answer to all the diseases that afflict advanced industrial societies. Moreover, the tone of moral superiority that pervaded the work of many democratic socialists began to irritate me. They continually advertised their concern for the poor, the sick, the aged, etc., and continually labelled those who disagreed with their prescriptions callous and venal. But I did not know how to go about questioning the premises of democratic socialism until I read more political theory, especially Friedrich Hayek's *The Constitution of Liberty* and a number of works by Raymond Aron. Hayek and Aron, I learned, belong to a tradition of skeptical Whiggism that includes such writers as Hume, Adam Smith, and Walter Bagehot, writers who offer a moderate and prudential defense of a market economy as the best means of preserving liberty, maintaining political stability, and spurring economic progress— progress that would benefit all levels of society, including the poor and the dispossessed.

Should I be called a skeptical Whig or a neoconservative? I prefer being called a neo-liberal—someone, that is, who does not categorically oppose governmental intervention but regards the expansion of government into many areas of modern life with skepticism and distrust. But I don't consider myself primarily a defender of free enterprise or capitalism. Shoring up liberal democracy, it seems to me, should be the central concern of all intellectuals, which means defending liberal democracy against the enthusiasts who praise capitalism and the enthusiasts who praise socialism. Capitalists are dangerous to liberal democracy because, as Sidney Hook has said, "for them freedom first means profit first" with an eye on profit and loss in the short term, they will supply the technical means and skills to totalitarian regimes that in the long run may ultimately destroy free cultures." Socialists are dangerous to liberal democracy because the state's takeover of all business will first seriously weaken productivity and then create a climate of bitterness, cynicism, and envy—a climate that will result in the erosion of liberty.

In their different ways both capitalists and socialists denigrate representative government. Capitalists—especially of the libertarian variety—abhor governmental intervention and regard politicians as corrupt men who meddle with their lives. Socialists want a society planned by an elite group of disinterested men who somehow speak for the people although they have not been elected by the people. Defending liberal democracy means defending the political vocation.

But to do so one needs to dust off the notion of civic virtue—not the idea of civic virtue, I should add, advanced by the likes of Ralph Nader or John Gardner, who radiate a smug assurance that they always know what is in the public interest. The civic virtue I have in mind would be modest in its pretension to understand the problems that beset us but would also be stern in its defense of liberal democracy. In practice, this means a willingness to engage in argument with democratic socialists like Irving Howe but a refusal to have anything to do with those, like Herbert Marcuse, who feel only contempt for democracy, who think that only they have "true consciousness." As Marcuse said in a recent interview: "It is most striking, the extent to which the ruling power structure can manipulate, manage and control not only the consciousness but also the subconscious and unconscious of the individual." But his consciousness, subconscious, and unconscious, of course, are not controlled by the "ruling power structure," which means that he has the right—and indeed the duty—to lead the people out of the desert of false consciousness and into the promised land of socialist freedom, a land where, as Marcuse said, "labour would no longer be the measure of wealth and value, and human beings would not have to spend their life in full-time alienated performances." But we have learned in the twentieth century that the dream of socialist freedom and solidarity leads to the nightmare of totalitarian slavery.

One cannot engage in argument with those enthralled by such utopian dreams. But the Herbert Marcuses, I hope, are few in number. Far more common are those liberals who are both smug and cynical—smug about their own moral superiority and cynical about the motives of others, especially politicians and businessmen. All too often they complacently inveigh against big corporations, the CIA, the FBI, and the Department of Defense without even attempting to consider how a liberal democracy should go about defending itself in a world that is not rich in liberal democratic regimes. All too often they protest their faith in democracy yet eagerly defend the idea of trade with China while abhorring the idea of trade with Chile or South Africa.

Let me end with an example. The wife of a democratic-socialist friend of mine was looking for a job. She knew several languages so I suggested to him that she apply to the CIA. He was aghast. His wife work for the CIA? God forbid. I asked him whether he thought the CIA should exist. He sort of nodded yes, then desperately changed the topic of conversation, since he didn't want to face up to the difficulties of his position. It was much easier for him to think of me as, well, a nice guy but strangely right-wing. Call his evasion a failure of nerve or a lack of civic virtue; it's an evasion that is commonplace among many people on the liberal-left who don't want to think about difficult questions lest they compromise their own moral self-regard. Their sense of virtue is the opposite of the civic virtue I have in mind. And their sense of virtue—both smug about themselves and cynical about others—is a luxury the country cannot afford.

W. Scott Thompson

How does a loud liberal of the sixties become a neoconservative of the seventies? Why did one student activist move incrementally rightward as his peer group moved crablike to the Left? I will account for my transition by reference to the influence, at least symbolic, of Nkrumah, Nozick, and Nitze, while confessing that mine may just be a perverse need to rub across the grain.

My genetically encoded liberalism—of civil rights and big government for everything but defense—went with me to Oxford in 1963, and from there to Africa for doctoral research on, as it happened, the efforts of a seemingly admirable syncretic Jacobin, Kwame Nkrumah, to unite his continent in a socialist paradise (with ample Soviet help, of course). He turned out to be an intellectual, ideological, and financial fraud, conclusions (published in my first book) unhelpful to my standing among the purveyors of what, in academe, then passed for thought on these matters.

Transforming those delicate systems called societies by wrenching them from their roots turned out to be more difficult than Nkrumah (or I) had envisaged. Ghana dissipated its substantial political and economic inheritance, becoming more a banana republic than the beacon Nkrumah intended. Even Lord Melbourne's admonition, "that most solutions would do more harm than good," looked better than the attempt to apply confused Marxist-Leninist formulae in alien soil. Radicalism had become a dead-end for me.

Where did a disillusioned liberal go in the ensuing years? "Conservatism stands, the Republican Party blocking the view," we might have paraphrased Spender in those days. But in the early 1970s I was moving, Nixon notwithstanding, to what seemed a new and intellectually vigorous conservatism. Nozick's *Anarchy, State, and Utopia* came at a good time for me as for many, as we sought to codify our instincts and lessons.

It was becoming clear to me as a social scientist that the state in fact seldom had any more claims on the citizen than it could enforce. Throughout my territory—the Third World—rebel cliques, corporals, and student mobs were overthrowing with abandon governments that didn't perform. These regimes' claims to legitimacy were just that, claims, of no higher standing than any others that could by whatever means be made to stick. Nozick in his own way brought all this into focus.

Our own state's claims were declining as its performance as a protection agency was flagging. Yet in my research I saw the world entering a new dark age, as Idi Amins and Pol Pots proliferated. Order, and hence liberty, were only possible for me and my kind anywhere if America remained strong. It was becoming weak, and weakness was being glorified. Kissinger's famous lament— "What in the name of God do you do with nuclear superiority?"—was the green light for the Soviets to dash for the number one spot. They knew, alas, what you did with it, having been on the underside during the preceding decades, when we enforced the peace through the superiority we then said we needed. (Today Jimmy Carter, who seeks to denuclearize the world and is proving only 50 percent successful, makes even Kissinger look tough.)

Enter Paul Nitze, strategist and *homme serieux.* He was trying to fix a SALT deal with the Russians at the time. It was eight years ago, at the scene of the talks. SALT was going to succeed, a friend asked, wasn't it? "I mean, you guys will defang the nuclear arms race and all that, won't you, in the interests of all humanity, for heaven's sake?" Nitze said he didn't know about any of that, since his instructions were in fact from the U.S. Government. "I'm simply trying to get the best deal possible for the United States."

It took a minute—or was it two years?—to digest that. What a shocking notion! The best deal possible for the U.S.? Not legislating for humanity? Of course I could not know then how much his successors would botch it, for America and thus for humanity.

So I became a defense analyst of sorts, looking at (and worrying about) what the Soviets were doing on my beat, from Luanda to Ho Chi Minh City, and debating SALT in Little Rock, Dallas, and Washington, as one of the hardy band guilty of the main charge of being on the side of the U.S.A.

Liberals can continue to feel virtuous rationalizing the problems they, through their weakness, helped to create—from the boat people in the China Sea to the Cubans in Africa. It is a self-sustaining circle. But not forever. That other liberal conceit, that in matters of war and peace all the world thinks like us, may have a frosty test in the 1980s. An all-powerful Politburo might decide that, with respect to détente, a joke is a joke but, since they are now the world's number one power (as codified in SALT II), the will of the party founders must be carried out. I reach this position from my earlier idealistic liberalism, not as a Saul on the road to Damascus, but through a lengthy and steady evolution, adjusting to what I think have been real trends in the world, not by contriving increasingly farfetched rationales to explain the realities of power in a barbaric world. We all have reason to hope that my analysis is wrong.

The Good Dog Richard Affair

(1981)

FRANK GANNON

What wouldn't you give to have been on Air Force One on that runway in Cairo when they closed the door, revved up the engines, and people suddenly noticed that Richard Nixon wasn't on board? Can't you just see it, as the seat belts were fastened and the tray tables locked securely in their upright positions and it sunk in that *he* was somewhere out there on his own doing God knows what.

Few people in our history have excited quite the same range of emotions as Richard Nixon. Nearing his seventieth birthday, and after six years of relative seclusion since he resigned the presidency, Nixon is still totem for some and taboo for others—still the man some love, the man some hate, and the man some love to hate. Why is this? Why should Nixon excite such extreme emotions? It would take many books—and Fawn Brodie's posthumously published *Richard Nixon: The Shaping of His Character* isn't one of them—to begin to answer that question.

One might begin by saying that Nixon has combined success with survivability while exhibiting apparent disregard for the approval—and even for the opinion—of the political and media establishment. From Jerry Voorhis to Archibald Cox, the list of those against whom Nixon has been pitted reads like the liberal pantheon of the last four decades. There is something almost superhuman about an individual who for thirty years could seek and survive such encounters. Indeed, at one point in Mrs. Brodie's book she questions whether his career wasn't assisted by "demonic forces."

As a Book of the Month Club selection, Mrs. Brodie's work deserves serious attention more for what it will become than for what it is. What it is is a very bad book, and had it been written by anyone else it would have sunk quietly into the fever swamps of the by now extensive eccentric Nixonphobic literature. But because of Mrs. Brodie's reputation as a best-selling biographer, and because her book purports to be so thoroughly researched and so full of undeniably memorable stories and details, it is bound to become a source for subsequent studies of Nixon.

Unfortunately, this is deadly serious stuff. This is Richard Nixon squirming spread-eagled on the merciless couch of psychobiography, written in a breathless, gossipy Hollywood style. You may laugh, you may cry, but you'll never forget the story they said couldn't be told: Nixon's mother, the castrating saint;

Nixon's father, the randy satyr who makes W. O. Gant look like Captain Kangaroo; Nixon's hatred of his dead brothers and guilt over profiting from their deaths; Nixon discovering that the reward for lying to everyone about everything is constantly higher political office; Nixon's bloodless, loveless marriage; Nixon's furtive attempts to cure his emotional wretchedness through psychotherapy; Nixon's increasing physical attraction to the swarthy Cuban, Bebe Rebozo; and finally Nixon triumphant: President of the United States, cut off by Pat, sustained by Bebe, overcoming all restraints of fratricidal guilt and glorying in the death he can rain on North Vietnam without anyone holding him personally responsible.

To advance her theories, Mrs. Brodie relies on the accumulative impact of scores of stories, anecdotes, and quoted sources. She skillfully paces her material and seeds her ground to condition the reader to accept her psychobiographical points. Her whole portrait of Nixon depends on being the sum of its parts, which is why the accuracy of each part is so important.

Richard Nixon is no stranger to psychobiography. He has been clinically diagnosed by scores of writers who have never met him. Bruce Mazlish *(In Search of Nixon)* wrote about what he saw as Nixon's self-absorption, capacity for denial, and excessive fear of being unloved. James David Barber *(The Presidential Character)* slotted Nixon as an "active-negative" type with the accompanying character traits of deviousness, secretiveness, and the tendency to fly off the handle in the face of overwhelming odds. Dr. Eli Chesen *(President Nixon's Psychiatric Profile: A Psychodynamic-Genetic Interpretation)* concluded that Nixon was a compulsive obsessive. Lloyd Etheredge ("Hard-ball Politics: A Model") described Nixon as suffering from a narcissistic personality disorder. And Dr. David Abrahamsen, in *Nixon vs. Nixon: An Emotional Tragedy,* found that the former president was a psychopathic personality, orally and anally fixated, and suffering from a severe character disorder.

There is no question that the circumstances of an individual's childhood, family, and upbringing, can and do play vital parts in adult outlook and behavior. One purpose of biography is to show how men and women develop personality and character from the raw materials of their early lives. But psychobiography takes this simple tool and beats its subjects to death with it. It is ludicrous to contend that something you did at age 5 will inexorably surface again at age 45. In the case of Mrs. Brodie's Nixon, she uses her research to build a straw man and then sets her Freudian dogs on him. Take, for example, her treatment of one of the staple biographical elements of Nixon's early life: the story of the prominent townswoman caught shoplifting in the Nixon market.

When the woman's crime was discovered, a family conference was held to decide what to do. Young Richard argued against subjecting her to the public humiliation of arrest. When Hannah Nixon confronted her indirectly, the mortified klepto offered to pay back everything she owed month by month so that the secret could be kept from her husband. Most biographers are content to accept this story as indicating Nixon's early maturity and compassion.

But Mrs. Brodie writes that "Preoccupation with shoplifting stayed with Nixon, and it infected an astonishing number of his jokes as President." As evidence she quotes speeches where Nixon told one group at a White House reception that they could have a cup of coffee but couldn't take anything else as a memento of their visit, and another group that they could take anything that wasn't nailed down as a souvenir. Just a few paragraphs later, these lame pleasantries have become "Nixon's preoccupation with thievery," and Mrs. Brodie suggests that

all through these adolescent years he never resolved the problem of what was really his in the store. . . . In any case, when Nixon finally became president, he found it impossible to distinguish between what was "mine and thine" in the presidential store. His problem with entitlement—"My father owns it, therefore I am entitled to it," translated into "I have been elected president, therefore I am entitled to it"—had never properly been resolved when he was very young.

For me, the paradigm of psychobiography's validity is the treatment of the famous "Good Dog Richard" letter which Nixon wrote on November 23, 1923, when he was almost eleven years old. It is worth reprinting in full:

My Dear Master:

The two boys that you left with me are very bad to me. Their dog, Jim, is very old and he will never talk or play with me.

One Saturday the boys went hunting. Jim and myself went with him. While going through the woods one of the boys triped and fell on me. I lost my temper and bit him. He kiked me in the side and we started on. While we were walking I saw a black round thing in a tree. I hit it with my paw. A swarm of black thing came out of it. I felt pain all over. I started to run and as both my eyes were swelled shut I fell into a pond. When I got home I was very sore. I wish you would come home right now.

Your good dog
RICHARD

Professor Barber suggests this letter was written "at a time when his mother was away with Harold"—although a simple command of the chronology indicates that his brother Harold's illness did not appear until years later. He continues:

The fantasy is full of symbols. Are the boys his brothers, kicking and hurting him? Is the old and neglectful dog Jim his father, who fails to protect him? . . . And what should be made of the "black round thing" which, when touched, releases dreadful stingers?

Dr. Abrahamsen exhibits no such hesitancy about interpreting these symbols. He states that the letter is highly revealing from a psychoanalytic point of view, because biting

is one of the most primitive responses we have. It is an animal reaction and belongs to the earliest stages of human development. . . . That Richard wrote that he bit one of the boys at an age when a child would normally have passed through this stage long before, reinforces our impression that the oral hostile aggression Richard harbored as an infant had been prolonged beyond the norm and had become fixated. The degree to which he regressed into a fantasy is abnormal. We can surmise therefore that the details were not incidental: they reflect an instinctive response which stayed with him long after he had learned that biting was not socially acceptable. Expressions of this kind of response appear in his adult behavior. In his political life, Nixon was often vindictive and revengeful. He was sarcastic, cutting, and caustic.

Mrs. Brodie, in turn, speculates that this plaintive letter was written to Hannah Nixon during one of the times when she supposedly returned to her family's home in order to escape the drudgery of life with her husband and sons. She states that "If nothing else, the letter demonstrates how early he had begun to exaggerate the wrongs inflicted on him by others—a compulsion that affected his whole life."

The actual facts surrounding the "Good Dog Richard" letter, however, are amusingly straightforward. Hannah Nixon kept two early examples of her second son's precocious writing ability. One was a letter, dated January 24, 1924, requesting a job as a delivery boy with the *Los Angeles Times*. The other was the "Good Dog" letter—a grade school composition exercise in which the students were told to pretend they were dogs whose masters were away from home, and to write him asking him to come back.

In putting her own particular spin on Nixon's psychobiography, Mrs. Brodie sees it as containing five elements: a history of lying from his earliest youth; the impact of death in advancing his career; a perverse delight in giving and taking physical and mental punishment; a failure to love; and the dark guilt of fratricide. Two examples will serve to illustrate her approach.

To begin with, Mrs. Brodie claims that Richard Nixon grew up in an atmosphere in which his father punished him physically and his mother punished him both mentally and emotionally. The resulting youngster adapted but was forever warped—cursed to a cold, secret, calculating adult life of taking punishment while awaiting the chance to give it back. "That Nixon was ambivalent about the punishment he received as a child is suggested by a comment he once made to Stewart Alsop. Discussing motivation in politics, he said, 'It's always good to have the whip on your back.'"

If this seems indirect, Mrs. Brodie has harder evidence. She points out that in the "Good Dog Richard" letter, Nixon complains about being kicked; in Peru in 1958 when Nixon was spat upon by a hostile demonstrator, he kicked him in the shin; after the 1962 gubernatorial defeat in California, he told reporters, "You won't have Nixon to kick around anymore"; in preparation for his 1969 inaugural address Nixon read TR's, Wilson's, FDR's, and JFK's inaugurals and told his speechwriter that the theme of each "was to kick hell out of someone else and tell the American people they're great"; Nixon asked John Dean, "Have you kicked a few butts around?"; and of his opponents in 1972 he said, "They got the hell kicked out of them in the election."

Bringing this significant litany together for the first time, Mrs. Brodie then raises the obvious question:

Did Frank Nixon kick his sons? The theme of kicking and of being kicked, appears early in Nixon's life, and surfaces repeatedly. . . . Whether Frank Nixon kicked his son or not is not as certain as that Nixon felt himself to be kicked around by his father. That the idea of kicking came easily to Frank Nixon his son made clear in *Six Crises.* After listening to his "Checkers" speech, Nixon wrote that Frank Nixon had observed, "It looks to me as if the Democrats have given themselves a good kick in the seat of the pants . . ."

The thread of fratricide, as unraveled by Mrs. Brodie, is an even more fascinating example of her method. And unlike some of Nixon's other hangups, this one is his very own:

But blame for the more sinister theme of fratricide, running like a lethal shadow through Nixon's life, should not rest with his parents. It was a development unique to him, which even now leaves me baffled and anguished. It surfaces too often to be accidental. Others have felt it. Theodore White, friendly to Nixon in 1972, castigated the liberal press for treating Nixon "as if the brand of Cain were on him."

Here, as Mrs. Brodie marches her evidence into serried ranks, the deadly pattern emerges. Nixon, she charges, profited from the deaths of his brothers Arthur and Harold both emotionally (advancing him in the affections of his parents) and financially (there would now be more money to spend on him and his education). Then, Nixon's maiden speech in Congress was "to encourage the destruction" of the Communist Eisler brothers. His "second act" in Congress (never mind Mrs. Brodie's chronology here, she's on a roll) was to attack Alger Hiss "and also Hiss's brother Donald, who bore the name of Nixon's own brother." Nixon, she says, started and encouraged the CIA movement to destroy Fidel Castro and his brother Raul as well. Then there were the assassinations of John and Robert Kennedy and Edward Kennedy's removal from the 1972 political scene by the events at Chappaquiddick. For good measure Mrs. Brodie throws in Martin Luther King, Jr., George Wallace, the Diem brothers, and the suicides of two of Nixon's early biographers which, she says, "must be added to the list of untimely deaths that touched Nixon's life."

Having thus proved beyond any shadow of doubt that the deaths of brothers, including his own, had played a pivotal role in his life and in his career, Mrs. Brodie admits, "What one does not know is whether or not Nixon suffered from an anxiety that the fate helping him was demonic and not divine." Fortunately, within just a few pages, she is able to answer even this tough question. Writing about the Christmas bombing of North Vietnam in 1972, she states: "Again, death was his ally, this time still more massive killing and mutilation. That he had come to delight in the slaughter and had no quarrel with God concerning it was clear enough . . ."

As Mrs. Brodie describes her research for this book, it sounds impressive. She lists the 150 individuals she interviewed; her bibliography fills six pages of minuscule type; her footnotes require 35 pages of closely printed double columns. But closer examination reveals that she has merely taken a long walk on the wilder side of the anti-Nixon literature. Time and again, her most telling points turn out to come from the same few books that are either overtly unfriendly (e.g., William Costello's seminal *The Facts About Nixon*) or marginally eccentric (e.g., Traphes Bryant's *Dog Days at the White House;* Bryant was keeper of the Executive Mansion's kennels and Mrs. Brodie quotes his professional judgment that Mrs. Nixon hugged the Irish Setter King Timahoe because she was starved for affection from her husband).

As for her use of new and otherwise uncorroborated materials about so chronicled and controversial a figure, only a naive or disingenuous historian could accept them so uncritically. From considerable exposure to the extant Nixonalia, I can assert that any new Nixon story must be subjected to the most rigorous scrutiny, particularly anything post-Watergate. Having read extensively in both pre- and post-Watergate oral history materials, I have observed that those who before Watergate remembered personally seeing Nixon walking on water afterwards had vivid and total recall of the times they saw him pulling the wings off flies. (In fact, it was decided that oral history material was so unreliable that, unless it could be independently corroborated, it would not be used in the Nixon memoirs.)

Mrs. Brodie seems not quite so discriminating, and some of the most important new stories in her book do not stand up to factual scrutiny. The story of Vita Remley, for example, is a dramatic addition to the Nixon canon, providing in microcosm the petty vindictiveness, pent-up rage, and violent emotional instability Mrs. Brodie sees in her subject.

The story is as follows: Vita Remley worked in the Los Angeles County Assessor's office. She was active in Democratic politics, and had been involved in the Nixon-Voorhis campaign in 1946. In 1952 she received a request for a veteran's property exemption from a Richard and Pat Nixon. At that time a married veteran owning less than $10,000 worth of property could qualify for a $50 reduction in his California taxes. Since Mrs. Remley knew from the papers that Nixon had just purchased a large new home in Washington, she knew he didn't qualify and therefore rejected his application. Drew Pearson somehow "indirectly" learned of this incident and ran it in his column.

Several weeks later, Nixon was giving a speech at the Long Beach Civic Auditorium and Mrs. Remley went to hear him. Mrs. Brodie dramatically relates what happened next:

Arriving late, she listened from near the open door. As he emerged he recognized her. In a sudden fit of rage he walked over and slapped her. His friends, horrified, hustled him away in the dark. There were no cameras or newsmen to catch the happening, and Mrs. Remley, fearful of losing her job, told only a few friends.

Mrs. Brodie hustles on to other matters, but the reader might want to linger over some of the more palpable improbabilities of this story. First, it depends on the coincidental geography that places Mrs. Remley and Nixon "near the open door" as he and his friends walk out. But the Long Beach Auditorium was a large public hall which held 2,000 people and had several entrances. Of course, it is possible that Nixon strode directly from the podium and through the crowd to where Mrs. Remley was standing. It's also possible that when he reached her he wasn't engulfed by the usual entourage of hosts, aides, supporters, and reporters which one would expect to surround the Vice President of the United States at a major appearance in his home state.

So there they are: face to face. Nixon instantly recognizes Mrs. Remley from the newspaper photos several weeks back and pastes her in the jaw. No one who saw it happen, and not one of the friends to whom the unaccountably frightened Mrs. Remley confided (after all, the damage had already been done by Pearson's column and the other publicity surrounding the exemption request), ever breaks his silence. Fortunately, Mrs. Remley felt safe enough 28 years later to give this episode to history by relating it to Mrs. Brodie. As the sole footnote for this remarkable story attests: "Vita Remley to FB, May 19, 1980."

It's a pity Mrs. Brodie didn't bother to complete the Vita Remley story. For one thing, the Remley refusal of Nixon's niggardly and patently unqualified request for a veteran's exemption was printed in Pearson's national column five days before the 1952 presidential election. Mrs. Brodie mentions neither this, nor the fact that three weeks after the election Pearson printed a retraction: The Richard and Pat Nixon who had filed the request just happened to have the same names as the vice president and his wife.

Apart from being uncritical of her sources, Mrs. Brodie is sometimes just wrong about them. She quotes "Kandy Stroud, on Pat Nixon's staff" as saying, "She gave so much and got so little of what was really meaningful to a woman. . . . Sometimes he was so brutally indifferent I wept for her." Coming from a member of Mrs. Nixon's staff this is powerful stuff. The problem here is that Kandy Stroud was the White House correspondent for *Women's Wear Daily.*

Trying to establish the point of Nixon's indifference to his wife, Mrs. Brodie cites the president's Daily Diary:

an astonishing record that chronicled what he did every moment of his life save for his trips to the bathroom. . . . At San Clemente, on July 6, 1972, for example, this president who had written with such emotion on the right to privacy seems not to have minded someone noting in a file that from 2:50 P.M. to 2:51 P.M. he spoke to his wife, that at 4:48 P.M. he met her at the pool area, that at 5:02 P.M. he returned to the compound residence. "Through the days and nights of his life," Jimmy Breslin noted, "his diaries showed he spent a half-hour, at the most up to an hour, a day with his wife."

If Mrs. Brodie had mastered her sources she would have known that the Daily Diary was a relatively selective document compiled by White House secretaries, telephone operators, and Secret Service agents. That it was called a "diary" undoubtedly leads to some confusion—not least because Nixon himself did keep a separate, tape-recorded personal diary (not to be confused with the White House tapes!) during the almost 19 months of his second term in office. The Daily Diary, however, was just a barebones outline of Nixon's schedule, phone calls, and whereabouts when he was anywhere outside the family quarters or residence area. Thus, the one minute conversation would have been a phone call logged by an operator. The fifteen minutes in the pool area would have been the daily afternoon swim the Nixons always took together in San Clemente. The pool was next to the residence, and the "return" there meant that the Nixons were now in their house for the evening and therefore off the logs.

In Mrs. Brodie's discussion of the 18 ½-minute gap, she states as absolute fact that

Eighteen and one half minutes of a crucial tape he destroyed totally. Prosecutor Leon Jaworski was certain of this, but Nixon, in his memoirs, continued to deny it, and said that the erasing might have been done accidentally by his lawyer. Fred Buzhardt by now was dead and unable to defend himself.

In fact, Fred Buzhardt died of a heart attack on December 16, 1978, eight months *after* the Nixon book was published. Besides, Mrs. Brodie makes it sound as if Nixon blamed Buzhardt for the erasure, but here is what Nixon actually wrote in his memoirs:

Haig told me that Garment and Buzhardt were completely panicked by the discovery of the 18 ½-minute gap. They suspected everyone, including Rose, Steve Bull, and me. Suspicion had now invaded the White House. I even wondered if Buzhardt himself could have accidentally erased the portion beyond the five-minute gap Rose thought she might have caused.

There is not time nor space enough to list all the errors and evasions in Mrs. Brodie's book. For each period of Nixon's life she dredges up every old canard and retells it in its most damning form as if it were gospel truth. Thus her version of the debate over the PAC endorsement in the 1946 campaign has Nixon snookering poor "nonpunishing and caring" Jerry Voorhis by entrapping him in a classic ploy of guilt by association. In fact, one of the revelations of the Nixon memoirs was the discovery of a newspaper report that Voorhis had actually been interviewed for that specific purpose by the organization whose endorsement he claimed was unsought and came as a complete surprise to him. Although Mrs. Brodie quotes from the Nixon memoirs regarding this campaign, she neglects to mention this new and devastatingly inconvenient fact.

Again, in the case of the 1952 Fund crisis, Mrs. Brodie states that Nixon lied in the Checkers speech when he said the Fund was not kept secret. But she does not explain how you keep secret a fund raised entirely from several thousand letters sent through the mails to past contributors.

Then, discussing the 1960 election, Mrs. Brodie asserts without proof that Nixon purposely arranged to go to Moscow in 1959 in order to bait Khrushchev and so demonstrate his ability to stand up to Communist leaders. And in a ridiculous version of the power relationships in the Eisenhower White House, she has Nixon virtually initiating and masterminding the plot to overthrow Castro as a means to assure his own election as president, all this despite contemporary documentary evidence that Nixon was undecided about Castro's intentions.

Because Mrs. Brodie makes so much of the friendship between Nixon and Bebe Rebozo, her errors in this regard are particularly noteworthy. For example, she writes that "Rebozo accompanied Nixon to the hospital when he had viral pneumonia in July 1973; a press photograph shows him saying to White House physician Dr. Tkach, 'Take good care of him.'" Given the relationship Mrs. Brodie implies existed between the two men, the tenderness conveyed here would seem to support her intimation. The footnote cites a page in *The Breaking of a President,* a rather bizarre compilation of Watergate material by Marvin

Miller, a California Nixon-phobe, published in 1975. The page does indeed show a photograph of Rebozo and Dr. Tkach, but the quotation "Take good care of him" is the caption Mr. Miller wrote for the photo in his book.

Mrs. Brodie introduces Rebozo as "a handsome, unmarried Florida native of Cuban descent who had a reputation for discretion," and notes that "Rebozo had been a beautiful youth, called 'the best looking boy' in his high school yearbook." She writes, without citation, that "one woman in the White House said he had 'the most beautiful eyes in Washington.' " And she cites no less an authority than Dan Rather as saying that Rebozo was "one of the most sensual men he had ever seen."

In order to explain away the fact that Rebozo was widely known as a man-about-town and was frequently seen in the company of attractive women, she turns to "the sensitive Jules Witcover," who saw this socializing "as a facade, and thought of Rebozo as being 'like Nixon, a loner and introvert.' " Finally, Mrs. Brodie produces Bob Greene of *Newsday* who said, "My own particular thought was that he was one of those guys who has an extremely low sex drive. He had a tendency to keep the company of whisky-drinking, fishing, rather masculine-type men, with the exception of Nixon."

Tying things together, Mrs. Brodie writes that after the resignation, "Rebozo's role in the complexities of the Nixon marriage for the first time became a matter of public comment." She observes that "Much about this friendship remains obscure but in one respect it was like a good marriage . . ." And she adds that "Nixon seems to have been willing to risk the kind of gossip that frequently accompanies close friendship with a perennial bachelor, this despite his known public aversion to homosexuals . . ." (Mrs. Brodie has already discussed Rebozo's marriage and remarriage, but that apparently doesn't affect perennial bachelorhood in her reckoning.) Lest any stone of innuendo be left unturned, Mrs. Brodie informs us that Rebozo stayed aloof from the so-called Palace Guard "led by Haldeman and Ehrlichman, who cracked the whip for the clean-cut handsome young staffers . . ."

It sure seems as if Mrs. Brodie is trying to tell us something here. Fortunately, her innate delicacy prevents her from coming right out with it, so it is up to the reader to fill in the blanks.

Mrs. Brodie is equally insinuative and misleading in her treatment of the relationship between Nixon and Dr. Arnold Hutschnecker. Dr. Hutschnecker was a Park Avenue internist who wrote a book called *The Will to Live,* which enjoyed considerable success in the early 1950s. It was of the self-help genre: Work-related stress was the cause of many psychosomatic ailments, and if people would tap into the vital life forces within them they would be happier and healthier.

Nixon was given a copy of the book by California Senator Sheridan Downey, the Democratic incumbent who endorsed Republican Nixon over fellow Democrat Helen Gahagan Douglas in 1950. Nixon liked the book, and when he was in New York he went to Dr. Hutschnecker for a checkup.

It is difficult for Mrs. Brodie to accept the fact that Dr. Hutschnecker was not a psychiatrist. When first we meet him, he is introduced correctly as "an internist with a special interest in psychosomatic illness, who treated Nixon for 'stress' when he was vice president . . ." Later, however, we are told that Dr. Hutschnecker was "called—not altogether incorrectly—'the President's shrink.'" Then, on page 333, Mrs. Brodie herself supplies the psychoanalytical diagnosis that Dr. Hutschnecker so unobligingly failed to provide: "We may assume that the doctor noted Nixon's 'neurotic hangups,' but these he cannot discuss." And in words that seem remarkably unenlightened coming from a psychobiographer, Mrs. Brodie declares that "No one goes to a doctor who specializes in emotional problems unless he is driven by a special wretchedness."

Finally, on page 503, we hit paydirt: Mrs. Brodie at last wrestles Nixon to the couch. She recounts a dream that Nixon mentioned in his personal tape-recorded diary and adds, "Sharing a dream is dangerous, as Nixon must certainly have recognized in therapy." *Therapy?*

Lest I leave the wrong impression, I want to assure potential readers that this is not a book without heroes and heroines. Fortunately the world compensates for people like the Nixons with people like the Kennedys. Mrs. Brodie is positively rhapsodic when she describes JFK as

a man of formidable natural gifts, who brought intellectuals swarming into his camp as had Franklin Roosevelt, and who charmed even the most cynical of reporters. Lean, athletic, handsome, a shock of boyish hair falling over his forehead, his cool gray eyes crinkling at the corners when he grinned, he caused palpable excitement among the women in every gathering, and his appearance on motorcades sent girls into paroxysms of shrieking and jumping.

And if she leaves you depressed reading about how banal poor Pat Nixon is and how badly she is ignored by her husband, Mrs. Brodie compensates with this portrait of Jackie Kennedy:

Her youth, offbeat piquancy, immense haunting eyes, and atypical beauty made her overnight an international sensation. Thanks to her maiden name, Bouvier, the French counted her peculiarly their own.

Richard Nixon: The Shaping of His Character is a sadly unbalanced book. Mrs. Brodie so actively despises her subject that she has none of the perspective good biography requires. She does not credit Richard Nixon, child, youth, or man, with one worthy achievement, one decent intention, one unselfish action, one normal motivation, one human instinct. It is a very bad book: the bitter legacy of a determined and passionate woman.

And what good has it done? Even as Mrs. Brodie's book begins inching toward the remainder stores, Richard Nixon seems once again on the verge of a fiery re-entry into the political atmosphere. His inclusion in the official delegation to President Sadat's funeral led the *Washington Post* to run a front-page story headlined "Nixon's Redemption—Mission in Middle East Could Be His Way Back From Elba." Mary McGrory, her worst fears confirmed, wrote that Nixon used the funeral as his "round-trip ticket to respectability" and the way to end "the hated obscurity of his exile in New Jersey." Joseph Kraft wrote that "the parish smirked his way back into the circle of grace."

Until Nixon's more passionate critics exorcise their own ghosts from the

35 years of bitter controversy that have surrounded him and meet him on the solid ground of historical fact, they will continue to flail at a bogey at least partly of their own imaginations, convinced that he is about to stage another successful comeback and at last achieve his goal of suppressing the Constitution.

Atlantic High
by William F. Buckley, Jr.

(1983)

LUIGI BARZINI

To dedicate one thick book to one Atlantic crossing on a sailboat with guests and crew is, for many reasons, a foolhardy enterprise. To dedicate two books to two similar crossings, as William F. Buckley, Jr. has done *(Airborne* and now *Atlantic High),* is downright temerarious. This is because there is practically nothing much to write about a long and well-organized sea voyage on a capacious yacht. That Buckley has managed to do it and to do it very well deserves high praise indeed.

There are many reasons why such literary efforts are forbidding. The first is the lack of suspense. Evidently the author has survived the ordeal, otherwise he wouldn't have been able to write what we read. You have the same reassuring sensation as when, watching an adventure film, you see the most expensive star risk his life in the first reel. You know nothing can happen to him that early. The second difficulty is that such crossings are boring for everybody except fanatic lovers of sailing cruises, like Buckley and me. Such voyages are, for most people, like war, long stretches of boredom interrupted by short intervals of drama and nail-biting worry, if not outright danger.

The conversation on good days is usually centered on what might be eaten at lunch or dinner and with what wine. Everybody who is not in charge lolls about and reads cheap thrillers. The fanatics milk the radio all day for weather reports, or pinpoint the boat's position on the chart with the help of all the necessary instruments, traditional or electronic. The incidents that can be written up on the logbook and recalled in tranquillity in later months are usually small matters, difficult to explain to the uninitiated.

There are seldom typhoons to describe. With a good knowledge of the meteorological conditions ahead they can usually be avoided. Nor are there long doldrums to survive (during which the sailors of old built miniature clippers inside bottles or braided lines into small bathroom mats). The engine takes care of the windless days.

There is also a limit to possible descriptions of the open sea. Buckley himself admits that it is almost everywhere the same. He writes: "A scene of a sailboat between the Azores and Gibraltar would, *coeteris paribus,* be identical with a scene of a sailboat in Block Island Sound or between Tasmania and New Zealand."

453

The principal difficulty for a writer is the practical impossibility to communicate by cold words on paper the ineffable beatitude sailing imparts to the aficionado. There is, for instance, the ecstatic moment when a good breeze rises. You recognize it from far away from the different color of the sea. It hits the sails and fills them. The boat lists against the water and gradually takes on speed. The engine is then turned off. Sudden deafening silence envelops the boat, broken only by the sound of water rushing by, what the French onomatopoetically call *clapotis.*

Or there is the sudden storm. You see it coming (a dark wall of clouds on the horizon). Everybody, wearing yellow slickers, comes on deck to tie reefs and shorten the mainsail. Hatches are tightly shut. You hold the wheel bravely, waiting for the impact. If the boat is your own (which was not the case of the *Sealestial,* on which Buckley made his second crossing) and not very new, you pass in mental review all the vital parts which you had carefully checked or replaced during the winter, to reassure yourself.

There are few of them, the stays that really absorb the force of the wind, the spots where the stays are attached to the body of the boat, the metal plate under the floors on which the lead keel is secured with nuts and bolts. To sail away across the Ocean on somebody else's boat, owned furthermore by a man one does not know at all well and who lives far from the sea (in Detroit, as was the case of the owner of the *Sealestial*), on a boat one has not examined inside and out in a boatyard, is a very courageous enterprise, almost a gamble.

It is also practically impossible to convey the immense pleasure of such long distance voyages or cruises to a layman. If you try, he looks at you as if you were mad. For it consists of this: the passionate anxiety to reach port when one is out at sea and the passionate anxiety to go out to sea when one is in port. There are days and days when one endures the lack of many elementary comforts. There is little fresh water. The bunks are narrow and hard, the intimacy with other people, their habits and mannerisms increasingly irritating, the menus forcedly monotonous (although Buckley is believed to manage gastronomic feats and a choice of the world's best wines on his voyages).

Then you reach a port. The boat is still. No danger is lurking. You go to a luxury hotel, to bask in the momentary solitude, enjoy a hot bath, a few wonderful meals with fresh vegetables and fruit, a wide and comfortable bed. Your companions become once more *simpatici.* Your clothes and the boat's sheets, towels, tablecloths, and napkins are laundered. Tanks are filled with fresh water and fuel. Little repairs are done. The stores of food and wine are replenished.

But, after a few days, you become impatient, and want to get on with the job, get out of the pestiferous little tourist town, and sail away toward one's goal. You long to be once again surrounded by water, facing the incertitude of every hour. Oh, the precious moment when, in the darkness of the night, you finally sight a distant lighthouse and, checking in the books, find it is the proper one, the one you were aiming at and not another, and that you have not made a mistake charting the course and currents have not made your boat drift too far.

Buckley has managed to convey the charm of the crossing in *Atlantic High* so effectively that landlubbers might be enticed to try the experience. He went from St. Thomas in the Virgin Islands via Bermuda and the Azores to Marbella in southern Spain, in June 1980 on a 71-foot ketch. He had gathered a group of companions, young and middle-aged, all of them agreeable. He asked each one to keep a diary and the excerpts from each, which he selected and incorporated in his personal narrative, make enticing reading. He also gives brief character sketches of each friend.

Nothing much happened during the voyage, thank God, and Buckley was not obliged to force on the reader a series of incomprehensible mishaps explained in sailor's jargon. The most adventurous moments were caused by his irrepressible progressivism, his American trust in improved gadgets that went often out of whack and seldom delivered what the ads and instruction books promised. But he is enough of an old-fashioned sailor to make do, in a pinch, very well if reluctantly, with ancient and well-tried instruments, those most non-Americans still use.

The technical moments of difficulty do not take up many pages. The book is filled with witticisms, bits of fascinating conversation, reflections, memories of other voyages, anecdotes, and souvenirs of life on land. Since Buckley has had a rich and many faceted life, his store of memories and experiences is vast, the number of interesting friends extensive, his expertise in many fields enviable and unique (music, politics, painting, skiing, Catholic theology, wines, food, debating techniques), the result is a book that anyone can read from cover to cover with pleasure.

Eric Hoffer
in San Francisco

(1983)

TOM BETHELL

I met Eric Hoffer in the lobby of the Raphael Hotel in October, 1980, just three weeks before President Reagan's election. He was sitting quietly in a corner armchair, looking out of place in his laborer's clothes. A flat workingman's cap was perched on his head. In his knobbly hands he clasped a knobbly walking stick. Earlier we had corresponded. I had been flattered to receive his letters, written in his artless, looping hand. "Come any time," he had written. "We shall eat, drink and talk."

We walked down the street to a coffee shop at the corner of Mason and Geary. He didn't exactly tap the ground with his stick but it was obvious that he saw only dimly. He spoke in a strong Bavarian accent. "It grows thicker as I grow older," he said. A couple walking by recognized him and stopped to acknowledge him and exchange a few words. Hoffer was obviously pleased to be recognized and to find that he still had some fans. Later on he told me how much as a writer he had wanted and needed to be praised.

I was unprepared for the contrast between his literary and his personal style. "I am a vehement person, a passionate person," he said. "But when I write, I sublimate. It's not natural for a passionate person like myself to write the way I write. I rewrite a hundred times, sometimes, so that it is moderate, controlled, sober. I need time to revise, time to change."

In his first book Eric Hoffer had written about "the true believer." Now I could see that he was himself part true believer, but that he had contrived a judicious disguise for himself in his books. He was in truth a "fanatic," he told me as we walked along. And his great cause was one rarely articulated by intellectuals in America: America itself.

"Do you know," he told me as we sat down, "I was never accepted by the San Francisco literary establishment. It was because I have praised America extravagantly." Herb Caen, the gossip columnist of the San Francisco *Chronicle*, particularly seemed to despise him, said Hoffer. He said of Caen that he had talent but that he had frittered it away. It seemed not to bother Hoffer that he had failed to win the affection of the local literati. On this he was detached, savoring the irony. We ordered coffee. As we waited he took issue with something I had written to the effect that America might now be in decline. He thought this was premature.

"America is a fabulous country," he said loudly. Heads at the lunch counter began to crane around in our direction. "It's not so conspicuous because the jetsam and the dirt are all on the surface. I remember when I first started to think about writing a book. I was going to go through my life and write down all the kindnesses done, right from the beginning. It is a really fabulous country. Consider the lengths people will go to to come here. And who built this country? Really nobodies. Nobodies. Tramps."

I said that I worried that an alliance of intellectuals had finally learned how to manipulate government to achieve the power they craved. They were slowly getting the grip that had so long eluded them.

"Well," he replied. "We'll see what Reagan does." He spoke highly of Reagan, saying that he had always been underestimated, just like America itself. "It is easy to underestimate America," he said. "We underestimate it, our friends underestimate it, our enemies thank God underestimate it. But somehow there is a tremendous vigor in this country. It is true that our intellectuals are becoming much more influential. They are shaping public opinion and so on. But that won't last. There will be a reaction against it. For years I wondered how and when the silent majority is going to wake up. And I didn't take the factor of religion into account. That's a beautiful situation right now. [Hoffer was referring here to the rise of the Moral Majority.] You see, there used to be a time when you had great leaders everywhere: here was de Gaulle, here was Churchill, here was Adenauer. Then all of a sudden there wasn't a great man on this planet. How come? What happened?"

He took out a pack of cigarettes and lit up, saying that he wasn't supposed to smoke but that he would anyway. "You see," he said, "you are going to have great leaders if it is possible to have power. But when the sources of power are so inconspicuous and so hard to manipulate, then leaders do not appear. Right now religion is the only source of power that's there. You have Pope John Paul, you have the Ayatollah Khomeini, you have them popping all over. And Reagan too is now tapping a religious strain."

He told me that he was working on a book he would call *Conversations With Quotations.* "If you ever come to my room you'll see. I have just an enormous number of cards. All my life I used to write down anything that I thought I wanted to remember. So I've got a thousand or maybe two thousand quotations. And every time, after that quotation, I am going to talk to that man."

It was soon time for Eric's long-time friend Lili Osborne to pick us up in her car. We would be going to a restaurant opposite the apartment building where he lived, overlooking the San Francisco docks. Lili turned out to be a motherly woman of Italian background. She taught school in Redwood City and had known Eric for about thirty years. Eric sat beside her, and as we drove along toward Market Street he pointed out a Unitarian Church as though it were a regular landmark on Eric Hoffer's Guided Tour of San Francisco. "That's where all the radicals go who have lost faith in radicalism," he said. Then for some reason the Pope once again crossed his mind. If he ever had a chance to meet the Pope he would tell him: "Go slow! The church has lasted so long. It has discovered the secret of survival."

As we drove toward the waterfront he said: "We forgot all about the human condition. We forgot what evil is. With Burke there is still a whiff of evil, in *Reflections on the French Revolution.* But with Freud, all we need is a little screwing. The man was a pervert I tell you! He admitted that he brainwashed little girls into saying that they wanted to play with him. He wants to infect us with his own sickness and then offer psychoanalysis as a cure."

When we entered the restaurant Hoffer put on a great display of bonhomie: the gourmand come to his feast. "Bon appetit!" But I wondered if it wasn't put on for show. Normally, surely, he didn't bother too much about material comforts. He was greatly amused because the restaurant, a fashionable one, was externally "French" but actually owned and run by Chinese—a people he much admired and wished would come to America in greater numbers.

The conversation soon turned to a recent CBS documentary about the rising political power of homosexuals in San Francisco. The producer, George Crile, had interviewed Hoffer for the program but had not used the footage, much to the relief of Lili, who was worried about the hostility his remarks surely would have evoked. What concerned Hoffer (as he apparently had said on camera) was the increasing shamelessness and militancy of the homosexuals.

"There cannot be civilized living without shame," he said, as slim waiters flitted by. "Shame means the acceptance of rules that cannot be enforced by coercion. If you have a shameless society you haven't got a society at all. In Russia for instance you accuse your father, your mother. Everybody accuses his friend. There is no shame, and no society. All you've got is a comglomerate of people held together by coercion. Hesiod has a beautiful saying: When the Goddess of Shame will depart, our society will fall apart. This is what bothered me about homosexuality: they were not ashamed to admit it. And they want to convert people to their oun thinking." (He pronounced "own" to rhyme with "noun.")

"Something different has happened in . . ." Lili began.

"All of a sudden our values are breaking down," Hoffer said. "Our norms are breaking down, and the rats are coming up from everywhere. They are a symptom of disintegration and decadence. I don't know if we can reverse it. The question always comes now, can we reverse things? It's an uphill battle. Of course, they always fall back on the Greeks. But the Greeks were a different kind of homosexual. There is a tremendous violence going hand in hand with the homosexuality in San Francisco. There is violence in the act there. They are hurting each other . . ."

The waiter at Hoffer's elbow was ready with his menu recital. "As an entree tonight I have angler . . ."

"Nothing is too good for us, remember that," said Hoffer. "I am floating through the air with the greatest of ease. It is good to be alive. Count your blessings." The last phrase was a favorite of his. He repeated it several times in my presence.

Eric Hoffer was born in the Bronx, supposedly in July, 1902. But he may really have been born a year or two earlier. There are hints in his writings and interviews that he may have changed his age, just as it is possible that some of the events of his early life, told and retold to interviewers, were imagined. The title of his posthumous memoir, *Truth Imagined,* suggests this. Lili Osborne also believes that Eric may have been born in Europe as they were never able to locate his birth certificate.

Eric told me that his father was a "small town atheist from Alsace." His parents came to America around 1900. "My father was a self-educated cabinet-maker," Hoffer wrote in *Truth Imagined.* "He had nearly a hundred books, in English and German, on philosophy, mathematics, botany, chemistry, music and travel. I spent passionate hours sorting the books according to size, thickness and the color of their covers. I also learned to distinguish between English and German books. Eventually I learned to sort according to contents. I might say, therefore, that I had learned to read both English and German before I was five."

When he was five (according to the oft-told story) his mother fell down a flight of stairs while carrying him. Two years later she died and he went blind. He recalled his father referring to him as the "blind idiot" or the "idiot child." He attended no school, recovered his sight when he was 15, and then began to read all he could lay his hands on (beginning with Dostoevsky's *The Idiot,* which seemed as though it might have been written with him in mind). In 1920 his father died, whereupon Hoffer set off for California. He proceeded to go through life "like a tourist," he said, because he had been told that, like his father, he would not live to be 50. He stayed in California for the rest of his life, very rarely leaving the state. A few uncomfortable minutes in a Mexican border town was his only trip outside the United States.

While doing part-time work as an agricultural worker and gold prospector in California, Hoffer discovered Montaigne's *Essays* in a public library. The thickness of the volume reassured him; it would last him through the season. He learned whole passages by heart and would recite them to his fellow hoboes in the San Joaquin Valley. "And then, every time something came up, like money or women, they would say, 'What does Montaigne say?' And I would quote him. There must be hundreds of hoboes going up and down San Joaquin Valley quoting Montaigne."

Hoffer read the Bible for the first time when he was 27, and this had an even greater influence on him than Montaigne. The Jewish nation and its role in history preoccupied him for the rest of his life, even though he wrote about the subject hardly at all. God, Hoffer said, was simply an invention of the Jews. But at table he usually asked someone to say grace. When the theory of evolution came up for discussion Hoffer said that he didn't believe it at all. "It is easier to believe in God," he said.

With the outbreak of World War II Hoffer found steady employment with the Longshoreman's Union in San Francisco, headed by Harry Bridges. Hoffer began to fill small notebooks, slowly piecing together *The True Believer.* He sent his only copy of the manuscript, in long-hand, to Harper & Row, receiving a telegram of acceptance several months later. When I asked him if he wasn't afraid that the manuscript might have been lost he said no—by then he knew it by heart. The book was published in 1951.

It was a *tour de force,* favorably reviewed by Bertrand Russell. Hoffer later became immensely antagonistic toward intellectuals, but in most respects he was one himself. Arthur Schlesinger Jr., praised *The True Believer,* and Richard

Rovere said in *The New Yorker* that it was the work of a "born generalizer." In an approximate one-sentence synopsis of *The True Believer* Hoffer wrote: "Faith in a holy cause is to a considerable extent a substitute for the lost faith in ourselves."

A later work, *Before The Sabbath* (1978), first attracted me to Hoffer. Here current events provided the stimulus for his thoughts about life and history. It is in the movement from the particular to the general that we find Hoffer at his best. (A possible criticism of *The True Believer* is that it is too inexorably general and too infrequently particular.) In *Before The Sabbath* he returned again and again to the anti-Americanism of the intelligentsia, attributing it to "leprous vanity . . . pretentious nonetities wanting to avenge themselves for being ignored." I wanted to meet him when I read that and so I wrote to him, receiving his reply within a week: "Come any time . . ."

The day after we had dinner he invited me to his apartment. He lived alone in a tenth-floor efficiency in a building with a doorman. His apartment overlooked the waterfront and San Francisco Bay. It was, as one might have guessed, spartan but sufficient for his needs: a bunk bed, a plain table, two chairs, a small bookcase containing only a few favorites: Dostoyevsky, Montaigne, his own books (with some foreign translations of *The True Believer*). He kept up with the *New York Times,* the *Jerusalem Post* (weekly edition), *Commentary, The Economist* and several other publications, but recently he had undergone an eye operation and he was beginning to find reading difficult. The view from his balcony brought back memories for Eric: he said he could smell his own sweat. At night, he said, he would sometimes dream he was back working on the docks, and then his muscles would ache when he woke up. That's why longshoremen are paid pensions, he said.

But he was not in a reminiscing mood today. He was holding one of his index cards, and he was trying to fathom, as though for the hundredth time, the quotation written on it.

America is the most aggressive power in the world, the greatest threat to peace, to national self-determination, and to international cooperation. What America needs is not dissent but denazification.   —Noam Chomsky

"Now," he said. "What do you do? This was during the heat of the Vietnam thing, I suppose. What do you do? You try to understand why they say these things. What do you think, Tom? You know them better than I do. You have been rubbing your brain against them. What is it that makes a man who is highly intelligent say such a thing? They call him a metaphysical grammarian. He was invited by Oxford to lecture. He couldn't be just a fraud. He's a very successful, prospering intellectual. What I know about his past is that he grew up in a highly orthodox Jewish household. Indeed, he says that all his ideas about grammar emerged from his familiarity with Hebrew grammar. He was born in this country. Somebody told me that he is good looking. I've been asking people about him, you know. Not only does he side with our enemies, he sides with the enemies of Israel: Arabs, Palestinians, dissenters in Israel. I am trying to say something reasonable, and what I probably will say will be this:

"Chomsky loves power. He is also convinced of his superiority over any politician or businessman alive in the United States. He sees the world being run by inferior people, by people who make money, by people without principle or ideology. He thinks that capitalism is for low-brows, you see, and that intelligent people should have a superior form of socialism, and so anybody who interferes with this program is a criminal."

Eric Hoffer went to sit on his bed. "Tom," he said, "what gives people like him the confidence that they really know everything, that they are superior to everybody else? Just knowledge doesn't give confidence. If you went to school and you looked at your professors you would see that the brighter they were the less confident they were that they knew everything. There's something *else* here, something else . . ."

Then, reflecting on the amazing ungratefulness of some who have done well in America, Hoffer said: "Gratefulness is not a natural thing. There are two sorts of people coming to America: both were nothing before they came, and both made good. One will say, I came as a barefoot boy, and look where I am now. What a good country it is! The other will say, I came as a barefoot boy, and look where I am now. What a bunch of idiots they must be! He sees his own rise as evidence of others' inferiority.

"There was a prototype for all this in Vienna," he went on, "toward the end of the Hapsburg Empire, before World War I. There was a group of very brilliant people, Jews and non-Jews, who were just glorying in the approaching doom. They knew that the end of the world was just around the corner. And I couldn't figure out how intelligent people, who liked to eat the good food of Vienna and sleep with the beautiful women of Vienna, should derive such tremendous pleasure from contemplating the approaching doom. And the answer is the same: they were so convinced that they were the fittest men to run the world that they wanted with all their hearts to wipe the floor and start from scratch. And they would show us how the world should be run."

Hoffer put the card down and said: "Well, I don't know. Maybe I should throw out Chomsky and not have any business with the sonovabitch. But he needs explaining. How come this hostility on the one hand, and this confidence on the other? Imagine what a disaster it was when we had the Depression and Roosevelt, that crippled aristocrat, got into power. He had a whole bunch of these chomskies and bomskies around him, telling him how to do things. These were people who didn't have the least idea what this country was all about. They knew that it wasn't built right, they called our Constitution a horse and buggy thing, and so everything had to be reformed. What a disaster that these intellectual swine had such a free hand! Roosevelt is a watershed in American history. The time will come when American history will be divided into B.R. and A.R. Before Roosevelt if something went wrong, you blamed yourself. After Roosevelt, you blamed the system—everybody but yourself."

Somehow Karl Marx came up. "All Marx's predictions turned out to be wrong," Hoffer said. "All his doctrines turned out to be wrong. And yet these wrong predictions and doctrines played a more fateful role in shaping events than anybody else's. Because all the slogans of recent revolutions came from Marx's wrong predictions and wrong doctrines." Here Hoffer emitted an unexpected cackle of laughter, followed by a great and mysterious groan. "That was

Marx's greatness. And of course the reason Marx had such great appeal was that he really hated humanity. Oh, that's their man, you see. You hate your own country, you hate your own species. You know Douglas, Justice Douglas? He said 'I finally came around. I am on the side of the fishes against the fisher.' That's his great achievement, in his old age. Nature is pure, it's healthy, salubrious. Man taints, pollutes the world. Oh, Tom. Get the book. See what Calvin says about humanity."

I read from his card index quoting Calvin: "The first man and woman brought sin into the world, and immersed all posterity in the most terrible pestilence, blunders, weakness, filthiness, emptiness and injustice."

Then I read Hoffer's written reply: "Is it possible to have ardent faith, even in man, without a loathing for man as he is? To a fanatically religious person the only sinful living being is a polluter of the universe."

Hoffer thought about this for a moment and added this coda: "To Chomsky, Kunstler, Douglas and all the others we are polluters. The moment we get in a forest we pollute with our breath, we pollute everything. They hate humanity. Humanity stinks in their nostrils. And they are our saviors, you see."

He suggested that I pick another card from the file, directing me to Arthur Bryant, the English historian. (Hoffer's cards were only indexed up to C.) He told me to read it aloud for his benefit: "There has never been a time in history when the Jews have not been news. And the periods during which the Jews have occupied and dominated Palestine have been the most exciting and significant in man's sojourn on this planet."

At this Eric gave a little sigh of pleasure. "Here you have a Wasp, an Anglo-Saxon, with not a drop of Jewish blood in him, saying something that no Jewish chauvinist would dare say!" He let out an odd, whinnying peal of laughter. "This is something I *can't* explain," he said, puzzled and serious once again. "The uniqueness of the Jews. I can describe their uniqueness, but why they became what they are I don't know. It's the greatest mystery in the world for me, and I have been preoccupied with the Jews since 1929. It's a special thing to be a Jew, and this is what most Jews don't know. They think they are like others, but they are not."

Hoffer said he had been invited to Israel many times but he didn't want to go because he was afraid that he would be "disappointed by reality." He said he knew the country "the way I know the palm of my hand. I can describe how you land in Jaffa or Haifa and how you go to Jerusalem. I can dexcribe the road exactly, as if I was there. Of course, I have seen photographs."

He fell silent for a while and seemed to be quite tired. He lay down on his bed. "The Jews have the atomic bomb," he said, "and they're going to use it if cornered." He opened his eyes and added: "I don't think Egypt will attack Israel there. The only place I . . . I think Russia will somehow stumble into it. If, let's say, Syria starts something, and the Israelis get in there and wipe the floor with Syria, then the Russians might send an army in and start to order the Israelis around. And the Israelis will say: What the hell. Let's see who blows up whom."

In the last year of his life, according to Lili Osborne, Hoffer became increasingly preoccupied with the Middle East, especially after one or two of his suppositions came true. In the course of a CBS television interview with Eric

Sevareid in 1967, Hoffer remarked that "If Israel fails then history can have no meaning."

When I first wrote to Hoffer, in 1979, I asked him something about the Soviet Union and its prospects. He replied as follows: "As to Russia: She will not change so long as the Occident remains dynamic. Only when the West declines and becomes negligible will Russia venture to experiment with democratic socialism or whatever. She may then even cast herself in the role of a modern Occidental power facing the primeval Chinese dragon."

Six months later I again went to see Eric Hoffer in his apartment. His health had noticeably deteriorated. He said he wanted me to entertain him a little, to read him a few pages from *The Idiot*. When he asked me if I had read the book and I said no he seemed disappointed in me. What were they saying about Reagan in Washington? he asked. He groaned when I said "simplistic." He lay on his bed with his eyes closed. I thought he was asleep when the buzzer rang and a voice announced that an old friend was downstairs: Selden Osborne.

Eric came to life immediately, sat up, and told me that here indeed was an interesting fellow—a "true believer," he said. They had known one another for many years. *The* true believer? Eric implied that Selden had contributed to a composite portrait. He and Selden had worked together as longshoremen on the waterfront. "He's a doctrinaire socialist," said Eric, just before Selden came into the room.

Selden was perhaps ten years younger than Eric. Slim and well preserved, with a trim beard, he was wearing a light khaki safari outfit.

"I was an active participant in the union," Selden told me. "Eric was more of an observer. He always said the table was laid for him."

"I appreciated it," said Eric.

"Eric was violently anti-Communist, but he gave credit to Harry Bridges," said Selden. "Bridges was afraid of educated longshoremen."

"No, he was afraid of longshoremen he couldn't use," said Eric, who was by now very much himself again.

"Eric always said that America is the country of the common man," said Selden. "I disagree. It's the most imperialistic country of all. Also the union under Bridges. I favored democracy in the union. Eric said it wasn't so important. Do you remember that, Eric? You said you never grew up with a sense of democracy because you never went to school."

Eric was leaning forward on his bed, and through the open window you could see the sailboats in San Francisco Bay leaning over in parallel. "Repeat what you said," he demanded. It was as though the years and decades had fallen away and they were back together, arguing on the waterfront.

Selden repeated it and added: "I think that the leadership of this country is hellbent to rule the world."

"His antagonism to this country is because it doesn't give him a role in leadership," Eric explained. "It's very difficult to become a leader . . ."

"Unless you have a lot of money."

"Nooooooooo-o-o-o. Bridges didn't have no money. You're not a democrat, Selden. You're an exclusivist. You resent any setup where an ignorant son of a bitch can run for office and get elected."

Then Eric lay down on his bed, coughing.

"Take Truman," he said, after a while. "He was an ignoramus and yet he made a good President. To me these things are all miracles." He challenged Selden to name a better country.

"Better country? I couldn't say. I might have said Australia or New Zealand. There is some advantage to a parliamentary form of government."

"I learned from Selden all the time," said Eric. "I classified him as a fanatic." He added that fanatics were often important and that "if you have a real cause that needs fighting you had better get some fanatics. Because you won't win without them."

"In those days I was a dissident Trotskyite," said Selden. "I remember I once took Eric to hear Max Schachtman. Most of the educated longshoremen were followers of Bridges. Bridges was a Communist and Eric anti-Communist. The union paper never acknowledges his existence, even after *The True Believer* came out."

"I never spoke a word to Bridges," said Eric from his bed. Finally he sat up and said: "I don't want to be nitpicking. But in my case it was not Bridges but America that set the table for me. I asked Lili to put on my tombstone: 'The good that came to him was undeserved.' Many times I had ignorant people correct me. I never found a common man who would agree with Henry Adams that America was created by a bunch of crooks. It was always axiomatic for the common man: America was the last stop. If you couldn't make it here, you couldn't make it nowhere. It's a sort of treason to complain about America. Selden's disagreement was crucial. But I love him."

I left with Selden. As we walked toward the center of San Francisco he told me: "My whole concern today is disarmament." There was a place where some friends of his lived, about fifty miles down the coast, set among the redwoods. An old property with a goodly acreage. He would be going there in a few days, and together they would have some good discussions about disarmament. He had graduated from Stanford University and later had shared an apartment with Clark Kerr in Palo Alto. He had joined the longshoreman's union because he believed at that time that the revolution would originate with the working class. But he now knew that this had been a mistaken belief. As for Eric Hoffer, Selden said: "All his conclusions are wrong—every one of them. But he writes beautifully and he asks the right questions."

That evening I was in the car again with Eric and Lili. She was driving him back to his apartment, where she would make up his lunch for the next day, and then leave him once again to contemplate his index cards in his customary and preferred solitude. Eric mentioned the hopeless impasse of all his arguments with Selden. Neither one could ever persuade the other of anything, and so it had been for over 30 years.

"Selden is so anti-American that it frightens you," he said. "Born and raised in America. If anyone is for America it should be him."

There was a silence, and Eric turned to me and asked: "Do you think he likes me—deep down?"

I hesitated. Lili Osborne had been married to Selden. Then, some years later she divorced him. It was Selden who had introduced her to Eric Hoffer at about the time that *The True Believer* was published.

Lili turned the wheel of the car, and changed the topic of the conversation. She said that Selden was a man of strong convictions. "He has gone to jail for what he believes."

"Of course, ready to sacrifice himself for the cause," said Eric, gripping his stick once again between his knees. On his head was the same old cloth cap that he seemed to wear everywhere.

"Not many people are willing to die for what they believe."

"Lili, I have told you a hundred times. It is easy to die for what you believe. What is hard is to live for what you believe."

George Will and the Contemporary Political Conversation

(1983)

JOSEPH SOBRAN

In early July, George Will underwent a sudden role change: all at once he was the object, rather than the transmitter, of moral indignation.

He had admitted having glimpsed the Purloined Briefing Book in the course of helping prepare candidate Ronald Reagan for his 1980 TV debate with Jimmy Carter.

Two weeks later, assorted Democrats, liberals, and Carterites were out-Pecksniffing Pecksniff in demanding that the *Washington Post* drop Will's column. (The *Post* didn't, but the *New York Daily News* did.) Lengthy stories in the *New York Times* and the *Wall Street Journal* abounded in phrases like "raises disturbing questions," "relationships between journalists and politicians," and so forth.

You would have thought George Will had been caught in a love nest. Actually, the press was still debating whether the papers themselves—let alone Will's trivial and marginal role in the story—constituted a bona fide scandal. The central fact, the Reagan team's illicit possession of Carter's briefing book, was out in the open for two weeks, and had been known to some for far longer, before anyone thought to make an issue of it. Why was Will retroactively expected to have reacted with electric outrage at the first touch of a document he had described as "excruciatingly boring"? True, stealing a boring document is as criminal as stealing a hot one; but the point is that Will didn't steal it. He was a bystander. Why should he have cared whether a dead horse had been stolen?

Something else was going on, though. The real event was aesthetic, not moral. The real issue, confusedly addressed, was not Will's character, but his persona. There was something incongruous about this conservative scourge of Nixon and Agnew finding himself in the thick of some dubious behind-the-scenes political dealing. It didn't match his aloof and starchy pose as the Pure Observer. It exposed him as a bit of—well, an operator. That was what really hurt him.

As it happened, I had recently roasted Will's latest book, *Statecraft as Soulcraft,* in the pages of *National Review.* I called his position "a toothless, coffee-table Toryism, nicely calculated for liberal consumption."

He wrote me a short, good-humored note about it, with however the complaint that my fierce tone had been "unseemly": "You could have ascribed my bad ideas to my bad thinking rather than my bad motives."

I could have, yes. But I didn't see bad thinking as the real problem. Bad motives—more precisely, bad intentions—had gotten in the way of his normally lucid thinking.

Aristotle, of course, condemned the ad hominem argument long ago, and he has been mindlessly echoed by people who don't stop to consider that Aristotle had a lot to hide: at least one illegitimate child, for instance. In his place, who *wouldn't* want to keep public discussion impersonal?

But the same Aristotle pointed out that rhetoric traffics constantly in motives. The orator has to persuade the audience of his good character. It was as rhetorical performance in this sense, not just as abstract argument, that I found Will's book interesting, and objectionable. *Statecraft as Soulcraft* is the work of an operator wearing the moralist's mask.

Will has always made it a point to establish his distance from other conservatives. He generally quotes them for the purpose only of contrasting them unfavorably with himself, notably on the score of that great motive and motif of today's political rhetoric, compassion. His, he has given us to understand, is the enlightened Toryism of Burke, Disraeli, and Shaftesbury, as opposed to the crass Manchester liberalism of "those who call themselves conservatives [nowadays]." For nowadays, in America, "there are almost no conservatives, properly understood."

In a 1975 column he launched his campaign against "the somewhat narrow and negative social prescriptions of American conservatism." If conservatives don't take "a quickened interest in the problem of poverty," he concluded, "it will be fair to assume that they have at least a mental skin too many, and have inadequate mental material beneath that skin."

In *Soulcraft* he defends the welfare state in principle—"irrefutably," he added in a subsequent column, though none of the reviewers seemed to agree—and complains that American conservatism has become "cranky and recriminatory." He asks: "Can there be conservatism with a kindly face?" He asserts: "A conservative doctrine of the welfare state is required if conservatives are even to be included in the contemporary political conversation."

"The conservatism for which I argue," he goes on, "is a 'European' conservatism. . . . It is the conservatism of Augustine and Aquinas, Shakespeare and Burke, Newman and T.S. Eliot and Thomas Mann." (Are these all the same thing?)

Well, it's a long way from Orange County, certainly. Nobody can accuse George Will of being obsessed with fluoridation or the Trilateral Commission. And he has certainly run with the compassion issue. Almost every policy debate in America tends to turn, alas, sooner rather than later, into a compassion contest, and conservatives, like Cordelia, have a poor won-lost record in these competitions of humanitarian histrionics.

Whether it is fair to hit them with Lacking Compassion on that account is another matter. It may be that they simply have a different conception of the role of the state, not to mention the constitutional limits of federal authority. But Will doesn't give this possibility a chance. He is talking *about,* not *to,* conservatives, and feels no obligation to answer them to their satisfaction. His relation to them is not of the I-thou variety. He is addressing another audience.

To understand what he is up to, we must see the board he is playing on, and watch his moves.

The full title of the book is *Statecraft as Soulcraft: What Government Does.* But its thesis is, as Adam Meyerson has noted in these pages, much narrower than the subtitle suggests. Will neither describes the full range of state activity (that would take a fat tome) nor defines the proper and specific purposes of government.

Instead he argues that whenever government acts, its actions have moral implications. It can't really be neutral about "values." It necessarily commits itself to some vision of the good, and thereby helps form the character of its citizens. "Statecraft is, inevitably, soulcraft." Therefore government ought to take into account the moral impact of its policies.

So far, so good. But beyond this point, the book is vague and confused. Because state policy has moral implications, it doesn't follow that the moral is the domain of the state. Nor does Will make quite so vast a claim for it. In fact he insists on what he has nicely called "the primacy of private life." But he never draws a helpful line of demarcation between public and private, and he drifts toward an ever-broader conception of the state's role.

As Will sees it, the American political system was begotten outside "the rich tradition of political philosophy, from Aristotle to Burke. Relatively recently—at the time of Machiavelli and Hobbes—we took a sharp fork in the intellectual road. It is time to retrace our steps, and rethink what we think."

Madison, Will contends, spoke for the Machiavellian tradition when he said that "neither moral nor religious motives can be relied on" against the abuse of power. "It is almost as though," Will comments, "the Founders thought they had devised a system so clever that it would work well even if no one had good motives—even if there was no public-spiritedness." Our Constitution itself was apparently a wrong turn.

Will calls for "a new, respectful rhetoric—respectful, that is, of the better angels of mankind's nature." A rhetoric, that is, of "virtue," which is to say, "good citizenship," including a "willingness to sacrifice private desires for public ends." The welfare state, properly understood, represents an "ethic of common provision" appropriate to this sort of virtue.

All this is questionable on several grounds. The Founders weren't building a new society from scratch, in utopian fashion, but striking a deal among preexisting polities. Madison wasn't being cynical, just realistic, when he said fine motives couldn't be "relied on" to prevent abuses of power. He insisted that republican government "presupposes" more virtue than other kinds of rule, but he had enough sense to know that even where there is a normal degree of virtue, human nature being what it is, institutional restraints are needed. If that isn't conservative sanity, I don't know what is.

For all his emphasis on property rights, Madison was anything but indifferent to virtue. "To suppose that any form of government will secure liberty or happiness without any virtue in the people," he argued in the Virginia ratifying debates in 1788, "is a chimerical idea." These are hardly the accents of Machiavelli and Hobbes. Strange as it may sound to modern ears, Madison, like most conservative thinkers, tended to associate property and character; acquisition requires providence and industry, and possession makes people rooted and responsible. (Tocqueville thought America owed much of its stability to its widespread, though unequal, distribution of property.) The pertinent question to ask ourselves is whether Madison would have thought the modern welfare state, on the evidence, more conducive to civic virtue than the Republic he so lovingly helped to design.

Meyerson has already pointed out that our own recent experience gives grounds for doubting that the size of the public sector is an index of our public-spiritedness. The number of pressure groups defining their own interests as "public ends" these days would surely confirm the Founders' worst apprehensions of rapacious "factions."

Will is echoing contemporary liberalism, not Burkean conservatism, when he reduces the private sector to "private desires" (in the sense of "appetites"). There is no correlation. The public sector has become the great arena of selfishness and greed. It is the triumph of liberal rhetoric to have disguised this truth, while portraying the competition for entitlements and the mass bribery of voters as the politics of "compassion." Meanwhile, it has been all but forgotten that property rights are the great *impediment* to greed, and to the greedy state; for greed consists in the desire for what is not one's own, especially the fruits of others' labor, which today's politics puts up for grabs.

That is why the great task of conservatism today is to restore the limits of the state, not to enlarge its claims. But Will shows no interest in this task. Instead he says, again and again, that we as a nation are "undertaxed." He says little about property rights, and less in their favor.

When he assigns the Founders to the Machiavellian tradition and calls on us to "retrace our steps, and rethink what we think," Will may seem to be throwing down a bold, even quixotic challenge to the status quo. But look again at that curious sentence—in my judgment, the key sentence of *Soulcraft:*

A conservative doctrine of the welfare state is required if conservatives are even to be included in the contemporary political conversation.

Odd. If Will can say we took a wrong turn as long ago as 1513, or even 1789, why can't other conservatives say we took a wrong turn as recently as 1932? If our entire national tradition is Machiavellian, wouldn't it really be much easier to retrace our steps from the New Deal than from *The Prince?*

Here is where we had best keep a careful eye on the actual framework of Will's rhetorical performance. He speaks from the strongholds of contemporary liberalism, in publishing, broadcasting, and education (*Soulcraft* began its life as the 1981 Godkin Lectures at Harvard), where the "contemporary political conversation" takes place. In terms of contemporaneity, if not political philosophy, 1932 is more *real* than 1513. Within the liberal strongholds, where Will finds the audience he is addressing primarily (and it is anything but a conservative audience), you can say what you like about 1513, as long as you watch what you say about 1932.

Under the circumstances, Will is gingerly in his approach to liberal pieties, but cavalier in his remarks about conservatives, who aren't "included" as he is. It would be one thing if he seriously criticized the principles he says they should abandon; but he doesn't even bother to state those principles carefully. In a book teeming with quotations, he never quotes an important conservative spokesman. The conservative position is represented by three-and-a-half sentences from Reagan campaign speeches.

He knows that a liberal audience will not object, as a conservative audience would, to such 1964-vintage japery as this: "If conservatives do not want to use government power in behalf of their values, why do they waste their time running for office? Have they no value other than hostility to government?" (If Goldwater doesn't *like* the government, why does he want to *run* it?)

Apart from assuming that conservatives are anarchists at heart, Will seems to think that misguided programs, once established, should be administered only by people foolish enough to believe in them. After issuing the grand invitation to all of us to rethink what we think, his practical advice to conservatives boils down to that sage reminder, "You can't turn back the clock."

Will oscillates erratically between two arguments for the status quo. In some moods he adopts the familiar tactic of falling back rhetorically on the simple fact that the welfare state exists: it is a "fact," it is a "reality," it is not "reversible," and so forth. This amounts to saying that whatever is, may as well be regarded as right. The virtue (such as it is) of this argument is that it spares one the trouble of specifying genuine norms of politics: approval of what currently obtains can be disguised as resignation to immutable conditions of existence. But why are they immutable? If the human will produced them, it can presumably change them. The refusal to criticize them because of their power is more in the spirit of Machiavelli than of the Great Tradition.

But in other moods, Will ventures a cloudily worded moral justification for welfarism: it represents an "ethic of common provision" or is an aspect of a "just society." He offers no helpful explanation. Instead he moralistically—and inaccurately—contrasts his communitarianism with libertarianism, which he defines as "the doctrine of [sic] maximizing freedom for private appetites."

The best answer to this familiar error is that of the ever-sensible Kenneth Minogue:

Like many other writers, Marx simply identified individualism with egoism, and a tendency to think in communal terms with altruism. An individualist, however, may well be altruistic to the point of self-abnegation; he merely wishes to choose his own way of acting. Similarly, egoism and selfishness can appear in the most communally minded people. That I should claim the right to own property might mean that I am greedy and wish to do in my fellow men; but it might also mean many other things—such as that I enjoy taking risks, investing, saving money, and so on. And if I should acquire a great deal of property, I may spend it on my own pleasure, or I may set up charitable foundations for art and science, or even (as some millionaires have done) spend it financing socialist revolutions, because such is my pleasure. There is, in other words, no logical relationship whatever between a right on the one hand, and a motive (such as egoism) on the other.

There is no telling, on a given day, whether Will is going to argue from Reality or Morality. In one frolicsome column, though, he recently announced the happy news that Mrs. Will had been confirmed by the Senate as Assistant Secretary of Education, a post that will annually diminish by a reported $68,000 the amount of money available for the gratification of the nation's private appetites. "I herewith disclose that I am sleeping with a government official," he joked amiably. Well, a man's sexual orientation is his own business. But conservatives should at least take note that the woman works for an agency with no constitutional warrant. Even the Supreme Court recognizes the problem of excessive entanglement.

Will, in short, neglects to *specify.* He is "for" government, "for" virtue, "for" somehow promoting virtue through government. But what is government itself for? The conservative, as Michael Oakeshott reminds us, "does not suppose that the office of government is to do nothing," but recognizes governing as "a specific and limited activity." The order of the words is subtly exact in its import: "specific," *then* "limited." Government exists, not to do nothing, but to do good; but good of a certain kind, and no other. *What kind?* That, I take it, is the central question of political philosophy. Mere general approval of the status quo is no answer to it.

"Conservatism in the modern age," Will has written, "has one fountainhead: Edmund Burke." In *Soulcraft* he derides with special sarcasm "today's *soi-disant* conservatives who have been so busy praising Burke they have not taken time to read, or at least comprehend, him." He continues: "It is perhaps marvelous that people who preach disdain for government can consider themselves the intellectual descendants of Burke, the author of a celebration of the state. But surely it is peculiar—worse, it is larcenous—for people to expropriate the name 'conservative' while remaining utterly unsympathetic to the central tenet of the greatest modern conservative."

Burke's "celebration of the state" that Will refers to is the (too-) familiar passage in which Burke says the state ought to be regarded as a transcendent partnership among the generations, not as a dissoluble partnership like those of the marketplace. But this is hardly an endorsement of everything states do: in fact it is (rather obviously) a rebuke to a particular state that breaks faith with citizen and alien, repudiates its debts, and confiscates property—namely, the new state Burke sees wreaking havoc in France.

There has been a long controversy as to the essence of "Burkean conservatism," so one wonders how Will can pluck out this particular passage and hold it up as Burke's "central tenet." Burke was a complex thinker, a devious man, and an occasional rather than a systematic writer. Even to talk of his "central tenet" this way is to betray an insensitivity to his wonderfully serpentine style.

Will is right to see the importance of the passage, just as he is right to notice Burke's stress on the key role of "manners" in society. But it is also necessary to weigh such passages against others that add fuller meaning to them. Burke did not mean that the state should regulate manners, but that it depends on them. Civilized government needs a civilized populace.

Quoting isn't learning, and Ellen Wilson scored a shrewd point when she wrote, reviewing *Soulcraft* for the *Wall Street Journal,* that Will's conservatism seems to be "the conservatism of *Bartlett's.*" You don't bag Burke for Toryism by quoting a few familiar paragraphs, any more than you bag Shakespeare by citing a few familiar lines from *Troilus and Cressida* ("Take but degree away, untune that string . . .").

Does Will really know Burke? He seems to think Burke can be claimed for the tradition of Tory paternalism; but nothing could be further from the truth. Burke was a Whig of the most rigorous laissez-faire stripe. To understand him fully we have to read not only the familiar quotations from the first half of his *Reflections,* but the passages on economics from the latter half, where he expresses his horror of confiscation and argues that "it is to the property of the citizen . . . that the first and original faith of civil society is pledged." There is nothing Burkean about Will's suggestion that "government's role in the generation of wealth" gives it the right to redistribute wealth as it sees fit (somewhere short of total leveling).

Even more vehemently than Madison, Burke holds that the rights of property (including its acquisition) take precedence over any financial needs of the state: "The claim of the citizen is prior in time, paramount in title, superior in equity." The operation of the market, moreover, is "the natural course of things," which it is "pernicious to disturb," even for the purpose of relieving the poor.

It may be fortunate that Will didn't get to know Burke in time for *Soulcraft:* he would have found an irresistible specimen of stony-hearted conservatism to whip for lacking compassion. In 1795, with famine spreading over England, Burke offered his "Thoughts on Scarcity" specifically to oppose government efforts to better the lot of the laboring poor. "To provide for us in our necessities," he wrote, "is not in the power of government."

The whole essay refutes the notion that "government's role in the generation of wealth" somehow creates a limitless sovereignty over the wealth of a nation. Burke understood that government creates necessary conditions for prosperity, but he did not think it a derogation of the state to distinguish between necessary and sufficient conditions. He also disliked humanitarian cant. Speaking of the common laborers who were suffering, he said: "Let compassion be shown in action—the more, the better—according to every man's ability; but let there be no lamentation of their condition."

To Burke the problem even had a theological aspect. He spoke of the duty "manfully to resist the very first idea, speculative or practical, that it is within the competence of government . . . to supply to the poor those necessaries which it has pleased the Divine Providence for a while to withhold from them." He went even further—further by far than Adam Smith. He called "the laws of commerce . . . the laws of Nature, and consequently the laws of God."

Mr. Will, meet Mr. Burke.

We are all impersonators of ourselves, says Ortega y Gasset; and Will has taken his characteristic posture so far in *Statecraft as Soulcraft* that several reviewers have found the book an exercise in "self-parody." His persona suffered a wound of a different kind when it transpired that he had seen the "pilfered" briefing book, hadn't told anyone, and, after helping prepare candidate Reagan for the debate, praised the performance as that of a "thoroughbred." Nobody could specify what he had done wrong—there was some huffing about "journalistic ethics"—but somehow everyone knew this wasn't the George Will we had thought we were seeing.

From now on it is going to be harder for Will to let on that he is to other conservatives as "Masterpiece Theater" is to "Dallas," and nearly impossible for him to climb back onto the moral pedestal from which he was wont to address the public. This is all to the good. He is, after all, a really excellent columnist, because he has one extraordinary gift: he can think straight. He can reduce an issue to its essentials.

He fails to do this only when he is preoccupied with making an impression of himself on the reader. His pseudo-Burkean affectations, his somewhat promiscuous quoting, his more-caring-than-thou postures—these are signs of distraction. He should write, as it were, anonymously; as if the point were to make the reader remember the argument and forget the author. "Read over your compositions," Dr. Johnson recalled a tutor instructing one of his pupils, "and whenever you meet with a passage which you think particularly fine, strike it out."

"Ethic of common provision," "contemporary political conversation," "the central tenet of the greatest modern conservative"—one has the horrible suspicion that in these phrases Will thinks he is being "particularly fine." Too bad. The pundit trade is already overstocked with what the editor of this journal has called "moral hams"; but there is no danger of a surplus of thinkers like Will in peak form. His real face is much handsomer than his mask.

The End of
Senator Joe McCarthy

(1983)

JOSEPH W. BISHOP, JR.

To most Americans today the name John Adams, if it means anything at all, means the second and sixth Presidents of the United States. Not one in a hundred knows that John Adams is a living lawyer practicing in Washington, D.C. But thirty years ago any citizen who could read a newspaper or owned a TV set knew who he was. At least 30,000,000 of them had seen and heard him on television and would have recognized him in the street. For John Adams, the General Counsel of the Army, had starred in the Army-McCarthy hearings of 1954, to this day the biggest TV spectacular in history, watched daily by 20 or 30 million people. It almost chased soap opera off the screen.*

On the other hand, most Americans in 1983 have at least a vague idea who Joe McCarthy was and what "McCarthyism" means, for the liberals and left-wingers will not let his memory die. In 1950 Joseph R. McCarthy, the junior senator from Wisconsin, was about as obscure as a United States senator can be. Those who knew anything about him, mostly newspapermen, thought very little of him; and many of them strongly suspected him of taking bribes from large corporations, such as Pepsi-Cola, to push bills they favored. His obscurity ended abruptly in February 1952, when he delivered a stump speech to the Ohio Valley Women's Republican Club at a Lincoln Day dinner in Wheeling, West Virginia. Looking for a good issue on which to seek re-election in 1952, Joe had hit upon the infiltration of the federal government by thousands of Communist spies. Specifically, he informed the ladies that there were no less than 205 Communists in the State Department alone, waving a sheet of paper which he said listed them by name. (Where the famous figure came from was never made clear, although Adams says he simply blew up some old figures given him by a reporter for the *Chicago Tribune* and someone in Richard Nixon's office. Even these figures did not refer to actual Communists but to people who had been investigated and in most cases cleared. None of those who had not been cleared was still employed by State in 1952. But it was Joe's way, when asked for substantiation of his charges, simply to leap to new accusations.) He got headlines beyond the dreams of political avarice.

*This essay is in large part based on Adams's book, *Without Precedent: The Story of the Death of McCarthyism.* W. W. Norton & Co.

For the next four years there were few days when Joe didn't make the front page and prime time. Some of this was due to the active cooperation of the press. There were in those days far-Right newspapers, such as the *Chicago Tribune* and the various Hearst papers, which enthusiastically supported McCarthy's crusade, but even liberal or leftish journals like the *New York Times* and the *Washington Post* printed uncritically his wildest charges. Reporters then, as now, were generally too busy (and sometimes too lazy) to check the facts. McCarthy made his announcements exactly in time to catch the next edition. It is always easier to get the media to broadcast sensational accusations than lackluster facts disproving them.

But the underlying causes of the Senator's immense success went deeper. Denouncing Communists (always called "red-baiting" by liberals) had been good politics since the days of Woodrow Wilson's attorney general, A. Mitchell Palmer. A succession of politicians and assorted rabble-rousers had done well with it in the thirties—Martin Dies, Karl Mundt (who later, as a senator, played a shabby role in the Army-McCarthy hearings), Father Coughlin, J. Parnell Thomas, Gerald L. K. Smith. All of them are now forgotten, as McCarthy is not, for none of them could match his talents at red-baiting. I do not mean to imply that there is anything wrong with condemning Communism. Communism, of course, really was and is an evil thing, but in those days most American Communists were more naive than vicious. Moreover, professional anti-Communists, up to and including Joe McCarthy, were rarely inclined to draw subtle distinctions between harmless, if idiotic, parlor pinks and genuine Stalinists. Joe hit upon a singularly fortunate time to revive the old fear and hatred of Bolshevism. The conviction of Alger Hiss had just demonstrated that there really were Americans ready and willing to spy for Stalin. (Adams, like almost everybody who writes about Hiss, describes him as "patrician." This has always been something of a mystery to me. Hiss was well-groomed and well-mannered, but I am not aware that his background was more than middle class. He was, to be sure, a graduate of the Harvard Law School, but that institution has always admitted plenty of people who, like me, were by no means aristocratic. He was dropped from *Who's Who* many years ago, so I haven't been able to check him out, but I'm pretty confident he is not an alumnus of Groton or St. Mark's or any equivalent prep school of his day. He got his undergraduate degree at Johns Hopkins, which is academically excellent, but not socially prestigious.) In addition, when McCarthy delivered his Wheeling speech, the evidence on Julius and Ethel Rosenberg was just coming to light. Though not patrician, they were far more dangerous spies than Hiss, for the information they gave the Russians confirmed that of Klaus Fuchs (like so many eminent moles, a British subject) and played a key role in the manufacture of the first Soviet atomic bomb. So the public was ready to take seriously a good red scare. Joe's rise to fame and power was meteoric.

As Joe became the nation's leading anti-Communist, he didn't always have to rely on his fertile imagination. He had his own corps of Daniel Ellsbergs, and occasionally the information they leaked to him was at least embarrassing to the government. For example, the "purloined letter," which purported to be a letter from J. Edgar Hoover to the Chief of Army Intelligence listing more than thirty suspected subversives employed at Fort Monmouth, was slipped to McCarthy by a member of what he called his "Loyal American Underground." (Actually it was an inaccurate two-and-a-half-page summary of a fifteen-page letter which did, in fact, list the names but furnished no real evidence against them—only the raw contents of FBI files, including hearsay, anonymous letters, and the like. Most of those named had already been investigated and cleared by the Army. But Hoover really had written such a letter, and what McCarthy got was about as close as he ever came to revealing genuine facts.)

The Senator was triumphantly re-elected in 1952. By that time he had laid the State Department waste. Unlike Nixon, he never caught a Communist, but he brought about the early retirement of several distinguished foreign service officers and demoralized other top men in the Department to the point where they simply avoided doing or saying anything that might attract his attention. As a target, State was pretty well played out by 1953. The Department of Justice was not adapted to his purposes, for its most powerful official, J. Edgar Hoover, and the second most important, Attorney General Brownell, were among his sympathizers. He turned to the Army. Unlike State, its officers included few Eastern establishment liberals and no striped-trousered cookie-pushers, but it had far more employees than State and was an even more obvious target for espionage. (The laws of statistical probability suggest that there were a few spies in the military establishment, but McCarthy and his assiduous aides never detected one.)

As it happened, I had been the Deputy General Counsel of the Army since 1952, and the Acting General Counsel since early 1953: when the administration changed I lined up a job with a Wall Street law firm, but agreed to stay with the Army until a Republican successor could be found. Thus I learned to know some of the *dramatis personae*—notably the new Secretary of the Army, Robert T. Stevens, McCarthy, and his closest adviser, a clever and unscrupulous young lawyer named Roy Cohn. Indeed, I fought in what was, to the best of my recollection, the opening skirmish of the Army-McCarthy war. McCarthy subpoenaed a Quartermaster Colonel commanding a depot in Brooklyn, demanding that he produce the loyalty-security files of several low-level civilian employees. When the Quartermaster General hollered for help, I shortly discovered that two Executive Orders of Harry Truman, which had never been revoked by President Eisenhower, forbade turning such files over to Congress without the authority of the President. In order to spare the Colonel from McCarthy's abuse and browbeating, I thought he ought to be furnished with an order from the highest possible authority to reject the Senator's demand. So I drafted one, calling the Colonel's attention to the Executive Orders and instructing him to refuse, with all possible courtesy, to hand over the files. But who would sign it? Secretary Stevens was officially out of town: I always thought he was really in Washington but unanxious to tangle with the Senator. The Secretary of Defense? Possibly even the President? I proceeded up the line to the office of the General Counsel of the Department of Defense, who informed me that the White House had let it be known that the problem was one for Defense or the Army to handle, and that the Defense Department preferred it to be the Army. So I drove across the river to the Justice Department, where I sought the help of the Assistant Attorney General in charge of writing the opinions of the Attorney General, one J. Lee Rankin. Did he agree with me that Truman's Executive Orders were still in effect? Yes. Would he or the Attorney General sign an opinion to that effect? No.

Back to the Pentagon. I was about ready to sign the letter myself when I wandered into the Secretary's dining room. There, eating a plate of ham and eggs, was Under Secretary Earl Johnson, also a holdover from the Truman Administration, with a good job in private industry waiting for him, and no fear of Senator McCarthy. Since Stevens was "out of town," Johnson was the Acting Secretary of the Army, and as such he signed the letter. The Colonel was armored when he went up to the Hill, and, for a wonder, McCarthy accepted the rebuff without vilifying either me or Johnson. (Later, however, in April 1954, months after I had left the Pentagon, McCarthy and Cohn included me as Item 17 in their bill of particulars against the Army—I had, they said, covered up for Fifth Amendment Communists. This was a singular piece of good fortune, though I was not grateful for it at the time. I am, in fact, a neoconservative, and whenever some *homme de gauche* or other, displeased by one of my pieces, accuses me of having been a McCarthyite—it has happened at least three times—I simply display my medal of honor and shut him up. My possession of the McCarthy medal has always graveled my left-liberal colleagues, for I am the only member of the Yale Law School faculty who was ever denounced by Joe McCarthy, though many of my colleagues were far more deserving than I.)

So I discovered, as John Adams was to discover by more painful experience (I was not surprised or disappointed, for I was only a holdover Democrat), that the Army would have to face McCarthy without support from any other part of the Administration. Even Eisenhower, though he indicated his dislike of the Senator in private, had no stomach for an open confrontation.

I also discovered, as Adams was to discover by more painful experience than mine, that Secretary Stevens could not be counted on either. When I told him about the episode above recounted, I gave him what I still think was excellent advice; so far as possible to conduct his relations with the Senator in writing and to let his lawyer draft the correspondence. Stevens gave me a disapproving, owlish stare and said in effect that he regarded McCarthy as playing on the same team as himself and intended to cooperate with him. I didn't argue; I thought he was headed for trouble, but there was nothing more I could do.

I was replaced by John Adams in October 1953. I gave him a brief and probably inadequate account of my experience, but I doubt that he perceived its applicability to himself. Adams, though repeatedly let down and ultimately fired by Stevens, is generally kind to him. He describes the Secretary's meek acceptance of McCarthy's chicanery, lies, and abuse as "gentlemanly forebearance." In some ways, Stevens *was* a gentleman, certainly when compared to McCarthy, a mucker if ever there was one. He was courteous, well dressed, a product of Andover and Yale, a member of good clubs. He was also very rich, having inherited the J.P. Stevens Company, one of the country's largest textile manufacturers. Adams says that, in order to avoid conflict of interest, "At a huge personal sacrifice, Stevens sold all his stock in the company." I doubt it; I think he sold or gave it to members of his family, with the understanding that it would revert to him when he left government service. Certainly when he resigned he promptly became again the company's chief executive, which probably would not have happened if he had really sold his control block to outsiders. But on the whole he was reasonably honest and honorable, as much so as most of those who are called "gentlemen."

Stevens, however, was conspicuously lacking in one essential characteristic of a gentleman: courage. He had not the backbone to take on the likes of Joe McCarthy. Robert P. Patterson, the last Under Secretary of War and the first Secretary of the Army, or John J. McCloy, Assistant Secretary of War under Henry L. Stimson, or Stimson himself, could have done it, and without getting down in the gutter with Joe, but Stevens could not. His attitude toward McCarthy was an odd combination of fear and naive trust, which led him to a course of regular appeasement and surrender. He ordered the general commanding Fort Monmouth to "cooperate" with Joe in investigating the alleged subversives there; he apologized to Roy Cohn when the latter, having no security clearance, was denied access to classified information; at Cohn's insistence he arranged special privileges for Cohn's dear friend, Private G. David Schine, when the latter had been drafted and was undergoing basic training at Fort Dix. The culmination was Stevens's abject surrender at the "Chicken Lunch" on February 24, 1954, when he signed a "Memo of Understanding" in which in effect he agreed to all McCarthy's demands that he had previously balked at, no matter how outrageous. For example, Stevens promised to make available for cross-examination (including abuse and insult) by McCarthy's committee—i.e., McCarthy—"everyone involved in the promotion and the honorable discharge of [Major Irving] Peress," an allegedly Communist dentist, including General Ralph Zwicker, the commandant at Camp Kilmer, where Peress had been filling teeth. (The answer to the question "Who promoted Peress?" was nobody but Congress—his promotion to major after a certain period of active duty was automatic under a statute providing for the drafting of doctors and dentists. Nor was there any ground at all for giving him a less than honorable discharge.) One picture is worth a thousand words, and Herblock drew it: Stevens handing his sword to McCarthy, with the caption, "Okay, bud, when I want you again I'll send for you." Stevens, otherwise so minor a figure in history as to be imperceptible, will be long remembered for his capitulation at the Chicken Lunch.

Adams thinks that even so McCarthy might have abandoned his assault on the Army—there were tougher men than Stevens among the generals and in the Department of Defense—in favor of, say, Communist infiltration of defense industry, if it had not been for Roy Cohn and Dave Schine. Schine was a handsome rich kid, a recent graduate of Harvard although rather lightly furnished in the upper story, with whom Cohn had become infatuated. The basis of the infatuation was never clear. Some people, of course, suggested a homosexual affair, but there was never any evidence of that, and Schine, at least, was clearly heterosexual. (He eventually married a former Miss Universe.) I speculated myself that Cohn, until he met Schine, simply did not know how to play; all work was making him a dull boy. Schine, with his good looks and money, had an entrée to one sort of cafe society, which Cohn enjoyed. Whatever the reason, Cohn got Schine a job with McCarthy's committee, constantly praised his talents at ferreting out Communists, and was genuinely outraged when Schine was drafted and threatened with basic training and even kitchen police. He demanded that Schine be commissioned and assigned to work with McCarthy's committee, perhaps sniffing out Communist propaganda in the textbooks used at West Point. Almost daily Cohn badgered Stevens, Adams, and anyone else he thought had influence to carry out his plans for Dave.

Adams says that McCarthy told him and Stevens that he didn't care what happened to Schine, but that Cohn could not be controlled. This may well have been true. But Cohn and Schine had leverage besides Cohn's increasing indispensability to the Senator. Their presence helped to dispel an anti-Semitic taint in McCarthy's record. In any event, the battle over Schine was the principal and immediate cause of the final confrontation between McCarthy and the Army. Adams disclosed the details of Cohn's incessant campaign to obtain special treatment for Dave: Cohn and McCarthy accused Stevens and Adams of holding Schine as a "hostage" to compel the committee to give up its investigation of and revelations about Communist infiltration of the Army. (There were many other similar charges, including one that Adams had offered to furnish dirt on homosexuality and subversion in the Navy and Air Force in exchange for immunity for the Army.)

So the Army-McCarthy hearings began on April 22, 1954, and lasted for 36 days. McCarthy resorted to all the tactics he had developed in eight years in politics—bullying witnesses, including the Secretary of the Army, turning purple and bellowing with rage and incredulity when he didn't like an answer. He introduced what purported to be carbon copies of memoranda to him from Cohn and other committee staffers which, had they been genuine, were accounts, made at the time, of the conduct of which he accused Adams. (Adams adduces convincing evidence that they were fakes, concocted for the hearings.) He also used a doctored photograph, cropped in such a way as to represent Stevens smirking benignly at Schine. He used, in fact, his whole capacious bag of dirty tricks. There were many dramatic moments, all good for two- and three-column headlines.

But only one is really worth chronicling here, the five minutes in which Joseph Welch, a Boston lawyer retained to act as counsel to the Army, permanently ended McCarthy's career. I saw it myself, along with uncounted millions of other watchers, and I saw it, of all places, in John Adams's office. (Usually my practice kept me too busy to watch the hearings, but this time I was serving in the Office of the General Counsel the annual two weeks of active duty required of me as an Army reservist. Adams had had a TV set installed in his office and there, not being much burdened by my military duties, I watched the hearings.)

On June 9, 1954, Welch's subtle mockery aroused McCarthy's wrath, and he started off on one of his characteristic (and entirely gratuitous) smears: ". . . I think we should tell [Mr. Welch] that he has in his law firm a young man named Fisher . . . who has been for a number of years a member of an organization which was named . . . as the legal bulwark of the Communist Party." (Fred

Fisher was an associate, and is now a senior partner, in Welch's firm, specializing in securities law. He had, in fact, some years before, when he was in law school, belonged to the National Lawyers' Guild, which, although founded by Jerome Frank and other honest liberals as a counterweight to the American Bar Association, had been infiltrated and finally dominated by Communists.) Cohn, who saw what McCarthy was doing to himself, grimaced and shook his head. But McCarthy ignored him and bulled ahead; Cohn shrugged his shoulders and sat back resignedly. After McCarthy finished, Welch stood up and delivered a short philippic which I regarded then and still regard as a masterpiece. (Adams thinks, as I have always thought, that Welch, anticipating the Senator's attack on Fisher, had prepared and memorized it well in advance.) Adams quotes it in full, which it deserves, but a few lines will convey its genius:

". . . Until this moment, Senator, I think I never really gauged your cruelty or your recklessness.

". . . Little did I dream you would be so reckless and so cruel as to do an injury to that lad. It is true he is still with Hale and Dorr. It is true that he will continue at Hale and Dorr. It is, I regret to say, equally true that I fear he shall always bear a scar needlessly inflicted by you. If it were in my power to forgive you for your reckless cruelty I would do so. I like to think that I am a gentle man, but your forgiveness will have to come from someone other than me."

McCarthy, who did not immediately realize that he had received a mortal wound, attempted to continue. Welch finished him off:

"Let us not assassinate this lad further, Senator. You have done enough. Have you no sense of decency, sir, at long last? Have you left no sense of decency?"

It is not often that one can pinpoint the precise moment at which a political career comes to a crashing end. But most of the millions who saw the scene realized that McCarthy was finished. In December 1954, after hearings by a Select Committee, the Senate voted in effect to censure McCarthy, although only for one of the most venial of his sins, abusing other senators. He stayed in the Senate until he drank himself to death in 1957, but his power was gone. He was a pariah; the Senate chamber emptied when he rose to speak. The media lost interest in him.

The sole result—and it was an important one—of the hearings was the destruction of Joe McCarthy. The only participants to emerge with credit were Welch and Adams, who had for the first time told the truth about McCarthy's dealings with the Army. When he died the Chaplain of the Senate praised his "sincerity." Only a clergyman, anxious to flatter a member of the body who paid his salary, could have made so fundamental a misjudgment of McCarthy's character, for his dominant quality was fraudulence. He would tell any lie, assassinate any character, to get a headline. He felt no personal animosity against his victims or even the Communist Party. If there had been a significant Communist vote in Wisconsin he would have said flattering things about Marx, Lenin, and Stalin. Liberals liked to describe him as an American Hitler, but he was nothing of the sort, if only because Hitler was sincere, a true believer in his own propaganda. McCarthy did not aspire to become a dictator. His basic motives were to be re-elected and to grab as many dishonest dollars as came within his reach. (He received very large sums of money, in amounts ranging from one to six figures, from his admirers. He did not, of course, spend these contributions on his crusade, but squandered most of the money speculating in soybeans and other commodities; his financial acumen was much less than his greed.) I believe that his goals were as simple as that.

In fairness it should be said that on at least one occasion he made an accusation that was substantially true, although he himself was probably indifferent to its truth or falsity. Adams calls "bizarre" McCarthy's 1949 charge that Army investigators had "tortured" a group of SS men accused of massacring American POWs at Malmedy in Belgium during the German Ardennes offensive of 1944. It was, however, a fact that their confessions had been extracted by third degree methods. The evidence is to be found in the record in *Everett on behalf of Bersin* v. *Truman,* 334 U.S. 824 (1949), a petition for habeas corpus denied for lack of jurisdiction by an evenly divided Supreme Court, and in the report of a Board of Investigation appointed by the Secretary of the Army. I doubt, however, that McCarthy had ever seen these documents.

From the perspective of thirty years later, how much harm did Senator McCarthy do? His false accusations caused emotional distress and some financial hardship to about fifty innocent people, notably the scientists employed at Fort Monmouth, although all were ultimately vindicated. His smear tactics brought about the defeat of at least two intelligent and honest members of the Senate. He harassed and abused hundreds of honest servants of the government, civilian and military. The truth is bad enough, although not quite the reign of terror attributed to him by the left-liberal version of the history of the period.

But in my view the worst thing he did was to make anti-Communism disreputable. To this day it is impossible to criticize the far Left without being accused of "McCarthyism."

At any rate, to tell McCarthy's story to people who never knew or have forgotten it, although they have heard of him, is to render a public service. John Adams has as much personal familiarity with that story as anyone alive, and he has done a lot of thorough research. He writes like a good lawyer, not elegantly but clearly and with less bias than would have been excusable. The more people who read *Without Precedent,* the less likely are we to contract the disease again.

The Death of
the Jackson Wing

(1984)

FRED BARNES

Former Vice President Walter F. Mondale is not exactly a stalwart of the Coalition for a Democratic Majority, the hawkish, anti-Communist, aggressively pro-Israel faction in the Democratic party. Yet by sounding slightly less dovish than usual, Mondale managed to elicit words of praise from CDM leaders last November. Penn Kemble, the chairman of CDM's executive committee, said he and others were "encouraged" by Mondale's "general tone of realism." Mondale is "less clearly left-wing" in foreign policy than Jimmy Carter and is "acceptable" to most CDM members, noted Austin Ranney, a leader of the organization.

The warming of the relationship between CDM and Mondale, surely an ideological odd couple, is a small thing by itself. But it touches on something bigger—on a trend of enormous significance in the Democratic party. That trend, now practically played out, is the decline and fall of the Jackson wing of the party. That's the late Senator Henry (Scoop) Jackson of Washington, not the Reverend Jesse. For two decades, Henry Jackson and his followers (mostly CDM members) exerted a hard-line influence on Democratic policy-making. They were often unsuccessful, failing miserably in attempts to steer Carter away from his meek, guilt-ridden foreign policy. But they had their moments even under Carter, pushing him toward a boost, not a cut, in military spending. Since Jackson's death last summer, however, no heir has stepped forward and the CDM faithful are left with trying to reconcile themselves to an old foe, Mondale. The Jackson-CDM grouping, says Democratic pollster Patrick Caddell, "isn't a wing; it's a feather." Caddell is right.

To see how this affects the Democratic party, you only need look at the fight for the presidential nomination. There used to be two magnetic poles in the party, Jackson and George McGovern, hard-line and accommodationist, tugging on the candidates during nomination struggles. Today there is only one, and as a candidate himself this year, McGovern boasts correctly of having drawn his colleagues to the left on such issues as the Middle East and Central America. All eight candidates found something critical to say about President Reagan's decision to invade Grenada. None liked the Kissinger Commission report. All seem to blame Reagan more than the Soviets for the lull in arms control talks. For six of the eight (except McGovern and Jesse Jackson), their only concession to the hard-line approach is support for a small increase in defense spending, one which would amount to a sharp reduction from Reagan's expenditure level.

A major factor in this leftward tilt is the makeup of the Democratic electorate in the caucuses and primaries. While two-thirds of the nation's Democrats identify themselves as moderates or conservatives, liberals dominate the presidential selection process. This obviously works against a hard-line presidential candidate, an unabashed anti-Communist, say, and it contributed to Jackson's pathetic showings in the 1972 and 1976 races. In 1984, it keeps potential hard-liners such as Senators John Glenn of Ohio and Fritz Hollings of South Carolina and former Governor Reubin Askew of Florida from articulating a hawkish position. They aren't doves, but they emphasize all the peace overtures and defense cuts they would make as President. Asked in Iowa last December if he favored deployment of Pershing missiles in West Germany, Glenn whispered hastily that he did, then launched into his plan for reneging on the commitment to deploy cruise missiles in Europe as well. And Glenn's first wave of campaign TV commercials played on fears of nuclear war—one showed a shrinking nuclear explosion—and cast him as a peace candidate.

The reflexively soft-line approach of the Democratic presidential candidates is a symptom of the crumbling of the Jackson wing. The causes lie elsewhere. One, of course, is the reform of party rules governing presidential delegate selection, which took power out of the hands of centrist Democratic leaders in the South, West, and cities and gave it to liberal activists. McGovern benefited immediately from this reform in capturing the presidential nomination in 1972. So did Carter four years later, his ambiguity leaving many liberals with the impression he was one of them. It turned out that on foreign policy he was, but not on domestic matters. In any case, the rules changes and the increase in the number of primaries (from 17 in 1968 to 35 in 1980) ruined Jackson's presidential bids in 1972 and 1976. It did not help that he was not charismatic. Leaders of the party-regular variety adored him, but they were vastly outnumbered by liberal activists, who prevailed.

Jackson lost ignominiously, and a political tradition evaporated with his defeats. It was the ideological tradition begun by Franklin Roosevelt and championed by Harry Truman, John Kennedy, and Lyndon Johnson. Charles Krauthammer, writing in *Time* recently, dubbed it "liberal internationalism"—strong defense and interventionist, anti-Communist foreign policy coupled with full-throttle, Great Society liberalism in domestic policy. Jackson was its last influential advocate. "Why has adopting the Jackson stance appealed to no presidential candidate's opportunism?" said Joshua Muravchik, former CDM executive director. "It must have something to do with his presidential campaign failures. The reason it's unattractive is that Jackson couldn't make it work."

But the decline of the Jackson wing involves more than the absence of a presidential contender. Jackson simply has no heir at all, candidate or otherwise, and this is important. Normally, it is individuals in politics who get press attention, not ideologies. This, in turn, gives their ideology national visibility, which serves to bring its adherents together as a movement. The logical heir to Jackson, of course, was Senator Pat Moynihan of New York. But Jackson's death was accompanied, Krauthammer notes accurately, by Moynihan's "abdication." In the 1970s, Moynihan was a more forceful and persuasive spokesman for the Jackson viewpoint than Jackson was, and many assumed that Moynihan's drift to the left was temporary and prompted only by re-election concerns in 1982. It wasn't. Once a neoconservative, then something of a neoliberal, Moynihan has emerged as a conventional, unadorned liberal, one who eagerly endorsed Mondale for President.

If Moynihan retains hawkish tendencies, he is successfully suppressing them. He opposed the invasion of Grenada, arguing that democracy couldn't be imposed at gunpoint. Later, he conceded he should have used different language to explain his opposition, but he remained opposed. Rather than invade, Reagan should have used events on Grenada, particularly the murder of Cuban-backed leader Maurice Bishop, as grounds for making overtures to Fidel Castro, he said. Moynihan endorsed the nuclear freeze, and said his re-election amounted to a mandate for pursuit of the freeze. He voted against the MX missile, calling it a first-strike weapon. He is sharply critical of American policy in Central America. He found flaws in the Kissinger report, complaining that it contained no evidence that the Soviet-Cuban influence in Central America was a serious threat to the United States. Moynihan says no one should be surprised by these positions, since the core of his foreign policy position had always been a "Wilsonian" concern for international law. The United States violated international law by invading Grenada, he said, but doesn't by backing the anti-Sandinista contras. The distinction Moynihan makes is that the Grenada invasion was not sanctioned by the Organization of American States while the activity of the contras is permissible under international law as a response to the export of revolution by the Sandinistas. So he backs continued aid to the contras.

Moynihan's abdication has troubled many of his former allies. One of them was recently reading his book about his experience as ambassador to the United Nations and was amazed—and saddened—by the contrast between his views then and now. Others are bluntly critical of him. Elliott Abrams, a one-time Senate aide to Moynihan and now the assistant secretary of state for human rights, attributes the demise of the Jackson wing to two factors: "Senator Jackson is no longer with us and Senator Moynihan is no longer with us." Moynihan was "the natural heir," Abrams said. "When he came to the Senate [in 1976], he was viewed as the natural heir. He has clearly abdicated that role. I don't know why. . . . What Pat is doing now is politically damaging to him. His fame and power comes from being Pat Moynihan. Liberals are a dime a dozen."

If Moynihan won't be Moynihan, why not John Glenn as heir? He, after all, has a military background, was dubious about SALT II (voting against it in committee), and supports a military buildup. The problem with Glenn is that he simply isn't enough of a party man; he's distrusted by party regulars, just as Carter, another military man, was. Some of the vigor of the Jackson wing came from its staunch support for Israel and for emigration of Soviet Jews. Glenn lacks the pro-Israel credential. And he also lacks the necessary affinity to organized labor, once a bulwark of the Jackson wing. Besides, Ben Wattenberg, the writer and CDM leader, says there are doubts over whether "Glenn understands the geo-political equation.'' People like Wattenberg and Abrams have never considered Glenn part of the Jackson wing.

Abrams himself represents another reason for the faltering of the Jackson wing. If Moynihan abdicated, Abrams and others who gave the Jackson wing much of its intellectual strength pulled out. Abrams has become a Republican, giving up on the Democratic party in 1976 after anyone associated with CDM was blackballed in the Carter Administration. ''That demonstrated to all of us that the Democratic party was a McGovernite party,'' he said. One of those barred from a Carter job was Jeane Kirkpatrick, who had been recommended as ambassador to Israel. A Carter aide boasted of blocking her nomination. Now, as President Reagan's UN ambassador, she wonders about ''the persistence of this peculiar Democratic resistance to the preferences of ordinary Americans [for] a strong defense and a reasonably but prudently assertive foreign policy.'' Others who didn't get posts under Carter but did under Reagan include Richard Perle, Jackson's defense expert who is an assistant defense secretary, and Charles Horner, a former Moynihan aide now at the State Department.

Apart from its intellectual elite, the Jackson wing has lost its base among labor leaders. AFL-CIO president Lane Kirkland is an anti-Communist, but not in the fashion of George Meany. He can't be. The unions—steel, building trades, crafts—which promoted Meany's hard-line positions have sagged in clout in the labor movement, and the liberal unions representing government workers and communications employees have gained influence. The AFL-CIO no longer plays a major foreign policy role. Kirkland, for instance, can't unabashedly back Reagan's policy in El Salvador because the Administration has failed to get the government there to bring to justice the murderers of two AFL-CIO officials. And Kirkland's stress is mostly on domestic policy anyway, namely combating Reaganomics.

Even before Jackson's death, Kirkland signaled the decline of the hard-line wing of the Democratic party. Though he was a founder of CDM, Kirkland largely abandoned his involvement in the group after the 1980 election. Instead, he threw in with the national Democratic party in spite of its dovishness, got labor officials installed on all its panels, and began clearing the way for the AFL-CIO's pre-primary endorsement of Mondale. Kirkland started a trend, Jackson's death accelerated it, Moynihan's actions did nothing to impede it, and CDM, all but irrelevant, merely followed suit. And the Jackson wing died.

Sidney Hook

(1987)

WILLIAM McGURN

Early this spring the *New York Times* published an op-ed piece by Sidney Hook on the ethical dilemmas in treating the critically ill. The subject holds more than theoretical interest for Hook, in that a few years back he suffered a heart attack, the treatment of which triggered a stroke. In the grey pages of the *Times* he described how, during a lucid moment, he pleaded with the doctor to end the agony. As might be expected in an article of this genre, the good doctor refused, the patient went on to make a satisfactory recovery, and, as he notes, the case is used as an argument against honoring requests by other patients *in extremis*. As also might be expected for those familiar with Hook, the gist of his article was to disagree: the doctor, he insists, ought to have let him die.

The incident is mentioned in the author's just-published memoirs, *Out of Step*. In nearly any other writer such a title would be an expression of vanity, but in the case of a man who indicts his doctor for having kept him alive it is an understatement. Nor is this nonconformity the outcome of any desire to *epater le bourgeois;* to the contrary, dissent for dissent's sake he forthrightly labels "mindless." It is simply the record, which shows Hook "prematurely antiwar in 1917–21, prematurely anti-fascist, prematurely a Communist fellow-traveller, prematurely an anti-communist, prematurely, in radical circles, a supporter of the war against Hitler, prematurely a cold warrior against Stalin's effort to extend the Gulag Archipelago, prematurely against the policy of detente and appeasement, prematurely for a national civil-rights program against all forms of discrimination, including reverse discrimination."

Whatever the merits of the particular case he might have been advancing at any given time, Hook has never stood accused of an unwillingness to put principle above self. Of course (as he would be the first to concede), this can have disastrous consequences if the principles themselves are not sound. The author's life, therefore, has been a constant testing of principles against reason and experience, and it exhibits a concomitant willingness to amend an initial assessment when that is the upshot of the exercise. Obversely, as the *Times* piece attests, he has also been willing to stick to his beliefs in the absence of any new objective evidence to the contrary. When Newman wrote that no man would be a martyr for a conclusion, he did not reckon on Sidney Hook.

Coupled with an old-fashioned sense of fair play, Hook's immoderate reasonableness makes easy criticism of his positions impossible. At the outset, for example, he admits to two main errors that distorted his vision for some time: a lack of appreciation for Zionism, and an underestimation of the regenerative powers of American capitalism. In fairness, he was not alone in these misjudgments and, when events proved him mistaken, he more than most displayed a willingness to re-examine his assumptions to find out where he had gone wrong. In light of this Hook's judgments in two other areas—god and socialism—are all the more incongruous.

Indeed, the most puzzling aspect of *Out of Step* memoirs is the author's continued affection, quite unlike him, for a socialism that does not now work anywhere and never has (with the possible exception of voluntary organizations like Christian religious orders and Israeli kibbutzim). At one point he explains this by noting that "the very meaning of socialism changed once we [socialist intellectuals] abandoned serious advocacy of collective ownership of *all* social means of production, distribution, and exchange." One smiles inwardly when contemplating the withering reply Hook would deliver to an adversary who tried to squeeze out of a problem by changing the definition.

To be sure, Hook's continued socialism is more implied than stated, and in the one part of the book where he does make his positive vestigial beliefs explicit he says he is "an unreconstricted believer" in "the welfare state," a far cry from the socialism that led him to vote Communist in 1932 or to help found the American Workers Party a few years later. He notes that few of his friends really considered socialism on its economic merits. In his case, for example, he was "drawn to socialism on ethical grounds," attracted by its "apparent rationality," its "sense of human fraternity," its "heroic element." Without ever endorsing the free market for its positive contributions, he confesses that the idea that extending such power to the state threatened freedom did not occur to these early socialists.

In most other men it would be enough to leave it at that. But Hook is so far above other men in both intellect and honesty that he ought to be pressed for a more exacting account. In the political and intellectual arenas, he has distinguished himself as a champion of freedom, a mature thinker who tolerates the inevitable distasteful excesses such freedom entails to preserve the precious core ("heresy, not conspiracy" is the good rule of thumb he proposes, the title of a book he wrote on the subject). Yet this same champion of freedom only grudgingly acknowledges similar arguments—and evidence—about the economic dimension.

Perhaps the most glaring reluctance of Hook and others is the failure to come to grips with the socialism of Nazi Germany, which most of them try to fob off as a product of the market in a confusion of big business with capitalism. That Hitler's party was called the National Socialist Workers Party does not seem to have discredited socialism in the least. True, Hook does at one point allude to Hitler's claim to socialism, but a more explicit reference talks of both Roosevelt's America and Hitler's Germany as "capitalist powers." How capitalism became confused with mere bigness is a paradox, given its key proposition: that the ability of those on the bottom to enter into the market acts as a wedge to prevent the abuses of the giant. Although fascism and corporatism are different from the Soviet or Chinese versions of the collective, the former are even further away from the free market philosophy Hook seems to find so abstract and antihuman.

In his defense, the language of free market partisans—this writer is no exception—often does not help. "Let the market decide" is one typical phrase, as though there were an identifiable "thing" as the market making that decision. The "magic of the marketplace" is another, conjuring up a mysterious system based on economic hocus-pocus. But Hook is smart enough to realize that letting the market decide means no more than to leave it to the free decisions of men and women to enter into agreements with one another. This is not to deny that the decisions of men and women at the bottom of this system are constrained, sometimes severely so. But then so are our political choices, at least in democracy. That Hook is so far off base here can be seen in a reference to a "reliance on laws that operate under ideal conditions," a charge more befitting of centrally planned economies. For capitalism, like democracy, sees the perfect as the enemy of the good.

Certainly Hook cannot be unaware of the arguments, especially having now taken shelter under the roof of the Hoover Institution. Perhaps that is why, sensing he is on weak ground, he shies away from outlining a specific economic arrangement. Instead he alternates between acknowledging the shortcomings of socialism and sniping at those who extol the virtues of capitalism. In the end he makes an uneasy peace with a free-enterprise system that includes Ronald Reagan's "safety net."

God is quite another matter. Now, a being in which the author clearly does not believe might not be expected to play much of a role in his memoirs, but the almighty, despite his nonexistence, nonetheless manages a remarkable, one might say miraculous, number of appearances. For Hook is no ordinary atheist, no bigot. Although he contends that "faith in the existence of an all-powerful and all-loving god has no more intellectual justification than faith in the existence of a cosmic Santa Claus," he equally holds that "the questions of God, freedom, and immortality are the most important of all questions that human beings can face." Still, there is a tendency to take the failure to prove God's existence as proof of his non-existence.

Although Hook does not flinch at the eternal silence of these infinite spaces, many of his erstwhile colleagues did, ultimately coming around to a deity, to Hook's great distress. This was the fate of, among others, James Burnham, William Barrett, Whittaker Chambers, and Will Herberg; even Delmore Schwartz "alarmed" Hook by confessing an attraction to the Church of Rome. When it comes to religion, Hook's powers of discrimination fail him. For example, despite all his disagreement with Roman Catholicism, he seems to take that as the only model of Christianity: Protestantism never gets a hearing; nor does he turn his attention to any religious aspect of Judaism. The treatment of Catholicism itself is odd, using as he does the positions of Mortimer Adler—a non-Catholic—and the church almost interchangeably.

This is not to deny that Hook's particular grievances vis-a-vis religion are valid. Early experiences with churchmen, particularly Roman Catholic hierarchy, who used their influence to block teachers like Bertrand Russell, evidently convinced him that faith is not compatible with intellectual freedom. Equally important is his opposition to the philosophical premise that only religion provides a basis for morality. Without using himself as an example (which example would be eminently justified), he insists that morality can be constructed outside religious faith.

There is no problem in conceding this point, as any number of faithful do. Indeed, if he weren't so dogmatically opposed to dogmas and so intent on forcing them into his own framework, he might find that many of the West's moral assumptions trace themselves to these dogmas, assumptions he by and large holds himself. But Hook rarely addresses religious propositions on their own terms. He argues, for example, that "men create God in their own image" whereas the Judeo-Christian tradition holds just the opposite; either position may be intellectually entertained but neither can be logically refuted. And like all ideas, that of being created in God's image, has profound consequences for how we may treat our fellow man.

Moreover, though religion is not logically essential to morals it has a better track record than most anything else. The alternatives propounded by philosophers over the ages have failed miserably, generally because they require populations of Marcus Aureliuses and Sidney Hooks to make them work. It's no secret, either, that the study of ethics today tends to undermine belief in a rational framework for morals, just as Hook's own memoirs bitterly attest to the lack of what he concludes is the pre-eminent virtue—moral courage—in the academy. To be sure, this does not constitute a logical proof. But it does go a long way toward establishing that "preponderance of evidence" the author suggests as a guide to conclusions.

All in all, Hook's objections to God appear downright, well, *scholastic;* he recounts an almost touching argument with Jacques Maritain over the mechanics of baptism that suggests a preoccupation with religious ritual, religious practice, and religious people that never quite gets to the strange but central claim of religion itself. By the same token, a religion that bases itself on a "hidden God" has no claim to be indignant when some fail to find him. It can only aim to show, via, for example, the Aquinate proofs that so fascinate and repel Hook, not that we can "prove" God but that his existence is not repugnant to reason. And, we might add, that faith in the alternative seems unreasonable.

To score Sidney Hook on such points is not an indictment of his character; nor, for that matter, does it have to do much with intellect. It is merely an argument about evidence, what we accept as evidence and what weight we attach to it. Unfortunately, in the case of a man whose hallmark was a courageous day-to-day commitment to freedom at the most trying times, focusing on areas of divergence can distort the entire picture. If these "failures" seem to loom large it is only because Hook's achievements are likewise disproportionate. "Besides," as he admits, "critical articles and reviews are more interesting as a rule than purely expository or interpretive ones."

A philosopher by trade, Hook naturally tends to attribute his successes to reason. But his memoirs suggest he underestimates his own horse sense, especially in light of the shameless causes so many other men of reason attached themselves to. From the first, one senses, Hook was saved from the philosophic pitfall of a personal *reductio ad absurdum* by an ability not only to see problems but to discriminate between them and act accordingly. Nor did he permit disagreement in one realm to lead him to denigrate another's achievements in other areas. It was the gift of perspective.

The outcome of this is an absence of black-and-white condemnation of even his enemies (and, for that matter, black-and-white praise for his friends). At the outset, for example, he mentions that the Irish gangs who beat up the Jewish boys in his neighborhood were nonetheless "chivalrous" in their fighting (the Sicilians score less well in this point). Later he recalls one of his high school students, a young tough who couldn't bring himself to repeat an obscenity in the classroom even though he had engaged in a knife fight over it; such a memory seems to heighten the outrage Hook felt when some NYU students disrupted a faculty meeting and one, pointing to the hat still on his head, said it remained there as a deliberate sign of disrespect for the teachers in the room (remarkably enough, the *teachers* applauded him for that). And although he clearly regarded Whittaker Chambers's digressions about God as bizarre, he credits Chambers with courage, even attributing it to his religious conversion.

It is precisely this abiding fairness that allowed him, time and again, to rise above particular disagreements to unite with others to address the larger issues. He explained this at a 1949 conference in Paris, where he characteristically paid homage to the higher value of human freedom:

I have more in common with a democrat who differs with me on economic questions, but who firmly believes in civil rights and a peaceful method of resolving his differences, than with any professed Socialist who would seize power by a minority coup, keep it by terror, and take orders from a foreign tyrant. Hitler and Stalin (both of whom invoke the term *socialism*) have written in letters of fire over the skies of Europe this message: Socialism without political democracy is not Socialism but slavery.

These were not mere words. At another congress, his cooperation with East European Catholic priests in support of a resolution in favor of philosophical freedom earned him an attack from Irving Howe on the unlikely charge that he had sold out to the Catholic church.

Of course, many of those who have been directly involved with Hook are no doubt bound to be rankled by the unsentimental dissection of past events and personalities. From Morris Cohen, whom he criticizes for a ruthless teaching style, to Albert Einstein, whose views on the Soviet Union he found absurd, to the *Partisan Review* crowd, whom he dismisses as "revolutionary comedians," to Ronald Reagan, whom he deems too irresolute in foreign affairs and too attached to ideology in domestic ones, neither friend nor foe escape. All are measured by their devotion to freedom, and, not surprisingly, all fall somewhat short.

In taking stock of his own life Hook subjects himself to the same standard. It does not have the virtue of seeing life whole, but the part that it does see takes us further than most. Over the course of eight decades it has even pushed its main proponent up to its outer boundaries, leading him to shift intelligence to second place after moral courage in his pantheon of virtues, as well as to deduce something suspiciously close to the concept of original sin to explain the rationally inexplicable. Having lived, by his own account, a happy and fulfilled life, marked by what he confesses is not a small measure of luck, he's almost even moved to prayer—but for the realization that this is impossible because "a world of chance rules out an author of nature." Like the Aquinas who maintained a sense of humor was logically incompatible with a deity, Hook might be better off not always taking things all the way to their logical conclusions. But the cause of freedom in our time has been advanced largely because he has, and it is the reason we can apply to Hook the same assessment, quoted in these memoirs, that Lionel Trilling gave to Whittaker Chambers: he was a man of honor.

Contributors

I. Media, Books, and Criticism

Roger Rosenblatt is a senior writer for *Time* magazine.

James Grant owns and edits *Grant's Interest Rate Observer* in New York.

William H. Nolte is C. Wallace Martin Professor of English at the University of South Carolina.

Philip Terzian is the deputy editorial page editor of the *Providence Journal.*

Rhoda Koenig is senior editor of *New York* magazine.

Michael Ledeen is senior fellow in international affairs at the Center for Strategic and International Studies. His book, *Grave New World,* was published by Oxford University Press.

Bryan F. Griffin is an essayist and writer of short fiction.

John P. Sisk is Arnold Professor of the Humanities at Gonzaga University in Spokane, Washington.

Thomas Sowell is a senior fellow at the Hoover Institution and author, most recently, of *A Conflict of Visions.*

Tom Wolfe is author of *In Our Time, The Right Stuff,* and, most recently, *The Bonfire of the Vanities.*

Geoffrey Norman is a contributing editor of *Esquire.*

II. Americana

John R. Coyne, Jr. is director of the creative writing service for Amoco Oil of Chicago.

E. T. Veal resides in Alexandria, Virginia.

Aram Bakshian, Jr., has served as an aide to three presidents and writes frequently on politics, history, and the arts.

Walter Goodman is a member of the editorial board of the *New York Times.*

Theo Lippman, Jr., is a columnist for *The Baltimore Sun.*

John O'Sullivan is chief editorial writer for the London *Times*. He is on leave to serve as Prime Minister Thatcher's chief speechwriter.

Joe Mysak is assistant managing editor of the *Daily Bond Buyer*.

Werner J. Dannhauser is professor of government at Cornell University.

Ben Stein is author of *'Ludes: A Ballad of the Drug and the Dream* and *Her Only Sin*.

Lewis H. Lapham is editor of *Harper's*.

P. J. O'Rourke is author of *Republican Party Reptile* (Atlantic Monthly Press) and *The Bachelor Home Companion* (Pocket Books). He is also International Affairs Desk Chief at *Rolling Stone* magazine.

Vic Gold, a native of New Orleans, is national correspondent for *The American Spectator*.

Malcolm Gladwell is a writer for the *Washington Post*.

Bruce Bawer is *The American Spectator*'s movie reviewer and author of *The Middle Generation* and *The Contemporary Stylist*.

III. The Sexes

George F. Will is a nationally syndicated columnist with the *Washington Post* and a commentator for "ABC News".

Michael Novak, Ledden Watson Distinguished Professor of Religion at Syracuse University, is a Resident Scholar at the American Enterprise Institute.

John Simon is drama critic for *New York* magazine and movie critic for *National Review*.

Tung Tung (pseudonym) is a short story writer and former leader of a major Red Guard faction in Shanghai.

Taki lives in London, New York, and Switzerland, where he writes for the *Spectator* of London, *Esquire,* and *National Review*.

Rachel Flick is a reporter for the *New York Post,* Washington Bureau.

Patrick J. Buchanan recently served as the Director of Communications and Assistant to President Reagan. J. Gordon Muir is a medical researcher.

William Tucker is *The American Spectator*'s New York correspondent and author of *Vigilante: The Backlash against Crime* (Stein and Day).

Andrew Ferguson is assistant managing editor of *The American Spectator*.

Colin Welch is a columnist for the London *Daily Mail*.

IV. Communism and Fellow Travelers

J. D. Lofton is a columnist for the *Washington Times*.

Hugh Kenner is Andrew W. Mellon Professor of the Humanities at the Johns Hopkins University.

Kenneth S. Lynn teaches U.S. History at the Johns Hopkins University.

Delba Winthrop is a lecturer at Harvard University.

Sidney Hook is Emeritus Professor of Philosophy, New York University, Senior Research Fellow at the Hoover Institution and author of the autobiography, *Out of Step: An Unquiet Life in the Twentieth Century* (Harper & Row).

Josef Škvorecký is a Czechoslovakian writer who lives in Canada and teaches American literature at the University of Toronto. His most recent novel is *Dvořak*.

Arnold Beichman is a Research Fellow at the Hoover Institution and a columnist with the *Washington Times*.

Matthew Stevenson, a former editor of *Harper's*, works in international banking.

Vladimir Bukovsky was expelled from the Soviet Union in 1976 after spending more than twelve years in Soviet labor camps, prisons, and psychiatric hospitals. Among his books is *To Build a Castle: My Life as a Dissenter*.

Rael Jean Isaac's most recent book (with Erich Isaac) is *The Coercive Utopians* (Regnery Gateway).

Liu Fong Da (pseudonym) is a visiting professor at the University of California, Berkeley. John Creger is a free-lance writer in Berkeley specializing in China.

Nicholas Rothwell was a reporter for the *Australian*.

Arch Puddington is on the staff of Radio Free Europe/Radio Liberty in New York.

V. America and the World

Peter W. Rodman serves on the National Security Council staff.

Stuart L. Koehl and Stephen P. Glick are practicing research analysts for a Washington-based defense consulting firm.

Stephen Rosen is a Secretary of the Navy Senior Research Fellow.

John Muggeridge teaches history at Niagara College in Welland, Ontario.

Walter Berns is the John M. Olin University Professor at Georgetown University.

H. J. Kaplan has been a foreign service officer, a corporate executive, a writer, and an editor of *Geo*.

Gregory A. Fossedal is a Media Fellow at the Hoover Institution and co-author (with Daniel O. Graham) of *A Defense That Defends* (Devin Adair).

Micah Morrison is *The American Spectator*'s former Israel correspondent and deputy director of the Committee for the Free World.

Richard Brookhiser is the managing editor of *National Review*.

VI. Conservatives

R. Emmett Tyrrell, Jr., is editor-in-chief of *The American Spectator*.

Harvey C. Mansfield, Jr., is professor of government at Harvard University.

Malcolm Muggeridge is the author of *Jesus: The Man Who Lives* and *Something Beautiful for God*. He has published two volumes of his memoirs, *Chronicles of Wasted Time*, and is presently writing the third.

David Niven (deceased 1985), a sailor of note, appeared in 90 motion pictures over 40 years. In 1958 he won the Academy Award for his performance in *Separate Tables*. Mr. Niven was the author of the best-selling memoir, *Bring on the Empty Horses*.

Roger Starr is a member of the editorial board of the *New York Times* and the author of *The Rise and Fall of New York City*.

—Elliott Abrams is assistant secretary of state for Inter-American Affairs.

—Tom Bethell has been *The American Spectator*'s Washington correspondent since 1979.

—Naomi Decter is a frequent contributor to *Contentions.*

—Christopher DeMuth is president of the American Enterprise Institute.

—Charles Horner is deputy director of the United States Information Agency.

—Roger Kaplan is senior editor for *Reader's Digest.*

—Rachel Mark lives in Washington, D.C.

—Adam Meyerson, former managing editor of *The American Spectator,* is editor of *Policy Review.*

—Stephen Miller is with Radio Free Europe in Washington, D.C.

—W. Scott Thompson is associate professor of international politics at the Fletcher School of Law and Diplomacy, Tufts University.

Frank Gannon, a former special assistant to President Nixon, is a segment producer for "Late Night with David Letterman."

Luigi Barzini (deceased 1984) was a distinguished Italian journalist and author of *The Italians* and *The Europeans.*

Tom Bethell is *The American Spectator*'s Washington correspondent.

Joseph Sobran is senior editor at *National Review* and author of *Single Issues.*

Joseph W. Bishop, Jr. (deceased 1985), was the Sam Harris Professor of Law at the Yale Law School.

Fred Barnes is a senior editor at the *New Republic.*

William McGurn is deputy editorial page editor of the *Asian Wall Street Journal.*

Index